ESPOSITO

ESPOSITO

INFORMATION SYSTEMS
IN BUSINESS MANAGEMENT

The Irwin Series in Information and Decision Sciences

Consulting Editors

Robert B. Fetter
Yale University

Claude McMillan
University of Colorado

INFORMATION SYSTEMS IN BUSINESS MANAGEMENT

with Software and BASIC Tutorials

James A. O'Brien

College of Business Administration
Northern Arizona University

Fifth Edition 1988

Homewood, Illinois 60430

Cover photo by Michel Tcherevkoff ©.

The previous editions of this book were published under the title of *Computers in Business Management: An Introduction.*

This book was set in Caledonia by Better Graphics, Inc.
The editors were Lawrence E. Alexander, Ann M. Granacki, Susan Trentacosti, Joan A. Hopkins.
The production manager was Carma W. Fazio.
The designer was Michael Warrell.
The drawings were done by Precision Graphics.
R. R. Donnelley & Sons Company was the printer and binder.

ISBN 0-256-05803-2

Library of Congress Catalog Card No. 87–82173

Printed in the United States of America
3 4 5 6 7 8 9 0 DO 5 4 3 2 1 0 9

To Him who makes all things possible

PREFACE

A fifth edition of an introductory text in the dynamic area of computers and information systems is unprecedented. Many texts have come and gone since the first edition of this text was introduced in 1975. This text has succeeded because it continues to offer its readers a unique combination of up-to-date technical, conceptual, and applications material set in a real-world business management context and presented in a well-organized, readable manner.

Therefore, the fundamental characteristics and concepts on which this book is based have been maintained and strengthened. However, this edition represents a major revision, as have all previous editions. Major changes have been made in response to recent developments in computers and information systems technology, conceptual foundations, and pedagogy. The change in the title of this edition emphasizes the extent of such changes. Let's take a brief look at what has changed, and what has remained the same.

WHAT HAS NOT CHANGED

This text continues to embody the following characteristics:

- [ ] A higher-level introduction to computers and information systems in business.
- [ ] An emphasis on real-world business applications, information system concepts, management of information system resources, and hands-on user computing.
- [ ] An emphasis on information system resources and activities as reflected in the integrative conceptual framework of the information systems model.
- [ ] A personal style, user's viewpoint, straightforward organization, and comprehensive content.

Unlike many introductory texts, this text continues to fulfill the requirements of providing a basic understanding of computers and information systems contained in curriculum standards recommended by the American Assembly of Collegiate Schools of Business (AACSB), the Association of Computing Machinery (ACM), and the Data Processing Management Association (DPMA). This includes (1) the AACSB standard requiring a basic understanding of "management information systems including computer applications"; (2) the coverage of topics recommended in Course IS1: Computer Concepts and Software Systems, and Course IS3: Information Systems in Organizations, of the ACM's model curriculum for undergraduate programs in Information Systems; and (3) the topics outlined in Course CIS-1: Introduction to Computer Information Systems, of the DPMA's model curriculum for undergraduate programs in Computer Information Systems.

Curriculum Standards

The first module of the text (Chapters 1, 2, and 3) is a true **core module.** It includes the foundation concepts of information systems, computer hardware, and software. This was done for two reasons. First, it allows instructors to assign *any other module or appendix* after completing the core module. Second, many instructors are now beginning classroom demonstrations of computer hardware and software and making application software lab assignments in the first few weeks of a course. They need a text that gives students an immediate yet fairly complete introductory coverage of the foundation concepts of information systems, computer hardware, and software. They don't need a text that makes them wait until the middle of the book for a software chapter or that has a skimpy introduction to such topics in an opening chapter, and then has to repeat itself in later chapters.

WHAT HAS CHANGED

The Core Module

Note that historical and future material is in a third section of the first chapter where it can be de-emphasized or deleted if necessary. However, such introductory material is important to give students a feel for *trends* in computing—where we came from and where we are going. Also note that the survey of programming languages material has been reduced and included as a third section of the introductory chapter on software (Chapter 3). This allows instructors to talk about programming languages when they talk about software. However, instructors can also de-emphasize or delete this section if they wish.

The Technology Module

Gathered together in a *technology* module (Chapters 4, 5, 6, 7, and 8) is more detailed treatment of how computer hardware and software support the information systems activities of processing, input/output, and storage. This includes concepts and applications in file and database processing and data communications. The core module and this module complete the coverage of the technology of information systems. This feature will thus support a range of instructor preferences and course objectives concerning the depth of coverage of CIS technology topics. For example, I prefer covering such chapters early in the course while also covering hands-on application software material, and before assigning students MIS and business application chapters. However, because of the modular approach, instructors with different preferences can accommodate a different order of coverage.

Microcomputer Coverage

Microcomputer concepts, considerations, and applications are integrated throughout the book, instead of being concentrated in one chapter. A single chapter on microcomputers is a simplistic, redundant, and unrealistic solution to the problem of including microcomputer content in a course. For example, in some schools, students may start using microcomputers in the first week of a course and continue to use them throughout the semester. In this text, microcomputer coverage is in the foundation chapters on information systems, computer hardware, and software; in the technology chapters on processing, input/output, and storage methods, and database and data communication systems; in the MIS chapters; in the management of information systems chapters; and in the hands-on appendix!

The Information Systems Model

The information systems model used throughout this text is a modified version of the one used in the fourth edition. It has been renamed and redefined to emphasize its importance in providing a conceptual framework that helps students understand and integrate the many facts and concepts that are part of information systems technology and applications. This simple yet comprehensive model makes it easier for students to learn how to analyze, evaluate, and manage computer-based information systems. Thus this model stresses that:

Information systems use the resources of hardware (machines and media), software (programs and procedures), and people (specialists and users) to perform input, processing, output, storage, and control activities that transform data resources into information products.

The coverage of MIS topics has been significantly reorganized. The American Assembly of Collegiate Schools of Business now requires that all business majors be exposed to substantial MIS and business applications coverage. This book has been one of the few introductory texts that always strongly supported this objective. To strengthen this support there has been a major revision of the opening MIS chapter (Chapter 9) to emphasize business and management concepts that many students have not had before taking an introductory CIS course.

MIS Coverage

Secondly, the conceptual organization of MIS topics in Chapter 9 and in the text has been revised. In the real world, information systems supply information to support either *operations* or *management*. Therefore, only two major types of conceptual information systems are emphasized: (1) *operations* information systems, and (2) *management* information systems. The text stresses that transaction processing systems, process control systems, and automated office systems are types of *operations information systems*. Likewise, management reporting systems, decision support systems, executive information systems, and expert systems are considered to be types of *management information systems*.

Notice that the chapter on systems development (Chapter 10) has been placed in this module. Business users and managers must learn to develop their own systems, as well as learning how to manage the systems development process. Only after students have covered foundation and technology concepts, and some basic MIS concepts, are they really ready to understand and apply systems development concepts to simple information problems in business. I don't believe they are ready for it early in the text or course. A simple case study has been added to demonstrate the use of several tools of analysis and design. Students should then be able to use such tools to analyze simple information problems and design simple solutions to those problems.

Finally, the depth of the chapters on functional information systems (Chapters 13 and 14) has been updated and strengthened. The chapter on office automation (Chapter 12) has been thoroughly revised and moved so that it is obvious that automated office systems are now a major type of computer-based information system.

This text continues to stress and has reorganized its coverage of the *management of information systems* (MOIS) and *information resource management* (IRM). Many business students will be future business managers. Therefore, they need a text that has a module that emphasizes that they must learn to manage data, information, and computer hardware, software, and people as

IS Management Coverage

valuable organizational resources. This includes issues of the control of information system resources, computer security and crime, privacy, and other effects of computers on society.

Software Tutorials

The software tutorials in Appendix A have been thoroughly revised by:

1. Adding a section on the use of the PC and DOS (Section I).
2. Dropping the sections on MORTGAGE and VISICALC.
3. Updating to the latest versions of WordStar (4.0), Lotus 1-2-3 (2.0), and dBASE III Plus (1.1).
4. Continuing the fourth edition concept of demonstrating fundamental generic activities that one does with productivity software packages. This is accomplished by using the most widely used commercial software packages as specific examples in figures of typical displays and in tutorial discussions of typical types of activities.

Software Development and BASIC

Introductory CIS and MIS courses are still being taught either with or without coverage of software development and a programming language. To accommodate these two approaches, the chapter on the software development process (Chapter 11) has been placed after the chapter on systems development, and an appendix containing introductory coverage of BASIC has been added (Appendix B). Thus instructors can better choose whether or not they want to cover such material. Dr. Jim Morgan, a colleague who teaches courses in BASIC, COBOL, and database, revised the BASIC appendix for this edition. Coverage of Pascal will still be available as a supplement in the Student Study Guide and has been revised by Professor Craig VanLengen to support the use of Turbo Pascal.

The Color Insert

In an effort to reduce costs and keep textbook prices from increasing out of sight, the fifth edition is printed in two colors, with a full-color photo insert included as the first section of Chapter 1. This 24-page insert contains *47 full-color photographs* organized into *four major topics*. All figures have several sentences of descriptive material as captions, and are referred to in subsequent chapters where appropriate. This color insert avoids arbitrary interruption of text material, emphasizes the presence of a color photo section, and makes it a real working section, not just a visual treat, as is the case in the multiple color inserts found in other texts.

Structure of the Text

One of the primary objectives of reorganizing the fifth edition was to simplify, shorten, and restructure the fourth edition text material. A significant effort was made to remove excess wordiness and to simplify the sentence structure and language used in the text. The text was reorganized into five modules and two appendixes. (See Figure 1.) Each chapter was also organized into two or three *sections*. This was done to provide better conceptual organization of the text and of each chapter and to reduce the number of chapters from 20 to 17. It also helps instructors spotlight material they wish to emphasize, make optional, or delete.

Figure 1 The modular organization of the text.

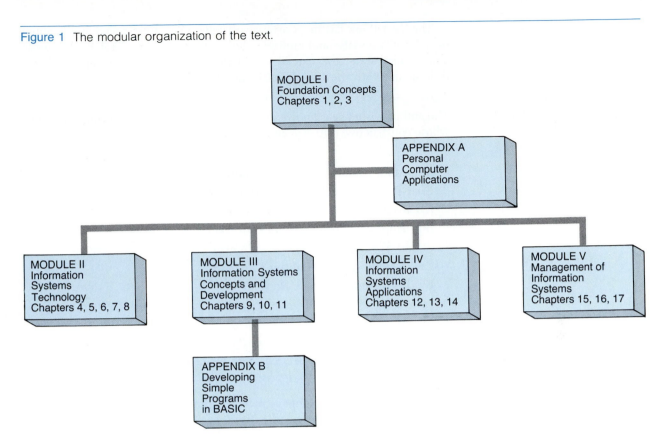

The practice of starting each chapter with an outline and learning objectives has been maintained. Real World Applications have been moved to the end of each chapter section. All Real World Applications are current and section-specific examples. Each chapter ends with Key Terms and Concepts, a new Review and Application Quiz tied directly to the Key Terms and Concepts, and Application Problems. The text also contains an extensive glossary of information systems terms.

SUPPORT MATERIALS

The **Student Study Guide** that supplements the text has been improved for this edition. It contains detailed chapter outlines, chapter learning objectives, chapter overviews, definitions of key terms and concepts, chapter test-yourself questions (true-false, multiple choice, fill-in-the-blanks, matching), answers to test-yourself questions, and short chapter assignments. It also contains an introductory programming appendix on Pascal. The study guide should thus be a valuable supplement to the main text.

An **Instructor's Guide** is available to instructors upon adoption of the text. It contains instructional aids and suggestions, answers to chapter questions and problems, solutions to the software appendix assignments, and answers and solutions to the questions and programming assignments in the BASIC appendix and the Student Study Guide. Transparency masters of important figures in the text are also provided.

The **Test Bank** has been extensively revised and improved and contains over 1,500 true-false and multiple choice questions. The Test Bank is available as a separate test manual and in computerized form on tape or floppy disk for use with the Irwin Test Generator Program.

ACKNOWLEDGMENTS

The author wishes to acknowledge the assistance of the following reviewers, whose constructive criticism and suggestions provided valuable input to this edition.

Augustine Brennan   *Erie Community College*

Elias R. Callahan, Jr.   *Mississippi State University*

J. Patrick Fenton   *West Valley College*

Bob Hopfe   *California State University—Sacramento*

Robert W. Law   *University of Denver*

Paul Leidig   *James Madison University*

Fred Lovgren   *Ferris State College*

Laurie MacDonald   *Bryant College*

Ron Murch   *University of Calgary*

Tom Pollack   *Duquesne University*

James Shannon   *New Mexico State University*

Victor Streeter   *University of Michigan—Dearborn*

A special acknowledgment is owed to Jim Morgan of Northern Arizona University, who coauthored the Student Study Guide and revised the BASIC appendix, Instructor's Guide, and the Test Bank. Craig VanLengen, also of Northern Arizona University, revised the Pascal appendix in the Student Study Guide. My thanks also to Toni Ohrn and Anne Bechard, whose word processing skills allowed me to complete the manuscript on time. The contributions of computer manufacturers and others who provided photographs and illustrations used in the text are gratefully acknowledged. Finally, but most importantly, I wish to thank the many instructors who have used my texts for their comments and suggestions that have helped me improve each edition of this book.

A Special Acknowledgment

A special acknowledgment is due the many business firms and other computer-using organizations that are the subjects of most of the **Real World Applications** in each chapter. In order of appearance in the text they are:

Chapter 2: The Travelers Corporation and Tenneco, Inc.
Chapter 3: San Diego Gas and Electric Company.
Chapter 4: Louisiana Geological Survey and Mobil Oil Corporation.
Chapter 5: Federated Investors, Inc. and West Point Pepperell.
Chapter 6: Microsoft Corporation and Richard T. Rodgers, Attorney-at-Law.
Chapter 7: Simmonds Precision Company and Citicorp, Inc.

Chapter 8: Canadian Imperial Bank of Commerce; Clairol, Inc.;
           and TRW International Distribution Services.
Chapter 9: Gillette Corporation and E. I. du Pont de Nemours &
           Co., Inc.
Chapter 10: The Gap, Inc.; Pacific Northwest Bell; and GTE Midwestern
           Telephone Operations.
Chapter 11: Romano Bros. Beverage Co. and IDS/American Express.
Chapter 12: United Telephone Company and Coca-Cola Foods.
Chapter 13: Dominick's Finer Foods, Inc.; Ex-Cell-O Corp.;
           and Canadian Broadcasting Company.
Chapter 15: Pillsbury Company and Ocean Spray Cranberry, Inc.
Chapter 16: The IBM Corporation.
Chapter 17: First Chicago Bank.

The real-life situations faced by these firms provide a valuable demonstration
of the benefits and limitations of using computer-based information systems
in modern organizations.

James A. O'Brien

CHAPTER AND SECTION CONTENTS

CONTENTS

APPENDIX B   DEVELOPING SIMPLE PROGRAMS IN BASIC   *B*

INFORMATION SYSTEMS
IN BUSINESS MANAGEMENT

FOUNDATION
CONCEPTS

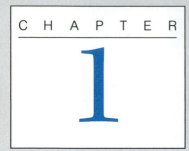

C H A P T E R

1

INTRODUCTION TO COMPUTERS AND INFORMATION SYSTEMS

Chapter Outline

Learning Objectives

The purpose of this chapter is to develop a basic understanding of the use of computers in information systems by analyzing (1) a pictorial overview of the uses of computers, (2) a fundamental conceptual framework of information systems, and (3) the development and impact of computers on information processing. After reading and studying this chapter, you should be able to:

1. Explain the importance of computers and information systems in today's society, and to your present and future activities.

2. Identify four basic advantages and related potential limitations of using computers for information processing.

3. Define the terms *computer, hardware, software, computer specialist*, and *computer user*.

4. Give an example to illustrate the difference between data and information.

5. Explain and give examples of the concept of information systems as systems which use the resources of hardware (machines and media), software (programs and procedures), and people (specialists and users) to perform input, processing, output, storage, and control activities that transform data resources into information products.

6. Identify the major changes that have occurred in each generation of computers, the trends that will continue into the future, and their effect on computer users.

7. Explain the impact of the microcomputer revolution in terms of
   a. microcomputer technology,
   b. distributed processing,
   c. personal computing, and
   d. smart products.

8. Use a personal computer and a software package to do one of the assignments in the section called "Using the PC and DOS" in Appendix A at the end of this book.

Figure 1–1 Levels of computer use. Which level would you like to be on?

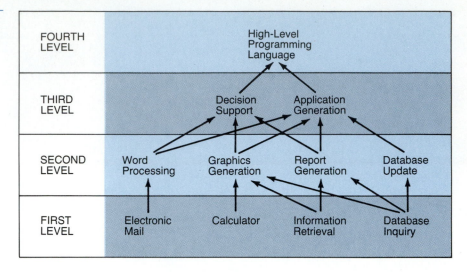

GETTING STARTED IN COMPUTERS

Today's computers and many of the programs that operate them are not difficult to use. A beginner can quickly learn to use them with a little bit of guidance and practice. Right now is a good time to start. You can move from a simple level of computer use to more complicated levels as you gain skills and experience. Figure 1–1 illustrates four levels of increasing sophistication in the use of computers. You should start at the first level and work your way up as far as you care to go. This text and its appendixes on using software packages and BASIC programming should help you accomplish most of the activities in each level of computer use.

Appendix A of this book, entitled "Personal Computer Applications," contains four sections. To start you should read the first section, which is called "Using the PC and DOS." Then use a personal computer and a prewritten program provided by your instructor. It should only take a few minutes to get accustomed to the peculiarities of your computer. After a few more minutes, you can begin to learn how to use simple programs on your computer. Try it, you'll like it!

Section I: Computers and Their Uses: A Pictorial Introduction

Sometimes pictures are worth more than words. Here for you is a visual introduction to:

☐ Computers in the Real World.
☐ Microcomputers and Other Computer Systems.
☐ Input, Output, and Storage Methods.
☐ Software Packages in Action.

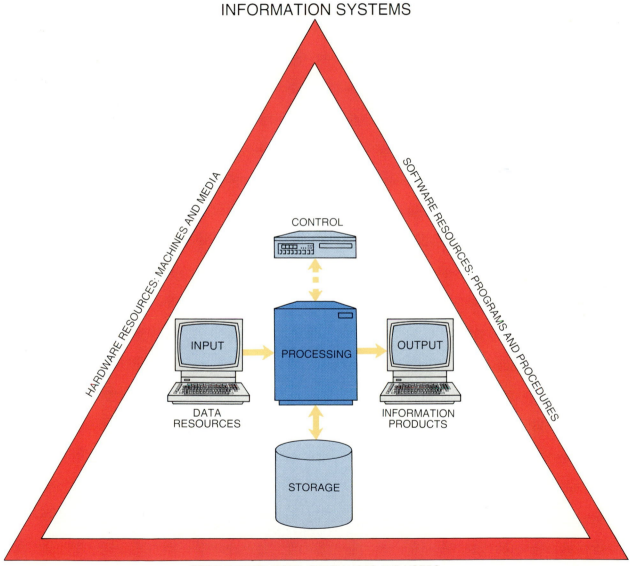

INFORMATION SYSTEMS

The Information Systems Model. This example of business graphics illustrates the components and activities of information systems. Notice that information systems use the resources of hardware (machines and media), software (programs and procedures), and people (specialists and users) to perform input, processing, output, storage, and control activities that transform data resources into information products. This important concept will be emphasized throughout this text.

COMPUTERS IN THE REAL WORLD

Computers in the Office. Computers have become an integral part of the modern office. They make possible a variety of automated office systems which can dramatically increase the efficiency and effectiveness of office activities and communications.

Computers in Manufacturing. Computer-aided manufacturing (CAM) systems help increase the efficiency and quality of manufacturing operations on the factory floor.

Computers and Robotics. Industrial robots use computer intelligence and computer-controlled physical capabilities to perform many production activities in automated factories, such as these welding robots on a Chrysler assembly line.

Computers in Distribution. Computers in warehouses and transportation centers help increase the efficiency of the transportation and distribution of raw materials and finished products to manufacturers, distributors, and consumers.

Computers in Retailing. Computers have automated the capture of sales transaction data with point-of-sale (POS) terminals that can use optical scanning "wands" to read merchandise tags.

Computers in Medicine. Computers are used in advanced diagnostic and treatment devices and in hospital information systems that automate patient monitoring and medical records processing.

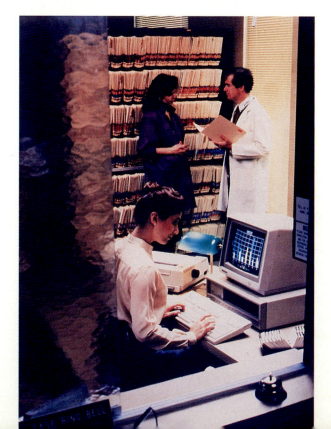

Computers in Education. Computers are becoming common educational tools as students and teachers rely on them for computer-assisted instruction (CAI) and problem solving.

Computers in the Home. Computers are becoming common home appliances as parents and children use them for home management, personal productivity, entertainment, and education.

Computers in Science and Engineering. Computers have become indispensable tools for scientific analysis, experiment monitoring, and engineering design.

Computers Need People. Users like you and specialists like the programmers and systems analysts shown here are the most important part of computer-based information systems.

MICROCOMPUTERS, MAINFRAMES, AND OTHER COMPUTER SYSTEMS

Video Monitor
(Output)

Printer
(Output)

Keyboard
(Input)

Main System Unit
(Processing, Primary Storage,
and Control. Also holds
Magnetic Disk Drives for
Secondary Storage.)

A Microcomputer System. A microcomputer is a system of input,
processing, output, storage, and
control components as identified
here. This is an IBM Personal Sys-
tem/2 Model 60 microcomputer.

Central Processing Unit
(Processing, primary
storage, and control)

Magnetic
Tape Units
(Secondary
storage
and I/O)

High-Speed
Printer
(Output)

Video and Printing Terminals
(Input/Output)

Magnetic
Disk Units
(Secondary
storage
and I/O)

A Mainframe Computer System. The
input, processing, output, storage,
and control components of a large
"mainframe" computer system are
identified here.

A Microprocessor, the Intel 80386. This new generation microprocessor is called a "mainframe on a chip." It is the central processing unit of the faster and more powerful models of advanced microcomputer systems.

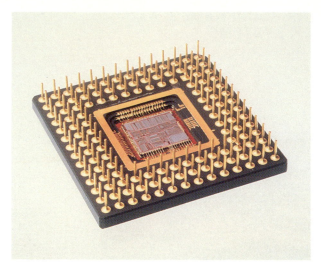

A microprocessor chip is mounted inside its carrier package and plugged into a circuit board along with memory and other chips.

The IBM Personal System/2 Model 80. This is a powerful new microcomputer that uses the Intel 80386 microprocessor chip. It is an advanced model of IBM's new line of micro-computer systems.

The COMPAQ DeskPro 386. A powerful model of a line of popular alternatives to IBM microcomputers. It uses the Intel 80386 microprocessor.

The Apple Macintosh. This popular
line of microcomputers are the successors to the original Apple
computers that began the microcomputer revolution.

The Hewlett-Packard Portable is an example of the many types of "lap-top" portable microcomputers that are available as smaller alternatives to the more common "desktop"
models.

This Prime 850 minicomputer system is an example of the powerful ''super minis'' that rival larger mainframe computers in speed and power.

The IBM 4341 is one of the most widely used medium-scale mainframe computer systems. Such computers serve as a major link between larger mainframes and networks of personal computers in large organizations.

IBM 3090 large-scale mainframe computer systems. Such computers can support hundreds of video terminals, personal computers, and other devices to meet the information processing requirements of large organizations.

The Cray XMP-4 Supercomputer System. This extremely powerful "supercomputer" system can process hundreds of millions of instructions per second as it works on projects requiring massive amounts of calculations.

INPUT, OUTPUT, AND STORAGE METHODS

Testing a voice recognition system to enter data and commands into a microcomputer system for word processing applications.

Using an electronic mouse to issue commands to an Apple Macintosh microcomputer.

This Hewlett-Packard "touchscreen" microcomputer allows you to issue commands by touching its touch-sensitive screen.

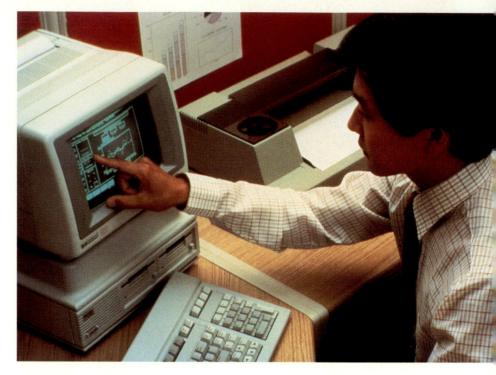

You can enter data into a computer by "writing" on its screen with a "light pen" as this engineer is doing, using an HP200 computer-aided-design workstation.

This engineer is using a graphics tablet, keyboard, and "joystick" to enter specifications data into a Prime engineering workstation used for computer-aided-design.

This is an example of the use of an optical scanning "wand" to read product bar codes using a portable data entry terminal with a liquid crystal display.

Using an Automated Teller Machine (ATM). Notice that this requires the use of a magnetic stripe plastic bank card and a small keypad for entry of data. A small video screen is used to display information.

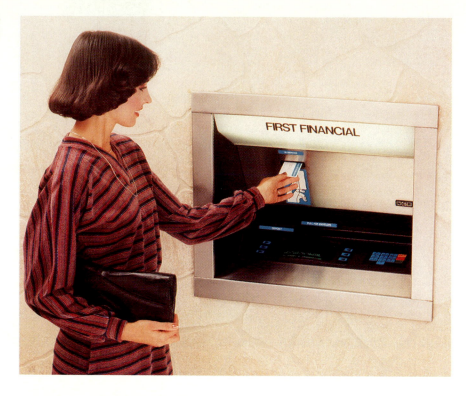

Printed paper reports and documents of all kinds are still a major form of computer output.

Computer graphics images can be displayed on a video screen or reproduced on paper using computer printers and plotters.

Portable microcomputers and terminals may use plasma display devices instead of traditional video display tubes when a compact flat visual display is needed.

This portable data terminal features a liquid crystal display. It uses "cellular radio" technology for data communications in urban areas.

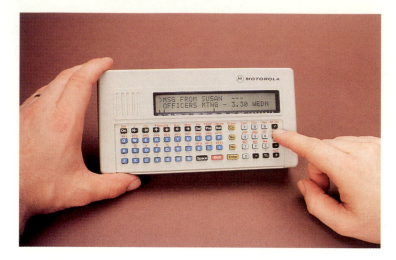

An advanced semiconductor memory chip for microcomputers that can hold one million bits of data or about 125,000 characters of information.

Magnetic disk units like these hold billions of characters of information on removable disk packs. This provides computer-based information systems with immediate access to the data resources of an organization.

Magnetic "floppy disks" are the most popular type of secondary storage media for microcomputers. They can store several hundred thousand to several million characters of information on flexible plastic disks.

Magnetic tape drives use reels or cartridges of magnetic tape which can store hundreds of millions of characters of data.

This "CD-ROM" optical disk unit for microcomputers uses lasers to read compact optical disks which can hold over 500 million characters of information.

SOFTWARE PACKAGES IN ACTION

This display of the WordPerfect word processing software package shows how you can create and edit a business letter with this computerized typing tool.

This display of the Lotus 1-2-3 spreadsheet package shows the layout of the electronic worksheet you can construct and manipulate to perform a variety of analysis and planning activities.

This display shows how the dBASE III Plus database management package gives you the ability to create files of data and produce reports which extract information from data files.

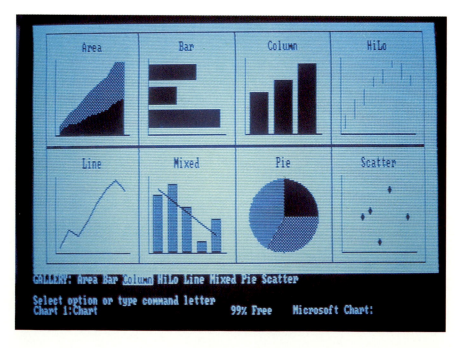

This Microsoft Chart graphics package display shows the selection of graphics alternatives you can choose when you wish to generate graphics displays.

This multiple window display of the TopView operating environment package shows how it helps integrate the use of several separate types of software packages.

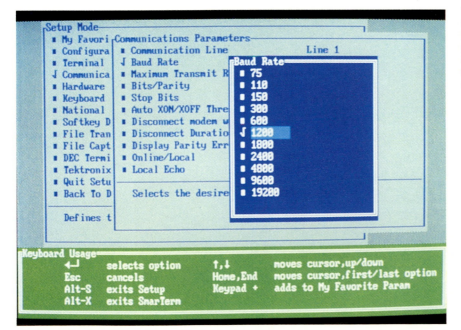

This is the multiple window display of the SmartTerm data communications package. It shows how you can use menus to select appropriate communications parameters for communicating with other computers and information networks.

This is a display of the Harvard Project Manager which shows a PERT chart constructed by this project management software package.

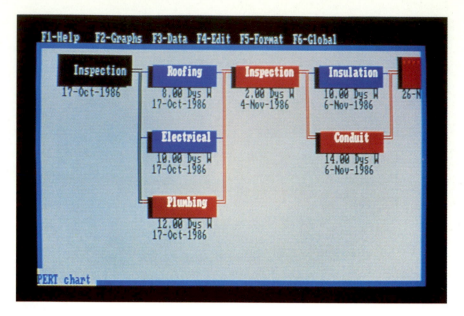

You can generate graphics displays like this when you use an investment analysis package like the Dow Jones Market Analyzer to help you analyze the performance of stocks and other securities.

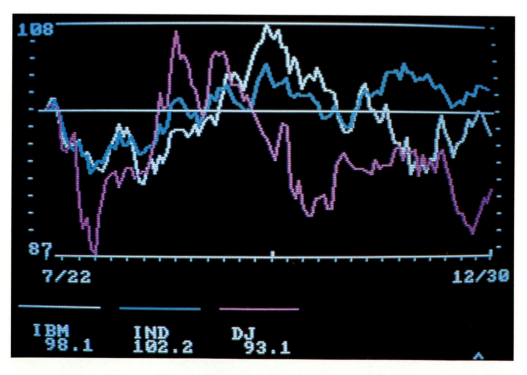

REAL WORLD APPLICATION 1-1

Computers in the Real World

It's remarkable how easily the computer has slipped into today's society. In just 25 years, people have made a necessity of the computer and its electronic progeny.

"Smart" products undreamed of a few decades ago now talk to schoolchildren, monitor vehicle performance, keep track of time, adjust camera lenses, and control home appliances. Others play blackjack and Space Invaders with kids at home or at the neighborhood arcade.

This awakening in everyone to the excitement of computer technology is but icing on a cake baked by business and industry. For if people now view the computer as fashionable, business and industry consider it heavy armament in a war against paper, inefficiency, and falling productivity. For example:

☐ Manufacturing designers routinely use computers and computer graphics to design parts and to generate programs for running numerically controlled machine tools. Now they are starting to use computers to tie design, manufacture, inventory control, and other functions into whole systems. The result: drastic drops in inventory-in-progress, quicker machine setup times, more commonality of parts.

☐ As the nursing force dwindles, health care industries use computers in patient monitoring and drug dosage calculation; doctors are discovering the potential for computerized diagnosis assistance.

☐ Retailers reap benefits by capturing stock data electronically, for reorder, pricing, and merchandising, using electronic point-of-sale terminals.

☐ Automated teller machines allow banks to stay open around the clock. Competing banks even share machines in cases where one bank's business alone won't generate enough traffic.

☐ Publishers shove deadlines closer to print runs by computerization from original typing—through editing, revision, layout, and pasteup, to automated phototypesetting.

☐ Robots are used widely by auto makers in spray painting and other nasty applications; whole automated factories are on stream.

☐ Energy management is suddenly worth computerizing. Computers track the sun in solar installations, cycle thermostats in office buildings, and even heat buildings as a by-product of operation.

☐ In the workplace, engineers, stockbrokers, factory workers, clerks, and executives punch the buttons of computerized workstations to help them design products, buy and sell securities, control assembly lines, keep track of millions of transactions, and make decisions with the advice of "expert systems."

☐ Offices everywhere are bursting with new automated equipment—word processors, copy machines, digital telephones, and microcomputer-based workstations. This is the start of an era where integrated word and data processing are commonplace, where voice, video, and data traffic all run on the same communications network.

The litany is endless. In every nook and cranny of the factory and the office, the computer—or some chip-based relative—is finding employment.

Application Questions

☐ Can you think of other uses of computers than those mentioned above?

☐ Which is the most important or appealing to you? Why?

☐ Do any computer uses upset you? Explain.

Source: Adapted from International Data Corporation.

Section II: Foundation Concepts

WHY LEARN ABOUT COMPUTERS AND INFORMATION SYSTEMS?

Why should you learn about computers and information systems? Here's why:

☐ Information, along with energy and materials, is a basic resource in today's world. We are living in an *information society* whose economy is heavily dependent on the creation and distribution of information by *knowledge workers.* We must learn to harness our information resources to benefit society. This includes finding ways to use information to make better use of our limited supplies of material and energy resources.

☐ A major tool in the production and use of information is the **computer.** The use of computers is vital to the operations and management of business firms, government agencies, and the rest of society. It has become even more so due to the rapidly growing use of *microcomputers.* We must learn to use such tools properly in order to harness the information resources in today's dynamic society.

☐ The proper flow and management of information is vital to the success of any organization. Thus, **information systems,** which transform data into information for users represent:

    ☐ A major part of the cost of doing business.

    ☐ A major factor in employee morale and customer satisfaction.

    ☐ A major source of information needed for effective decision making by the managers of an organization.

    ☐ A vital, dynamic, and expanding career opportunity for millions of men and women.

Therefore, you can increase your opportunities for employment and advancement by becoming a knowledgeable user of computers and information systems. Business firms and other organizations need people who can help them manage these valuable resources. As an informed user or information specialist, you can play a major role in seeing that information system resources are used efficiently and effectively for the benefit of the entire organization. This text is designed to help you achieve that goal.

WHY USE COMPUTERS FOR INFORMATION PROCESSING?

Business firms and other organizations are faced with information requirements of increased complexity. Ever-increasing volumes of data must be processed. That is why so many firms, both large and small, have turned to the use of computers for information processing. What has caused this growth in complexity and volume of processing requirements? Three reasons stand out:

☐ Most organizations are faced with growth in the size, complexity, and scope of their operations. Many firms are providing more products and services to more customers at more locations with more employees. Thus their need for information has increased.

☐ Managers and other users of information are demanding more kinds of information to support the management and operations of their organizations. The information demanded must be accurate, timely, and tailored to the needs of the manager or user.

☐ Business firms must respond to increased requirements for information from local, state, and federal governmental agencies. Such demands have become a major political issue as well as a major information processing problem.

Thus, for many firms, using computers for information processing is an absolute necessity. For example, banks, stock exchanges, and airlines would not be able to process the millions of money transfers, stock trades, and travel requests made each day. Thousands of business firms in many other industries could not operate without the basic information concerning their customers, suppliers, inventories, and finances provided by their computerized information systems.

Why can computers meet the present and future information processing requirements of such business firms? The answer lies in four basic advantages of properly managed computerized systems compared to manual processing methods.

Speed

Computers are capable of executing millions of instructions per second. Thus, it takes a computer only seconds to perform millions of data processing functions that human beings would take years to complete. This processing speed of the computer allows information systems to provide information in a *timely* manner to the managers and other users of information within a business firm. This is a major benefit of such systems.

However, poorly designed computerized information systems will not provide timely information. Improving the quality of hardware, software, and people resources may be required to ensure that the speed capability of the computer is properly used.

Accuracy

Computers can accurately process large volumes of data according to complex and repetitive processing procedures. This contrasts with manual processing systems, where the constant repetition of the same processing tasks by human beings becomes a cumbersome and tedious chore, and is extremely susceptible to errors. This is not to say that computers always produce accurate information. However, computer errors are minimal compared to the volume of data being processed and are frequently the result of human error.

For example, errors in management reports or customer statements are usually the result of incorrect data input supplied by humans, or errors in a computer program developed by a human programmer. Thus the term *garbage in, garbage out* (GIGO), is used by computer professionals to emphasize that incorrect input data or programs will result in incorrect output from the computer. It also emphasizes the importance of *control* procedures to ensure accuracy of such systems.

Figure 1–2 The declining cost of computer processing compared to the rising cost of using people for information processing.

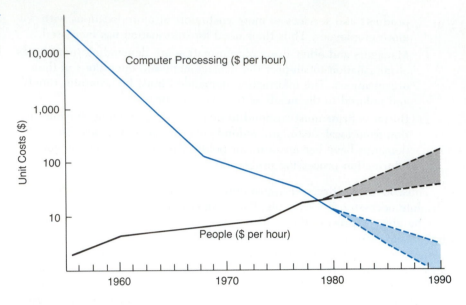

Reliability

The accuracy of computerized information systems is directly related to the exceptional reliability of computers and their electronic circuitry. Modern computers consistently and accurately operate for long time periods without failure. Their electronic circuitry is inherently reliable and includes self-checking features that ensure accuracy and automatically diagnose failure conditions. Such built-in "diagnostics" and regular preventive maintenance checks help ensure consistent reliability.

Computers do "go down" or "crash" (stop working). However, such *downtime* is usually only a fraction of a percent of the operating time of most systems. Backup systems and protective measures can also be used to minimize the effects of such failures.

Economy

The speed, accuracy, and reliability of computers would be available to only a few large organizations if it were not for the very real economy of computer usage. Except for very simple and low-volume tasks, computerized information processing is more economically justifiable than manual processing for most firms. This cost advantage continues to increase as new developments in computer technology continue to drive down the historical cost of computer processing. See Figure 1–2.

Of course, as in other areas of business activity, the cost of information processing for a business firm can go out of control. Proper procedures must be developed by management to control such costs.

WHAT IS A COMPUTER?

Before we get any further, let us define what we mean by the term **computer.** There are several varieties of computers and each has a variety of characteristics. However, in information processing, in the computer industry, and in the popular literature the term *computer* typically has the following meaning:

A computer is a device that has the ability to accept data, internally store and automatically execute a program of instructions, perform mathematical, logical, and manipulative operations on data, and report the results.

In the next chapter we will see that there are digital and analog computers, special-purpose and general-purpose computers, microcomputers, minicomputers, and many large computer systems, including *supercomputers!* In the remaining chapters of this text, we will explore fundamental concepts of the hardware, software, and uses of computers for information processing.

WHAT IS INFORMATION PROCESSING?

It is important to understand computers in the context of their use in **information processing,** which is also called **data processing.** Computers are now the primary tool in the production of information for users. Thus, to really understand the uses of computers discussed in this text, you need to understand several fundamental concepts of information processing, which we will now explain.

Data versus Information

The word *data* is the plural of *datum*, though data is commonly used to represent both singular and plural forms. **Data** can be defined as *facts* or *observations*, typically about physical phenomena or business transactions. For example, a spacecraft launch or the sale of an automobile would generate a lot of data describing these events. Data usually take the form of numbers, words, or codes composed of numerical or alphabetical characters or special symbols. However, data can also take the form of lines on a graph or other types of visual or audible representation.

The terms *data* and *information* are often used interchangeably. However, it is helpful to view data as raw material *resources* that are *processed* into finished information *products*. **Information** can then be defined as *data* that has been *transformed* into a *meaningful and useful form* for *specific human beings*.

Example   Names, quantities, and dollar amounts recorded on sales forms represent data about sales transactions. However a sales manager does not consider them to be information. Only when such facts are properly organized and manipulated can meaningful sales information be provided, such as the amount of sales by product type, sales territory, or salesperson.

Of course, data may not require processing before constituting information for a particular human user. However, data is usually not useful until subjected to a "value-added" process where (1) its form is manipulated and organized, (2) its content is analyzed and evaluated, and (3) it is placed in a proper context for a human user. Thus you should view information as processed data placed in its proper context to give it value for specific human users. See Figure 1–3.

Figure 1–3 Data versus information. Notice that information is processed data placed in its proper context to give it value for specific human users.

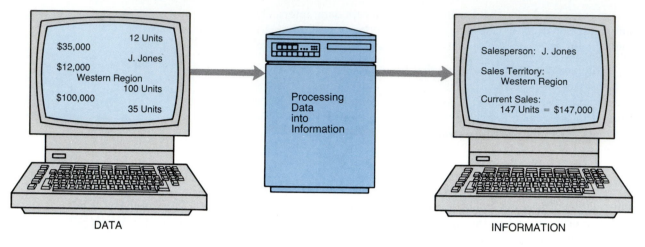

DATA   INFORMATION

Data and Information Processing

Data processing has traditionally been defined as the processing of data to transform it into information. Thus, **data processing** consists of actions that make data usable and meaningful (i.e., transforms data into information). However, the term **information processing** is gradually replacing the term *data processing*. Information processing is a more generic term that emphasizes the following concepts:

☐ The production of *information products* for users should be the focus of processing activities.

☐ The concept of *word processing* is part of information processing. In word processing, *text data* (words, phrases, sentences, and paragraphs) are processed into letters, memos, reports, and other documents.

☐ The raw material resources being processed no longer consist only of numeric and alphabetic data. Other forms such as *text material, graphic and video images,* and *voices* must also be processed.

Example Your reading of this text is one type of data or information processing. Your eyes are transmitting the text data of letters and words to your brain, which transforms these images into information by organizing and evaluating them and storing them for later use.

WHAT IS A SYSTEM?

The activity of information processing can be viewed as a **system.** What is a system? A system can be very simply defined as a *group of interrelated or interacting elements forming a unified whole.* Many examples of systems can be found in the physical and biological sciences, in modern technology, and in human society. Thus, we can talk of the physical system of the sun and its planets, the biological system of the human body, the technological system of an oil refinery, and the socioeconomic system of a business organization. However, the following generic concept of a system is typically used in computer and information systems technology.

A system is a group of interrelated components working together toward a common goal by accepting inputs and producing outputs in an organized transformation process.

Such a system (sometimes called a "dynamic system") has three basic functional components that interact to form a system:

- **Input** involves capturing and assembling elements that enter the system so they can be processed. *Examples:* Raw materials, energy, data, and human effort must be secured and organized for processing.
- **Processing** involves "transformation" processes that convert input into output. *Examples:* a manufacturing process, the human breathing process, data calculations.
- **Output** involves transferring elements that have been produced by the transformation process to their ultimate destination. *Examples:* Finished products, human services, and management information must be transmitted to their human users.

Examples A manufacturing system accepts raw materials as inputs and produces finished goods as output. An *information processing system,* or more simply, an **information system,** can be viewed as a system that accepts *data resources* as *input* and *processes them* into *information products* as *output.* See Figure 1–4.

Feedback and Control

The systems concept can be made even more useful by including two additional components: *feedback* and *control.* Figure 1–5 illustrates a system with feedback and control components. Such a system is sometimes called a "cybernetic" system, that is, *a self-monitoring, self-regulating* system.

- **Feedback** is data or information concerning the performance of a system.
- **Control** is a systems component that monitors and evaluates feedback to determine whether the system is moving toward the achievement of its goal. It then makes any necessary adjustments to the input and processing components of the system to ensure that proper output is produced.

Note that the feedback function is frequently included as part of the control function of a system. The responsibility of the control function then is to *develop* as well as monitor and evaluate feedback and make necessary adjustments to a system. We will use this concept of the control function in this text.

Examples A familiar example of a self-monitoring and self-regulating system is the thermostatically controlled heating system found in many homes, which automatically monitors and regulates itself to produce a desired temperature. Another familiar example is the human body, which can be considered an adaptive cybernetic system that automatically monitors and adjusts many of its functions, such as temperature, heartbeat, and breathing.

Figure 1–4 A fundamental system concept applied to manufacturing and information systems.

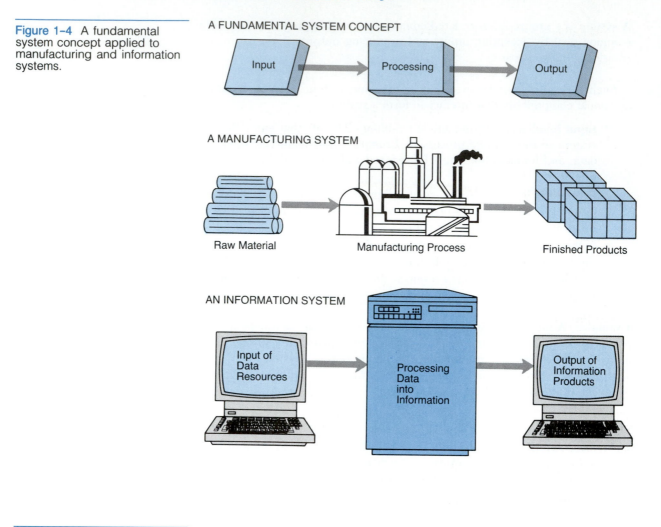

A FUNDAMENTAL SYSTEM CONCEPT

Input → Processing → Output

A MANUFACTURING SYSTEM

Raw Material   Manufacturing Process   Finished Products

AN INFORMATION SYSTEM

Input of Data Resources → Processing Data into Information → Output of Information Products

Figure 1–5 A fundamental system concept with feedback and control components.

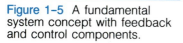
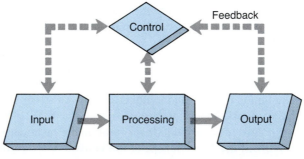

Control   Feedback

Input   Processing   Output

The feedback-control concept can also be applied to information systems. *Feedback* would consist of information describing the input, processing, and output activities of the system. *Control* would involve monitoring and evaluating feedback to determine if the system is operating according to the established information processing procedures and is producing the proper output. If not, the control function would make necessary adjustments to input, processing, and output activities so proper information products would be produced.

Example If *subtotals* of sales amounts in a sales report do not add up to *total sales*, then input or processing procedures may have to be changed to accumulate correctly all sales transactions.

A final basic component found in information systems is the *storage* function.

The Storage Function

☐ **Storage** is the system function in which data and information are stored in an organized manner for further processing or until needed by users of the system. Figure 1–6 summarizes a common method of organizing stored data for information processing.

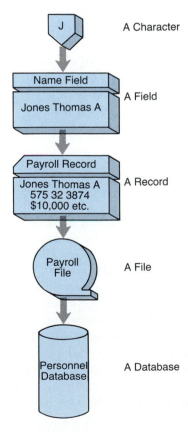

A Character

A Field

A Record

A File

A Database

Data and information must be organized in some systematic way for proper information processing, whether manual or computerized methods are used. We will discuss the topic of *data organization* in detail in Chapter 7 but you need to be introduced to some basic concepts now. Just as written text material is typically organized into letters, words, sentences, and paragraphs, data is commonly organized in the following *hierarchy* of **common data elements** in modern information systems.

☐ A **character** consists of a single alphabetic, numeric, or other symbol. Examples are the letters of the alphabet, numbers, and special symbols, such as dollar signs and decimal points.

☐ A **field** is a grouping of characters that represent a characteristic of a person, place, thing, or event. That is, your *name field* would consist of the alphabetic characters of your name, while your social security number, annual salary, and home address *fields* would each consist of a combination of numbers, letters, and special characters.

☐ A **record** is a collection of interrelated fields. For example, an employee's *payroll record* might consist of a name field, a social security number field, a department field, and a salary field.

☐ A **file** is a collection of interrelated records. For example, a *payroll file* might consist of the payroll *records* of all employees of a firm.

☐ A **database** is a collection of interrelated files and records. For example, the *personnel database* of a business might contain payroll, personnel action, and employee skills files.

Figure 1–6 The common data elements in information processing.

Example Sales data is accumulated and stored for subsequent processing, which produces daily, weekly, and monthly sales analysis reports for management.

WHAT IS AN INFORMATION SYSTEM?

We have said that an information system is a system that accepts data resources as input and processes them into information products as output. But how does an information system do this? That's what the **information systems model** in Figure 1–7 shows you. It illustrates that:

Information systems use the resources of hardware (machines and media), software (programs and procedures), and people (specialists and users) to perform input, processing, output, storage, and control activities that transform data resources into information products.

Figure 1–7 expresses in a few words and a simple figure a fundamental conceptual framework or *model* of information systems. This concept is so important that it will be emphasized in every chapter of this text. It will help you tie together the many facts and concepts involved in the study of computers and information systems.

The information systems model emphasizes three major concepts:

☐ Hardware (machines and media), software (programs and procedures), and people (specialists and users) are the resources needed to accomplish information processing activities in information systems.

☐ Information processing consists of input, processing, output, storage, and control activities.

☐ Data resources are transformed into a variety of information products by the information processing activities of information systems.

Information System Activities

In the previous section, we outlined the basic system functions of input, processing, output, storage, and control. Let's summarize how they apply to information systems.

☐ **Input** of data resources. Data about business transactions and other events must be captured and prepared for processing by *data entry* activities such as recording, coding, classifying, and editing. This may involve recording data on paper forms (**source documents**), magnetic disks and tapes, or entering it directly into a computer system using a keyboard or other device. The goal of the input function is to provide correct and complete data for processing.

☐ **Processing** of data into information. Data is typically manipulated by activities such as calculations, comparisons, sorting, and summarizing. These activities organize, analyze, and manipulate data so that it is transformed into information for users. The quality of stored data and information must also be *maintained* by a continual process of correcting and updating.

Figure 1–7 The information systems model. Information systems use the resources of hardware (machines and media), software (programs and procedures), and people (specialists and users) to perform input, processing, output, storage, and control activities that transform data resources into information products.

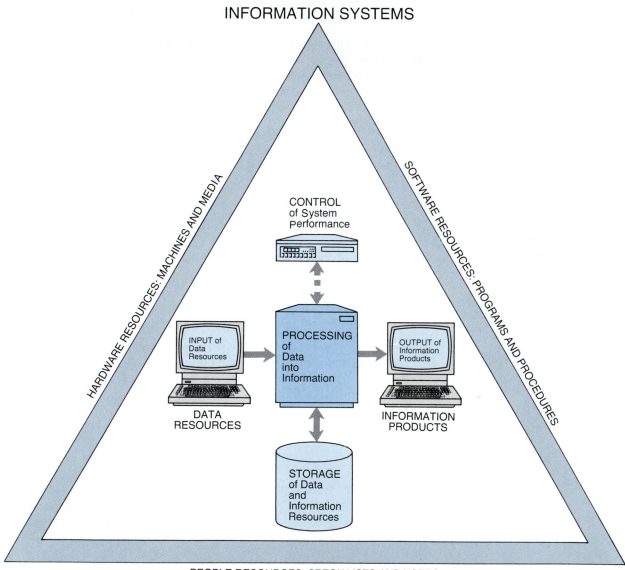

INFORMATION SYSTEMS

□ **Output** of information products. Information in various forms is transmitted to users. Information products may be in the form of printed reports and documents, video displays, audio responses, graphics, and so on.

□ **Storage** of data and information resources. Data and information must be stored in an organized manner. This facilitates its later use in processing or its retrieval as output to users.

☐ **Control** of system performance. Feedback about all input, processing, output, and storage activities must be monitored and evaluated. Then these activities must be adjusted and directed so that proper information products are produced for users.

Hardware Resources

The concept of **hardware resources** includes *all physical devices and materials* used in information processing. Specifically, this should include not only **machines,** such as computers or calculators, but also all data **media—** that is, *all tangible objects on which data is recorded*, whether a sheet of paper or a magnetic disk. Examples of hardware are:

☐ The *central processing unit* (CPU) of a computer system.

☐ *Computer terminals* and *personal computers*, which use a keyboard for input of data and a video screen or printer for output of information.

☐ *Magnetic disk media*, which can store millions of items of data as magnetic spots on circular metal or plastic disks.

Software Resources

The concept of **software resources** includes *all sets of information processing instructions*. Specifically, this includes not only the sets of operating instructions called **programs** which direct and control computer hardware, but also the sets of information processing instructions needed by people, called **procedures.** The following are examples of such software:

☐ *System software*, such as an *operating system* program, which controls and supports the operations of a computer system.

☐ *Application software*, which are programs that direct processing for a particular use of the computer. Examples are an inventory program, a payroll program, or a word processing program.

☐ *Procedures*, which are operating instructions for the people who will operate and use an information system.

People Resources

Did you notice that people are pictured in most of the photographs of computers in the opening pictorial section of this chapter? That's because computers need people more than people need computers! People are required for the operation of all information systems. These **people resources** include *computer specialists* and *computer users*.

☐ **Specialists** are people who develop and operate information systems. They include systems analysts, programmers, computer operators, and other managerial, technical, and clerical personnel. Basically, *systems analysts* design information systems based on the information requirements of users; *programmers* prepare computer programs based on the specifications of systems analysts; and *computer operators* operate the computer. The job activities of such specialists are discussed in the Managing Information Services section of Chapter 15.

☐ **Users** or **end users** are people who use an information system or the information it produces. They can be accountants, salespersons, engineers, clerks, customers, or managers. Most of us are information system users.

Data Resources

In the opening pages of this section, we defined and gave examples of the concept of data. Data is a very important resource to individuals and organizations. There are at least six major types of data: (1) traditional *alphanumeric data* composed of numbers and alphabetical and special characters that describe business transactions and other events and entities; (2) *text data* consisting of sentences and paragraphs used in written communications; (3) *image data*, such as graphic shapes and figures; (4) *audio data*—the human voice and other sounds; (5) *tactile data*—generated by touch-sensitive materials; and (6) *sensor data* provided by a variety of sensors used in the control of physical processes.

Data resources are typically recorded and stored on paper, magnetic, optical, film, or electronic media. Examples are paper documents, magnetic disks, optical disks, microfilm, and electronic circuit chips. *Note:* **Source documents** are input media that are the original written records of an activity. Examples are paper forms such as purchase orders or sales receipts on which data about individual purchases or sales are recorded.

Information Products

The production of **information products** for users is the only reason for the existence of all information resources and activities. Information is provided to users in a variety of forms. Such information products include *video displays, audio responses, messages, prompts, menus, forms, documents, reports*, and *listings*. We use such information products to provide us with information to improve our personal and professional performances as we live and work in society. We will give examples of many types and uses of information products in the rest of this chapter.

UNDERSTANDING INFORMATION SYSTEMS

There are many kinds of information systems in the real world. Some are simple *manual* information systems where people use simple tools such as pencils and paper, or even machines such as calculators and typewriters to transform data into information. Others are **computer-based information systems** that use computers to process data automatically. These are frequently called **electronic data processing** (EDP) systems. However, whether they are manual or computer-based systems, you should be able to use the information systems model to help you understand the systems that you encounter in the real world. Let's see if we can do this right now by analyzing examples of a manual system, a microcomputer-based system, and a large computer-based system.

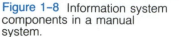

Figure 1–8 Information system components in a manual system.

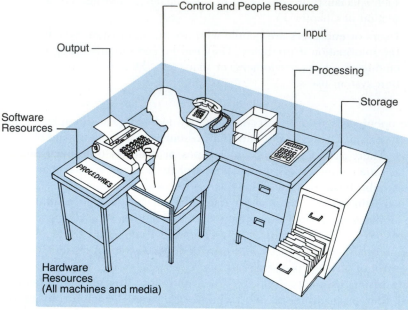

A Manual System

Figure 1–8 illustrates the components of a manual information system. Data is received as input by telephone or mail. An electronic calculator is used for processing by a clerk who controls the process according to written operating instructions. Data and information storage are provided by a filing cabinet. Typewritten reports are the output of this manual system.

The hardware resources of the system includes several machines (typewriter, telephone, calculator, filing cabinet, and so on) and media such as paper reports and file folders. Software includes the procedures contained in the reference manual which must be followed. People resources consists of the clerk who is both the operator and user of the system.

A Microcomputer-Based System

Figure 1–9 illustrates a microcomputer-based information system. Hardware resources include machines, like the microcomputer and its keyboard, video monitor, printer, and magnetic disk drives, and media of magnetic diskettes and printer paper. Software resources include programs used by the microcomputer and procedures followed by the user. People resources include the user who is operating the system, and specialists who developed its hardware and software.

Data resources are entered into the system as input through the keyboard by a user. Processing is done by a microprocessor and other circuitry in the microcomputer. Programs of computer instructions and procedures followed by the user control the system. Output of information products is accomplished by video monitor displays and printed paper reports. Storage of data and information resources is provided by microelectronic memory chips and magnetic diskettes.

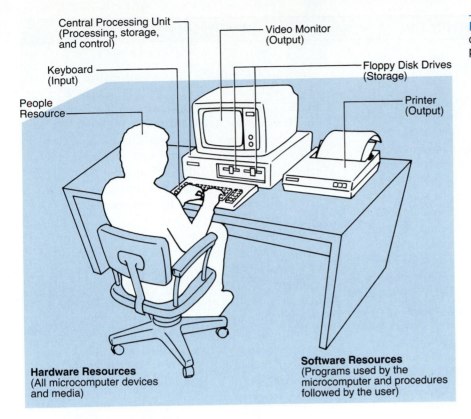

Central Processing Unit
(Processing, storage,
and control)

Video Monitor
(Output)

Keyboard
(Input)

Floppy Disk Drives
(Storage)

People
Resource

Printer
(Output)

Hardware Resources
(All microcomputer devices
and media)

Software Resources
(Programs used by the
microcomputer and procedures
followed by the user)

Figure 1–9 Information system components in a microcomputer-based system.

A Large Computer-Based System

Real World Application 1–2: ABC Department Stores is a simple business example that shows how resources, activities, and products are used in a computerized information system in the real world. It illustrates these components in action in a business firm (ABC Department Stores) that needs to know and use information about one of its important activities (sales). The information processing jobs that need to be done are frequently called *sales transaction processing* and *sales analysis*.

Sales transaction processing involves collecting, processing, and storing facts and figures about each sales transaction made by the company. Sales analysis involves the manipulation and organization of such data resources to produce a variety of reports for the managers of the company concerning its sales activities. Managers use the knowledge gained from such information products to help them make decisions to improve the sales performance of the company. Figure 1–10 and the following analysis spotlight many examples of the resources, products, and activities of the information system described in Real World Application 1–2. How many of them did you identify?

REAL WORLD APPLICATION 1–2

ABC Department Stores

ABC Department Stores is a regional chain of small department stores in the Southwest. It uses computers for various information processing jobs, such as processing sales transactions, analysis of sales performance, employee payroll processing, and preparation of monthly customer statements. Here's what happened on a typical day in an ABC Department Store. Marsha Johnson walked up to the customer service counter and presented an automatic toaster she wanted to buy, along with her plastic credit card, to the salesclerk, Dave Kent. Dave used a point-of-sale (POS) terminal (an electronic cash register terminal) to record the sale. He entered the details of the transaction (product, department, and store codes) into the store's computer system using a handheld optical scanning *wand* to scan the special coding on the toaster's merchandise tag. The correct recording of this data was signaled by an audible "beep" from the POS terminal.

Information about the sale was immediately shown on the terminal's display screen. Dave inserted Marsha's credit card into a slot in the POS terminal. The terminal read her customer account number from the magnetic stripe on the back of the card. This data was transmitted to the store's computer along with information about her purchase. The computer checked her customer record, which was stored on its magnetic disk units. Then it completed the rest of the tasks required by the instructions in the *sales transaction program* it was following. This included changing Marsha's customer record to reflect the details of the sale and causing a sales receipt to be printed by Dave's POS terminal. Dave then taped the receipt to the boxed toaster and handed it to Marsha.

Meanwhile, Jennifer Baker, the store buyer, was using her video display terminal to find out which types of small appliances were the most popular with the store's customers. "DISPLAY ALL SALES OF APPLIANCES FOR TYPE = SMALL AND YEAR = 1989" she typed, using the keyboard of her terminal. Instantly, the information was displayed on her video screen. The computer had translated and acted on her request by following the instructions in a *database management* program that extracted sales data from the company's computerized files.

While this was going on, Joan Alvarez, the store manager, was talking to Jim Klugman, vice president for information systems of the company. "I need more information about sales than I am getting from these reports that the computer keeps printing," she was saying. "When will the systems analyst and programmer be done with the new sales analysis program and procedures they're developing? It's taking me too long to interpret our sales analysis reports."

Jim Klugman responded: "We will be done soon. We lost some time yesterday when one of our computer operators erased the wrong magnetic disk. Luckily, our backup and recovery procedures and our operating system control program got us running again quickly."

Joan replied, "I hope the new sales analysis system is operational by the end of this month. If not, I'm going to have to use an electronic spreadsheet program and my personal computer to try to get the information I want from our sales data that way."

Application Questions

☐ Identify the basic system components (the input, processing, output, storage, and control activities) of the information system for ABC Department Stores.

☐ Can you identify the hardware, software, people, and data *resources*, and the information *products* of this information system? Try it. Then read the rest of this section and try it again.

Figure 1–10 Analysis of the sales information system at ABC Department Stores using the information systems model.

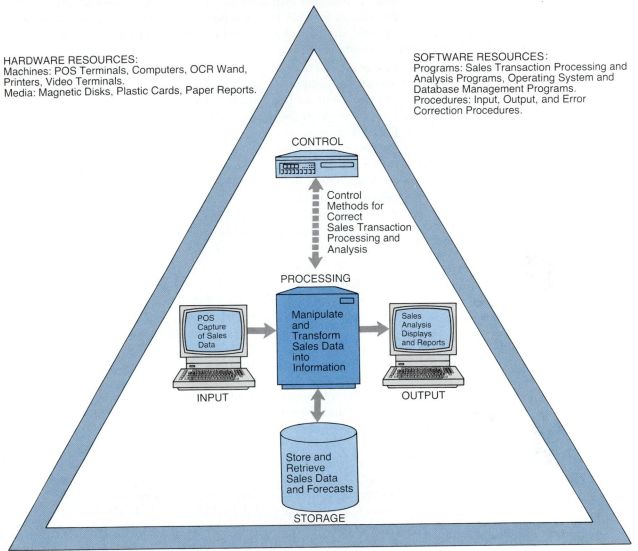

HARDWARE RESOURCES:
Machines: POS Terminals, Computers, OCR Wand, Printers, Video Terminals.
Media: Magnetic Disks, Plastic Cards, Paper Reports.

SOFTWARE RESOURCES:
Programs: Sales Transaction Processing and Analysis Programs, Operating System and Database Management Programs.
Procedures: Input, Output, and Error Correction Procedures.

CONTROL

Control Methods for Correct Sales Transaction Processing and Analysis

PROCESSING

POS Capture of Sales Data

Manipulate and Transform Sales Data into Information

Sales Analysis Displays and Reports

INPUT

OUTPUT

Store and Retrieve Sales Data and Forecasts

STORAGE

PEOPLE RESOURCES:
Specialists: Computer Operator, Systems Analyst, Programmer.
Users: Customer, Salesperson, Buyer, Store Manager.

☐ **Hardware Resources.**

Machines: point of sale (POS) terminals; store computer; personal computer; optical scanning wand; magnetic disk drives; video display terminals; printers.

Media: magnetic disks; paper merchandise tags; plastic credit card with magnetic stripe; paper sales receipts; paper reports.

Analysis of the Sales Information System at ABC Department Stores

☐ **Software Resources.**
Programs for sales transaction processing, sales analysis, system control, database management, and electronic spreadsheets. Procedures for POS terminal input, error correction, credit authorization, computer backup and recovery, and sales analysis interpretation.

☐ **People Resources.**
Specialists: computer operators; systems analysts; programmers; vice president for Information Systems.
Users: customers; salesclerks; buyers; store manager.

☐ **Data Resources.**
Customer data; product data; salesperson data; department data; store data; company data. Some data are captured by input activities. Other data are stored as records in computerized files.

☐ **Information Products.**
Video displays for salesclerks, buyers and managers; paper reports for managers; paper documents (sales receipts) for customers; audible signals for salesclerks.

Analysis of Information System Activities

☐ **Input Activities.**
Data describing individual sales transactions is collected by salesclerks using POS terminals and other devices and entered into the information system according to established procedures.

☐ **Processing Activities.**
The sales data is manipulated and organized by a computer according to instructions contained in sales transaction processing and analysis programs and in other programs. The company's customer and sales data in storage is updated, and information products are prepared for output.

☐ **Output Activities.**
Sales analysis displays and reports are produced for managers and buyers. These information products reveal important trends in sales activity, organized according to such categories as customer, product, salesperson, and department. Audible signals and visual displays of data entry are provided to sales clerks. Sales receipts are produced for customers.

☐ **Storage Activities.**
Sales data are stored as organized records and files on magnetic disk units. This data, along with historical sales data and sales forecasts, are updated and retrieved by the processing function.

☐ **Control Activities.**
Various methods are used to control information system performance. For example, hardware contains circuitry that can detect errors during *processing*, and programs contain instructions that can detect errors during *input* activities. Procedures help the salesclerks detect and correct errors during input using audible signals and video displays. Even the sales receipt allows customers to monitor the accuracy of the system.

Section III: The Past, Present, and Future

You have been introduced to the concepts of information system hardware, software, and people resources—and their use in processing data resources into information products. We will cover these topics in more detail in subsequent chapters. Now it's time for us to take a brief look at how computers developed into the vital tools they are today. It is important to examine each major stage or **generation** in the development of computers. This should help you discover several major trends that have developed in the past and are expected to continue into the future.

Take a look at Figure 1–11. It outlines the major trends and developments of the computer generations. All of the terms used in this figure are explained in this text. Refer to the Glossary and Index at the back of this text if you want to look up some of these terms now.

Figure 1–11 Major trends and developments of the computer generations. This figure indicates when each development first became a major characteristic of information systems technology. It also spotlights the major trends that have developed and are expected to continue into the future.

Major Characteristics	First Generation	Second Generation	Third Generation	Fourth Generation	Fifth Generation?
COMPUTER CIRCUITRY	Vacuum Tubes	Transistors	Integrated Semiconductor Circuits	Large-Scale Integrated (LSI) Semiconductor Circuits	Very Large-Scale Integrated (VLSI) Superconductor Circuits
TREND: Towards Smaller, Faster, More Reliable, and Lower Cost Computers.					
MAIN MEMORY	Magnetic Drum	Magnetic Core	Magnetic Core	LSI Semiconductor Circuits	VLSI Superconductor Circuits
TREND: Towards Large Capacities Using Smaller Microelectronic Circuits.					
SECONDARY STORAGE	Magnetic Tape Magnetic Drum	Magnetic Tape Magnetic Disk	Magnetic Disk Magnetic Tape	Magnetic Disk Floppy Disk Magnetic Bubble Optical Disk	Optical Disk and Card Magnetic Disk
TREND: Towards Massive Capacities Using Magnetic and Optical Media.					
INPUT MEDIA/ METHOD	Punched Cards Paper Tape	Punched Cards	Key to Tape/Disk	Keyboard Data Entry Direct Input Devices Optical Recognition	Speech Input Tactile Input
TREND: Towards Direct Input Devices that Are Easy to Use.					
OUTPUT MEDIA/ METHOD	Punched Cards Printed Reports	Punched Cards Printed Reports	Printed Reports Video Displays	Video Displays Audio Responses Printed Reports	Graphics Displays Voice Responses
TREND: Towards Direct Output Devices that Communicate Quickly and Clearly.					
SOFTWARE	User-Written Programs Machine Language	Packaged Programs Symbolic Languages	Operating Systems High-Level Languages	Database Management Systems Fourth-Generation Languages Microcomputer Packages	Natural Languages General-Purpose Integrated Packages
TREND: Towards Easy-to-Use Application Packages and Natural Programming Languages.					
OTHER DEVELOPMENTS	Batch Processing	Overlapped Processing Realtime Processing Data Communications	Time Sharing Multiprogramming Multiprocessing Minicomputers	Microprogramming Virtual Memory Distributed Processing Microcomputers	Parallel Processing Knowledge-Based Systems Intelligent Computers and Robots
TREND: Towards People Having Immediate Access to Computers Anytime and Anywhere for Any Uses.					

TIME CAPSULES

Volumes could be written on the past, present, and future of computers. Instead, this section provides you with the following brief **time capsules**. Read them for an understanding of the high points of developments and trends in computing.

- ☐ The Origin of Computing Machines
- ☐ Computer Pioneers
- ☐ The First Three Generations
- ☐ The Present Fourth Generation
- ☐ The Microcomputer Revolution
- ☐ The Future Fifth Generation

TIME CAPSULE: THE ORIGIN OF COMPUTING MACHINES

The modern computer has many origins, some well known, some lost in antiquity. Early manual computing devices and the use of machinery to perform arithmetic operations were important advancements. However, these and other devices were not computers, though they were important contributions to the development of machine computation.

- ☐ The earliest data processing devices included the use of fingers, stones, and sticks for counting, and knots on a string, scratches on a rock, or notches in a stick as record-keeping devices. The Babylonians wrote on clay tablets with a sharp stick, while the ancient Egyptians developed written records on papyrus using a sharp-pointed reed as a pen and organic dyes for ink. The earliest form of manual calculating device was the abacus. The use of pebbles or rods laid out on a lined or grooved board were early forms of the abacus and were used for thousands of years in many civilizations. The abacus in its present form originated in China and is still used as a calculator.

- ☐ The use of machinery to perform arithmetic operations is frequently attributed to Blaise Pascal of France and Gottfried von Leibnitz of Germany for their development of the *adding machine* and the *calculating machine*, respectively, in the 17th century. (The programming language **Pascal** is named in honor of Blaise Pascal.) However, the inventions of Pascal and Leibnitz incorporated some ideas similar to

those used in the clockwork mechanism and the odometer, both of which had been developed as far back as the Greek and Roman civilizations. It must also be recognized that the calculators of Pascal and Leibnitz—and other early mechanical data processing devices—were not reliable machines. The contributions of many persons were necessary during the next two centuries before practical, working data processing machines were developed.

- ☐ The use of *electromechanical punched card machines* for the automatic processing of data recorded by holes punched in paper cards was another major development in machine computation. Punched cards were developed in France by Joseph Jacquard during the 18th century to automatically control textile weaving equipment. However, their use in data processing originated with the work of the statistician Dr. Herman Hollerith during the 1880s. He was hired by the U.S. Bureau of the Census to develop new ways to process census data. The 1880 census report had not been completed until 1887, and it became evident that the processing of the 1890 census might not be completed before the 1900 census would get under way.

  Dr. Hollerith developed a punched paper card for the recording of data, a hand-operated card punch, a sorting box, and a tabulator that allowed the 1890 census to be completed in less than three years. Dr. Hollerith then left the Census Bureau to start a business firm to produce punched card machines. The International Business Machines Corporation (IBM) is a descendant of Dr. Hollerith's Tabulating Machine Company.

- ☐ Improvements in punched card machines led to their widespread use in the late 1930s. These machines could "read" the data from punched cards when electrical impulses were generated by the action of metal brushes making electrical contact through the holes punched in a card. Data processing operations were "programmed" by an externally wired removable control panel. Electromechanical punched card machines continued to be the major method for large-scale "automatic data processing" (ADP) in business and government until the late 1950s, when they were made obsolete by the development of computers.

An abacus: The first manual calculator.

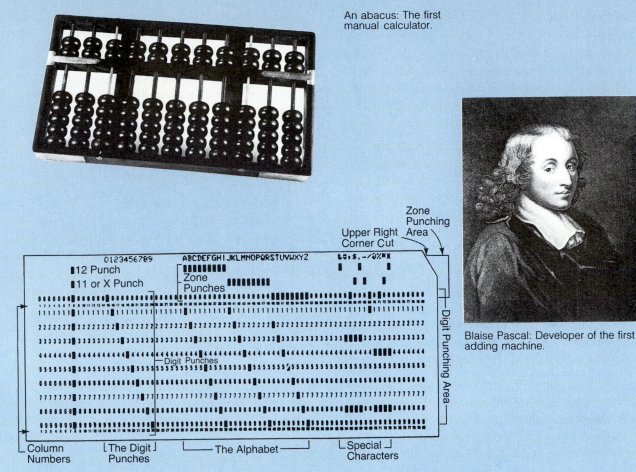

Blaise Pascal: Developer of the first adding machine.

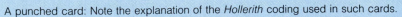

A punched card: Note the explanation of the *Hollerith* coding used in such cards.

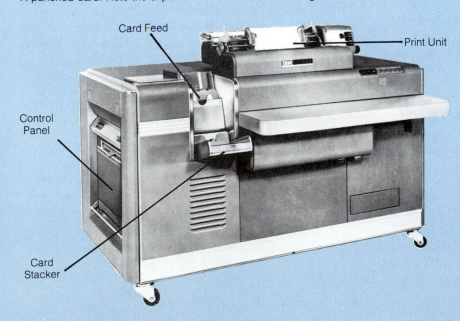

An electromechanical punched card accounting machine.

TIME CAPSULE: COMPUTER PIONEERS

Charles Babbage is generally recognized as the first person to propose the concept of the modern computer. He designed and partially built a steam-driven mechanical calculator called the "difference engine" with the help of a grant from the British government. In 1833, this English mathematician outlined in detail his plans for an "analytical engine," a mechanical steam-driven computing machine that would accept punched card input, automatically perform any arithmetic operation in any sequence under the direction of a mechanically stored program of instructions, and produce either punched card or printed output. He produced thousands of detailed drawings before his death in 1871, but the machine was never built. Babbage had designed the world's first general-purpose, stored-program, digital computer, but his ideas were too advanced for the technology of his time.

Many of Babbage's ideas were recorded and analyzed by Lady Augusta Ada Byron, Countess of Lovelace, the daughter of Lord Byron, the famous English poet. She is considered by some to be the world's first computer programmer. The programming language **Ada** is named in her honor.

Almost a hundred years passed before the ideas outlined by Babbage began to be developed. Highlights of this pioneering period include:

- Vannevar Bush of the Massachusetts Institute of Technology (MIT) built a large-scale electromechanical analog computer in 1925.
- Konrad Zuse of Germany built an electromechanical digital computer in 1941. Called the Z3, it used electrical switches (relays) to perform its computations.
- The first large-scale electromechanical digital computer was developed by Howard Aiken of Harvard University with the support of IBM in 1944. Aiken's Automatic Sequence Controlled Calculator, nicknamed MARK I, used electrical relays instead of mechanical gears. It relied heavily on the concepts of IBM's punched card calculator developed in the 1930s.
- The first working model of an electronic digital computer was built by John Atanasoff of Iowa State University in 1942. The ABC (Atanasoff-Berry Computer) used vacuum tubes instead of electrical relays to carry out its computations.

- The first operational electronic digital computer, the ENIAC (Electronic Numerical Integrator and Calculator), was developed by John Mauchly and J. P. Eckert of the University of Pennsylvania in 1946. The ENIAC weighed over 30 tons and utilized over 18,000 vacuum tubes instead of the electromechanical relays of the Mark I. The ENIAC was built to compute artillery ballistic tables for the U.S. Army; it could complete in 15 seconds a trajectory computation that would take a skilled person with a desk calculator about 10 hours to complete. However, the ENIAC was not a "stored program" computer and utilized the decimal system. Its processing was controlled externally by switches and control panels that had to be changed for each new series of computations.
- The first stored-program electronic computer was EDSAC (Electronic Delayed Storage Automatic Computer) developed under the direction of M. V. Wilkes at Cambridge University, England, in 1949.
- The EDSAC and the first American stored-program computer, the EDVAC (Electronic Discrete Variable Automatic Computer), which was completed in 1952, were based on concepts advanced in 1945 by Dr. John von Neumann of the Institute for Advanced Study in Princeton, New Jersey. He proposed that the operating instructions, or *program*, of the computer be stored in a high-speed internal storage unit, or *memory*, and that both data and instructions be represented internally by the *binary* number system rather than the decimal system. These and other computer design concepts form the basis for much of the design of present-day computers.

Several other early computers and many individuals could be mentioned in a discussion of the pioneering period of computer development. However, the high points discussed should illustrate that many persons and many ideas were responsible for the birth of the computer.

The difference engine: A mechanical calculator built by Babbage.

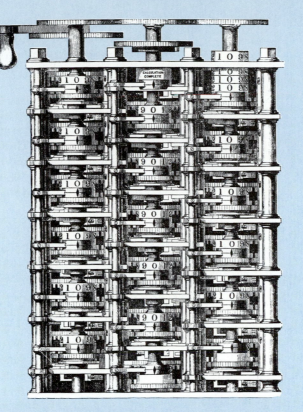

Charles Babbage: He first proposed the concept of a computer.

The ENIAC computer: The first general-purpose electronic digital computer. Also shown is one of its inventors, J. P. Eckert.

Augusta Ada Byron: Considered to be the first computer programmer.

TIME CAPSULE: THE FIRST THREE GENERATIONS

The UNIVAC I (Universal Automatic Computer), the first general-purpose electronic digital computer to be commercially available, marks the beginning of the **first generation** of computers. Highlights of this generation include:

☐ The first UNIVAC was installed at the Bureau of Census in 1951. The UNIVAC I became the first computer to process business applications when it was installed at a General Electric manufacturing plant in Louisville, Kentucky, in 1954. An innovation of the UNIVAC I was the use of *magnetic tape* as an input and output medium.

☐ Another first-generation computer, the IBM 650, was an intermediate-size computer designed for both business and scientific applications. It had a *magnetic drum* memory and used punched cards for input and output.

☐ Computers developed before the first generation were special-purpose one-of-a-kind machines, whereas 48 UNIVAC Is and almost 2,000 IBM 650s were built.

☐ The first generation of computers were quite large and produced enormous amounts of heat because of their use of **vacuum tubes.** They had large electrical power, air conditioning, maintenance, and space requirements.

The **second generation** of computers was introduced in 1959. Highlights of this generation include:

☐ Vacuum tubes were replaced by **transistors** and other *solid state, semiconductor* devices. Transistorized circuits were a lot smaller, generated little heat, were less expensive, and required less power than vacuum tube circuits. Second-generation computers were thus significantly smaller and faster and more reliable than first-generation machines.

☐ The use of *magnetic cores* as the primary internal storage medium, and the introduction of removable *magnetic disk packs* were other major hardware developments of the second generation. Magnetic tape emerged as the major input/output and *secondary* storage medium for large computer installations, with punched cards continuing to be widely used.

The introduction of the IBM System/360 series of computers in 1964 signaled the arrival of the **third generation** of computers. Highlights of this generation include:

☐ Transistorized circuitry was replaced by **integrated circuits** in which all the elements of an electronic circuit were contained on a small silicon wafer or *chip.* These microelectronic circuits were smaller and more reliable than transistorized circuits and significantly increased the speed and reduced the size of third-generation computers.

☐ The *family* or *series* concept, which provides standardization and compatibility between different models in a computer series, was developed. Manufacturers claimed to have developed computers that could handle both business and scientific applications and process programs written for other models without major modifications.

☐ The emergence of *time-sharing* (where many users at different terminals can share the same computer at the same time), *data communications* applications, and the ability to process several programs simultaneously through *multiprogramming* were other features of the third generation.

☐ The third generation marked the growth in importance of software as a means of efficiently using computers. **Operating systems** programs were developed to supervise computer processing. High-level programming languages, such as FORTRAN and COBOL, greatly simplified computer programming, since they allowed program instructions to be expressed in a form that resembles human language or the standard notation of mathematics.

☐ **Application software packages** (prewritten programs for users) proliferated as the number of independent software companies grew rapidly. This was the result of the *unbundling* of software and hardware in 1969 by IBM and other manufacturers. They began to charge separately for software and other services instead of including them in the price of the hardware.

☐ The first **minicomputer** was marketed by the Digital Equipment Corporation in 1965. These small computers had greater computing power than larger second-generation systems and came into widespread use.

The UNIVAC I: The first commercially available electronic digital computer. Also shown is J. P. Eckert and newscaster Walter Cronkite.

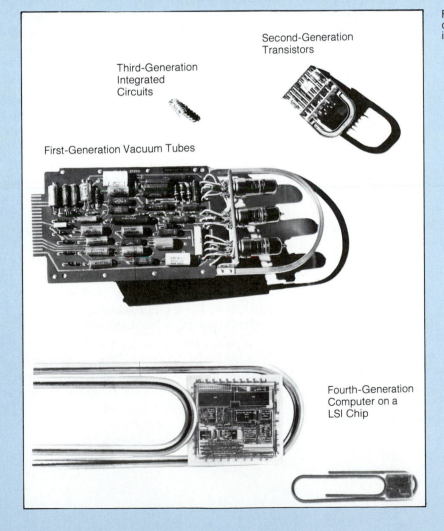

Four generations of computer circuitry. Notice the major changes in the size of these circuits.

Second-Generation Transistors

Third-Generation Integrated Circuits

First-Generation Vacuum Tubes

Fourth-Generation Computer on a LSI Chip

TIME CAPSULE: THE PRESENT FOURTH GENERATION

The **fourth generation** began in the 1970s and continues to the present time. The following developments are highlights of the fourth generation:

☐ A major technological development was the use of LSI (**large-scale integration**) semiconductor circuits for both the *logic* and *memory* circuitry of computers. The use of such microelectronic **semiconductor memories** was a dramatic change from the *magnetic core* memories used in second- and third-generation computers. LSI semiconductor technology enables thousands of electronic components to be placed on a tiny chip of silicon.

☐ LSI technology led to the development of a **microprocessor** in 1971 by a team led by M. E. Hoff of the Intel Corporation. All of the circuitry for the main processing unit of a computer was placed on a single chip! This was followed by the development of the Intel 8080 microprocessor in 1974, which was used in the first commercially available **microcomputer** system, the Altair 8800 in 1975. However, microcomputer sales and uses did not grow dramatically until the development of the Apple® II by Steve Jobs and Steve Wozniak in 1978, and the IBM® Personal Computer® in 1981.

☐ Main memory capacity of fourth-generation computers increased dramatically. For example, a medium-size second-generation business computer like the IBM 1401 had a memory of 4,000 to 16,000 character positions of storage. In comparison, the fourth-generation IBM 4361 medium-size computer has a main memory capacity of 4 to 16 *million* characters of storage. Even microcomputers soon had memories with hundreds of thousands of positions. The cost of such memory capacity dropped in the same period from about $2 per character to only a fraction of a cent per character of storage.

☐ The trend toward increased microminiaturization significantly reduced the cost, size, and power requirements of fourth-generation computers, and greatly increased their processing speeds. Processing speeds in billionths of a second and in millions of instructions per second are common. The decrease in computer hardware costs is remarkable. The computing power of third-generation business computers costing hundreds of thousands of dollars can be purchased with fourth-generation professional microcomputers costing only a few thousand dollars.

☐ Another trend was the increased use of *direct input/output* devices to provide a more natural *user interface*. Data and instructions were increasingly entered into a computer system directly through a keyboard or other input devices such as the *electronic mouse, light pens, touch screens, data tablets,* and *optical scanning wands*. Direct output of information through video displays of text and graphics and audio (voice) response devices also became commonplace.

☐ The trend toward programming languages that were easy to use and more like human languages continued. *Database management systems (DBMS)* and *natural* or *fourth-generation* languages (4GL) not only make programming computers easier for programmers but reduce the need for traditional programming. Users do not have to tell the computer *how* to do a task, but only *what* task they want accomplished.

☐ Easy-to-use software packages for microcomputer users, such as *electronic spreadsheet* and *word processing* programs were developed. The development of the VisiCalc® electronic spreadsheet program and the WordStar® word processing package in 1979, and the dBASE II® database management package and the LOTUS® 1-2-3® integrated package in 1982 contributed to the purchase of millions of software packages by microcomputer users.

☐ Computers have come into such widespread use that by the mid-1980s millions of computer systems were in use. Most of these computers were not large "mainframes" but were microcomputer and minicomputer systems.

IBM 3090: A large-size fourth-generation computer system.

	First Generation	Second Generation	Third Generation	Fourth Generation	Fifth Generation
SIZE (Typical computers)	Room Size	Closet Size	Desk-Size Minicomputer	Typewriter-Size Microcomputer	Credit Card-Size Micro?
DENSITY (Components per circuit)	One	Hundreds	Thousands	Hundreds of Thousands	Millions?
SPEED (Instructions/second)	Hundreds	Thousands	Millions	Tens of Millions	Billions?
RELIABILITY (Failure of circuits)	Hours	Days	Weeks	Months	Years?
MEMORY (Capacity in characters)	Thousands	Tens of Thousands	Hundreds of Thousands	Millions	Billions?
COST (Per million instructions)	$10	$1.00	$.10	$.001	$.0001?

Trends in computer characteristics and capabilities.

TIME CAPSULE: THE MICROCOMPUTER REVOLUTION

The development of **microcomputers** is being heralded not only as a major development of the fourth computer generation, but as a major technological breakthrough that has started a "second computer revolution."

Are such claims justified? It appears that they are. The microcomputer revolution can be described as a technological breakthrough that is bringing computer power to both *people* and *products*. The four major dimensions of this revolution are (1) microcomputer technology, (2) distributed processing, (3) personal computing, and (4) smart products.

Microcomputer Technology

The development of microcomputers represents a major revolution in computer science and technology due to accelerating trends in microelectronics. Microcomputers range in size from a "computer on a chip" to typewriter-size units. Thus, computers of small size and cost—but of great speed, capacity, and reliability—are now a reality. Therefore, microprocessors and microcomputers are changing the design and capabilities of computer hardware and software.

Microcomputer technology requires a complex and delicate process for the production of microelectronic circuit chips. Since only a single speck of dust can ruin a chip, the entire process is done in "clean rooms," where workers are dressed in surgical-type clothing and the air is constantly filtered.

Distributed Processing

Distributed processing is a new type of information processing made possible by a network of computers dispersed throughout an organization. Microprocessors and microcomputers now allow many data input, output, storage, and communication devices to become powerful "intelligent" processors or terminals with their own computer capability. Though started by the minicomputer, the microcomputer thus makes truly possible the dispersion of computer processing away from a central computer and out to the users in an organization. Distributed processing in branch offices, retail stores, factories, office buildings, remote locations, and other worksites is the result of this development.

Personal Computing

Personal computing involves the use of microcomputers as personal computers by individuals for business, professional, educational, recreational, home management, and other personal applications. Thus, the power of computerized data processing is now finally available to everyone. Microcomputers are small, affordable, powerful, and easy to use. Millions of these computer systems are currently in use. Personal computing at home, at work, or at play is the result of this development. Much of this text and its photographs emphasize the role played by microcomputers for personal computing.

Smart Products

It is now economically and technologically feasible to use microprocessors to improve and enhance a host of industrial and consumer products and to create many new ones. **Smart products** with "intelligence" provided by built-in microcomputers or microprocessors that significantly improve their performance and capabilities are the result of this development. Smart consumer products range from electronic games and toys (some with "talking" microprocessor chips) to microwave ovens and automobiles with microprocessor intelligence, and even "smart cards"—credit cards with microprocessor chips embedded in them! Smart commercial and industrial products range from talking calculators and smart copying machines to industrial robots.

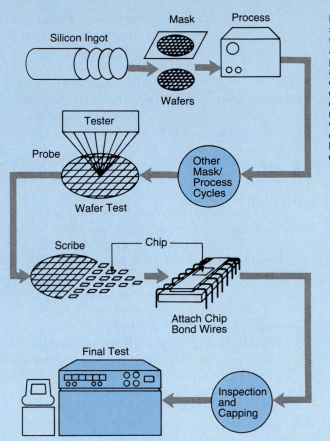

How microelectronic chips are made. Crystals of pure silicon are grown in the laboratory and sliced into paper-thin *wafers*. Microscopic circuits are etched on the silicon wafer in a series of layers in a complex photolithographic process. This process involves repeatedly bathing the wafer in chemicals and exposing it to ultraviolet light through circuit patterns called *masks*. Gradually, the process results in a complex grid of circuits composed of transistors, resistors, capacitors, and other circuit elements. Several firms have begun to produce microelectronic circuits by drawing them directly on a wafer with a computer-controlled electron beam! After testing the circuits on the wafer it is sectioned into several hundred chips. Defective chips are discarded and good chips are sealed with external wiring in individual packages.

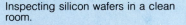

Inspecting silicon wafers in a clean room.

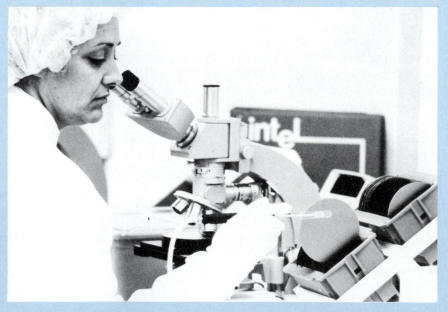

TIME CAPSULE: THE FUTURE FIFTH GENERATION

Developments in the present computer generation and the microcomputer revolution indicate the continued revolutionary impact of computers on business and the rest of society. It is apparent that several major trends will continue into a future **fifth generation** of computing.

- *Intelligent computers* with the ability to see, listen, talk, and think are the goal of the fifth generation! The United States, Japan, and others hope to produce such computers with a *parallel processing* computer architecture that is different from the traditional *von Neumann design* of current computers. Fifth-generation computers will process data and instructions in *parallel* (many at a time), instead of *serially* (one at a time) as done by today's computers. The development of intelligent computer systems is one of the main goals of the science of *artificial intelligence* (AI).

- The fifth generation will also accelerate the trend toward direct input/output of data and instructions. Voice and visual input will be coupled with voice and visual output to make obsolete most present methods of communicating with a computer.

- Computer hardware costs and sizes will continue to decrease steadily. This will be a major effect of the increased use of VLSI (very large-scale integration) technology where hundreds of thousands and even millions of circuit elements are placed on a microelectronic chip. This trend will accelerate with the development of **superconductor** circuit materials which do not need super-cold temperatures to dramatically increase the speed of electronic circuits.

- Also on the horizon are *optical computers* that use *photonic* or optoelectronic circuits rather than electronic circuits. They process data using pulses of laser light instead of electronic pulses, and operate near the speed of light. Further into the future are extremely small, fast, and powerful *biocomputers* grown from organic materials using individuals cells as circuits!

- Computer software will continue to grow in its ease of use and versatility. Users will converse with computers in natural human languages. Application software packages will become integrated general-purpose programs that can easily handle a variety of tasks for nontechnical users.

- Use of microcomputers and microprocessors will continue to increase dramatically. Smart products—especially industrial *robots*—will multiply as microcomputer intelligence is built into more and more consumer, commercial, and industrial products.

- The office of the future will become a reality by blending computerized word processing, data processing, and telecommunications. Distributed networks of *intelligent workstations* and other computerized office devices will create *automated office* typing, dictation, copying, and filing systems, as well as *electronic mail* and message systems.

- Advanced information systems will merge the transmission and processing of data, images, and voices. This will involve extensive use of earth satellites, *fiber optics*, and *laser/optical disk* technology in advanced telecommunication systems.

- Computers and computerized workstations will become integrated into everyday business operations in offices, small business firms, wholesale and retail outlets, warehouses, and factories. Managers will rely heavily on computer-based management information systems (MIS), decision support systems (DSS), and *expert systems* based on artificial intelligence to help them make better business decisions.

- Society as a whole will become increasingly reliant on computers in many areas. Everyday use of computer-based systems—such as *electronic funds transfer* (EFT) systems in banking, *point-of-sale* (POS) systems in retailing, *computer-assisted instruction* (CAI) systems in education, and *videotex* systems for electronic shopping, banking, and information services in the home—will increase dramatically.

REAL WORLD APPLICATION 1–3

Toward the Fifth Generation

It is 1995 and the popular images of science fiction have been transformed into fact: intelligent humanoid machines in the form of robots; computers that see, hear, speak, and reason; knowledgeable systems that are nourished by the input of a genius's storehouse of wisdom, able to hold and use that knowledge forever.

This script for tomorrow, however, is not from a Hollywood dream factory or the pages of an Isaac Asimov novel. These images are the very practical perceptions of researchers in both academia and industry, and the boundary between fact and fiction has grown increasingly hazy. The future is no longer measured in space odyssey fantasies but in the price/performance specifications of an industry waiting to explode. This is the fifth generation, the next significant step in the evolution of computing; the leap forward that, if successful, will bring the future in.

The computer industry coined the fifth-generation term to describe the goal of creating powerful, intelligent computers by the mid-1990s. Since then, fifth generation has become an umbrella description encompassing work being done in the fields of parallel processing, artificial intelligence, expert systems, robotics, natural language, vision systems, and more.

The fifth generation is not without controversy, however. Debate has raged around artificial intelligence (AI), for example, since serious work in that field began in the 1950s. Not only technological but moral and philosophical questions about the concept of intelligent, "thinking" machines abound. Though pioneering work has been done in many of the subgroups that fall under the AI mantle, critics claim that devising many of the algorithms needed to impart true humanlike capabilities is simply not possible.

Fifth-generation computers, which will either depart from or drastically alter current architectures, are under development in the United States, Europe, and Japan. These new supercomputers, employing parallel rather than serial processing, promise to bring about massive change in the computer industry during the next quarter century.

Besides the goal of creating intelligent knowledge processing machines, fifth-generation computers will perfect the following current developments in AI:

☐ Expert systems—software that attempts to duplicate the decision-making process of human experts in a given field such as geology, medicine, engineering, or business.

☐ Natural language software—programs that allow the user to query the computer and access data in a conversational style as opposed to specific computer commands.

☐ Visual and tactile recognition—software and hardware being developed primarily for applications associated with robotics, allowing a robot to discern particular objects, shapes, or components by the senses of sight and touch.

☐ Voice recognition—hardware and software designed to analyze the sound of and identify each spoken word.

Application Questions

☐ How will fifth-generation computers differ from current computers?

☐ What developments in the field of artificial intelligence will be part of fifth-generation computing?

Source: Adapted from Glenn Rifkin, "Towards the Fifth Generation," *Computerworld*, May 6, 1985, Update, pp. 3–8.

SUMMARY

☐ An understanding of computers and information systems is very important today. These are major tools by which we can properly use information resources for the benefit of society. The speed, accuracy, reliability, and economy of using computers for information processing has become a necessity for the operation and management of business firms and other organizations.

☐ The computer is a device that has the ability to accept data; internally store and automatically execute a program of instructions; perform mathematical, logical, and manipulative operations on data; and report the results.

☐ A system is a group of interrelated components working toward the attainment of a common goal by accepting inputs and producing outputs in an organized transformation process. Feedback is information concerning the components and operations of a system. Control is the component that monitors and evaluates feedback to determine whether the system is moving toward the achievement of its goal, and then makes necessary adjustments to the input and processing components to ensure that proper output is produced.

☐ An information system uses the resources of hardware (machines and media), software (programs and procedures), and people (specialists and users) to perform input, processing, output, storage, and control activities that transform data resources into information products. Data is first collected and converted to a form that is suitable for processing (input). Then the data is manipulated or converted into information (processing), stored for future use (storage), or communicated to its ultimate user (output) according to correct processing procedures (control).

☐ The concept of hardware resources includes both machines and media used in information processing. Software resources include both computerized instructions (programs) and instructions for people (procedures). People resources include both information systems specialists and users. Data resources include both traditional numeric and alphabetic data, and text, image, and audio data. Information products produced by an information processing system can take a variety of forms, including paper reports, visual displays, documents, messages, menus, graphics, and audio responses.

☐ The development of microcomputers in the fourth computer generation has been acclaimed as a revolution because it is bringing computer power to both people and products. Computer processing capability is being brought to the users in an organization through distributed processing and to everyone in society through personal computing and smart products.

☐ Major trends expected in a future fifth generation of computing are the development of intelligent computers, continued decreases in the size and cost of computer hardware, and the growth of general-purpose, easy-to-use software. Smart products will multiply, automated offices and factories will become a reality, managers will use computer-assisted decision systems, and the everyday use of computers in society will accelerate.

☐ Major trends and developments in computers and information systems during the five computer generations are summarized in Figure 1–11.

These are the key terms and concepts of this chapter. The page number of their first explanation is in parenthesis.

KEY TERMS AND CONCEPTS

1. Benefits of computer use (33)
2. Common data elements (39)
   a. Character
   b. Field
   c. Record
   d. File
   e. Database
3. Computer (35)
4. Computer generations (49)
5. Computer-based information system (43)
6. Data or information processing (36)
7. Distributed processing (58)
8. Information system activities (40)
   a. Input
   b. Processing
   c. Output
   d. Storage
   e. Control
9. Information system resources (42)
   a. Hardware
   b. Software
   c. People
   d. Data
10. Information products (43)
11. Information system (40)
12. Integrated circuit (54)
13. Machines (42)
14. Media (42)
15. Microcomputer (58)
16. Personal computing (58)
17. Procedure (42)
18. Program (42)
19. Smart products (58)
20. Source document (43)
21. System (37)

Match one of the **key terms and concepts** listed above with one of the brief examples or definitions listed below. Look for the "best" fit for answers that seem to fit more than one key term or concept. Defend your choices.

REVIEW AND APPLICATION QUIZ

_____ 1. Major stages in the development of computers.
_____ 2. Programs and procedures.
_____ 3. A set of instructions for a computer.
_____ 4. A set of instructions for people.
_____ 5. A device that can accept data, automatically execute a program of instructions, and report the results.
_____ 6. Automobiles with automatic fuel injection.
_____ 7. Machines and media.
_____ 8. The IBM PC or the Apple Macintosh®.
_____ 9. Computer disk drives, video monitors, printers, and so on.
_____ 10. Magnetic disks, magnetic tape, paper forms, and so on.

_____ 11. Individuals using computers at home, school, or work.

_____ 12. Computer systems analysts, programmers, operators, and users.

_____ 13. Many electronic circuits on a tiny silicon chip.

_____ 14. A network of cooperating computers in an organization.

_____ 15. Using the keyboard of a computer to enter data.

_____ 16. Having a sales receipt to document a purchase you made.

_____ 17. Printing a letter you wrote using a computer.

_____ 18. Saving a copy of the letter on a magnetic disk.

_____ 19. Computing loan payments.

_____ 20. Your name, social security number, and address.

_____ 21. The name, social security number, and address of everyone in an organization.

_____ 22. A collection of related data files.

_____ 23. Transforming data into information.

_____ 24. A group of interrelated components working together toward the attainment of a common goal.

_____ 25. Facts or observations.

_____ 26. Printed reports and documents or graphics displays for users.

APPLICATION PROBLEMS

1. If you have not already done so, read and answer the questions after the three Real World Applications in this chapter.

2. Get started in the use of computers. Complete the assignment suggested at the beginning of this chapter entitled "Getting Started in Computers."

3. Have you read and done one of the assignments of the first section of Appendix A at the end of this text? Its purpose is to give you a "hands-on" experience with using a personal computer. Now you should apply the *information systems model* explained in this chapter to your experience. What are the hardware, software, people, and data resources you used? Identify the input, processing, output, storage, and control activities involved. What information products did you produce?

4. Each statement below gives an example of information system resources, products, or activities. Identify which of these are involved and explain each answer.

   a. A fire occurs in the data center, and all data stored on magnetic tapes or disks in the data center are lost. However, copies of these files have been stored in the vault at a local bank.

   b. Sales reports are not only printed on paper but are also written on magnetic tape.

   c. In the general ledger accounting system, each account (i.e., payroll expense) is given a number.

   d. The sales order processing system will not allow anyone to enter an order unless the quantity sold is present.

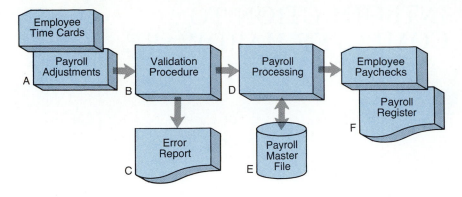

Figure 1–12 Flowchart of a payroll information system.

    e. A special report is printed listing customers in order of greatest sales volume to least sales volume.

5. Each major activity of an information system (input, processing, output, storage, and control) appears in the flowchart of a computerized payroll system shown in Figure 1–12. Each letter represents a different activity. Match each letter with one of the following activities:

    a. Input.   *d.* Storage.
    b. Processing.   *e.* Control (procedure).
    c. Output.   *f.* Control (feedback).

6. The Holiday Cheer Company, a manufacturer of Christmas ornaments and artificial Christmas trees, has been having problems with sales order processing. Currently the system is totally manual. The company has a competitive edge in the marketplace because of its outstanding designs and efficiency in production. The growth in sales has been 20 percent per year. The problems in sales order processing stem from a high volume of sales transactions and a lack of time to respond. Customers order 70 percent of their merchandise in the spring. Once they see what is selling during the fall, they order the remaining 30 percent of their merchandise. Most problems occur in processing these fall orders. Several days are required to process an order through the accounting department. Also the inventory records often indicate sufficient stock is on hand to fill an order when it really isn't. Once production receives an order it can take up to 10 days to fill. Should this company convert from manual processing to computerized information processing? Justify your answer.

7. Analyze a manual or computerized information system that you are familiar with using the information systems model. For example, you could analyze your use of an information system at a retail store, supermarket, school, or bank. Refer to the examples of the analysis of manual, microcomputer, and large systems given in Section Two of this chapter to help you in your analysis.

8. Refer to Figure 1–11. Can you think of different examples of new computer developments that fit each of the seven major trends shown in that figure? Give it a try, even if you have to speculate on future developments. Explain your choices.

INTRODUCTION TO COMPUTER HARDWARE

Chapter Outline

Learning Objectives

The purpose of this chapter is to promote a basic understanding of modern computers by analyzing (1) the components and functions of a computer system, (2) the basic types of computer hardware, and (3) microcomputers and other types of computer systems. After reading and studying this chapter, you should be able to:

1. Identify the components and functions of a computer system.
2. List the major types of computer hardware used for input, processing, output, and storage, especially for microcomputer systems.
3. Name the most commonly used computer storage capacity and time elements.
4. Outline the major differences and uses of microcomputers, minicomputers, and mainframe computers.
5. Identify the major characteristics and uses of supercomputers, analog computers, special-purpose computers, scientific computers, and multiprocessor computer systems.

THE COMPUTER SYSTEM CONCEPT

It would be easy to think of a microcomputer as a combination typewriter/TV set, or a large computer as a group of electronic devices in metal cabinets. However, it is absolutely vital to your effective use of computers to understand that the computer is not a solitary electronic data processing "black box." Nor is it an unrelated grouping of electronic devices performing a variety of information processing activities.

You should learn to understand the computer as a **system.** That is, a computer is an interrelated grouping of components that perform the basic system functions of **input, processing, output, storage,** and **control,** thus providing you with a powerful information processing tool. Your understanding of the computer as a **computer system** is one of the most important basic objectives of this text. For example, you should be able to visualize any computer (from a microcomputer to a supercomputer) as a system of hardware devices organized according to the following system functions:

☐ **Input.** The input devices of a computer system include keyboards, touch screens, electronic "mice," optical scanners, and so on. They convert data into electronic form for input into the computer system.

☐ **Processing.** The *central processing unit* (CPU) is the main processing component of a computer system. In particular, the *arithmetic-logic unit*, one of its major components, performs the arithmetic and logic functions required in computer processing.

☐ **Output.** The output devices of a computer system include video display units, printers, audio response units, and so on. They convert electronic information produced by the computer system into a *human-intelligible* or machine-readable form.

☐ **Storage.** The storage function of a computer system takes place in the *primary storage unit* of the CPU and in *secondary storage* devices such as magnetic disk and tape units. These devices store data and program instructions needed for processing.

☐ **Control.** The *control unit* of the CPU is the control component of a computer system. It interprets computer program instructions and transmits directions to the other components of the computer system.

Figure 2–1 illustrates this concept of the functions and hardware components of a computer system. Also refer to Figures 2–6 and 2–12 and to page 13 of the pictorial section in Chapter 1. They identify the system functions of devices used in microcomputers and large computer systems.

COMPUTER SYSTEM FUNCTIONS

You have now been introduced to the concept of the computer as a system of hardware devices. Let's take a closer look at how the system functions of input, processing, output, storage, and control are implemented in the hardware components of a computer system. Refer to Figure 2–1 if necessary, for a visual summary of these functions.

Figure 2–1 The computer system concept: A computer is a system of hardware components and functions.

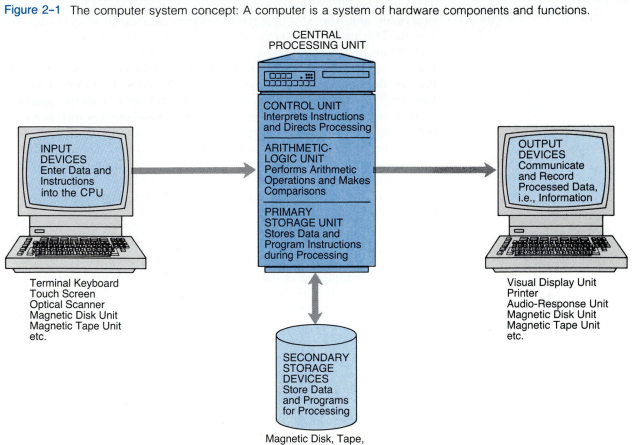

Data and program instructions are entered into the computer in the input function. Data and instructions may be entered directly into the computer system (through the keyboard of a computer terminal, for example) or may first be converted into a machine-readable input medium, such as magnetic disks or tape. For example, data from source documents could be recorded on magnetic disks and then be entered into the computer system through a magnetic disk unit. Most computer systems automatically control the flow of data and instructions into the computer from many types of **input devices,** such as keyboards, disk drives, and optical scanners. These input devices convert program instructions and data into electrical impulses that are then routed to the primary storage unit where they are held until needed.

The function of **output devices** is to convert processed data (information) from electronic impulses into a form that is intelligible to human beings or into a machine-readable form. For example, output devices such as high-speed printers produce printed reports; video terminals produce visual displays; and audio response units produce audible sounds and speech as output. Other devices record output in machine-readable code on media such as magnetic disks and tape. Most computers can automatically control several types of output devices.

Input/Output

**The CPU: Control,
Processing, and Storage**

The processing function of a computer system is performed by the **central processing unit,** the most important hardware component of any computer system. This unit is also known as the CPU, the *central processor,* or the **mainframe** in large computers, and as the *microprocessor* or MPU in a microcomputer. This is the unit that accomplishes the processing of data and controls the other parts of the system. The CPU consists of three subunits known as the **arithmetic-logic unit,** the **control unit,** and the **primary storage unit.** It also includes specialized circuitry and devices such as input/output interface devices and specialized processors. Examples are processors for arithmetic operations, input/output, and data communications. Such processors assist the CPU in its processing tasks. Chapter 4 will go into more detail on the various types and capabilities of computer processors and specialized processor devices. Let's now take a brief look at how the CPU performs its system functions.

The Control Unit

Every other component of the computer system is controlled and directed by the **control unit.** The control unit obtains instructions from the primary storage unit. After interpreting the instructions, the control unit transmits directions to the appropriate components of the computer system, ordering them to perform the required data processing operations. The control unit tells the input and secondary storage devices what data and instructions to read into memory; tells the arithmetic-logic unit where the data to be processed is located in memory, what operations to perform, and where in memory the results are to be stored. Finally, it directs the appropriate output devices to convert processed data into machine or human-readable output media.

The Arithmetic-Logic Unit

Arithmetic and comparison operations occur in the **arithmetic-logic unit** (or ALU). Depending on the application being processed, data may be transferred from primary storage to the arithmetic-logic unit and then returned to storage several times before processing is completed. The arithmetic-logic unit also performs such operations as shifting and moving data. Through its ability to make comparisons, it can test for various conditions during processing and then perform appropriate operations.

The arithmetic-logic unit allows a computer to perform the arithmetic operations of addition, subtraction, multiplication, and division, and identify whether a number is positive, negative, or equal to zero. It can thus compare two numbers to determine which is higher than, equal to, or lower than the other. This ability of the computer to make comparisons gives it a *logic* capability. It can make logical changes from one set of program instructions to another based on the results of comparisons made during processing.

For example, in a payroll program, the computer can test if the hours worked by employees exceed 40 hours per week. Payments for such overtime would be computed using a different sequence of instructions than that used for employees without such overtime. We will explain this process in more detail in Chapter 4.

Primary Storage

The computer can store both data and instructions internally in its "memory." This internal storage enables the computer to "remember" the details of many assignments and to proceed from one assignment to another automatically, since it can retain data and instructions until needed. The ability of the computer to store its operating instructions internally (the *computer program*) allows the computer to process data *automatically*, that is, without continual human intervention.

The storage function of computer systems takes place in the **primary storage unit** of the CPU and in **secondary storage devices.** All data and programs must be placed in the primary storage unit (also called main memory or main storage) before they can be used in processing. The primary storage unit is also used to hold data and program instructions between processing steps, and after processing is completed, but before release as output.

In modern computers, the primary storage unit consists of microelectronic semiconductor storage circuitry. As we will discuss further in Chapter 6, this takes the form of either RAM or ROM storage chips. Most of the memory capacity of a computer consists of **random access memory (RAM)**, in which data and instructions are stored temporarily during processing. The rest of memory is composed of **read only memory (ROM)** chips, in which software, such as parts of the operating system program and several other programs, can be permanently stored. Unlike RAM, the programs in ROM cannot be erased. ROM is not *volatile* like RAM, which loses its contents when electrical power is interrupted.

Primary storage is subdivided into many small sections called *storage positions* or *storage locations*. Primary storage is frequently compared to a group of mailboxes, where each mailbox has an address and is capable of storing one item of data. Similarly, each position of storage has a specific numerical location called an *address* so that data stored in its contents can be readily located by the computer. In most modern computers, each position of storage can usually hold at least one character, including alphabetic, numeric, and special characters.

Secondary Storage

Data and programs can also be stored in **secondary storage devices,** such as magnetic disk and tape units, and thus greatly enlarge the storage capacity of the computer system. However, the contents of such secondary storage devices cannot be processed without first being brought into the primary storage unit. Thus, external secondary storage devices play a supporting role to the primary storage unit of a computer system. Typically, programs and files of data are stored until needed on either "floppy" magnetic diskettes or hard magnetic disks in microcomputer systems and large magnetic tape and disk units on larger computer systems.

It should be emphasized that secondary storage devices such as magnetic disk and tape perform both an input/output function and a secondary storage function. For example, data can be recorded on a magnetic diskette and entered into a computer system (input), then stored on magnetic disk units until needed (secondary storage). After processing, information can be recorded by the computer on magnetic disks (output).

OTHER HARDWARE CONCEPTS

You should now be able to see that a **computer system** is the single most important **hardware resource** of the computer-based **information systems** introduced in Chapter 1. Be sure you don't confuse these two important concepts. A computer-based information system needs more than the *hardware* resources of a *computer system*. It also requires *software* and *people* resources in order to transform *data resources* into *information products*. Figure 2–2 emphasizes several important hardware concepts. It gives you an overview of the major types of hardware found in many computer systems. These devices will be explained in the first three chapters of Module 2 of this text.

Peripheral Equipment and Media

Peripheral equipment and media include all devices that are separate from, but are (or can be) **online,** that is, electronically connected to and controlled by the central processing unit. Peripherals include a wide variety of input/output (I/O) equipment (such as video display terminals) and secondary storage devices (such as magnetic disk and tape drives), which depend on a direct connection or communication link to the CPU. The media used by peripheral equipment consists primarily of magnetic disks and tape, and paper documents. Notice how many types of peripherals and media are mentioned in Figure 2–2.

Many types of computer peripherals and media can be used for both input and output or for all three functions of input, output, and secondary storage. For example, magnetic disk equipment uses magnetic disks as a data medium and performs all three functions of input, output, and secondary storage. However, as Figure 2–2 illustrates, some peripheral devices do not need to use *data media* for input or output. For example, many computer terminals consist of a keyboard to enter data directly into the computer system and a video screen to directly display visual output. Since such peripherals do not use data media, they are called **direct input/output** devices. We will discuss input, output, and secondary storage devices in more detail in Chapters 5 and 6. Refer back to pages 19–26 of the pictorial section in Chapter 1 for color photographs of such devices.

Auxiliary Equipment and Media

Auxiliary equipment and media include equipment that is **offline,** that is, equipment separate from and *not* under the control of a central processing unit. Auxiliary equipment and media support the input, output, and storage functions of computer systems. It includes offline data entry equipment, such as key-to-disk machines that convert data from source documents into magnetic disks for later entry into a computer system. Offline output and storage equipment, such as copiers and filing devices, and data processing supplies, such as paper forms are other examples.

Figure 2–2 Overview of hardware in a computer system. Notice that computer hardware includes both *machines* (processors and peripheral equipment) and *media* (disks, tape, paper documents, etc.).

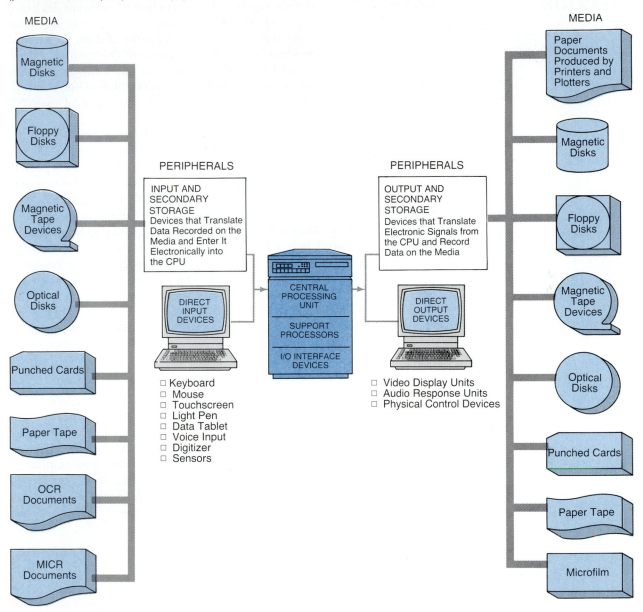

COMPUTER STORAGE CAPACITY AND TIME ELEMENTS

Computer Storage Capacities

How big are computer storage capacities? There is a lot that can be said about this topic, most of which is covered in Chapters 4 and 6. But for now, let's just say that the storage capacity of most computer hardware devices is usually expressed in terms of **bytes.** At this point, think of a byte as a funny term for a storage capacity that can hold one **character** of data. So for now, every time you see the word *byte*, you can substitute the term *character.* For example, suppose you have a floppy disk that has a capacity of over 360,000 bytes. This means that it can hold over 360,000 alphabetic, numeric, and other characters of data. This would be the equivalent of over 200 double-spaced pages of typewritten material.

Storage capacities are typically measured in **kilobytes** (abbreviated as KB or K) or **megabytes** (abbreviated as MB or M). Although "kilo" means one thousand in the metric system, the computer industry uses K to represent 1,024 (2^{10}) storage positions. Therefore, a memory size of 256K, for example, is really 262,144 storage positions, rather than 256,000 positions. However, such differences are frequently disregarded in order to simplify descriptions of storage capacity. Thus a **megabyte** is roughly 1 million bytes, while a **gigabyte** is roughly 1 billion bytes of storage, and a **terabyte** represents 1 trillion bytes of storage! Typically, computer primary storage capacities might range from 64K bytes (65,536 bytes) for small microcomputer memories to 40M bytes (40 megabytes or approximately 40 million bytes) of memory for a large computer system. Magnetic disk capacities might range from 360K bytes (368,640 bytes) to over three megabytes for floppy disks. Large magnetic disk units can supply several gigabytes of online storage. See Figure 2–3.

Computer Time Elements

Do you know how fast a computer works? Computer operating speeds that were formerly measured in **milliseconds** (thousandths of a second) are now being measured in the **microsecond** (millionth of a second) and **nanosecond** (billionth of a second) range, with **picosecond** (trillionth of a second) speed being attained by some computers. Such speeds seem almost incomprehensible. For example, an average person taking one step each nanosecond would circle the earth about 20 times in one second! Advanced micro- and minicomputers and most mainframe computers operate at nanosecond

Figure 2–3 Computer capacity and time elements.

Storage Elements (approximate capacities)	Computer Time Elements
Kilobyte = One thousand bytes or characters	Millisecond = One thousandth of a second
Megabyte = One million bytes or characters	Microsecond = One millionth of a second
Gigabyte = One billion bytes or characters	Nanosecond = One billionth of a second
Terabyte = One trillion bytes or characters	Picosecond = One trillionth of a second

speeds and can thus process several million instructions per second (MIPS). However some supercomputers have been clocked at 900 MIPS and more!

What do these speeds mean in terms of a computer's information processing capabilities? If you have a microcomputer, you can do your personal and professional information processing chores much faster than you ever could. In fact, you can type, file, analyze, and display information in ways that were not even possible before the development of personal computers. Users who rely on larger computer systems for business information processing also depend on the processing speed of their systems. See Figures 2–3 and 2–4.

Figure 2–4 The speed and power of the computer: an example.

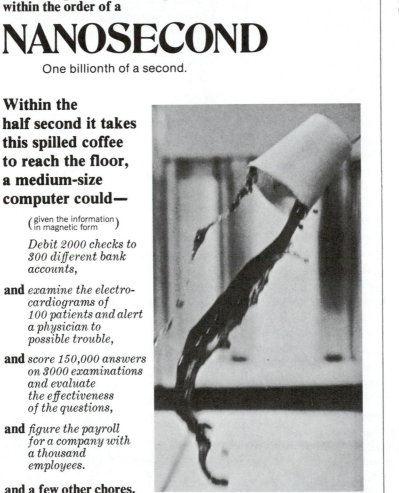

In the computer, the basic operations can be done within the order of a

NANOSECOND

One billionth of a second.

Within the half second it takes this spilled coffee to reach the floor, a medium-size computer could—

$\left(\begin{array}{l}\text{given the information}\\\text{in magnetic form}\end{array}\right)$

Debit 2000 checks to 300 different bank accounts,

and *examine the electro-cardiograms of 100 patients and alert a physician to possible trouble,*

and *score 150,000 answers on 3000 examinations and evaluate the effectiveness of the questions,*

and *figure the payroll for a company with a thousand employees.*

and a few other chores.

REAL WORLD APPLICATION 2–1

Computers in Small Business

Small businesses enjoying increased productivity because of the power of a personal computer can be found from coast to coast.

☐ John L. Scott Real Estate in Bellevue, Washington now has 600 agents working out of 20 branch offices as it grows along with the greater Seattle area. This is big business. The reality, however, is that each of the branch offices represents a small community-centered business. And now each of the 20 branches uses a Hewlett-Packard 150 microcomputer to track client follow-up information and print client mailings and newsletters.

Computer development manager Melody Bowman believes that the company has only scratched the surface with the most obvious benefits generated from improved client/agent benefits. They do make more contacts, of course. The quality of service is enhanced, and the agents benefit from the information stored in the in-house database on magnetic disks. This provides complete historical information on clients who are potential leads for repeat business.

☐ Allen Hughes, owner of Dairy Management Records Consulting in New Hampshire, packs a GM utility van with a multiuser, UNIX™-based computer and a printer. He visits his clients once a month to input weight records and other production factors that are a part of a dairy farmer's daily records. If he starts early in the morning, by afternoon he can sit in his mobile office with the farmer and bring to the screen his recommendations for optimal herd feed mixture. During the consultation the farmer presents various "what if" postulations and Hughes can show him the results. The farmer has immediate results of feed testing, based on the monthly ongoing record of quantity and quality of production. Hughes' service provides guidelines for nutritional programs and individual cow and herd maintenance. It maintains medical and production records and helps with pricing and profit predictions.

☐ Tom Mee, president of Mee Industries, Inc., of San Gabriel, California, sells fog for a living. The company's custom fog machines help farmers maintain an ideal growing environment for their crops, regardless of the season. Mee's COMPAQ computers help him design more efficient fogging systems and provide customers with quick and accurate price information. "We are engineers and scientists so it is natural for us to get involved with computers," he says, "but we couldn't afford them until PCs came along. I bought my first one [PC] in 1980 and now we have more than 20 computers for only 30 people."

In the offices of Mee Industries, salesmen use their COMPAQ personal computers to write their own letters and proposals. Company employees also wrote their own software program so that the sales staff could instantly do quotes for their clients. "It used to take us six to eight man weeks of engineering merely to prepare a quote," Mee says. "With the computer it takes five minutes to type it in and get an answer." Mee continues: "That's one of the magical things. The microcomputer has revolutionized the way we do business—and it did it instantly."

Application Questions

☐ What computer system functions do you recognize in these three brief case histories?

☐ How have computers benefited these businesses?

Source: Tom Badgett, "Revitalizing the Small Business," *Personal Computing*, October 1986, pp. 141–43.

Section II: Microcomputer Systems

Microcomputers have blossomed into commonplace personal and professional appliances. They come in all shapes and sizes, from devices that are as small as chips, pockets, and notebooks, to models that are as big as briefcases, typewriters, and TV sets. With millions of these computing appliances in use, there is no question that the microcomputer revolution is in full force. People are using microcomputers in their homes and schools, in businesses and factories, and in laboratories and the great outdoors. They are using them to play video games, type letters, keep records, learn their lessons, compose music, do accounting, perform financial analysis and modeling, draw pictures, send electronic mail, and yes, even crunch a few numbers. Obviously, we had better take a hard look at the device responsible for all of this activity, the microcomputer.

What is a **microcomputer?** A microcomputer is the smallest current type of computer. It usually consists of a **microprocessor** (a central processing unit on a chip) and associated control, primary storage, and input/output circuitry on one or more circuit boards, plus a variety of input/output and secondary storage devices.

THE MICROCOMPUTER SYSTEM

Microcomputers are given a lot of other names. They come in a variety of sizes and shapes, and are used for a variety of purposes. For example, microcomputers categorized by *size* may be called single chip, pocket, handheld, lap-size, portable, transportable, desktop, and floor-standing microcomputers. Or based on their *use*, they may be called special-purpose, home, personal, professional, and small-business microcomputers. The most popular alternative name for microcomputers right now is **personal computer** or **PC.** However, microcomputers have become much more than small computers used by individual persons. They have become powerful *professional workstations* for use in business firms and other organizations.

What hardware does a microcomputer system have? That depends on its size and use. However, the typical hardware components of a personal computer are shown in Figure 2–5. Figure 2–6 emphasizes that a microcomputer is a **computer system** and uses a variety of devices to perform the system functions of *input, processing, output, storage,* and *control.* Typical personal computer components are summarized below and discussed in more detail in the next few sections. Also, refer to pages 13–16 of the pictorial section in Chapter 1 for pictures of microcomputer systems and their hardware.

- ☐ Input—keyboard (plus *electronic mouse* and other devices).
- ☐ Processing and control—main system unit containing the main microprocessor and other devices on circuit boards.
- ☐ Storage—*primary storage:* RAM and ROM chips on the circuit boards in the main system unit; *Secondary storage:* floppy disk drives (plus hard disk drives and other devices), which can be part of the main system unit or be externally connected.
- ☐ Output—video display monitor and printer (plus audio speaker and other devices).

Figure 2-5 A hardware diagram of a microcomputer system.

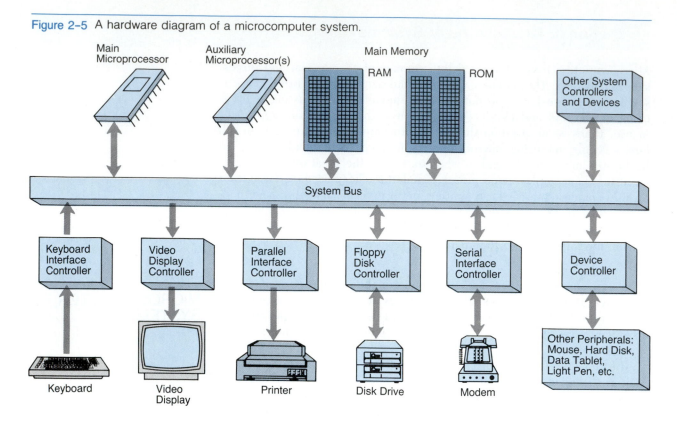

Figure 2-6 The input, processing, output, storage, and control
components of a microcom-
puter system.

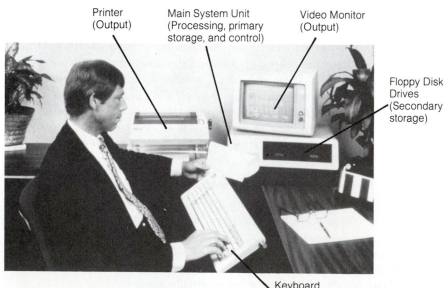

IBM Custom VLSI Chips   Floppy Disk Connector   Sockets for 1-Megabyte Memory

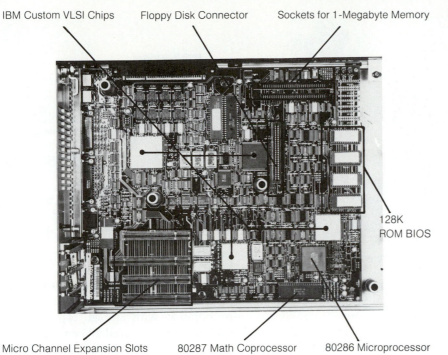

Figure 2–7 The main circuit board of the IBM Personal System/2 Model 50 microcomputer with its major components identified.

128K
ROM BIOS

Micro Channel Expansion Slots   80287 Math Coprocessor   80286 Microprocessor

Let's look at what's inside a popular microcomputer to get a better idea of what makes a microcomputer tick. Figure 2–7 is a picture of the main circuit board of the IBM Personal System/2 Model 50 microcomputer, with its major components identified. Integrated circuit chips are enclosed in rectangular plastic packages fitted with electrodes. They are interconnected with other chips by a pattern of conductors printed on the circuit board. The main chip is the Intel 80286 microprocessor, which is the central processing unit of the microcomputer. Other microprocessors include an optional Intel 80287 *coprocessor* for faster mathematical calculations and custom *VLSI* microprocessors to control video displays, disk drives, and other input/output functions. We will explain microprocessors in more detail in Chapter 4.

The memory chips on the circuit board include read only memory (ROM) chips for permanent storage of the basic input/output system (BIOS) of the operating system control program. The major share of primary storage chips are for random access memory (RAM) where programs and data are stored during processing. Other devices, such as timing and clock circuits, input/output *ports*, memory access circuits, and connectors for a keyboard, magnetic disk drives, an electronic mouse, and a speaker are also included. The Model 50 also has three *expansion slots*, which can be used for additional circuit boards to support more memory and input/output devices.

PROCESSING AND CONTROL HARDWARE

STORAGE HARDWARE

Microcomputers use integrated circuit memory chips plugged into their circuit boards for **primary storage** or memory. Storage capacity typically ranges from 64K bytes to several megabytes.

Figure 2–8 Microcomputer storage devices: Floppy disks are the most popular secondary storage media.

The most popular **secondary storage** devices for microcomputers are magnetic disk drives using flexible magnetic diskettes or **floppy disks.** The 5¼-inch (diameter) size is the most popular, with storage capacities of several hundred thousand to over a million characters available on each disk. However, the 3½-inch size is gaining popularity since it is used in the Apple Macintosh and IBM Personal System/2 microcomputers. **Magnetic hard disk** devices have become popular for business and professional users of microcomputers. Though they are more expensive, such devices offer 10 to 100 million positions of storage and are much faster than floppy disks. Other devices include **magnetic bubble** plug-in cartridges and plug-in **RAM cards** (circuit boards) that provide additional storage capability much faster than other media. Finally, **magnetic tape cassette** and **cartridge** devices may be used for backup storage. We will discuss these types of storage media further in Chapter 6. See Figure 2–8.

INPUT HARDWARE

The most popular input device for microcomputers is the familiar **keyboard,** which can be part of the main system unit or be a separate device. Keyboards come in a variety of styles and capabilities. Some keyboards have 10-key *numeric pad,* (for numeric input), *cursor control* keys (to move the cursor on the screen), and special *function keys,* which reduce the number of keystrokes needed to enter selected commands into the computer.

Other input devices are available that are easier to use than a keyboard when you are moving a *cursor,* making selections from a *menu* display, entering commands, or doing specialized tasks. (The cursor is a point of light that indicates the position on the screen where the next entry will appear.) Apple microcomputers emphasize use of the **electronic mouse.** It is a small device connected to the computer that you move by hand on a flat surface (a desktop). This moves the cursor on the screen in the same direction. The buttons on the mouse allow you to make a selection or issue a command. Hewlett-Packard microcomputers emphasize use of a **touch-sensitive screen** to accomplish similar functions. Other specialized hardware include *optical*

Figure 2–9 Microcomputer input devices: This personal computer uses a keyboard, light pen, mouse, and joystick as input devices.

scanning wands, light pens, graphic tablets, joysticks, game paddles, digitizers, and *voice recognition units.* We will discuss the functions of these and other input devices in Chapter 5. See Figure 2–9.

OUTPUT HARDWARE

The two most common microcomputer output devices are the **video display monitor** and the **printer.** The video display monitor allows you to see the output of the computer, as well as your input, while you are entering instructions or data. Inexpensive microcomputers include a device called an RF modulator, which allows you to use a TV set as a monitor. Better microcomputers assume you will use a specially designed monochrome or color monitor that allows a sharper image to be displayed. Video monitors come in various types and costs, depending on the clarity and number of colors displayed. For example, a full-color monitor for graphics displays will cost several times as much as a monochrome monitor for viewing text and numeric output.

If you are a serious microcomputer user, you will want a *hard copy* of some of your output printed on paper. That's where printers come in. An inexpensive (and quiet) *thermal* (heat transfer) printer can be purchased at low cost for portable computers. The most popular types of printers print one character at a time using a *dot matrix* or *daisy wheel* print head. Speeds range from 15 to 300 characters per second, though 100 characters a second is common. The speed, quality, and cost of printers varies widely. For example, *draft quality* printers are cheaper than *correspondence quality* printers.

Other output devices include **audio speakers, voice synthesizers,** and **graphic plotters.** An important input/output device that should also be

Figure 2–10 Microcomputer output devices: A video monitor and printer are the most widely used output devices.

mentioned is the **modem.** It allows a microcomputer to engage in data communications over telephone lines with other computers. This capability can be built into one of a microcomputer's circuit boards, or it can be an external device. We will discuss input/output devices in more detail in Chapter 5. See Figure 2–10.

MICROCOMPUTER APPLICATIONS

What can you do with a microcomputer? The answer to the question of what **applications** (uses) can be accomplished by a microcomputer is tied directly to the **software packages** (computer programs) available. Fortunately, a wide variety of software packages are available for purchase at reasonable prices for many microcomputers. Of course, you could always write your own programs, but this is not necessary for most microcomputer users. Thus, microcomputers can do most of the things that larger computers can do, only they do it just for you!

Figure 2–11 spotlights the types of applications that are most popular with today's microcomputer users. These include:

- ☐ **Word processing**—automated electronic typing and editing.
- ☐ **Electronic spreadsheets**—computerized worksheet analysis and modeling.
- ☐ **Database management**—electronic record-keeping, interrogation, and report generation.
- ☐ **Graphics**—generation of charts and other graphic images.
- ☐ **Communications**—telecommunications with other computers, databanks, information services, and electronic mail networks.
- ☐ **Personal and home**—entertainment, home management, personal finance, education, and so on.

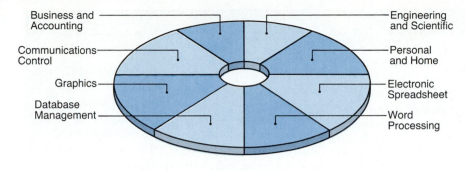

Figure 2–11 Popular micro-computer applications. Word processing, spreadsheet analysis, and database management are the most popular applications.

☐ **Business and accounting**—common accounting and business information processing, and managerial decision support.

☐ **Engineering and scientific**—using powerful microcomputers for computer-aided design and analysis.

We will go into detail on the functions and characteristics of major types of computer software packages available for microcomputers in the next chapter. Also, a hands-on introduction to the use of several types of popular software packages for microcomputers is provided in Appendix A at the back of this book.

In Chapter 16, Acquiring Information System Resources, we will discuss selection criteria, costs, and sources of microcomputers and other computer system resources. For now, you should understand the following major points:

COST AND SOURCES

☐ The cost of microcomputer systems is steadily decreasing due to intense competition and advances in technology. Costs range from a few hundred dollars for home computers to several thousand dollars for more advanced professional models.

☐ Costs depend primarily on such factors as (1) brand name, (2) type of main microprocessor and support electronics, (3) number and capabilities of input, output, and storage devices included, (4) the amount and types of software packages purchased, and (5) any provision for support services (such as education and maintenance).

☐ The leading manufacturers of microcomputers are IBM Corporation and Apple Computer, Inc. IBM makes several models of the IBM Personal Computer (PC) and the newer Personal System/2 (PS/2). Apple has several models of the Apple II and the Macintosh. The IBM PC and PS/2 have become standards for business and professional use, while Apple leads in the nonbusiness and education markets.

☐ There are a host of other manufacturers including AT&T, Atari, Commodore, COMPAQ, Tandy, and Zenith, and numerous compatible "clone" makers. Microcomputers are sold to major corporations by their manufacturers, and to the rest of us by computer retail stores and mail-order houses.

REAL WORLD APPLICATION 2–2

The Travelers Corporation

For a corporation that proudly describes itself as a "staid New England insurance company," The Travelers Corp., of Hartford, Connecticut, has been far from conservative in its commitment to personal computers.

While other companies impose policies to control PC proliferation, Travelers executives are holding firm to their plans to put a PC on the desktop of every one of the company's 30,000 employees by 1990.

While many corporate data processing departments cling stubbornly to "dumb" terminals that serve as slaves to a host computer, at Travelers, intelligent PCs will be the workstation of choice for communicating with mainframe computers.

While executives at many companies talk vaguely about exploring network technology, Travelers is linking its PCs by installing IBM's Token-Ring Network cabling in every one of its offices nationwide.

Travelers has made the personal computer a key part of its data processing strategy because management is convinced that the most profitable and strongest financial services firms will be those with the best information technology, according to Joseph T. Brophy, senior vice president of data processing. "If we didn't have [the latest information technology], I can tell you one thing: We wouldn't be in business. That's for sure. We would die around here. We couldn't possibly do the work and gather the information that we need to make the type of investment decisions we make every day," Mr. Brophy said.

Travelers caused a stir in corporate data processing in mid-1982 when it ordered 10,000 IBM Personal Computers—at that time the largest single order of IBM Personal Computers ever made. To date, Travelers has installed more than 17,000 micros in its headquarters and field offices.

According to Mr. Brophy, computers are going to cause "a very significant shift in our demographic profile, from clerical to professional." Travelers will no longer employ an army of clerks shuffling papers, searching for folders, and updating files. "We are going to be a society of knowledge workers"—professionals who understand how to use the information managed by the company's computer systems, to make decisions and how to share that information.

Clerical tasks, such as compiling lists of different Travelers policies held by the same person, are disappearing—computers have streamlined the task of gathering and organizing data. Information about customers, policies, and investments are entered into the system once, at the point of origin. After the information is entered into the system, it is available to anyone who needs to access it. The mountain of paper that was maintained by clerks is now maintained electronically.

Travelers records more than a billion transactions a year, maintains 3,500 internal databases, and accesses 4,000 external databases. But the amount of paper processing is decreasing 20 percent a year as it is replaced by computer processing, said Mr. Brophy.

Travelers has chosen to develop a two-tiered network of computers in which personal computers communicate directly with its large computers. Travelers has found that there is no need to connect personal computers to a midrange departmental computer that manages communication with mainframe systems.

Application Questions

☐ How and why is Travelers using microcomputers?

☐ How has the use of computers affected their employees and information processing tasks?

Source: John Pallatto, "A PC per Desktop Remains Objective of Travelers Corp.," *PC Week*, November 11, 1986, pp. 69–88.

Section III: Mainframes and Other Computer Systems

What is a **mainframe computer?** That's the name given to computers that are larger and more powerful than microcomputers and minicomputers. *Larger* is understandable, but what does *more powerful* mean? Let's just say that mainframe computer systems frequently have:

☐ One or more central processors with larger instruction processing capacities and greater processing speed (several millions of instructions per second).

☐ Large primary storage capacities (millions of storage positions) and greater secondary storage capacities (billions of positions of online magnetic disk and tape storage).

☐ The ability to service many users at once (up to several hundred!). That's because they can process many programs and handle many peripheral devices (terminals, disk and tape drives, printers, etc.) at the same time.

Several large computer manufacturers produce *families* or *product lines* of mainframe computers that have models ranging in size from small to medium to large. This allows them to provide a range of choices to their customers, depending on their information processing needs. Most models in a family are compatible (i.e., programs written for one model can usually be run on other models of the same family with little or no change). This allows customers to move up to larger models of the same mainframe family as their needs grow.

It should be emphasized that the development of microcomputers and minicomputers has erased many of the traditional distinctions between various sizes of computers. For example, *supermini* computers may be less expensive and more powerful than some medium-size mainframe computers. These developments have weakened the traditional size distinctions between full-scale computer systems. However, mainframe computers are still a major force in the computer industry. See Figure 2–12 and refer to pages 13 and 18 of the pictorial section in Chapter 1.

MAINFRAME COMPUTER SYSTEMS

Applications

Microcomputers and minicomputers are typically used by one individual or a few people. Mainframe computers, however, are designed to handle the information processing needs of organizations in business, government, and education with many employees and customers or complex computational problems. Small and medium sizes of mainframe computers can handle the processing chores of smaller organizations or the regional divisions of larger organizations. They can handle the processing of thousands of customer inquiries, employee paychecks, student registrations, sales transactions, and inventory changes, to name a few. You can't beat such computers when it comes to processing large volumes of data. They can also handle large numbers of users needing access at the same time to the centralized databases and libraries of application programs of *time-sharing* networks.

Figure 2–12 The input, processing, output, storage, and control components of a large mainframe computer system, the IBM 3090.

Magnetic Tape Units (Secondary storage and I/O)

Central Processing Unit (Processing, primary storage and control)

Magnetic Disk Units (Secondary storage and I/O)

Video Consoles (Input/Output)

Large mainframe computer systems are used by major corporations and government agencies, which have enormous and complex data processing assignments. For example, large computers are necessary for organizations processing millions of transactions each day, such as major national banks or the national stock exchanges. Large mainframes can also handle the great volume of complex calculations involved in scientific and engineering analysis and simulation of complex design projects, such as the design of aircraft and spacecraft. A large computer can also act as a *host computer* for *distributed processing networks* that include many smaller computers. Thus, large mainframe computers are used in the national and international computing networks of such major corporations as airlines, banks, and oil companies.

Cost and Sources

The cost of mainframe computers can range up into the millions of dollars. Therefore, many mainframes are leased instead of purchased outright. Of course, costs will vary greatly depending on such features as the amount of primary memory, input/output *channels,* and data communications *ports,* as well as the number and types of input, output, and secondary storage devices included in the system. Purchase prices for small mainframes may vary from $50,000 to $250,000, with monthly rentals from $1,000 to $5,000 per month. Medium-size mainframes may cost between $200,000 and $1 million, and rent for between $5,000 and $20,000 per month. Large mainframes have purchase prices that may vary from about $1 million to $5 million, and rent for between $20,000 to $200,000 per month.

Mainframe computers are manufactured by several large firms, including IBM, Control Data, Unisys, NCR Corporation, Honeywell-Bull, Digital Equipment Corporation (DEC), Hewlett-Packard Company, Tandem, and Amdahl. They produce a variety of small, medium, and large mainframe computers. Examples of some current small mainframes are the IBM 9370, most of Hewlett-Packard's 3000 series, and DEC's VAX 8800. Medium-size mainframes include the IBM 4381 and the Unisys 4700. Examples of large mainframes include the IBM 3090 series, the Honeywell-Bull 7000 series, and the Amdahl 5890.

MINICOMPUTER SYSTEMS

Minicomputers are small computers that are larger and more powerful than most microcomputers but are smaller and less powerful than most of the models of mainframe computer systems. However, this is not a precise distinction. High-end models of microcomputer systems (*supermicros*) are more powerful than some minicomputers. High-end models of minicomputers (*superminis*) are more powerful than some small and medium-size mainframe computers. Thus some experts predict that minicomputers will disappear as a separate computer category, leaving only mainframes and microcomputers of various sizes. But for now, minicomputers have a wide range of processing capabilities and hardware characteristics.

Minicomputers can perform all of the functions of mainframe computers but are typically smaller, lower-cost machines. They might have slower processing speeds, smaller memories, and less input/output and data communication capabilities. Smaller minicomputers might be limited to a few video terminals, a slow-speed printer, and floppy disk secondary storage. Larger minicomputers use more peripherals, such as multiple video terminals, larger capacity hard magnetic disk units, faster line printers, and magnetic tape devices. Typically, video terminals are used for keyboard input and video displays, and small printers are used for paper output. Magnetic floppy disks and removable disk packs provide secondary storage. Smaller versions of standard magnetic tape and disk units, faster printing devices, and many other peripheral devices are available.

Minicomputers were designed to handle a limited set of jobs and peripheral devices. Thus they can be physically smaller and less costly than mainframe computers. Most minicomputers can also function in ordinary operating environments, do not need special air conditioning or electrical wiring, and can be placed in most offices and work areas. In addition, since they are comparatively easy to operate, the smaller models of minicomputers do not need a staff of data processing professionals but can rely on properly trained regular employees. Therefore, large numbers of users purchased and continue to acquire minicomputer systems. See Figure 2–13. Also refer to page 17 of the pictorial section in Chapter 1.

Applications

Minicomputers are quite versatile. They are being used for a large number of business data processing and scientific applications. Minicomputers first became popular for use in scientific research, instrumentation systems, engineering analysis, and industrial process monitoring and control. Minicomputers can easily handle such uses because these applications are narrow in scope and do not demand the processing versatility of mainframe systems. Minicomputers are now being used as *end-user* computer systems in distributed processing networks. They serve as industrial process-control and manufacturing plant computers, where they play a major role in computer-assisted manufacturing (CAM). They also serve as powerful individual *engineering workstations* for computer-assisted design (CAD) applications.

Figure 2-13 A minicomputer system: The VAX 11/730, by Digital Equipment Corporation.

They are also being used as *front-end* computers to control data communications networks and large numbers of data-entry terminals. Minicomputers are also being used as *departmental* or *office* computers. They are being used to tie together the microcomputer workstations, word processing terminals, and other computerized devices found in large departments and automated offices. In addition, minicomputers are used as small-business computers. They provide more processing power and online storage and can support more users at the same time than microcomputers used for business applications.

Cost and Sources

The wide variation of minicomputer capabilities is reflected in a wide range of prices for minicomputer systems. The majority of minicomputers cost between $10,000 and $50,000, though prices between $50,000 and $100,000 and even higher must be paid for some supermini systems. Like microcomputer systems, the cost of input/output and secondary storage peripheral devices frequently exceed the cost of the minicomputer CPU. Each unit of software needed must also be purchased unless it is "packaged" along with the computer hardware.

The leading manufacturers of minicomputers include Digital Equipment Corporation (DEC), IBM, Honeywell-Bull, Hewlett-Packard, Data General, Wang Laboratories, Prime Computer, Datapoint, Perkin-Elmer, and Texas Instruments Incorporated. Examples of some popular minicomputers include the DEC VAX 8200, the Wang VS100, the Data General Eclipse series, the IBM System/36 and 38, and some models of the Hewlett-Packard HP3000 series. Minicomputers can be purchased directly from a local or regional office of the larger computer manufacturers or through independent distributors who represent minicomputer manufacturers who do not sell directly to end users.

Figure 2-14 The Cray 2 supercomputer.

Though most computers fit into the micro, mini, and mainframe categories, several other classifications of computers exist. They include **supercomputers, analog** computers, **special-purpose** computers, **scientific** computers, and **multiprocessor computer systems.** Let's take a brief look at these computers to round out our coverage of the major types of computer systems in use today.

OTHER TYPES OF COMPUTERS

The term **supercomputer** has been coined to describe a category of extremely powerful mainframe computer systems. A small number of supercomputers are built each year for large government research agencies, military defense systems, national weather forecasting agencies, large time-sharing networks, and large corporations. The leading maker of supercomputers is Cray Research, which produces the Cray I, CRAY X-MP, and CRAY 2, the most widely used supercomputers. These models can process from 80 to over 900 million instructions per second! Expressed another way, they can perform arithmetic calculations at a speed of 160 million to 1.7 billion *floating-point operations per second* (FLOPS)! Control Data is the other major manufacturer of supercomputers. Its Cyber 205 supercomputer is capable of 200 million floating-point operations per second. Purchase prices for many supercomputers are in the $5 million to $15 million range. However, the development of powerful microprocessors ("mainframes on a chip") and developments in parallel processing have spawned a new breed of *mini-supercomputers* with prices below $1 million. Thus, supercomputers continue to advance the state of the art for the entire computer industry. See Figure 2–14 and page 18 of the pictorial section in Chapter 1.

Supercomputers

Analog Computers

Most computers in use today are **digital computers,** which *count* discrete units (digits) as they perform their arithmetic and logical operations. However, there also are electronic **analog** computers, which perform arithmetic operations and comparisons by *measuring* physical changes. For example, analog computers may measure changes in magnitude of a continuous physical phenomenon, such as electronic voltage. The change in voltage represents, or is "analogous" to, the numerical values of the data being processed. Analog computers are used on a limited basis to process the data arising from scientific or engineering experiments, manufacturing processes, and military weapons systems. For example, the temperature changes of a chemical process can be converted by the analog computer into variations in electronic voltage and mathematically analyzed. The results of the processing could be displayed on dials, graphs, or TV screens or be used to initiate changes in the chemical process.

Special-Purpose Computers

Computers used for information processing are typically **general-purpose computers,** which are designed to process a wide variety of applications. For example, applications ranging from scientific and engineering analysis to business data processing are possible merely by changing the program of instructions stored in the machine. A **special-purpose computer** is specifically designed to process one or more specific applications. Some of these computers are so specialized that part or all of their operating instructions are built into their electronic circuitry. However, the use of built-in microprocessors and microelectronic memories makes it possible to easily customize computers for specific uses.

Special-purpose computers have been built for both military and civilian applications (such as aircraft and submarine navigation, and for aircraft, missile, and satellite tracking), airline reservation systems, and industrial process control. Special-purpose computers are widely used as *front-end* processors for the control of data communication networks. They also are used as *back-end* processors for management of database systems. Some of the computerized word processors for automatic typing and text editing are special-purpose computers found in modern offices. Other examples are electronic video game computers, computerized robots, computers used for computer-assisted design and manufacturing (CAD/CAM), and microprocessors used in a multitude of smart products, from digital watches and automatic cameras to microwave ovens and automobiles.

You should also realize that a general-purpose computer can be "dedicated" or committed to a particular data processing task or application, even though it is capable of performing a wide variety of other tasks and applications. Such **dedicated computers** are frequently used to perform such jobs as data communications network control, database management, input/output control for larger computer systems, transaction processing, and automated manufacturing. The development of minicomputers and microcomputers has accelerated the trend toward the use of dedicated computers. It has become economically feasible to dedicate these small yet powerful general-purpose computers to more specific data processing tasks, such as word processing or small business accounting applications.

Present general-purpose computers can be programmed to operate for either scientific data processing or business data processing. However, scientific computers are still being built for the high-speed processing of numerical data involving complex mathematical calculations. Some scientific computers are large supercomputers, while others are powerful special-purpose processing units called *array processors*, which can be attached to a CPU to vastly increase the arithmetic processing power of a computer system. Scientific computers are typically designed with limited input, output, and storage capabilities. But they have advanced "number crunching" computational power in order to handle the large amount of computations that are typical of scientific applications.

Scientific Computers

Many fourth-generation computers (from microcomputers to mainframes) can be classified as **multiprocessor computer systems** since they use multiple processors for their processing functions. Instead of having one CPU with a single control unit, arithmetic-logic unit, and primary storage unit (called a **uniprocessor design**), the CPUs of these computers contain several types of processing units. The major types of multiprocessor architecture involve:

Multiprocessor Computer Systems

- ☐ **Support processor systems.** The key to this multiprocessor design is the use of microprocessors to control the operations of several major processing functions. Special-purpose microprocessors may be used for input/output, primary storage management, arithmetic operations, and data communications, thus freeing the main central processor (sometimes called the *instruction processor*) to do the major job of executing program instructions. Such microprocessors are now widely used in microcomputers, as well as minicomputers and mainframes.

- ☐ **Coupled processor systems.** This multiprocessor design uses multiple CPUs, or CPU configurations consisting of multiple arithmetic-logic and control units that share the same primary storage unit. These systems can therefore execute instructions from several different programs at the same time.

- ☐ **Parallel processor systems.** This new multiprocessor design uses hundreds or even thousands of instruction processors organized in clusters or networks. These systems can therefore execute many instructions at a time in *parallel*. This is a major departure from the traditional Von Neumann design of current computers, which execute instructions *serially* (one at a time). Many experts consider such systems as the key to providing artificial intelligence capabilities to fifth-generation computers.

- ☐ **Subsidiary processing systems.** One or more separate computer systems handle specific functions (such as input/output) for and under the complete control of a larger computer system. For example, a large *master* computer may utilize smaller *slave* computers to handle "housekeeping chores" such as input/output operations. In other cases, several computers may be intercon-

Figure 2–15 Multiprocessor computer systems. Notice the variety of multiprocessor architectures shown.

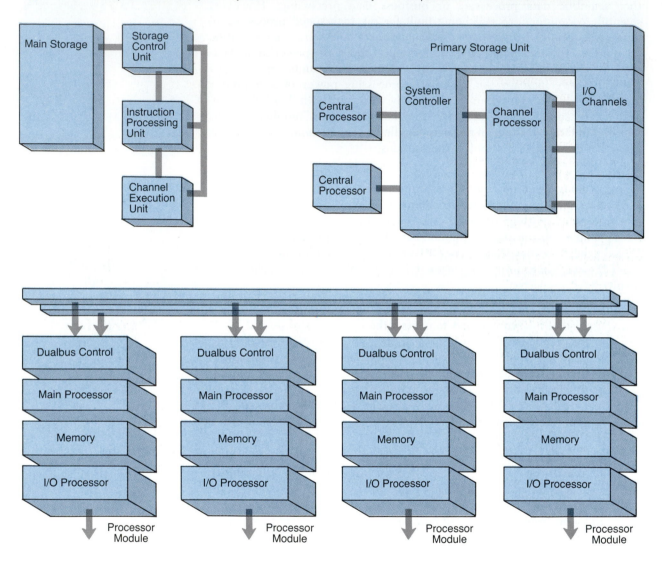

nected in order to handle large processing assignments and to provide a backup capability that would not be present if only one large computer was used. This *fault-tolerant* capability is a major benefit of multiprocessor systems. See Figure 2–15.

Computer manufacturers are moving toward multiprocessor architectures primarily because of the availability of powerful, low-cost microprocessors, which can be dedicated to handle specific CPU functions. Therefore, attaining the advantages of multiprocessing has become technologically and economically feasible. Multiprocessor computer systems do cost more than uniprocessor systems and may require more expensive and advanced operating systems. However, they have the following benefits:

REAL WORLD APPLICATION 2–3

Tenneco, Inc.

While many organizations are installing departmental minicomputer systems to fill the gap between micros and mainframes, Tenneco, Inc.'s only oil refinery is sticking to its mainframe guns.

The Tenneco refinery uses an IBM 4381 dual processor mainframe computer system. "We run all the general-type financial applications, such as payroll, accounts payable, general ledger, inventory, and maintenance work order processing on that system," said Warren V. Camp, supervisor of information services for the refinery operations of Tenneco Oil Process and Marketing, a division of Tenneco, Inc.

Tenneco has no immediate plans to change. "Those applications are going to stay on the mainframe. It is easier to manage, and all those systems are used by people throughout the refinery. We also have users in Houston that use our system," Camp said.

Nor is the Tenneco refinery about to install a raft of departmental minicomputer systems to service particular work groups. "As far as departmental type machines, I think we are either going to stick with PCs, or, if we need more processing, we will be looking at a PC networking type of thing," Camp said.

Of the refinery's 750 employees, some 300 currently use some type of computing device, either a terminal or personal computer, Camp stated. That number is expected to increase with terminals leading the charge, at least in the short term. "There are probably more terminals being added than PCs, but that is going to slow, and they will pretty much even up in the future," Camp said.

The growth in the number of PCs is not expected to reduce the load on the firm's mainframe. "Those applications were just done manually before, and some were done using a computer service time-sharing," Camp said.

Despite increasing the number of applications running on PCs, the organization also expects to increase the use of its mainframe. "Where the application is just within a given department, such as drafting, we are looking at putting them on PCs. Where they have refinerywide application, we try to put them on the mainframe," Camp said.

Application Questions

☐ How does the Tenneco Refinery use its mainframe computer?

☐ On which type of computer system will future applications be placed? Why?

Source: Adapted from "Sticking to Their Mainframe Guns," *Computerworld,* January 5, 1987, p. 6.

☐ Significantly greater and faster processing capability.

☐ Better use of primary storage, since processors share primary storage units.

☐ More efficient use of input/output and secondary storage peripheral devices.

☐ Increased reliability, since multiple processors provide a backup (fault-tolerant) capability as well as help to meet peak-load processing.

☐ Reduced software problems, since processors may share the same system control and service programs.

☐ A more economical arrangement than having several independent computer systems share processing responsibilities.

SUMMARY

☐ A computer is a system that performs input, output, storage, arithmetic-logic, and control functions, thus providing users with a powerful information processing tool. The hardware components of a computer system include input devices, a central processing unit, storage devices, and output devices. The major functions and types of computer system hardware are summarized in Figures 2–1 and 2–2. Computer capacity and time elements are summarized in Figure 2–3.

☐ Microcomputers are being used as personal home computers, and as professional computers, intelligent workstations, and small business computers. The typical microcomputer uses a keyboard for input, a system unit containing the main microprocessor for processing and control, semiconductor RAM and ROM circuits for primary storage, floppy disk drives for secondary storage, and a video display monitor and printer for output. A wide variety of other hardware devices are also available. Thousands of application software packages are available. Most popular are packages for word processing, electronic spreadsheets, database management, graphics, communications, common business applications, and personal and home applications.

☐ Minicomputers are small general-purpose computers that are larger and more powerful than most microcomputers. They are used by small groups of users for many business data processing and scientific applications. Mainframe computers are larger and more powerful than most minicomputers. They are usually faster, have more memory capacity, and can support more input/output and secondary storage devices. They are designed to handle the information processing needs of organizations with many customers and employees, or complex computational problems.

☐ Supercomputers are a special category of extremely powerful mainframe computer systems designed for massive computational assignments. Analog computers measure continuous physical magnitudes, such as electronic voltage, while digital computers count discrete units (digits). A special-purpose computer is specifically designed to process a specific application, while a general-purpose computer is designed to process a wide variety of applications. Scientific computers are designed for the high-speed processing of numerical data involving complex mathematical calculations.

☐ Many current computers are multiprocessor computer systems, which have CPUs that contain several types of processing units. Some computers use microprocessors to handle subsidiary functions in support of the CPU, while others involve several separate CPUs that are interconnected and share the same primary storage.

These are the key terms and concepts of this chapter. The page number of their first explanation is in parenthesis.

1. Analog computer (*90*)
2. Arithmetic-logic unit (*70*)
3. Auxiliary equipment (*72*)
4. Central processing unit (*70*)
5. Computer system (*68*)
6. Control unit (*70*)
7. Digital computer (*90*)
8. General-purpose computer (*90*)
9. Input devices (*69*)
10. Mainframe computer (*85*)
11. Microcomputer (*77*)
12. Microprocessor (*77*)
13. Minicomputer (*87*)
14. Multiprocessor computer systems (*91*)
15. Offline (*72*)
16. Online (*72*)

17. Output devices (*69*)
18. Peripheral equipment (*72*)
19. Primary storage unit (*71*)
    a. RAM
    b. ROM
20. Secondary storage devices (*71*)
21. Special-purpose computer (*90*)
22. Supercomputer (*89*)
23. Storage capacity elements (*74*)
    a. Kilobyte
    b. Megabyte
    c. Gigabyte
    d. Terabyte
24. Time elements (*74*)
    a. Millisecond
    b. Microsecond
    c. Nanosecond
    d. Picosecond

Match one of the **key terms and concepts** listed above with one of the brief examples or definitions listed below. Try to find the "best fit" for answers that seem to fit more than one term or concept. Defend your choices.

_____ 1. Contains the arithmetic-logic unit, control unit, and primary storage unit.

_____ 2. Performs computations and comparisons.

_____ 3. Interprets instructions and directs processing.

_____ 4. Stores instructions and data during processing.

_____ 5. Magnetic disk and tape drives.

_____ 6. Video monitor and printer.

_____ 7. Keyboard and optical scanner.

_____ 8. Connected to and controlled by a CPU.

_____ 9. Separate from and not controlled by a CPU.

_____ 10. The central processing unit of a microcomputer.

_____ 11. Used as a personal and professional productivity machine.

_____ 12. Between a microcomputer and a mainframe computer.

_____ 13. Handles the information processing needs of large organizations.

_____ 14. Can have several interconnected CPUs.

_____ 15. Counts discrete units of data.

_____ 16. Measures changes in physical magnitudes.

_____ 17. Can process a wide variety of applications.

_____ 18. The most powerful type of computer.

_____ 19. Online computer devices.

_____ 20. Offline copiers for computer output.

_____ 21. One billionth of a second.

_____ 22. One billion characters of storage.

_____ 23. Permanently stores programs in primary storage.

_____ 24. Most of primary storage consists of this type of storage circuits.

APPLICATION PROBLEMS

1. If you have not already done so, read and answer the questions after the three Real World Applications in this chapter.

2. Have you had an opportunity for a hands-on experience with a computer yet? Did you use a microcomputer or larger computer system? Indicate the hardware (equipment and media) you used to perform the system functions listed below.
   a. Input.   *d.* Storage.
   b. Processing.   *e.* Control.
   c. Output.

3. Natalie Dreste, an enterprising young college student, has just started a mail-order catalog business selling silk blouses. She processes all orders manually but plans to purchase an IBM PS/2 to handle order processing as soon as possible. Natalie places all orders to be processed in a special in-box. On her desk she has a copy of the catalog to look up prices, colors, and so on, and a calculator to calculate the total of the order. When finished with the order, she places it in a special out-box and also places a copy of the order in the customer's file. Natalie has all the customer files alphabetically stored in a file cabinet. When a customer calls with a question, she can retrieve the file from the file cabinet and answer the question. When Natalie buys her IBM PS/2, all the components of her manual system will exist in the hardware components of the computer system. Match each component of the manual system with the corresponding component of the computer hardware system.
   1. Natalie.   *a.* Input device.
   2. Calculator.   *b.* Control unit.
   3. Catalog.   *c.* Arithmetic-logic unit.
   4. File cabinet.   *d.* Primary storage unit.
   5. In-box.   *e.* Secondary storage devices.
   6. Out-box.   *f.* Output devices.

4. Have you used a microcomputer yet? If you have, explain what applications you accomplished. Were the microcomputer's hardware and software capabilities appropriate for the jobs you performed? Explain.

5. Have you used a mainframe or minicomputer? What jobs did you perform? Were the computer's capabilities sufficient for the jobs you had to do? Explain.

6. Jim Klugman is the vice president of Information Systems of ABC Department Stores, described in Real World Application 1–2 in Chapter 1. Jim has recommended that the company ban the purchase of microcomputers by individual stores. He feels that point-of-sale terminals and video display terminals (tied to the firm's central mainframe computer) are sufficient. What do you think of this recommendation? Explain.

7. Joan Alvarez, a store manager for ABC Department Stores, disagrees with the vice president of Information Systems. She is trying to decide on a computer purchase for her store. The top competing proposals involve a purchase of several microcomputer systems versus the purchase of a minicomputer system that can support up to 20 users simultaneously. What are some of the major factors that she should consider in choosing between these two proposals?

8. Are minicomputers on their way out? Both the Travelers Corporation and Tenneco, Inc. (Real World Applications 2–2 and 2–3) are deliberately choosing not to use such computers. Yet there is a big market for departmental or office computers that can tie together microcomputer workstations and other computer devices, and communicate with mainframes. What do you think? Explain the reasons for your answer.

3

INTRODUCTION TO COMPUTER SOFTWARE

Chapter Outline

Learning Objectives

The purpose of this chapter is to promote a basic understanding of computer software by analyzing the functions, benefits, and limitations of major types of system and application software packages and programming languages. After reading and studying this chapter, you should be able to:

1. Identify several major types of system and application software.
2. Outline the functions of an operating system.
3. Describe the role of database management systems, data communications monitors, and programming language translator programs.
4. Identify and explain the purpose of several popular microcomputer software packages.
5. Determine the various types of system and application software available for use on your microcomputer system or at your computer center.
6. Explain the differences between machine, assembler, high-level, and fourth-generation languages.
7. Summarize several major characteristics, benefits, and limitations of BASIC, COBOL, and Pascal.

INTRODUCTION

By now, you should have a good idea of the role of **software** in information systems and computer systems. In this chapter, we will explore in more detail the major types of software you will depend on as you work with computers. We'll discuss their major characteristics and purposes, and give examples of their use. This should provide you with the knowledge you need to learn to use the many types of software that are an indispensable part of modern information systems.

First, let's summarize three different ways that software can be categorized to give you a good overview of this important topic. We have said that information systems rely on *software resources*, as well as *hardware* and *people* to transform *data resources* into a variety of *information products*. Software must support the *input, processing, output, storage,* and *control* activities of such systems. In this context software resources consist of:

- □ **Programs** of instructions used to direct the operation of the *hardware* of computer systems.
- □ **Procedures** used to direct the activities of the *people* who operate and use computer systems.

We have also said that computer software consists of two major types of programs:

- □ **System software**—programs that control and support the operations of a computer system as it performs various information processing tasks.
- □ **Application software**—programs that direct the performance of a particular use or *application* of computers to meet the information processing needs of users.

Finally, you should realize that computer software can be subdivided into two other categories, depending on whether it is developed by users themselves or acquired from external sources.

- □ **Software packages**—programs acquired by users from various software vendors that are developed by computer manufacturers, independent software companies, or other users.
- □ **User-developed software**—programs developed by users or the professional programmers of a computer-using organization.

Let's begin our analysis of software by looking at an overview of the major types and functions of software available to computer users. Look at Figure 3–1. This figure summarizes the major categories of system and application software that we will discuss in this chapter. Of course, this is a conceptual illustration. The actual types of software categories that you may experience depend, first of all, on the manufacturer and model of computer you use; and second, on which additional software is acquired to increase your computer's performance or to accomplish specific tasks for you and other users.

Figure 3–1 Overview of system and application software. Notice the many types and uses of system and application software.

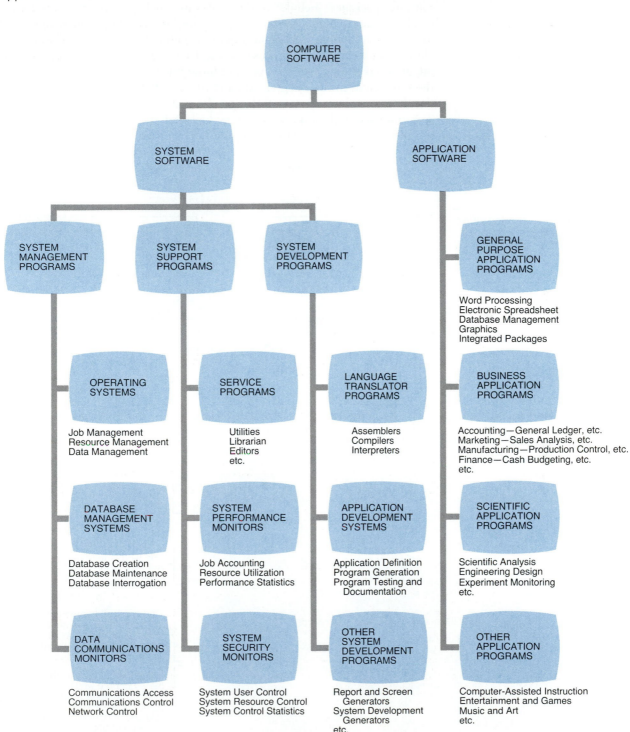

For example, if you are a microcomputer user, you probably will use only a few software packages most frequently. The most popular microcomputer software packages include system software such as operating systems, database management systems, programming language translators, and communications monitors. Popular microcomputer applications software includes packages for word processing, electronic spreadsheets, graphics, and integrated packages that do several of these functions. We will discuss all of these packages in this chapter. Most of them will also be explained in more detail in later chapters or in the appendixes at the back of the book. Figure 3–2 summarizes these packages. Now look at Figure 3–3. It illustrates the use of several types of software in one microcomputer display. You should also refer back to pages 27–30 in the pictorial section of Chapter 1 for color video displays of software packages in action.

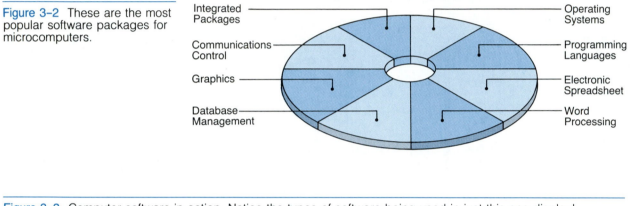

Figure 3–2 These are the most popular software packages for microcomputers.

Integrated Packages

Operating Systems

Communications Control

Programming Languages

Graphics

Electronic Spreadsheet

Database Management

Word Processing

Figure 3–3 Computer software in action. Notice the types of software being used in just this one display!

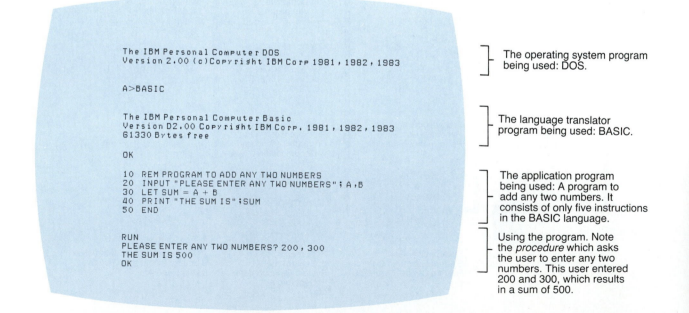

```
The IBM Personal Computer DOS
Version 2.00 (c)Copyright IBM Corp 1981, 1982, 1983


A>BASIC


The IBM Personal Computer Basic
Version D2.00 Copyright IBM Corp. 1981, 1982, 1983
61330 Bytes free

OK

10  REM PROGRAM TO ADD ANY TWO NUMBERS
20  INPUT "PLEASE ENTER ANY TWO NUMBERS"; A,B
30  LET SUM = A + B
40  PRINT "THE SUM IS"; SUM
50  END


RUN
PLEASE ENTER ANY TWO NUMBERS? 200, 300
THE SUM IS 500
OK
```

The operating system program being used: DOS.

The language translator program being used: BASIC.

The application program being used: A program to add any two numbers. It consists of only five instructions in the BASIC language.

Using the program. Note the *procedure* which asks the user to enter any two numbers. This user entered 200 and 300, which results in a sum of 500.

Section I: System Software

System software consists of computer programs that control and support a computer system and its information processing activities. As shown in Figure 3–1, system software includes a variety of programs such as operating systems, database management systems, communications monitors, service programs, and programming language translators. Notice, however, that such programs can be grouped into three major functional categories:

- ☐ **System management programs**—programs that *manage* the use of the hardware, software, and data resources of the computer system during its execution of the various information processing jobs of users. Major system management programs are operating systems, database management systems, and communications monitors.

- ☐ **System support programs**—programs that *support* the operations, management, and users of a computer system by providing a variety of support services. Major support programs are service programs, performance monitors, and security monitors.

- ☐ **System development programs**—programs that help users *develop* information system programs and procedures and prepare user programs for computer processing. Major development programs are language translators and application development systems.

Each of these programs performs important functions in modern computer systems and should be understood by knowledgeable computer users. Therefore, we will examine system software in this section. Such programs serve as a vital software *interface* between computer system hardware and the application programs of users. See Figure 3–4.

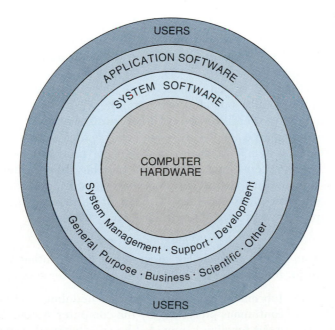

Figure 3–4 The system and application software interface between users and computer hardware.

OPERATING SYSTEMS

The most important system software package for any computer is its **operating system.** An operating system is an integrated *system* of programs that supervises the *operations* of the CPU, controls the input/output and storage functions of the computer system, and provides various support services as the computer executes the application programs of users.

The primary goal of the operating system is to maximize the productivity of a computer system by operating it in the most efficient manner possible. An operating system minimizes the amount of human intervention required during processing by a computer operator. An operating system also simplifies the job of computer programmers, since it includes programs that perform common input/output and storage operations and other standard processing functions. If you have done any of the hands-on exercises of Appendix A or any other jobs on a computer, you know that you must load and use the operating system before you can accomplish any other task. This emphasizes that operating systems have become the most indispensable component of the software interface between users and the hardware of their computer systems.

Many operating systems are designed as a collection of program *modules*, which can be organized in several combinations to form operating systems with various capabilities. Such operating systems can be tailored to fit the processing power and memory capacity of a computer system and the type of processing jobs that need to be done. For example, some operating system packages include a selected number of service programs, language translator programs, and even some application programs!

Popular microcomputer operating systems are PC-DOS™ and OS/2 by IBM, CP/M by Digital Research, and MS-DOS® and XENIX by Microsoft. CP/M was the most widely used operating system for 8-bit microcomputers. PC-DOS, MS-DOS, and OS/2 were all developed by Microsoft and are the most popular operating systems for 16-bit micros, especially the IBM PC, PS/2, and similar computers. The XENIX operating system is a microcomputer version of the AT&T UNIX system for larger computers. Several versions of such popular operating systems are available. Which version you should use depends primarily on the main microprocessor in your microcomputer.

Figure 3–5 is an example of the programs that are or can be included in three popular operating systems. The UNIX operating system was developed by AT&T. Versions of UNIX are being used in many supermini and supermicro computers because UNIX is such a powerful and *portable* operating system. Also shown are the major program modules and functions of the MVS operating system used by many IBM mainframe computers. Of course, many operating systems for microcomputers do not include so many different programs. Like PC-DOS, they usually consist of a main control program and several service and utility programs.

Operating System Management Programs

The system management programs of an operating system perform three major functions in the operation of a computer system.

- ☐ **Job management**—preparing, scheduling, and monitoring jobs for continuous processing by the computer system. The job management function is provided by an integrated system of programs that schedules and directs the flow of jobs through the computer

Figure 3-5 Three popular operating systems. Notice the variety of program modules and their functions.

THE UNIX OPERATING SYSTEM

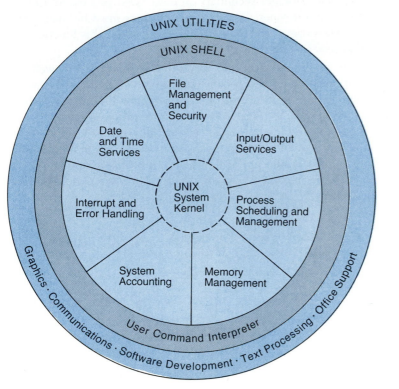

THE IBM PERSONAL COMPUTER
OPERATING SYSTEM

THE MVS OPERATING SYSTEM
FOR IBM MAINFRAME COMPUTER SYSTEMS

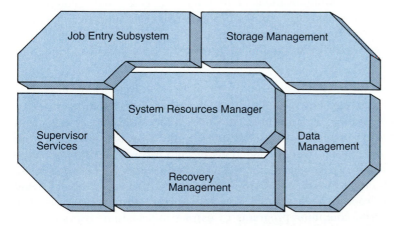

system. Job management activities include interpreting job control language (JCL) statements, scheduling and selecting jobs for execution by the computer system, initiating the processing of each job, terminating jobs, and communicating with the computer operator.

☐ **Resource management**—controlling the use of computer system resources by the other system software and application software programs being executed by the computer system. These resources include primary storage, secondary storage, CPU processing time, and input/output devices. Since these resources must be managed to accomplish various information processing tasks, this function is also called *task management*.

☐ **Data management**—controlling the input/output of data as well as their location, storage, and retrieval. In some operating systems, the programs that perform this function are called the *input/output control system (IOCS)*. This is a collection of programs that performs all of the functions required for the input and output of data. Data management programs control the allocation of secondary storage devices, the physical format and *cataloging* of data storage, and the movement of data between primary and secondary storage devices.

The Supervisor

In some operating systems, some of the functions of resource, job, and data management are handled by a group of programs called the **supervisor** (also known as the *executive,* the *monitor,* or the *controller*). The supervisor directs the operations of the entire computer system by controlling and coordinating (1) the other operating system programs, (2) other system and application software packages, and (3) the activities of all of the hardware components of the computer system. Portions of the supervisor reside in primary storage whenever the computer is operating, while other supervisor segments are transferred back and forth between primary storage and a magnetic disk drive.

The supervisor monitors input/output activities and handles interrupt conditions, job scheduling and queuing, program fetching, and primary storage allocations. It coordinates the use of other system management software, such as communications monitors and database management systems. The supervisor also communicates with the computer operator through a video display console concerning the status of computer system operations, and records information required for proper job accounting. See Figure 3–6.

DATABASE MANAGEMENT SYSTEMS

A **database management system** (DBMS) is a set of computer programs that control the creation, maintenance, and use of the *databases* of users and computer-using organizations. A DBMS is a system software package that helps you use the integrated collections of data records and files that are known as databases. It allows different user application programs to easily access the same database. A DBMS also simplifies the process of retrieving information from databases in the form of displays and reports. Instead of having to write computer programs to extract information, users can ask simple questions in the *query language* provided by most DBMS. Microcomputer versions of *file management* and database management programs have become so popular that they are now viewed as *general-purpose application programs* like word processing and spreadsheet packages.

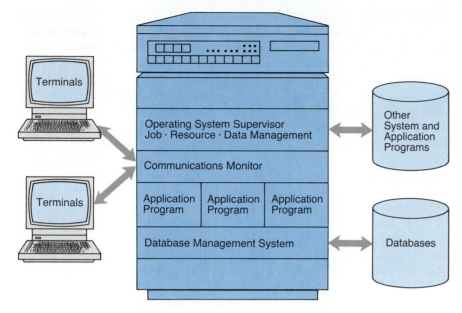

Figure 3–6 The functions of system management software: (1) job, resource, and data management, (2) communications management, and (3) database management.

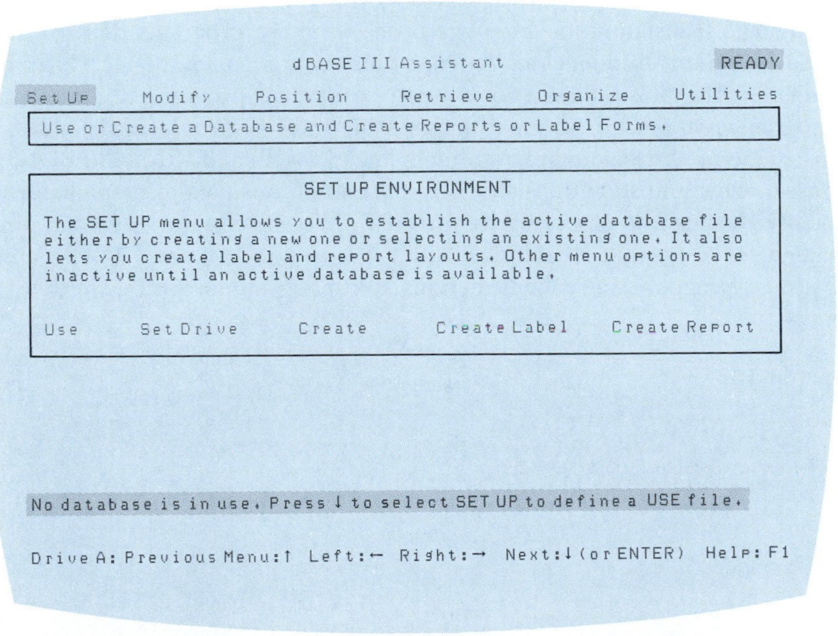

Figure 3–7 Using DBMS packages. Notice how this dBASE III display allows you to create or select a database file, or create reports or labels.

Examples of popular mainframe DBMS include DB2 by IBM and IDMS-R by Cullinet. Popular microcomputer database management systems are dBASE III Plus by Ashton-Tate and R:base System V by Microrim. We will explore the use of DBMS in modern information systems in Chapter 7. A hands-on tutorial on the use of microcomputer DBMS packages (using dBASE III Plus as an example) is presented in Appendix A at the back of the book. Figure 3–7 and page 28 of the pictorial section of Chapter 1 illustrate the use of popular microcomputer DBMS packages.

COMMUNICATIONS MONITORS

Modern information processing relies heavily on data communications systems, which provide for the transmitting of data over electronic communication links between one or more computer systems and computer terminals. This requires data communications control programs called **communications monitors** (or **teleprocessing** monitors). They are used by a main computer (called the *host*) or in specialized communications control processors (*front-end* computers). Communications monitors and other similar programs perform such functions as connecting or disconnecting communication links between computers and terminals, automatically checking terminals for input/output activity, assigning priorities to data communications requests from terminals, and detecting and correcting transmission errors. Thus they control and support the data communications activity occurring in a communications network.

Even microcomputers have versions of such software that help them communicate with other personal computers and mainframes in a network. For example, Figure 3–8 and page 29 of the pictorial section of Chapter 1 illustrate menu displays of data communications software packages. Such packages help users access personal computer information networks. (We will discuss data communications software in more detail in Chapter 8.)

LANGUAGE TRANSLATOR PROGRAMS

Language translators (or *language processors*) are programs that translate other programs into *machine language* instruction codes the computer can execute. They also allow you to write your own programs by providing program creation and editing facilities. Computer programs consist of sets of instructions written in programming languages like BASIC, COBOL, or Pascal, which must be translated into the computer's own machine language before they can be processed by the CPU. We will discuss these and other languages in Section III of this chapter.

Most programming language translator programs are called either *as-*

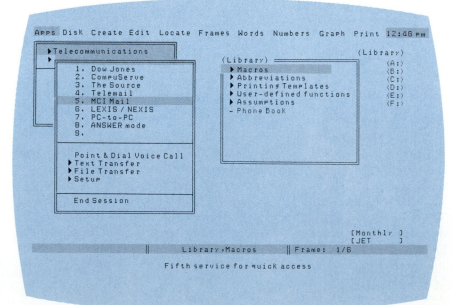

Figure 3–8 Accessing personal computer information networks with the data communications module of the Framework integrated software package.

semblers, *compilers*, or *interpreters*. An **assembler** translates the symbolic instruction codes of programs written in an assembler language into machine language instructions. A **compiler** translates the high level language statements of a program into machine language instructions the computer can execute. An **interpreter** is a special type of compiler that translates and executes each program statement one at a time, instead of first producing a complete machine language program, like compilers and assemblers do. The language translation process is called *interpreting* when an interpreter is used, *compiling* when a compiler is used, and *assembling* when an assembler is used. Language translators include extensive diagnostic capabilities that assist the programmer by recognizing and identifying programming errors.

Figure 3–9 illustrates the typical language translation process. A program written in a language like BASIC or COBOL is called a *source program*.

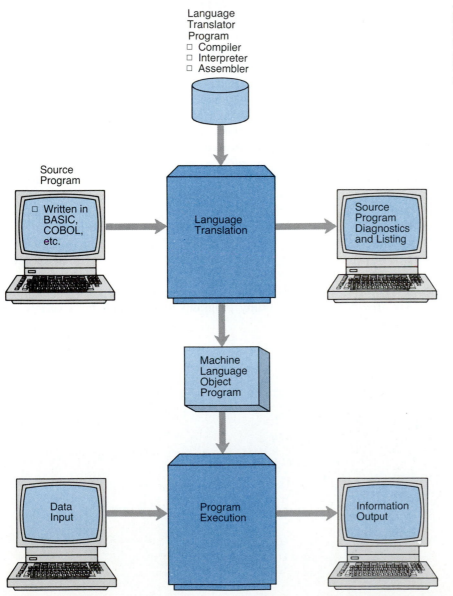

Figure 3–9 The language translation process: A program is first translated into machine language. Then it is executed to transform data input into information output.

When the source program is translated into machine language, it is called the *object program*. The computer then executes the object program. Besides the object program, most translators can produce a listing or display of the source program, and error messages (called *diagnostics*), which identify programming errors recognized by the translator program.

The most popular microcomputer language translators are those for the BASIC and Pascal programming languages. Other popular language translators are those for the Assembler, C, FORTRAN, and COBOL programming languages. The major categories and types of programming languages are covered in Section III of this chapter.

SERVICE PROGRAMS

Service programs are specialized programs that perform common routine and repetitive functions and are made available to all of the users of a computer system. For example, service programs, language translators, and most control programs and applications programs are usually maintained in *program libraries*. In addition, there is usually a *system library* of commonly used programs and subprograms *(subroutines)* shared by all users of a large computer system. Therefore, an important service program usually provided is the **librarian,** which catalogs, manages, and maintains a directory of the programs that are stored in the various libraries of the computer system. Another service program is the **linkage editor,** which edits a program by defining the specific storage locations it requires. It also links together programs and subroutines needed to accomplish specified user applications.

Finally, a major category of service programs is **utility programs** or *utilities*, which are a group of miscellaneous programs that perform various "housekeeping" and file conversion functions. *Sort-merge* programs are important utility programs that perform the sorting and merging operations on data that are required in many information processing applications. Utility programs also clear primary storage, load programs, record the contents of primary storage (memory dumping), and convert a file of data from one storage medium to another, such as from tape-to-disk. Many of the operating system commands used with microcomputers and other computer systems provide users with utility programs and routines for a variety of chores. See Figure 3–10.

Figure 3–10 Examples of operating system commands for utilities of the Microsoft DOS operating system.

```
                  DOS COMANDS

      COPY = Copy File
      DIR = Display Directory
      DISKCOPY = Copy Disk
      ERASE = Delete File
      FORMAT = Format Disk
      MODE = Change Display Option
      RENAME = Change File Name
      TYPE = Display File Contents
```

REAL WORLD APPLICATION 3–1

San Diego Gas and Electric Company

At San Diego Gas and Electric Company, the data processing department has established an "information center" for end-user computing assistance. Managers there use the center to free department programmers for strategic DP tasks. "Because of the information center, the end user is able to do tasks that we had to provide in the past," says Tom Ilas, information systems supervisor. "We used to have to be a jack-of-all-trades, taking the applications idea, developing it, and working with end users to define the requirements. Now, with the help of information center staff, users identify the need and develop the actual business case, as well as the detailed requirements for new systems."

As a result, the data processing staff has been freed from what Ilas calls "basic" backlog items such as reporting from the data base. Users can do this themselves with the aid of the mainframe's database management system. Now, programmers can spend their time on more sophisticated projects, like using the DBMS to refine the database or developing a complex tracking application in COBOL. These applications increase the productivity of the company as a whole.

The information center's 12-person staff of user consultants supports about 2,500 users who operate workstations, terminals, and personal computers. They use a wide range of applications packages from word processing and electronic spreadsheets to engineering and accounting programs. With their equipment, users can access two IBM 3081 mainframe computer systems, one of which runs the VM operating system and the other of which runs the MVS operating system.

IBM's TSO communications package is used to allow terminal workstations and personal computers to communicate with the mainframes. There are about 1,200 workstations and 230 IBM Personal Computers located within the company. Eighty percent of the PCs operate as stand-alone devices, using the PC-DOS operating system and a variety of leading software packages for spreadsheet analysis, word processing, database management, and graphics.

Application Questions

□ Identify the system software and application software used by San Diego Gas and Electric.

□ Briefly identify the functions of each of these packages.

Source: Adapted from Michael Sullivan-Trainor, "Utility's Info Center Frees DP Staff for Sophisticated Projects," *Computerworld*, August 11, 1986, p. 55.

OTHER SYSTEM SOFTWARE PACKAGES

Let's take a brief look at several other important system software packages that we will explain in greater detail in later chapters of this book.

Application development systems provide interactive assistance to programmers in the development of application programs. *Application generators* such as IBM's DMS (development management system) or ADS/ONLINE by Cullinet help simplify and automate the programming process. An application development system does this by providing *software tools*— programs that support interactive program editing, coding, testing, debugging, and maintenance. We will discuss application development systems further in Chapter 11.

System performance monitors are programs that monitor the processing of jobs on a computer system. They monitor computer system performance and produce reports containing detailed statistics concerning the use of system resources such as processor time, memory space, I/O devices, and system and application programs. Such reports are used to plan and control the efficient use of a computer system. We will discuss the role of such programs again in Chapter 15.

System security monitors are programs that monitor the use of a computer system to protect the computer system and its resources from unauthorized use, fraud, and destruction. Such programs provide the *computer security* needed to allow only authorized users to access the system. For example, identification codes and passwords are frequently used for this purpose. Security monitors also control use of the hardware, software, and data resources of a computer system. For example, even authorized users may be restricted to the use of certain devices, programs, and data files. Finally, such programs monitor use of the computer and collect statistics on any attempts at improper use. They produce reports to assist in maintaining the security of the system. System security monitors are discussed further in Chapter 17.

Section II: Application Software

Application software consists of programs that direct computers to perform specific information processing activities for users. These programs are called *application programs* because they direct the processing required for a particular use or *application* of computers. Remember that a **computer application** is the use of a computer to solve a specific problem or to accomplish a particular job for a computer user. Thousands of application programs are available because there are thousands of different jobs that users want computers to do. The use of personal computers has multiplied the growth of such programs. We will briefly explain the most popular types of application packages in this section.

But first, refer back to Figure 3–1. Notice that application software includes a variety of programs that are segregated into the following categories.

☐ **General-purpose application programs**—programs that can perform common information processing jobs for users from all application areas. For example, word processing programs, spreadsheet programs, database management programs, integrated packages, and graphics programs are popular with microcomputer users for home, education, business, scientific, and many other purposes.

☐ **Business application programs**—programs that can accomplish the information processing tasks needed to support important business functions or industry requirements. Examples of several business functions and corresponding applications are accounting (general ledger), marketing (sales analysis), finance (cash budgeting), manufacturing (material requirements planning), operations management (inventory control), and personnel (employee benefits analysis).

☐ **Scientific application programs**—programs that perform informa-tion processing tasks for the natural, physical, social, and behavioral sciences, for mathematics, engineering, and all other areas involved in scientific research, experimentation, and development. Some broad application categories include scientific analysis, engineering design, and monitoring of experiments.

☐ **Other application programs**—there are so many other application areas of computers that we lump them all into this category. Thus we can talk of computer applications in education, entertainment, music, art, law enforcement, medicine, and so on. Some specific examples are computer-assisted instruction (CAI) programs in education, video game programs in entertainment, and computer-generated music and art programs.

WORD PROCESSING PACKAGES

Word processing packages are built around programs that automate the creation, editing, and printing of *documents* of all kinds, including letters, memos, reports, and so on. They electronically process *text data* (words, phrases, sentences, paragraphs) you provide through the keyboard of a microcomputer or terminal. The text material is simultaneously stored in memory and displayed on your video screen so you can easily correct, change, and manipulate it. You can then print a document on your printer and save a copy of it on your system's magnetic disk unit.

Sounds simple, doesn't it? It is, with a little bit of study and practice. Word processing and the use of word processing packages (like WordStar®, WordPerfect™, and MultiMate) are described in detail in Appendix A at the back of this book. Figure 3–11 and page 27 of the pictorial section in Chapter 1 illustrate video displays generated by popular word processing packages.

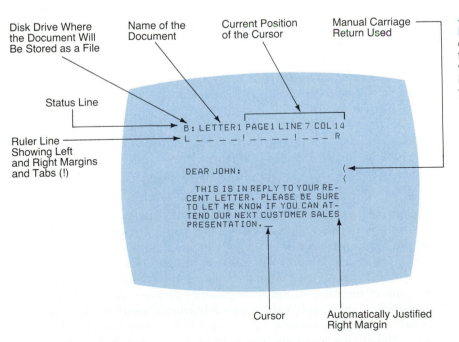

Disk Drive Where the Document Will Be Stored as a File

Name of the Document

Current Position of the Cursor

Manual Carriage Return Used

Status Line

Ruler Line Showing Left and Right Margins and Tabs (!)

B: LETTER1 PAGE1 LINE 7 COL 14
L _ _ _ _ ! _ _ _ _ ! _ _ _ R

DEAR JOHN:

    THIS IS IN REPLY TO YOUR RE-
CENT LETTER. PLEASE BE SURE
TO LET ME KNOW IF YOU CAN AT-
TEND OUR NEXT CUSTOMER SALES
PRESENTATION.

Cursor

Automatically Justified Right Margin

Figure 3–11 Using a word pro-cessing package. Notice how this video display shows you what you have typed and other information about the document you are creating.

Many word processing packages provide advanced features or can be upgraded with supplementary packages. One example is a **spelling checker** program that uses built-in dictionaries to help you identify and correct spelling errors in your document. Another example is a **thesaurus** program that helps you find a better choice of words to express your ideas. **Style checker** programs can be used to identify and correct grammar and punctuation errors, as well as suggest possible improvements in your writing style. Another text productivity tool is an **idea processor** or **outliner** program. It helps you organize and outline your thoughts before you prepare a document or develop a presentation. Also popular is a **mail-merge** program that allows you to automatically merge the names and addresses in a mailing list file with your letters and other documents.

ELECTRONIC SPREADSHEET PACKAGES

Electronic spreadsheet packages are application programs used for analysis, planning, and modeling. They provide an electronic replacement for more traditional tools such as a paper worksheet, pencil, and calculator. They generate an electronic spreadsheet, which is a worksheet of rows and columns that is stored in the computer's memory and is displayed on its video screen. You use the computer's keyboard or other devices, such as an electronic mouse or touch screen, to enter data and relationships (formulas) into the worksheet. This results in an *electronic model* of your problem. In response to your commands the computer quickly performs necessary calculations based on the relationships you defined in the spreadsheet. Then results are immediately displayed for you to see.

How do you use the worksheet created by electronic spreadsheet packages? Think of the worksheet as a *visual model* of a particular business activity or other operation. It can thus be used to record and analyze past and present activity. However, it can also be used as a decision-making tool to answer "what if" questions. For example, "**What** would happen to net profit **if** advertising expense increased by 10 percent?" To answer this question, you would simply change the advertising expense figure on an income statement worksheet. Then the affected figures would be recalculated, including a new net profit figure.

Once an electronic spreadsheet has been developed, it can be stored on a floppy disk or other storage device for later use, or be printed out as a paper report on your computer's printer. The use of electronic spreadsheet packages like Lotus 1-2-3, Multiplan, and SuperCalc are explained in Appendix A at the back of this book. Refer to Figure 3–12 and page 27 of the pictorial section of Chapter 1 for examples of spreadsheet displays.

GRAPHICS PACKAGES

Graphics packages transform numeric data into graphics displays such as line charts, bar charts, and pie charts. These are displayed on your video monitor, or printed copies can be made on your system printer or plotter. Not only are such graphic displays easier to comprehend than numeric data, but multiple color displays can more easily emphasize strategic differences and trends in the data. To use some graphics packages (like BPS Graphics, PFS: GRAPH, and GraphPlan), you merely enter through the keyboard the categories of data you want plotted in response to prompts displayed on your screen. The graphics program then analyzes the file of data you specify and

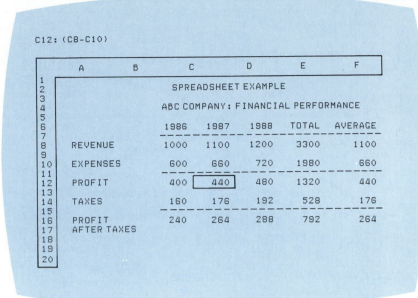

Figure 3–12 A simple financial spreadsheet. Note that *cell* C12 is highlighted by a *cell pointer*. This cell displays the quantity 440. However, it contains the formula (C8–C10) as shown on the top of the screen. This indicates that the value of cell C12 is the result of subtracting the value of cell C10 from cell C8. In this example, this is 1100 − 660 = 440. This *relationship* expressed in words is: Revenue Minus Expenses Equals Profit.

Figure 3–13 Using a graphics package. The first video display shows how you would enter graphics specifications using BPS Graphics. The second display shows the resulting bar chart.

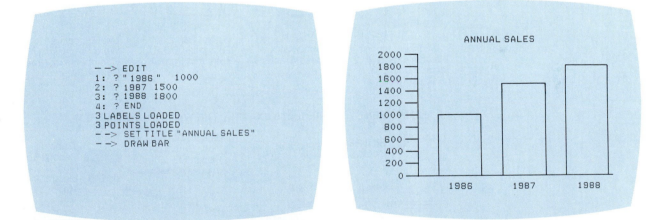

generates the requested graphics. See Figure 3–13 and refer to page 28 of the pictorial section in Chapter 1 for graphics program displays.

INTEGRATED PACKAGES

Integrated packages combine the ability to do several general-purpose applications in one program. This really benefits you if you wish to perform a variety of information processing jobs using the same file of data. The alternative would be to use separate programs, entering each program and the same data file each time you used a different program. To make it worse, some programs will refuse to work with data files created by other programs!

Figure 3–14 Using an integrated package. Notice the many activities you can do with one software package.

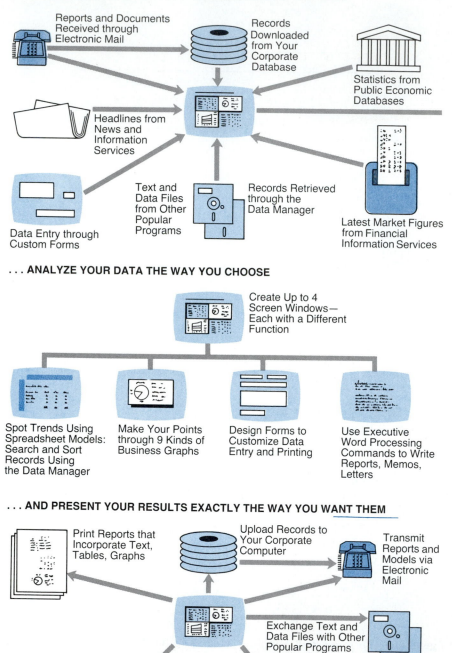

. . . GATHER INFORMATION FROM ALL THE SOURCES YOU NEED

Reports and Documents Received through Electronic Mail

Records Downloaded from Your Corporate Database

Statistics from Public Economic Databases

Headlines from News and Information Services

Data Entry through Custom Forms

Text and Data Files from Other Popular Programs

Records Retrieved through the Data Manager

Latest Market Figures from Financial Information Services

. . . ANALYZE YOUR DATA THE WAY YOU CHOOSE

Create Up to 4 Screen Windows—Each with a Different Function

Spot Trends Using Spreadsheet Models: Search and Sort Records Using the Data Manager

Make Your Points through 9 Kinds of Business Graphs

Design Forms to Customize Data Entry and Printing

Use Executive Word Processing Commands to Write Reports, Memos, Letters

. . . AND PRESENT YOUR RESULTS EXACTLY THE WAY YOU WANT THEM

Print Reports that Incorporate Text, Tables, Graphs

Upload Records to Your Corporate Computer

Transmit Reports and Models via Electronic Mail

Exchange Text and Data Files with Other Popular Programs

Create or Update Records in Data Files

Plot or Print Presentation-Quality Business Graphs

Generate Custom Forms to Display Information

Integrated packages have solved the problems caused by the inability of individual programs to communicate and work together with common files of data. However, most integrated packages require significant amounts of additional memory capacity. Also, they have had to compromise on the speed, power, and flexibility of some of their functions in order to achieve integration. Therefore, users may prefer single function packages for applications that they use heavily.

Examples of popular integrated packages include Symphony, Framework, Enable, and the Smart System. Such packages combine some of the general-purpose application software functions of electronic spreadsheets, word processing, and graphics with the system software functions of database management and data communications. Thus you can process the same file of data with one package, moving from one function to the other by pressing a few keys on your keyboard. You can view displays from each one separately or together on multiple *windows* on your video screen. Figure 3–14 and page 29 of the pictorial section in Chapter 1 illustrate the use of integrated packages.

Some of the advantages of integrated packages can be derived by using an **operating environment** package, like TopView, Windows, and Desqview. These provide an additional *software interface* between users, the operating system, and their application programs. These packages serve as a *shell* to interconnect several separate application packages so they can communicate and work together and share common data files. They also allow the outputs of several programs to be displayed at the same time in *multiple windows*. Finally, several of these packages support some type of *concurrent processing*, where several programs or tasks can be processed at the same time. (Concurrent processing is explained in Chapter 4.) These *software integrator* packages have become popular with users who prefer to integrate a variety of single function programs. See Figure 3–15.

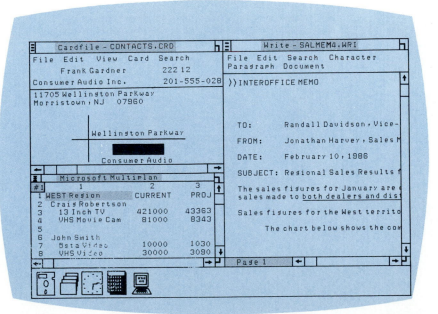

Figure 3–15 Using an operating environment package. Microsoft Windows allow you to use word processing, spreadsheet, file management, and other programs in multiple window displays.

Figure 3–16 A summary of common business application packages. Notice how computers can help businesses perform these typical activities.

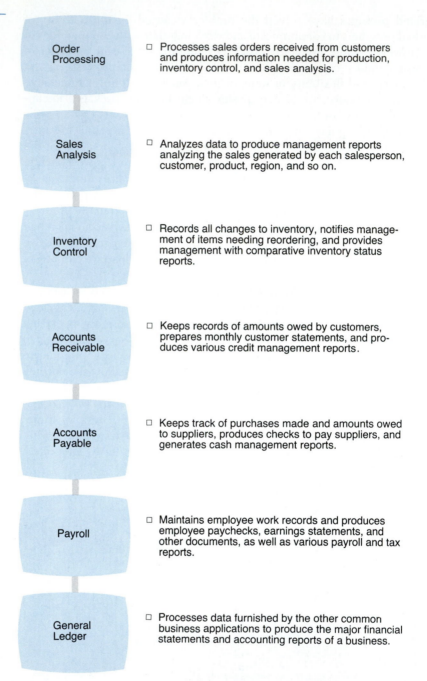

Order Processing
□ Processes sales orders received from customers and produces information needed for production, inventory control, and sales analysis.

Sales Analysis
□ Analyzes data to produce management reports analyzing the sales generated by each salesperson, customer, product, region, and so on.

Inventory Control
□ Records all changes to inventory, notifies management of items needing reordering, and provides management with comparative inventory status reports.

Accounts Receivable
□ Keeps records of amounts owed by customers, prepares monthly customer statements, and produces various credit management reports.

Accounts Payable
□ Keeps track of purchases made and amounts owed to suppliers, produces checks to pay suppliers, and generates cash management reports.

Payroll
□ Maintains employee work records and produces employee paychecks, earnings statements, and other documents, as well as various payroll and tax reports.

General Ledger
□ Processes data furnished by the other common business applications to produce the major financial statements and accounting reports of a business.

Common business packages are programs that accomplish the information processing tasks required by accounting and other business activities. Applications like sales analysis, accounts receivable and payable, inventory control, order processing, general ledger, and payroll need to be accomplished whether a business is large or small. So businesses need software packages that help them perform such activities efficiently and effectively. Examples for microcomputers are Dac-Easy Accounting, Solomon III, and Easy Business Accounting, to name a few. Figure 3–16 summarizes the most important of these common business and accounting applications. They are all discussed in more detail in Chapter 14.

COMMON BUSINESS PACKAGES

We could spend a lot more time discussing the many application packages available for mainframes, minicomputers, and microcomputers. In fact, one of the attractions of microcomputers is that many low cost software packages are available to support a variety of uses. This includes using microcomputers for applications such as personal finance, home management, video games, education, and information services. Other application packages support more professional and business uses such as project management, investment analysis, and desktop publishing. Still other packages (like *desktop organizers*) support computer users by helping them organize and accomplish routine tasks. We will discuss these and other software packages in later chapters on data communications, financial information systems, and office automation.

OTHER APPLICATION PACKAGES

REAL WORLD APPLICATION 3–2

Popular Software Packages

In the real world, the most widely used software packages for spreadsheets, word processing, database management, graphics, and communications are the following:

Lotus 1-2-3 Electronic Spreadsheet Package

Solve complicated numerical problems with this electronic spreadsheet program, which also provides sophisticated graphics and simple data management. Lotus 1-2-3 combines the convenience and familiarity of a pocket calculator with the powerful memory and electronic display capabilities of your personal computer. You can build spreadsheets up to 256 columns and over 8,000 rows in size! Later modifications are automatically recalculated throughout the entire spreadsheet. With a simple change of data elements, you can also compute a variety of "what if" situations and graphically display the results for quick and easy comparisons.

WordStar Word Processing Package

WordStar provides comprehensive word processing capabilities. Your editing commands are easily accomplished. You can insert, delete, move, and copy text. You can choose a variety of margin settings and font styles such

Continued on page 120

REAL WORLD APPLICATION 3–2

Continued from page 119

as boldface and italics. WordStar now allows you to "undo" mistaken commands and can automatically index a document. Also included is an online spelling checker and thesaurus to help you use the right words correctly.

dBASE III Plus Database Management Package

Use your personal computer to create, update, and interrogate a database of files and records. With dBASE III Plus you'll be able to work with up to 15 files at once; manipulate a database, and update and revise data. Use the report function to organize data and produce printed reports. This advanced relational database management system includes an extensive programming language. However, untrained office personnel can use it because dBASE III Plus has an "assistant" mode that provides a series of menus that simplifies its operations.

Microsoft Chart Business Graphics Package

Quickly and easily produce multicolored charts and graphs. Eight major chart types and 45 predesigned formats are provided. Use simple commands to key in data or extract data to be graphed from programs, reports, and documents. Create your own graphic formats, then store the commands to automatically update or generate graphic reports.

Crosstalk Communications Package

Crosstalk lets you dial into a host computer system and act as terminal to that system. You can also easily exchange or transfer any size or type of file with compatible systems. Crosstalk supports most popular autodial modems.

Symphony Integrated Package

Get this powerful package and you'll have word processing, data management, electronic worksheet analysis, sophisticated graphics, and communications capability in a single program! With Symphony you get a flexible worksheet, expanded mathematical functions, "what if" analysis, and instant Help. You also get text entry and editing, simple data management, easy but powerful graphics, and a helpful communications access program.

Application Questions

☐ Which of these software packages would you (or do you) find most useful? Why?

☐ Have you used these or any similar packages? Which were easiest to use? Why?

Source: Ashton-Tate (dBASE III Plus); Microsoft Corporation (Microsoft Chart); Lotus Development Corporation (Lotus 1-2-3 and Symphony); Microstuff, Inc. (Crosstalk); and Micropro International Corp. (WordStar).

Section III: Programming Languages

A proper understanding of computer software requires a basic knowledge of **programming languages.** Programming languages allow the instructions in software packages to be written in a language that is mutually understandable to both people and computers. To be a knowledgeable computer user, you should know the basic characteristics of several popular programming languages. Then you should have the experience of using one to develop a few simple programs of your own. Many different programming languages have been developed, each with its own unique vocabulary, grammar, and uses. We will briefly analyze several major languages in this section. However, let us first examine the four major types shown in Figure 3–17.

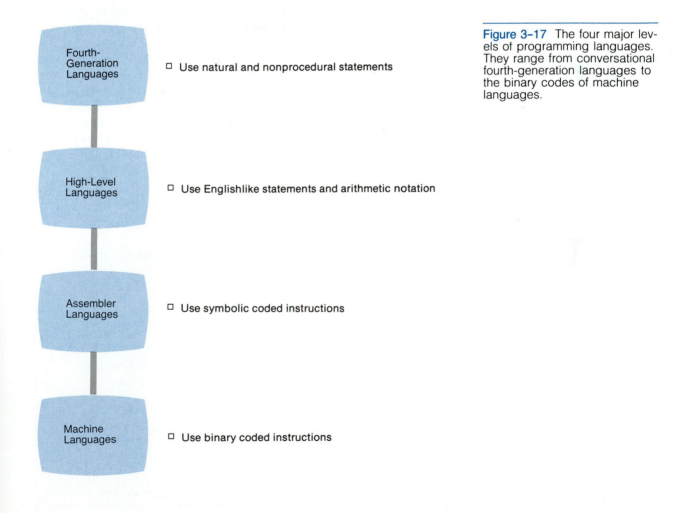

Figure 3–17 The four major levels of programming languages. They range from conversational fourth-generation languages to the binary codes of machine languages.

MACHINE LANGUAGES

Machine languages are the most basic level of programming languages. In the early stages of computer development, all program instructions had to be written using *binary codes* unique to each computer. (Binary codes are discussed in Chapter 4.) This type of programming involved the difficult task of writing instructions in the form of strings of ones and zeros. Programmers had to have a detailed knowledge of the internal operations of the CPU they were using. They had to write long series of detailed instructions to accomplish even simple processing tasks. Programming in machine language requires specifying the storage locations for every instruction and item of data used. Instructions must be included for every switch and indicator that is used by the program. These requirements make machine language programming a difficult and error-prone task.

A machine language program that would add two numbers together in the accumulator and store the result $(X = Y + Z)$ might take the form shown in Figure 3–18. Like many computer instructions, these instructions consist of an *operation code*, which specifies what is to be done, and an *operand*, which specifies the address of the data or device to be operated upon.

ASSEMBLER LANGUAGES

Assembler languages are the next level of programming languages and were developed to reduce the difficulties in writing machine-language programs. The use of assembler languages requires the use of language translator programs called *assemblers*, which allow a computer to convert the instructions of such languages into machine instructions. Assembler languages are frequently called symbolic languages, because symbols are used to represent operation codes and storage locations. Convenient alphabetic abbreviations

Figure 3–18 Examples of four levels of programming languages. These programming language instructions might be used to compute the sum of any two numbers, as expressed by the formula X = Y + Z. The last two levels also demonstrate how Englishlike instructions can be, if X is defined as GROSSPAY, Y as SALARY, and Z as COMMISSIONS.

MACHINE LANGUAGE

Operation Code	Operand	
1010	11001	(Replace the current value in the accumulator with the value Y at location 11001)
1011	11010	(Add the value Z at location 11010 to the value Y in the accumulator)
1100	11011	(Store the value X in the accumulator at location 11011)

ASSEMBLER LANGUAGE

Operation Code	Operand	
LD	Y	(Load Y into the accumulator)
AD	Z	(Add Z to the accumulator)
ST	X	(Store the result X)

HIGH-LEVEL LANGUAGE

FORTRAN: X = Y + Z
  COBOL: COMPUTE X = Y + Z

FORTRAN: GROSPAY = SALARY + COMMIS
  COBOL: ADD SALARY, COMMISSIONS GIVING GROSSPAY

FOURTH-GENERATION LANGUAGE

SUM THE FOLLOWING TWO NUMBERS
COMPUTE THE GROSSPAY OF ALL SALESPERSONS BY SUMMING THEIR SALARY AND COMMISSIONS

called *mnemonics* (memory aids) and other symbols are used to represent operation codes, storage locations, and data elements. For example; the computation $(X = Y + Z)$ in an assembler language program might take the form shown in Figure 3–18.

Notice how alphabetical abbreviations that are easier to remember are used in place of the actual numeric addresses of the data. This greatly simplifies programming, since the programmer does not need to know or remember the exact storage locations of data and instructions. However, assembler language is still *machine-oriented*, since assembler language instructions correspond closely to the machine language instructions of the particular computer model being used. Also, notice that each assembler instruction corresponds to a single machine instruction so the same number of instructions are required in both illustrations. This is a major limitation of some assembler languages.

Assembler languages are still widely used as a method of programming a computer in a machine-oriented language. Most computer manufacturers provide an assembler language that reflects the unique machine-language *instruction set* of a particular line of computers. This characteristic is particularly desirable to *systems programmers*, who program systems software (as opposed to *applications programmers*, who program applications software) since it provides them with greater control and flexibility in designing a program for a particular computer. They can then produce more *efficient* software, that is, programs that require a minimum of instructions, storage, and CPU time to perform a specific processing assignment.

High-level languages are also known as *compiler languages*. The instructions of high-level languages are called *statements* and closely resemble human language or the standard notation of mathematics. Individual high-level language statements are really **macro instructions.** That is, each individual statement generates several machine instructions when translated into machine language by high-level language translator programs called *compilers* or *interpreters*.

High-level language statements resemble the English language or mathematical expressions required to express the problem or procedure being programmed. The *syntax* (vocabulary, punctuation, and grammatical rules) and the *semantics* (meanings) of such statements do not reflect the internal code of any particular computer. For example, the computation $(X = Y + Z)$ would be programmed in the high- level languages of FORTRAN and COBOL as shown in Figure 3–18. It also illustrates how close to the English language high-level language statements can be.

A high-level language is obviously easier to learn and understand. It takes less time and effort to write an error-free computer program or to make corrections and revisions that may be required. However, high-level language programs are usually less efficient than assembler language programs and require a greater amount of computer time for translation into machine instructions.

Since many high-level languages are machine-independent, programs written in a high-level language do not have to be reprogrammed when a new computer is installed, and computer programmers do not have to learn a new language for each computer they program. High-level languages have less rigid rules, form, and syntax, thus reducing the potential for errors.

HIGH-LEVEL LANGUAGES

Figure 3–19 Comparing third- and fourth-generation languages. Notice how brief, nonprocedural, and conversational INTELLECT is compared to COBOL.

```
NATURAL LANGUAGE (INTELLECT):
FOR THE MENS AND WOMENS DEPARTMENTS, COMPARE THE ACTUAL
AND FORECASTED SALES FOR LAST MONTH.


COBOL (PROCEDURE DIVISION):
  MAIN-PARAGRAPH.
    PERFORM INITIALIZATION.
    PERFORM PROCESSING UNTIL END-OF-FILE.
    CLOSE IN-FILE, OUT-FILE,
    STOP RUN.

  INITIALIZATION.
    OPEN INPUT IN-FILE, OUTPUT OUT-FILE.
    PERFORM READ-RECORD
    MOVE "87 MAY ACT SALES   87 MAY EST SALES   DIFFERENCE   % CHANGE"
      TO LINE OUT.
    WRITE OUT-REC AFTER ADVANCING 1 LINE.

  PROCESSING.
    SUBTRACT MAY_87_ACT_SALES FROM MAY_87_EST_SALES GIVING DIFFERENCE.
    COMPUTE CHANGE = 100*DIFFERENCE/MAY_87_ACT_SALES.
    MOVE MAY_87_ACT_SALES TO MAY_87_ACT_SALES_PRT.
    MOVE MAY_87_EST_SALES TO MAY_87_EST_SALES_PRT.
    MOVE DIFFERENCE TO DIFFERENCE_PRT.
    MOVE CHANGE TO CHANGE_PRT.
    WRITE OUT-REC FROM PRT-REC AFTER ADVANCING 1 LINE.
    PERFORM READ-RECORD.

  READ-RECORD
    READ IN-FILE AT END MOVE "Y" TO EOF-FLAG.
```

FOURTH-GENERATION LANGUAGES

The term **fourth-generation language** (4GL) is used to describe a variety of computer-using languages. This includes **natural language, very high-level languages** (VHLL), **nonprocedural languages, actoral languages,** and so forth. *Application* and *program generators* are also considered to be fourth-generation languages, as are the *query, report generator*, and *data manipulation* languages provided by most current database management systems. These languages are called fourth-generation languages (4GL) to differentiate them from machine languages (first generation), assembler languages (second generation), and high-level languages (third generation).

Note: Some industry observers have begun to use the term **fifth-generation language** to describe languages using artificial intelligence techniques to accomplish results for users.

Natural languages are a type of 4GL that are very close to English or other human languages. Much research and development activity is still underway to develop languages that are as easy to use as ordinary conversation in one's natural language. Development of the complex language translator programs (sometimes called *intelligent* compilers) required to translate such natural languages into structured machine-language programs is also involved. Some fourth-generation languages are called **nonprocedural languages,** because they do not require users to write detailed procedures that tell the computer *how* to do a *process* to produce a desired result. Instead, such languages allow users to simply tell the computer *what* result they want.

Figures 3–18 and 3–19 compare fourth-generation languages with earlier generation languages. In Figure 3–19, notice how brief, nonprocedural, and

4GL	SUPPLIER
Query Languages and Report Writers	
ADRS II, QBE, SQL CLOUT DATATRIEVE EASYTRIEVE HAL INTELLECT	IBM Microrim DEC Panasophic Lotus Development Artificial Intelligence
Decision Support Generators	
EXPRESS IFPS MODEL SYSTEM W	Mgt. Decision Systems Execucom Lloyd Bush Compushare
Application Generators	
ADF, CSP, DMS ADS/ONLINE FOCUS IDEAL LINC, MAPPER MANTIS MARK V NATURAL NOMAD 2 RAMIS II	IBM Cullinet Info. Builders ADR Unisys Cincom Informatics Software AG Thomson SA Mathematica

Figure 3–20 Examples of popular fourth-generation languages.

conversational INTELLECT is compared to COBOL when you wish to accomplish a simple sales analysis task. Many other software packages that feature fourth-generation languages are available, such as SAVVY, FOCUS, SQL/DS, and CLOUT. This includes several microcomputer versions. Many more are being developed and will be introduced in the coming years. Indications are that such languages will one day make computer programming as easy for you as ordinary conversation. Of course, there are major differences in the ease of use and technical sophistication of these products. For instance, INTELLECT and CLOUT impose no rigid grammatical rules, while SQL/DS requires concise structured statements. Figure 3–20 outlines some of the major categories of fourth-generation languages.

EXAMPLES OF PROGRAMMING LANGUAGES

Hundreds of programming languages have been developed, many of them with humorous names, ranging from FRED and LOLITA to STRUDL and SYNFUL! The number of programming languages and different versions or "dialects" is growing rapidly. However, let's take a closer look at three of the most widely used languages: BASIC, COBOL, and Pascal. A brief analysis and illustration of each language is presented in the remainder of this section. Figure 3–21 is a summary of these and other major programming languages.

Figure 3–21 A summary of major programming languages. Notice the differences in the major characteristics and purposes of each language.

Ada: Named after Augusta Ada Byron, considered the world's first computer programmer. Developed in 1980 for the U.S. Department of Defense as a standard "high-order language" to replace COBOL and FORTRAN. It resembles an extension of Pascal.

ALGOL: (ALGOrithmic Language). An international algebraic language designed primarily for scientific and mathematical applications. It is widely used in Europe in place of FORTRAN.

APL: (A Programming Language). A mathematically oriented interactive language originated by Kenneth Iverson of IBM. It utilizes a very concise symbolic notation designed for efficient interactive programming of analytical business and scientific applications.

BASIC: (Beginner's All-Purpose Symbolic Instruction Code). A simple procedure-oriented language developed at Dartmouth College. It is used for interactive programming on time-sharing systems and has become a popular language for minicomputer and microcomputer systems for small business use and personal computing.

C: A low-level structured language developed by Bell Laboratories as part of the UNIX operating system. It resembles a machine-independent assembler language and is presently popular for system software programming and microcomputer packages.

COBOL: (COmmon Business Oriented Language). Designed by a committee of computer manufacturers and users (CODASYL) as an Englishlike language specifically for business data processing. It is the most widely used programming language for business applications.

FORTRAN: (FORmula TRANslation). The oldest of the popular high-level languages. It was designed for solving mathematical problems in science, engineering, research, business, and education. It is still the most widely used programming language for scientific and engineering applications.

LISP: (LISt Processing). A procedural list processing language developed by John McCarthy of MIT. Programs in LISP consist of linked lists of functions within parenthesis. LISP has long been a popular language for artificial intelligence applications.

LOGO: An interactive graphical language used as a tool for learning a variety of concepts (color, direction, letters, words, sounds, and the like) as well as learning to program and use a computer. Forms and figures are used (sprites and turtles), which a child learns to move around on the screen to accomplish tasks.

MODULA-2: Developed by Nicholas Wirth as a successor to Pascal for general-purpose applications. Allows large and complex programs to be in self-contained modules.

Pascal: Named after Blaise Pascal. Developed by Niklaus Wirth of Zurich as a powerful successor to ALGOL, and designed specifically to incorporate structured programming concepts and to facilitate top-down design. Pascal has become a popular language for both large computers and microcomputers.

PILOT: (Programmed Inquiry, Learning Or Teaching). A special-purpose language designed to develop CAI (computer-aided instruction) programs. It is a simple interactive language that enables a person with minimal computer experience to develop and test interactive CAI programs.

PL/1: (Programming Language/1). A general-purpose language developed by IBM. It was designed to combine some of the features of COBOL, FORTRAN, ALGOL, and other special languages. It is thus a highly flexible "modular" general-purpose language that can be used for business, scientific, and specialized applications.

PROLOG: (PROgramming in LOGic). A nonprocedural language developed by Alain Colmerauer of France. Programs in PROLOG consist of declarations that define quantities and relationships between objects. Logical inferences result from such programs, thus making PROLOG a popular language for developing expert systems and other AI applications.

RPG: (Report Program Generator). A problem-oriented language that generates programs that produce reports and perform other data processing tasks. It is a popular language for report preparation, file maintenance, and other business data processing applications of small computer users.

BASIC (Beginner's All-purpose Symbolic Instruction Code) is a widely used programming language for time-sharing applications and microcomputer systems for small business use and for personal computing. BASIC was developed in the early 1960s at Dartmouth College as a simple, easily learned language that would allow students to engage in interactive (conversational) computing, using a time-sharing computer system. BASIC resembles a shortened and simplified version of FORTRAN. With only a few hours of instruction, a computer user can solve small problems by "conversing" with a computer. BASIC has proven so easy to learn and use that it has quickly become a widely used programming language.

Several versions of BASIC have been developed. Such "extensions" of BASIC have transformed it into a more powerful language that can handle a wide variety of data processing assignments. The extensions of BASIC have not been standardized. However, the specifications for the most essential and widely used parts of BASIC (called Standard Minimal BASIC) were standardized in 1978. Versions with more advanced features (frequently called "Extended" BASIC) are more likely to contain differences in specifications and usage.

BASIC is a "friendly" language that is easy to learn and use for several reasons. Entering data is easy because input is comparatively "free form" (i.e., no rigid input format is necessary). Output formats are also provided, if desired. Many BASIC translator programs are really interactive interpreters that translate each BASIC statement immediately after it is typed in, and provide helpful diagnostics if an error is sensed in a statement. These benefits must be balanced against its lack of strong support for "structured programming" (see Chapter 11) and its limited ability to handle large database processing applications. However, recent compiler versions of BASIC have been developed that rectify these limitations.

BASIC

There are five major categories of statements in fundamental versions of BASIC:

BASIC Statements

- ☐ *Arithmetic statements*. Arithmetic operations can be accomplished through the use of LET statements such as LET X = Y + Z. Arithmetic expressions may also be contained in a PRINT statement.

- ☐ *Input/output statements*. Fundamental input/output statements are READ, DATA, INPUT, and PRINT. READ statements read the contents of specific data fields from input data provided by DATA statements. INPUT statements accept input data directly from the keyboard, while PRINT statements type output to a video monitor or printer.

- ☐ *Control statements*. Fundamental control words are GO TO, IF–THEN, FOR, NEXT, WHILE, WEND, and END. GO TO and IF–THEN statements alter the sequential execution of program statements by transferring control to another statement. FOR and WHILE statements command the computer to repeatedly execute a series of statements (a "program loop") that are part of the

Figure 3–22 A sample BASIC program. This simple program computes an average exam score.

```
OK
10 REM PROGRAM TO COMPUTE AN AVERAGE EXAM SCORE
20 LET COUNTER = 0
30 LET TOTAL = 0
40 READ SCORE
50 WHILE SCORE <>9999
60    LET COUNTER = COUNTER + 1
70    LET TOTAL = TOTAL + SCORE
80    READ SCORE
90 WEND
100 LET AVERAGE = TOTAL / COUNTER
110 PRINT "AVERAGE SCORE IS"; AVERAGE
120 DATA 64, 87, 43, 95, 66, 75, 59, 97, 67
130 DATA 9999
140 END
RUN
AVERAGE SCORE IS 72.5555
OK
```

computer program. NEXT and WEND statements are used to end program loops formed by FOR and WHILE statements, while an END statement terminates a BASIC program.

☐ *Other statements.* Two other BASIC statements are frequently used even in simple BASIC programs. REM statements are not translated by the compiler or executed by the computer. They are merely remarks and comments of the programmer that help document the purpose of the program and only appear in the program listing. The DIM statement is used in BASIC to specify the "dimensions" (rows and levels) or "arrays" of data items. It reserves the memory locations required to store each element in an array.

☐ *System commands.* BASIC system commands are not BASIC program statements but are commands to the operating system of the computer. They control the use of the BASIC compiler and the processing of BASIC programs. Two examples are RUN (tells the computer to execute a program), and LIST (a printed or displayed listing of the statements in the program).

Sample BASIC Program

Figure 3–22 illustrates a simple BASIC program that computes an average exam score (arithmetic mean) of the scores received on an exam by students in a class. It shows the statements of the BASIC program, the input data of exam scores, and the output of the computed average exam score. Figure 3–23 is a brief analysis of how the program works. It includes a **flowchart** that illustrates the logic of the program. An introduction to programming in the BASIC language is provided by Appendix B at the back of this text.

COBOL

COBOL (Common Business Oriented Language) is the most widely used programming language for data processing applications in business. It is an Englishlike language that was specifically designed to handle the input, processing, and output of large volumes of alphanumeric data from many data files that is characteristic of business transaction processing. COBOL

Figure 3-23 The explanation and flowchart of the sample BASIC program in Figure 3-22.

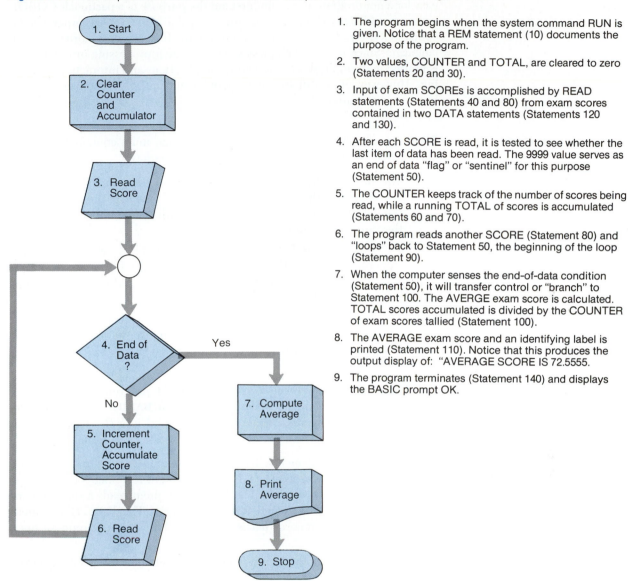

1. The program begins when the system command RUN is given. Notice that a REM statement (10) documents the purpose of the program.

2. Two values, COUNTER and TOTAL, are cleared to zero (Statements 20 and 30).

3. Input of exam SCOREs is accomplished by READ statements (Statements 40 and 80) from exam scores contained in two DATA statements (Statements 120 and 130).

4. After each SCORE is read, it is tested to see whether the last item of data has been read. The 9999 value serves as an end of data "flag" or "sentinel" for this purpose (Statement 50).

5. The COUNTER keeps track of the number of scores being read, while a running TOTAL of scores is accumulated (Statements 60 and 70).

6. The program reads another SCORE (Statement 80) and "loops" back to Statement 50, the beginning of the loop (Statement 90).

7. When the computer senses the end-of-data condition (Statement 50), it will transfer control or "branch" to Statement 100. The AVERGE exam score is calculated. TOTAL scores accumulated is divided by the COUNTER of exam scores tallied (Statement 100).

8. The AVERAGE exam score and an identifying label is printed (Statement 110). Notice that this produces the output display of: "AVERAGE SCORE IS 72.5555.

9. The program terminates (Statement 140) and displays the BASIC prompt OK.

was developed and is maintained by the Conference on Data Systems Languages (CODASYL), which is composed of representatives of large computer users, government agencies, and computer manufacturers. The specifications of the COBOL language are, therefore, subject to periodic revision and updating. The American National Standards Institute (ANSI) has developed standards for COBOL that recognize different "levels" and "modules" of COBOL. Standards for a Minimum Standard COBOL and Full Standard COBOL have also been developed.

COBOL's use of Englishlike statements facilitates programming, makes it easy for a nonprogrammer to understand the purpose of a particular COBOL program, and gives a "self-documenting" capability to COBOL programs. Of course, COBOL does have several limitations. It is a "wordy" programming language. Since it has a data processing and batch processing orientation, it is limited in its applicability to scientific applications and interactive processing. However, it is still the most popular and heavily used language for business applications.

The COBOL Divisions

Every program written in the COBOL language must contain four major parts called "divisions," which are summarized below.

1. *The Identification Division.* Identifies the program by listing such information as the name of the program, the name of the programmer, the date the program was written, and other comments that identify the purpose of the program.

2. *The Environment Division.* Specifies the type of computer and peripheral equipment that will be used to process the program.

3. *The Data Division.* Describes the organization and format of the data to be processed by the program.

4. *The Procedure Division.* Contains the COBOL statements (called "commands") that describe the procedure to be followed by the computer in accomplishing its data processing assignment.

COBOL Procedure Division Statements

The Procedure Division is the section of a COBOL program that is most like programs written in languages like FORTRAN or BASIC. The major statements in this division of COBOL can be grouped into the following four categories:

1. *Input/output statements.* The OPEN statement is used to prepare files to be read or written. The CLOSE statement terminates the processing of a file in a program. The READ statement reads a single record from a file that is named in the statement. The WRITE statement writes a single record that is named in the statement onto an open output file.

2. *Data movement statements.* The MOVE statement transfers data from one area of storage to another.

3. *Arithmetic statements.* The COMPUTE statement is used to perform arithmetic operations that are expressed in the form of a mathematical formula. The ADD, SUBTRACT, MULTIPLY, and DIVIDE statements also perform arithmetic computations.

4. *Control statements.* The PERFORM statement transfers control temporarily to other parts of the program, while the STOP statement halts the execution of the program.

Sample COBOL Program

Figure 3–24 illustrates the statements of a simple COBOL program that computes an average exam score similar to the previous BASIC example.

Notice the large number of statements required by the first three COBOL divisions. However, notice how easy it is to read the Englishlike statements that detail the processing procedures required by the program.

```
IDENTIFICATION DIVISION.
PROGRAM-ID. AVERAGE.
AUTHOR. JOSEPH SILICON.

ENVIRONMENT DIVISION.
CONFIGURATION SECTION.
SOURCE-COMPUTER. IBM-370.
OBJECT-COMPUTER. IBM-370.
INPUT-OUTPUT SECTION.
FILE-CONTROL.
     SELECT IN-FILE ASSIGN TO UR-S-SYSIN.
     SELECT OUT-FILE ASSIGN TO UR-S-SYSPRINT.

DATA DIVISION.
FILE SECTION.
FD    IN-FILE
      LABEL RECORDS ARE OMITTED.
01    IN-REC.
      02 NAME-IN                     PIC X(40).
      02 SCORE                       PIC 999.

FD    OUT-FILE
      LABEL RECORDS ARE STANDARD.
01    OUT-REC                        PIC X(133).

WORKING-STORAGE SECTION.
01    TEMP-REC.
      02 STORE-NUMBER                PIC 999 VALUE IS ZEROS.
      02 STORE-SCORE                 PIC 99999 VALUE IS ZEROS.
      02 EOF-FLAG                    PIC X VALUE 'N'.
         88 END-OF-FILE              VALUE 'Y'.

01    PRINTER-LINE.
      02 FILLER                      PIC X.
      02 NAME-OUT                    PIC X(40).
      02 FILLER                      PIC X(5).
      02 SCORE-OUT                   PIC ZZ9.
01    AVERAGE-LINE.
      02 FILLER                      PIC X(46).
      02 AVERAGE                     PIC 99.99.

PROCEDURE DIVISION.
MAIN.
     PERFORM INITIALIZATION.
     PERFORM PROCESS-RECORDS UNTIL END-OF-FILE.
     PERFORM END-OF-JOB.

INITIALIZATION.
     OPEN INPUT IN-FILE.
     OPEN OUTPUT OUT-FILE.
     PERFORM READ-RECORD.

PROCESS-RECORDS.
     ADD SCORES TO STORE-SCORE.
     ADD 1 TO STORE-NUMBER.
     MOVE NAME-IN TO NAME-OUT.
     MOVE SCORE TO SCORE-OUT.
     WRITE OUT-REC FROM PRINTER-LINE
          AFTER ADVANCING 1.
     PERFORM READ-RECORD.

END-OF-JOB.
     DIVIDE STORE-NUMBER INTO STORE-SCORE GIVING AVERAGE.
     WRITE OUT-REC FROM AVERAGE-LINE
          AFTER ADVANCING 2 LINES.
     CLOSE IN-FILE.
     CLOSE OUT-FILE.
     STOP RUN.

READ-RECORD.
     READ IN-FILE
          AT END MOVE "Y" TO EOF-FLAG.
```

Figure 3–24 A sample COBOL program: Computing an average exam score. Notice how Englishlike the program statements are.

PASCAL

Pascal is a programming language named after the noted mathematician and philosopher Blaise Pascal (1623–1662), who invented a practical calculating machine at age 19. Pascal was developed in the late 1960s by Niklaus Wirth of Zurich, who was looking for an ideal language to teach the concepts of "structured programming" and "top-down design" (explained in Chapter 11). The small number of types of Pascal statements and the simplicity of its syntax have enabled systems programmers to develop fast, powerful Pascal compilers that occupy a minimal amount of memory. Turbo Pascal by Borland International is a popular example. This, together with its appeal as a logically complete and easy-to-learn language, explains the popularity of Pascal for use on microcomputers.

One of the major contributions of Wirth's work is his formalization of the concept of "type" as used in Pascal. Each item of data must have its type specified explicitly or implicitly in the module in which it appears. As data is passed from one module to another, its type must not change, and any attempt to write a program that violates this principle results in an error message generated by the compiler. The main disadvantages of Pascal are the lack of a variable dimension facility for arrays and the lack of flexible file handling capabilities. Some later versions of Pascal, however, have provided extensions to the language that overcome these deficiencies. *Note:* The study guide for this text contains an appendix on programming in Pascal.

Pascal Statements

A Pascal program consists of a program statement followed by declaration statements, which in turn are followed by executable statements. Statements are separated by semicolons, and the program is terminated with a period. Declaration statements are used to assign constants to identifiers. They are also used to declare the "type" of each variable, and to define procedures and functions. Executable statements are described below:

- □ *Assignment* statements are used to assign a new value to a variable, usually as a result of a calculation.
- □ *Input/Output* statements move data between variables and either external devices or internal files defined by the user. Files are declared, specifying the "type" of data they are to contain. *Textfiles* represent data as a string of characters, such as English letters, or as decimal digits. Other files may hold numerical data.
- □ *Compound statements*—a sequence of statements enclosed between BEGIN and END is considered to be a single statement in the logic of a program.
- □ *Conditional statements* choose an alternative flow of control based on the value of some expression. Pascal includes the IF–THEN, the IF–THEN–ELSE and, for multiple alternatives, the CASE statement.
- □ *Repetitive statements* repeat the execution of a statement or sequence of statements until some condition is met. These "structured statements" include the WHILE–DO, the REPEAT–UNTIL, and the FOR statement.

COBOL and the 4GLs

For some time now, COBOL's detractors have been keen on painting the venerable computer language as an aging warrior ready to be retired. Much to the chagrin and surprise of many, however, COBOL has been busy pumping iron to get back into shape. COBOL, in fact, is drawing on some major strengths to flex new muscle on several market fronts.

The critical mass of COBOL mainframe applications and the sheer numbers of programmers well versed in the language have swelled during the past 25 years. It has been estimated that more than 75 percent of existing mainframe applications have been written in COBOL. Supported by its widespread user base, COBOL has proven tenacious in resisting the change to fourth-generation languages (4GL) that appear to be the heirs apparent to COBOL and other third-generation languages.

The increased activity in the COBOL marketplace has centered on three broad thrusts: (1) restructuring the language and existing mainframe COBOL programs; (2) migrating COBOL's core building blocks to run on microcomputers; and (3) using 4GL and artificial intelligence–expert systems techniques to generate COBOL programs.

☐ The first movement has its base in the work done by the American National Standards Institute (ANSI). ANSI's COBOL 74 and COBOL 85 standards made COBOL a more structured programming language. Then software vendors began supplying COBOL retrofit packages to larger mainframe installations that are experiencing trouble upgrading older COBOL programs. These firms provide tools to get the programs up to what is deemed an acceptable structured COBOL level.

☐ COBOL programming on microcomputers is not a new phenomenon, but recent advances in microcomputer hardware and software are ready to break it wide open. The big push will come from the onrush of microcomputers based on the Intel 80386 microprocessor. The large memory and increased speed of these machines are naturals for programmers. Another catalyst will be Microsoft Corp.'s new operating systems that will overcome the memory limitations of existing MS-DOS operating systems. These developments are promising to boost the microcomputer a quantum leap into the realm of COBOL programming.

☐ Ironically, this gradual shift of COBOL applications onto micros might pose yet another stumbling block for fourth-generation language vendors. "But it's not going to be an either/or situation at the micro level," claims Mike McCandless, telemarketing sales manager at Micro Focus, Inc. "Software developers are always looking for better ways of programming for business applications. That includes fourth-generation languages." McCandless claims that 4GLS are being integrated into COBOL code generator packages now on the market. "In spite of all of these activities within the COBOL market" he explains, "it's good to remember that COBOL is still a language for programmers. While all these COBOL improvements are aimed at hiking programmer productivity, they might also be clearing the path for fourth-generation languages to fulfill their destiny as programming tools for end users."

Application Questions

☐ What three developments are revitalizing COBOL?

☐ What roles will COBOL and fourth-generation languages play in the future?

Source: Stan Kolodziet, "COBOL Shapes Up," *Computerworld*, January 7, 1987, Focus pp. 13–14.

Figure 3–25 A sample Pascal program: Computing an average exam score with another popular programming language.

```
PROGRAM averagescore{infile,outfile};

VAR score,sum,average,count : real;
    infile,outfile : text;

BEGIN
    sum:=0.0; count:0.0;
    REPEAT
        read{infile,score};
        sum:=sum + score;
        count:=count + 1.0
    UNTIL eof{infile};
    average:=sum/count;
    write{outfile,'Average score is',average}
END.
```

Sample Pascal Program

To illustrate Pascal programming, Figure 3–25 shows another program that finds the average of exam scores.

SUMMARY

☐ The software resources of an information system consist of (1) programs of instructions used to direct the operation of the hardware of a computer system and (2) procedures used to direct the activities of the people who operate and use computer systems. Computer software consists of two major types of programs: (1) system software, which controls and supports the operations of a computer system as it performs various information processing tasks; and (2) application software, which directs the performance of a particular use or application of computers to meet the information processing needs of users. Computer software can also be subdivided into (1) software packages, which are acquired by users from various software vendors; and (2) user-developed software, which is developed by users or professional programmers of a computer-using organization. Refer to Figure 3–1 for an overview of the major types of software.

☐ System software can be subdivided into system management programs, system support programs, and system development programs. System management programs manage the use of the hardware, software, and data resources of the computer system during its execution of information processing jobs. Major system management programs are operating systems, database management programs, and communications monitors. System support programs support the operations, management, and users of computer systems by providing a variety of support services. Major support programs are service programs, performance monitors, and security monitors. System development programs help users develop information processing programs and procedures and prepare user programs for computer processing. Major development programs are language translators and application development systems.

☐ The most important system software package for any computer is its operating system. An operating system is an integrated system of programs that supervises the operation of the CPU, controls the input/output and storage functions of the computer system, and provides various support services. The management programs of an operating system perform the three major functions of job management, resource management, and data management. Other programs that could be part of the operating system, or that can be acquired as separate programs, are language translators and service programs. Language translator programs convert programming language instructions into machine-language instruction codes. Service programs are specialized programs that perform common support functions for the users of a computer system.

☐ Database management systems control the creation, maintenance, and use of a database. A DBMS simplifies the use of the data and information in a database for both users and programmers. Data communications monitors monitor, control, and support the data communication activities between the computers and terminals in a data communications network.

☐ Application software includes a variety of programs that can be segregated into general-purpose, business, scientific, and other application program categories. General-purpose application programs can perform common information processing jobs for users. Examples are word processing, electronic spreadsheet, and graphics programs. Business application programs can accomplish information processing tasks that support important business functions or industry requirements. Scientific application programs perform information processing tasks for the sciences, engineering, and all other areas involved in scientific research, experimentation, and development. The other application programs category includes programs in education, entertainment, music, and art.

☐ Programming languages are a major category of system software. They allow computer instructions to be written in a language that is understandable to both people and computers. The four major levels of programming languages are machine languages, assembler languages, high-level languages, and fourth-generation languages. High-level languages such as BASIC, COBOL, and Pascal are the most widely used programming languages for business applications. However, the use of natural, nonprocedural, fourth-generation languages is growing. Refer to Figure 3–21 for a summary of major programming languages.

KEY TERMS AND CONCEPTS

These are the key terms and concepts of this chapter. The page number of their first explanation is in parentheses.

1. Application development system *(111)*
2. Application software *(112)*
3. Assembler language *(122)*
4. BASIC *(127)*
5. COBOL *(128)*
6. Common business package *(119)*
7. Computer application *(112)*
8. Data management *(106)*
9. Communications monitor *(108)*
10. Database management system *(106)*
11. Electronic spreadsheet package *(114)*
12. Fourth-generation language *(124)*
13. General-purpose application program *(112)*
14. Graphics package *(114)*
15. High-level language *(123)*
16. Integrated package *(113)*
17. Job management *(104)*
18. Language translator program *(108)*
19. Machine language *(122)*
20. Macro instruction *(123)*
21. Natural language *(124)*
22. Nonprocedural language *(124)*
23. Operating system *(104)*
24. Pascal *(131)*
25. Resource management *(106)*
26. Service program *(110)*
27. Software packages *(100)*
28. Supervisor *(106)*
29. System development programs *(103)*
30. System management programs *(103)*
31. System performance monitor *(111)*
32. System security monitor *(112)*
33. System software *(103)*
34. System support programs *(103)*
35. User-developed software *(100)*
36. Word processing package *(113)*

REVIEW AND APPLICATION QUIZ

Match one of the **key terms and concepts** listed above with one of the brief examples or definitions listed below. Try to find the "best fit" for answers that seem to fit more than one term or concept. Defend your choices.

_____ 1. Programs that control and support the operations of computers.

_____ 2. Programs that direct the performance of a specific use of computers.

_____ 3. An integrated system of programs that manages the operations of a computer system.

_____ 4. Managing the flow of information processing jobs through a computer system.

_____ 5. Managing the use of CPU time, primary and secondary storage, and input/output devices.

_____ 6. Managing the input, output, storage, and retrieval of data.

_____ 7. Manages and supports the use of databases and files.

_____   8. Manages and supports data transmissions in a network.

_____   9. Translates high-level instructions into machine language instructions.

_____   10. Performs "housekeeping" chores for a computer system.

_____   11. Provides software tools for programmers.

_____   12. Monitors and reports on computer system performance.

_____   13. Monitors and protects computers from misuse.

_____   14. The use of a computer to accomplish a particular job for a user.

_____   15. A category of application programs that performs common information processing tasks for all types of users.

_____   16. Allows you to create and edit documents.

_____   17. Creates and displays a worksheet for analysis.

_____   18. Produces line, bar, and pie charts, and other displays.

_____   19. Combines the ability to do several general-purpose applications in one program.

_____   20. Performs sales analysis, order processing, inventory control, payroll, and so on.

_____   21. Uses instructions in the form of coded strings of ones and zeros.

_____   22. Uses instructions consisting of symbols representing operation codes and storage locations.

_____   23. Uses instructions called statements that resemble human language or the standard notation of mathematics.

_____   24. A single instruction that generates several machine instructions.

_____   25. Also called a very high-level language.

_____   26. You don't have to tell the computer how to do something, just what result you want.

_____   27. As easy to use as ordinary conversation.

_____   28. A popular language for beginning microcomputer users.

_____   29. The most widely used language for large business application programs.

_____   30. A popular structured programming language.

APPLICATION PROBLEMS

1. If you have not already done so, read and answer the questions after each Real World Application in this chapter.

2. Have you completed any of the exercises or assignments in the use of software packages from the Appendix? Remember, you need hands-on experience with these packages to be a knowledgeable computer user. Briefly describe the advantages and disadvantages of one of the packages you have used so far.

3. Have you used one of the software packages mentioned in this chapter? How would such a package help you in a present or future job situation? How would you improve the package you used?

4. Make a list of 10 of the major types of software packages mentioned in this chapter. Then briefly explain (one sentence each) the purpose of each package.

5. ABC Department Stores would like to acquire system software that could do the tasks listed below. Identify what system software packages they need.
   a. Control data communications with many remote terminals;
   b. Control access and use of the hardware, software, and data resources of the system;
   c. Monitor and record how the system resources are being used;
   d. Make it easier to update and interrogate its databases.

6. Suppose you wanted to do the following:
   a. Type correspondence and reports;
   b. Analyze rows and columns of figures;
   c. Store and access business records;
   d. Develop line, bar, and pie charts;
   e. Transmit data to other computers.

   What individual application software packages would you need for each activity?

7. A software expert commented that integrated packages like Symphony, Framework, and Enable were not a new generation of software, but the last of the present software generation. He feels that operating environment packages like TopView and Windows, which make it easy for users to integrate the operations of a variety of individual packages, are the real wave of the future. What do you think? Explain.

8. Compare and contrast the major characteristics of BASIC, COBOL, and Pascal. Which language would you recommend for business data processing? For your own use? Explain.

9. Look at Figure 3–21. Have you used any of these programming languages to write a simple program? If you have, evaluate this language in terms of its business orientation, ease of use, and closeness to natural language.

10. Look at Figures 3–18 and 3–19. Explain what they tell you about the differences in the major types of programming languages. Where does a language you may have used or might use fit in?

MODULE

II

INFORMATION SYSTEMS TECHNOLOGY

PROCESSING CONCEPTS AND METHODS

Chapter Outline

Learning Objectives

The purpose of this chapter is to promote a basic understanding of the capabilities of computer-based information systems. After reading and studying this chapter, you should be able to:

1. Identify several CPU and input/output interface components and their functions.
2. Describe how a computer executes an instruction.
3. Explain how a computer represents data and why it is based on the binary number system.
4. Differentiate between a bit, a byte, and a word.
5. Identify several major types of computer processing and the capabilities they provide to computer users.
6. Provide several reasons for the use of batch processing, realtime processing, interactive processing, and time-sharing.
7. Use examples to illustrate several levels of realtime processing systems.
8. Explain the concept of distributed processing and its major applications in information processing.

Section I: How Computers Work

Does a computer user really have to know how a computer works in order to use one effectively? The answer to that question is similar to what you might answer if someone asked you whether you had to know how a car works in order to drive one properly. Yes, you need to know some basic facts and concepts about computer operations. This will help you be a more productive user of computers when things are going well. It will also help you when you run into problems operating and using computers. That doesn't mean that you have to become a computer scientist or technician. Your goal should be to become an informed user of computer resources.

CPU COMPONENTS

In order to know how a computer works, you must know something about what goes on inside a CPU. The internal architecture of a CPU or microprocessor can be quite complex. A detailed knowledge of the circuitry and scientific principles involved is beyond the scope of this book. However, you should understand the basic functions of the arithmetic-logic, control, and primary storage units of the CPU as they were described in Chapter 2. In addition, you should realize that a CPU or microprocessor includes several types of special-purpose circuitry, such as *registers, counters, adders, decoders,* and the like. These electronic circuitry elements serve as temporary work areas, analyze instructions, or perform required arithmetic and logical operations. The number, function, and capacity of such circuits depends on the internal architecture of each particular computer. Figure 4–1 shows some of these components and functions in a microprocessor used in advanced microcomputers. Figure 4–2 summarizes some of these CPU components. We will briefly mention the functions of these components as we explain how a computer works.

HOW COMPUTERS EXECUTE INSTRUCTIONS

Computers work by executing instructions in a program. The specific form of a computer instruction depends on the type of programming language and computer being used. However, a machine language instruction usually consists of:

☐ An **operation code** that specifies what is to be done (add, compare, read, etc.).

☐ One or more **operands,** which specify the primary storage addresses of data or instructions, and/or indicate which input/output and secondary storage devices will be used.

The operation code and operands of the instruction being executed, as well as data elements affected by the instruction, are moved through the special-purpose circuitry of the CPU or microprocessor during the execution of an instruction. A fixed number of electrical pulses emitted by the CPU's timing circuitry or *internal clock* determines the timing of each basic CPU operation. The time period to accomplish each basic operation is called a

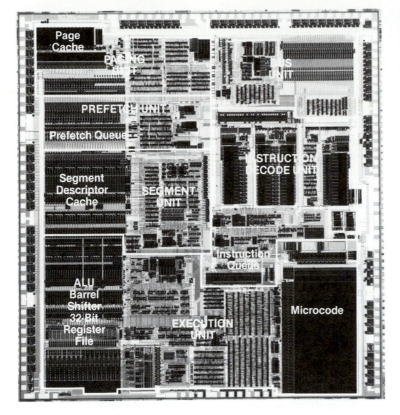

Figure 4–1 A new generation microprocessor. The Intel 80386, a 32-bit microprocessor "mainframe on a chip." Note the functions performed by major parts of the chip.

Registers. Small high-speed storage circuitry areas used for temporary storage of an individual instruction or data element during the operation of the control and arithmetic-logic units.

Counters. Devices whose contents can be automatically increased or decreased by a specific amount, thus enabling them to "count" the number of particular computer operations.

Adders. Circuits that perform the arithmetic operations of the arithmetic-logic unit.

Decoders. Circuits in the control unit that analyze the instructions of a computer program and start their execution.

Internal clock. Circuits that emit electrical pulses at frequencies ranging from several million to billions per second. This energizes the circuitry of the CPU and insures the exact timing necessary for its proper operation.

Buffer. A high-speed temporary storage area for storing parts of a program or data during processing or I/O operations.

I/O interface or port. Circuitry for the interconnection ("interface") required for access to input/output devices.

Bus. A set of conducting paths (for movement of data and instructions) that interconnects the various components of a CPU or microprocessor.

Channels. Special-purpose processors that control the movement of data between the CPU and input/output devices.

Figure 4–2 Other central processing unit components. The control unit, arithmetic-logic unit, and primary storage unit use such components in their operations.

machine cycle. We will see examples of such basic operations shortly. The number of machine cycles required to execute an instruction varies with the complexity of the instruction.

During each machine cycle, electrical pulses generated by the internal clock energize special-purpose circuitry elements that sense and interpret specific instructions and data and move them (in the form of electrical pulses) between the various specialized circuitry components of the CPU summarized in Figure 4–2. One of the most important of these are **registers,** which are small high-speed storage circuit areas used for the temporary storage of an individual instruction or data element during the operation of the control and arithmetic-logic units.

The execution of an instruction can be divided into two segments, the *instruction cycle* and the *execution cycle*. Simply stated, the **instruction cycle** consists of processes in which an instruction is *fetched* from primary storage and *interpreted* by the control unit. The **execution cycle** consists of *performing* the operations specified by the instruction that was interpreted during the instruction cycle. Let's look at a simplified illustration and explanation of what happens in a CPU during the instruction and execution cycles.

Figure 4–3 illustrates and explains the execution of a typical instruction by a computer. First let's state the instruction in conversational English, then in a form more like the machine language instructions executed by computers. Then you should follow the steps used by the computer to execute this instruction as shown in Figure 4–3.

English Instruction: Add the amount of hours worked today by an employee to his or her total hours worked this week.

Computer Instruction: Add the amount stored in primary storage at address 006 to the amount contained in the *accumulator register* and store the result in primary storage location 008.

The Order of Execution

The computer automatically repeats instruction and execution cycles until the final instruction of a program is executed. Usually, instructions are sequentially executed in the order in which they are stored in primary storage. An *instruction counter*, which automatically advances or "steps" in sequential order to the address of the next instruction stored in memory, is used to indicate what instruction is to be executed next.

Sometimes, a *branch instruction* is brought from storage. It tells the control unit that it may have to execute an instruction in another part of the program, instead of the next sequential instruction. This change in the sequence of instructions can be *unconditional* or *conditional*. A conditional branch is usually the result of a *test* or *comparison* instruction, which can cause a change in the sequential order of processing if a specified condition occurs. For example, in a payroll program, a different sequence of instructions is typically used for employees whose hours worked exceeded 40 hours

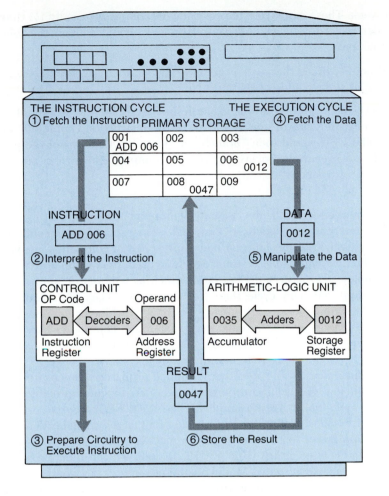

Figure 4–3 How computers execute an instruction. Notice the steps involved in this example.

THE INSTRUCTION CYCLE

1. First, an instruction is *fetched* from its location in primary storage and temporarily stored in the registers of the control unit. In this example, the instruction had been stored in primary storage location 001. The operation code part of the instruction (ADD) is moved to an instruction register, and its operand portion (006) is moved to an address register.

2. Next, the instruction is *interpreted* by the circuitry of the control unit. This involves decoding the operation code and operands of the instruction. Specialized decoder circuits interpret the operation code and operand of the instruction.

3. Finally, the control unit prepares electronic circuitry "paths" within the CPU to carry out the required operations. For example, this may involve activating the circuits that will "read" the data stored in the memory location (006) described in the operand of the instruction.

THE EXECUTION CYCLE

4. First, the data to be processed is fetched from its locations in primary storage and temporarily stored in a storage register of the arithmetic-logic unit. In this example, storage location 006 contained a value of 0012 (12 hours).

5. Next, the operations specified by the operation code of the instruction are performed (addition, subtraction, comparisons, and so on). In this example, the contents of the storage register (0012) are added to the contents of an important register known as the accumulator by the use of specialized circuitry called adders. For this example, let's assume that the amount of hours worked this week (0035) was stored in the accumulator by a previous instruction.

6. Finally, the result arising from the manipulation of the data is stored in primary storage. In this example, the contents of weekly hours worked will be 0047. This amount will be transferred to primary storage at address 008 when the operand specifying this address is executed.

per week. These employees have earned *overtime pay* (usually 1½ times the regular pay rate). Thus, the payroll program could contain the following instruction:

If hours worked this week is greater than 40, **then** execute the instruction at storage address 020 next.

Since the employee in our example in Figure 4–3 has worked 47 hours this week, the control unit would reset the instruction counter to address 020. The CPU would then "branch" or "jump" to that part of the program and begin executing the instructions for computing overtime pay, rather than the instructions for computing regular pay.

The Speed of Execution

As we mentioned in Chapter 2, many computers now operate at *nanosecond* speeds and can thus execute several *million instructions per second* (MIPS). Other measures of the internal operating speed of computers are *machine cycle time* and *memory cycle time*. **Machine cycle** time is the time necessary to complete one basic CPU operation (such as fetching or interpreting an instruction). **Memory cycle** time is the time necessary for a computer to recall data from one primary storage position. Machine cycle times are now below 20 nanoseconds for some large mainframe computers like the IBM 3090 series, which operates in the 50 MIPS range. Memory cycle times below 100 nanoseconds are common for such systems.

One final measure of speed that is applied primarily to microprocessors is the frequency of machine cycles as generated by microprocessor timing circuits. Let's look at a few examples. The Intel 8088 microprocessor used in the IBM Personal Computer has a basic rating of 4.7 **megahertz** (MHz), or 4.7 million cycles per second. It has a machine cycle time of 210 nanoseconds, and is rated at less than ½ MIP. In contrast, the Intel 80286 used in the IBM Personal System/2 Model 50 microcomputer has a basic rating of 10 MHz. It has a machine cycle time of 100 nanoseconds and is rated at 2.5 MIPS. Finally, one version of the high-powered Intel 80386 microprocessor used in the IBM PS/2 Model 80 microcomputer is rated at 16 MHz and 4 MIPS, and has a machine cycle time of 62.5 nanoseconds.

The speeds of such microprocessors can be increased by adjusting their timing circuits, typically by using a faster quartz clock crystal. Therefore, many microcomputers allow you to select a faster "turbo" mode. For example, this can increase the speed of the 8088 to 8 megahertz, the 80286 to 16 megahertz, and the 80386 to 20 MHz and higher.

INPUT/OUTPUT SUPPORT FOR THE CPU

The CPU needs help with input/output activities in order to carry out its processing assignments quickly and efficiently. **Input/output interface devices** are computer components that provide such support. They can be physically part of the CPU, a separate unit, or can be built into an input/output or storage device. The main purpose of devices, such as *buffers*, *channels*, and *input/output control units*, is to assist the CPU in its input and output assignments. These devices have been developed to provide a uniform, flexible, and efficient *interface* or connection between the CPU and its input/output units. They provide mainframe computer systems with the

Figure 4–4 Input/output interface devices support input and output activities between the CPU and peripheral devices.

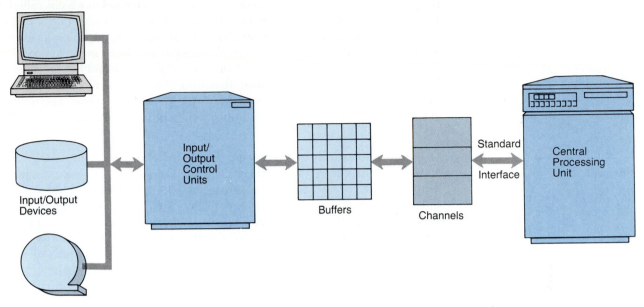

Input/Output Devices

Input/ Output Control Units

Buffers

Channels

Standard Interface

Central Processing Unit

ability to carry out many input and output functions simultaneously. At the same time they allow the CPU to carry out other processing functions, since it no longer must directly control I/O devices. Figure 4–4 shows how such devices support the input/output function.

Buffers are high-speed storage circuits that are used for the temporary storage of input or output data to reduce the demands of input/output operations on the CPU. Buffers are sometimes built into the CPU or into the input/output device, or they may be housed separately in a peripheral unit. When buffers are used, the CPU does not have to wait for the input or the output of data but can initiate an input or output command and then return to other processing. Data can then move from the input device into the buffer or from the buffer into an output device without tying up the CPU. High-speed transfer of data occurs when an input buffer transfers data to a CPU or when a CPU can transfer data into an output buffer.

Buffers

Channels are special-purpose microprocessors or miniprocessors that control the movement of data between the CPU and input or output devices. Channels are housed within the CPU or can be separate peripheral units and may contain buffer storage. Once the channel receives an input or output command from the CPU, it can control the operations of several input/ output units simultaneously without disturbing the CPU. Only when the input or output operation is completed will the channel "interrupt" the CPU to signal the completion of its assignment.

Channels

There are two main types of channels, each of which can handle several input or output units. The *selector channel* selectively allows each input or output device temporarily to monopolize the entire channel in what is called the *burst mode* of data transmission. *Multiplexor channels* can control data input or output from several slower devices simultaneously in a *multiplex mode*. Most multiplexor channels can also operate in a burst mode to service high-speed input/output devices. Some multiplexor channels are called *block multiplexor channels*, since they can transmit or receive data in "blocks" of several bytes of data, rather than one byte at a time. The high-speed data transmission of these units is called *data streaming*.

Input/Output Control Units

Channels are normally not connected directly to an input/output device but to **input/output control units.** These can be built into the CPU or an input/output device, or be housed as a separate unit that controls several input/output devices. The job of such I/O controllers is to decode the input/output commands from the CPU or channel and to control operation of the appropriate input/output device. This includes the coding, decoding, and checking of data transmitted from the CPU. Buffer storage units are part of the controllers of some input/output devices.

HOW COMPUTERS REPRESENT DATA

The letters of the alphabet in this book are symbols that when properly organized or "coded" into the English language will "represent" data that you, the reader, can process into information. Thus, we can say that words, numbers, and punctuation are the human-sensible code by which data is represented in this book. Similarly, data must be represented in a machine-sensible code before it can be processed by a computer system.

Data is represented in a computer system by either the presence or absence of electronic or magnetic "signals" in its circuitry or in the media it uses. This is called a **binary** or "two state" representation of data, since the computer is indicating only two possible states or conditions. For example, transistors and other semiconductor circuits are either in a conducting or nonconducting state. Media such as magnetic disks and tapes indicate these two states by having magnetized spots whose magnetic fields can have two different directions or *polarities*. These binary characteristics of computer circuitry and media are the primary reason why the **binary number system** is the basis for data representation in computers. Thus, for electronic circuits, the conducting *(ON)* state represents a *one* and the nonconducting *(OFF)* state represents a *zero*. For magnetic media, the magnetic field of a magnetized spot in one direction represents a *one*, while magnetism in the other direction represents a *zero*.

COMPUTER NUMBER SYSTEMS

The binary number system has only two symbols, 0 and 1, and is, therefore, said to have a *base* of two. The familiar decimal system has a base of 10, since it uses 10 symbols (0 through 9). The binary symbols 0 and 1 are commonly called **bits,** which is a contraction of the term *binary digits*. In the binary

Binary Position Values							
2^6	2^5	2^4	2^3	2^2	2^1	2^0	
64	32	16	8	4	2	1	
Binary Numbers							Examples of Equivalent Decimal Numbers
0	0	0	0	0	0	0	0
0	0	0	0	0	0	1	1
0	0	0	0	0	1	0	2
0	0	0	0	0	1	1	3
0	0	0	0	1	0	0	4
0	0	0	0	1	0	1	5
0	0	0	0	1	1	0	6
0	0	0	0	1	1	1	7
0	0	0	1	0	0	0	8
0	0	0	1	0	0	1	9
0	0	0	1	0	1	0	10
0	0	0	1	1	1	1	15
0	0	1	0	0	0	0	16
0	0	1	0	0	0	1	17
0	0	1	1	1	1	1	31
0	1	0	0	0	0	0	32
0	1	0	0	0	0	1	33
0	1	1	1	1	1	1	63
1	0	0	0	0	0	0	64
1	0	0	0	0	0	1	65

Figure 4–5 Examples of how the binary number system represents decimal values. Can you determine that the decimal number 34 is equivalent to 0100010 in binary?

number system, all numbers are expressed as groups of binary digits (bits), that is, as groups of zeros and ones.

Just as in any other number system, the value of a binary number depends on the position or place of each digit in a grouping of binary digits. Values are based on the right-to-left position of digits in a binary number, using powers of 2 (2^0, 2^1, 2^2, 2^3, and so on) as position values. Therefore, the rightmost position has a value of 1 (2^0), the next position to the left has a value of 2 (2^1), the next position a value of 4 (2^2), the next, 8 (2^3), the next 16 (2^4), and so forth. Thus the value of any binary number consists of adding together the values of each position in which there is a binary *one* digit, and ignoring those positions that contain a binary *zero* digit. Figure 4–5 gives a simple illustration of how the binary number system can represent decimal values.

The **octal** (base 8) and the **hexadecimal** (base 16) number systems are used as a shorthand method of expressing the binary data representation within many modern computers. The binary number system has the disadvantage

Figure 4-6 Examples of the equivalents of decimal numbers in the binary, octal, and hexadecimal number systems. Can you tell that the decimal number 21 would be equivalent to 10101 in binary, 25 in octal, and 15 in hexadecimal?

Decimal	Binary	Octal	Hexadecimal
0	0	0	0
1	1	1	1
2	10	2	2
3	11	3	3
4	100	4	4
5	101	5	5
6	110	6	6
7	111	7	7
8	1000	10	8
9	1001	11	9
10	1010	12	A
11	1011	13	B
12	1100	14	C
13	1101	15	D
14	1110	16	E
15	1111	17	F
16	10000	20	10
17	10001	21	11
18	10010	22	12
19	10011	23	13
20	10100	24	14

of requiring a large number of digits to express a given number value. The use of octal and hexadecimal number systems, which are proportionately related to the binary number system, provides a shorthand method of reducing the long "string" of ones and zeros that make up a binary number. This is also helpful in simplifying computer codes based on the binary number system, as we will see shortly. For example, one popular computer code uses eight bit positions to represent a character. The hexadecimal equivalent would need only two positions to represent the same character. This helps programmers and computer operators who frequently have to determine the data or instruction contents of primary storage.

Figure 4–6 shows examples of the binary, octal, and hexadecimal equivalents of the decimal numbers 0 through 20. Using the relationships in Figure 4–6, you should be able to determine that the decimal number 21 would be expressed by the binary number 10101, the octal number 25, and the hexadecimal number 11, and so on. Several methods can be used to convert decimal numbers to a binary, octal, or hexadecimal form, or vice versa, or to use them in arithmetic operations, but they are beyond the scope of this text.

COMPUTER CODES

The internal circuitry of a computer needs to represent only binary ones and zeros in its operations. However, several coding systems have been devised to express the *machine language* instruction codes executed by the CPU, and to represent the characters of *data* processed by the computer. These codes make the job of communicating with a computer easier and more efficient. They should be considered as shorthand methods of expressing the binary patterns within a computer. These computer codes can also be thought of as methods of organizing the binary patterns within a computer to more efficiently use its arithmetic, logic, and storage capabilities.

The most basic computer code would be the use of the "pure" binary number system to represent data for all computer operations. Some scientific and special-purpose computers do use the pure binary code as their only method of internal data representation. However, most modern computers, though they may use a pure binary code for some operations, use special codes based on the binary, octal, or hexadecimal number systems.

Many common computer codes are versions of the *binary coded decimal* (BCD) coding system. In this system, decimal digits are expressed in a binary form using only the first four binary positions. Referring back to Figure 4–6, we see that the decimal digits 0 through 9 can be expressed by using only the first four binary positions. Therefore, any decimal number can be expressed by stringing together groups of four binary digits. For example, the decimal number 1987 would be expressed in BCD form as shown below.

Decimal Form	1	9	8	7
BCD Form	0001	1001	1000	0111

The **Extended BCD Interchange Code (EBCDIC)** (pronounced *eb-si-dick*) is used by many current mainframe computers and can provide 256 (2^8) different coding arrangements. Figure 4–7 shows that this eight-bit code consists of four *numeric* bits and four *zone* bits. The letters of the alphabet or special characters can be represented when combinations of zone and numeric bits are used.

Another popular code is the **American Standard Code for Information Interchange (ASCII)** (pronounced *as-key*). This was originally a seven-bit code which could represent 128 (2^7) different characters. However, eight-bit versions (sometimes called ASCII-8) which can represent 256 characters are now more widely used. It is a standardized code first developed for data communications between computers and input/output devices. However, it is used by most microcomputers and minicomputers, and many larger computers. Because of the differences between EBCDIC and ASCII codes, computers must be able to convert from one code to the other. ASCII has been adopted as a standard code by national and international standards organizations. Its use is expected to continue to grow in the future. Figure 4–7 shows a common eight-bit version of ASCII.

Most computer codes include an additional bit called the *check bit*. The check bit is also known as a *"parity"* bit and is used for verifying the accuracy or validity of the coded data. Many computers have a built-in checking capacity to detect the loss or addition of bits during the transfer of data between components of a computer system. For example, the computer may be designed to continuously check for an *odd parity*, that is, an odd number of *binary one* (electronically *ON* bit positions) in each character of data that is transferred. In such cases, a check bit is turned on when needed to ensure that an odd number of electronically *ON* bit positions is present in each character of data in storage. Thus the check bit allows the computer to automatically determine whether the correct number of bit positions representing a character of data have been transferred.

Figure 4-7 Examples of two common computer codes: EBCDIC and ASCII.

Character	EBCDIC		ASCII	
	Zone Bits	Numeric Bits	Zone Bits	Numeric Bits
0	1111	0000	0011	0000
1	1111	0001	0011	0001
2	1111	0010	0011	0010
3	1111	0011	0011	0011
4	1111	0100	0011	0100
5	1111	0101	0011	0101
6	1111	0110	0011	0110
7	1111	0111	0011	0111
8	1111	1000	0011	1000
9	1111	1001	0011	1001
A	1100	0001	0100	0001
B	1100	0010	0100	0010
C	1100	0011	0100	0011
D	1100	0100	0100	0100
E	1100	0101	0100	0101
F	1100	0110	0100	0110
G	1100	0111	0100	0111
H	1100	1000	0100	1000
I	1100	1001	0100	1001
J	1101	0001	0100	1010
K	1101	0010	0100	1011
L	1101	0011	0100	1100
M	1101	0100	0100	1101
N	1101	0101	0100	1110
O	1101	0110	0100	1111
P	1101	0111	0101	0000
Q	1101	1000	0101	0001
R	1101	1001	0101	0010
S	1110	0010	0101	0011
T	1110	0011	0101	0100
U	1110	0100	0101	0101
V	1110	0101	0101	0110
W	1110	0110	0101	0111
X	1110	0111	0101	1000
Y	1110	1000	0101	1001
Z	1110	1001	0101	1010

Figure 4-8 Example of data representation using the EBCDIC code: The letter C.

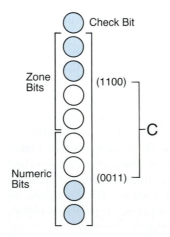

Figure 4–8 concludes this section on data representation with an illustration of how data is physically represented in many modern computers. Assuming the use of the EBCDIC or eight-bit ASCII code, Figure 4–8 reveals that one character (in this case the letter C) can be represented by an eight-bit code. The circles represent semiconductor circuit elements or other forms of storage media. The shaded circles represent an electronic or magnetic *ON* state, while the nonshaded circles represent the *OFF* state of binary devices.

You should now realize that each storage location of computers using the EBCDIC or eight-bit ASCII codes consists of electronic circuit elements or magnetic or optical media positions that can represent at least eight binary digits. Thus each storage location can hold one character. This grouping of eight binary digits is commonly known as a **byte.** Also notice that in the case of the letter C in Figure 4–8, the ninth or check bit is *ON* to make *odd parity;* that is, an odd number of bits (five) are turned on. If the check bit was *OFF*, this would result in *even parity;* that is, an even number of bits (four) would be turned on.

COMPUTER DATA ELEMENTS

The organization of data within a computer is a function of the internal design of the computer circuitry and of the coding system used. Let's limit our discussion to data elements based on the use of the ASCII and EBCDIC codes used by most computers. Computers that use other schemes of data organization differ in the size and names of the data elements used, rather than in the basic concepts required.

Bits

Figure 4–9 illustrates the hierarchy of data elements used by many computers. The smallest element of data is the **bit,** or binary digit, which can have a binary value of either zero or one.

Bytes

A **byte** is a basic grouping of bits that the computer operates on as a single unit. It typically consists of eight bits and is used to represent a character by such coding systems as EBCDIC and ASCII. As we mentioned in Chapter 2, the capacity of a computer's primary storage and its secondary storage devices are usually expressed in terms of bytes. The byte is thus the basic unit of data in most modern computer systems.

Name	Size
BIT	One binary digit.
BYTE	Eight bits (EBCDIC and ASCII-8)
WORD	8, 16, 32, or 64 bits.

Figure 4–9 Examples of typical computer data elements.

Words

The next major computer data element is the **word.** A word is a grouping of binary digits (usually larger than a byte) that is transferred as a unit between primary storage and the registers of the arithmetic-logic unit and control unit. Thus a computer with a 32-bit word length might have registers with a capacity of 32 bits, and transfer data and instructions within the CPU in groupings of 32 bits. It should process data faster than computers with a 16-bit or 8-bit word length.

However, actual word size does not depend solely on the capacity of the registers in the CPU or microprocessor. It also depends on the capacity or "width" of the *data path* or *data bus* on which data and instructions are moved through the circuitry of the CPU or microprocessor. Thus, some large computers that typically have 32-bit registers may move data in *half words* of 16 bits or *double words* of 64 bits. Also, some microprocessors use a *bit slice* design, in which data is moved in "slices" of 2 bits or 4 bits (called a *nibble*) within the circuits of the microprocessor.

Therefore, computers with a large word size that have large register capacities and wide data paths can have the following benefits:

☐ Faster processing speeds. For example, many current microcomputers have microprocessors with 16-bit registers, but still have data paths that are only 8 bits wide. Thus their "true" word size is said to be 8 bits, since they must make two 8-bit transfers of data from memory to fill a 16-bit register. Obviously, this reduces their processing speed compared to microprocessors with 16-bit data paths and registers.

☐ Larger instruction sets. CPUs and microprocessors with larger registers and data paths can interpret and execute a larger variety of basic machine instructions. This can increase their processing speed and flexibility since they can execute more complex instructions with less machine cycles. However, a large instruction set can also slow down a processor. Too much time can be spent accessing specific machine instruction circuits. This limitation is the basis for the development of *reduced instruction set computers* (RISC). They increase processing speed by optimizing the use of a smaller number of basic machine instructions.

☐ Greater arithmetic precision. Larger registers and data paths and a larger instruction set allow a computer to perform arithmetic operations on larger or more precise numbers more quickly with greater accuracy.

☐ Larger memory capacity. The larger a computer's address registers, the more memory positions with unique storage location addresses it can directly access. For example, several popular 8-bit microprocessors can directly access only about 64K bytes of memory. On the other hand, many 16-bit microcomputers can have from one million to 16 million bytes of directly addressable memory. Full 32-bit microprocessors can address from 16 million to four billion bytes of main memory!

REAL WORLD APPLICATION 4–1

John Johnston—Louisiana Geological Survey

John Johnston's heavy database management and spreadsheet work as chief of energy and mineral resources at the Louisiana Geological Survey made him keenly aware of his speed—or, more accurately, his lack of it. As a result, Johnston methodically evaluated each microcomputer system component with an eye toward maximizing performance. The result was an overhaul worthy of the Chrysler Corporation—Johnston increased his system's speed by 40 percent, thereby increasing his personal productivity at the same time.

Johnston's calculation-intensive spreadsheet and database applications often left him staring at his screen waiting as his system processed data, even on his IBM Personal Computer AT, which ran at 6 MHz. So Johnston decided to optimize his system's performance, initially by replacing the crystals that govern microprocessor speed. "The first thing I did was to buy the Ariel (Flemington, N.J.) clock crystals," says Johnston. When installed, the $20 crystals replace the standard AT crystals controlling the Intel 80286 microprocessor's operating speed. The result was an increase of 2 MHz, so that his AT ran at 8 MHz—one third again as fast as the original AT.

In spite of the faster processor speed, the AT's Intel 80287 math coprocessor chip, which reduces the time required for certain math calculations, was too slow for Johnston. He would have to wait—sometimes for hours—for his data to recalculate. So Johnston bought a 287 Turbo board from MicroWay (Kingston, Massachusetts).

Once Johnston finished the work on his system, he found the hard disk the biggest bottleneck to increased speed. Many of Johnston's applications, such as database management, required constant disk access when reading or writing data. The computer's processor sits idle during this time; thus, with so many disk accesses, he loses his speed advantage.

To circumvent this problem, Johnston made his most costly purchase, a $1,395 20-megabyte Plus hard disk from Core International (Boca Raton, Florida). Core's disks are reputedly the fastest on the market, with average access times for data between 15 and 20 milliseconds. They operate twice as fast as even the speedy AT disks. But since the computer needs to access the disk only intermittently to find data (some data is already stored in memory buffers from previous accesses), the speed gained with a faster disk is more like 35 to 40 percent.

The faster processor, the math coprocessor, and the Core hard disk provided the bulk of Johnston's speed increase. He also replaced the standard 150-nanosecond RAM memory chips with faster 120-nanosecond RAM to ensure that memory speed kept pace with the faster processor. Finally, he provided added speed boosts through software. For instance, Johnston uses a disk-organizing program to improve file access time and disk buffer software to load programs in RAM and reduce the number of disk accesses. All told, Johnston spent about $1,000 to speed up his system (not including the cost of the hard disk, which he had planned to purchase anyway.)

Johnston revamped his system's speed from its original 6MHz to between 9.5 and 10 MHz. By recognizing the benefits of speed through system improvements, Johnston realizes benefits in both the quantity and quality of his work.

Applications Questions

☐ How did John Johnston increase the instruction processing speed of his microcomputer?

☐ How did he increase the speed of primary and secondary storage devices?

Source: Cheryl Spencer, "Saga of a Speed Upgrade," *Personal Computing,* January 1987, p. 75.

SECTION II: COMPUTER PROCESSING CAPABILITIES

Several major types of computer-based information systems are available to satisfy your information needs. Each of these can use one or more basic processing methods, and each has some basic advantages and disadvantages. Look at Figure 4–10. Its purpose is to emphasize the processing capabilities of modern information systems.

Figure 4–10 spotlights the changes that have occurred since manual information systems were replaced by computer-based information systems that relied on **batch processing** methods. Then **realtime processing systems** began to appear, along with *remote-access batch processing systems*. This trend accelerated with the development of **distributed processing systems** of microcomputers, minicomputers, intelligent terminals, and other computers dispersed throughout an organization and interconnected by **data communications networks.** Other developments included **database processing systems,** which integrate the use and storage of data; and **automated office systems,** where computers automate typing and other office communications. Thus modern information systems have begun to integrate the transmission, processing, and storage of data, words, images, and voices.

The diversity of information processing capabilities mentioned in the preceding paragraph and illustrated in Figure 4–10 can seem overwhelming. It is the cause of some of the confusion concerning the use of computers. However, such diversity is really the key to the amazing versatility of computers and the wide range of problems that they can handle. The goal of such capabilities is to provide users with *immediate access* to *computing resources anywhere* and *anytime* for *any information processing tasks!*

Figure 4–10 also illustrates that computer systems can have several basic processing capabilities, such as **concurrent processing, overlapped processing, dynamic job processing, multitasking, multiprogramming,** and **multiprocessing.** It is important that you gain a basic understanding of these capabilities, since they make possible the efficient and effective use of computers for modern information processing.

What is the basic objective of these different capabilities? *Efficient use of computer system resources* is the answer. The problem is this: The CPU of a computer system or the microprocessor of a microcomputer works so quickly (in nanoseconds) that it can easily spend too much of its time waiting. Do you realize how slow the fastest keyboard user, disk drive, or printer is, compared to the processing speed of a microprocessor or CPU? Hundreds of thousands of *nanoseconds* can go by while the processor waits for a user to key in a single one-character command! High-speed printers and disk drives don't do much better, comparatively speaking.

Figure 4–10 The capabilities of computer-based information systems. Notice the many types of processing capabilities that are possible.

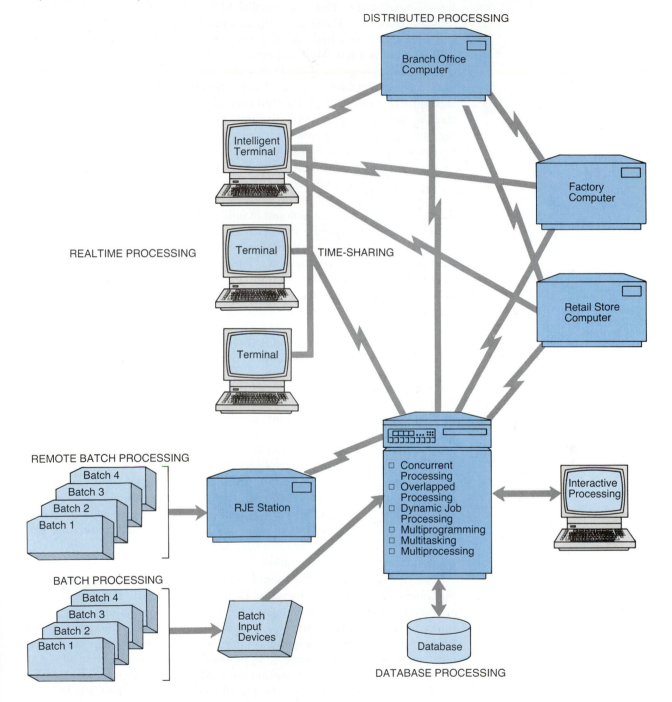

CONCURRENT PROCESSING

What is the solution to this problem? **Concurrent processing** is the answer. Computers can be given the capability of working on more than one task at a time *(concurrently)*. This is accomplished by a combination of hardware and software resources. Hardware with advanced capabilities—advanced CPUs and microprocessors, high-speed storage devices, and input/output interface devices—are needed. Most importantly, control programs that can manage the use of the computer system's resources by more than one task, program, or user are an absolute necessity. Concurrent processing, however, is a basic capability that can be implemented several ways. More specific capabilities, such as overlapped processing, dynamic job processing, spooling, multitasking, multiprogramming, and multiprocessing, are alternative ways that concurrent processing can be implemented. We shall examine the role played by each of these capabilities in this section.

Concurrent processing solves the problems of inefficient use of computer resources, and increases the *throughput* of a computer system. Throughput can be defined as the total amount of fully completed information processing occurring during a specific time period. Thus the efficiency of a computer system is gauged not by the speed of its input, processing, or output equipment but by its throughput. Concurrent processing also helps reduce the time it takes to complete an information processing assignment, which is called *turnaround time*. Concurrent processing techniques greatly increase the throughput of most business information systems and reduce turnaround time because most business applications require many input/output operations, which can waste large amounts of CPU time.

OVERLAPPED PROCESSING

A computer system with an **overlapped processing** capability can increase the use of its central processing unit by overlapping input/output and processing operations. Input/output interface hardware (such as buffers, I/O control units, and channels) and system software (data management programs of an operating system) make such processing possible. Overlapped processing is the opposite of *serial processing*, where the processing function cannot take place until the input function is completed, and the output function must wait until the processing function is completed. A computer system is said to be *input/output bound* if its CPU must wait while its input/output equipment carries out its functions, and it is *process-bound* (or CPU-bound) if the input/output devices have to wait while the CPU is involved in computations and other operations. See Figure 4–11.

Overlapped processing frequently involves an activity known as **spooling** (Simultaneous Peripheral Operation Online), which allows input and output operations to occur simultaneously with processing operations. Input data from low-speed devices are stored temporarily on high-speed secondary storage units. On large computer systems, this is typically magnetic disk or tape units. On microcomputers, it is usually a reserved section of RAM circuits. Data forms a *queue* (waiting line), which can be quickly accessed by the CPU. Output data can also be transferred quickly by the CPU to high-speed storage units and form another queue waiting to use slow-speed devices such as a printer or a card punch. The operating system needs to have a special utility program to control the spooling process, or it must be purchased as a separate software package. See Figure 4–12.

Figure 4–11 Serial versus overlapped processing. Notice that in the fourth time period, the serial processing method has completed the output of the first data record, and is accomplishing the input of the second data record. The overlapped processing method, on the other hand, has completed the output of data records one and two, and is accomplishing the processing of data record three and the input of data record four.

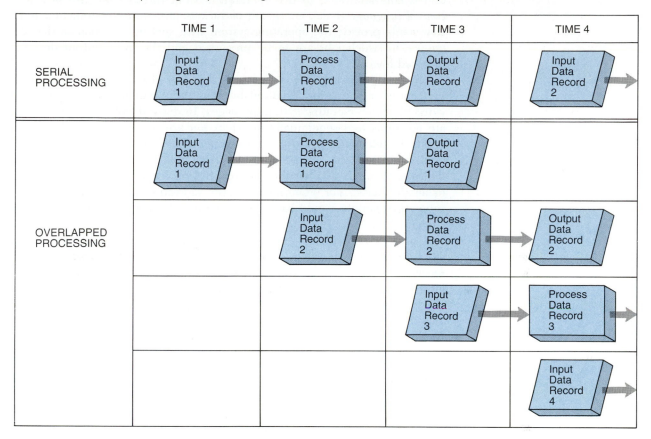

	TIME 1	TIME 2	TIME 3	TIME 4
SERIAL PROCESSING	Input Data Record 1	Process Data Record 1	Output Data Record 1	Input Data Record 2
OVERLAPPED PROCESSING	Input Data Record 1	Process Data Record 1	Output Data Record 1	
		Input Data Record 2	Process Data Record 2	Output Data Record 2
			Input Data Record 3	Process Data Record 3
				Input Data Record 4

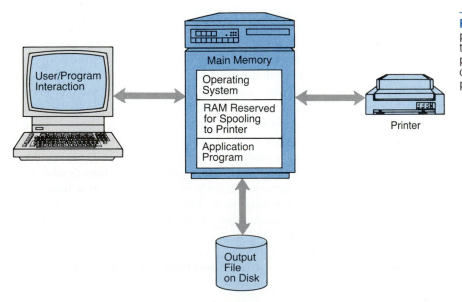

Figure 4–12 The spooling process: A user can continue to interact with an application program while output stored on disk is *spooled* to the printer.

DYNAMIC JOB PROCESSING

Some operating systems allow computers to perform *stacked job processing*, in which a series of data processing jobs are executed continuously without operator intervention being required between each job. Necessary information is communicated to the operating system through the use of a *job control language* (JCL), consisting of various job control statements. JCL statements provide the operating system with such information as the sequence in which jobs are to be processed and the input/output devices required for each job.

Dynamic job processing is a term used to describe the constantly changing computer operations required by many information systems and provided by many operating system packages. In dynamic job processing, jobs are not processed sequentially in stacks but are processed according to a constantly changing *priority interrupt system*. A system of priorities is established for jobs, job steps, and various operational situations, which indicate when the CPU can be "interrupted" in its processing and diverted to another task. For example, an error indication or a signal from the computer operator would have a higher priority than a payroll processing computation.

A priority interrupt system usually requires *time slicing*, in which each job is allocated a specified "slice" of CPU time (frequently a fraction of a second) as measured by the electronic clock of the computer. Jobs are interrupted if they exceed their allocated time slice, are replaced with a waiting job, and are assigned another priority for later processing. A priority interrupt system usually results in a waiting line or queue of jobs that may be stored in primary storage or in direct access storage devices called "swapping" storage. Thus, dynamic job processing involves the continual swapping of jobs and job steps between primary storage and swapping storage. This requires that a continually revised queuing and priority interrupt schedule be maintained by the operating system.

MULTIPROCESSING, MULTIPROGRAMMING, AND MULTITASKING

Multiprocessing is the ability of a *multiprocessor* computer system to execute several instructions simultaneously. As we said in Chapter 2, multiprocessor computer systems may have two or more interconnected central processing units. Thus they can execute two or more instructions simultaneously, one in each processor. Multiprocessing is common on large mainframe computer systems designed for continuous *fault-tolerant* transaction processing. It is also the basis for the operation of fifth-generation *parallel processor* computer systems, where clusters of processors execute many instructions at a time in parallel. Thus this form of multiprocessing is also called *parallel processing*.

Multiprogramming can be defined as the ability of a *uniprocessor* computer system to process two or more programs in the same period (i.e., *concurrently*). In multiprogramming, only one instruction at a time is executed by the central processing unit. However, the CPU switches so quickly from executing the instructions of one program to existing instructions from another program that it gives users the appearance of simultaneous operation. Multiprogramming is accomplished by storing all or part of several programs in primary storage and then switching from the execution of one program to another. An enhanced operating system or operating environment program transfers entire programs or segments of programs and data into and out of main memory from secondary storage devices. Also, arithmetic or logic operations for one program can be performed while simultaneously performing input/output or storage operations for several other programs.

Another way to accomplish concurrent processing is **multitasking.** This involves the concurrent use of the same computer to accomplish several different information processing *tasks.* Each task may require the use of a different program, or the concurrent use of the same copy of a program by several users. Each task in this context is defined as a unit of work involving the execution of a separate program, subprogram, subroutine, I/O operation, and so on. Multitasking is not limited to large computer systems. More powerful microprocessors, operating systems, and operating environment packages have brought multitasking capabilities to many microcomputer systems.

A multiprogramming or multitasking capability allows a computer system to better utilize the time of its central processing unit, since a large part of a CPU's time can be wasted if it has to wait between jobs. However, a multiprogramming or multitasking operating system can allocate portions of primary storage among various jobs and job segments. It subdivides primary storage into several fixed or variable *partitions* or into a large number of **pages.** This allows several programs to be processed during the same period of time. See Figure 4–13.

Figure 4–13 shows the allocation of primary storage into three *partitions:* one for the operating system, a *foreground* partition for high-priority programs, and a *background* partition for low-priority programs. Typically, high-priority programs have extensive input/output requirements but require only small amounts of CPU processing time. Low-priority jobs usually have extensive CPU processing requirements or are routine jobs that do not

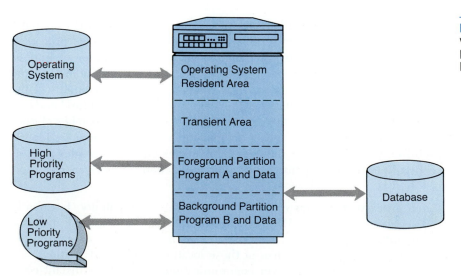

Figure 4–13 Multiprogramming with memory partitions: Two application programs are being processed concurrently.

require immediate processing. For example, a time-sharing system with many remote terminals may use the foreground partition, while stacked job processing might take place in the background partition. Figure 4–13 also shows that application programs and parts of the operating system are stored on magnetic disk and tape devices so they can be shuttled back and forth between primary and secondary storage devices.

BATCH PROCESSING

In a **batch processing system,** data are accumulated over a period of time and then processed periodically. Batch processing usually involves:

☐ Gathering *source documents* originated by business transactions such as sales orders or invoices into groups called *batches*.

☐ Recording transaction data on an *input medium*, such as magnetic disks or magnetic tape.

☐ Sorting the transactions in a *transaction file* into the same sequence as the records in a sequential *master file*.

☐ Computer processing that results in an updated master file and a variety of *documents* (such as customer invoices or paychecks) and *reports* (such as control and management reports).

In batch processing, not only are the data for a particular application or job accumulated into batches but usually a number of different jobs are accumulated and *run* (processed) periodically (daily, weekly, monthly). The rationale for batch processing is that data and jobs should be grouped into batches and processed periodically according to a planned schedule to efficiently use the computer system, rather than allowing data and jobs to be processed in an unorganized, random manner. Of course, this efficiency, economy, and control are accomplished by sacrificing the immediate processing of data for computer users. In a typical example of batch processing, the banking industry usually accumulates all checks that are deposited at banks during the day into batches for later processing each evening. Thus, customer bank balances are updated on a daily basis and many management reports are produced daily.

Figure 4–14 illustrates a batch processing system where batches of data, computer programs, and master files for several different jobs are processed periodically according to a schedule set up by the computer operations department of an organization. The master files are updated by making any necessary changes to the records in the files based on the contents of the batches of input data. Output takes the form of required reports and updated master files. For example, the data could be in the form of batches of sales transactions, income and expense figures, or units of production. Reports produced could be reports required by management, such as sales analysis reports, income and expense reports, or production status reports.

Remote Access Batch Processing

Batch processing systems can have a remote access capability, frequently called *remote job entry* (RJE). Batches of data can be collected and converted into an input medium at remote locations that are far away from the computer. Input/output devices at these locations (called RJE stations) are then used to transmit data over communications circuits to a distant com-

Figure 4–14 A batch processing system example. Batches of data are accumulated for several applications and processed periodically according to a schedule.

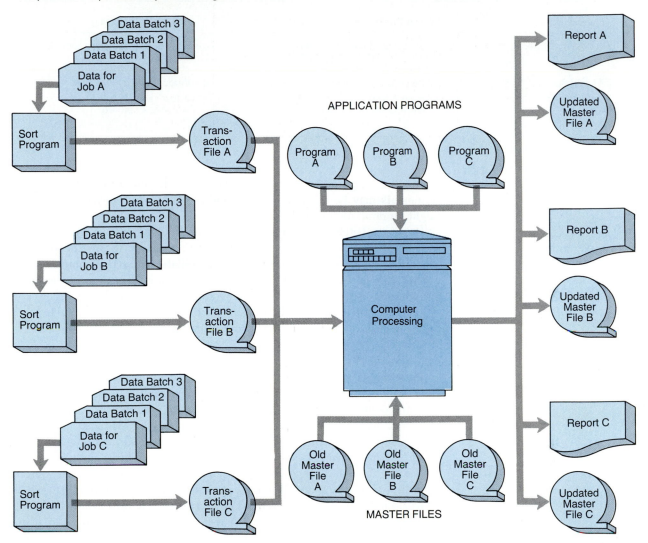

puter. The batches of data are then processed, thus producing updated master files as well as information that is transmitted back to the remote terminal. Remote access batch processing can also involve *remote offline input/output*. For example, data can be transmitted from the keyboard of a terminal to an offline magnetic tape unit, where they are accumulated for subsequent batch processing.

Batch processing is an economical method when large volumes of data must be processed. It is ideally suited for many applications where it is not necessary to update files as transactions occur, and where documents and

Advantages and Disadvantages

Figure 4–15 Batch versus realtime processing. Notice the major differences.

Characteristics	Batch Processing	Realtime Processing
Processing of transactions	Transaction data is recorded, accumulated into batches, sorted, and processed periodically	Transaction data is processed as generated
File update	When batch is processed	When transaction is processed
Response time/turnaround time	Several hours or days after batches are submitted for processing	A few seconds after each transaction is captured

reports are required only at scheduled intervals. For example, customer statements may be prepared on a monthly basis, while payroll processing might be done on a weekly basis.

However, batch processing has some real disadvantages. Master files are frequently out-of-date between scheduled processing, as are the periodic scheduled reports that are produced. Immediate updated responses to inquiries cannot be made. For these reasons, more and more computer applications use realtime processing systems. However, batch processing systems are still widely used, and some of their disadvantages are overcome by using realtime processing for some of their data processing functions.

REALTIME PROCESSING

Realtime processing systems process data immediately after they are generated and can provide immediate output to users. In full-fledged realtime processing systems, data are processed as soon as they are originated or recorded, without waiting to accumulate batches of data. Data are fed directly into the computer system from *online terminals*, without having to be sorted, and are always stored *online* in *direct access files*. The master files are always up-to-date since they are updated whenever data are originated, regardless of its frequency. Responses to user inquiries are immediate, since information in the direct access files can be retrieved almost instantaneously. Heavy use is made of remote terminals connected to the computer using *data communications* links. A summary of the important capabilities that differentiate batch processing and realtime processing is shown in Figure 4–15.

An example of a realtime processing system is shown in Figure 4–16. Notice how POS terminals are connected by data communications links for immediate entry of sales data and control responses (such as customer credit verification). The online direct access customer, inventory, and sales master files are all immediately updated to reflect the effect of sales transactions. The application programs required for sales transactions processing, file updates, and inquiry/response processing are brought into the CPU from a direct access program file as needed. Finally, management personnel use data communication links to terminals located throughout the organization to make inquiries and receive displays concerning customer sales potential, inventory status, and salesperson performance.

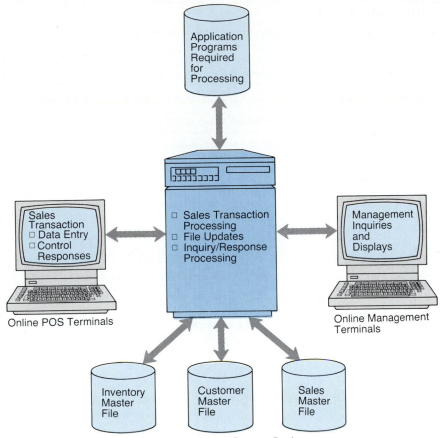

Online POS Terminals

Online Management Terminals

Online Direct Access Storage Devices

Figure 4–16 Example of a real-time sales processing system. Notice that sales transaction processing, management inquiries and responses, and file updates are accomplished immediately using online devices.

Realtime processing is frequently called *online*, or *direct access* processing, since both of these capabilities are required of realtime processing systems. However, use of such terms can be misleading because we have seen that batch processing systems can use online direct access files in the processing of batches of data. As a compromise, experts may use the term *online realtime* (OLRT) processing.

Levels of Realtime Processing

Part of the reluctance to use the term *realtime* stems from its former narrow meaning as promoted by the U.S. Department of Defense. In that context, not only had data to be processed immediately but the results of processing had to be instantly available to control an ongoing process. That definition could then be used to describe only a limited number of applications, typically process control and military defense systems. However, advances in computer hardware and software capabilities have made a realtime capability applicable to many of the functions of modern information systems. In this context, *realtime processing* means that not only is input data processed immediately, but output results are available fast enough to meet the immediate information needs of users. Many modern information systems can easily meet this criterion, whether they rely on microcomputers or mainframe computer systems.

Figure 4–17 Levels of realtime processing, with examples.

Level of Realtime Processing	Business Examples
INQUIRY/RESPONSE	Request customer balance in bank checking accounts using online audio-response terminals. Request number of parts on hand in inventory using online visual display terminals.
DATA ENTRY	Collect sales data with online terminals and record on magnetic tape for later processing. Capture checking account transactions handled by bank tellers and record on temporary file for control purposes.
FILE PROCESSING	Update customer files due to sales transaction data captured by online terminals. Update work-in-process inventory files due to production data captured by data recording terminals on the factory floor.
FULL CAPABILITY	Process airline reservations using online video terminals and update online flight reservation files. Process data arising from the purchase or sale of securities using online terminals and update online securities transaction files.
PROCESS CONTROL	Control petroleum refinery process with online sensing and control devices. Control of electric power generation and transmission.

Other writers refer to *interactive processing* to emphasize the interactive capability of many realtime systems, or use the term *transaction processing* to emphasize that individual transactions are processed as they occur and are not accumulated into batches. Some of the semantic confusion arises from the fact that there can be different combinations of realtime and batch processing capabilities, depending on the information system functions to be performed. Thus many current information systems are combinations of batch and realtime processing. Again, a pertinent example is the banking industry, which typically updates checking accounts on a daily batch basis, but uses realtime processing to allow immediate response to inquiries concerning customer bank balances stored on online direct access files.

To help clarify this situation, you should understand that realtime processing can be subdivided into the five levels illustrated in Figure 4–17 and summarized below.

☐ **Inquiry/response systems.** The main function of an inquiry system is information retrieval. The user of a realtime inquiry system wishes a quick response to a request for information; for example, the current balance in a particular bank checking account.

☐ **Data entry systems.** The main function of a data entry system is the immediate but temporary collection and recording of data until they can be processed at a later date. Thus the realtime data entry system is designed to perform only collection, conversion, and storage activities, leaving processing activities to a batch processing system. For example, some retail stores use online point-of-sale terminals to capture and record sales data on magnetic tape or disk during the day for subsequent remote batch processing at night.

☐ **File processing systems.** File processing realtime systems perform all of the activities of information systems except output. Thus, data are collected, converted, manipulated, and then stored—resulting in an immediate and continual updating of files. The output activity may be performed by subsequent batch processing, which produces reports and other output, or by a realtime inquiry system, which interrogates the files. For example, customer files could be updated immediately by POS terminals, but customer statements and credit reports could be done only on a periodic basis.

☐ **Full capability systems.** The full capability realtime processing system provides immediate and continuous performance of all of the activities of information systems. It can thus perform the services of the other levels of realtime systems. Example: the reservation systems of the major airlines are full capability systems, since they process passenger reservations in realtime using online terminals at airline offices and airports. Realtime processing systems with a full processing capability are being installed or developed by almost all users of large or medium-scale computers.

☐ **Process control systems.** A particular type of full capability realtime processing system is the process control system, which not only performs all information system activities but, in addition, uses its information output to control an ongoing physical process. Examples are industrial production processes in the steel, petroleum, and chemical industries.

Realtime processing systems provide immediate updating of files and immediate responses to user inquiries. Realtime processing is particularly important for applications where there is a high frequency of changes that must be made to a file during a short time to keep it updated. Input data does not need to be sorted, and only the specific records affected by transactions or inquiries need to be processed. Also, several files can be processed or updated concurrently, since transaction data does not have to be sorted into the sequence of any particular file.

Advantages and Disadvantages

Realtime processing has its disadvantages. Because of the online, direct access nature of realtime processing, special precautions must be taken to protect the contents of data files. Thus many realtime systems have to use magnetic tape files as *control logs* (to record all transactions being made) or as *backup files* (by periodically making a magnetic tape copy of a file). Also, more controls have to be built into the software and data processing procedures to protect against unauthorized access or accidental destruction of data. Thus the many advantages of realtime processing must be balanced with the extra costs and security precautions that are necessary. However, most computer-using firms are willing to pay this price, since the use of realtime processing continues to increase in modern information systems.

INTERACTIVE PROCESSING

An important characteristic of many realtime processing systems is that they provide an **interactive processing** capability. You can use a microcomputer or online terminal to interact with a computer on a realtime basis. The four major applications of interactive processing are:

☐ **Inquiry/response** applications, where a request for information is entered through the keyboard and the answer is immediately displayed on the screen.

☐ **Conversational computing,** which uses interactive software packages to carry on a dialogue and help a user solve a problem or accomplish a particular job on the computer.

☐ **Online data entry,** which provides data entry assistance to operators. For example, a data entry system can be a *menu-driven* approach, which prompts and guides the data entry operator with menu-selecting choices, specialized formats that help an operator with prompting messages, and sophisticated editing with error-control reminders.

☐ **Interactive programming,** where a programmer uses a terminal to develop and test the instructions for a program with the realtime assistance of a computer. It has become the primary form of programming for professional programmers.

TIME–SHARING

Want to share the use of a computer in realtime? Then use a **time-sharing** system. Time-sharing is the sharing of a computer system by many users in different locations at the same time through the use of online input/output terminals. Time-sharing systems "interleave" the data processing assignments of many users by giving each user a small, frequently repeated "slice" of time. Time-sharing systems operate at such fast speeds that each user has the illusion that he or she alone is using the computer, because of the seemingly instantaneous response. The ability of time-sharing systems to service many users simultaneously is sometimes hard to comprehend. However, one must remember that a computer operating in nanoseconds speeds can process millions of instructions per second.

Remote batch processing and realtime processing can be accomplished using time-sharing systems. A time-sharing user could accumulate batches of data and periodically process them, using input/output devices ranging from small terminals to larger batch processing stations, to small satellite computer systems. However, time-sharing systems are currently used primarily for realtime processing applications. Time-sharing systems can easily handle the inquiry/response, data entry, and file processing types of realtime processing assignments from users at work sites throughout an organization or geographical area. Time-sharing thus relies heavily on data communications hardware and software to provide instantaneous responses to many users using remote terminals and personal computer workstations.

Types of Time-Sharing

Special-purpose time-sharing systems exist that have been designed for a specific application, such as airline reservation systems. The American Airlines Sabre system or the United Airlines Apollo system are examples. More prevalent, however, are general-purpose time-sharing systems, which can be used internally within an organization, such as a large business firm or university, where many remote time-sharing terminals allow simultaneous use of the computer by many users throughout the organization.

The other major form of general-purpose time-sharing is the time-sharing services offered by data processing service centers and national time-sharing companies. Time-sharing services are provided to many subscribers, representing various business firms and organizations. Subscribers pay for time-sharing by paying an initial installation charge, basic monthly charges, and transaction charges, which vary according to the amount of computer resources used. Firms offering such time-sharing services are sometimes referred to as computer or information "utilities." Nationwide time-sharing services are offered to business firms by such companies as GE, Control Data, Tymeshare, and Telenet. Time-sharing services are also available to personal computer users from networks like *The Source* and *CompuServe*.

Distributed processing is also called distributed data processing (DDP). It is a form of information processing made possible by a network of computers dispersed throughout an organization. Processing of user applications is accomplished by several computers interconnected by a data communications network. Users no longer rely on one large *centralized* computer facility, or on the *decentralized* operation of several independent computers. Computers may be dispersed over a wide geographic area, or may be distributed to user departments in a limited *local area network* (LAN). Distributed processing systems rely heavily on a network composed of microcomputers, minicomputers, and mainframes controlled by computer users throughout an organization. These computer users can thus perform many of their own information processing tasks. They can communicate with similar computers and share hardware, software, and data resources in the network, if necessary. See Figure 4–18.

Distributed processing is a movement away from a centralized processing approach, which relies on large central computers and a centralized information processing department. However, it is not the same as traditional decentralized processing. That would involve completely independent user computer systems with independent databases, programs, applications, budgets, and information system development efforts. Instead, distributed processing is:

□ A *system* of user department and headquarters computers.
□ *Interconnected* by a data communications network.
□ *Integrated* by a common database-oriented approach.

The use of distributed processing systems can be subdivided into five application categories: (1) distributed information processing, (2) central site processing, (3) distributed data entry, (4) distributed database processing, and (5) distributed communications networks.

DISTRIBUTED PROCESSING

Distributed Processing Applications

Figure 4–18 Centralized, decentralized, and distributed processing. Notice how distributed processing differs from the centralized and decentralized alternatives.

CENTRALIZED PROCESSING: Centralized Computer Processors and Resources

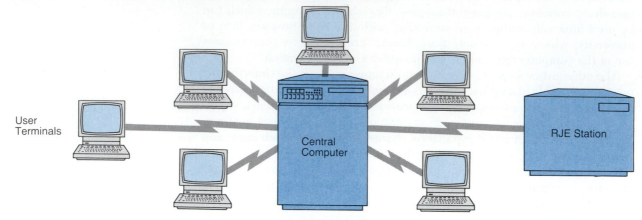

DECENTRALIZED PROCESSING: Independent Computer Processors and Resources

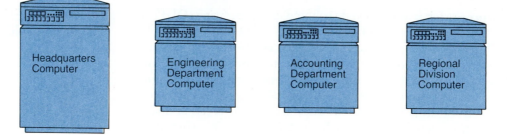

DISTRIBUTED PROCESSING: A Network of Dispersed Computer Processors and Resources

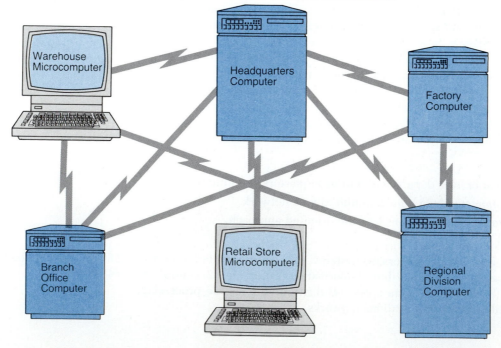

Distributed Information Processing

With distributed information processing, local users can handle a broad range of information processing tasks. These include data entry processing and local database inquiry and response systems. Also included is fully independent transaction processing, which involves updating local databases and generating necessary output reports. One rule of thumb states that if 70 to 80 percent of the information needed by users can be produced locally, then users should have their own computer systems. Thus data can be completely processed locally, where most input and output (and errors and problems) must be handled, anyway. This should provide computer processing more tailored to the needs of users, and increase information processing efficiency and effectiveness as users become more responsible for their own application systems.

Central Site Processing

With DDP, large central site computers can be applied to those jobs they can best handle, such as large highly structured and repetitive batch applications, communications control for the entire distributed processing network, maintaining large corporate databases, and providing sophisticated planning and decision-making support for corporate management. Users at local sites might typically access a central computer to receive corporatewide management information or transmit summary transaction data reflecting local site activities.

Distributed Data Entry

Data entry using terminals connected to a local computer helps generate *clean data* from source documents at their point of origin for local processing or transmittal to a central site. Data that contain errors and require editing and preprocessing *(dirty data)* can usually be cleaned better at the site where it originated. Local personnel are more familiar with the local conditions, which may have caused the errors, and feel more responsible for having them corrected.

Distributed Database Processing

There are many kinds of data that may be of interest to only one local site. Thus specialized local databases, containing data unique to user departments, can be distributed to local sites. In such *distributed database processing systems*, all transaction data, or just summary data, may be sent to a central computer for storage in a common database. Distributed database systems can provide faster response times, better user control of data structures and access, and lower communication costs, because data are closer to users. We will discuss distributed databases further in Chapter 7.

REAL WORLD APPLICATION 4–2

Mobil Oil Corporation

Backed by an MIS department independent of the mainstream corporate MIS establishment, Mobil Oil Corp.'s U.S. Refining and Marketing Division has for the last five years spent a considerable amount of time, energy, and money bringing up a nationwide point-of-sale (POS) network.

According to Johnathan Briggs, Mobil's POS project manager, the Fairfax, Virginia–based division uses a number of Tandem Non-Stop Fault-Tolerant computer systems to drive its network of POS systems at 3,600 service stations nationwide. All 3,600 cashier terminals communicate through leased lines to the main data processing center in Kansas City, Missouri, which uses an IBM mainframe.

The Tandem POS network does what Briggs calls negative file lookups, meaning it runs a credit check against bad customer accounts before issuing credit card authorizations. The POS network also gathers customer billing data on Mobil's own credit card users.

The Tandem network performs all online transaction processing (OLTP) tasks, then at night off-loads the information to an IBM mainframe computer running proprietary Mobil allocations, according to Briggs. OLTP systems can play an important strategic role in keeping a company ahead of its competition. At Mobil, credit authorization is the key to keeping that edge. Briggs says Mobil is planning for the *cashless society* that the advent of debit cards and regional banking cards might

bring. Mobil is considering adding these capabilities sometime next year.

Already, the firm is devoting part of the Tandem's processing capabilities to communications switching between Mobil's own credit card authorization and those for other major credit cards. The needed credit information is collected by the system at the service station, enters the network, and is passed through to the appropriate third-party credit card authorization facilities.

The next step will be for Mobil to switch all debit card transaction requests through its own system to a corresponding OLTP system at local banks. Once there, the transaction request would check the current cash balance of the customer's account and either approve or deny the transaction. If approved, the appropriate amount would be automatically deducted from that account and passed onto Mobil accounts. With an on-line foundation already in place, such electronic funds transfers (EFT) should not be difficult.

Application Questions

☐ Is Mobil's online transaction processing (OLTP) system an example of batch processing or realtime processing? Explain.

☐ Identify the benefits of this system to Mobil. What problems might such a system have?

Source: Philip J. Gill, "On-Line Transaction Processing," *Computerworld*, September 29, 1986, p. 49.

Distributed Communications Networks

Several computers and many terminals can typically be interconnected by a local area network (LAN) at each large local site. These LANs can be connected by communications channels to each other and to headquarters computers. We will discuss these and other distributed processing networks in Chapter 8 when we analyze data communications networks.

SUMMARY

- A CPU or microprocessor contains several types of special-purpose circuitry elements such as registers, adders, and decoders. They serve as temporary work areas, analyze instructions, or perform arithmetic and logical operations. In addition, the CPU relies on several types of interface devices to support its use of input/output peripheral equipment.

- The execution of a computer instruction can be subdivided into an instruction cycle (when the computer prepares to execute an instruction) and an execution cycle (when it actually executes the instruction).

- Data is represented in a computer in a binary form because of the two-state nature of the electronic and magnetic components of the computer. Most computers use special codes based on the binary number system, including the EBCDIC and ASCII codes.

- Within the computer, data is usually organized into bits, bytes, and words. Each position of storage can store one byte, and has a specific numerical location so the data stored in its contents can be readily located.

- Several types of computer processing capabilities are available to meet the information needs of an organization. This includes concurrent processing—the ability of a computer system to work on more than one job at the same time. Concurrent processing can be implemented by such techniques as overlapped processing, spooling, dynamic job processing, multiprocessing, multiprogramming, and multitasking.

- Two basic categories of information systems are batch processing systems, in which data are accumulated and processed periodically, and realtime processing systems, which process data immediately. Realtime processing systems can be subdivided into several levels: inquiry, data entry, file processing, full capability, and process control systems.

- Realtime processing systems provide an interactive processing capability, in which users at online terminals can interact with a computer on a realtime basis. This may take the form of inquiry/response, conversational computing, online data entry, or interactive programming. Time-sharing systems are a major form of realtime processing systems, which allow many users in different locations to share a computer system at the same time through the use of online input/output terminals.

- Distributed processing is a form of decentralization of information processing made possible by a network of computers dispersed throughout an organization. Processing of user applications is accomplished by several computers interconnected by a data communications network, rather than relying on one large centralized computer facility, or on the decentralized operation of several independent computers. Distributed processing systems are used for five major application areas: (1) distributed data processing, (2) central site processing, (3) distributed data entry, (4) distributed database processing, and (5) distributed communications networks.

KEY TERMS AND CONCEPTS

These are the key terms and concepts of this chapter. The page number of their first explanation is in parenthesis.

1. Batch processing (*163*)
2. Binary number system (*150*)
3. Binary representation (*150*)
4. Computer codes (*153*)
   a. EBCDIC
   b. ASCII
5. Computer data elements (*155*)
   a. Bit
   b. Byte
   c. Word
6. Concurrent processing (*160*)
7. Distributed processing (*171*)
8. Dynamic job processing (*162*)
9. Execution cycle (*146*)
10. Input/output interface devices (*148*)
11. Instruction cycle (*146*)
12. Interactive processing (*170*)
13. Multiprocessing (*162*)
14. Multiprogramming (*162*)
15. Multitasking (*163*)
16. Overlapped processing (*160*)
17. Realtime processing (*166*)
18. Registers (*146*)
19. Time-sharing (*170*)

REVIEW AND APPLICATION QUIZ

Match one of the **key terms and concepts** listed above with one of the brief examples or definitions listed below. Try to find the "best fit" for answers that seem to fit more than one term or concept. Defend your choices.

_____ 1. Assist the CPU in its input/output assignments.

_____ 2. An individual data or instruction element is stored here in the CPU.

_____ 3. Fetching and interpreting an instruction.

_____ 4. Fetching and manipulating data.

_____ 5. The presence or absence of electric current or magnetism in computer circuitry or media.

_____ 6. A zero or a one.

_____ 7. Typically equals eight bits.

_____ 8. Equals 16 bits for most current microcomputers.

_____ 9. An eight-bit computer code.

_____ 10. The generic term for computers doing several things at the same time.

_____ 11. Doing input, processing, and output activities at the same time.

_____ 12. Information processing jobs are executed according to a constantly changing priority system.

_____ 13. Executing more than one instruction at the same instant.

_____ 14. Concurrent processing of several programs by quickly switching from one to another, thus giving the appearance of simultaneous execution.

_____ 15. Concurrent performance of several information processing activities using one or more programs.

_____ 16. Concurrent use of the same computer by several users.

_____ 17. Collecting and periodically processing data.

_____ 18. Processing data immediately after it is captured.

_____ 19. Users have a dialogue with a computer.

_____ 20. Computers at central and local sites interconnected by a network.

1. If you have not already done so, read and answer the questions after the two Real World Applications in this chapter.

2. Use Figure 4–2 to help you match the following terms with the appropriate sentences below:

   a. Register.   d. Port.
   b. Buffer.   e. Bus.
   c. Channel.

   _____ 1. Circuitry for the connection of I/O devices to the CPU.

   _____ 2. A special-purpose processor that controls the movement of data between the CPU and I/O devices.

   _____ 3. Small high-speed storage circuitry areas in the CPU for storing an individual instruction or data element.

   _____ 4. A temporary storage area for storing parts of programs or data during processing or I/O operations.

   _____ 5. A set of conducting paths for movement of data and instructions.

3. For the following computer instructions, identify which parts are:

   a. operation code.
   b. operands.

   1. Read data from disk to addresses 01, 02, 03, 04.

   2. Read contents of address 01 into arithmetic-logic unit.

   3. Multiply contents of arithmetic-logic by contents of address 04, store result in address 18.

   4. Write contents of address 18 on printer.

4. If the EBCDIC character M, which represents 11010100, is transferred from a CRT to the CPU using odd parity, what value will the parity bit have? In even parity, what value will the parity bit have? If the ASCII-8 character 8, which represents 0111000, is transferred from a CRT to the CPU using odd parity, what value will the parity bit have? In even parity, what value will the parity bit have?

5. Use Figures 4–5 and 4–7 to help you match the following answers with the statements below:

   a. 1100000.   c. 1000010.
   b. 00111111.   d. 11111100.

   _____ 1. Represents 66 in binary.

   _____ 2. Represents 96 in binary.

   _____ 3. Represents 12 in EBCDIC.

   _____ 4. Represents 15 in ASCII.

6. Match the following terms with the appropriate sentence below:
   a. Stacked job processing.   e. Dynamic job processing.
   b. Multiprocessing.   f. Distributed processing.
   c. Multiprogramming.   g. Time-sharing.
   d. Multitasking.   h. Interactive processing.

   _____ 1. One operating system in control of more than one
              CPU.
   _____ 2. One or more programs used to perform several ac-
              tivities concurrently.
   _____ 3. Several users access the same CPU via terminals and
              receive what seems to be simultaneous results.
   _____ 4. The ability to switch from one program to another so
              rapidly that it appears that many programs are running
              at the same time.
   _____ 5. Works on the basis of an interrupt feature.
   _____ 6. A network of cooperating computers.
   _____ 7. A conversational type of computing.
   _____ 8. Allows for automatic job to job transition.

7. For each example below of an information system, state whether the
   system is most probably batch or realtime. If realtime, specify one of
   the following levels of realtime processing:
   a. Inquiry/response.   d. Full capability.
   b. Data entry.   e. Process control.
   c. File processing.

   1. A computerized tax program designed to catch up with individ-
      uals and businesses who have evaded city tax payments has
      resulted in the collection of millions of dollars in New York City.
      The system matches various types of files; the city has been able
      to detect evaders of the commercial rent tax, or of unpaid
      business income taxes and delinquent individual taxpayers.
   2. A large chain of pharmacies has automated its order entry and
      customer billing functions. Pharmacists enter orders via terminals
      located in each retail store. When an order is entered, charge
      information is automatically generated, captured, and stored by
      the computer. The information is passed to the main computer on
      a daily basis. The main computer reads pharmacy data, posts
      charges to the proper accounts, and generates customer bills.
   3. In an accounts payable system, all transactions are currently
      driven by interactive user menus. It takes about one minute to
      update an invoice.
   4. A large warehouse is taking inventory. The stock clerks carry
      small handheld terminals. As they count the number of items in
      each bin, they enter the stock code and the quantity on hand
      onto the terminal. The handheld terminals are then linked to the
      computer to update the inventory.

8. Match the following terms with the appropriate example shown below:
   a. Centralized processing.
   b. Decentralized processing.
   c. Distributed processing.

   _____ 1. The accounting, marketing, and engineering departments each have their own independent computer systems and databases.

   _____ 2. The accounting, marketing, and engineering departments have video display terminals and remote printers tied in a time-sharing network to the headquarters computer and central database.

   _____ 3. The accounting, marketing, and engineering departments each have computer systems and local databases interconnected by a data communications network to other users and the headquarters computer and central database.

9. New operating systems, operating environment programs, and advanced microprocessors have caused such terms as *multiuser,* *multitasking,* and *concurrent processing* to be applied to some microcomputers. Explain what these capabilities might provide to users of such microcomputer systems.

10. ABC Department Stores uses POS terminals connected to a minicomputer in each store to capture sales data immediately and store them on a magnetic disk unit. Each night the central computer in Phoenix *polls* each store's minicomputer to access and process the day's sales data, update the corporate database, and produce management reports. The next morning, managers use their terminals to interrogate the updated store and corporate databases.

    Identify how each of the following types of computer processing are occurring in the example above:
    a. Batch.   e. Interactive.
    b. Realtime.   f. Data entry.
    c. Online.   g. Distributed.
    d. Transaction.

CHAPTER

5

INPUT/OUTPUT CONCEPTS AND METHODS

Chapter Outline

Section I: Input/Output Concepts

The User Interface
Data Entry Concepts
Traditional Data Entry
Source Data Automation
Computer-Assisted Data Entry
Data Output Concepts
Changing Output Methods
Computer Graphics
Real World Application 5–1: Federated Investors, Inc.

Section II: Input/Output Methods

Visual-Supported Input/Output
Printed Output
Voice Input/Output
Optical Scanning
Magnetic Media Data Entry
Micrographics
Real World Application 5–2: West Point Pepperell

Learning Objectives

The purpose of this chapter is to promote a basic understanding of computer input and output by analyzing (1) important input/output concepts, and (2) the characteristics, functions, benefits, and limitations of major methods of input and output.

After reading and studying this chapter, you should be able to:

1. Explain several major input/output concepts, including:
   a. Traditional data entry versus source data automation.
   b. Computer-assisted data entry.
   c. Changing output methods, including the use of computer graphics.
2. Outline the advantages and disadvantages of several major input/output methods.
3. Identify the input and output devices of any microcomputers you use, as well as other computers used by your school or business. Also, determine their basic physical and performance characteristics.

Section I: Input/Output Concepts

How do computer users communicate with a computer? Typically, they will (1) issue commands, (2) enter data, and (3) ask questions of the computer, and it will respond in a variety of ways. Such communication relies on the information system functions of *input* and *output*. Data has to be collected, converted to a form the computer can understand, and entered into the computer system in the **input** function. After processing is completed, information has to be converted to a form you can understand and be presented to you by the computer in the **output** function. In this chapter we will discuss how this occurs, concentrating on some important concepts and on the variety of methods that enable us to communicate with computers.

Why are there so many methods of input/output? Refer back to Figure 2–2 in Chapter 2 and pages 19–26 of the pictorial section of Chapter 1. Notice how many types of media and devices are used to communicate with computers. Then take a look at Figure 5–1. It shows you the equipment, media, major functions, speed, advantages, and disadvantages of several important input/output methods. Look specifically at the advantages and disadvantages summarized in the last column. This should emphasize that the perfect input/output device does not exist. They all have their advantages and disadvantages, especially given the many different users and environments that we have for computers. So the computer industry has responded by developing the many different input/output devices we will discuss in this chapter.

THE USER INTERFACE

The computer industry is making a major effort to develop better input/ output methods and devices for users. Their goal is to develop a better **user interface** between users and computers. (An *interface* is a connection or boundary between systems or parts of systems.) In this chapter, we will show you how the computer industry is using such developments as source data automation, computer-assisted data entry, keyboard aids, video display aids, computer graphics, and many other input/output devices and methods to assist you in using computers. A major effort is being made to use the science and technology of **ergonomics** (also called *human factors engineering*) to produce hardware and software that will be **user friendly** (i.e., safe, comfortable, and easy to use). Figure 5–2 summarizes many of the input/ output features being developed to improve the interface between users and computers.

DATA ENTRY CONCEPTS

The **input** activity in information systems frequently involves a process called **data entry.** In this process, data is captured or collected by recording, coding, and editing activities. Then data may be converted to a form that can be entered into a computer system. Data entry activities have always been a bottleneck in the use of computers for information processing. We have always had a problem getting data into computers correctly and quickly enough to match their awesome processing speed. Thus traditional *manual* methods of data entry that make heavy use of *data media* are being replaced

Figure 5–1 Characteristics of important input/output methods. Notice especially the advantages and disadvantages of each method.

Peripheral Equipment	Media	Primary Functions	Typical I/O Speed Range	Major Advantages and/or Disadvantages
VIDEO DISPLAY TERMINALS	None	Keyboard input and video output	250–50,000 characters per second output	Conventional and inexpensive, but limited display capacity and no hard copy
PRINTERS	Paper	Printed output of paper reports and documents	10–600 characters per second: Character printer. 200–3,000 lines per minute: Line printer. 250–20,000 lines per minute: Page printer.	Hard copy, but inconvenient and bulky. Many printers are relatively slow.
VISUAL-SUPPORTED INPUT/OUTPUT DEVICES	None	Input by mouse, joystick, light pen, touch screen, and digitizers. Video output.	Not applicable	Input devices are easy to use and inexpensive, but have limited applications and software
VOICE INPUT/ OUTPUT DEVICES	None	Voice input and output	Input: Noncontinuous speech. Output: Normal human speech.	Easiest I/O but is slow, has limited vocabulary, and accuracy problems
OPTICAL SCANNERS	Paper documents	Direct input from written or printed documents	100–3,600 characters per second for Optical Character Recognition (OCR) readers.	Direct input from paper documents, but some limitations on input format
MAGNETIC INK CHARACTER RECOGNITION (MICR) READERS	MICR paper documents	Direct input of MICR documents	700–3,200 characters per second. 180–2,000 documents per minute.	Fast, high-reliability reading, but documents must be preprinted and the character set is limited
MICROGRAPHICS DEVICES	Microfilm	Microfilm input or output	Computer-output microfilm (COM) recorders: 500,000 characters per second and 60,000 lines per minute.	Fast, compact media, but relatively expensive peripherals

Figure 5–2 These technical and ergonomic developments are making the interface between users and computers more user friendly: Safe, comfortable, and easy to use.

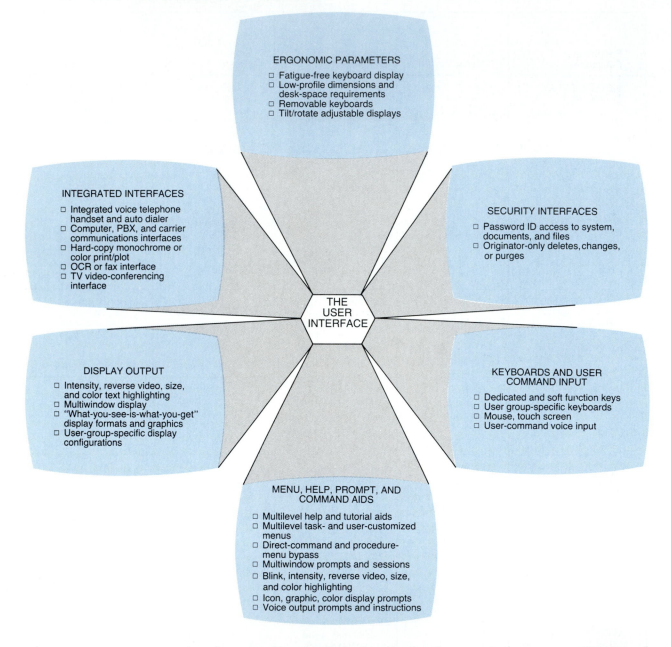

ERGONOMIC PARAMETERS

- Fatigue-free keyboard display
- Low-profile dimensions and desk-space requirements
- Removable keyboards
- Tilt/rotate adjustable displays

INTEGRATED INTERFACES

- Integrated voice telephone handset and auto dialer
- Computer, PBX, and carrier communications interfaces
- Hard-copy monochrome or color print/plot
- OCR or fax interface
- TV video-conferencing interface

SECURITY INTERFACES

- Password ID access to system, documents, and files
- Originator-only deletes, changes, or purges

THE USER INTERFACE

DISPLAY OUTPUT

- Intensity, reverse video, size, and color text highlighting
- Multiwindow display
- "What-you-see-is-what-you-get" display formats and graphics
- User-group-specific display configurations

KEYBOARDS AND USER COMMAND INPUT

- Dedicated and soft function keys
- User group-specific keyboards
- Mouse, touch screen
- User-command voice input

MENU, HELP, PROMPT, AND COMMAND AIDS

- Multilevel help and tutorial aids
- Multilevel task- and user-customized menus
- Direct-command and procedure-menu bypass
- Multiwindow prompts and sessions
- Blink, intensity, reverse video, size, and color highlighting
- Icon, graphic, color display prompts
- Voice output prompts and instructions

by more *direct automated* methods. These methods are more efficient and reliable and are known as **source data automation.** Let's take a look at these methods.

TRADITIONAL DATA ENTRY

Traditional methods of data entry typically rely on the users of the information system to capture data on **source documents** such as purchase orders, payroll time sheets, and sales invoices. The source documents are then usually accumulated into batches, and transferred to data processing profes-

Figure 5–3 A traditional data entry example: Sales transaction processing. Notice that source documents are: (1) manually edited, (2) batched, (3) converted to another media, (4) entered into a computer system, (5) edited again, (6) rejected data is corrected and reentered, (7) sorted, and (8) accepted into the computer system.

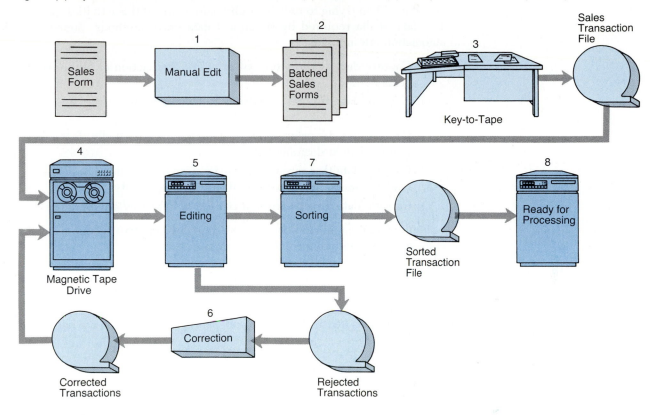

sionals who specialize in data entry. Periodically, the source documents are subjected to one of the following additional data entry activities:

☐ The data is converted into a **machine-readable media,** such as punched cards, magnetic tape, or magnetic disks. Typically, this means using such devices as keypunch machines, key-to-tape machines, and key-to-disk systems. The media are then read by input devices that enter the data into a computer.

☐ The data from source documents could alternatively be directly entered into a computer system, using a **direct input** device (such as the keyboard of a video terminal) without the use of machine-readable media.

Figure 5–3 illustrates this traditional data entry process, using sales transaction processing as an example. Notice the use of sales forms as source documents, and their conversion to magnetic tape media. Notice also the many data entry activities involved. It should not be surprising, then, to discover that there has been a major shift away from traditional data entry. First, it requires too many activities, people, and data media. Second, it results in high costs and increases the potential for errors. Therefore, the response of both users and the computer industry has been to move toward *source data automation.*

SOURCE DATA AUTOMATION

The use of automated methods of data entry is known as **source data automation.** Several methods have been developed to accomplish this automation, though very few completely automate the data entry process. They are all based on trying to reduce or eliminate many of the activities, people, and data media required by traditional data entry methods. Source data automation attempts to:

☐ Capture data *as early as possible* after a transaction or other event occurs.

☐ Capture data *as close as possible* to the *source* that generates the data.

☐ Capture data by using *machine-readable media* initially, instead of written source documents.

☐ Capture data that rarely changes by *prerecording* it on machine-readable media, or by *storing* it in the computer system.

☐ Capture data directly *without the use of data media* if possible.

Figure 5–4 is an illustration of an automated data entry process, using the entry of sales data into a computer system as an example.

Figure 5–4 An automated data entry example: Sales transaction processing. Notice how few steps are needed compared to traditional data entry.

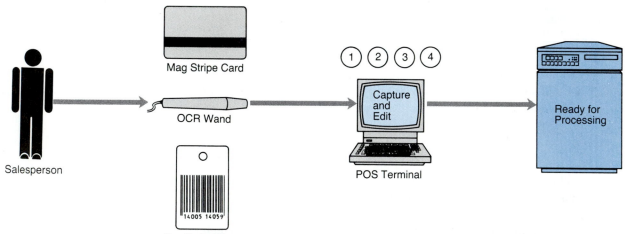

1. Sales data is captured as soon as sales occur by *POS (point-of-sale) terminals.* They are not batched for later processing, and no sorting is necessary.

2. Sales data is captured by sales personnel right at the store, not by data processing personnel at another location. They edit their own input just once.

3. Sales data is captured partially by the use of machine-readable data media, on which product or customer data has been prerecorded. This includes bar-coded merchandise tags, which are read by *optical scanning wands*, and a plastic credit card with a *magnetic stripe*, which can be read by POS terminals. Thus no written source documents are used.

4. Other sales data is entered directly into the computer system without the use of any type of data media by using the *keyboard* of the POS terminal.

The example in Figure 5–4 reveals some of the types of equipment and media used in current source data automation. Major types of such hardware include:

- **Transaction terminals** and data collection terminals, such as POS terminals and keyboard/video display terminals.
- **Optical character recognition** (OCR) devices, such as optical scanning wands.
- **Magnetic ink character recognition** (MICR) devices, such as MICR reader/sorters used in banking for check processing.
- Other technologies, including the **electronic mouse, light pens, magnetic stripe cards, voice input,** and **tactile input.** We will discuss each of these technologies in the rest of this chapter.

A fast growing area of source data automation is called **electronic data interchange** or EDI. This involves the electronic transmission of source documents between the computers of different companies. Source documents representing a variety of business transactions (such as purchase orders, invoices, and shipping notices) are electronically transmitted using standard document message formats. Thus, EDI is an example of the complete automation of the data entry process. Transaction data is transmitted directly between computers, without paper documents and human intervention. Companies in the automotive, chemical, grocery, and transportation industries were the earliest users of this technology, but it has spread to many manufacturing and retailing companies. Some of the benefits of EDI are reductions in paper, postage, and labor costs; faster flow of transactions; reductions in inventory levels; and better customer service.

Electronic Data Interchange

Besides attempts to automate data entry, the computer industry is continually developing methods and devices to use the computer itself to assist a user or data entry operator. **Computer-assisted data entry** can assist traditional methods of data entry, as well as source data automation systems. Let's take a look at the many ways this can be accomplished using computer terminals, microcomputers, and other computer systems.

COMPUTER-ASSISTED DATA ENTRY

Most keyboards now provide specialized *function keys* and *control keys*, which reduce the number of keystrokes needed to accomplish data entry tasks. Pressing one or two keys may accomplish what formerly took several keystrokes to accomplish. The functions of these keys may be controlled by hardware circuits or software. The advantage of function keys controlled by software *(soft keys)* is that they can be controlled to accomplish different tasks, depending on the application program being processed. Examples of function keys are *deposit* and *withdrawal* keys on a bank teller terminal, or *boldface* and *italic* keys on a microcomputer using a word processing package. Examples of typical control keys include *cursor control* keys, and *delete, backspace,* and *numeric mode* keys. See Figure A1–2 in Appendix A for an example of special keys on a common computer keyboard.

Keyboard Aids

Figure 5–5 A formatted screen assists data entry. Notice how this data entry screen helps you enter the proper data.

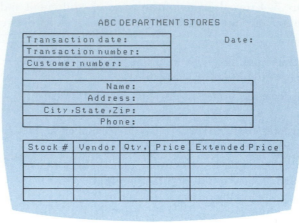

Video Display Aids

Video display terminals are widely used data entry devices. Keyed-in data can be displayed and visually edited and corrected before input into a computer system. Most video display units use a variety of features to assist data entry. These features include blinking cursors and characters, highlighting displayed material, and split screen windows.

A **cursor** is a point of light which assists users by indicating the position of data to be entered or changed. It may look like a short blinking underline or other shape. **Highlighting** is a feature that brightens areas of the screen where data is to be entered. Sections of text material can also be highlighted. Many software packages also allow a display screen to be split into several sections called **windows.** This enables a user to see several different displays at the same time in each window.

Video display terminals can be programmed to project a **formatted screen,** which displays a document or report format. An operator can then fill out this electronic form by using the keyboard to fill in the blanks, guided by the cursor. When both the computer and user agree the form is properly filled out, the data is entered into the computer system. See Figure 5–5.

Many software packages provide menu displays and operator prompting. A **menu** is a *list of available options* from which users can select the functions they wish to perform. In a **menu-driven** approach, the operator makes choices from a series of menus until the selected processing function is performed. Many terminals also provide **prompts,** which are helpful messages that assist the operator in performing a particular job. This would include error messages, correction suggestions, prompting questions, and other messages that guide an operator through the work in a series of steps. Thus computer software can make the input activity a lot easier for users. See Figure 5–6.

Icons and Mice

A major development in video display aids for microcomputers is the use of *icon displays* for output and the *electronic mouse* for input. This provides a "point and click" capability for computer users as an alternative to the use of a keyboard and text displays to issue commands and provide responses.

Menu

Prompt

Figure 5–6 A menu and prompt display. Users are prompted to make a selection from the menu.

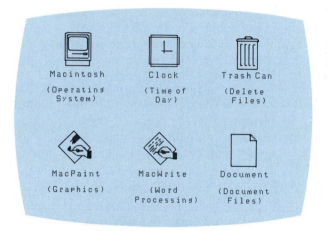

Figure 5–7 An icon-based display. For example, you could move the cursor with a mouse to the document symbol to retrieve a document file and then to the trash can to delete it.

Icons are small figures that look like familiar devices, such as a file folder (for storing a file), a wastebasket (for deleting a file), a calculator (for switching to a calculator mode), and so on. Icons were developed by Xerox for the STAR line of workstation computers in 1978. The Apple Macintosh computers and operating environment software like Microsoft Windows emphasize the use of icons displays. Using icons helps simplify computer use, since they are easier to use for some input operations than text-based displays.

The **electronic mouse** is a device used to move the cursor on the screen, as well as to issue commands and make icon and menu selections. It is connected to the computer and contains a roller ball, which moves the cursor in the direction the ball is rolled. For example, you would move the mouse on your desktop with your hand in the direction you want the cursor to go on the screen. You then move the cursor next to the icon you want to select from those displayed on the screen. Then press a button on the mouse to begin the activity represented by the icon you selected. See Figure 5–7.

Other Aids

Other devices and methods are used to simplify data entry. These include *audio prompts*, in which an audio "beep" or other sound (including computer-generated speech) alerts the user. Also included in this category are several specialized input devices we will describe shortly, such as voice input, light pens, joysticks, and touch-sensitive screens. All of these devices are designed to simplify the job of entering data into computer systems by reducing the use of manual keyboard methods for data entry.

DATA OUTPUT CONCEPTS

The **output** function involves converting processed data (information) from electronic impulses or magnetic and optical media into a form that users can understand. It also involves presenting such information to users in a variety of *information products* such as paper documents and reports, visual displays, or audio responses. Forms and methods of output are changing in computer-based information systems, paralleling the changes taking place in data entry. Let's take a brief look at several major developments that are occurring in methods of output.

CHANGING OUTPUT METHODS

The goal of the changes taking place in output methods is to reduce the bottleneck of output activities that slows the speed of computerized processing, as well as making computer-generated output more attractive and easy to use. Several important trends can be identified:

- ☐ Replacing or supporting printed paper output with **visual displays** from video display terminals or **voice output** from **audio response** devices.
- ☐ Replacing punched paper cards and tapes, as well as printed paper output, with machine-readable media such as magnetic tape and disks, optical disks, or microfilm media. They are faster to use for retrieval or processing, and take up much less space.
- ☐ Reducing the amount of standardized printed paper reports produced on a regular basis with visual displays tailored to users and furnished to them instantly, but only at their request.
- ☐ Reducing the use of *monochrome* displays of numeric data or text material with *color displays* of various forms of *graphics*, such as line, bar, and pie charts, or other more attractive **graphics displays.**

Figure 5–8 illustrates the variety of changes taking place in the methods, equipment, and media found in modern information systems. Notice how printed sales documents and reports are being replaced by visual displays, audio responses, and magnetic and microfilm media. We will discuss the equipment and media used in traditional and newer methods of output in this chapter. But first, let's take a closer look at one of the major developments in computer-generated output, *computer graphics.*

COMPUTER GRAPHICS

Which type of output would you rather see—columns of figures or a graphic display of the same information? Most people find it difficult to quickly and accurately comprehend numerical or statistical data that is presented in a purely numerical form (such as rows or columns of figures). That is why

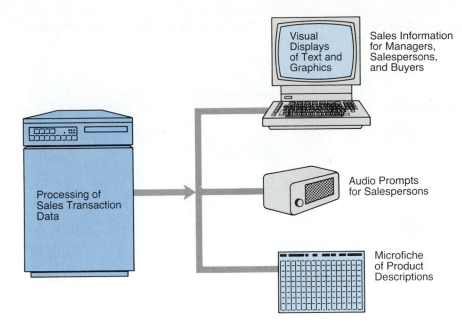

Figure 5–8 Output methods example. In sales transaction processing, paper output is being replaced by visual displays of text and graphics, audio responses, and other methods.

Visual Displays of Text and Graphics

Sales Information for Managers, Salespersons, and Buyers

Processing of Sales Transaction Data

Audio Prompts for Salespersons

Microfiche of Product Descriptions

charts and graphs are typically used in technical reports and business meetings. This graphics capability is now being offered by *graphics terminals* using video displays as well as *graphics plotters* and *graphics printers*, which draw or print graphs on paper and other materials. Most computer systems, including most microcomputer systems, now offer some degree of graphics capability.

Many graphics features require additional hardware capabilities and special *graphics software packages*. For example, advanced graphics terminals use special microprocessor chips, called *display processors*, and additional buffer memory. However, the rapid decrease in the cost of microprocessor and memory chips has moved computer graphics capabilities down to the range of small, low-priced systems, including microcomputers and their relatively inexpensive printers.

Color graphics displays are replacing monochrome (one color) displays of graphics. This, too, requires additional hardware and software capabilities. Color displays provide a more normal and natural people-computer interface. This should make using a video terminal a more attractive and comfortable experience and should result in fewer errors and more productivity. Color is a very effective way of categorizing displayed information. Color helps draw attention more easily to selected items and can be used to link related items in the display. For example, if an operator changes a data item that affects other data items in a display, the affected data items can be programmed to change color, alerting the operator to the relationships that exist.

Computer graphics has been used for many years for engineering design applications called *computer-aided design* (CAD) used in the aircraft, automobile, machine tool, electronics, and other industries. Computer graphics assists engineers in designing complex structures, researchers in analyzing

Figure 5–9 Business graphics displays. Notice the use of line and bar graphs, pie charts, three dimensional graphs, and multiple window graphics.

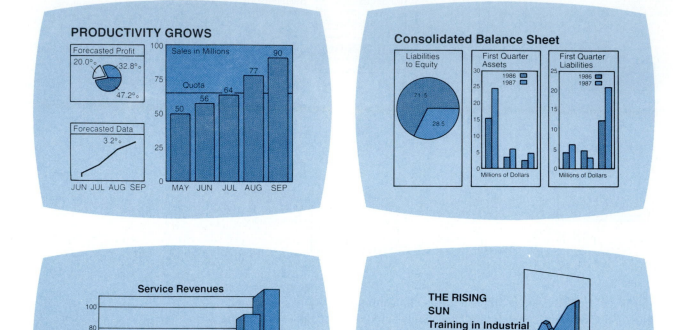

volumes of data, and process control technicians in monitoring industrial processes. However, its use to help managers analyze business operations and make better decisions is now being emphasized. Instead of being overwhelmed by large amounts of computer-produced data, graphics displays assist managers in analyzing and interpreting data.

Graphics displays do not totally replace reports or displays of numbers and text material. Such methods are still needed to present the detailed information required in many applications. However, trends, problems, or opportunities hidden in data are easier to spot when using graphic displays. For example, computer graphics would make it easier for a marketing manager to see complex market trends and analyze market problems and opportunities such as product line, sales outlet, and salesperson performance. These capabilities indicate that computer graphics are an important management tool. See Figure 5–9, and pages 23 and 28 of the pictorial section in Chapter 1.

REAL WORLD APPLICATION 5–1

Federated Investors, Inc.

In a two-pronged thrust, Federated Investors, Inc. of Pittsburgh is revamping the online system that institutional investors use to buy and sell its mutual funds. By replacing dumb terminals with personal computers and rewriting software, Federated aims to make the network more flexible and easier to use, company officials say. Roughly 1,500 bank trust departments and other money managers nationwide use the system.

Federated, which manages nearly $2 billion in assets, is in the midst of replacing Digital Equipment Corp. terminals used in the Tandem Computers, Inc.–based system with IBM PC AT microcomputers and rewriting part of the system software. That should reduce the transmission time and effort required for clients to make transactions, according to Paul Angell, a Federated vice president and the firm's director of data processing.

Angell says Federated is rewriting the software to accommodate the changes but leaving users' procedures intact. "We wanted to make sure we didn't cause any confusion at the bank level," he adds. The ATs with the new software validate the client's transaction themselves, rather than relying on the mainframe at Federated's headquarters, and transmit orders at 1,200 bits/second rather than 300 bits/second, according to Angell.

The new system also avoids the need for users to key in numbers to identify their bank, the fund they are trading, and their account, requiring only menu selections, a dollar amount, and indication of whether the transaction is a buy or a sell, he says. "With the PC we have the intelligence in the field to be able to do that. That is a major improvement to our world."

The number of transactions the firm handles each business day has grown from about 300 in 1982 to roughly 15,000, totaling approximately $800 million a day, according to Angell. A staff of 50 handles the transactions, most of which take place between 10:30 A.M. and noon, he says. "There would be no way you could support those transactions in a manual mode," Angell says.

Before the new system was in place, Federated clients called orders in to Pittsburgh by telephone, where a data entry clerk keyed them into a computer for validation. If the order was good, the computer sent it to Federated's bank servicing agent, State Street Bank and Trust Co. of Boston. There the order was keyed into a Federal Reserve Bank system, which transmitted cash to or from the client. If the order was not valid, the Federated operator would not know about it until hours later.

The online system automatically validates orders with Federated's system, providing clients with hard-copy printout, posts them with State Street Bank and Trust, and sends them to the Federal Reserve wire system. In addition to speeding up transactions, the online system has cut the costs of order entry in half, Angell says. It also provides clients with information on their investments, current interest rates, and Federated products.

Application Questions

☐ How is Federated Investors improving the user interface of its transaction processing system?

☐ What are the benefits of the new system?

Source: David A. Ludlum, "Federated Invests in PC ATs," *Computerworld,* September 1, 1986, pp. 63–65.

Section II: Input/Output Methods

We have now examined several important input/output concepts and how they affect computer users. We can thus begin our coverage of input/output methods, both the equipment involved and the media they utilize. Notice that in each case we also briefly analyze the advantages and disadvantages for computer users of each major input/output method.

VISUAL–SUPPORTED INPUT/OUTPUT

What is the most widely used method of communicating with computers? Using microcomputers or terminals connected to mainframes and minicomputers typically involves the use of a **keyboard** for direct entry of data without the use of data media. A **video display screen** (or *video monitor*) is the major method of output for users. However, video displays are also used to guide users or operators in the process of data entry or other uses. This is what is meant by the term **visual-supported input/output.** In this section we will briefly explain several major types of visual-supported input/output devices and methods.

Computer Terminals

Computer terminals of various types are the most widely used form of input/output hardware. Most of them are connected directly or by communications lines to mainframes or minicomputers. Any input/output device that can directly enter data into a computer or directly receive computer output is called a *terminal*. The major categories of computer terminals are summarized in this section. They are illustrated in Figure 5–10 and on pages 23 and 24 of the pictorial section of Chapter 1.

Visual Display Terminals

Terminals that use a keyboard for input and a TV-like screen for visual output are called **visual** (or video) **display terminals** (VDT) or, more popularly, CRT (cathode ray tube) terminals. They allow the display of alphanumeric data and graphic images. They are the most widely used type of computer terminal.

Intelligent Terminals

Smart terminals have built-in microprocessors so they can perform their own error checking and input/output communications control functions. (*Dumb terminals* do not have such capabilities.) **Intelligent terminals** are really microcomputers or minicomputers with input/output and data communications capabilities, which can also act as *stand-alone* computers and independently perform information processing tasks.

Data Entry Terminals

Typically used for traditional data entry tasks, **data entry terminals** use a keyboard for entry of data. They also use a video display screen to support data entry. Data can be displayed and corrected before it is recorded on

Figure 5-10 Four major types of computer terminals.

A videodisplay terminal.

A portable printing terminal.

A graphics terminal.

A financial transaction terminal.

magnetic disks or entered into a computer system. These terminals differ from **transaction terminals** in that they may be offline devices not connected directly to the main computer system. Also, they are typically used to convert data taken from source documents into computer-readable media (such as magnetic disks) for later entry into a computer system. Thus they are primarily used for data entry in batch processing systems.

Graphics Terminals

Graphics terminals and graphics programs allow operators to transform numeric data into **graphics displays.** Numeric data can be entered through the use of the terminal keyboard or a variety of other devices we will discuss shortly. Numeric data can be transformed into bar charts, pie charts, line graphs, three-dimensional graphs, or the multitude of drawings found in engineering design, architecture, and even *computer art!* Advanced graphics terminals allow the operator to *zoom* in and out, and to *pan* (turn) the drawing up or down, right or left, in order to better analyze and modify the graphics display.

Transaction Terminals

Transaction terminals are widely used in banks, retail stores, factories, and other worksites for source data automation. They are used to capture transaction data at its point of origin. They typically use a keyboard or small *pad* for data entry. Either a printer or video display unit is used for output. A variety of other input/output methods and media may also be used. Thus most of these terminals can be classified as special-purpose terminals. For example, many transaction recorders might include a slot into which badges, plastic cards, inventory tags, or prepunched cards can be inserted for data input. Some terminals may use an OCR (optical character recognition) **wand** to directly enter printed data into a computer system. Three examples are summarized below:

- ☐ **Automated teller machines** (ATMs), also called *cash machines*, are transaction terminals that seem to be everywhere. Typically, they require you to insert a bank card with a magnetic stripe into the machine and use a small keypad to enter a security code plus data on your transaction. Output is by a small video display and printed receipts.

- ☐ **A factory transaction terminal** could use an employee's plastic badge, prepunched cards, and a keyboard to enter data directly into a manufacturing control system.

- ☐ **Point-of-sale (POS) terminals** connected online to a computer serve as electronic cash registers and allow instant credit verification and immediate automated capture of sales transaction data for entry into a computer system. Magnetic stripe credit cards and OCR wands are typically used to capture sales data.

Visual Output Methods

Cathode ray tubes (CRTs) are used in most visual display monitors and terminals for display of output. They use a picture tube similar to those used in home TV sets, though a variety of technologies are used to provide different levels of picture clarity. These video display devices are available in monochrome (typically white, green, blue, or amber displays) or multiple-color models. Usually, the clarity of a color display depends on the quality of the video monitor you use and the graphics circuit board or *video adapter* installed in a microcomputer. This can provide a variety of *graphics modes* of increasing capability. (Examples are IBM's EGA (Enhanced Graphics Adapter) or VGA (Video Graphics Array) graphics standards.) Also, video adapters and monitors that use analog instead of digital video signals can provide more shades of color. (For example, the IBM PS/2 microcomputers offer monochrome displays of 64 shades of gray and color displays of 256 colors out of 256,000 possible shades.)

Most CRT video monitors use a *raster-scan* process in which an electron gun generates an electron beam that *scans* across a phosphor-coated screen in a series of parallel lines known as a *raster*. The computer sends signals to circuits (including a display control microprocessor) that control the direction and the intensity of the electron beam. This causes the phosphors to emit light of various intensities and colors, thus causing images to form on the screen. This scanning process must be repeated 30 to 70 or more times per second to *refresh* the image so that it will not flicker or fade away. Most standard monitors show a display of 25 lines (rows) with 40 to 80 characters (columns) per line. Each character on the screen is composed of *picture elements* called **pixels.** For example, a typical character might be composed of 128 (8×16) pixels.

Video monitors used primarily for displays of text material (numeric, alphabetic, and special characters) are less expensive but have lower *resolution* (clarity) than monitors used primarily for graphics displays. Low-resolution monitors typically use a *character addressable* display, where the screen is divided into a specific number of addressable character locations, and each character is composed of a predefined matrix of pixels. High-resolution monitors usually rely on a *bit-mapped display,* where each pixel is a directly addressable bit or dot location on the screen. The clarity of this *dot addressable* display is therefore much higher and is limited only by the number of pixel locations provided. For example, a medium-resolution graphics displays might contain 307,200 pixels (640×480 pixels), while a high-resolution graphics workstation might display over one million pixels ($1,000 \times 1,000$ pixels)! Such displays require special video microprocessor controllers and additional amounts of primary storage.

Liquid crystal displays (LCDs), such as those used in electronic calculators and watches, are also being used to display computer output. Their biggest use is to provide a visual display capability for portable microcomputers and terminals. Advances in technology have improved the clarity of such displays, which were hard to see in bright sunlight or artificial light. This includes "backlighting" with supplementary light sources and a "supertwist" LCD technology that significantly improves liquid crystal display performance.

Plasma display devices are replacing CRT devices in providing visual displays in a limited number of applications. Plasma displays are generated by electrically charged particles of gas (plasma) trapped between glass plates. Plasma display units are becoming more popular, but are still more expensive than CRT units. However, they are being used in applications where a compact, flat visual display is a critical factor, such as in portable terminals and microcomputers. See pages 21 and 24 of the pictorial section in Chapter 1.

Visual-Supported Input Methods

The video display screens of microcomputers and many video terminals can now support input as well as output. A variety of devices allow graphic or alphanumeric data to be entered directly into the computer system. Users can write directly on a video screen or on the surface of other devices and see the results on their video screens. Visual-supported input has been used for many years in military applications, engineering and architectural design, scientific research, cartography (mapmaking and analysis), and is now being used in many business applications. See Figure 5–11 and pages 19–21 of the pictorial section in Chapter 1 for illustrations of the following devices.

Figure 5–11 Major types of visual-supported input methods. Pictured are a touch-sensitive screen, electronic mouse, graphics pen and tablet, and keyboard.

Using a touchscreen.   An electronic mouse.

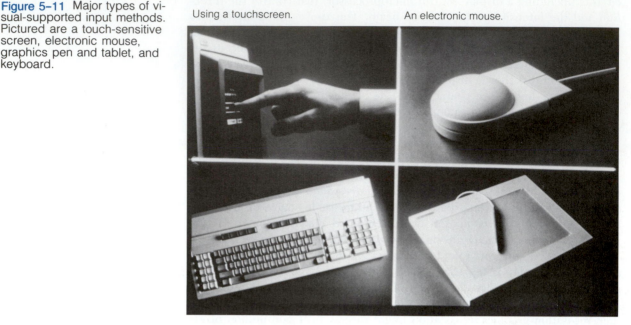

An advanced keyboard.   A graphics pen and tablet.

The **electronic mouse** is a recent input device for microcomputers. It is also being used with some video display terminals of large computer systems. The use of such devices was explained in the previous section on video display aids for input.

The **joystick** and the **trackball** are devices that are used to move the cursor on the display screen. A joystick looks like a small gear shift lever set in a box. Joysticks are widely used for computer-assisted design, and are also popular control devices for microcomputer video games. A trackball is related to the mouse since it is a roller ball device with just its top exposed outside its case. You use your finger to spin the trackball in the direction you want the cursor to move on the display screen.

The **light pen** is a pen-shaped device that uses photoelectric circuitry to enter data into the computer through a video screen. A user can *write* on the video display, because the light-sensitive pen enables the computer to calculate the coordinates of the points on the screen being touched by the light pen, even though the video screen may contain over one million points of light.

Touch-sensitive screens are *tactile input* devices that allow operators to enter data into a computer system by touching the surface of a sensitized video display screen with a finger or pointer. For example, you could indicate your selection on a menu display by just touching the screen next to that menu item.

Digitizers of several types are used to convert drawings and other graphic images on paper or other materials into digital data and to enter it into a computer system. Digital data can then be displayed on a video screen and be processed by the computer system. One form of digitizer is the *graphics tablet*, which has sensing devices embedded in a special tablet on which material to be digitized must be placed. A *graphics pen* (also called an *electronic stylus*) is pressed on the material placed on the graphics tablet to draw or trace figures that appear simultaneously on the video screen. A small hand-held device called a *spatial cursor*, with a small round viewing window with cross hairs etched on the glass, is another form of digitizer. It can be passed over the surface of a drawing or graphic image to convert it to digital data. Some graphic pens are *sonic digitizers*, which use sonic impulses (sound waves) to digitize drawings laid on a graphics tablet.

Visual display units are much faster and quieter than printing devices and do not flood users with rivers of paper. A specific piece of information or an entire page of data can be displayed instantly in either alphanumeric or graphic form. The ability to correct or edit input data displayed by a VDT before entry into a computer system is a major benefit. The light pen and other digitizers provide a valuable method of visual/graphic input.

Advantages and Disadvantages

Visual-supported input/output is a popular method of people-computer communication, but does have several limitations. Special video display circuitry and software may be needed to provide the high-quality video images needed by some users. Additional equipment is required to produce the hard copy that visual display units do not provide. In addition, there has been some controversy concerning the possible harmful effects of radiation generated by CRT units. Recent studies have shown that such radiation is minimal and not harmful, but research is continuing to investigate these and other complaints concerning the long-term use of visual display devices.

PRINTED OUTPUT

After video displays, **printed output** is the most common form of computer output. Most computer systems use printing devices to produce permanent *(hard copy)* output in human-readable form. You need such printed output if you want copies of output to take with you away from the computer and to share with others. Hard copy output is also frequently needed for legal documentation. Thus computers can produce printed reports and documents such as sales invoices, payroll checks, bank statements, and forms of all kinds.

Some types of printed output are designed to be read by magnetic or optical scanning equipment. Forms produced in this manner are known as **turnaround documents** because they are designed to be returned to the sender. For example, many computer-printed invoices consist of a turnaround portion, which is returned by a customer along with his or her payment. The turnaround document can then be automatically processed by optical scanning devices. Thus computer printers can perform an *input preparation* function.

Printers can be classified as impact or nonimpact printers; as character, line, or page printers; and as slow-speed and high-speed printers. **Plotters** that draw graphics displays on paper also produce printed paper output. Figure 5–12 illustrates several types of computer printing methods. Figure 5–13 shows several types of printers, as do many of the photographs in the pictorial section in Chapter 1.

Figure 5–12 Major types of computer printing methods include print chain, dot matrix, and laser printing.

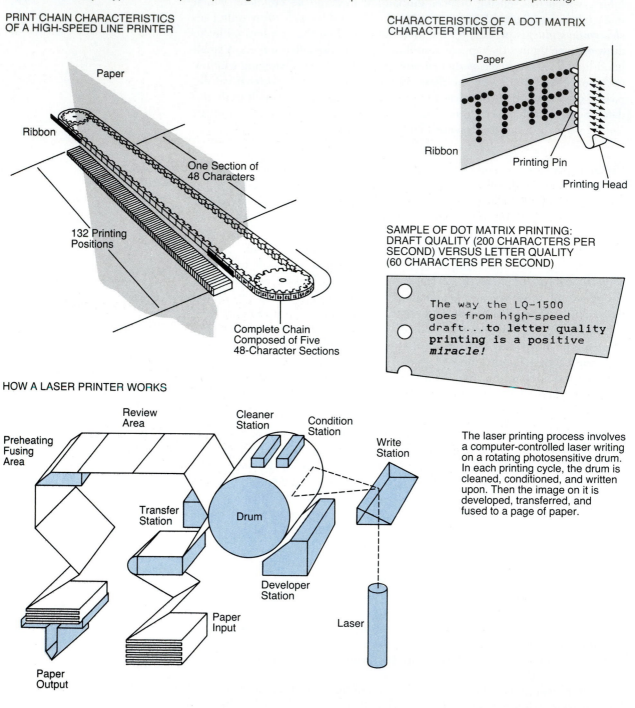

PRINT CHAIN CHARACTERISTICS
OF A HIGH-SPEED LINE PRINTER

Paper

Ribbon

One Section of
48 Characters

132 Printing
Positions

Complete Chain
Composed of Five
48-Character Sections

CHARACTERISTICS OF A DOT MATRIX
CHARACTER PRINTER

Paper

Ribbon

Printing Pin

Printing Head

SAMPLE OF DOT MATRIX PRINTING:
DRAFT QUALITY (200 CHARACTERS PER
SECOND) VERSUS LETTER QUALITY
(60 CHARACTERS PER SECOND)

The way the LQ-1500
goes from high-speed
draft...to letter quality
printing is a positive
miracle!

HOW A LASER PRINTER WORKS

Review
Area

Cleaner
Station

Condition
Station

Write
Station

Preheating
Fusing
Area

Transfer
Station

Drum

Developer
Station

Laser

Paper
Input

Paper
Output

The laser printing process involves
a computer-controlled laser writing
on a rotating photosensitive drum.
In each printing cycle, the drum is
cleaned, conditioned, and written
upon. Then the image on it is
developed, transferred, and
fused to a page of paper.

Figure 5–13 Four major types of computer printers.

A small ink-jet printer—the Quad Jet.

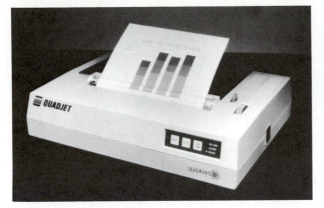

A small laser printer—the HP Laser Jet.

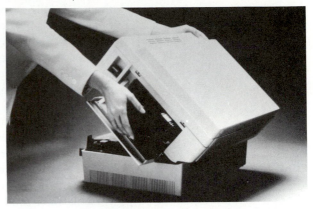

A dot matrix printer.

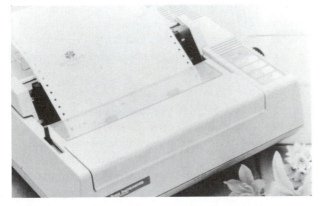

A high-speed line printer.

All computer printing devices print a character at a time, a line at a time, or a page at a time. **Character printers** (also called serial printers) print *serially* (one character at a time) as typewriters do. Thus many character printers print at the relatively slow speed of between 60 to 200 characters per second. **Line printers** print an entire line at a time (up to 132 characters) and, therefore, are much faster than a character printer, reaching speeds of 3,000 lines per minute. **Page printers** print an entire page at a time and can reach speeds exceeding 20,000 lines per minute.

Character, Line, and Page Printing

Impact printers form characters and other images on paper through the impact of a printing mechanism that presses a printing element (such as a print wheel or cylinder) and an inked ribbon or roller against the face of a continuous paper form. Multiple copies can be produced because the impact of the printing mechanism can transmit an image onto several layers of

Impact Printers

multiple copy forms. Slow-speed impact printers are typically used in micro-computer and minicomputer systems and as slow-speed *printing terminals*. They cost much less than high-speed printers (from a few hundred to a few thousand dollars) and yet are fast enough for most small computer applications. Speeds of such printers range from 15 to 400 characters per second.

Most slow-speed printers are *character printers*, which print one character at a time. The **daisy wheel** printing element consists of characters at the end of the spokes of a wheel. It rotates to print a solid character. **A dot matrix** printing element consists of short *print wires* that form a character as a series (or *matrix*) of dots. Solid character printing is usually of higher quality than dot matrix printing. Thus, printers with solid character (*solid font)* print mechanisms (like the daisy wheel) are frequently used for correspondence quality or letter quality printing jobs.

Dot matrix printers are typically used for high-speed draft quality printing. However, dot matrix printing is much faster, more reliable, and more versatile than solid font printing. Increases in the number of print wires (from 9 to 24) have improved dot matrix printing to near letter quality. Printers can be adjusted and programmed to print a variety of type fonts, type sizes, and foreign or special characters. They can also easily produce printed graphics images developed by graphics software packages.

High-speed line impact printers can print up to 3,000 lines per minute. A moving metal chain or cylinder of characters is used as the printing element. Speed is heavily dependent on the size and type of character set used by the printing element. Costs for such printers depend on speed and print quality but can range from $3,000 to over $100,000.

Nonimpact Printers

Nonimpact printers may use specially treated paper that forms characters by thermal (heat), electrostatic, or electrochemical processes. Other nonimpact printers use plain paper and inkjet, laser, or xerographic technologies to form an image. Nonimpact printers are usually much quieter than impact printers, since the sound of a printing element being struck is eliminated. However, they cannot produce multiple copies like impact printers.

Slow-speed nonimpact printers include **ink-jet printers,** which spray tiny ink particles from fast-moving nozzles against paper. Electrostatic charges placed on the paper attract the ink, which forms characters of high-print quality. Ink-jet printers can print at speeds of over 200 characters per second. **Thermal printers** are slow-speed nonimpact character printers that print a character on heat-sensitive paper by using heated wires to produce a character similar to the dot matrix printing element.

Laser printers have become a popular method of producing high-quality printed output that rivals some of the printing done by commercial printers. Companies can now produce their own business forms as well as formal reports and manuals. We will discuss such microcomputer "desktop publishing" applications in Chapter 12. High-speed laser printers can print over 40,000 lines per minute. Costs for such printers range from $150,000 to $300,000. However, less-expensive but slower laser printers are available, at prices ranging from $2,000 to $20,000; with speeds from 5 to 120 pages per minute. The lowest priced laser printers print 5 to 12 pages per minute, and have become popular high-performance printers for microcomputer systems.

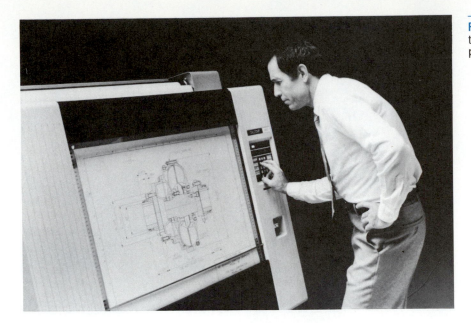

Figure 5–14 A computer plotter. This is a large electrostatic plotter.

Hard Copy Graphics

Hard copy graphics devices reproduce graphic computer displays on paper or other materials. This requires such equipment as printers, plotters, copying machines, or photographic devices. **Plotters** produce graphic displays using a pen-and-ink process, electrical inscribing, or electrostatic nonimpact techniques. Some plotters have mechanical arms containing one or more pens: They draw lines on paper as directed by a computer. See Figure 5–14.

Printers can also produce hard copy graphics of reasonable quality. Thus graphics software packages allow even dot matrix printers to produce hard copy graphics. Ink-jet and laser printers are also used to produce high-quality printed graphics.

Advantages and Disadvantages

Printing devices provide a computer system with the ability to produce printed reports and forms of all kinds. Printing of excellent quality can be done at high speeds. However, the speed factor is the cause of two contradictory problems. Computers can now produce printed reports so quickly that managers can be buried in mountains of paper. The ability of managers to use the information in computer-printed reports to assist their decision making is diminished by the rapid flow of volumes of paper. On the other hand, high-speed printers are not fast enough output devices for most computer systems, thus causing an "output-bound" condition. For example, the data transfer rate of high-speed printers is over 4,000 characters per second, which is quite slow compared to over 300,000 characters per second for magnetic tape output. This problem is being solved by the use of visual display terminals, offline magnetic tape to printer operations, and microfilm output devices.

Figure 5–15 Using a voice input system with a personal computer. A user can (1) issue commands, (2) enter data, and (3) ask questions with such systems.

VOICE INPUT/OUTPUT

Computer users can now talk or listen to computers. Applications of **voice input/output** devices have been limited in the past but are now growing rapidly. Microprocessor chips that synthesize human speech are being used to give voice output capabilities to everything from children's toys to telephone communication systems. Voice input hardware has not developed as fast as voice output devices. However, the use of voice input terminals with limited speed recognition capabilities is growing steadily in applications ranging from sales data entry to manufacturing quality control.

Voice Input

Speech is the easiest, most natural means of human communication. When voice input is perfected, it will be the easiest method of data entry and conversational computing. Voice input of data into a computer system is now at the frontier of people-computer communication, but it has become technologically and economically feasible for a variety of applications. *Voice data entry terminals* are now being used that allow the direct entry of data into a computer system by verbal communication of a human operator. A typical configuration might consist of one or more portable voice recognition units, microphones, and a CRT terminal for visual display of spoken input. Such systems can have over a 1,000-word vocabulary and support several users simultaneously. Other voice-recognition devices place all of the required circuitry on a single circuit board, including a vocabulary of several hundred words. They are being incorporated in visual display terminals and microcomputer systems. See Figure 5–15 and page 19 of the pictorial section in Chapter 1.

Voice input units rely on **voice recognition** (or *speech recognition*) microprocessors, which analyze and classify acoustic speech patterns and transform them into electronic digital codes for entry into a computer system. The process is directed by speech recognition programs that compare the

Figure 5–16 How voice recognition works.

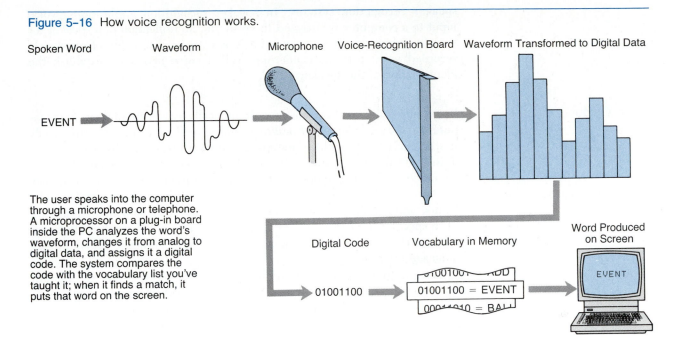

Spoken Word   Waveform   Microphone   Voice-Recognition Board   Waveform Transformed to Digital Data

EVENT

The user speaks into the computer through a microphone or telephone. A microprocessor on a plug-in board inside the PC analyzes the word's waveform, changes it from analog to digital data, and assigns it a digital code. The system compares the code with the vocabulary list you've taught it; when it finds a match, it puts that word on the screen.

Digital Code   Vocabulary in Memory   Word Produced on Screen

01001100   01001100 = EVENT   EVENT

speech input to previously stored voice reference patterns that are kept on a secondary storage device, such as a magnetic disk. Most voice input systems require "training" the computer to recognize a limited vocabulary of standard words for each individual using the system. Operators train the system to recognize their voices by repeating each word in the vocabulary about 10 times. Trained systems regularly achieve over a 99 percent word recognition. *Speaker-independent* voice recognition systems are being developed that allow a computer to understand a voice it has never heard before. Development of such systems would eliminate the need for training. See Figure 5–16.

Voice input devices are now being used in work situations where operators need to perform data entry without using their hands to key in data or instructions, or where it would provide faster and more accurate input. For example, voice recognition systems are being used by several manufacturers for the inspection, inventory, and quality control of a variety of products, and by several airlines and parcel delivery companies for voice-directed sorting of baggage and parcels. In another application, a major U.S. oil company uses a voice recognition system to receive oil exploration data over the telephone that are called in from exploration centers around the country. This application demonstrates that voice recognition technology can transform the telephone into a voice input terminal. Voice recognition units for microcomputers have recently become available that enable users to develop and use electronic spreadsheet and other standard software packages using voice input.

Besides data entry and computerized machinery control, other voice recognition applications include information retrieval from data banks, telephone network control, computer use by the physically handicapped, and speaker recognition systems. In speaker recognition applications, voice input to a computer is analyzed to verify the identification of a speaker for security purposes. The speaker's voice is compared to a file of previously recorded voice patterns (sometimes called *voice prints*) to establish the identification of the speaker.

Voice Output

Voice output devices have changed dramatically as a result of the microcomputer revolution. Computer **audio-response** units have shrunk dramatically in size and cost. Microelectronic *speech synthesizers* are now being used that fit the devices necessary to synthesize human speech onto a single integrated circuit chip. "Talking" chips are being used to provide computerized speech for toys, games, greeting cards, consumer appliances, automobiles, elevators, and a variety of other consumer, commercial, and industrial uses. Such speech synthesizing microprocessors are also being used in electronic calculators, in digital watches, and in hand-held computers and foreign language translators.

Voice output devices allow the computer to verbally guide an operator through the steps of a task in many types of activities. They are also used to allow computers to respond to inquiries and other input over the telephone. In many present applications, input of data is accomplished by pressing the buttons of a Touch-Tone telephone while output is in the form of a voice produced by an audio-response device controlled by a computer system and transmitted over the telephone lines. This application is found in bank pay-by-phone bill-paying services, stock quotation services, and customer credit and account balance inquiries.

Advantages and Disadvantages

Voice input/output devices provide the quickest and easiest method of people-computer communications. Every telephone becomes a potential computer terminal. Voice output devices are small and inexpensive, while voice input devices are now feasible for many applications. Chief limitations concern the quality of synthetic speech and the limited vocabulary and training required by most voice recognition systems. These limitations should be overcome with the continued development of electronic voice technology.

OPTICAL SCANNING

Optical scanning devices read text or graphics and convert it into digital input for a computer. This includes **optical character recognition** (OCR) equipment which can read alphabetic, numeric, and special characters that are printed, typed, or handwritten on ordinary paper. Optical scanning thus provides a method of direct input of data from source documents into a computer system.

Many scanners can read graphic images, though graphic scanning is not as advanced as OCR technology. Scanning of graphic images is especially popular in *desktop publishing* applications, as we will discuss in Chapter 12. There are many types of optical readers, but they all employ photoelectric devices to scan the characters being read. Reflected light patterns of the data

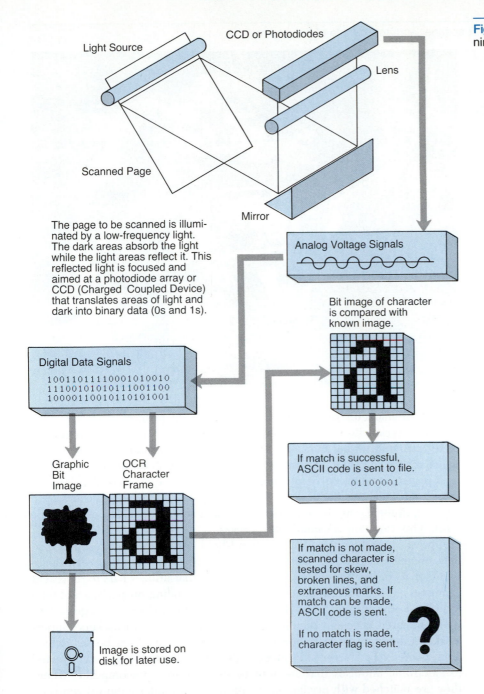

Figure 5–17 How optical scanning works.

are converted into electronic impulses that are accepted as input into the computer system. Devices can now read many types of printing and graphics. Progress is continually being made in improving the reading ability of scanning equipment. The technology of optical scanning is shown in Figure 5–17.

Figure 5–18 A supermarket OCR scanner and an example of bar coding.

This Universal Product Code (UPC) identifies the item as a grocery product (the 0 on the left) of the Green Giant Company (specified by the 20000), which in this instance is a 10-ounce frozen package of baby lima beans in butter sauce (specified by the 12190).

Optical character recognition devices can read printed characters produced by typewriters, word processors, computer printers, cash registers, credit card imprinters, and so on. They can even read handwriting, provided the characters meet OCR standards. Thus optical scanners are being used to read pages of text for entry into word processing systems, as well as into the more traditional reading of documents printed in OCR standard characters. OCR equipment can also read pencil marks made in specific positions of a form. This variation is called *mark-sensing*.

Optical scanning devices such as hand-held **wands** are being used to read data on merchandise tags and other media. Such devices can read documents that contain **bar coding,** which is a code that utilizes bars to represent characters. Universal Product Code (UPC) bar coding on packages of food items and other products has become commonplace, since it is required for the automated checkout scanners installed at many supermarkets. Supermarket scanners (like that shown in Figure 5–18) emit laser beams, which are reflected off a Universal Product Code. The reflected image is converted to electronic impulses that are sent to the in-store minicomputer, where they are matched with pricing information. Pricing information is returned to the terminal, visually displayed, and printed on a receipt. It happens as fast as the item can be moved past the scanning window.

Advantages and Disadvantages

The major benefit of optical scanning is that it provides a method of direct input of data from source documents into a computer system. It thus eliminates much costly input preparation activity and increases the accuracy and speed of an information system. OCR-based optical scanning systems are extensively used in the credit card billing operations of credit card companies, banks, and oil companies. They are also used to process utility bills, insurance premiums, airline tickets, and cash register machine tapes. OCR scanners are used to automatically sort mail, score tests, and process a wide variety of forms in business and government. A major limitation of optical scanning for some applications has been high document rejection and reading error rates. However, recently developed optical scanners can read printing of a variety of type fonts with satisfactory accuracy.

MAGNETIC MEDIA DATA ENTRY

Magnetic disk and tape systems can be used for the data entry function, in which data from source documents (such as sales invoices) is recorded on magnetic media. Large **key-to-disk** systems use many keyboard/CRT terminals that input data simultaneously to a central magnetic disk unit. These systems are usually offline from a large computer system but are controlled and supported by a minicomputer. Large key-to-disk systems are expensive and can only be justified for batch processing applications with large volumes of data from many sources. The major advantage of these systems over **key-to-tape** methods is that they do not require the merging and sorting of magnetic tapes that is characteristic of key-to-tape systems.

Magnetic diskettes or *floppy disks* are also used for inexpensive data entry by microcomputer and minicomputer systems. Data is typically entered via a keyboard, visually verified by a video display, and recorded on a diskette. Finally, we have previously mentioned **magnetic stripe cards.** They provide limited customer information automatically for bank and retail store transaction terminals. They are being replaced in some applications by cards using laser-optical technology *(optical cards)* or cards with imbedded microprocessor chips *(smart cards).*

Magnetic Ink Character Recognition

Magnetic ink character recognition (MICR) technology allows the computer systems of the banking industry to magnetically read checks and deposit slips. Computers can thus sort, tabulate, and post checks to the proper checking accounts. Such processing is possible because the identification numbers of the bank and the customer's account number are preprinted on the bottom of checks with an iron-oxide based ink. The first bank receiving a check after it has been written must encode the amount of the check in magnetic ink on its lower right-hand corner. The MICR system uses 14 characters (the 10 decimal digits and 4 special symbols) of a unique design.

MICR characters can be preprinted on documents or can be encoded on documents using a keyboard-operated machine called a *proof-inscriber*. This device also segregates checks into batches and accumulates batch totals. Equipment known as MICR *reader-sorters* read a check by first magnetizing the magnetic ink characters and then sensing the signal induced by each character as it passes by a reading head. Data is thus electronically captured by the computer system. The check is then sorted by directing it into one of the pockets of the reader-sorter. Reader-sorters can read over 2,000 checks per minute, with a data transfer rate of over 3,000 characters per second. See Figures 5–19 and 5–20.

Figure 5–19 A check with MICR encoding. The MICR characters on the bottom of the check on the left are preprinted. Those on the right are encoded after a check is deposited.

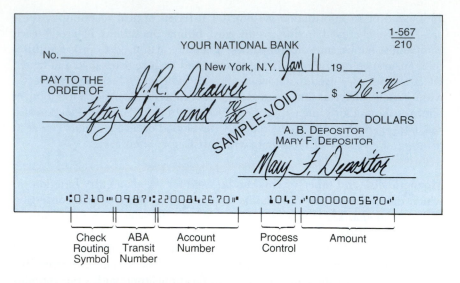

Check Routing Symbol	ABA Transit Number	Account Number	Process Control	Amount

Figure 5–20 A MICR reader-sorter. It automatically reads and sorts over 2,000 checks per minute.

Advantages and Disadvantages

Magnetic ink character recognition has greatly benefited the banking industry. Banks would be hard pressed to handle the processing of checks without such computer technology. MICR documents are human-readable as well as machine-readable. MICR has proved to be a highly accurate and reliable method for the direct entry of data on a source document. Major limitations are the lack of alphabetic and other characters and the necessity to encode the amount of the check in a separate manual processing step. These limitations are the impetus for research and development in methods of optical scanning for check processing. They have also promoted the growth of electronic funds transfer (EFT) methods that make checks unnecessary.

Figure 5–21   How Computer-Output-Microfilm (COM) works.

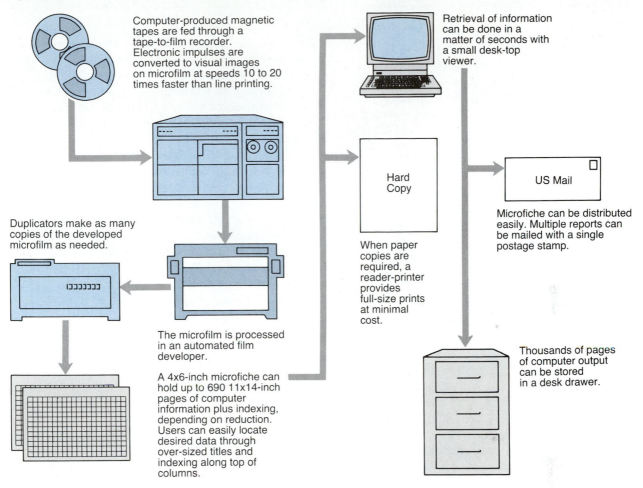

Computer-produced magnetic tapes are fed through a tape-to-film recorder. Electronic impulses are converted to visual images on microfilm at speeds 10 to 20 times faster than line printing.

Retrieval of information can be done in a matter of seconds with a small desk-top viewer.

Hard Copy

US Mail

Duplicators make as many copies of the developed microfilm as needed.

When paper copies are required, a reader-printer provides full-size prints at minimal cost.

Microfiche can be distributed easily. Multiple reports can be mailed with a single postage stamp.

The microfilm is processed in an automated film developer.

A 4x6-inch microfiche can hold up to 690 11x14-inch pages of computer information plus indexing, depending on reduction. Users can easily locate desired data through over-sized titles and indexing along top of columns.

Thousands of pages of computer output can be stored in a desk drawer.

The use of computers in the field of **micrographics** involves:

□ **Computer-output-microfilm,** or COM, in which microfilm is used as a computer output medium. High-speed microfilm recorders are used to electronically capture the output of computer systems on microfilm, microfiche, and other *microforms*.

□ **Computer-input-microfilm,** or CIM, where microfilm is used as an input medium. CIM systems use OCR devices to scan microfilm for high-speed input of data.

□ **Computer-assisted-retrieval,** or CAR, in which special-purpose computer terminals are used to locate and retrieve automatically a microfilm copy of a document.

Micrographics hardware includes microfilm recorders, hard copy printers, microfilm readers, and micrographics terminals. See Figure 5–21.

MICROGRAPHICS

REAL WORLD APPLICATION 5–2

West Point Pepperell

In factories and warehouses, recording quality control and inventory data while work proceeds can promote efficient shop management. Ideally, having workers themselves record this information should cut expenses and increase accuracy. But for personnel who load pallets or check parts on an assembly line, the idea of simultaneously entering data with a keyboard is absurd. In such situations, a voice recognition system makes sense.

Atlanta's West Point Pepperell, a fabric manufacturer for major garment makers such as Levi Strauss, uses PC-based voice recognition on the factory floor to enhance customer service. Pepperell ships its material in massive rolls, whose price depends on the number and severity of defects in the fabric. Pepperell inspectors scrutinize each roll and read their findings into a wireless headset mike. A receiver on the PC plugs in to a phone jack on Votan's VPC 2000 VoiceCard, one of the few PC-based voice recognition circuit boards that can parse continuous speech. The board translates spoken information about fabric defects and their locations into ASCII data, which is transferred to a custom database application that Votan developed for the company.

The database application automatically calculates each roll's price and produces a spreadsheetlike map of the defects. The map is then delivered to the customer, who uses it to plan the cutting of the roll into sections, thus avoiding the flagged flaws and reducing waste. Pepperell has found the VPC 2000 to be extremely accurate, even with background noise as high as 100 decibels—loud enough for the Occupational Safety and Health Administration to require that workers wear ear protection.

Pepperell also employs Votan's voice recognition system for warehouse inventory control. Formerly, when a length of fabric was cut from a roll, forklift drivers had to drive it to a location reserved for that type of fabric. Now drivers simply set the fabric in the nearest available space and send the location via wireless mike to the VPC 2000, which reads the data into an inventory control program. An inventory report provides a directory of fabric locations, yielding more efficient use of both warehouse space and forklift time. According to Gaines Nichols, senior engineer for Pepperell, "We've had a 30 percent increase in work production. Also, accuracy in quality and inventory control have improved significantly."

Application Questions

☐ What are the reasons West Point Pepperell uses a voice recognition system instead of other methods of data entry?

☐ What benefits have occurred because of the voice recognition system?

Source: Thais Mazur and Ives Brant, "The PC Hear and Now," *PC World*, November 1986, pp. 226–28.

Advantages and Disadvantages

Micrographics hardware is used to replace computer printing devices that are too slow and produce too much paper. COM recorders can have a data transfer rate up to 500,000 characters per second and "print" up to 60,000 lines per minute, which is much faster than most high-speed printers and equals or exceeds the output rate of magnetic tape or disk units. Microfilm output also takes up only 2 percent of the space of paper output. Micrographic output thus is a lot faster and takes up much less space than paper output. The storage, handling, and retrieval of microfilm files are substantially easier and cheaper than paper documents.

COM is used to sharply reduce the volume of computer-printed paper. This is true even though some COM users record *all* transaction data instead of merely producing printed "exception reports." Such users claim that they can provide better customer service and better information for management. The computer provides them with up-to-date microfilm records of all transactions, recording only exception items on paper. The major limitation of COM has been its high hardware cost, which limited it to high-volume applications or the COM facilities of computer service centers. However, advances in *microimage* technology have made micrographics much more cost effective and widely used.

SUMMARY

☐ Traditional data entry methods that require too many activities, people, and forms of data media are being replaced by more direct automated methods known as source data automation. The high cost and potential for errors of traditional data entry methods can be minimized if source data automation is used to capture data as early and as close as possible to the source that generates the data. Data is captured by using machine-readable media, prerecording data, or capturing data directly without the use of data media. Electronic data interchange methods allow direct electronic transmission of source documents between companies.

☐ Whether traditional or automated methods of data entry are used, the computer can still be used to assist the data entry process. Special keyboards can be used, and video displays can provide features such as cursors, menus, prompts, and icons. Or other devices and methods can be used, such as audio prompts, the electronic mouse, touch-sensitive screens, and so on. All of these devices are designed to simplify the job of entering data in the computer systems by reducing the use of manual keyboard methods for data entry.

☐ Computer output methods are also changing. Printed paper output is being replaced by visual displays. Microfilm media are replacing printed paper documents. Standardized printed reports produced on a regular basis are being replaced by visual displays tailored to users and furnished to them at their request. Finally, displays of numeric data or text material are being replaced by graphics displays.

☐ Figure 5–1 can be used to help you summarize the types of input and output methods that have been discussed in this chapter.

KEY TERMS AND CONCEPTS

These are the key terms and concepts of this chapter. The page number of their first explanation is in parentheses.

1. Audio-response (206)
2. Cathode ray tube (196)
3. Computer-assisted data entry (187)
4. Computer terminal (194)
5. Cursor (188)
6. Data entry terminal (194)
7. Digitizers (198)
8. Direct input/output (186)
9. Electronic data interchange (187)
10. Electronic mouse (189)
11. Ergonomics (182)
12. Formatted screen (188)
13. Graphics displays (191)
14. Icons (189)
15. Intelligent terminal (194)
16. Joystick (198)
17. Key-to-disk (209)
18. Light pen (198)
19. Liquid crystal displays (197)
20. Machine-readable media (186)
21. Magnetic ink character recognition (209)
22. Menu (188)
23. Menu-driven (188)
24. Micrographics (211)
25. Optical character recognition (206)
26. Optical scanner (206)
27. Plasma display (197)
28. Plotters (203)
29. Point-of-sale (POS) terminal (196)
30. Printers (199)
    a. Character, line, and page
    b. Impact and nonimpact
    c. Dot matrix
    d. Laser
31. Prompt (188)
32. Source data automation (186)
33. Touch-sensitive screen (198)
34. Trackball (198)
35. Traditional data entry (184)
36. Transaction terminal (196)
37. Turnaround documents (199)
38. User friendly (182)
39. User interface (182)
40. Visual display terminal (194)
41. Voice input/output (204)
42. Wand (206)
43. Windows (188)

REVIEW AND APPLICATION QUIZ

Match one of the **key terms and concepts** listed above with one of the brief examples or definitions listed below. Try to find the "best fit" for answers that seem to fit more than one term or concept. Defend your choices.

_____ 1. Computer input/output methods and devices for users.
_____ 2. Human factors engineering.
_____ 3. Systems that are safe, comfortable, and easy to use.
_____ 4. Too many activities, people, media, costs, and errors.
_____ 5. The automatic capture of data at the time and place of transactions.
_____ 6. Capture data or communicate information without media.
_____ 7. The electronic transmission of source documents between companies.
_____ 8. A point of light that assists your input activities.
_____ 9. A display of a list of options for your selection.

_____ 10. A message is displayed to assist you in using the computer.

_____ 11. Small figures are displayed to help you indicate activities to be performed.

_____ 12. The screen is divided into several sections, each with its own display.

_____ 13. A visual display of a blank form for you to fill out.

_____ 14. Easier to understand than columns of figures.

_____ 15. A device that provides keyboard input plus video output for computers.

_____ 16. A microcomputer used as a terminal.

_____ 17. An automated teller machine (ATM) is an example.

_____ 18. Helps you write on the video screen.

_____ 19. Moving this on your desktop moves the cursor on the screen.

_____ 20. You can communicate with a computer by touching its display.

_____ 21. Produces hard copy output such as paper documents and reports.

_____ 22. May use a mechanical arm with several pens to draw hard copy graphics output.

_____ 23. Part of a customer's invoice is returned for automated data entry.

_____ 24. Promises to be the easiest, most natural way to communicate with a computer.

_____ 25. The computer talks to you.

_____ 26. Optical scanners may use this technology.

_____ 27. Bank check processing uses this technology.

_____ 28. A hand-held device that reads bar coding.

_____ 29. Another name for an electronic cash register terminal.

_____ 30. Using microfilm for input, output, and storage.

APPLICATION PROBLEMS

1. If you have not already done so, read and answer the questions after the two Real World Applications in this chapter.

2. Outline the functions, advantages, and disadvantages of three input/output devices, indicating whether they perform input and/or output functions and the type of media they use. Use Figure 5–1 to help you.

3. Which method of input would you recommend for the following activities? Explain your choices.
   a. Entering data from printed questionnaires.
   b. Entering data from telephone surveys.
   c. Entering data from bank checks.
   d. Entering data from merchandise tags.
   e. Entering data from engineering drawings.

4. Which method of output would you recommend for the following information products? Explain your choices.

    a. Visual displays for portable microcomputers.
    b. Legal documents.
    c. Engineering drawings.
    d. Financial results for top executives.
    e. Responses for telephone transactions.

5. A chain of eight department stores processes sales by recording each sale on a sales order form. Daily these forms are sent to the central computer department for recording on magnetic tape. Monthly customers are billed, and inventory and sales reports are sent to store managers. The managers receive their reports about seven days after the end of the month. The managers have been complaining about the infrequency and untimeliness of these reports. Could new input/output methods alleviate the problem? Identify specific input and output devices that could be used. Identify where they would be located, what they would do, and who would use them. Justify the benefits of each device you propose.

6. Robertson Manufacturing has been using printed paper output in its computer systems. Now it is facing mountains of paper. What other devices could be used to cut down on this excessive volume of paper?

7. Intelligent terminals cost more than *dumb* terminals. Name two advantages of using intelligent terminals that help to justify the added cost.

8. Name two devices that can read characters printed on source documents and convert these characters directly into computer-usable format. Identify a current use for each device.

9. Which of the input/output devices described in this chapter do you personally use? Which devices are most widely used by people in organizations with whom you come into contact on a regular basis? (For example, the banks, retail stores, supermarkets, and restaurants you may use.) Evaluate three such devices from this personal perspective in terms of ease of use. Suggest any improvements that could be made.

CHAPTER 6

STORAGE CONCEPTS AND METHODS

Chapter Outline

Learning Objectives

The purpose of this chapter is to promote a basic understanding of computer storage by analyzing (1) important storage concepts and (2) the characteristics, functions, benefits, and limitations of major storage devices. After reading and studying this chapter, you should be able to:

1. Explain the following storage concepts:
   a. Storage media cost/speed/capacity trade-offs.
   b. CPU storage areas.
   c. Firmware versus software and hardware.
   d. Direct and sequential access.
   e. Virtual memory.
2. Outline the functions, advantages, and disadvantages of semiconductor, magnetic disk, magnetic tape, magnetic bubble, and optical disk storage media and devices.
3. Identify the types of storage devices used in your personal computer or by other computer systems at your school or business. Determine their basic physical and performance characteristics.

Section I: Computer Storage Concepts

OVERVIEW OF STORAGE MEDIA

What storage devices do modern information systems need? In Chapter 1 we introduced the concept of **storage** as one of the basic functions of any information system. Data and information need to be stored after input, during processing, and before needed as output. In Chapter 2 we said that a computer system accomplishes the storage function by the use of **primary storage** in the CPU, as well as in **secondary storage** hardware such as magnetic disk and tape devices and media. Now it's time to take a closer look at the concepts and methods that provide the storage function in today's computers.

Why are there so many types of storage media and devices? Take a look at Figure 6–1. It illustrates the speed, capacity, and cost of several alternative primary and secondary storage media. Notice the cost/speed/capacity trade-offs as one moves from semiconductor memories, to moving surface magnetic media such as magnetic disk and tape, and then to optical disks. Figure 6–1 emphasizes that the "perfect memory" does not exist. High-speed storage media cost more per byte and provide lower capacities. Large capacity storage media cost less per byte but are slower. That's why we have different kinds of storage media.

Figure 6–1 also emphasizes that there isn't enough room in the primary storage circuits of most computers to store all the data and programs required to meet the information processing needs of users. That's a major reason why computers use secondary storage devices to enlarge their storage capacity. Also, primary storage circuits usually lose their contents when electric power is turned off. So secondary storage media provide a more permanent type of storage. However, remember that the contents of secondary storage devices must be transferred into the primary storage unit before being processed by the CPU.

Figure 6–1 Storage media cost, speed, and capacity trade-offs. Notice how cost increases with speed, and how it decreases as capacity increases.

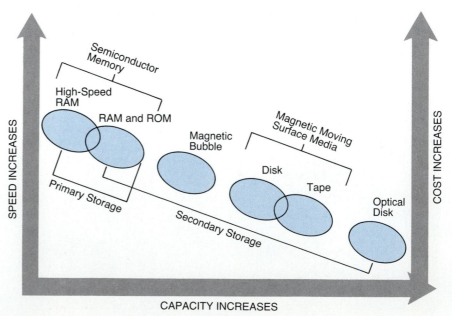

Figure 6–1 shows that at the present time, semiconductor memories are being used mainly for primary storage, though they are finding increasing use as high-speed secondary storage devices. Magnetic bubble memories, on the other hand, are currently being used mostly in secondary storage applications, as are magnetic disk and tape and optical disk devices.

Figure 6–2 summarizes the functions, speed, storage capacities, and advantages and disadvantages of important computer storage devices. We'll take a look at each of these devices in this chapter. But first, there are some other important computer storage concepts you need to understand.

Figure 6–2 Characteristics of important computer storage methods. Notice the advantages and disadvantages of each method.

Peripheral Equipment	Media	Primary Functions	Typical I/O Speed Range	Typical Storage Capacity	Major Advantages and/or Disadvantages
MAGNETIC DISK DRIVE	Magnetic disk Disk pack Disk cartridge Fixed disk	Secondary storage (direct access) and input/output	Data transfer: 200,000– 2,000,000 bytes per second Access time: 10–100 milli- seconds	Over 500 mil- lion characters per disk pack and several billion charac- ters per drive	Large ca- pacity, fast, direct ac- cess storage device (DASD), but expensive
FLOPPY DISK DRIVE	Magnetic dis- kette 8-, 5¼-, and 3½-inch diameters	Secondary storage (direct access) and input/output	10,000–30,000 bytes per second Access time: 100–600 milliseconds	150,000 to 3,500,000 characters per disk	Small, inex- pensive, and convenient, but slower and smaller capacity than other DASDs
MAGNETIC TAPE DRIVE	Magnetic tape reel and car- tridge	Secondary storage (sequential access), input/ output, and disk backup	15,000– 1,250,000 bytes per second	Up to 200 mil- lion characters per tape reel or cartridge	Inexpensive, with a fast transfer rate, but only sequential access
MAGNETIC STRIP STORAGE UNIT	Magnetic strip cartridge	Mass second- ary storage (direct/se- quential access)	Data transfer: 25,000– 55,000 bytes per second Access time: up to several seconds	Up to 500 bil- lion bytes per unit	Relatively inexpensive, large capac- ity, but slow access time
OPTICAL DISK DRIVE	Optical disk (CD–ROM: 4.72–5¼-inch diameters)	Secondary storage (direct access) and archival storage	Data transfer: 150,000– 500,000 bytes per second Access time: 200–600 milli- seconds	Up to 600 mil- lion characters per CD–ROM disk	Large ca- pacity, high- quality stor- age of data, text, and images. Primarily a read-only medium

Figure 6–3 Types of CPU storage. Notice the functions of the different types of storage areas.

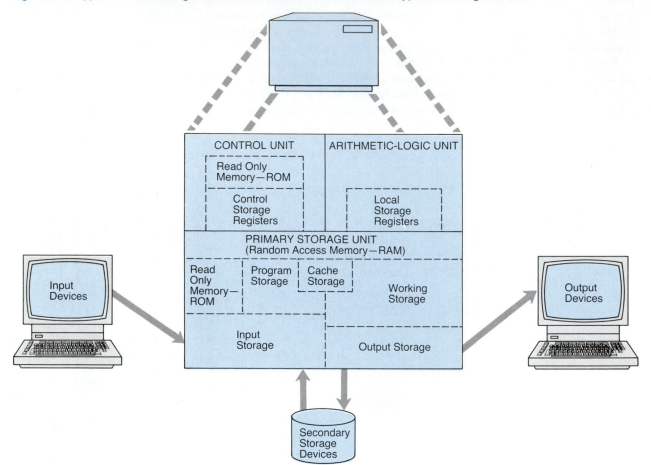

CPU STORAGE AREAS

Several types of storage exist within the CPU, depending on the particular storage function being performed. Figure 6–3 is a conceptual illustration of the types of storage areas that might exist within the CPU of modern computers. Let's examine each of them briefly.

Primary Storage Areas

The primary storage unit can be conceptually subdivided into several types of storage. *Input storage* receives data from input devices, *program storage* contains program instructions, and *output storage* contains information waiting for transfer to output devices. *Working storage* holds information being processed, as well as intermediate processing results. The primary storage units of many larger computers also include a small, very high-speed *buffer* or *cache* storage area. It is sometimes called *scratch pad memory*, because it is used to temporarily store data, instructions, and intermediate results during processing.

Arithmetic-Logic and Control Storage Areas

Other categories of CPU storage include *local storage*, which consists of the high-speed registers of the arithmetic-logic unit, and *control storage*, which consists of the registers and *read only memory* (ROM) circuits of the control unit. Remember that **registers** are small high-speed storage circuit areas used for the temporary storage of an individual instruction or data element during the operation of the control and arithmetic-logic units. *General-purpose registers* carry out a variety of register functions, while *special-purpose registers* perform specific functions. In Chapter 4 we saw the use of several types of registers in the execution of an instruction. For example, a *storage register* temporarily holds data or instructions taken from or being sent to primary storage. An *address register* may hold the address of the storage location of data, or the address of an input/output device or a control function. An *instruction register* contains the instruction being executed by the CPU. An *accumulator register* accumulates the results of arithmetic operations.

Firmware Storage

The CPUs of most computers today contain special storage circuitry modules where certain programs *(software)* are permanently stored in semiconductor ROM chips *(hardware)*. This permanent storing of selected programs or instructions in ROM storage circuits is known as **firmware.** Firmware has two major functions in a CPU:

☐ In the primary storage unit, firmware replaces the temporary storage of system and application programs in RAM storage circuits. Firmware provides permanent storage of machine language versions of selected programs in ROM circuits.

☐ In the control unit, firmware replaces electronic logic circuitry, which is designed to accomplish particular tasks (such as perform an arithmetic operation). Instead, firmware consists of *microprograms* of elementary control instructions stored in memory circuits.

Firmware and Primary Storage

Important programs that do not need frequent changes are placed in ROM chips in the primary storage unit. This protects them from accidental erasure or loss if electric power is interrupted. It also significantly increases the speed of program execution since programs are stored in high-speed micro-electronic circuits in the form of machine language instruction codes.

Remember from Chapter 2 that many current computers contain ROM chips in which selected programs or parts of programs have been permanently stored. In microcomputers, this usually consists of parts of the operating system program of the computer, a programming language translator program (typically a BASIC interpreter), and selected application programs. For example, most models of the IBM Personal System/2 microcomputer have 128K bytes of ROM storage. Another example is the HP 110 "laptop" portable microcomputer from Hewlett-Packard. It has 384K bytes of ROM, which contains its operating system, and spreadsheet, word processing, and communications programs.

Firmware and Control Storage

The control units of many current computers contain ROM modules or other read only storage areas, where elementary machine instructions called *microinstructions* or *microcode* are stored. Sets of microinstructions (called **microprograms**) interpret the machine language instructions of a computer program and decode them into elementary microinstructions, which are then executed. This changes how elementary operations of the control unit (such as clearing and loading a register) are executed. Operations that formerly were executed by hardware (hardwired logic circuits) are now executed by **firmware,** that is, software (microprograms) stored in ROM circuits. Also, firmware and **microprogramming** (the use of microprograms) increase the versatility of computer systems by allowing various degrees of customizing of the *instruction set* of a CPU.

DIRECT AND SEQUENTIAL ACCESS

Primary storage media such as semiconductor storage chips are called **direct access** or *random access memories* (RAM). Magnetic disk devices are frequently called *direct access storage devices (DASD).* On the other hand, media like magnetic tape devices are known as *sequential access devices.* There are also magnetic bubble and other devices that have a combination of direct access and sequential access properties. What do the concepts of direct access, random access, and sequential access mean in terms of the capabilities of storage media? Let's see.

Direct access is frequently called **random access.** Both terms describe the same concept. They mean that any element of data or instructions (bit, byte, or word) can be directly stored and retrieved by randomly selecting and using any of the locations on the storage media. It also means that each storage position (1) has a unique address, and (2) can be individually accessed in approximately the same length of time without having to search through other storage positions. For example, each memory cell on a microelectronic semiconductor RAM chip can be individually sensed or changed in the same length of time. The same holds true for magnetic disk media. Any data record stored on such a direct access storage device (DASD) can be accessed directly in approximately the same time period. See Figure 6–4.

Figure 6–4 Sequential versus direct access storage. Magnetic tape is a typical sequential access medium. A magnetic disk is a typical direct access storage device (DASD).

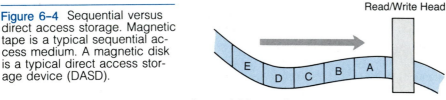

Sequential Access Storage Device

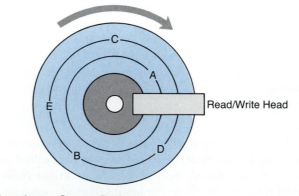

Direct Access Storage Device

An example of direct access from the world of popular music media might clarify this concept. Consider what happens when you decide to play a stereo phonograph record on a record turntable unit. The direct access process is similar to directly selecting a specific song on a phonograph record that is spinning on a turntable. You can pick up the tone arm and move it directly to the track where the song you want to hear begins. That's direct access.

Sequential access storage devices use media such as magnetic tape whose storage locations do not have unique addresses and cannot be directly addressed. Instead, data must be stored and retrieved using a sequential or serial process. Thus data are recorded one after another in a predetermined sequence (such as a numerical or alphabetical order) on a storage medium. Locating an individual item of data requires starting at the beginning of a tape and searching all of the recorded data until the desired item is located. This is similar to using *fast forward* or *rewind* on a home tape recorder/player to find a specific song or conversation.

VIRTUAL MEMORY

Virtual memory is the ability to treat secondary storage devices as an extension of the primary storage of a computer. This gives the "virtual" appearance of a larger main memory than actually exists. Virtual storage enables only parts of a program or data file to be in primary storage during processing. That's because data and programs are subdivided into segments which are transferred between main memory and secondary storage devices by the computer's operating system. Thus it appears that the computer has a larger real memory than it actually has. Therefore, the computer system can be used as if it had "virtually" unlimited primary storage. For example, one recent computer model with a *real memory* (primary storage) capacity of 8 megabytes can act as though it has a memory size of 256 megabytes through its use of secondary storage on magnetic disks and its virtual memory operating system.

Virtual memory requires a form of memory transfer called *paging*. Primary storage is subdivided into a large number of segments called **pages** whose contents and location are automatically controlled by the virtual memory operating system and the use of special registers. Programs and data are subdivided automatically into pages. They are moved to and from secondary storage devices and are retrieved as needed. See Figure 6–5.

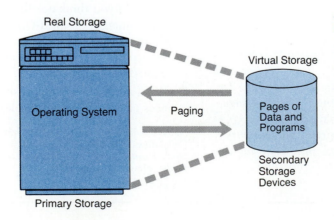

Real Storage

Virtual Storage

Operating System   Paging   Pages of Data and Programs

Primary Storage

Secondary Storage Devices

Figure 6–5 The virtual memory process. Pages of data and programs are shuttled between primary storage and secondary storage during processing. This gives the CPU a virtual memory capacity much larger than its real memory.

REAL WORLD APPLICATION 6–1

Microsoft Corporation

No one will ever accuse the Microsoft Corporation, of Redmond, Wash., of being boring hosts. Microsoft convened its Second International Conference on CD-ROM technology during the first week of March 1987. At that time the company, a leading manufacturer of software for personal computers, announced the release of its first CD-ROM software product—the $295 Microsoft Bookshelf. In this world of computer-related hyperbole, Microsoft Bookshelf qualifies as a stunning product.

CD-ROM stands for "compact disk, read-only memory." It refers to a computer memory system that allows users to retrieve stored information but will not accept the entry of new information. CD-ROM uses laser-optical technology that makes it possible to store a roomful of data on a plastic "optical disk" that looks just like an audio compact disc. Each ROM compact disk has the capacity to catalog up to 550 megabytes, the equivalent of 270,000 pages of text.

The Bookshelf is intended for use by professional journalists, academics, and other professionals who may require instant online access to a dictionary, thesaurus, zip code lookup table, famous quotations, or an almanac. In concert with a CD-ROM drive (which costs about $1,000) connected to a personal computer, customers will have instant (and we mean *instant*) access to the following full-text publications: *The American Heritage Dictionary*, *Roget's II: The New Thesaurus*, *The World Almanac and Book of Facts*, *Bartlett's Familiar Quotations*, *The Chicago Manual of Style*, *Houghton Mifflin's Spelling Verifier and Corrector*, *Forms and Letters*, *The U.S.A. Zip Code Directory*, *The Houghton Mifflin Usage Alert*, and *Business Information Sources*.

The lightning-quick program, which operates by means of "hot keys," pull-down menus, and dialog box selections, is compatible with most popular MS-DOS word processing programs. When using the memory-resident Bookshelf, users have access to information that can easily be cut and pasted from the CD-ROM format into a word processing file.

Few dispute the power of optical disk technology or its wide-ranging applications. The variety of CD-ROM disks has expanded. Currently, about 300 titles are available, and the list is growing. Other CD-ROM disks now available include complete databases on federal and state environmental regulations; abstracts from psychological, behavorial, agricultural, medical, and legal research journals; and the 20-volume Academic American Encyclopedia by Grolier.

The immediate beneficiaries of the technology will be reference libraries, industry research and marketing firms, and anyone who needs access to large amounts of data quickly. Newspapers and other information-generating businesses are looking at the technology to store years' worth of articles on a bookshelf. Manufacturers hope the technology becomes a staple research tool for colleges and universities.

"Most of the key work we need to do in the next year is in the software area. We see this as a great business opportunity," said William Gates, chairman and chief executive officer of Microsoft Corp.

Application Questions

☐ What do you think are the advantages and disadvantages of CD-ROM optical disks compared to other storage media, such as semiconductor chips or magnetic disks and tape? Refer to Figure 6–2.

☐ What are some of the present and future uses of this storage technology?

Source: Adapted from "CD-ROM with a View," *Personal Computing*, May 1987, p. 27; and Bob Webster, "Disk Holds More Than 250,000 Pages of Data," *Arizona Republic*, March 23, 1987, p. C3.

With virtual memory, large programs can be easily processed, since programs do not have to reside entirely in main memory. Subdividing large programs into segments or overlays is no longer necessary. Efficient use is made of primary storage, since pages of programs can be placed wherever space is available. Many more programs can be run simultaneously when paging is used. That's because only those parts of a program containing the specific instructions and data actually being processed are stored in memory.

Of course, virtual memory systems have several limitations. Applications may take longer to process and use more total memory space. Proper system controls are needed to minimize the increase in "overhead" (i.e., time and memory space) that can result from the use of virtual memory.

Section II: Types of Computer Storage

The primary storage of most modern computers consists of microelectronic semiconductor circuits. Groups of these circuits (each group representing eight bits plus a check bit, for example) make up each position of storage. Thousands of **semiconductor storage** circuits are etched on large-scale integrated (LSI) circuit chips. Remember that the chips originated from semiconducting silicon crystal wafers. Each memory chip may be less than an eighth of an inch square and contains thousands of storage positions. For example, a 64K bit memory chip contains 65,536 bit positions, for a storage capacity (including check bits) of almost 7K bytes. Memory chips with capacities of 256K bits and 1 million bits (1 megabit) are now being used in many computers. See Figure 6–6 and page 24 of the pictorial section in Chapter 1.

SEMICONDUCTOR STORAGE

Figure 6–6 A semiconductor memory chip with a capacity of one million bits.

Figure 6-7 Diagram of a semi-conductor memory chip segment. The individual bit being accessed is at location 53 (column 5, row 3).

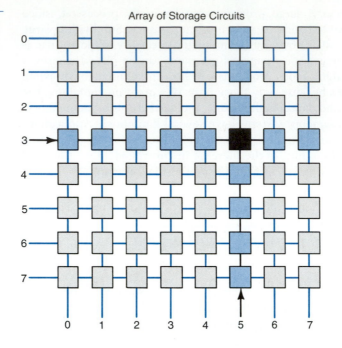

Array of Storage Circuits

Each storage position (cell) consists of a microelectronic switch or "flip-flop" circuit. The direction of the electronic current passing through each cell determines whether the switch is in an *ON* or *OFF* position. Thus the binary digits 0 and 1 can be represented. The *state* of each storage position (ON or OFF) can be electronically sensed without altering that state. Semiconductor storage is known as a random access memory (RAM) or direct access storage medium because each memory cell can be individually sensed or changed in the same length of time irrespective of its location. Figure 6–7 illustrates an eight-by-eight array that can store 64 bits.

Semiconductor memories currently use two basic types of LSI technology—bipolar and metal oxide semiconductor (MOS)—with many variations of these two technologies being used. High-speed semiconductor memory uses bipolar circuits that are faster but more costly and, therefore, are used primarily for high-speed buffer (cache) storage. Most semiconductor main memories use MOS-type circuits. Access times for high-speed memories are below 50 nanoseconds and into the picosecond range. Speeds from 70 to 300 nanoseconds are common for other semiconductor memories.

Research and development is continuing to improve present silicon chip performance, or to develop substitutes for silicon. One alternative silicon technology is CMOS (complimentary metal oxide semiconductor), which allows production of microprocessor and memory chips that are smaller, faster, and consume much less power than standard MOS chips. A promising silicon substitute is a chip made from a costly rare mineral called *gallium*. The *gallium-arsenide chip* offers speeds up to five times faster than silicon, doesn't overheat as much, and uses a fraction of the power that silicon chips need. Recent discoveries of *superconducting* oxide compounds promise even faster and smaller chips operating at normal temperatures. Refer back to the "Microcomputer Revolution" time capsule in Chapter 1 if you want to review chip manufacturing technology.

Some of the major attractions of microscopic semiconductor storage are small size, great speed, shock and temperature resistance, and low cost due to mass production capabilities. One major disadvantage of most semiconductor memory is its **volatility.** Uninterrupted electric power must be supplied or the contents of memory will be lost. Therefore, emergency transfer to other devices or standby electrical power (battery packs or emergency generators) is required if data must be saved. Another alternative would be to more permanently "burn in" the contents of semiconductor devices so they could not be erased by a loss of power. Let's take a closer look at several alternative semiconductor memories.

As we said in Chapter 2, there are two basic types of semiconductor memory: **random access memory (RAM)** and **read only memory (ROM).** Variations of these two basic types are being used for electronic computers and other devices requiring electronic storage of data or instructions.

- ☐ **RAM: random access memory.** Most widely used for primary storage. Each memory position can be both sensed (read) or changed (write) so it is also called read/write memory. This is a *volatile* memory of two basic types. *Dynamic* RAM chips need their electrical charges continually refreshed by special regenerator circuits. *Static* RAM chips do not need such regeneration, and require less power. However they still need to be supplied with a continuous electrical current. In addition, they need several additional circuits for each storage position and thus are larger and more expensive. Therefore dynamic RAM chips (DRAM) are the most commonly used semiconductor storage devices.

- ☐ **ROM: read only memory.** This is a type of *nonvolatile* random access memory used for permanent storage. It can only be read, not "written" (i.e., changed). Frequently used control instructions in the control unit and programs in primary storage (such as parts of the operating system are permanently "burned in" to the storage cells during manufacture.

- ☐ **PROM: programmable read only memory.** This is a type of ROM chip that can be programmed after manufacture. Several versions can only be written in (programmed) once after their manufacture.

- ☐ **EPROM: erasable programmable read only memory.** This is a type of ROM chip that can be erased and reprogrammed indefinitely. Erasure of memory requires a special technique, such as exposing the circuits to ultraviolet light. These memories are useful for storage of contents that will be changed infrequently. A version that can be erased by applying a larger electrical charge is known as *electronically erasable read only memory*, or EEPROM.

Semiconductor storage chips are now being used as direct access secondary storage media for both large and small computers. For example, if you own a microcomputer, you could add a plug-in circuit board containing up to several megabytes of semiconductor storage chips (a RAM card). You could use this for additional primary storage, but you could also use it for secondary storage. Additional software can then make the main microprocessor and the operating system program think that you have added another disk drive

Semiconductor Secondary Storage

Figure 6-8 Adding a microcomputer circuit board for up to
a million bytes of additional
semiconductor storage.

Figure 6-8 Adding a micro-computer circuit board for up to a million bytes of additional semiconductor storage.

to your system! What you have instead is a very high-speed semiconductor secondary storage capability, sometimes called a RAM disk. Some semiconductor secondary storage devices are also marketed as competition for magnetic disk units used on mainframe computers. See Figure 6–8.

MAGNETIC DISK STORAGE

Magnetic disk media and equipment are now the most common form of secondary storage for modern computer systems. They provide a direct access capability and high storage capacities at a reasonable cost. The two basic types of magnetic disk media are conventional (hard) metal disks and flexible (floppy) diskettes. Several types of magnetic disk peripheral equipment are used as direct access storage devices (DASDs) in both small and large computer systems.

Characteristics of Magnetic Disks

Magnetic disks are thin metal or plastic disks that resemble phonograph records and are coated on both sides with an iron oxide recording material. Several disks may be mounted together on a vertical shaft, which typically rotates the disks at speeds of 2,400 to 3,600 revolutions per minute (rpm). Electromagnetic read/write heads are positioned by access arms between the slightly separated disks to read or write data on concentric circular **tracks.** Data is recorded on tracks in the form of tiny magnetized spots to form binary digits arranged in serial order in a code such as EBCDIC. Thousands of bytes can be recorded on each track, and there are several hundred data tracks on each disk surface. Each track contains the same number of bytes, because data is packed together more closely on the small inner tracks than on the large outer tracks.

Figure 6–9 illustrates some of the physical storage characteristics of magnetic disks. This illustration shows a disk assembly consisting of 11 disks, which provide 20 recording surfaces since the unprotected top surface of the

Figure 6–9 Characteristics of magnetic disks. Notice especially the concepts of cylinders, tracks, and sectors.

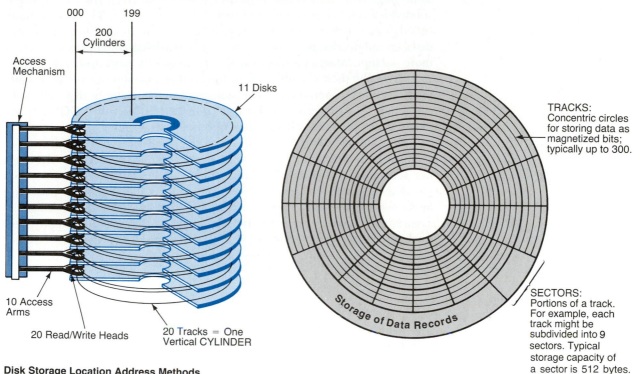

000   199

200
Cylinders

Access
Mechanism

11 Disks

10 Access
Arms

20 Read/Write Heads

20 Tracks = One
Vertical CYLINDER

Storage of Data Records

TRACKS:
Concentric circles
for storing data as
magnetized bits;
typically up to 300.

SECTORS:
Portions of a track.
For example, each
track might be
subdivided into 9
sectors. Typical
storage capacity of
a sector is 512 bytes.

Disk Storage Location Address Methods

☐ By cylinder (or track), surface, and data record number.
   Example: Cylinder 199, surface 15, record 08.
☐ By sector and data record number.
   Example: Sector 74, record 02.

top disk and bottom surface of the bottom disk are not used to record data. An access mechanism with 20 read/write heads is shown, providing one head for each recording surface. This illustration shows a *moving-head* access mechanism that moves in and out between the disks to position the read/write heads over the desired track. Other types of magnetic disk units may use *fixed-head* (or *head-per-track*) access mechanisms, which do not move because they provide a read/write head for each track of each disk.

Figure 6–9 also illustrates the concept of a **cylinder,** which is one of the basic methods of organizing data on magnetic disks. In this illustration, each cylinder is composed of the 20 circular tracks that are on the same vertical line, one above the other, on each of the 20 recording surfaces. Thus a cylinder is sometimes defined as the collection of tracks that can be read when the read/write heads are stationed in a position between the disks. In Figure 6–9, each disk surface contains 200 tracks, which means that the disk units shown can store data in 200 cylinders. When the cylinder method of organization is used, the location of an individual data record is determined by an address consisting of the cylinder number, the recording surface number, and an individual data record number.

Another popular method of disk organization used for floppy disks and some large disk units is also shown in Figure 6–9. Each track on a disk is subdivided into a fixed number of **sectors** or *fixed blocks*. This is sometimes called *fixed block architecture*. Typically, tracks on microcomputer floppy disks are subdivided into nine sectors, while hard disks might have 16, 32, or more sectors. Magnetic disks can be permanently organized into "hard" sectors during their manufacture, or they can be magnetically organized into "soft" sectors by operating system commands to the magnetic disk drives of a computer. For example, the Format command of Microsoft DOS 2.0 will magnetically organize a floppy disk into nine soft sectors.

Sector storage capacities for 5¼-inch floppy disks can be 128 bytes per sector (single density), 256 bytes per sector (double density), or 512 bytes per sector (quad density). Sectors seem to subdivide the disk surface into pie-shaped or wedge-shaped areas, since sectors at the large outer tracks are larger than sectors at the smaller inner tracks. However, each sector has the same storage capacity since data is packed together more closely on the inner tracks of a disk. When the sector method of organization is used, each sector in the entire disk unit is assigned a unique number. Thus, the location of data is identified by an address consisting of the sector number and an individual data record number.

Types of Magnetic Disks

There are several types of magnetic disk arrangements including removable disk packs and cartridges as well as fixed disk units. The removable disk devices are the most popular, because they can be used interchangeably in magnetic disk units and stored offline when not in use. See Figures 6–10 and 6–11, and page 25 of the pictorial section of Chapter 1.

☐ **Disk packs** are easy to handle; one popular type contains 11 disks, each 14 inches in diameter, is about 6 inches high, weighs about 20 pounds, and can store over 300 million characters.

☐ **Hard disk drives** combine magnetic disks, access arms, and read/write heads into a sealed module. Removable cartridge versions are also available. This arrangement (known as "Winchester" disk technology) reduces exposure to such airborne contaminants as smoke or dust. It significantly increases speed, capacity, and reliability, compared to open disk packs. Such hard disk drives contain one or more magnetic disks and can store from 10 to over 100 million bytes. They have become a popular option for high-speed, large-capacity secondary storage for microcomputers.

☐ **Disk cartridges** are a popular alternative to hard disk drives, especially for microcomputers. *Bernoulli boxes* use one or two flexible eight-inch disks, each of which is enclosed in a removable plastic cartridge. When the disk is rotated, the air under the disk creates enough *aerodynamic lift* to lift the disk toward the read/write heads. This is known as the *Bernoulli effect* of aerodynamics. Each disk typically contains 10 or 20 megabytes. Internal disk cartridge drives are a competing product for microcomputers. They use a small removable cartridge containing a four-inch hard disk

Figure 6–10 Magnetic disk media. Notice the different types and sizes of hard and floppy disks. This includes 5¼- and 3½-inch floppy disks and a hard magnetic disk pack and disk cartridge.

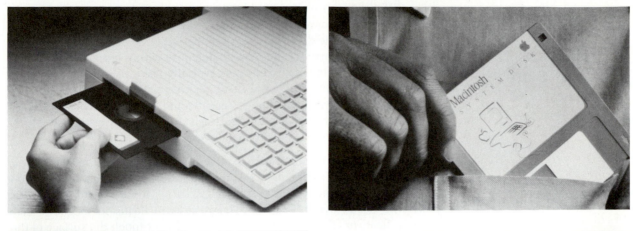

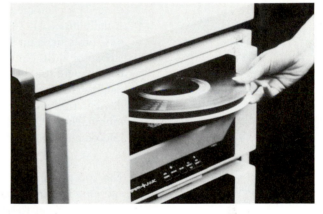

Figure 6–11 Inside a hard disk drive. Note the arrangement of disks and read/write heads.

with a capacity of 15 megabytes. Removable disk cartridge devices are a popular but more expensive alternative to nonremovable hard disk drives for microcomputers.

☐ **Fixed disk,** nonremovable magnetic disk assemblies are used in some magnetic disk units. This allows higher speeds, greater data-recording densities, and closer tolerances within a sealed, more stable environment. Fixed disks typically use a fixed-head access mechanism (one read/write head per track) and thus have great speed as well as high storage capacity and reliability. One typical fixed disk unit contains six eight-inch disks and has a storage capacity of more than 500 megabytes.

Sealed disk modules and fixed disk drives have grown in popularity. Their control of the disk environment results in a faster, more reliable operation and more compact, high-density storage capacity. This is a result of very low read/write head "flying heights." The read/write heads in magnetic disk devices "float" or "fly" on a cushion of air and do not touch the surface of the disk. The clearance between the read/write head and the disk surface is usually less than 50 microinches (millionths of an inch). Thus all magnetic disk units have air filtration systems to remove airborne particles, such as smoke or dust. Such particles could cause the read/write head to come in contact with the disk (called a *head crash*), which usually results in the loss of data on that portion of the disk. This explains the increased use of hard disk devices that are sealed and filtered to eliminate particles greater than 17 microinches. Thus the read/write head of such devices can fly less than 20 microinches above the disk surface. See Figure 6–12.

Capabilities of Magnetic Disks

The speed of magnetic disk units is expressed by their *average access time* and *data transfer rate*. The **average access time** refers to the time it takes a read/write head to access a specific data location on a magnetic disk. The average access time of moving-head disks includes the time required to move the read/write head into position over the track where the data is stored *(seek time)*. It also includes the time it takes the disk to rotate until the desired data is under the read/write head *(rotational delay)*. Of course, since fixed-head disks provide a read/write head for every track on the disk, seek time is eliminated. Thus their average access time equals the rotational delay time. Average access times for moving-head disks range from about 30 to 60 milliseconds and from 15 to 30 milliseconds for fixed-head disk units. The **data transfer rate** of magnetic disk units refers to the speed by which data can be transferred between the disk unit and the CPU. Data transfer rates vary from 100,000 to over 3 million bytes per second.

Storage capacity of magnetic disk units varies depending on the type, number, and arrangement of magnetic disks in a unit. Magnetic disk units may contain one or more disk drives, each of which accommodates one removable disk pack or module, or may contain a permanent grouping of fixed disks. The storage capacity of individual disk packs, modules, or fixed disk drives ranges from several million bytes to over 500 megabytes. Large magnetic disk units containing multiple disk drives can store several billion bytes (gigabytes). See Figure 6–13. The use of microcomputers has encour-

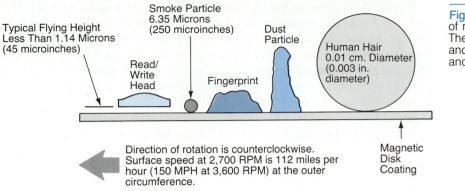

Smoke Particle
6.35 Microns
(250 microinches)

Typical Flying Height
Less Than 1.14 Microns
(45 microinches)

Dust
Particle

Human Hair
0.01 cm. Diameter
(0.003 in.
diameter)

Read/
Write
Head

Fingerprint

Direction of rotation is counterclockwise.
Surface speed at 2,700 RPM is 112 miles per
hour (150 MPH at 3,600 RPM) at the outer
circumference.

Magnetic
Disk
Coating

Figure 6–12 Comparative size
of magnetic disk contaminants.
They can cause "head crashes"
and damage the disk surface
and the read/write head.

Figure 6–13 A large magnetic
disk unit. Notice the storage
containers for the removable
disk packs used by this unit.

aged increases in the capacity of both hard and floppy disks, while their size has been reduced. *Half-height* drives that are half the height of full-size drives are widely used.

The magnetic *diskette*, or **floppy disk,** is a small, flexible magnetic disk that consists of a polyester film covered with an iron oxide compound. A single disk is mounted and rotates freely inside a protective plastic jacket, which has access openings to accommodate the read/write head of a disk drive unit. Floppy disk drives rotate the disks at between 300 to 400 revolutions per minute. Average access time is 100 to 300 milliseconds. Data can be recorded on one or both sides (single or double-sided disks). Recording densities range from 3,200 to 12,800 bits per inch (bpi) and higher.

Floppy Disks

Floppy disks come in 8-inch, 5¼-inch, and 3½-inch sizes, with the 5¼-inch size being the most popular. Figure 6–14 shows some of the characteristics of the 5¼-inch disk. However, the 3½-inch size is expected to become a standard since it has been adopted by the Apple Macintosh and IBM Personal System/2 microcomputers. This disk is protected by a hard plastic jacket and a metal cover for its read/write opening. Typical storage capacities are 1 to 2.5 megabytes for 8-inch disks, 360K to 720K bytes for 5¼-inch disks, and 720K to 1.44 megabytes for 3½-inch diskettes. Thus a 3½-inch disk could store the equivalent of 720 double-spaced typewritten pages.

Advantages and Disadvantages

Floppy disks have become a popular secondary storage and input/output medium for microcomputer systems. They provide an economical and convenient form of direct access storage. They are also removable and interchangeable with other diskettes and can be conveniently stored offline when not being used. The major attraction of hard magnetic disks is that they are superb direct access secondary storage devices. They are thus superior to magnetic tape for many current applications that require the immediate access capabilities of direct access files. Removable disk devices provide large storage capacities at a relatively low cost, and they can be easily stored offline.

A major limitation of magnetic disks is the possible loss of data due to contamination and head crashes. Another limitation is their cost. A large magnetic disk pack may cost over $1,000, while a large-capacity magnetic tape reel may cost less than $100. For microcomputers, a hard disk drive may cost several hundred dollars more than a floppy disk drive. Magnetic disks may also be slower and more expensive than magnetic tape for applications where large sequential access files are used.

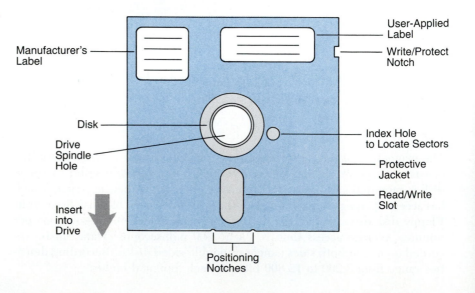

Figure 6–14 Characteristics of a 5¼-inch floppy disk. Notice that the actual magnetic disk is contained inside a square protective plastic jacket.

Magnetic tape is a widely used input/output and secondary storage medium. Data is recorded in the form of magnetized spots on the iron oxide coating of a plastic tape somewhat similar to that used in home tape recorders. Magnetic tape is usually subdivided into nine horizontal tracks or channels to accommodate a check bit and the eight-bit EBCDIC code, though the ASCII code is also used. Blank spaces, known as "gaps," are used to separate individual data records or blocks of grouped records. Most magnetic **tape reels** contain tape ½-inches wide and 3,600-feet long wound on plastic reels about 10 inches in diameter. The density of the data that can be recorded on such tape is frequently either 1,600 or 6,250 bytes per inch. Thus a reel of magnetic tape could contain over 180 million bytes. A recent advance in magnetic tape technology is the high-capacity magnetic **tape cartridge** and drive unit. For example, the IBM 3480 magnetic tape cartridge system for mainframe computers uses cartridges that can hold over 200 million bytes.

Magnetic tape also comes in the form of small **cassettes** and **cartridges.** Cassettes have a capacity of up to 60 megabytes. Small cartridges can store over 100 million characters. Magnetic tape cassettes and small magnetic tape cartridges are becoming a popular means of providing a backup capability for microcomputers using hard disk drives. See Figures 6–15 and 6–16.

MAGNETIC TAPE STORAGE

Nine-Track Tape (EBCDIC Code)

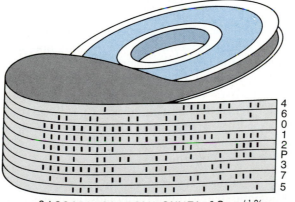

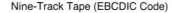

0 1 2 3 4 5 6 7 8 9 A B C M N O X Y Z ' + & S . — / ' %

Figure 6–15 Magnetic tape data storage format. Notice how numbers, letters, and other characters can be represented by the EBCDIC code on this nine-track tape.

Figure 6–16 Magnetic tape reel and cartridge. The familiar tape reel is being challenged by a new cartridge with a capacity of over 200 million bytes! Shown is the IBM 3480 magnetic tape cartridge.

Magnetic Tape Peripherals

Devices that can read and write data on magnetic tapes are called **magnetic tape drives.** Electromagnet read/write heads record data on each channel in the form of magnetic spots on the tape during writing operations. The read/write heads are also used in the reading operation to sense the magnetized spots on the tape and convert them into electronic impulses that are transmitted to the CPU. Reading and writing speeds range from 15,000 to 180,000 bytes per second using standard magnetic tape and up to 1,250,000 bytes per second for high-density tape. Small magnetic tape *cartridge drives* can read data at the rate of 85,000 bytes per second. Magnetic tape *cassette decks* can read or write data at speeds ranging from 300 to 5,000 bytes per second. See Figure 6–17.

Magnetic Strip Hardware

Magnetic strip hardware combines the inexpensive high-capacity benefits of magnetic tape with the direct access advantages of magnetic disks. These advantages are offset to some extent by a slower access time. Magnetic strip units offer mass storage capacity and random access storage at a lower cost than magnetic disks. They are used for applications that do not require fast access times, such as for a large inventory file in a batch processing system.

For example, the IBM 3850 Mass Storage System uses magnetic strips similar to magnetic tape but about 3 inches wide and up to 770 inches long. Several hundred strips are mounted in removable cartridges and stored in a honeycomblike arrangement of "cells." The magnetic strip mass storage system allows the computer to select an individual strip, move it under a read/write head, and return it to its cartridge. Such units may store from 16 to 500 billion bytes of data! Access times are quite slow, however, ranging from a fraction of a second to several seconds. Data transfer rates vary between 25,000 to 55,000 characters per second. See Figure 6–18.

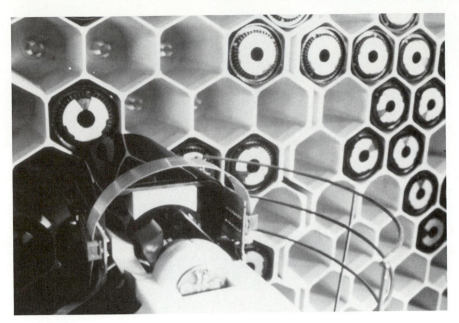

Figure 6–18 Magnetic strip cartridge in a data cell unit. This device is used for mass storage—up to 500 billion bytes per unit.

Magnetic tape is a high-speed input/output medium as well as a high-density secondary storage medium. In comparison to large magnetic disk units, magnetic tape is less expensive and can store more data on a single reel or cartridge. The limitations of magnetic tape include the fact that it is not human-readable, and is vulnerable to dust particles. Also it is a sequential access storage medium and thus slower than direct access media like magnetic disks.

Advantages and Disadvantages

Magnetic bubble storage chips have been developed that use thin slices of garnet crystals on which tiny magnetized areas known as magnetic bubbles or "domains" can be generated. The data is represented by groupings of these magnetic bubbles, which can be moved across the surface of the crystal slices by electrical currents or magnetic fields. Magnetic bubble chips with capacities up to 1 megabit (1 million bits) are now in use. Though magnetic bubble memory is slower than semiconductor memory, it has the important advantage of retaining data being stored even when electric power is cut off. Though it has not been able to compete with magnetic disk devices, it continues to be used as a specialized secondary storage medium.

A major application of bubble memory chips has been in numerical control of machine tools. Dust and chemicals in the atmosphere make moving magnetic media unsuitable. Bubble memory chips are used in portable terminals, where resistance to shock is important. They are also being used as either a built-in or removable cartridge type of secondary storage medium in microcomputers, and as "buffer" memory for such devices as data entry terminals. For example, one portable microcomputer offers 128K bytes of secondary storage in the form of a plug-in magnetic bubble cartridge, while another has 384K bytes of built-in magnetic bubble secondary storage. See Figure 6–19.

MAGNETIC BUBBLE STORAGE

Figure 6–19 A one million-bit magnetic bubble chip.

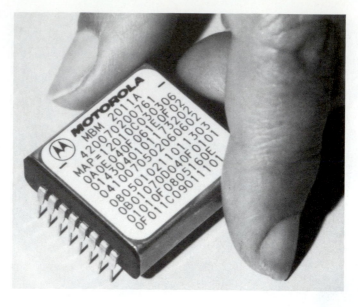

OPTICAL DISK STORAGE

Optical disks are a new mass storage medium. They are also called *compact disks, laser optical disks,* or *video disks.* They use a laser device to read binary codes caused by microscopic pits permanently impressed on the surface of plastic disks. Video disks were introduced for entertainment and educational use in homes, schools, and industry. In these applications, video disks compete with video cassette systems. Video disks can hold several hours of high-quality movie and television pictures and sound or the equivalent of over 50,000 35 mm photographic slides.

However, the use of optical disks as a secondary data storage medium for information processing is still in its early stages. Some versions use 8- and 12-inch plastic disks with capacities of several billion bytes of information. A version designed for use with microcomputers is called CD-ROM (compact disk-read only memory). It uses 12 centimeter (4.7-inch) or 5¼-inch compact disks (CDs) similar to those used in stereo music systems. Each disk can store from 500 to 600 megabytes. This is the equivalent of over 270,000 double-spaced typewritten pages or 1,500 5¼-inch floppy disks! Data is recorded by using a laser to burn microscopic pits in a spiral track into a master disk from which compact disks can be mass produced. This track is over three miles long and results in a density of 16,000 tracks per inch! Data is typically organized in blocks or sectors containing 2 kilobytes of data and 288 bytes of error detection and correction codes. The data transfer rate of CD-ROM disk drives is 150 to 500 kilobytes per second, with access times of 200 to 600 milliseconds. See Figure 6–20.

A more recent version is known as *write once read many* (WORM) technology. This allows microcomputers with the proper optical disk drive unit to record their own data once on an optical disk, but then be able to read it indefinitely. An example of this WORM technology is the optical disk drive available for the IBM Personal System/2 microcomputers. It uses 5¼-inch optical disks with a capacity of 200 megabytes. One of the major

Figure 6-20 Optical data disks. Each of these CD–ROM disks can store as much data as 1,500 floppy disks.

limitations of these and other optical disk systems is that recorded data cannot be erased. However, new erasable optical disk systems have been announced, so this technology looks like a promising alternative to magnetic disks.

One of the major uses of optical disks is in *image processing*, where long-term *archival storage* of historical files of document images must be maintained. Thus financial institutions and others are using optical scanners to capture digitized document images and store them on WORM optical disks as an alternative to microfilm media. However, the major use of CD-ROM disks is to provide microcomputer users with direct access to reference materials and data banks. Examples are encyclopedias, directories, periodical abstracts, parts listings, and statistical databases of business and economic activity. Interactive educational and industrial training applications have also been developed for CD-ROM disks.

SUMMARY

☐ Figures 6–1, 6–2, and 6–3 should be used to summarize the many types of computer storage discussed in this chapter. These figures show there are many types of storage media and devices, each with their own cost/speed/capacity characteristics. This includes integrated circuit semiconductory memory for primary storage, and magnetic disk, magnetic tape, magnetic bubble, and optical disk devices for secondary storage.

☐ Also introduced in this chapter are the major concepts of firmware, microprograms, direct and sequential access, and virtual memory. Firmware is the permanent storing of programs (software) in ROM circuits (hardware) in primary storage. It also includes the storing of microprograms of elementary machine instructions in ROM circuits of the control unit of the CPU. Direct access devices (like semiconductor

REAL WORLD APPLICATION 6–2

Richard T. Rodgers, Attorney-at-Law

As a lawyer, I've got a lot invested in my computer system. Not just money, but information. Programs, data, and access to specific information when I need it have turned my computer into the cornerstone of my law operation.

As I came to depend on my computer for more of my daily activities, my need for data storage increased proportionately. It wasn't long before I outgrew the storage capacity of my floppy disks. In spite of relentless efforts to keep my floppy disk library organized, I could never be certain that I'd be able to locate the data I needed or the form letter I was looking for.

A hard disk, I thought, would be the answer. One disk could store all my programs and data in one place and keep them from being lost on a little-used floppy. So I transferred everything to a hard disk—spreadsheet, word processing, and database management programs, all my data files, everything. And when the process was complete, I still had nearly 6 million bytes of storage space left. It was just too good to be true.

But now I had the opposite problem. I had to play "Where is it?" on a disk with a massive directory. Although I could use wild-card searches and other tricks that gave me more selective access to the directory contents, locating information was still overwhelming. The situation was even worse when my operator wanted to run something. My hard disk, which was supposed to make life easier for me, actually increased the amount of time I spent messing around in the disk operating system (DOS), pulling directories, and so on. In one stroke, the hard disk had obliterated the neat divisional lines I had established between the floppy disks in my library.

I needed a way to organize my hard disk so I could find and run the programs I wanted without becoming too chummy with the DOS. After some thrashing around, I found I could do it with Profile Plus, my all-purpose database management system. You can probably do the same thing with your own database system. I divided my disk into sections that an operator can invoke by simply pressing one key. The programs and data on my hard disk fall into seven categories. Using these categories, I developed a main menu with these options: Accounting, Word Processing, Information Management, Communication, Substantive System, Games/Recreation and Utilities, and an option to exit to DOS. Each option on the main menu leads to a submenu that I also created. This has saved an enormous amount of time and, as an added benefit, has made the hard disk system easier to use than floppy disks.

Application Questions

☐ Why did Mr. Rodgers switch from floppy disks to a hard disk drive?

☐ What problems arose when he began using a hard disk drive? How did he solve those problems?

Source: Adapted from Richard T. Rodgers, "How to Organize Hard Disk Data," *Popular Computing,* May 1984, p. 123. Reprinted with permission.

memory or magnetic disks) give computers the ability to store and retrieve data in any storage position on a storage medium in approximately the same length of time. Sequential access involves the use of a serial or sequential process to store and retrieve data on a storage medium like magnetic tape. Finally, a virtual memory capability allows computers to treat direct access secondary storage devices as an extension of primary storage. This gives computers a larger effective memory than their real memory capacity.

KEY TERMS AND CONCEPTS

These are the key terms and concepts of this chapter. The page number of their first explanation is in parentheses.

1. CPU storage areas *(222)*
2. Direct access *(224)*
3. Firmware *(223)*
4. Magnetic bubble memory *(239)*
5. Magnetic disks *(232)*
   a. Disk pack or cartridge
   b. Hard disk
   c. Fixed disk
   d. Floppy disk
6. Magnetic disk characteristics *(231)*
   a. Cylinder
   b. Sector
   c. Track

7. Magnetic tape *(237)*
   a. Tape reel
   b. Tape cartridge
   c. Tape cassette
   d. Strip cartridge
8. Microprogramming *(223)*
9. Optical disk storage *(240)*
10. Semiconductor storage *(227)*
11. Sequential access *(224)*
12. Storage media trade-offs *(220)*
13. Types of
    a. RAM *(229)*
    b. ROM *(229)*
14. Virtual memory *(224)*
15. Volatility *(229)*

REVIEW AND APPLICATION QUIZ

Match one of the **key terms and concepts** listed above with one of the brief examples or definitions listed below. Try to find the "best fit" for answers that seem to fit more than one term or concept. Defend your choices.

_____ 1. Storage media cost, speed, and capacity differences.

_____ 2. Storage areas in the arithmetic-logic, control, and primary storage units.

_____ 3. Software is permanently stored in hardware.

_____ 4. You cannot erase the contents of these storage circuits.

_____ 5. You can read and write data on these storage circuits.

_____ 6. Is data lost or retained when power fails?

_____ 7. The use of elementary machine instructions stored in ROM circuits of the control unit.

_____ 8. Each position of storage can be accessed in approximately the same time.

———— 9. Each position of storage can be accessed according to a predetermined order.

———— 10. Secondary storage devices can be treated as an extension of primary storage.

———— 11. Microelectronic storage circuits on silicon chips.

———— 12. Uses magnetic spots on semiconductor chips.

———— 13. Uses magnetic spots on metal or plastic disks.

———— 14. Uses a laser to read microscopic pits on plastic disks.

———— 15. Concentric circles for storing data on magnetic disks.

———— 16. Subdivisions of a track on a magnetic disk.

———— 17. Large capacity, sequential storage devices.

———— 18. Large capacity, fast, removable direct access storage devices for mainframes.

———— 19. Small, inexpensive, and relatively slow direct access storage devices for microcomputers.

———— 20. Use this to add larger, faster magnetic disk storage to a microcomputer.

APPLICATION PROBLEMS

1. If you have not already done so, read and answer the questions after the two Real World Applications in this chapter.

2. Refer to Figure 6–1. Which storage devices are the fastest? Which have the greatest capacity? Which have the lowest cost? Taking cost/speed/capacity trade-offs into consideration, which storage device do you think is the best? Explain.

3. Refer to Figure 6–2. Outline the functions, advantages, and disadvantages of semiconductor, magnetic disk, and magnetic tape storage, and indicate the equipment and the media involved.

4. Refer to Figure 6–3. What are the functions of the following types of CPU storage?
   a. Control storage.   d. Control unit ROM.
   b. Local storage.   e. Primary storage ROM.
   c. RAM storage.   f. Cache storage.

5. Give the biggest advantage of using magnetic disks over magnetic tape. Then give two reasons why one might still use magnetic tape instead of magnetic disks.

6. How would you answer each of the following arguments for using magnetic tape instead of magnetic disk?
   a. No backup files exist when one uses magnetic disk.
   b. Disks are more expensive than tapes.
   c. Disks are too expensive for historical storage.
   d. Disks require the use of terminals.
   e. Disks can be easily damaged by dust and fingerprints.

7. Joan Alvarez, a store manager for ABC Department Stores, is trying to decide whether to replace one of the floppy disk drives on her microcomputer with a 20 MB hard disk drive. She says she needs more storage capacity, but is worried about backing up the files and programs stored on the hard disk. What would you advise Joan to do? Explain your recommendation.

8. Indicate which secondary storage medium you would use for each of the following storage tasks. Select from the choices at the right:
   1. Long-term archival storage.
   2. Small business microcom-
      puter storage.
   3. Personal computer files.
   4. Large files for occasional
      processing.
   5. Secondary storage for
      portable computers.
   6. High-speed secondary
      storage.

   a. Magnetic hard disk
   b. Floppy disk
   c. Magnetic tape
   d. Magnetic bubble
   e. Semiconductor storage
   f. Optical disk

9. Explain the difference between the use of WORM optical disks by financial institutions for image processing and CD-ROM optical disks by business microcomputer users.

C H A P T E R

7

DATABASE CONCEPTS AND APPLICATIONS

Chapter Outline

Learning Objectives

The purpose of this chapter is to promote a basic understanding of how data resources are organized, stored, and accessed in information systems by analyzing basic concepts and applications of file and database processing systems. After reading and studying this chapter, you should be able to:

1. Provide examples to illustrate each of the common data elements.
2. Differentiate between the following concepts:
   a. Physical versus logical elements.
   b. Sequential versus direct file organization.
   c. Sequential access versus direct access file processing.
   d. File processing systems versus database processing systems.
3. Discuss the development and use of database processing systems.
4. Explain the functions of database management system software in terms of users, programmers, and database processing applications.

Section I: Data Organization and File Processing

Just imagine how difficult it would be to get any information from an information system if data and information were stored in an unorganized way, and if there was no systematic way to retrieve them. Therefore, in all information systems, data resources must be organized and structured in some logical manner so that they can be processed efficiently and managed properly. That's why the topics of *data organization, file processing,* and *database processing* are so important. *Data structures* ranging from simple to complex have been devised to logically organize data in information systems. Understanding and implementing these concepts properly is important if a business or other organization wants to do a better job of *information resource management* (IRM). This concept stresses that data and information must be managed as valuable organizational resources. We will discuss the IRM concept further in Chapter 15.

COMMON DATA ELEMENTS

A *hierarchy* of several levels of data has been devised that differentiates between the most simple elements of data and more complex data elements. Thus, data are organized into **characters, fields, records,** and **files,** just as writing may be organized in letters, words, sentences, and paragraphs. We introduced you to these **common data elements** in Chapter 1. Now let's review and expand our knowledge of these concepts. Examples of the common data elements are shown in Figure 7–1.

Figure 7–1 Examples of the common data elements in information processing. Notice especially the examples of data fields, records, files and a database.

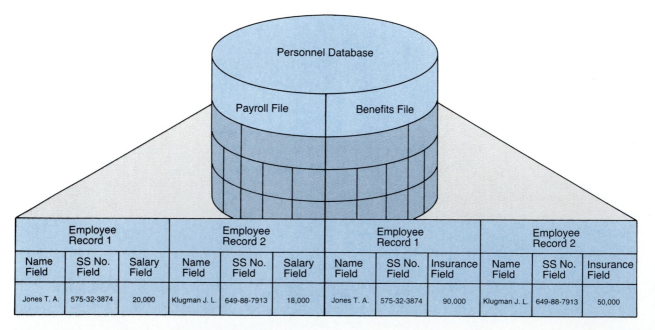

Employee Record 1			Employee Record 2			Employee Record 1			Employee Record 2		
Name Field	SS No. Field	Salary Field	Name Field	SS No. Field	Salary Field	Name Field	SS No. Field	Insurance Field	Name Field	SS No. Field	Insurance Field
Jones T. A.	575-32-3874	20,000	Klugman J. L.	649-88-7913	18,000	Jones T. A.	575-32-3874	90,000	Klugman J. L.	649-88-7913	50,000

The most basic data element is the **character,** which consists of a single alphabetic, numeric, or other symbol. One could argue that the **bit** or **byte** is a more elementary data element. But remember that those terms refer to computer data elements (along with **words**) as explained in Chapter 4. From a user's point of view, the character is the most elementary element of data that he or she can observe and manipulate.

Character

The next higher level of data is the **field.** It consists of a grouping of characters. For example, the grouping of alphabetical characters in a person's name forms a *name field*, and the grouping of numerical characters in a sales amount forms a *sales amount field*. A data field represents an **attribute** (a characteristic or quality) of some **entity** (objects, people, places, or events). For example, a person's age could be a data field that represents one attribute of an individual.

Field

Related fields of data are grouped to form a **record.** Thus a record represents a collection of *attributes* that describes an *entity*. An example is the payroll record for a person, which consists of data fields such as his or her name, social security number, and rate of pay. *Fixed-length* records contain a fixed number of fixed-length data fields. *Variable-length* records may contain a variable number of fields and field-lengths.

Record

A group of related records is known as a data **file**. Thus a *payroll file* would contain the payroll records for all of the employees of a firm. Files are frequently classified by the application for which they are primarily used, such as a *payroll file* or an *accounts receivable file*. Files are also classified by their permanence. For example, a payroll *master file*, as opposed to a payroll *weekly transaction file*. A **transaction file,** therefore, would contain records of all transactions occurring during a period and would be used periodically to update the permanent records contained in a **master file.** A *history file* is an obsolete transaction or master file retained for backup purposes or for long-term historical storage called *archival storage*. A **program file** (as opposed to a data file) is a file that contains a computer program. For example, floppy disks for microcomputer systems are frequently used to store both data files and program files.

File

A **database** is an integrated collection of logically related records or files. A database consolidates records previously stored in separate files into a common pool of data records for many applications. For example, a personnel database consolidates data formerly segregated in separate files such as a payroll file, personnel action file, and employee skills file. The term **data bank** is sometimes used to describe a collection of several databases.

Database

A distinction should be made between "logical" and "physical" data elements. The common data elements just discussed are logical data elements, not physical data elements.

LOGICAL AND PHYSICAL DATA ELEMENTS

Figure 7-2 Examples of logical and physical data elements.

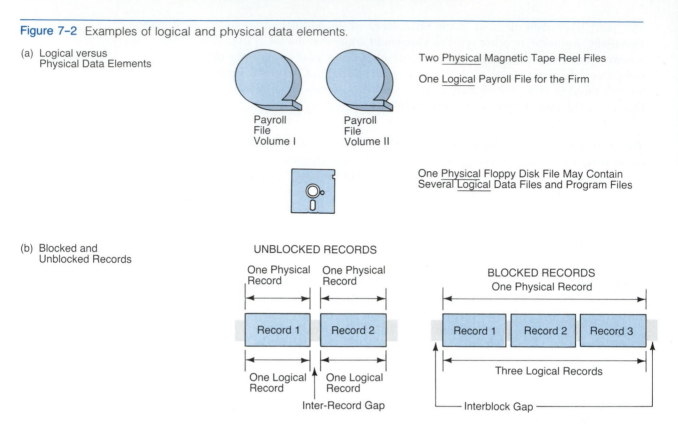

(a) Logical versus
    Physical Data Elements

Two <u>Physical</u> Magnetic Tape Reel Files

One <u>Logical</u> Payroll File for the Firm

Payroll
File
Volume I

Payroll
File
Volume II

One <u>Physical</u> Floppy Disk File May Contain
Several <u>Logical</u> Data Files and Program Files

(b) Blocked and
    Unblocked Records

UNBLOCKED RECORDS

One Physical
Record

One Physical
Record

Record 1   Record 2

One Logical
Record

One Logical
Record

Inter-Record Gap

BLOCKED RECORDS
One Physical Record

Record 1   Record 2   Record 3

Three Logical Records

Interblock Gap

☐ **Physical data elements** are related to the individual physical data media or devices on which logical data elements are recorded. For example, a single reel of magnetic tape or a single magnetic disk each represents a single physical file.

☐ **Logical data elements** are independent of the data media on which they are recorded. For example several reels of magnetic tape (several physical files) may be needed to store the payroll data file (one logical file) of a large business firm. Or several data files and program files (several logical files) may be stored on one floppy disk (one physical file). See Figure 7-2(a).

Another example: A magnetic tape or disk file may contain blank spaces (*gaps*) between groups (*blocks*) of logical records. A block of logical records on magnetic tape or disk is considered a physical record. Interrecord or interblock gaps are required, since a certain amount of blank space between records or blocks is needed to allow for such mechanical operations as the start/stop time of a magnetic tape unit. Most files group logical records into blocks to conserve file space instead of leaving gaps between each logical record. See Figure 7-2(b).

FILE ORGANIZATION: ACCESS AND PROCESSING

Files are stored on various types of storage media and are usually organized in some manner to make it easier to **access** (store, locate, and retrieve) the data records they contain. Let's review several important concepts of file organization, access, and processing.

File Storage Media Sequential access storage devices Direct access storage devices	**File Organization Methods** Sequential organization Direct organization
File Access Methods Sequential Indexed sequential Key transformation Indexed Linked list Inverted file	**File Processing Methods** Sequential access Direct access

Figure 7–3 Important concepts of file media, organization, access, and processing.

☐ In the previous chapter, we described two basic types of storage media, **sequential access storage devices** such as magnetic tape, and **direct access storage devices** (DASDs) such as magnetic disks. Refer back to Figure 6–4 to refresh your memory if necessary. In this chapter, we will discuss several ways that data can be organized, accessed, and processed when stored on such devices.

☐ The data records in a file can be physically organized on a storage device in two basic ways, **sequential file organization** (in a physical sequence next to each other) and **direct file organization** (in no particular physical sequence). The direct file organization is also called the *random* or *nonsequential* method of file organization.

☐ Various methods have been developed to access data records stored in files. These **file access methods** include the *sequential access* method and the *indexed sequential access* method for files organized sequentially, and the *key transformation* method, the *linked list* method, and various *indexing* methods for files using a direct method of organization.

In common usage, file access methods are frequently called **file organization** methods. For example, one popular file access method that is typically called a method of file organization is the *indexed sequential file access method* (ISAM). It is a way to directly access records stored sequentially on a direct access storage device using an index. Thus, file access methods can be viewed as methods that *logically* organize the records in a file. That is why file access methods are frequently referred to as methods of logical file organization. Keep this fact in mind when looking at Figure 7–3, which summarizes some of the major concepts involved in file (and database) organization and processing. We will discuss these concepts and their use in information systems in this chapter. However, let's first explain three basic tools used to help organize data in files and databases.

Key

Each record in a file or database contains one or more identification fields or **keys,** which are used when searching or sorting a file. For example a social security number might be used as the key for identifying each employee's data record in a payroll file.

Pointer

Records may contain other identifying fields (called **pointers**) that help in cross-referencing the contents of a file or database. Thus each record cold contain a *pointer field*, which contains the storage location address of a related record in the file or database. For example, the payroll record of an employee could include the address of the payroll record for another employee who works on the same project.

Index

A file or database may contain an **index,** somewhat similar to an index in a book. The index is a listing of record keys and their associated storage location addresses. It helps locate records in a file or database. For example, an index could consist of a listing of employee social security numbers (record keys) along with the corresponding storage address for each employee's payroll record.

SEQUENTIAL FILE ORGANIZATION AND PROCESSING

Sequential File Organization

One of the basic ways to organize the data in a file is to use a **sequential** methodology. Records can be physically stored in a predetermined sequence. Records are arranged in a specified order according to a record key. For example, payroll records could be placed in a payroll file in a sequential manner according to a numeric order based on employees' social security numbers or an alphabetical order based on employees' last names. The sequential file organization is a simple method of data organization that is fast and efficient when processing large volumes of data that do not need to be processed except on a periodic basis. However, the sequential file organization requires that all records be sorted into the proper sequence before processing. The entire file must be searched to locate, store, or modify even a small number of data records. Thus this method is too slow to handle applications requiring immediate updating or responses.

Sequential Access File Processing

When sequentially organized files are stored on sequential access storage devices, they must be processed using a methodology called **sequential access file processing.** Figure 7–4 is an example that illustrates sequential access file processing.

Notice that the old master file resulting from sequential access file processing can be stored offline and used for backup purposes. Usually, several *generations* of master files are kept for control purposes. Thus, for example, if the sequential access file processing is being done on a weekly basis, master files from the three most recent weeks' processing (known as the *child, parent,* and *grandparent* files) might be kept for backup purposes. Depending on the application, even more backup files might be required.

DIRECT FILE ORGANIZATION AND PROCESSING

Direct File Organization

The **direct** method is also called *random, nonsequential,* or *relative* file organization. Records are physically stored in a file in a random or nonsequential manner; that is, they are not arranged in any particular sequence. However, the computer must keep track of the storage location of each record in the file using such data organization aids as keys, pointers, indexes, and other methods so data can be retrieved when needed. For example, payroll records could be placed in a payroll file in no particular sequence.

Figure 7–4 Sequential access file processing. This is an example of the processing of sequentially organized files stored on sequential access storage devices.

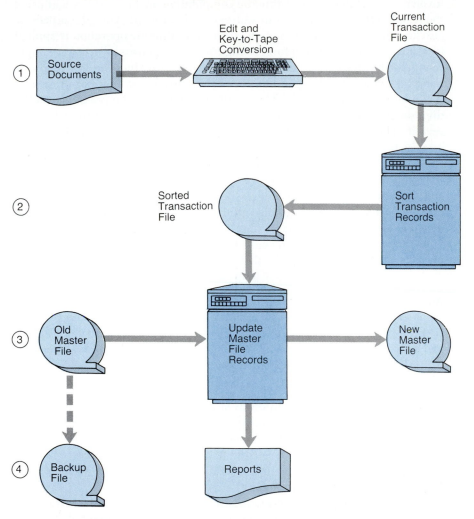

1. The transaction data from source documents (such as sales invoices) are captured and edited for correctness using a key-to-tape device. This records the data on a magnetic tape transaction file.
2. The current transaction file is then sorted into the same sequence as the master file (such as a sales order master file).
3. A master file update program uses the transactions data from the sorted transaction file to update the records in the old master file. This requires sequentially reading the entire master file. A new updated master file is produced, which incorporates all the changes to records that were affected by the data in the transaction file.
4. Various reports are also produced, such as control listings, activity reports, and analytical reports for management. The old master file is usually stored offline for backup purposes.

The computer system could use each record's key field to assign and keep track of the storage locations of each record in the file. In direct file organization, input data does not have to be sorted, and processing that requires immediate responses or updating is easily handled. There are a number of ways to access (assign storage locations, locate, and retrieve) the records in the random file organization. Let's take a look at each of them.

Key Transformation Access Method

One common technique of file access is called **key transformation.** It uses a *transform algorithm* (also called a *randomizing* or *hashing* algorithm), which involves performing some arithmetic computation on a record key and using the result of the calculation as an address for that record. Thus the process is also known as a key transformation, since an arithmetic operation is applied to a key to transform it into a storage location address. To use a simple example, the transform algorithm might involve dividing the key field of a record (such as an employee number) by the maximum number of records that might be stored in a file. The resulting number (or the *remainder* of the division process) would be used as the storage location address for that record. Thus the computer can use record keys and a key transformation process to randomly store and directly locate the data records in a file.

Sometimes the transformation computation results in the same address (the same answer) for two different keys. This occurrence is called a *collision*, and the keys with the same address are called *synonyms*. One method of handling such collisions is to place the record in the next available storage location. To minimize collisions, randomly organized files may be kept only 60 to 70 percent full. Thus the speed of this method of accessing a file must be balanced with the file space that is wasted.

Indexed Access Method

Another basic access method used to store and locate records for a direct file organization involves the use of an index of record keys and related storage addresses. A new record is stored at the next available location and its key and address are placed in an index. The computer uses this index whenever it must access a record. See Figure 7–5.

Indexed Sequential Access Method

In this method, records are physically stored in a sequential order on a direct access storage device (such as a magnetic disk) based on the key field of each record. However, each file also contains an index that references one or more key fields of each data record to its storage location address. Thus any individual record can be directly located by using its key fields to search and locate its address in the file index.

The **indexed sequential access method** (ISAM) combines the advantages of both the sequential and direct file organizations. The sequential organization provided by this method is used when large numbers of records must be processed periodically, as in *batch processing systems*. However, if a few records must be processed quickly (as in *realtime processing*), the file index is used to directly access the records needed. The indexed sequential

Figure 7–5 An example of an index that allows quick access to employee records.

Record Key (Employee number)	Record Address
28541	101
35879	102
47853	103
50917	104

organization does have several disadvantages. It is slower than the direct organization, because the index is usually stored on secondary storage devices and not in main memory. Another disadvantage is the cost of creating, storing, and maintaining the indexes, including the extra storage space this requires.

List Access Method

This method uses pointers to locate related records stored in a nonsequential manner. This data structure is called a **list** (or *linked list*), because pointers (also called *link fields*) are used to express data relationships as *lists* of data records. Each data record contains a pointer field, which gives the address of the next logical record. Thus all logically related records can be linked together by means of pointers. A grouping of records related by pointers is called a *list*, or *chain*. Since the records in a file can have many possible relationships (for example, employees' ages, sex, or department), each record can contain several pointers. These pointers form chains throughout the file or database. This allows records with the same particular attributes (such as all male employees over age 55) to be located. See Figure 7–6.

In many cases, an index containing the addresses of the first record in each list is used. The pointer in the first record will point to the address of the next logical record in the list, thus allowing the computer to follow a chain of pointers to locate related records in a file. A pointer field may also

Figure 7–6 An example of pointers linking records within a file and between two files. Notice how pointers can link an employee record in a personnel file with the same employee's record in the payroll file, as well as linking the records of employees who belong to the same department.

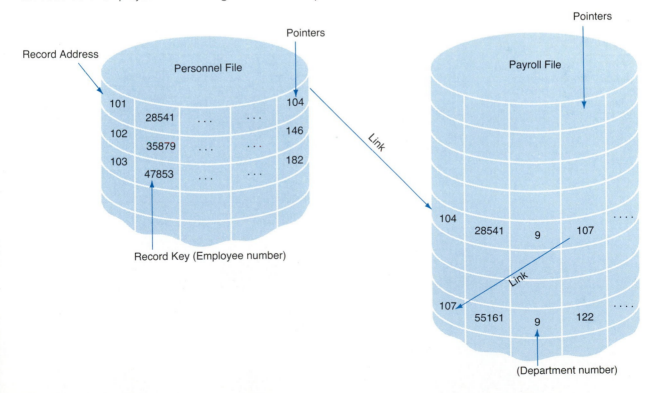

indicate the address of a related record in another file. For example, the payroll record for an employee in the payroll file might include a pointer linking it to the same employee's record in a personnel action file. Thus the list organization uses pointers to easily access records having multiple relationships. A disadvantage of this method is that pointers may become too numerous and the lists or chains may become too long, thus increasing access time and storage requirements.

Inverted File Access Method

This approach uses an index called an **inverted file.** Each inverted file lists the addresses or keys for all records having the same attribute. For example, an inverted index might indicate the record addresses of all employees between the ages of 18 to 25, 26 to 30, 31 to 35, and so forth. Several inverted files might be needed if we wish to locate the records for many alternatives (such as age, gender, or marital status). Thus inverted files greatly facilitate searching a file for records sharing many attributes. However, this advantage is attained at the cost of creating, storing, and continually updating multiple inverted files. The data needed to express relationships and addresses of the records referenced by inverted files is known as *overhead data.* Such overhead data may be several times as great as the original data it describes! Figure 7–7 provides an inverted file example.

Direct Access File Processing

We have now explained several major ways that the records in files can be accessed directly. Such files are processed, using **direct access file processing** methods similar to the example illustrated in Figure 7–8.

Figure 7–7 An inverted file example. An inverted file helps access records sharing similar attributes, such as age categories.

Portion of Personnel File			Inverted File by Age	
Record Address	Employee Number	Age	Age	Record Address
101	28541	43	18–25	104, . . .
102	35879	27	26–35	102, 103, . . .
103	47853	32	36–45	101, . . .
104	50917	24		

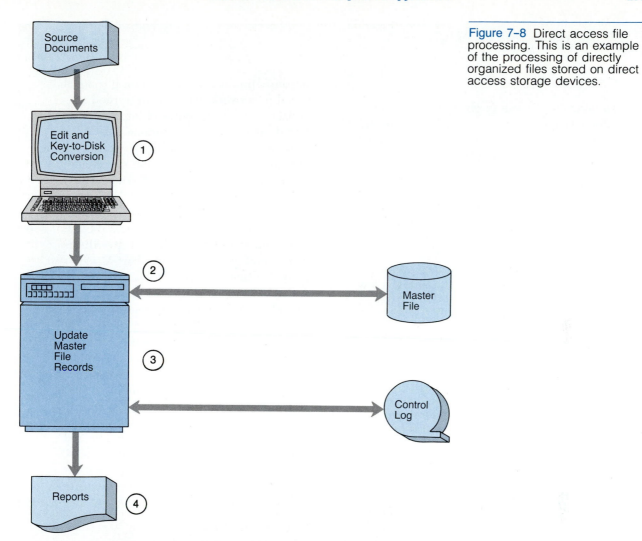

Figure 7-8 Direct access file processing. This is an example of the processing of directly organized files stored on direct access storage devices.

1. Input source documents, such as sales orders or sales invoices, are edited and entered into the system. A key-to-disk conversion process using a *data entry* terminal with a keyboard and video display is used.
2. Since a direct access master file is used, there is no need to sort input data before updating the master file. Thus the master file is immediately updated.
3. Direct access file processing does not result in old master files that can be used for backup purposes. Therefore, backup copies of the direct access files are obtained by periodically copying of *dumping* the contents of a direct access file to a magnetic tape file. This backup file is then stored for *control* purposes. Another method is to keep a magnetic tape *control log*, which records all transactions.
4. The master file update program also produces several reports, such as control listings, summary reports, exception reports, and analytical reports for management.

REAL WORLD APPLICATION 7–1

Simmonds Precision Company

The ongoing pursuit of obtaining and managing information often puts personal computer users in large companies face to face with the limits of desktop technology: It doesn't all fit in the box. The multiple megabytes of memory and hard disk storage in the most accommodating of personal computers can't begin to herd the gigabytes (and beyond) of data moving through many corporations. But that's what the company mainframe computer is for—so the information you need, carved into portions your database can digest, is stored just a few keystrokes away. Thus your desktop database management program can become the window through which you view—and manipulate—a vast universe of information.

Quality control engineers at Simmonds Precision, a Vermont manufacturer of fuel measurement devices for military and commercial aircraft, require such a window. In tracking the testing and repair of fuel gauge systems, engineers in Simmonds' product assurance department use the IMS database management system software to draw upon the company's huge database of customer records and equipment history that resides in its IBM mainframe computer system. The selective retrieval of mainframe information enables them to use database management software like dBASE III Plus and R:base System V on their IBM and COMPAQ personal computers to produce test reports for internal and external review.

Typically, a faulty fuel gauge system is returned by an aircraft manufacturer like Boeing or McDonnell Douglas to Simmonds. The company's product support group fills out the needed paperwork, which is forwarded to the data center to be entered into the sales order database on the mainframe. The exact nature of the problem and the corrective action taken are entered into the same mainframe database by each engineer. All data entries are accomplished with the aid of the IMS software. Finally, drawing on the base of customer history in the mainframe, engineers use the sorting and reporting features of dBASE or R:base—and the graphics of Chart-Master—to summarize their findings. These reports tell customers what is being done about the problem and enable company managers to better assess equipment failures.

In addition to acting as a funnel for a sea of vital information, the microcomputer-to-mainframe connection at Simmonds ensures that the resulting reports are complete and accurate, according to Dave Fredenburg, the department's data systems manager. Without the communication between mainframe and personal computer, he says, engineers (and other workers) could not access updated records from the company "bible"—the central database on the mainframe.

Application Questions

☐ Use this example to explain why microcomputer users may need to access a central database on a mainframe computer system.

☐ Explain the roles of the mainframe and microcomputer database management software packages in this example.

Source: Christopher O'Malley, "Call in the Mainframe," *Personal Computing,* January 1986, p. 105.

Section II: Database Processing Systems

How would you feel if you were an executive of a computer-using company and were told that some information you wanted about some of your employees was too difficult and too costly to obtain? Suppose the vice president of information services gave you the following reasons:

☐ The information you want is stored in several different files, each organized in a different way.

☐ Each file has been organized to be used by a different application program, none of which produces the information you want in the form you need.

☐ No application program is available to help get such information from these files.

Figure 7–9 shows a summary of the information you want and its related files and programs.

As a company executive, you would probably be frustrated and disenchanted with computer-based processing if it could not provide you with information for such a simple request. Well, that's how users are frequently frustrated by file processing systems, such as those described in the previous section. Data are organized, stored, and processed in *independent files* when file processing systems are used. In **database processing systems,** on the other hand, files are consolidated into a common pool of records available to many different application programs. In addition, an important system software package called a **database management system** (DBMS) serves as a software interface between users and databases. This helps users easily access the records in a database. For example, if all data about an employee were stored in a common database, you could use the query language feature of a DBMS and a computer terminal to easily obtain the employee information you want. See Figure 7–10.

REASONS FOR DATABASE PROCESSING

For many years, information systems had the file processing orientation illustrated in the previous example. Data needed for each user application was stored in independent data files. Processing consisted of using separate computer programs that updated these independent data files and used them to produce the documents and reports required by each separate user

Information Requested	File	Application Program
Employee Salary	Payroll File	Payroll Program
Educational Background	Employee Skills File	Skills Inventory Program
Salary Increases and Promotions	Personnel Action File	Personnel Action Program

Figure 7–9 An example of independent files and programs for information on employees.

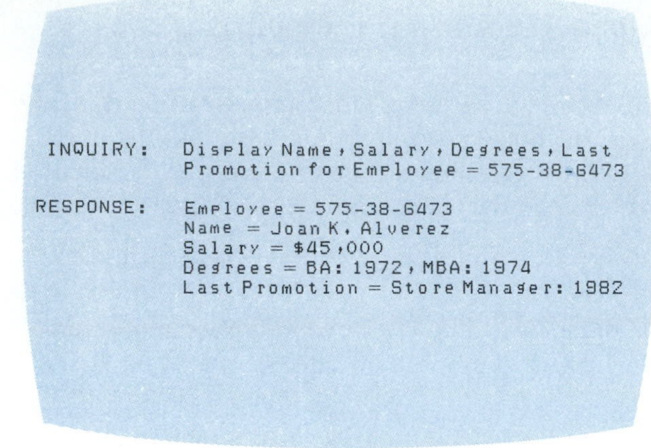

Figure 7-10 An example of
inquiry and response using a
database management system
program and a common
employee database (instead
of independent files and
programs).

```
INQUIRY:     Display Name, Salary, Degrees, Last
             Promotion for Employee = 575-38-6473

RESPONSE:    Employee = 575-38-6473
             Name  = Joan K. Alverez
             Salary = $45,000
             Degrees = BA: 1972, MBA: 1974
             Last Promotion = Store Manager: 1982
```

application. This file processing approach is still being used, but has several
major problems that limit the efficiency and effectiveness of computer-based
information systems.

Duplication of Data

Independent data files include a lot of duplicated data. The same data (such
as a customer's name and address) was recorded and stored in several files.
This *data redundancy* caused problems when data had to be updated, since
separate *file maintenance* programs had to be developed and coordinated to
insure that each file was properly updated. This was a time-consuming and
costly process, which increased the secondary storage space requirements of
computer systems.

Unintegrated Data

Independent data files made it difficult to provide users with information
that required processing data stored in several different files. Special computer programs would have to be written to retrieve data from each independent file. This was so difficult, time-consuming, and costly for some
organizations that it was impossible to provide users or management with
such information. Some users had to manually extract the required information from the various reports produced by each separate application.

Program/Data Dependence

Computer programs typically contained references to the specific *format* of
data stored in the files that they used. Thus any changes to the format and
structure of data and records in a file required that changes be made to all of
the programs that used that file. This *program maintenance* effort, due to
changes to the format of data, is a major burden of file processing systems.

THE DATABASE PROCESSING CONCEPT

The concepts of **databases** and **database processing** were developed to solve
the problems of file processing systems. We have defined a database as an
integrated collection of logically related records or files. It consolidates
records previously stored in independent files, so that it serves as a common

pool of data to be accessed by many different application programs. The data stored in a database is independent of the computer programs using it and of the type of secondary storage devices on which it is stored. Database processing sytems are information systems that use databases for both the *storage* and *processing* of data.

Common databases are developed in the database processing approach. *Data structures* are used to organize the data to ensure integrity, consistency, processing efficiency, and reliability. The data needed by many different applications in an organization are consolidated and integrated into several of these common databases, instead of being stored in many independent data files. For example, customer records and other common data are needed for several different applications in banking, such as check processing, automated teller systems, bank credit cards, savings accounts, and installment loan accounting. This data can be consolidated into a common customer database, rather than being kept in separate files for each of those applications.

Database Storage

Information processing no longer consists of updating and using independent data files to produce information needed for each user's application. Instead, information processing consists of three basic activities:

Database Processing

- ☐ Updating and maintaining a common database.
- ☐ Providing information needed for each user's application by using computer programs that share the data in the common database. This is accomplished through a common *software interface* provided by a **database management system** (DBMS) package.
- ☐ Providing an inquiry/response capability through a DBMS package so users can easily interrogate the database and receive quick responses to their requests for information.

Figures 7–11 and 7–12 contrast the file processing and database processing approaches with examples from the banking industry.

Let's take a closer look at the capabilities provided by database management systems. We said in Chapter 3 that a database management system is a set of computer programs that control the creation, maintenance, and use of the databases of computer users. A DBMS is a software package that provides a vital software interface between users and their computerized databases. Figure 7–13 illustrates the components of a typical DBMS.

DATABASE MANAGEMENT SYSTEMS

A database management system works in conjunction with the data management programs of an operating system, which are primarily concerned with the physical transfer of data during processing. Advanced computer systems may even use a *back-end processor* or *database machine*, which is a special-purpose computer that contains the DBMS. The four major uses of a DBMS are illustrated in Figure 7–14.

Figure 7–11 Examples of file processing systems in banking. Notice the use of separate computer programs and independent data files in a file processing approach to the savings, installment loan, and checking account applications.

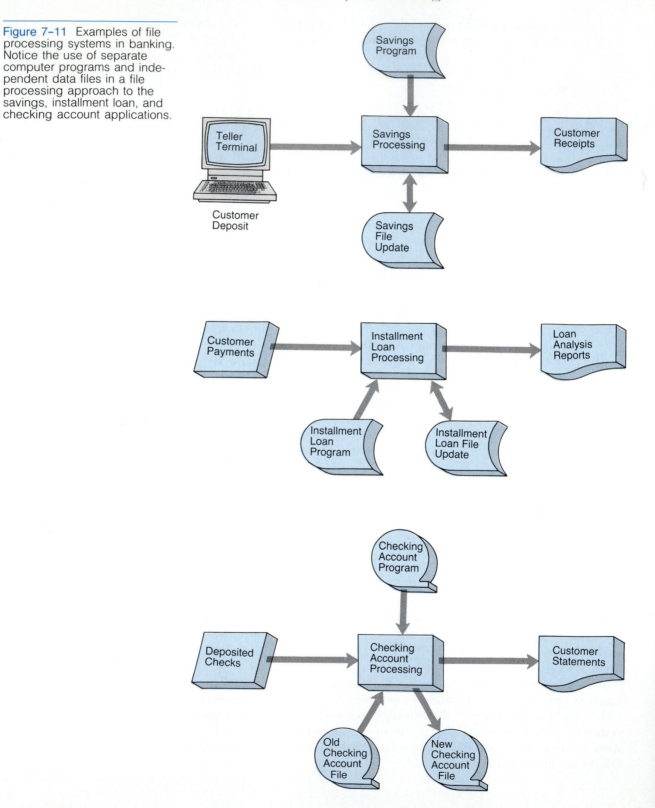

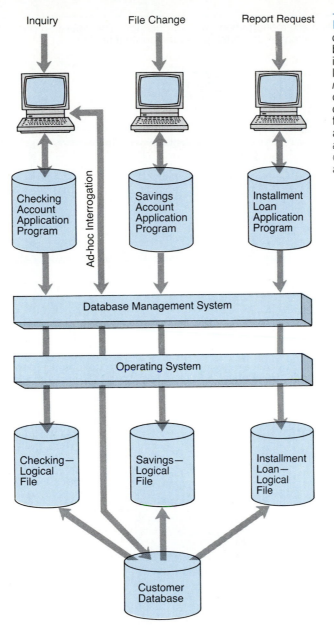

Inquiry   File Change   Report Request

Ad-hoc Interrogation

Checking Account Application Program

Savings Account Application Program

Installment Loan Application Program

Database Management System

Operating System

Checking— Logical File

Savings— Logical File

Installment Loan— Logical File

Customer Database

Figure 7–12 An example of a database processing system in banking. Notice how the savings, checking, and installment loan programs use a *database management system* to share a customer database, as if it were organized into separate logical files. Note also that the DBMS allows a user to make a direct *ad hoc interrogation* of the database without using an application program.

Figure 7-13 Components of a database management system package. This figure emphasizes that a DBMS is a system of programs that perform a variety of database management functions.

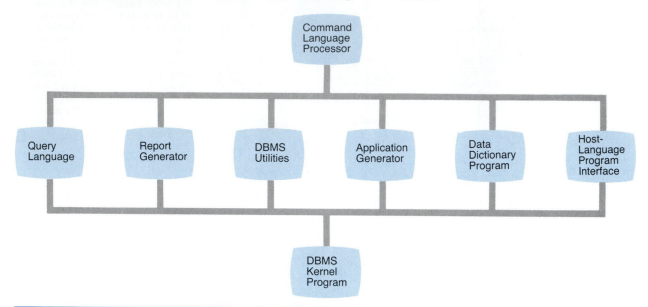

Figure 7-14 The four major uses of a DBMS package: (1) database interrogation and reporting, (2) application programming, (3) database access and maintenance, and (4) database creation and modification.

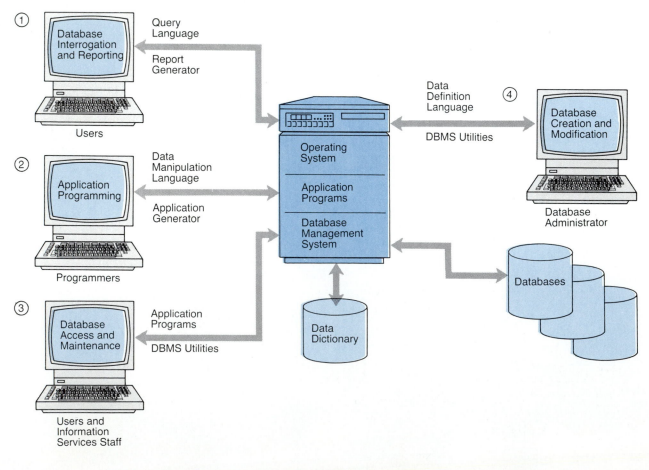

1. Database Interrogation and Reporting

End users can use a DBMS by asking for information from a database using a simple Englishlike **query languge** or a **report generator.** They can receive an immediate response in the form of video displays or printed reports. No difficult programming is required. This database processing capability is a major benefit to ordinary end users. The query language feature lets you easily obtain immediate responses to spontaneous inquiries: You merely key in a few short inquiries on a microcomputer or computer terminal. The report generator feature allows you to quickly specify a report format for information you want presented as a report. See Figure 7–15.

Figure 7–15 Examples of using query languages and a report generator. Notice how computers can understand conversational inquiries and respond with appropriate displays of information. Also notice how you can specify the format of a report without programming, and then have it produced by a report generator.

Using a natural mainframe query language: INTELLECT.

Using a natural microcomputer query language: CLOUT.

Using a report generator from dBASE III Plus.

The report produced.

Figure 7–16 Data manipulation language statements and a DBMS application generator.

Using data manipulation language statements in a COBOL program segment. These are COBOL/DL Data Manipulation Language statements of the Datacom/DB database management system.

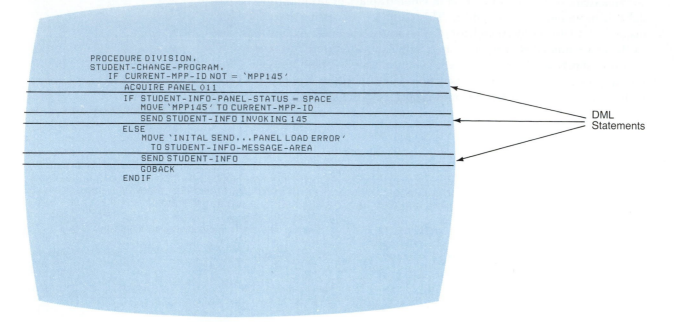

```
PROCEDURE DIVISION.
STUDENT-CHANGE-PROGRAM.
   IF CURRENT-MPP-ID NOT = 'MPP145'
      ACQUIRE PANEL 011
   IF STUDENT-INFO-PANEL-STATUS = SPACE
      MOVE 'MPP145' TO CURRENT-MPP-ID
      SEND STUDENT-INFO INVOKING 145
   ELSE
      MOVE 'INITAL SEND...PANEL LOAD ERROR'
         TO STUDENT-INFO-MESSAGE-AREA
      SEND STUDENT-INFO
      GOBACK
   ENDIF
```

DML
Statements

Using a DBMS application generator: Applications EXPRESS from R:base System V. In this example, a user is going to develop or modify an Order Entry program by responding to a series of menus, prompts, and formatted screens. The application generator will generate the required program code.

```
══════════ Classical Computer Company ══════════

              (1) Order Entry
              (2) Invoicing
              (3) Inventory Tracking
              (4) Print Sales Reports
              (5) Exit


═══════ Select action for this menu selection ═══════

 Load  Edit  Delete  Modify  Select  Print  Custom  Macro  Template
 Menu  Password  Exit


    [F3] Review [F5] Reset value [F10] Help


 Database COMPUCO —Changing Application Compco —Menu MAIN
```

2. Application Programming

A DBMS facilitates the job of programmers, since they do not have to develop detailed data-handling procedures using a conventional programming language (a *host* language, such as COBOL) each time they write a program. Instead, they can include several simple *data manipulation language* (DML) statements in their application programs, which let the DBMS perform necessary data-handling activities. Programmers can also use the internal programming language provided by many DBMS packages or a built-in application generator program to develop complete application programs. Figure 7–16 shows a sample of DML statements in an actual COBOL program segment and the use of an application generator.

3. Database Access and Maintenance

Users and the information services department can access and update the data in selected databases of an organization. This is accomplished by the use of business application programs containing DML statements or various *utilities* (specialized service programs), which are provided by the DBMS.

4. Database Creation and Modification

A DBMS removes the major databases of an organization from the control of individual programmers and computer users. Responsibility for them is placed in the hands of a specialist called a **database administrator** (DBA) and other *data administration* specialists. This improves the integrity and security of the databases. The database administrator uses a data definition language (DDL) to specify the content, relationships, and structure of each database and to modify it when necessary. Such information is cataloged and stored in a file called a **data dictionary** (see Figure 7–17), which is maintained by the DBA. Figure 7–18 lists some of the popular DBMS programs available today.

Microcomputer DBMS Packages

As we said in Chapter 3, many database management packages are available for microcomputer systems. A lot of them are really file management programs, and not true database management systems. They allow users to set up files of data records on their personal computer systems. Most DBMS microcomputer packages are used to perform three primary jobs:

- ☐ Create and maintain (change or update) data files.
- ☐ Selectively retrieve and dispay records from one or more files to provide users with information they need.
- ☐ Print information from these files in various formats to provide printed reports and documents.

Some DBMS microcomputer packages provide a fourth major capability. They contain their own built-in programming language or application generator that allows users to develop programs that use the database for more complex jobs. For example, users can develop programs for inventory,

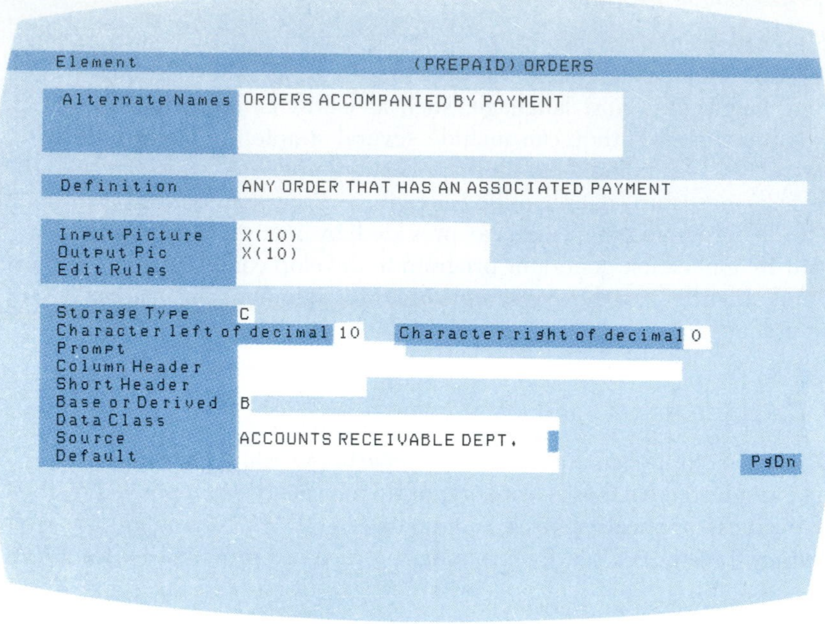

Figure 7–17 A display of part of the information in a data dictionary for an accounts receivable application.

```
Element                        (PREPAID) ORDERS

Alternate Names  ORDERS ACCOMPANIED BY PAYMENT


Definition       ANY ORDER THAT HAS AN ASSOCIATED PAYMENT

Input Picture    X(10)
Output Pic       X(10)
Edit Rules

Storage Type     C
Character left of decimal 10    Character right of decimal 0
Prompt
Column Header
Short Header
Base or Derived  B
Data Class
Source           ACCOUNTS RECEIVABLE DEPT.
Default                                                    PgDn
```

Figure 7–18 Examples of current database management system packages.

Microcomputer DBMS	Supplier
dBASE III Plus	Ashton-Tate
Knowledgeman 2	Micro Data Base Systems
Paradox	Ansa
R:base System V	Microrim
Reflex	Borland
Mainframe DBMS	**Supplier**
ADABAS	Software AG
DATACOM DB	Applied Data Research
IDMS, IDMS-R, SUPRA	Cullinet
IMS, SQL/DS, DB2	IBM
Model 204	Computer Corp. of America
RAMIS II	Mathematica
System 2000	Intel
TIS, TOTAL	Cincom

payroll, and accounting systems involving multiple files, menu-driven input, and complex reports. Refer back to Figure 3–7 in Chapter 3 and page 28 of the pictorial section in Chapter 1 for examples of DBMS packages in use. Appendix A at the back of this book includes a section, "Doing Database Management and Report Generation," that shows you how to use such packages.

The databases of many organizations are collections of integrated records and files involving complex record relationships. They use many variations of the data organization and access methods we described in the first section of this chapter. The relationships between the many individual records stored in databases are based on one of several *logical data structures* or *models.* Database management system packages are designed to use a specific data structure to provide computer users with quick and easy access to information stored in both small and large databases. The three fundamental database structures or models are **hierarchical, network,** and **relational.** Simplified illustrations of these three database structures are shown in Figure 7–19.

DATABASE STRUCTURES

In the **hierarchical** model, the relationships between records form a *hierarchy* or *tree* structure. In this structure, all records are dependent and arranged in multilevel structures, consisting of one *root* record and any number of *subordinate* levels. Thus all of the relationships between records are *one-to-many*, since each data element is related to several records below it, but only one data element is above it. The data element or record at the highest level of the hierarchy (the *department* data element in this illustration) is called the *root* and is the point of entry into the hierarchy. Data elements are stored and located by moving progressively downward from a root and along the *branches* of the tree until the desired record (for example, the employee data element) is located.

Hierarchical Structure

The **network** model can represent more complex logical relationships. It allows *many-to-many* relationships between records. Thus the network structure allows entry into a database at multiple points, because any data element or record can be related to any number of other data elements. For example, in Figure 7–19, departmental records can be related to more than one employee record, and employee records can be related to more than one project record. Thus one could locate all employee records for a particular department, or all project records related to a particular employee.

Network Structure

The **relational** model is the most recent of the three database structures. It was developed in an attempt to simplify the representation of relationships between data elements in large databases. In this approach, all data elements within the database are viewed as being stored in the form of simple tables. Figure 7–19 illustrates the relational database model with two tables representing some of the relationships among departmental and employee records. Other tables or *relations* for this organization's database might represent the data element relationships between projects, divisions, product lines, and so on. Database management system packages based on the relational model can link data elements from various tables to provide information to users. Such relational DBMS packages are the fastest growing segment of the market for microcomputer, minicomputer, and mainframe database management software.

Relational Structure

Figure 7–19 Examples of three fundamental database structures. They represent three basic ways to develop and express the relationships among the data elements in a database.

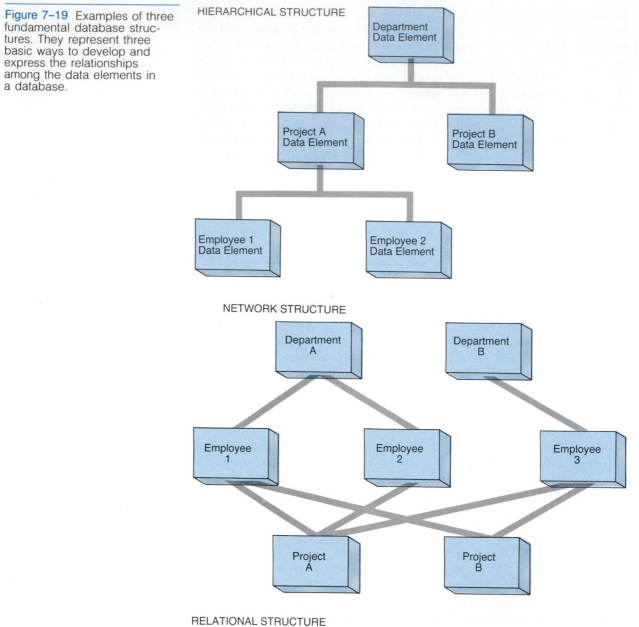

HIERARCHICAL STRUCTURE

Department
Data Element

Project A
Data Element

Project B
Data Element

Employee 1
Data Element

Employee 2
Data Element

NETWORK STRUCTURE

Department
A

Department
B

Employee
1

Employee
2

Employee
3

Project
A

Project
B

RELATIONAL STRUCTURE

Department Records

Dept No	D Name	D Loc	D Mgr
Dept A			
Dept B			
Dept C			

Employee Records

Emp No	E Name	E Title	E Salary	Dept No
Emp 1				Dept A
Emp 2				Dept A
Emp 3				Dept B
Emp 4				Dept B
Emp 5				Dept C
Emp 6				Dept B

Developing small personal databases is easy using microcomputer database management packages. You will see this for yourself if you use the database management tutorial in Appendix A at the back of this book. However, developing a large database based on the hierarchical and network models is a complex task. Even the more simple relational model may require the development of hundreds of tables of record relationships in a large database. So there is much work to do by users, programmers, and systems analysts. In many companies, developing and managing the database is the primary responsibility of a **database administrator** (DBA), and database design analysts. They work with users, programmers, and analysts to determine what data should be included in the database and what structure or relationships exist between the data elements. Figure 7–20 outlines the major stages of logical database design.

DEVELOPING A DATABASE

Figure 7–20 The steps in designing a major database for an organization.

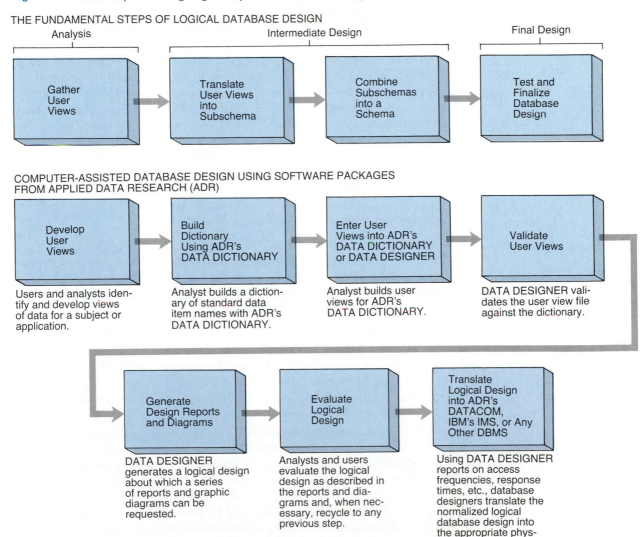

Schema

Defining the structure of the logical relationships between data in a database results in the development of a database **schema.** The schema is an overall *conceptual* or *logical* view of the relationships between the data in the database. For example, the schema would describe what types of data elements (fields, records, files, etc.) are in the database, the relationships between the data elements (pointer fields, linking records, etc.), and the structure of data relationships (hierarchical, network, or relational database structures).

Subschema

Once the schema is designed and documented, a **subschema** must be designed for each user application program that will access the database. A subschema is typically a subset of the database schema. However, it may also contain field and record types not described in the schema. Obviously, each program does not have to access the entire database, but only a portion (subschema) of its logical data elements and relationships. For example, the subschema for a bank's checking account program would not include all of the record types and relationships in a customer database but only those records and files that were related to the operation and management of the checking account activity.

It must be emphasized that both the schema and subschema are *logical* views of the data and relationships of the database. The *physical* view of the data (also called the *internal view*) describes how data is physically arranged, stored, and accessed on secondary storage devices of a computer system. The actual physical arrangement of data (such as their storage locations on a magnetic disk unit) may be quite different from the logical data relationships defined in the schema and subschema (frequently called *user's views*). The physical arrangement and placement of data on secondary storage devices is one of the primary tasks performed by the data management programs of an operating system. Figure 7–21 shows the multiple database views and software interface of a bank database processing system.

TYPES OF DATABASES

The growth of distributed processing, microcomputer-based executive work-stations, and decision support systems has caused the development of several major types of databases. Figure 7–22 illustrates five major types of databases for computer-using organizations:

☐ **Common operational databases.** These databases store detailed data generated by the operations of the entire organization. Thus they are also called *transaction* databases or *production* databases. Examples might include a customer database, personnel database, accounting database, and other common databases containing data generated by business operations.

☐ **Common user databases.** These databases store data and information extracted from selected operational and external databases. They consist of summarized data and information most needed by the organization's managers and other end users. Thus they are also called *information* databases or *management* databases. These are the common databases accessed by personal computer/executive workstation users as part of the *decision support systems* (DSS) that support managerial decision making, discussed in Chapter 9.

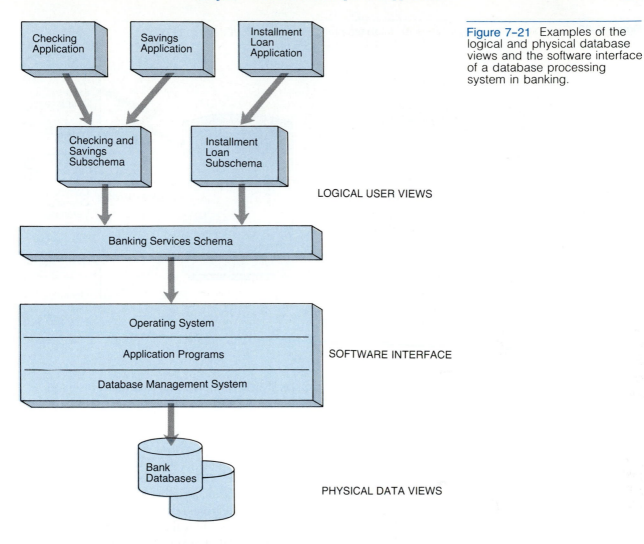

Figure 7-21 Examples of the logical and physical database views and the software interface of a database processing system in banking.

□ **Distributed local databases.** These are databases at local work-places, such as regional offices, branch offices, and manufacturing plants. These databases can include segments of both common operational and common user databases, as well as data generated and used only at a user's own site. The next section discusses several important concepts of such **distributed databases.**

□ **Personal user databases.** These local databases consist of a variety of data files developed by personal computer/executive workstation users to support their individual professional activities. For exam-ple, they may have their own electronic copies of documents they have generated by using word processing packages or received by electronic mail. Or they may have their own data files generated from using electronic spreadsheet and microcomputer DBMS packages.

□ **External databases.** Access to large, privately owned databases is available for a fee to computer users. These **data banks** contain a wealth of economic information that can help support the manage-

Figure 7–22 Examples of the major types of databases that an organization can have.

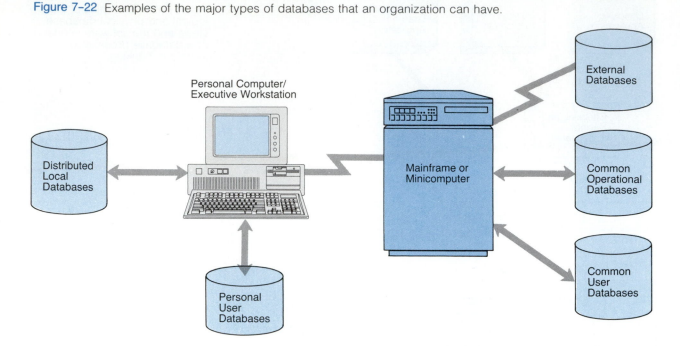

ment of an organization if it is properly analyzed and presented. The types of information provided by such data banks will be discussed in Chapter 8.

Distributed Databases

The concept of **distributed databases** is a major consideration when developing databases for an organization that uses *distributed processing systems.* As we mentioned in Chapter 4, data as well as computing power must be distributed to the user departments in an organization. Thus data that needs to be used and processed only at a user's site (called *local data*) is stored in *local databases,* while data needed by all or several of the local and central computer systems (called *global data*) is frequently stored in *common databases.* However, part or all of the common database can be duplicated at one or more local sites. Thus global data can be *centralized* in one common database, or *partitioned* into *segments* that are distributed to several processing sites. Also, all or part of the global data in the common database can be duplicated and distributed to various processing sites.

Obviously, any of these methods of distributing databases has its advantages and disadvantages and requires careful planning and design. For example, centralizing all global data is the simplest arrangement but may involve potential problems of performance and reliability, since all computers in the network are dependent on the computer system where the common database is stored. These problems can be eliminated if the global data are replicated and copies of the data are distributed to several processing sites. However, this arrangement involves potential problems in insuring that all copies of the global data are properly and concurrently updated every time they are affected by transactions or other changes. The complex

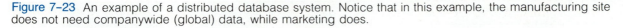

Figure 7–23 An example of a distributed database system. Notice that in this example, the manufacturing site does not need companywide (global) data, while marketing does.

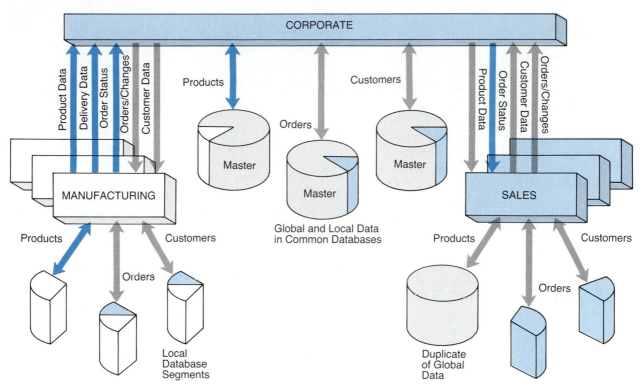

database management software required is still not fully developed. Thus developing a distributed database system frequently requires trade-offs between service to users, processing and communications costs, and processing performance and control. See Figure 7–23.

Text databases are a natural outgrowth of the use of computers to create and store documents electronically in *word processing systems*. They are also a result of the development of commercial *data banks* of business, economic, and other information stored in large text databases or provided on CD-ROM optical disks. Major corporations and government agencies have developed large mainframe computer-based text databases of documents of all kinds. They use **text database management systems** software to help them create, store, search, retrieve, modify, and assemble documents stored as text data in such databases. Microcomputer versions of such software have also been developed to help users manage their own text databases. Such *text management* applications are part of the *automated office systems* discussed in Chapter 12.

Several advantages of database processing systems have already been mentioned. Database processing systems reduce the duplication of data and integrate data so they can be accessed by multiple programs and users.

Text Databases

ADVANTAGES AND DISADVANTAGES

REAL WORLD APPLICATION 7–2

Citicorp, Inc.

Tony Peters, vice president and product manager for municipal leasing at Citicorp in New York, uses his database management package to help him develop and sell capital equipment financing agreements to investors. This process requires a number of complex calculations, including present value, rates of return, and profit margins on resale. It also requires a great deal of cross-checking to locate leases that satisfy all of a potential investor's requirements.

"In a typical case," Peters says, "an investor might tell me he's looking for deals in the $1 million to $5 million range that have a remaining lease life of five to seven years, but then add that they can only be located in California.

Current database management packages are ideal for this sort of inquiry because they let you dictate so many conditions of data retrieval information that meet specific criteria. "I have one screen," Peters says, "where I can select up to 15 different parameters and, even at that, I don't think I'm operating near the limit."

Thanks to a command statement in dBASE III Plus, Peters can perform conditional calculations on records and include the results in a report. When he creates a report on leases that are resale prospects, this capability lets him set up "if/then" conditions for math operations like monthly payments. "I can use this statement to have the program automatically check the total dollar value of contracts included in a report," says Peters. "And then, depending on the size of the contract, either divide the total value by the number of months or else plug in the minimum monthly payment we require for any contract under $100,000."

Developing calculations this way lets Peters look at factors like his own cost and profit requirements in relation to deals meeting customer specifications. "It is just a nifty feature, being able to combine all of this in one report," Peters says. "Before, I would have needed at least two separate reports to get the same kind of information."

And Peters' secretary can design a report with nothing more than "a little direction. It is a point, sketch, and drag kind of system," says Peters. "After you have your database set up, all your fields are listed down one side of the screen and all you have to do is point at the one you want and drag it over to the proper location."

Application Questions

☐ Explain how Tony Peters' database management package helps him in (1) data retrieval, (2) conditional report calculations, and (3) report generation.

☐ What benefits can you see in this example?

Source: Joanne Kelleher, "Data Bases: Why They're Finally Usable," *Personal Computing*, October 1986, p. 85.

Programs are not dependent on the format of data and the type of secondary storage hardware being used. Users are provided with an inquiry/response capability that allows them to easily obtain information they need without having to write computer programs. Computer programming is simplified, because programs are not dependent on either the logical format of data or its physical storage location. Finally, control and security of the data stored in databases can be increased, since all access to data is controlled by a database management system and a database administrator.

Disadvantages and limitations of database processing systems arise from the increased complexity of the database concept. Developing a large database and installing a DBMS can be difficult and expensive. It is not a simple or easy task. More hardware capability is required, since storage requirements for the organization's data, overhead control data, and the DBMS programs are greater. Finally, if an organization relies on one central database, its vulnerability to errors and failures is increased. We will discuss the major *information resource management* challenge this poses to the managers of computer-using organizations in Chapters 15 and 17.

SUMMARY

☐ Data must be organized in some logical manner so that it can be efficiently processed. Thus data is commonly organized into characters, fields, records, files, and databases, and can be described as either physical or logical elements. Data files can be organized in either a sequential or direct manner, and files can be processed by either sequential access or direct access file processing methods.

☐ Access methods for the two basic file organization methods include the indexed sequential access method, in which records are organized sequentially but referenced by an index; the list file organization, which uses pointers to locate related records stored in a nonsequential manner; and the inverted file access method. Database structures are used to organize the complex relations between the individual records stored in large databases. Three fundamental database structures are the hierarchical, network, and relational models.

☐ For many years, information processing had a file processing orientation, in which separate computer programs were used to update independent data files and produce the documents and reports required by each user application. This caused problems of data duplication, unintegrated data, and program/data dependence. The concepts of databases and database processing were developed to solve these problems.

☐ Database processing systems use databases for both the storage and processing of data. The data needed by different applications is consolidated and integrated into several common databases, instead of being stored in many independent data files. Also, information processing consists of updating and maintaining a common database, having users' application programs share the data in the database, and providing an inquiry/response capability so users can easily receive quick responses to requests for information.

☐ Database management systems are software packages that simplify the creation, use, and maintenance of databases by users. They provide a software interface between users and programmers and databases.

☐ Developing a large database is a complex task that is the responsibility of users, programmers, systems analysts, and the database administrator. The schema or structure of the logical relationships between data elements in the database must be developed, as well as the subschema, which is a subset of the schema required of a particular user application.

□ Several types of databases can exist in computer-using organizations. They include a variety of central, local, user, and external databases.

□ Developing distributed databases requires trade-offs between service to users, processing and communications costs, and processing performance and control.

KEY TERMS AND CONCEPTS

These are the key terms and concepts of this chapter. The page number of their first explanation is in parentheses.

1. Common data elements (248)
   a. Character
   b. Field
   c. Record
   d. File
   e. Database
2. Data bank (249)
3. Data dictionary (267)
4. Data organization aids (251)
   a. Key
   b. Pointer
   c. Index
5. Database administrator (267)
6. Database management system (261)
7. Database processing (261)
8. Database structures (269)
   a. Hierarchical
   b. Network
   c. Relational
9. Direct access file processing (256)
10. Distributed databases (274)
11. File organization (252)
    a. Direct
    b. Sequential
    c. Indexed sequential
    d. List
    e. Inverted file
12. Logical and physical data elements (250)
13. Query language (265)
14. Schema (272)
15. Sequential access file processing (252)
16. Subschema (272)
17. Text databases (275)
18. Types of databases (272)
    a. Operational
    b. User
    c. Local
    d. External

REVIEW AND APPLICATION QUIZ

Match one of the **key terms and concepts** listed above with one of the brief examples or definitions listed below. Try to find the "best fit" for answers that seem to fit more than one term or concept. Defend your choices.

_____ 1. A customer's name.

_____ 2. A customer's name, address, and account balance.

_____ 3. The names, addresses, and account balances of all of your customers.

_____ 4. An integrated collection of all of the records of your business activities.

_____ 5. A collection of several large databases.

_____ 6. It takes two reels of magnetic tape to store one payroll file.

_____ 7. An identification field in a record.

_____ 8. A cross-reference field in a record that indicates where the next related record is.

_____   9. A listing of record keys and record addresses.

_____ 10. Records are organized in ascending order by social security number.

_____ 11. Transactions must be sorted before processing.

_____ 12. Records do not have to be organized in a particular order.

_____ 13. Records are organized sequentially and referenced by an index.

_____ 14. Unsorted transactions can be used to update a master file.

_____ 15. Reduces data duplication, integrates data, and breaks the dependency between programs and data formats.

_____ 16. Software that allows you to create, interrogate, and maintain a database.

_____ 17. A specialist in charge of the databases of an organization.

_____ 18. A file that specifies the structure and relationships of a database.

_____ 19. This DBMS feature allows users to easily interrogate a database.

_____ 20. A treelike structure of records in a database.

_____ 21. A tabular structure of records in a database.

_____ 22. An overall conceptual view of the relationships between data in a database.

_____ 23. Databases are dispersed throughout an organization.

_____ 24. Your own personal databases.

_____ 25. Databases of documents.

APPLICATION PROBLEMS

1. If you have not already done so, read and answer the questions after the two Real World Applications in this chapter.

2. Refer to Figure 7–3. Given the following examples of files, what file organization and access method would most likely be in use? Why?
   a. A payroll masterfile.
   b. A checking account masterfile at a bank.
   c. An accounts receivable masterfile at a large retail store.
   d. A student registration file used for online registration at a major university.

3. Refer to Figure 7–6, which shows a personnel and payroll file being linked together via pointers. Assume that using this pointer method has become too cumbersome. Numerous pointers are being stored and the access time has doubled. Therefore, the company is preparing to combine its payroll and personnel files into a single file. For producing paychecks, the file will be processed in a batch mode once a week. For meeting personnel needs, the file will be accessed on an ad hoc basis to answer such questions as "which of our data processing personnel can speak Spanish?"
   a. What type of file (by permanence, not by organization) will the combined payroll and personnel file be?
   b. Can one file be used or accessed in the two different ways indicated? Why or why not?

    c. When processing payroll in batch mode, should sequential or direct access be used? What criteria must be considered to make this decision?

    d. What file organization should be used in establishing the combined file? Why?

    e. On what medium should the file be stored?

4. A partial inventory file is shown below. Complete the forward and backward links (pointers) for this file.

Inventory Item Number	Warehouse Number	Quantity	Unit Price	Forward Warehouse Link or Pointer	Backward Warehouse Link
438	3	50	1.50		
450	2	610	6.00	463	472
452	1	750	7.50		
463	2	112	.50	472	450
469	3	425	9.00		
472	2	62	4.75	450	463
473	3	30	3.25		

5. Using the partial inventory file in problem 4, create an inverted file:
    a. By warehouse.
    b. By unit price using two categories 0–5.00; and 5.01–10.00.

6. Refer to Figure 7–14. Briefly explain each of the four major uses of database management system software and how it affects business users.

7. A database management system (DBMS) may have three different types of languages: data manipulation language (DML), data definition language (DDL), and query language. For each of the examples given below, identify which of these three languages would most probably be used:
    a. A programmer writes a COBOL program to update fields of accounts receivable records contained in the database.
    b. The field for ZIP code in the database is expanded to handle a 10-digit number.
    c. The president of the company requests and receives an ad hoc report detailing the company's debt structure.
    d. The database administrator documents the content, relationships, and structure of the database.

8. What database structures do the diagrams shown here represent? Explain your answer.

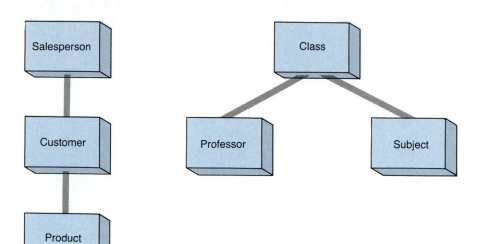

CHAPTER

8

DATA COMMUNICATIONS CONCEPTS AND APPLICATIONS

Chapter Outline

Learning Objectives

The purpose of this chapter is to promote a basic understanding of data communications and the role it plays in information systems. After reading and studying this chapter, you should be able to:

1. Identify the functions and components of a data communications system.
2. Explain the functions of data communications hardware and software.
3. Identify the major types of data communications media.
4. Use examples to illustrate how you could benefit from using several types of data communications networks.

Section I: Data Communications Hardware and Software

INTRODUCTION

People need to communicate. Computer users are no exception. They need to transmit and receive data and information between themselves and their computer systems. This wasn't easy in the early years of computing, when all the computer resources of an organization may have been located in a single room. But today's computing environment is a lot different. Computer terminals, personal computers, minicomputers, and mainframe computers seem to be everywhere. They are *dispersed* both geographically and organizationally throughout computer-using organizations. That's why we need *data communications*.

Data communications systems provide for the transmitting of data over communication links between one or more computer systems and a variety of input/output terminals. These can range from simple telephone communication links to complex communications networks involving earth satellites and communications control computers. Data communications are part of the general area of **telecommunications.** That term refers to all types of long-distance communication (i.e., voice, data, and images) including telephone, radio, and television transmission. Finally, note the frequently used term **teleprocessing.** It is a combination of the terms *telecommunications* and *data processing* and has more of an information processing emphasis. However, in this text, we will continue to use the more popular term of *data communications.* Let's first look at the components of data communications systems. Then we will discuss the major ways such systems are used in today's dynamic computer environment.

A DATA COMMUNICATIONS SYSTEM MODEL

It would be easy for anyone to be overwhelmed by the large numbers of devices and complex technologies involved in modern data communications. However, a simple *system model* can help us organize and understand this important area of computer use. Look at Figure 8–1. It shows you that a data communications system consists of the following five major components:

- ☐ **Terminals,** such as video display terminals. Of course, any input/ output device that uses communications channels to transmit or receive data is a terminal. This includes microcomputers, telephones, and the many types of terminals discussed in Chapter 5.
- ☐ **Data communications processors** (such as *modems, multiplexers,* and *front-end processors*), which support data transmission between terminals and computers. These devices perform a variety of support functions on both ends of a communications channel. For example, they convert data from digital form to analog and back, code and decode data, and control and maximize the communications flow between computers and terminals in a data communications network.
- ☐ **Communications channels and media** over which data are transmitted and received. Communications channels can consist of combinations of media, such as telephone lines, coaxial cables, fiber optic cables, microwave systems, or earth satellite systems.

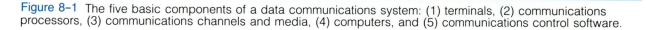

Figure 8-1 The five basic components of a data communications system: (1) terminals, (2) communications processors, (3) communications channels and media, (4) computers, and (5) communications control software.

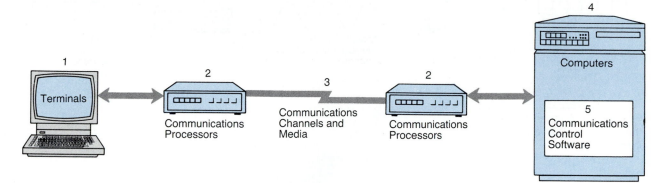

- **Computers** of all sizes and types use data communications to carry out their information processing assignments. Many times there is one larger general-purpose computer that serves as the *host computer* and contains the main communications control programs that manage the data communications network.

- **Communications control software** consists of control programs that reside in the host computer system and other communications control computers. They control input/output activities involving the data communications system, and they manage the functions of communications networks.

Modems are the most common type of communications processor. They convert the *digital* signals from a computer or transmission terminal at one end of a communications link into *analog* frequencies, which can be transmitted over ordinary telephone lines. A modem at the other end of the communications line converts the transmitted data back into digital form at a receiving terminal. This process is known as *modulation* and *demodulation*, and the word *modem* is a combined abbreviation of these two words. Modems are necessary because ordinary telephone lines were primarily designed to handle continuous analog signals, such as the human voice. Since data from computers are in digital form, devices are necessary to convert digital signals into appropriate analog transmission frequencies and vice versa. However, *digital communications networks* that transmit digital signals are rapidly being developed. Modems that only perform the digital/analog conversion function are not required when such channels are used. See Figure 8-2.

Intelligent modems use special-purpose microprocessors to support additional capabilities, such as simultaneous data and voice transmission, transmission error detection, automatic dialing and answering of calls to and from remote terminals, conversion from EBCDIC to ASCII codes and back, and automatic testing and selection of transmission lines. Modems can also vary in their data communications speed capacity. Typically, speeds vary from

DATA COMMUNICATIONS PROCESSORS

Modems

Figure 8–2 Modems perform a modulation-demodulation process that converts digital signals to analog and back.

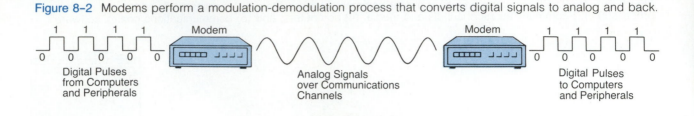

Digital Pulses
from Computers
and Peripherals

Modem

Analog Signals
over Communications
Channels

Modem

Digital Pulses
to Computers
and Peripherals

Figure 8–3 A stand-alone modem used with a microcomputer.

300 bits per second (BPS) for connecting low-speed printing terminals, to 1,200 or 2,400 BPS, for use with medium-speed video terminals, and up to 9,600 BPS or higher, for high-speed peripheral devices.

If you have a microcomputer you will need a modem if you want to communicate with other computers or use personal computer networks and data banks. To connect to a modem, your computer will have to have a communications interface circuit board with a *serial* (one bit at a time) interface *port* and an RS232C connection. RS232C is a standard 25-pin connector arrangement used to connect modems to terminals and personal computers. It includes pins for data, control signals, and timing circuits. You will need a 300, 1,200, or 2,400 BPS modem (or one that provides several speeds). Cost typically ranges between $200 and $700 but can go higher.

Modems come in three major forms: (1) stand-alone, (2) board-level, and (3) acoustic coupler. The stand-alone modem is a separate unit that is connected between a terminal or microcomputer and the telephone line. The board-level modem consists of a circuit board, with appropriate chips and circuits, that plugs into one of the expansion slots inside the microcomputer or terminal. The acoustic coupler modem has a special holder or cradle into which the telephone handset is placed. This acoustically connects the modem to the telephone line so the modem can process audible analog tones. See Figure 8–3.

There are many types of data communications processors besides modems. These include devices known as multiplexers, concentrators, communications controllers, cluster controllers, protocol converters, data encryptors, communications processors, and front-end processors! However, the fastest growing category of communications control device is the **multiplexer.** A multiplexer is an electronic device that allows a single communications channel to carry simultaneous data transmissions from many terminals. Typically, a multiplexer merges the transmissions of several terminals at one end of a communications channel, while a similar unit separates the individual transmissions at the receiving end. This is accomplished in two basic ways. In *frequency division multiplexing* (FDM), a multiplexer effectively divides a high-speed channel into multiple slow-speed channels. In *time division multiplexing* (TDM), the multiplexer divides the time each terminal can use a high-speed line into very short time slots or time frames. The most advanced and popular type of multiplexer is the *statistical time division multiplexer*, most commonly referred to as a **statistical multiplexer** or *stat mux*. Instead of giving all terminals equal time slots, it dynamically allocates time slots to only active terminals based on priorities assigned by a user.

Statistical multiplexers are rapidly making all other types of multiplexers obsolete. They are also being used to perform the functions of other devices. By their use of microprocessors and memory circuits, **intelligent multiplexers** can now perform many communications interface functions. For example, advanced models have such capabilities as error monitoring, diagnostics and correction, modulation-demodulation, data compression, data coding and decoding, protocol conversion, message switching, port contention, buffer storage, and use of internally stored programs. Some models can even manage communications with satellite and other advanced communications networks!

Many of these communications processing capabilities were formerly found only in other advanced devices. For example, devices known as **concentrators** and **communications controllers** have microprocessor intelligence, stored communications programs, and buffer storage. They *concentrate* many slow-speed lines into a high-speed line and *control* transmission activities among several terminals. However, since some intelligent multiplexers can now perform such functions, they are sometimes called concentrators and controllers by their manufacturers. See Figure 8–4.

A **front-end processor** is typically a special-purpose minicomputer that is dedicated to handling the data communications control functions for large mainframe computer systems. It can perform many of the functions of other communications processors and can be programmed to perform additional functions. For example, a front-end processor has its own memory, which is used to store its data control programs and to provide temporary buffer storage. Its functions may include coding and decoding data, error detection, recovery, recording, interpreting, and processing of control information that is transmitted (such as characters that indicate the beginning and

Multiplexers and Other Communications Processors

Front-End Processors

Figure 8–4 A multiplexer. This communications processor allows a single communications channel to carry simultaneous transmissions from several terminals.

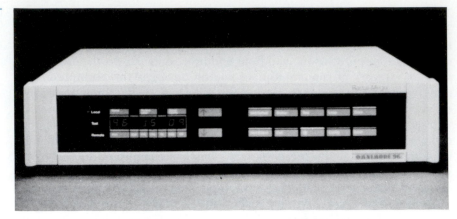

end of messages). It can also *poll* remote terminals to determine if they have a message to send or are ready to receive a message.

However, a front-end computer has more advanced responsibilities. It controls access to a network and allows only authorized users to use the system, assigns priorities to messages, logs all data communications activity, computes statistics on network activity, and routes and reroutes messages among alternative communication links. Thus the front-end processor can relieve the host computer of its data communications control functions. It has been estimated that the use of front-end processors and other advanced communications processors can provide up to 30 percent additional processing time for a large host computer system.

Private Branch Exchange

Large offices and other work areas have been using a telephone switching device called the **private branch exchange** (PBX) for decades. A PBX is a *switchboard* that serves as an interface device between the many telephone lines within a work area and the local telephone company's main telephone lines or *trunks*. In recent years, PBXs have become electronic computerized devices with built-in microprocessor and stored program intelligence. They not only route telephone calls within an office but also provide other services, such as automatic forwarding of calls, conference calling, and least-cost routing of long-distance calls.

However, the PBX has recently become a major new *data communications processor* to connect and control the terminals, computers, and other information processing devices in modern offices and other work areas. These computerized PBXs can handle the switching of both voice and data in the **local area networks** (**LANs**) that are needed in such locations. They allow computer users to share data and information processing capabilities with each other.

A computerized PBX typically consists of five major components: (1) a main microprocessor, (2) semiconductor memory, (3) a stored program, (4) interface circuits, and (5) switching circuits. The main microprocessor controls the network by following a program of instructions stored in the memory unit. Interface circuits and support microprocessors perform such functions as *digitizing* analog voice communications before transmission over digital networks. Then they convert such digitized voice messages back into normal *analog* form. They also handle feedback and control messages between the main microprocessor, the other components of the PBX, and the telephone devices in the system. Lastly, the switching circuits and support microprocessors in the PBX are used to switch both voice and data calls between internal and external telephone lines. We will discuss the role of the PBX further in an upcoming section on local area networks.

Communications channels (also called communications *lines* or *links*) are the means by which data and other forms of communications are transmitted between the sending and receiving devices in a communications network. A communications channel makes use of a variety of **communications media,** such as ordinary telephone lines, coaxial cables, fiber optic cables, microwave systems, and earth satellite systems, to transmit and receive data. You should have a basic understanding of the major types of communications media that are used in modern communications channels. See Figure 8–5.

DATA COMMUNICATIONS MEDIA

Ordinary telephone lines, consisting of copper wire twisted into pairs *(twisted pair wire)*, are used extensively for data communications. These lines are widely used in established communications networks throughout the world for both voice and data transmission. This includes privately leased lines, which can be conditioned to reduce distortion and error rates and thus allow faster transmission rates.

Standard Telephone Lines

Coaxial cable consists of groups of copper and aluminum wires that are wrapped to insulate and protect them. This minimizes interference and distortion of the signals they carry. These high-quality lines are usually buried underground or laid on the floors of lakes and oceans. They allow high-speed data transmission and are being used as replacements for twisted pair wire lines in high-service metropolitan areas, for cable TV systems, and for short-distance connection of computers and peripheral devices. They are thus used in office buildings and other work sites for local area networks. There are two basic coaxial cable technologies. In *baseband*, all devices share one communications channel. *Broadband* provides over 10 times the channels of baseband cable but costs up to twice as much.

Coaxial Cable

Fiber optics uses cables consisting of thousands of very thin filaments of glass fibers. They can conduct light pulses generated by *lasers* at transmission frequencies that approach the speed of light. Lasers are very concentrated high-frequency beams of light that are capable of transmitting about 100,000 times as much information as microwaves. Fiber optics has demonstrated digital transmission speeds about a thousand times faster than microwave transmission. Fiber optic cables provide substantial size and weight reductions as well as increased speed and greater carrying capacity. A half-inch diameter fiber optic cable can carry up to 50,000 channels, compared to

Fiber Optics

Figure 8–5 An example of the communications media in a communications channel. Notice the use of a communications satellite, earth stations with dish antennas, microwave links, and fiber optic and coaxial cable.

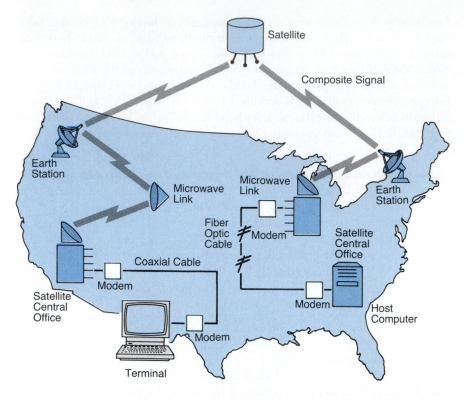

Figure 8–6 Glass fibers from a fiber optic cable conducting light from a laser.

about 5,500 channels for a standard coaxial cable. In another comparison, a one and one-half pound fiber optic cable can transmit as much data as 30 pounds of copper wire. Fiber optic cables have already been installed in many parts of the U.S. Lasers and fiber optics are expected to replace many other communications media in the near future. See Figure 8–6.

Figure 8–7 A communications satellite in earth orbit.

Terrestrial (earth-bound) microwave systems transmit high-speed radio signals in a line-of-sight path between relay stations spaced approximately 30 miles apart. Microwave antennas are usually placed on top of buildings, towers, hills, and mountain peaks, and are a familiar site in many sections of the country.

Microwave Systems

An exciting data communications media is the use of **communications satellites** for microwave transmission. There are several dozen communications satellites from several nations placed into stationary "parking orbits" approximately 22,000 miles above the equator. Satellites are launched by NASA and other organizations and weigh several thousand pounds. They are powered by solar panels and can transmit microwave signals at a rate of several hundred million bits per second. They serve as relay stations for communication signals transmitted from *earth stations*. Earth stations beam microwave signals to the satellites, which amplify and retransmit the signals to other earth stations thousands of miles away. While communications satellites were used initially for voice and video transmission, they are capable of high-speed transmission of large volumes of data. Present communications satellite systems are operated by several firms, including AT&T, Western Union, American Satellite Company, and Intellsat, an international consortium of over 100 nations. Large corporate and other users are developing their own networks using small satellite dish antennas to connect their many work sites, thus *bypassing* communications networks provided by communications carriers. See Figure 8–7.

Communications Satellites

Cellular radio is a new radio communications technology that divides a metropolitan area into a honeycomb of *cells*. This greatly increases the number of frequencies and users that can take advantage of mobile phone service. Each cell has its own low-power transmitter, rather than having one high-powered radio transmitter to serve an entire city. The number of radio frequencies available for mobile phone service using this technology increases dramatically: from 14 to 333! However, a powerful central computer and other communications equipment is needed to coordinate and control the transmissions of thousands of mobile phone users as they drive from one

Cellular Radio

cell to another. Cellular radio is expected to become an important communications medium for mobile voice and data communications. Page 24 of the pictorial section in Chapter 1 shows a portable data communications terminal for cellular radio networks.

DATA COMMUNICATIONS SOFTWARE

Software is a vital component of all data communications systems. Data communications control software includes programs stored in the host computer or in front-end computers and other communications processors. They control and support the communications occurring in a data communications network. Data communications software packages for large computer networks are frequently called *communication monitors,* or *teleprocessing* (TP) *monitors.* Local area networks (LANs) rely on software called *network operating systems.* Many communications software packages are also available for microcomputers. Figure 8–8 illustrates the tasks performed by a communications monitor for a mainframe computer.

Figure 8–8 An example of a communications monitor. Notice the various activities performed by the program modules that make up this software package.

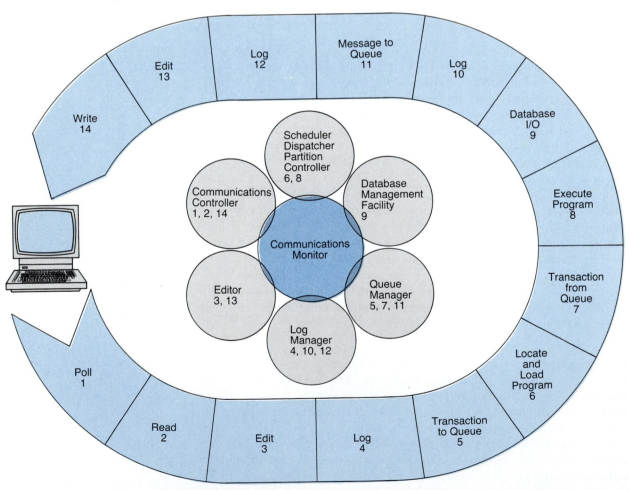

Data communication software packages provide a variety of communications support services. The number and type of terminals, computers, communication processors, and communications activities involved determine the capabilities of the programs required. Several major functions can be provided.

☐ **Access control.** This function establishes the connection between terminals and computers in the network. The software works with a communications processor (such as a modem) to connect and disconnect communications links and establish communications parameters such as transmission speed, mode, and direction. (See Section III of this chapter for details on these parameters.) This function may also involve automatic telephone dialing and redialing, logging on and off with appropriate account numbers and security codes, and automatic answering of telephone calls from another computer.

☐ **Transmission control.** This function allows computers and terminals to send and receive commands, messages, data, and programs. Some error checking and correction of data transmissions may also be provided. Data and programs are usually transmitted in the form of files, so this activity is frequently called *file transfer*.

☐ **Network control.** This function manages communications in a network. The software determines transmission priorities, routes (switches) messages, polls the terminals in the network and forms waiting lines *(queues)* of transmission requests. It also logs statistics of network activity and resource use, and detects and corrects errors.

☐ **Error control.** This function involves detection and correction of transmission errors. Errors are usually caused by distortions in the communications channel such as line noise or power surges. Parity checking (mentioned in Chapter 4) is one common method of checking for errors. Other methods involve the use of error check codes with each group or a *packet* of data being transmitted. (We will discuss these methods in Section III.) Error correction methods typically involve retransmission. A signal is sent to the computer or terminal to retransmit the previous message. Other methods involve activating correction procedures while transmission continues.

☐ **Security control.** This function protects a communications network from unauthorized access. Access control software and other types of programs restrict access to data and the computing resources in the network. This usually involves control procedures that limit access to all or parts of a network by various categories of users. Automatic disconnection and call back procedures may also be used. Data transmissions can also be protected by coding techniques called **encryption.** Data is "scrambled" into a coded form before transmission and decoded upon arrival. Thus banks, government agencies, and others use a Data Encryption Standard as the basis for data encryption.

Microcomputer Communications Software

Data communications software packages for microcomputers provide several of the control functions mentioned above. Such packages will connect a microcomputer equipped with a modem to public and private networks. We will discuss those networks shortly. Communications control packages such as Crosstalk, Access, and Smartcom provide microcomputer users with several major communications capabilities.

☐ **Terminal emulation.** The microcomputer can act as a generic *dumb terminal* that can only send, receive, and display data one line at a time. It can also act as a generic *intelligent terminal* and transmit, receive, and store on disk entire files of data and programs. Finally, some packages allow a microcomputer to *emulate* (act like) a specific type of smart terminal such as the DEC VT-220 or IBM 3101 terminals used with large computer systems.

☐ **File transfer.** Files of data and programs can be *downloaded* from a host computer to a microcomputer and stored on disk. Or files can be *uploaded* from the microcomputer to a host computer. Some programs even allow files to be transferred automatically between unattended computer systems.

☐ **Script language.** Several packages provide their own limited programming language. This allows users to add additional features. For example, a user might develop an automatic sequence of commands to access a particular computer system or network.

Communication packages for microcomputers are fairly easy to use. Once you load the program, you are usually provided with a display that asks you to set communications parameters (transmission speed and mode, type of parity, etc.). Then you dial the computer system or network you want, or have it done automatically for you. Most networks will provide you with a series of prompts or menus to guide you in sending or receiving messages, information, or files. We will give you more examples shortly. See Figure 8–9 and page 29 of the pictorial section in Chapter 1.

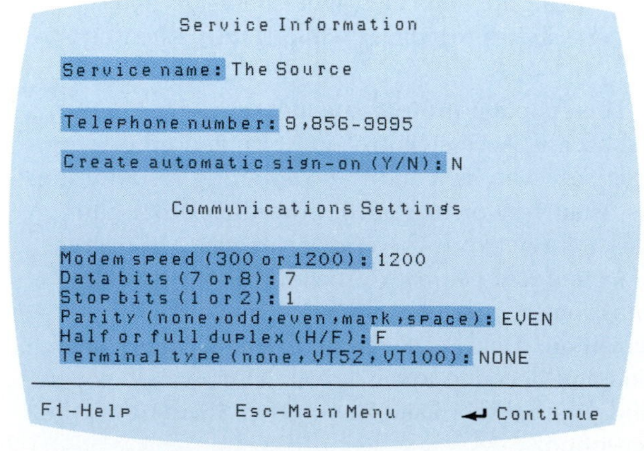

Figure 8–9 Using a microcomputer communications package. This display allows a user to establish a data communications link with a personal computer network service.

```
                Service Information

Service name: The Source

Telephone number: 9,856-9995

Create automatic sign-on (Y/N): N

            Communications Settings

Modem speed (300 or 1200): 1200
Data bits (7 or 8): 7
Stop bits (1 or 2): 1
Parity (none,odd,even,mark,space): EVEN
Half or full duplex (H/F): F
Terminal type (none,VT52,VT100): NONE
_____

F1-Help          Esc-Main Menu      ↵ Continue
```

REAL WORLD APPLICATION 8–1

Canadian Imperial Bank of Commerce

IBM calls it "the largest network of its kind that we know about." Frank Dzubeck, president of Communications Network Architects, Inc., of Washington, D.C., says, "that many PCs connected that way is absolutely unique." The network they're talking about belongs to the Canadian Imperial Bank of Commerce (CIBC), Canada's third-largest bank. CIBC has nearly 8,000 Personal Computers and 2,000 Personal Computer ATs networked locally in its branches across Canada that are connected over leased communications lines to two 308X IBM mainframe computer systems at headquarters in Toronto.

The CIBC has over 1,500 branches that spread from the Atlantic to the Pacific to the Arctic oceans. It has been highly computerized since 1969, when it originally installed COLT, the Canadian On Line Teller system, that supports basic banking transactions and is in use by four of Canada's big-five national banks. The COLT system interacted with IBM 1970 banking terminals (dumb teletypewriters) in the bank's branches through minimally intelligent controllers in each branch and through low-speed communications links.

An upgrading program was begun in 1980, motivated by the expense and obsolescence of the old technology and by the need to support new services introduced by the banks and not included in COLT. The new banking system is called COINS (Commerce Online Information Network System).

The bank chose Personal Computers from IBM as tellers' workstations for the new system. Each PC drives an Olivetti passbook printer. Having decided on PCs for workstations, the bank needed some type of intermediary between the PCs and the mainframe. IBM suggested Series 1 minicomputers, but as the bank was evaluating solutions, IBM introduced the PC Cluster Adapter and associated software, and shortly thereafter, the Personal Computer AT. Together, they provided an inexpensive way to connect and control the PCs in the branch offices, and to link them to the bank's central computers. Each AT also has an adapter for communication with the bank's mainframe computers.

The PCs are used as intelligent workstations, and the ATs as controllers, file servers, and communications links rather than for any real processing. The bank uses an AT to handle up to seven PCs, although the average is between three and four. Some large branches have multiple clusters of PCs, so the total number of clusters in the bank's 1,500 branches is 2,000.

The communications link is via voice-grade telecommunications links between each branch cluster and one of nine regional data centers. Here, IBM 3725 controllers collect and concentrate data and send it via data links to equivalent controllers at the bank's central computer facility in Toronto.

The software on the ATs and the PCs in a branch is called Intelligent Controller Facility (ICF), and consists of a collection of programs written by the bank. The ICF software in the AT handles communication with the mainframe and controls the local PC cluster. It also includes transaction-processing "dialogues"— menu-driven simple user interfaces—for ordinary teller functions like savings and checking deposits and withdrawals, as well as more complex transactions like foreign exchange, mortgages, and term deposits.

Application Questions

☐ Identify examples of the five basic components of a data communications system in the COINS banking system.

☐ What are the functions of each of these components?

Source: John Helliwell, "Pioneering a Unique PC Network on a Grand Scale," *PC Week,* November 11, 1986, pp. 55–58.

Section II: Data Communications Networks and Applications

Data communications systems are not solitary single-user, single-purpose systems. They require **data communications networks.** Such networks consist of interconnected hardware, software, and communications channels that support data communications activity for a variety of users. Let's take a look at several examples of networks and the applications they provide to individuals and business users.

COMMUNICATIONS CARRIERS AND NETWORKS

Data communications networks are provided by many companies. Several companies have traditionally offered a broad range of communications services, including American Telephone and Telegraph (AT&T), the operating companies that were formerly part of the Bell system, General Telephone and Electronics, Western Union, and many independent telephone companies. These **common carriers** provide communications networks that are used by most computer-using firms and individuals. They have traditionally been authorized by government agencies to provide a variety of communication services. For example, besides voice and data communications, carriers may provide standard radio and television transmission, facsimile, teleconferencing, electronic mail, and cellular radio networks.

Private communications networks used by major business firms and government agencies are a growing communications alternative. However, most data communications activity still takes place in public networks. This includes companies known as *specialized common carriers*. They sell high-speed voice and digital data communications services in high-density areas of the country and internationally. Examples of such specialized carriers are ITT World Communications, Southern Pacific Communications Company, and MCI Communications Corporation. In addition, these and other companies are called *value-added carriers*. They may lease communications facilities from the common carriers and combine messages from customers into groupings called packets for transmission. These *packet switching* networks are also known as *value-added networks*—VAN. They add "value" to their communications facilities by adding advanced hardware and software to provide packet switching and other data communication services. Examples of value-added companies include GTE Telenet and Tymnet by Tymeshare. Two other major communications carriers that provide networks for personal computing are CompuServe and The Source.

WIDE AREA NETWORKS

Data communications networks covering a large geographic area are called **wide area networks** (WANs). Such networks are becoming a necessity for carrying out many business, government, and individual activities. Let's look at several examples.

□ *Inquiry/response systems* depend on data communications networks. Inquiries and responses can be transmitted in realtime to and from distributed database systems. This provides up-to-date information for business operations and management throughout an organization. It also provides access to national data bank services that provide economic, demographic, and financial data to individual and corporate users.

☐ *Online data entry* and *remote job entry* are made possible by data communications networks. Data are captured and transmitted to a computer system immediately after being generated by business transactions. Networks of terminals in business offices, retail stores (POS terminals), and distribution centers minimize manual data entry, thus cutting costs and reducing errors.

☐ *Remote realtime computer use* is provided by data communications networks. They link users, terminals, and computer systems spread over a large geographic area. This includes time-sharing systems, personal computing, and interactive programming applications. This also includes multinational corporations that communicate with their branch offices, manufacturing plants, and distribution centers throughout the world using national and international networks. These networks can be provided by communications carriers, or can be *private networks* which *bypass* the carrier's networks.

☐ *Electronic funds transfer* (EFT) systems of the banking industry would not exist without data communications networks. Bank data communications systems support *teller terminals* in all branch offices, and *automated teller machines* (ATMs) at remote locations throughout a city or state. Also included is *pay-by-phone* services, which allow bank customers to use their telephones as computer terminals to electronically pay their bills. Large networks also connect POS terminals in retail stores to bank EFT systems.

☐ *Airline and hotel reservation systems* are another example. Computer terminals are installed all over the world at airline offices and ticket counters, in the offices of travel agents, rental car agency offices, and hotels and motels. The SABRE system of American Airlines or the Holidex system of Holiday Inns are examples. These national and international data communications systems provide realtime inquiries and responses concerning the status of travel reservations. They also provide realtime file updating to reflect reservations made or other transactions.

LOCAL AREA NETWORKS

Why can't you just plug a microcomputer or terminal into a wall outlet and communicate with other computers in an office building or anywhere in the world? You can in many organizations. One of the bottlenecks was right in the office. But this is changing because of the rapid growth of privately owned **local area networks** (LANs). Local area networks connect information processing devices within a limited physical area, such as an office building, manufacturing plant, or other worksite. LANs use either regular telephone lines and a computerized PBX, or coaxial cables and other communications processors. Local area networks interconnect computer terminals, personal computers, other computer systems, and a variety of computer peripheral devices. For example, they may share a powerful microcomputer with a large hard disk capacity (called a *file server*), which contains the network control program and distributes copies of common data files and software

Figure 8–10 A local area network (LAN) connecting personal computers (PCs), shared peripherals, and a departmental minicomputer and its terminals. Notice how this LAN allows users to share hardware, software, and data resources.

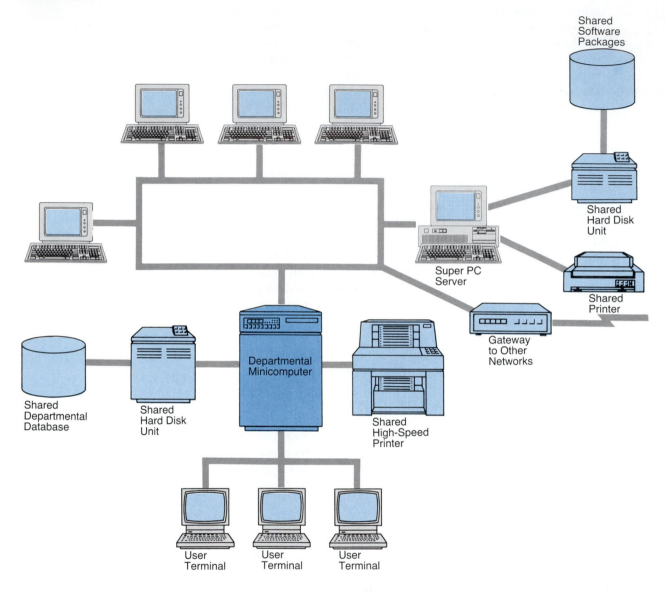

packages to the other microcomputers in the network. They may also share a common high-speed, high-quality printer (called a *print server*) for fast, high-quality printing. These local networks are connected to larger external networks by communications processors that form a common interface called a *gateway*. See Figure 8–10.

Several competing technologies are vying for dominance in providing the communications channels for local area networks. Two examples are **coaxial cable** and **PBX-based networks.** Coaxial cable networks rely on baseband or broadband cable strung throughout an office building or other worksite.

Computers, peripheral devices, and office equipment are connected to this cable and can thus communicate with each other. PBX-based systems use standard telephone wiring to interconnect all devices. They rely on advanced computerized PBXs to control both voice and data communications.

Ethernet, a joint development of Xerox, Digital Equipment Corporation, and Intel Corporation, is an example of a popular local area network using baseband coaxial cable technology. Many companies are also experimenting with broadband technology. Wangnet by Wang Laboratories and Lan/1 by 3M Corporation are examples of broadband coaxial cable networks. Other companies are turning to computerized PBX-based networks, because they allow use of regular phone lines. Examples of advanced computerized PBXs are CBX II by Rolm Corporation and SLI by Northern Telecom. However, baseband or broadband coaxial channels are still needed to handle high-speed/high-capacity applications such as mainframe-to-mainframe computer input/output, or CAD/CAM and video teleconferencing transmissions.

There are several major techniques and types of network control software for controlling communications within a local area network still being developed. Three basic technologies are now vying for supremacy: (1) *collision detection and avoidance* systems, such as the Ethernet system; (2) *token passing* systems, such as those developed by IBM; and (3) *star* systems, which have been developed at AT&T. Figure 8–11 describes and illustrates these three LAN communications control methods.

INFORMATION SERVICES NETWORKS

Another major group of communications networks is information services networks. This includes the large public networks used by services such as CompuServe and The Source. These networks offer a variety of information services to anyone with an appropriately equipped personal computer or computer terminal. They offer such services as electronic mail, financial market information, use of software packages for personal computing, electronic games, home banking and shopping, news/sports/weather information, and a variety of specialized data banks.

Gaining access to such services is easy if you have a personal computer; but it must be equipped with a communications interface board, a modem, and a communications software package. Figure 8–12 shows you how to access the CompuServe network. It shows a series of menus furnished by CompuServe that lead you to their electronic mail service. It should also give you a good idea of the variety of services available on such personal computer networks.

DATA BANKS AND VIDEOTEX NETWORKS

Data communications and a *data bank* or *videotex* service can provide users with information on a variety of topics. **Data banks** are large, privately owned computerized databases available to the computer-using public for a fee. All you need is a computer terminal or microcomputer with data communications capability. Data and information are available in the form of statistics on all types of economic and demographic activity from statistical data banks. Or you can receive abstracts from hundreds of newspapers, magazines, and other periodicals from bibliographic data banks. Some of the data bank services even provide software for a fee. This allows you to

Figure 8–11   Three competing LAN communications control methods.

THREE WAYS TO LINK TOGETHER THE AUTOMATED OFFICE AND FACTORY

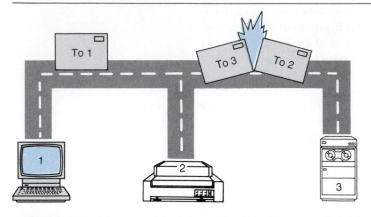

Collision avoidance and detection: Technically known as carrier-sense multiple access with collision detection, or CSMA/CD. This scheme, used by Ethernet, operates like a one-lane highway with two-way traffic. It requires all computer equipment to monitor the network, then send a message on to the data highway in packages whenever the road appears clear. If two packages collide, they must go back and try again. Because the electronics controlling this net are simple, it is relatively inexpensive. But when traffic is heavy, it is more difficult to send a package down the highway.

Token passing: Computer equipment attached to this kind of network must wait for a coded electrical signal, called a token, to pass by. Then the equipment attaches its information package to that token and moves it on to the data highway. After delivering the package, the token is passed along to the next device. The token scheme comes in two configurations: a linear approach pioneered by Datapoint and a ring design adopted by IBM.

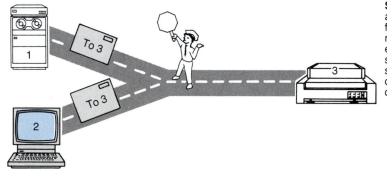

Star: All information packages must pass through a central controller, which directs them to their final destination. Because this network functions much like a central telephone switchboard, it is easy to piggyback on to existing office telephone systems without having to do any new wiring. This scheme is somewhat easier to maintain than the others because of centralized control, but if the central switch fails, the network does too.

manipulate their data for such purposes as investment analysis or economic forecasting. Figure 8–13 shows you the contents of some of the major computerized data banks.

Another way you can get information using a computerized telecommunications system is **videotex.** In its simplest form *(teletext)* it is a one-way, repetitive television broadcast of pages of text and graphics information to your TV set. This method uses cable, telephone lines, or standard TV transmission. A control device allows you to select the page you want to

Figure 8–12 Using the CompuServe personal computer network for an electronic mail service. Also notice the other services offered.

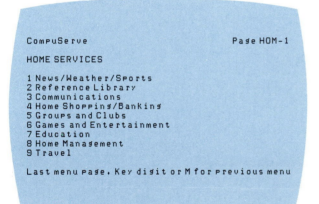

①

```
CompuServe                        Page CIS-1

CompuServe Information Service

1 Home Services
2 Business & Financial
3 Personal Computing
4 Services for Professionals
5 User Information
6 Index

Enter your selection number or H for more
information
```

Once your personal computer or terminal is connected to a modem you're ready to connect to the CompuServe Information Service. Dial the access number for your area. CompuServe will respond with this main menu of services.

② To get here, you entered #1 from the main menu. Now, enter #3 and...

```
CompuServe                        Page HOM-1

HOME SERVICES

1 News/Weather/Sports
2 Reference Library
3 Communications
4 Home Shopping/Banking
5 Groups and Clubs
6 Games and Entertainment
7 Education
8 Home Management
9 Travel

Last menu page. Key digit or M for previous menu
```

③ ...this will appear: Select #1 (Electronic Mail) and...

```
CompuServe Page                        HOM-30

COMMUNICATIONS

1 Electronic Mail
  {user to user messages}
2 CB Simulation
3 National Bulletin Board
  {public messages}
4 User Directory
5 Talk to Us
6 Lobby Letters of America
7 Ask Aunt Nettie
8 CB Society

Last menu page. Key digit or M for previous menu
```

④ ...CompuServe will guide you to Electronic Mail's main menu.

```
CompuServe                        Page HOM-26

Welcome to EMAIL, the user-to-user
message system from CompuServe.
EMAIL allows you to communicate with
other users of the information service.
Instructions and options are included on
each page. You are prompted for all
required information. If you are not sure of
what to do, key H {for help} and receive
further instructions.

Key S or {ENTER} to continue
```

⑤ Now you're ready to read or send mail electronically!

```
CompuServe                        Page EMA-1

ELECTRONIC MAIL MAIN MENU

1 Read mail
2 Compose and send mail

Last menu page. Key digit or M for previous menu
```

Figure 8–13 The computerized data banks of these information services allow you to access many types of data and information on many topics.

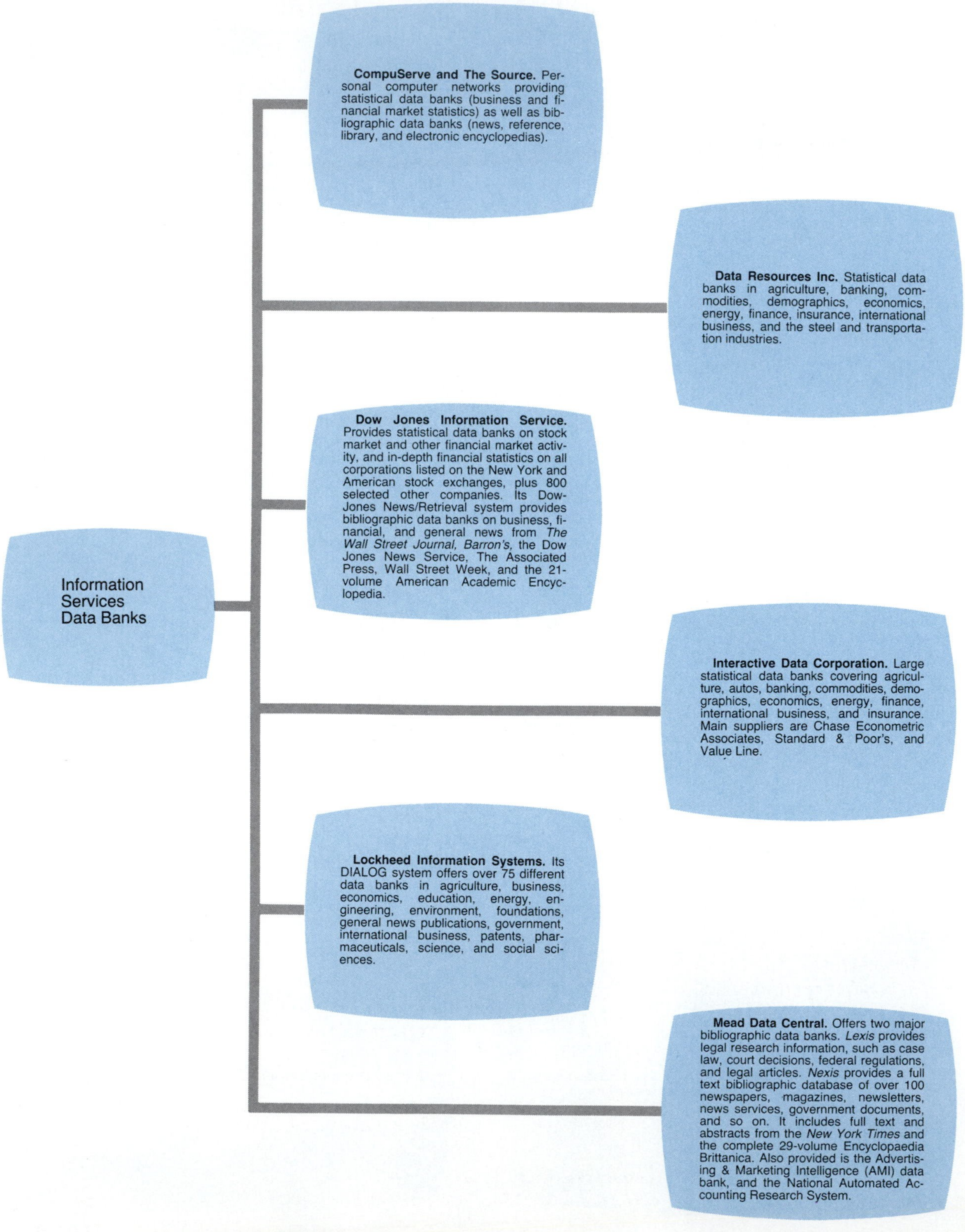

Information Services Data Banks

CompuServe and The Source. Personal computer networks providing statistical data banks (business and financial market statistics) as well as bibliographic data banks (news, reference, library, and electronic encyclopedias).

Data Resources Inc. Statistical data banks in agriculture, banking, commodities, demographics, economics, energy, finance, insurance, international business, and the steel and transportation industries.

Dow Jones Information Service. Provides statistical data banks on stock market and other financial market activity, and in-depth financial statistics on all corporations listed on the New York and American stock exchanges, plus 800 selected other companies. Its Dow-Jones News/Retrieval system provides bibliographic data banks on business, financial, and general news from *The Wall Street Journal, Barron's,* the Dow Jones News Service, The Associated Press, Wall Street Week, and the 21-volume American Academic Encyclopedia.

Interactive Data Corporation. Large statistical data banks covering agriculture, autos, banking, commodities, demographics, economics, energy, finance, international business, and insurance. Main suppliers are Chase Econometric Associates, Standard & Poor's, and Value Line.

Lockheed Information Systems. Its DIALOG system offers over 75 different data banks in agriculture, business, economics, education, energy, engineering, environment, foundations, general news publications, government, international business, patents, pharmaceuticals, science, and social sciences.

Mead Data Central. Offers two major bibliographic data banks. *Lexis* provides legal research information, such as case law, court decisions, federal regulations, and legal articles. *Nexis* provides a full text bibliographic database of over 100 newspapers, magazines, newsletters, news services, government documents, and so on. It includes full text and abstracts from the *New York Times* and the complete 29-volume Encyclopaedia Brittanica. Also provided is the Advertising & Marketing Intelligence (AMI) data bank, and the National Automated Accounting Research System.

Figure 8–14 Using videotex for shopping at home.

display and examine. Videotex, however, is meant to be an *interactive* information service provided over phone lines or cable TV channels. You can select specific video displays of data and information (such as electronic *Yellow Pages*, or your own personal bank checking account register). You can also use a special terminal or personal computer to do your banking and shopping electronically! Many banks, telephone companies, large retailers, newspaper publishers, television networks, and equipment manufacturers are testing videotext services. Such services are already available from several sources, including personal computer networks (such as the CompuServe Bank-at-Home and Shop-at-Home services). See Figure 8–14.

DISTRIBUTED PROCESSING NETWORKS

In Chapter 4, we described how distributed processing involves dispersing computers throughout an organization, rather than relying on one central computer facility. These distributed computers (microcomputers, minicomputers, or mainframe computers) are typically interconnected by data communications channels to form **distributed processing networks.**

Figure 8–15 illustrates the three basic *topologies* or structures of distributed processing networks. A **star network** ties end-user computers to a large central computer. In a **ring network,** local computer processors are tied together in a ring on a more equal basis. A **bus network** is a variation of the ring network in which local processors share the same *bus* or communications channel. In many cases, star networks take the form of *hierarchical networks*. In these networks a large headquarters computer at the top of the company's hierarchy is connected to medium-size computers at the divisional level. These are then connected to smaller computers at the departmental or local level. Ring and bus networks are also called *peer networks*. In most cases, computers operate autonomously for local processing, but also cooperate as equal partners or *peers*. A variation of the ring network is the *mesh network*. This uses direct communication lines to connect some or all of the computers in the ring to each other. Another variation is the *tree network* which joins several bus networks together.

In most cases, distributed processing systems use a combination of star, ring, and bus approaches. Obviously, the star network appears to be more centralized, while ring and bus networks have a more decentralized approach. However, this is not always the case. For example, the central

Figure 8-15 The star, ring, and bus network topologies. Notice how local processors use communications channels to a central computer or to each other.

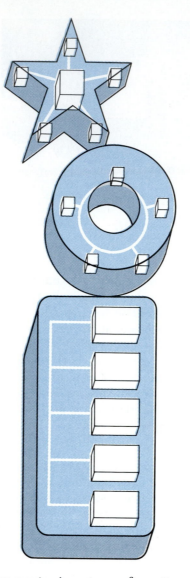

computer in a star configuration may be acting only as a **switch** or message-switching computer that handles the data communications between autonomous local computers. Figure 8–16 illustrates a simple combination of star and ring approaches. Figure 8–17 outlines the hierarchical DDP network of a large manufacturing firm.

Star, ring, and bus networks differ in their performance, reliability, and cost. These factors depend on the type of organization structure and information processing required. There is no simple answer to what network will provide the best performance. A pure star network is considered less reliable than a ring network, since the other computers in the star are heavily dependent on the central host computer. If it fails, there is no backup processing and communications capability. The local computers will then be cut off from the corporate headquarters and each other. Therefore, it is essential that the host computer be highly reliable. Having some type of *multiprocessor architecture* to provide a backup capability is a common solution.

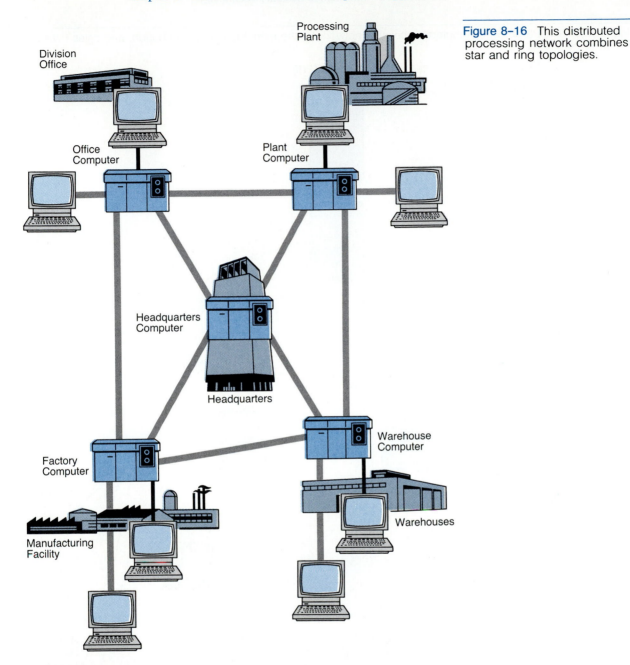

Division
Office

Processing
Plant

Office
Computer

Plant
Computer

Headquarters
Computer

Headquarters

Factory
Computer

Warehouse
Computer

Manufacturing
Facility

Warehouses

Figure 8–16 This distributed processing network combines star and ring topologies.

Star network variations are most common, because they can support the *chain-of-command* and hierarchical structure of most organizations. Ring and bus networks are most common in *local area networks*. Ring networks are considered more reliable and less costly when there is a low level of communications between the computers in the ring. That's because they do not have a host computer to handle communications control assignments. Also, if one computer in the ring goes down, the other computers can continue to process their own work as well as to communicate with each other.

Figure 8–17 A hierarchical distributed processing network for the manufacturing, distribution, and sales divisions of a large company.

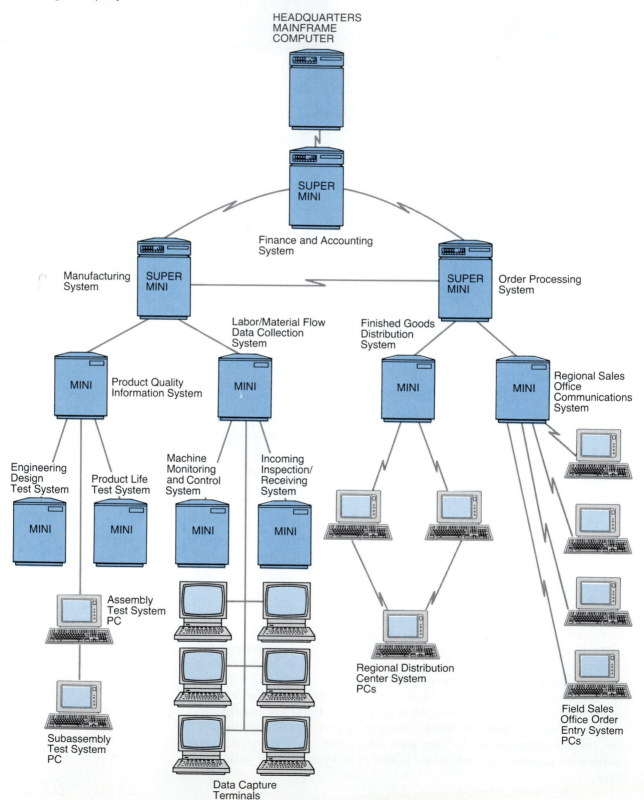

REAL WORLD APPLICATION 8–2

Clairol, Inc.

Linking a small department with a local area network (LAN) can increase the department's productivity, but it also means that the department manager must assume new responsibilities. Wayne Markowitz, manager of finance for the consumer products division of Clairol, Inc., has lived both sides of this experience. His department handles the budget process for Clairol's consumer products division, and it recently installed a local area network after years of doing budgetary work on a mainframe.

"We decided on the network because it gave us everything we had before and more," Markowitz says. "We still can connect to the mainframe, but now we have the network link, which gives us central departmental databases, distributed programming—all our analysts can be working on the same file—and yet they can also do stand-alone work with programs like Lotus 1-2-3."

Five finance departments currently share Clairol's 11-node system. Markowitz's is the largest, with four IBM Personal Computer AT local nodes. The four other finance departments use two ATs and five IBM Personal Computers between them. A Nestar Plan 5000 microcomputer (a Motorola 68000-based processor) with a 289Mb hard disk stores shared data and software resources, thus acting as the system's file server. Nestar File Server software controls network functions. The system is physically configured as a star network, with the file server in the center and the nodes radiating out from it in a star pattern. But the system's configuration is logically a ring network since it supports node-to-node communications. This configuration is unique to Clairol—other users can configure Nestar in a number of ways. Clairol links its nodes with coaxial cable, although here again they could have chosen another cable type.

Markowitz's department benefits from the LAN in concrete ways. Most of the work Markowitz's staff does involves the consumer division's annual budget. Each month, the staff updates the budget with reports that compare actual income and expenses to projections. With the LAN, says Markowitz, "Any of my analysts can get into the database and get what they need when they need it." The LAN lets staffers do more what-if financial analyses, produce more comprehensive profit-and-loss reports than before, and communicate electronically between floors.

Clairol's New York information services department wrote the applications that run on the network with a multiuser programming and database language called Focus. Markowitz worked hand-in-hand with the information services staff, so the applications would do what the finance people wanted. The LAN has also saddled Markowitz with one more management responsibility: the LAN itself, which a full-time systems administrator handles under Markowitz's aegis. In addition, Markowitz functions as guide to the finance managers in other departments. While his role has given him the greatest say in the design of the system, he also bears the greatest burden. He has developed disaster scenarios in case the system breaks down, and he checks with the system's administrator to make sure the administrator backs up data files and handles data fixes.

"Whatever effort I've put into the system, and continue to put in, is more than outweighed by the benefits," Markowitz says. "My department is able to do its normal work so much more efficiently. Plus we can support other departments. For example, we help the marketing people with financial plans for testing or introducing a new product, and also analyze the competition. We can even make those reports more dramatic by using graphics."

Application Questions

□ What type of LAN technology characteristics can you identify in this example?

□ What are the benefits of this LAN approach to Clairol?

Source: Henry Fersko-Weiss, "Powerful Ways to Link the Small Department," *Personal Computing*, August 1986, p. 82.

Section III: Data Communications Technical Characteristics

Data communications is a highly technical, rapidly developing field of computer technology. Most business computer users will not become involved in decision making about data communications alternatives. Therefore, they do not need a detailed knowledge of its technical characteristics. However, it is important that business computer users become familiar with the basic characteristics of data communications networks. This should help them become better managers of the computing resources of their organizations. This section should help achieve that goal.

COMMUNICATIONS ARCHITECTURES AND PROTOCOLS

Communications Network Architectures

Until quite recently, there was a lack of sufficient standards for the interface between the hardware, software, and communications channels of data communication networks. Therefore, it is quite common to find a lack of compatibility between the data communications hardware and software of different manufacturers. This situation has hampered the use of data communications, increased its costs, and reduced its efficiency and effectiveness. Since the mid-1970s, computer manufacturers and national and international organizations have developed standards called **protocols** and have been working on master plans called **network architectures** to support the development of advanced data communications networks.

The goal of network architectures is to promote an open, simple, flexible, and efficient data communications environment. This will be accomplished by the use of standard protocols, standard communications hardware and software interfaces, and the design of a *standard multilevel interface* between end users and computer systems. The International Standards Organization (ISO) has developed a seven-layer Open System Interconnection (OSI), model to serve as a standard model for network architectures. By dividing data communications functions into seven distinct layers, the ISO hopes to promote the development of modular network architectures. This would assist the development, operation, and maintenance of large data communications networks. Network architectures currently being developed and implemented include IBM's System Network Architecture (SNA), the Digital Network Architecture (DNA) of the Digital Equipment Corporation, and a local area network architecture for automated factories sponsored by General Motors and other manufacturers called the Manufacturing Automation Protocol (MAP). Figure 8–18 illustrates the multilevel interface of IBM's SNA as compared to the OSI model.

Related to the development of these network architectures is the development of a set of standards called ISDN—the Integrated Digital Services Network. This is a still-developing set of international standards for global telecommunications of voice, data, text, and images in digitized form. This standard is being developed by the International Telegraph and Telephone Consultative Committee (CCITT) in Geneva, Switzerland. Many communications carriers are developing and testing the communications technology needed to implement these standards.

Figure 8-18 Communications network architectures. The OSI model is recognized as an international standard. IBM's SNA is the leading network architecture for mainframe data communications networks.

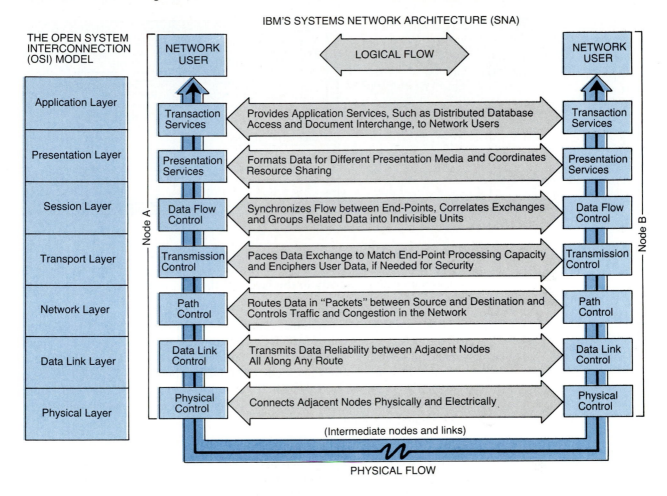

A **protocol** is a standard set of rules and procedures for the control of communications in a network. However, these standards may be limited to just one manufacturer's equipment, or to one type of data communications. Thus there are many competing and incompatible protocols in use today. Part of the goal of communications network architectures is to create more standardization and compatibility in communications protocols. We have already mentioned one example of a protocol—the RS232C standard for physical connection of terminals and computers to modems and communications lines. Another example is the X.25 protocol for packet switching networks described in the next section. Protocols frequently establish the communications control information needed for *handshaking*. This is the process of exchanging predetermined signals and characters to establish a

Protocols

Figure 8–19 Protocols used in data communications networks. Notice their use in the layers of the OSI model for network architectures.

Physical Interconnection Protocols (Layer one)	Data Link Control Protocols (Layer two)	Network Connection Management Protocols (Layer three)	End-to-End Data Transport Protocols (Layer four)
RS232C MIL-STD-188 RS449 V.24 X.21 bis X.21 V.35 303 (All specify the characteristics of interconnecting devices.)	Start-Stop BSC: Binary Synchronous HDLC SDLC ⎤ UDLC ⎥ High-Level BDLC ⎢ Data Link ADCCP ⎦ Control CSMA CSMA/CD ⎤ LAN Token Passing ⎦ Control	X.21: Circuit Switching X.25: Packet Switching Request-Response Autodial Gateway Protocols X.75: Packet Networks IP: Internet Protocol GGP: Gateway-to-Gateway	TCP: Transmission Control Protocol TP: International Transport Protocol

connection between communications terminals and computers. Figure 8–19 summarizes some of the protocols in use today and shows how they apply to communications activity in the layers of the OSI model.

Communications Control Codes

Data communications systems typically use the American Standard Code for Information Interchange (ASCII) to represent the characters of data being transmitted. However, most IBM computers use the Extended Binary Coded Decimal Interchange Code (EBCDIC). Therefore, the ASCII code is typically translated into the EBCDIC code by communications processors prior to entry into such computer systems. These computer codes were illustrated in Chapter 4.

Communications Error Control

Communications software and processors control errors in transmission by several methods, including *parity checking*. As described in Chapter 4, parity checking involves determining whether there is an odd or even number of *binary one* digits in a character being transmitted and received. If a transmission error is detected, it is usually corrected by retransmitting the message. Besides parity bits, additional *control codes* are usually added to the message itself. This includes information indicating the destination of the data, their priority, the beginning and ending of the message, plus additional error detecting and correcting information. For example, in packet switching networks, packets are preceded and followed by control codes, which are necessary to manage their routing through the network and to detect transmission errors. Thus a *protocol layer*, or *envelope*, of control information "packages" the user data during transmission. See Figure 8–20.

DATA TRANSMISSION ALTERNATIVES

The communication capabilities of communication channels can be classified by *bandwidth*. This is the frequency range of the channel, which determines the channel's maximum transmission rate. Data transmission rates are typically measured in bits per second (BPS). This is sometimes referred to as the *baud rate*, though **baud** is more correctly a measure of signal changes in a transmission line.

Transmission Speed

Figure 8–20 An envelope of protocol layer control information. This helps minimize transmission and routing errors in data communications.

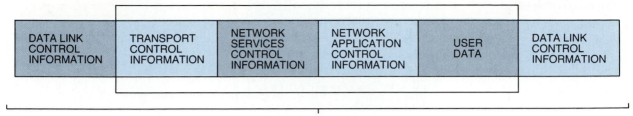

Complete Envelope Transmitted
from One Node to an Adjacent Node

☐ *Narrowband* or *low-speed* channels allow transmission rates of up to 300 bits per second (BPS). They are used primarily for teletypewriters and other low-speed printing terminals.

☐ *Voiceband* or *medium-speed* channels are "voice grade" communication lines commonly used for voice communications. Data transmission rates of up to 4,800 BPS are attainable. Rates of up to 9,600 BPS are achieved with the use of specially conditioned leased lines. These medium-speed lines are typically used for CRT terminals, microcomputers, and medium-speed printers.

☐ *Broadband* or *high-speed* channels allow transmission rates at specific intervals from about 20,000 BPS to more than a million BPS. They typically use microwave, fiber optics, or satellite transmission. An example is the T1 communications channels developed by AT&T and used by many large private communications networks. They have transmission rates up to 1.54 million BPS.

Transmission Mode

The two modes of transmitting data are called *asynchronous* and *synchronous* transmission. Asynchronous transmission transmits one character at a time with each character preceded by a *start bit* and followed by a *stop bit*. Asynchronous transmission is normally used for low-speed transmission at rates below 2,000 BPS. Synchronous transmission transmits groups of characters at a time, with the beginning and ending of a character determined by timing circuitry of a modem or other communications processor. Synchronous transmission is normally used for high-speed transmission exceeding 2,000 BPS.

Transmission Direction

Communications channels can provide three types of data transmission direction. A *simplex* channel allows data to be transmitted in only one direction, such as just receiving transmissions or just sending transmissions. A *half-duplex* channel allows transmission in either direction, but in only one direction at a time. This is usually sufficient for many low-speed terminals (such as transaction terminals). Alternating sending and receiving is a typical characteristic of their normal communications activities. The *full duplex* channel allows data to be transmitted in both directions at the same time. It is used for high-speed communications between computer systems. See Figure 8–21.

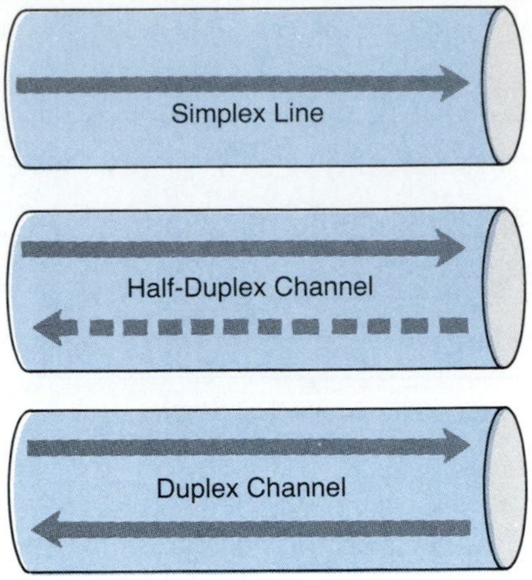

Figure 8–21 Simplex, half-duplex, and duplex channels. Notice the direction of data transmission allowed.

Packet Switching

Packet switching involves subdividing communications messages into groups called *packets*, typically 128 characters long. The packet switching network carrier uses minicomputers and other communications processors to control the packet switching process and transmit the packets of various users over its leased lines. Packet switching networks are also known as *X.25 networks*, which is the international standard or protocol governing the operations of public packet switching networks.

Point-to-Point versus Multidrop Lines

The two basic types of communication links in data communications networks are *point-to-point* and *multidrop*. When point-to-point lines are used, each terminal is connected by its own individual line to a computer system. When multidrop lines are used, several terminals share each data communications line to a computer. Obviously, point-to-point lines are more expensive than multidrop lines. All of the communications capacity and equipment of a data communications line is being used by a single terminal. Thus point-to-point lines are used only if there will be continuous communications between a computer and a terminal or other computer system. A multidrop line decreases communications costs, because each line is shared by many terminals.

Multidrop lines allow more than one terminal on the line to receive data at the same time. However, only one terminal at a time can transmit data to the computer system. There are several ways to get around this limitation. In the **contention** approach, line use is on a first-come, first-served basis, where a terminal can transmit data if the line is not in use, but must wait if it is busy. In the **polling** approach, the computer or communications processor polls (contacts) each terminal in sequence to determine which has a message to send. The sequence in which the terminals are polled is based on the communications traffic expected from each terminal. Thus the transmission of each terminal is based on a "roll call" of each terminal on the line. Polling is widely used because the speed of computers allows them to poll and control transmissions by many terminals sharing the same line. Thus users at many terminals can share the same line, especially if their typical communications consist of brief messages and inquiries. See Figure 8–22.

Figure 8–22 Multidrop lines allow terminals to share a communications line. Point-to-point lines provide a separate communications line for each terminal.

MULTIDROP LINES   POINT-TO-POINT LINES

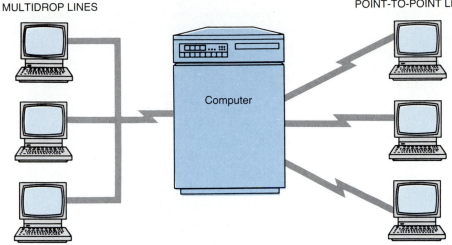

Multidrop lines are usually *leased lines* (or *direct lines*). A specific communications circuit is leased (or acquired) and used to connect terminals with a computer system. Typically, a user can begin using a terminal connected to a leased line by merely turning the terminal on and entering appropriate identification messages. Point-to-point lines may use leased lines or a *switched line*. This method uses the telephone lines and switching service of the regular telephone system. A user wanting to begin using a terminal on a switched line must dial the telephone number assigned to the communications processor, which establishes contact with the computer system.

Leased versus Switched Lines

SUMMARY

☐ Data communications systems provide for the transmitting of data over electronic communications links between one or more computer systems and a number of input/output terminals at some physical distance away from the computer. Modern use of computers is heavily dependent on data communications systems for remote access batch processing, most realtime processing, and many personal computing, industrial, and office communication systems.

☐ The major components of a data communications system consist of (1) terminals, (2) communications processors, (3) communications channels and media, (4) computers, and (5) communications control software. Data communications hardware consists of modems, multiplexers, and various communications processors. Data communications software consists of computer programs that control and support the communications occurring in a data communications network.

☐ Communications channels include such media as ordinary telephone lines, coaxial cables, fiber optic cables, microwave systems, cellular radio, and communications satellite systems. Use of these channels is provided by companies called common carriers and private carriers. They offer a variety of data communications services.

REAL WORLD APPLICATION 8–3

TRW International Distribution Services

TRW International Distribution Services (IDS) uses a global computer network to move information quickly among its three offices, located in the United States, Europe, and Asia. The network provides enough flexibility to help the company capture market share and remain profitable in the dynamic automotive parts aftermarket.

Ray A. Weaver, the business systems coordinator for IDS and the designer of its network, faced the challenge of coordinating three principle control centers. The Independence, Ohio center is responsible for sales to South America; offices in Antwerp, Belgium and Geneva handle European sales; and a center in Nagoya, Japan, near Tokyo, covers the Far East. Each center has different equipment. The American operation has a mixture of IBM Personal Computers and mainframes; the European operation is exclusively on mainframes; and the Japanese base has a single PC.

Mr. Weaver was also responsible for installing the equipment in the Ohio office. There, eight PCs are tied together with a local area network and are also connected to an IBM mainframe. Each trade coordinator downloads information from the mainframe to his or her PC to determine the best possible routing for orders. The coordinator also uses the host to determine which supplier has sufficient inventory and to track purchase orders and invoices. "In the past, TRW had many divisions around the world working autonomously," Mr. Weaver said. TRW needed to network the three offices so as to move parts and financial paperwork quickly.

Mr. Weaver's solution was to connect the three offices through General Electric's Mark III data network system. There were several reasons for his decision. First, GE was the only network to offer store-and-forward capabilities for data communications messages. This was essential due to the extreme time differences among the three offices. "Nagoya and Independence are 14 hours apart; Antwerp and Independence, six. GE's store-and-forward abilities help bridge the time-zone gap," said Mr. Weaver.

Also, "GE could provide us with a compliance check that verifies the integrity of data once it gets up into the GE system. It also verifies compliance with Automotive Industry Action Group (AIAG) standard, which is the standard that the auto parts industry has adopted," Mr. Weaver explained. "That's important for us because we want to interchange data with other makers of auto parts." GE also provides access to a wider range of network locations, particularly in the Far East. The network has greatly sped up communications among the three offices.

"If someone needs Japanese parts in Germany and his order is so large that it cannot be filled out of our Antwerp office, it gets put on the network. Within 15 minutes the order is filled by Japan," Mr. Weaver explained. "It immediately gets verified for correct part numbers, and an acknowledgment is sent back to show that the order was received." The combined order is let out by the one office most familiar with suppliers of that item. The larger order volume gives that office more leverage in arranging the best price. "Now, with our network, we can consolidate information at one location. With greater quantities, we can get better prices," Mr. Weaver said.

Mr. Weaver estimated that, with the network, TRW IDS has trimmed 10 to 15 percent of its costs. Just as important are the savings in time. Noted Mr. Weaver, "Getting purchase orders between shipper and supplier used to take three days. Now the paperwork is handled within minutes over the network."

Application Questions

☐ What data communications capabilities are evident in this example?

☐ What benefits does this global network have for IDS?

Source: Winn L. Rosch, "Firm Has Parts for Global Network, *PC Week,* February 3, 1987, p. C/5.

☐ Data communications networks include the worldwide networks of multinational corporations, regional distributed processing networks, local area networks in office buildings and other worksites, personal computer networks, and videotex and data bank networks.

These are the key terms and concepts of this chapter. The page number of their first explanation is in parentheses.

KEY TERMS AND CONCEPTS

1. Cellular radio *(291)*
2. Coaxial cable *(281)*
3. Communications carrier *(296)*
4. Communications channels and media *(289)*
5. Communications control software *(292)*
6. Communications network architecture *(308)*
7. Communications processors *(285)*
8. Communications satellites *(291)*
9. Data banks *(299)*
10. Data communications system *(284)*
11. Distributed processing networks *(303)*

12. Encryption *(293)*
13. Fiber optic cables *(289)*
14. Front-end processors *(287)*
15. Host computer *(285)*
16. Local area networks *(297)*
17. Modems *(285)*
18. Multiplexers *(287)*
19. Personal computer networks *(299)*
20. Private branch exchange *(288)*
21. Protocol *(309)*
22. Videotex *(300)*
23. Wide area networks *(296)*

Match one of the **key terms and concepts** listed above with one of the brief examples or definitions listed below. Try to find the "best fit" for answers that seem to fit more than one term or concept. Defend your choices.

REVIEW AND APPLICATION QUIZ

_____ 1. Includes terminals, communications processors, channels and media, computers, and control software.
_____ 2. Includes modems, multiplexers, and front-end processors.
_____ 3. Includes programs for control of communications access, transmission, networks, errors, and security.
_____ 4. A common communications processor for microcomputers.
_____ 5. Helps a communications channel carry simultaneous data transmissions from many terminals.
_____ 6. The main computer in a data communications network.
_____ 7. A minicomputer dedicated to handling communications functions.
_____ 8. Handles the switching of both voice and data in a local area network.
_____ 9. Provide a variety of communications networks and services.
_____ 10. Includes coaxial cable, microwave, fiber optics, and satellites.

_____ 11. A communications media which uses pulses of laser light in glass fibers.

_____ 12. Supports mobile data communications in urban areas.

_____ 13. A communications network covering a large geographic area.

_____ 14. A communications network in an office, a building, or other worksites.

_____ 15. Offer a variety of services to microcomputer users.

_____ 16. Computerized databases available for a fee to computer users.

_____ 17. An interactive information service over phone lines or cable TV channels.

_____ 18. Includes star, ring, and bus network structures.

_____ 19. Coding techniques for data communications security.

_____ 20. A master plan for a standard multilevel data communications interface.

_____ 21. A standard set of rules and procedures for control of communications in a network.

APPLICATION PROBLEMS

1. If you have not already done so, read and answer the questions after the three Real World Applications in this chapter.

2. Apply the data communications system model to the data communications networks of the Canadian Imperial Bank of Commerce, Clairol, Inc., and TRW IDS as described in the Real World Applications of this chapter. That is, identify as many of the five basic components of a data communications system that you can find in these networks.

3. Users of the mainframe computer at ABC Department Stores are experiencing very slow response times at their terminals. Some users are speculating that the modems they are using are too slow. The mainframe vendor's sales rep says that it needs more ports so more terminals can be directly connected. Somebody from the information services department says that ABC needs to add a front-end processor. A data communications consultant advises ABC to purchase several multiplexers. Identify the functions of the communications processors in this example. Explain why each could be responsible for the slow response times.

4. The corporate headquarters for ABC Department Stores wants to install a local area network in its present 10-year-old, five-story office building. They are trying to decide between a baseband or broadband coaxial cable network, or a PBX-based LAN. They want to tie together the computer peripheral devices, personal computers, and terminals in the building. What would you advise them to do? Identify the functions of the communications media involved. Then explain the recommendation you would make in this case.

5. The data communications network used by TRW International (described in Real World Application 8–3) must use a variety of communications media. Describe how they could use almost all of the communications media mentioned in this chapter in their communications channels.

6. A personal computer user tells you that she uses a local area network to share resources in her office, a private network to communicate with the corporate headquarters computer, and a wide area network to access several data banks. Explain what she is doing and the benefits she is probably deriving from using each network mentioned.

7. Match one of the following types of communications network structures with the statements listed below.
   a. Bus network.   *d.* Ring network.
   b. Hierarchical network.   *e.* Star network.
   c. Mesh network.

   _____ 1. Ties end-user computers to a large central computer.

   _____ 2. Ties computers together on an equal basis.

   _____ 3. A combination of star and ring approaches.

   _____ 4. A variation of the ring network.

   _____ 5. A variation of the star network.

8. Match one of the following communications architectures or protocol with one of the examples listed below.
   a. Integrated Digital Services Network (ISDN).
   b. Manufacturing Automation Protocol (MAP).
   c. Open Systems Interconnection (OSI).
   d. RS 232C protocol.
   e. Systems Network Architecture (SNA).
   f. X.25 protocol.

   _____ 1. Developed by the International Standards Organization as a model communications network architecture.

   _____ 2. IBM's communications network architecture.

   _____ 3. General Motors and others developed this local area network architecture standard for factories.

   _____ 4. An international standard for joint transmission of voice, data, text, and images.

   _____ 5. A protocol for packet switching networks.

   _____ 6. A protocol for the physical connection between terminals and modems.

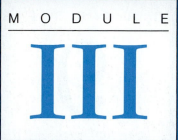

MODULE

III

INFORMATION SYSTEMS CONCEPTS AND DEVELOPMENT

INFORMATION SYSTEMS CONCEPTS

Chapter Outline

Learning Objectives

The purpose of this chapter is to promote a basic understanding of the role of information systems in business operations and management by analyzing (1) a business as a system, (2) the information requirements of a business firm and its managers, and (3) the major types of information systems. After reading and studying this chapter, you should be able to:

1. Identify the basic system components of a business.

2. Explain how the information requirements of management are affected by
   a. the functions of management,
   b. managerial roles,
   c. levels of management,
   d. information quality,
   e. internal versus external information, and
   f. past versus future information.

3. Explain how the three major types of operations information systems support the operations of a business.

4. Identify the major types of management information systems, and discuss the reasons for the development of the MIS concept for computer use in business.

5. Explain the decision support system concept, how it differs from traditional operations and management reporting systems, and how it is related to executive information systems and expert systems.

Section I: Foundation Concepts: Business and Management

Everyone needs information to survive and thrive. Organizations and their managers are no exception. That's why organizations need several varieties of **information systems.** This chapter will demonstrate the vital role played by information systems in modern business organizations. But before we get any further, let's review some basic concepts of business and management in this section. This will help us better understand the organizational requirements of information systems in a business environment.

A BUSINESS AS A SYSTEM

Information systems play a *feedback* role in many types of organizations. Figure 9–1 illustrates this concept. A *business system* consists of the following interrelated components that must be controlled and coordinated toward the attainment of organizational goals such as profitability, market share, return on investment, and social responsibility.

Input

Resources such as people, money, material, machines, land, facilities, energy, data, and information are entered into the business. They are the resources that are used in the processing activities of the business system.

Processing

The business system uses various kinds of organizational processes, including production, marketing, finance, and personnel activities, known as the **functions of business.** Other processes are also used to transform inputs into outputs. This includes engineering, research and development, and legal services.

Output

The firm produces products, services, payments to employees and suppliers, dividends, interest, taxes, and contributions, information, and other effects.

Feedback

An organization's information systems are its *feedback* component. Two major categories are necessary. **Operations information systems** collect, process, and store data generated by business transactions and other operations of the business. **Management information systems** refine the data and information provided by the operations information systems of the organization and gather information from the business environment. They then provide information needed to support decision making by managers.

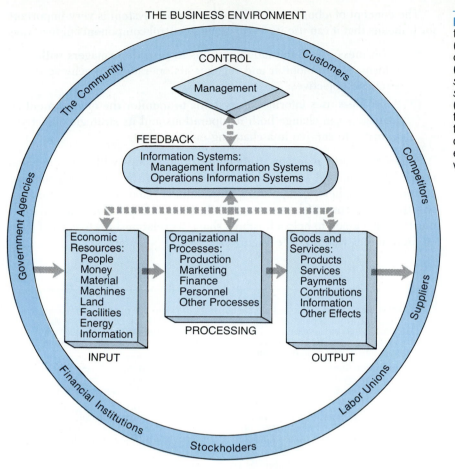

THE BUSINESS ENVIRONMENT

Figure 9–1 A business is a system where *economic resources* (input) are transformed by various *organizational processes* (processing) into *goods and services* (output). *Information systems* provide information (feedback) on the operations of the system to *management* for the direction and maintenance of the system (control), as it exchanges inputs and outputs with the business environment.

Control

The management of an organization consists of managers at all organizational levels who are engaged in planning, organizing, staffing, directing, and controlling activities (called the **functions of management**), as well as other managerial roles and activities. They control the operations of the business system based on feedback provided by the firm's information systems.

Environment

A business is a *subsystem* of society and is surrounded by the other systems of the **business environment.** It exchanges inputs and outputs with its environment, and is therefore called an *open system*. In addition, a business is an *adaptive system* (i.e., it has the ability to adjust to the demands of its environment).

The concept of a business as an open, adaptive system is very important, for it means that it can use its feedback and control components in two ways:

☐ A business uses information systems to provide managers with information to monitor and regulate its operations to achieve its strategic objectives.

☐ A business uses information systems to monitor the environment so managers can change both its operations and its strategic objectives in order to survive in a changing environment.

A business must maintain proper interrelationships with the other economic, political, and social subsystems in its environment. This includes customers, suppliers, competitors, stockholders, labor unions, financial institutions, governmental agencies, and the community. Information systems must be developed to help a business shape its relationships to each of these environmental systems. See Figure 9–2.

Figure 9–2 The information requirements of the business environment. Notice the importance of information systems in each of these environmental systems.

Customer Systems. Information systems should help the business firm understand what consumers want and why they want it, so *consumers* can be converted into *customers.* Such "marketing information systems" support marketing activities such as advertising, selling, pricing, distribution, product development, and market research.

Competitor Systems. Information systems must provide management with information on present and potential *competitors,* why they are competitors, and what their competitive activities are and will be. Such information helps management shape its competitive strategy.

Supplier Systems. *Suppliers* provide a business firm with goods and services. Information systems must support the purchasing function so that the business firm can minimize its purchasing cost and maximize the value of goods and services that it procures.

Labor Union Systems. Though employees are a vital component of the business firm, they are frequently represented by an environmental system—the *labor union.* Information systems must provide management, employees, and labor unions with information on employee compensation and labor productivity within the firm and competing business systems.

Stockholder Systems. Though *stockholders* are the owners of business firms that are organized as corporations, they can be considered as an environmental system because many business firms are owned by many different and distant stockholders. Information systems must provide information concerning dividends and financial and operating performance to management and stockholders.

Financial Institution Systems. Financial institutions (such as banks) provide the business system with money, credit, and various financial services. Information systems must provide management and financial institutions with information on the financial and operating performance of the firm, and the state of the financial markets.

Governmental Systems. Business firms are governed by laws and regulations of *government agencies* at the city, county, state, federal, and foreign government levels. The information systems of a business firm must supply a wide variety of information to various governmental agencies concerning many aspects of the operations of the firm. Management also needs information on political, legal, and legislative developments so that it can effectively deal with changes in laws and regulations.

Community Systems. The business firm resides in local, regional, national, and world *communities.* Information systems must provide the management of business firms with information concerning how well they are meeting their responsibilities as good citizens of these communities.

People in business perform several basic business functions. We have just explained that a business firm uses the **functions of business,** such as production, marketing, finance, and personnel activities, to transform economic resources into goods and services. Having a good understanding of these basic business functions helps us understand how computers and information systems are used by people in business. We will take a brief look at them now, and go into more detail in the chapters of Module Four. Of course, there are other functions in a business that people have to perform. Some examples are research and development, engineering, legal services, and so on. But let's concentrate on the following major functions.

WHAT PEOPLE DO IN BUSINESS

Marketing

Products and services have to be marketed, or they will just sit on the factory floor or on the shelves of retail stores. The marketing function is a system of people and activities that plans, prices, promotes, sells, and distributes products and services to customers. It also includes the development of new products and services for new markets to better serve present and potential customers. So you see, there is a lot more to marketing than just selling or advertising products.

Production/Operations

Somebody has to turn ideas for new products and services into reality. Products and services have to be *produced* in a form acceptable to a firm's customers. The production/operations function includes all people and activities concerned with the planning, monitoring, and control of the processes that produce goods and services. This includes *manufacturing* activities that transform raw materials into finished products. But it also includes activities that plan, monitor, and control the *operations* of non-manufacturing firms. For example, retail stores use the production/operations function to manage the purchases, inventories, and flows of goods and services in their organizations.

Accounting

Managers and others must be kept informed about a firm's financial position and performance. Therefore, the business transactions and changes occurring in a firm must be forecasted, recorded, and reported. So people in the accounting function have two main jobs. First, accounting involves legal and historical record-keeping and the production of accurate financial statements. Secondly, accounting assists the planning and control of business operations through the development of financial budgets and other forecasts of projected financial performance. Then reports are produced for management that show how well the business met those budgets and forecasts.

Finance

Where do businesses get the money they need to produce and market products and services? Most firms get it from investments by stockholders, loans from financial institutions, and profits plowed back into the business. Thus, one of the main jobs of people in the finance function is to find the best sources and methods of raising money for a business. Once this money is raised, it is spent on projects and proposals that have been evaluated as most profitable to the firm. Thus the other important job of people in the finance function is to evaluate proposals that require funding to determine how they will affect the financial performance and financial position of the business.

Personnel

A business needs good employees to produce and market products and services. How does a firm recruit and keep good people? That is the job of people in the personnel function, also called *human resource management*. People in the personnel function are concerned with the recruitment, placement, evaluation, compensation, and professional development of the employees of an organization. The human resource management concept emphasizes *planning* to meet the personnel needs of a business. It also emphasizes the *control* of all personnel policies and programs, so that effective and efficient use is made of the *human resources* of the company.

WHAT COMPUTERS DO IN BUSINESS

There are as many ways to use computers in business as there are business activities to be performed, business problems to be solved, and business opportunities to be pursued. Therefore, no one can acquire a complete understanding of all computer applications in business. However, as a computer user, you should have a *general* understanding of the major ways the computer is used in business. You should also have a *specific* understanding of how computers affect a *particular business function* (marketing, for example) or a *particular industry* (banking, for example) that is directly related to your *career objectives*. Thus someone whose career objective is a marketing position in banking should have a basic understanding of how computers are used in banking and how computers support the marketing activities of banks and other firms.

Figure 9–3 illustrates how major computer applications can be grouped into business function categories. Figure 9–4 gives examples of computer applications in a variety of industries. Applications in the chapters of Module Four will thus be discussed according to the business function they support (marketing, production/operations, finance, accounting, and personnel) or according to the industry in which they are utilized (retailing, banking, insurance, etc.).

Trends in Computer Use in Business

In the early years of computer use, the computer was applied to the solution of information processing problems in a piecemeal fashion. Most computer applications involved the computerization of clerical and record-keeping

PRODUCTION/ OPERATIONS	MARKETING	FINANCE	ACCOUNTING	PERSONNEL
Computer-Aided Manufacturing	Market Research	Capital Budgeting	Billing and Accounts Receivable	Personnel Record-Keeping
Material Requirements Planning	Sales Forecasting	Cash Management	Payroll	Labor Analysis
Inventory Control	Advertising and Promotion	Credit Management	Accounts Payable	Employee Skills Inventory
Purchasing and Receiving	Sales Order Processing	Portfolio Management	General Ledger	Compensation Analysis
Process Control	Sales Management	Financial Forecasting	Fixed Asset Accounting	Training and Development Analysis
Numerical Control	Product Management	Financing Requirements Analysis	Cost Accounting	Personnel Requirements Forecasting
Computer-Aided Engineering	Marketing Management	Financial Performance Analysis	Tax Accounting	
Robotics			Budgeting	
			Auditing	

Figure 9–3 Computer applications in business. Notice how they support the major functions of business.

tasks. Such tasks (1) were comparatively simple, (2) were already organized for manual data processing, (3) could show immediate cost savings, and (4) posed the most pressing information processing problems in terms of sheer volumes and growth. The trend of computer applications since that time has been to develop a computer *applications portfolio* (diversified collection of applications). The main goals of such applications are to provide information services that support management decision making or that help a firm gain a strategic advantage over its competitors.

Figure 9–5 illustrates three levels of computer applications in computer-using business firms.

☐ Computers are applied to *record-keeping* activities in accounting and other functions (using centralized batch systems). The payoff is frequently an immediate reduction in costs.

☐ Computers are applied to *operations control* functions in manufacturing and distribution (using realtime distributed/database systems). These have a less immediate payoff. Operating improvements provide less tangible benefits.

☐ Firms with sufficient computer experience or expertise move to a third level. Interactive executive computing systems are used to support the *strategic planning* functions of management. It may take years to recognize strategic benefits that give a firm a comparative advantage in its industry.

Figure 9–4 Computer applications by industry categories. Notice the variety of applications in each industry.

Industry Segment	Basic Applications	Advanced Applications
Manufacturing	Production accounting Production planning Purchasing and receiving Inventory control	Computer-aided manufacturing Computer-aided engineering Process control Numerical control Robotics
Business and Personal Services	Service bureau functions Tax preparation Accounting Client records	Econometric models Time-sharing Engineering analysis Financial planning
Banking and Finance	Demand deposit accounting Check processing Proof and transit operations Cost accounting	Online savings Electronic funds transfer Portfolio analysis Cash flow analysis
Insurance	Premium accounting Customer billing External reports Reserve calculation	Actuarial analysis Investment analysis Policy approval Cash flow analysis
Utilities	Customer billing Accounting Meter reading Inventory control	Rate analysis Line and generator loading Operational simulation Financial models
Distribution	Order processing Inventory control Purchasing Warehouse control	Vehicle scheduling Merchandising Forecasting Store site selection
Transportation	Rate calculation Vehicle maintenance Cost analysis Accounting	Traffic pattern analysis Automatic rating Tariff analysis Reservation systems
Health Care	Patient billing Inventory accounting Health care statistics Patient history	Lab/operation scheduling Nurses' station automation Patient monitoring Computerized diagnostics
Retail	Customer billing Sales analysis Accounting Inventory reporting	Point-of-sale systems Sales forecasting Merchandising Cash flow analysis
Printing and Publishing	Circulation Classified ads Accounting Payroll	Automatic typesetting Desktop publishing Media analysis Page layout

Applications Level	Applications Technology	Applications Benefits
Record-Keeping Applications	Batch centralized systems	Immediate payoff Reduced clerical cost Improved speed and accuracy
Operations Control Applications	Realtime distributed/database systems	Intermediate payoff Improved service and control Reduced asset levels and operating costs
Strategic Planning Applications	Interactive executive computing systems	Improved information and decisions Slow recognition of strategic benefits

Figure 9–5 Three levels of computer applications in business.

Before we discuss what information a manager needs, we should define what the term *management* means. Figure 9–6 summarizes three basic ways to answer the question, "What does a manager do?" For example, management is traditionally described as a process of leadership involving the *management functions* of planning, organizing, staffing, directing, and controlling. A manager should *plan* the activities of the organization, *staff* it with required personnel, *organize* its personnel and their activities, *direct* the operations of the organization, and *control* its direction by evaluating feedback and making necessary adjustments.

WHAT A MANAGER DOES

☐ **Planning** involves the development of long- and short-range plans that require the formulation of goals, objectives, strategies, policies, procedures, and standards. It also involves the perception and analysis of opportunities, problems, and alternative courses of action, and the design of programs to achieve selected objectives.

☐ **Organizing** involves the development of a structure that groups, assigns, and coordinates activities by delegating authority, offering responsibility, and requiring accountability.

☐ **Staffing** involves the selecting, training, and assignment of personnel to specific organizational activities.

☐ **Directing** is the leadership of the organization through communication and motivation of organizational personnel.

☐ **Controlling** involves observing and measuring organizational performance and environmental activities and modifying the plans and activities of the organization when necessary.

Figure 9–6 What a manager does. This figure summarizes (1) the four decision-making stages of managers, (2) the five functions of management, and (3) the ten major roles played by managers.

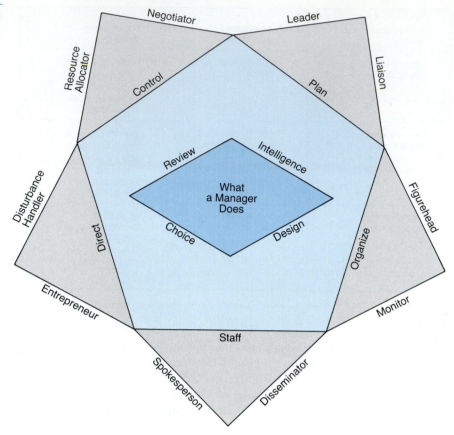

Figure 9–6 What a manager does. This figure summarizes (1) the four decision-making stages of managers, (2) the five functions of management, and (3) the ten major roles played by managers.

The functions of management presented above were developed by Henri Fayol a long time ago. They have given us a valuable way to think about what managers do. However, another useful management model is that of Henry Mintzberg. This model views management as the performance of a variety of roles. These **managerial roles** can be used in response to the question, "What do managers do?" A manager has the authority and status to play the following roles:

☐ **Interpersonal roles.** A manager should be (1) a *leader* of subordinates, (2) a *liaison* with the external environment, and (3) a *figurehead* when ceremonial duties arise.

☐ **Informational roles.** A manager should be (4) a *monitor* of information on organizational performance, (5) a *disseminator* of valuable information within the organization, and (6) a *spokesperson* to the external environment.

☐ **Decisional roles.** A manager should be (7) an *entrepreneur* in making innovative changes that affect the organization, (8) a *disturbance handler* when major unanticipated events occur, (9) a *resource allocator* in determining the distribution of financial and other resources within the organization, and (10) a *negotiator* who resolves both internal and external disputes.

The decisional roles of management mentioned above lead to our final way of looking at what managers do. Managers make decisions! How do they make decisions? Herbert Simon answered that question with another useful model. Managers go through four stages of decision-making activities:

- ☐ **Intelligence activity.** Managers search the environment for events and conditions requiring a decision.
- ☐ **Design activity.** Managers develop and then analyze possible courses of action.
- ☐ **Choice activity.** Managers select a particular course of action from the alternatives available.
- ☐ **Review activity.** Managers evaluate the results of their past choices.

INFORMATION NEEDS OF MANAGERS

Information is an indispensable ingredient in each of the management functions and roles just discussed. But what information do managers need? Managers cannot possibly absorb all of the information that can be produced by information systems. Therefore, we should understand several basic concepts that guide the determination of the information needed by managers. Figure 9–7 summarizes some of the major characteristics of such information.

Quality Information

High-quality information must possess several major characteristics in order to effectively support managerial decision making. For example, quality information should be:

- ☐ **Timely.** Information should be provided when needed by the manager.
- ☐ **Accurate.** Information should be free from errors.
- ☐ **Complete.** As much as possible, all the information needed by a manager to make a decision should be provided.
- ☐ **Concise.** Only the information needed to make a decision should be provided. This avoids flooding the manager with unnecessary information.
- ☐ **Crucial.** As a minimum, managers need information about a few key factors that are crucial or critical to the success of their organizations. These **critical success factors** (as John Rockart calls them) must be identified by executives as crucial to their success in meeting the objectives of their organization. Information should be provided that helps managers measure changes in these critical factors, both within the firm and in its environment.

Figure 9–7 The information requirements of management. This figure summarizes some of the major characteristics of the information needed by managers.

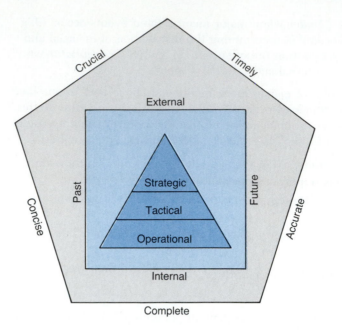

Past versus Future Information

Future information is another important concept that has to be emphasized in determining the information needs of management. It means that managers must be provided with information that helps them see future trends and determine their impact on their decision-making responsibilities. It's not enough to provide managers with historical (backward-looking) information and analysis. Future (forward-looking) information and analysis concerning trends developing inside the organization or in the business environment must also be provided. For example, an analysis of *past* sales performance may not provide management with adequate information. Sales management reports should also provide forecasts of *expected* trends in sales and factors that might affect sales performance.

Internal versus External Information

Management should also be provided with information about the internal operations of the business firm as well as the developments in the business environment. Refer back to Figure 9–2 and ahead to Figure 9–8. They summarize the types of external and internal information needed by management.

Levels of Management

Finally, the information requirements of management depend heavily on the **management level** involved. Figure 9–8 illustrates how management can be subdivided into three major levels: (1) *strategic management*, (2) *tactical management*, and (3) *operational management*. These levels are related to the traditional management levels of top management, middle management,

Figure 9–8 The activities and information requirements of the three major levels of management.

Management Levels	Primary Activities	Activity Results	Activity Examples	Information Requirements
Strategic Management	Long-range planning and goal setting Determine organizational resource requirements and allocations	Goals and strategic objectives Company policies Long-range plans and other strategic decisions	Policy on industry and product diversification Social responsibility policy Major capital expenditure policy	Forecasts Simulations Inquiries External reports One-time reports Condensed internal reports
Tactical Management	Allocate assigned resources to specific tasks Make rules Measure performance Exert control	Budgets Procedures Rules and other tactical decisions	Personnel practices Capital budgeting Marketing mix	Forecasts and historical data Regular internal reports Exception reports Simulations Inquiries
Operational Management	Direct the utilization of resources and the performance of tasks in conformance with established rules	Directions Commands Actions and other operational decisions	Production scheduling Inventory control Credit management	Regular internal reports Detailed transaction reports Procedures manuals Current and historical data Programmed decisions

and operating management. The activities and results of each management level are summarized in Figure 9–8, as well as the types of information required by level.

Figure 9–8 emphasizes that the information requirements of management are directly related to the types of activities that predominate in each level of management. For example, the strategic management level requires more summarized special one-time reports, forecasts, and external reports to support its heavy planning and policy-making responsibilities. The operational management level on the other hand, may require more regular internal reports emphasizing detailed current and historical data comparisons that support its control of day-to-day operations.

REAL WORLD APPLICATION 9–1

Gillette Corporation

Do you know the first 10 questions your chief executive officer will ask upon returning from a three-week vacation? Will he or she question sales results? Inventory levels? Cash balances? New order activity? Currency fluctuations? Stock market indexes? Better yet, do you help to provide the answers to your CEO's questions? Will your system quickly and easily correlate, track, and display the specific information that CEOs look for?

Executive information systems (EIS) claim to do just that. EIS applications primarily monitor and track strategic corporate business. They typically consist of easily operated, executive-to-system software interfaces that connect to both external data sources and internal corporate databases.

Prepackaged EIS software products include Comshare's Commander EIS and Pilot Executive Software's Command Center software. In addition, users are taking advantage of widely installed DSS products like Execucom Systems' IFPS or they are custom-designing proprietary systems. Let's look at one example.

To support executives who wanted an EIS that identifies, tracks, and analyzes data critical to the success of the company, Don Palmer, controller of Gillette Corp. of Boston, implemented a system that includes status monitoring with ad hoc query capabilities. Palmer, responsible for providing an EIS for all of Gillette's executives in North America, invested in Command Center, an EIS shell made by Pilot Executive Software, Inc. of Boston, and then set his staff to work making the system meet the corporation's requirements.

Currently, between 25 and 35 Gillette executives access Command Center using IBM Personal Computers linked to a Digital Equipment Corp. VAX 8600 superminicomputer. Information available through the EIS includes the Dow Jones News/Retrieval service, national and foreign news accounts, corporate financial results, market share information,

sales figures, and customer share information.

The system is built around critical success factors, which are indicators of how well business is going. Ninety-eight percent of this information is displayed graphically. "Ease of access is an important feature. You really don't need to be familiar with a keyboard except in terms of transmitting electronic messages," Palmer says. His staff made Command Center available as a menu item on the executives' Personal Computers, accessible after the user enters an appropriate password. The system menu is divided into external and internal categories, which can be examined further through the use of a mouse.

A key factor in the company's successful implementation of the package was the identification and preparation of the data the executives needed to access. "From the beginning, we saw EIS as a way of having a clearer insight on our performance against some key measures that were inherent in our whole strategic planning process," Palmer explains. "For this reason, we spent a fair amount of time identifying what our critical success factors were and how to measure them, as opposed to simply taking the existing reporting system and attempting to replicate that on a PC. Once that was done, it was not a difficult process to accomplish the technical implementation," he adds. However, to make Command Center accessible to the users, the company had to invest the programming time to enhance the user interface and add significant computer resources.

Application Questions

☐ What characteristics of information needed by managers are mentioned above? Give examples of each.

☐ What advantages or disadvantages do you see for the use of EIS to provide information to top management?

Source: Damien Rinaldi and Ted Jastremski, "Executive Information Systems," *Computerworld,* October 27, 1986, pp. 37–38.

Section II: Foundation Concepts: Information Systems

In Section I of this chapter we introduced the concept of the business firm as a system. We stressed the vital *feedback* role played by information systems. We also mentioned major types of information systems that provide feedback for business operations and management. Now let's look at each of these systems more closely to see how this is done.

In Chapter 1, we defined an information system as any system that uses the resources of hardware (machines and media), software (programs and procedures), and people (specialists and users) to perform input, processing, output, storage, and control activities that transform data resources into information products. Figure 9–9 illustrates a model of the resources and activities of information systems in computer-using organizations. Notice the following system components:

TYPES OF INFORMATION SYSTEMS

- ☐ **Input**—Data and information from within the organization or from the societal environment are entered into the system.
- ☐ **Processing**—Computer systems and other hardware, software, and people resources transform data resources into a variety of information products.
- ☐ **Output**—A variety of information products are produced by *operations* and *management* information systems.
- ☐ **Storage**—Data, information, models, and knowledge are stored for retrieval and processing.
- ☐ **Control**—*Information resource management* activities monitor and adjust the use of hardware, software, people, and data resources for optimum information system performance.

Figure 9–10 illustrates in more detail the major types of information systems in many organizations. This includes the following categories of *operations* and *management* information systems.

Operations information systems process data generated by and used in business operations. Major subsystems provide the following outputs:

- ☐ A variety of information products for internal and external use result from the processing of business transactions. This is accomplished by **transaction processing systems.**
- ☐ Operational decisions that control physical processes are produced by **process control systems.**
- ☐ Office communications are accomplished by **automated office systems.**

Management information systems provide information to support management decision making. Major subsystems provide the following outputs:

- ☐ Management reporting is accomplished by **management reporting systems.**
- ☐ Managerial decision support is accomplished by **decision support systems.**

Figure 9–9 The resources and activities of information systems in computer-using organizations.

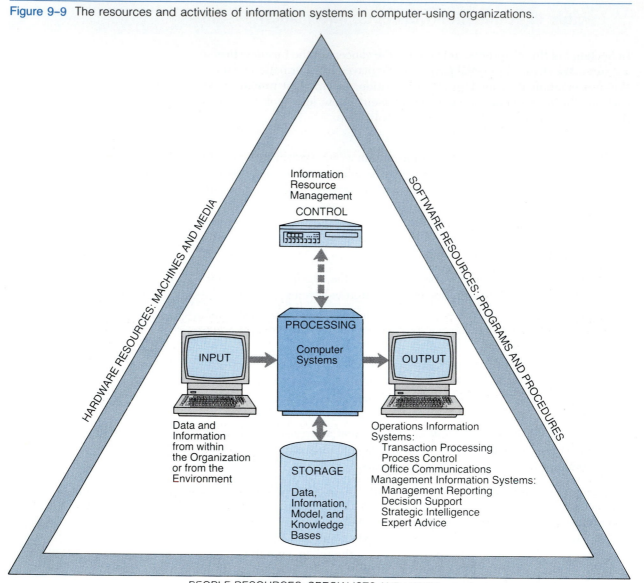

PEOPLE RESOURCES: SPECIALISTS AND USERS

☐ Strategic intelligence for top management is provided by **executive information systems.**

☐ Expert advice is provided by **expert systems** and other **knowledge-based systems.**

OPERATIONS INFORMATION SYSTEMS

Operations information systems process data that is generated by business operations (sales transactions, production results, employee payroll, etc.) but do not produce the kind of information that can best be used by management. Further processing by a management information system is usually required. Figure 9–11 shows how a manufacturing firm's operations information systems are related to its basic *physical operations* system.

Figure 9-10 Types of information systems. Notice the types of information systems included in the two major categories of operations and management information systems. Also note the main purpose of each type of information system.

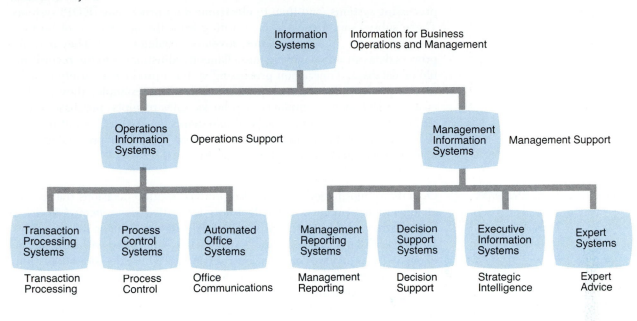

Figure 9-11 Examples of the operations information systems of a manufacturing firm. Notice how they are related to its physical operations system.

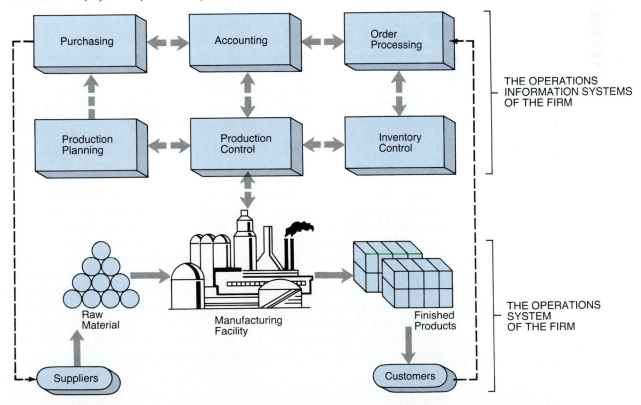

Transaction Processing Systems

Operations information systems include **transaction processing systems.** Transaction processing systems are the earliest type of information system. They evolved from manual information systems, to machine-assisted data processing systems, and then to **electronic data processing** (EDP) systems. These subsystems process data resulting from the occurrence of business transactions (i.e., sales, purchases, inventory changes, etc.). They may also process data caused by making miscellaneous adjustments to the records in a file or database. Transaction processing systems produce a variety of information products for internal or external use. For example, they produce customer statements, employee paychecks, sales receipts, purchase orders, dividend checks, tax forms, financial statements, and so on. They also update the databases of an organization that are used for further processing by its management information systems. See Figure 9–12.

Process Control Systems

Operations information systems also produce routine decisions that control an operational process. Such decisions are called *programmed decisions* because they are automated (programmed) by basing them on decision rules. Decision rules outline the actions to take when confronted with a certain set of events. This includes **process control systems,** where decisions adjusting a physical production process are automatically made by computers. For example, a petroleum refinery or the assembly lines of an automated factory use such systems. They monitor a physical process, capture and process data detected by sensors, and make realtime adjustments to a process. We will discuss such systems further in Chapter 13.

Automated Office Systems

Another major type of operations information system is transforming traditional manual office methods and paper communications media. **Automated office systems** collect, process, store, and transmit data and information in the form of electronic office communications. These automated systems rely on word processing, telecommunications, and other information system technologies. Typical subsystems include word processing, electronic mail, desktop publishing, teleconferencing, records management, micrographics, electronic calendars, and so on. We will discuss automated office systems in detail in Chapter 12.

MANAGEMENT INFORMATION SYSTEMS

When information systems are designed to provide information needed for effective decision making by managers, they are called **management information systems.** The concept of management information systems (MIS) originated in the 1960s and became the byword (and the "buzzword") of almost all attempts to relate computer technology and systems theory to data processing in business. During the early 1960s it became evident that the computer was being applied to the solution of business problems in a piecemeal fashion, focusing almost entirely on the computerization of clerical and record-keeping tasks. The concept of management information systems was developed to counteract such *inefficient* development and *ineffective* use of computers. The MIS concept is vital to efficient and effective computer use in business for two major reasons:

Figure 9-12 Examples of information products produced by transaction processing systems. Customer statements must be prepared and mailed to customers on a monthly basis. The cash requirements register lists the checks that must be prepared in payment of amounts owed to vendors.

LANG CORPORATION

STATEMENT OF CUSTOMER ACCOUNT

CUSTOMER NO. 554385

DATE 9/30/--

HITTON CORPORATION
138 MARSHALL DR.
PO BOX 851
LONG PORT, CA 94134

DATE			INVOICE NUMBER	REFERENCE NUMBER	DESCRIPTION	AMOUNT
MO	DY	YR				
					PRIOR BALANCE	$7.565.46
09	08	--	185163		INVOICE	1,685.91
09	10	--	075126		PAYMENT	1,856.00CR
09	15	--		091531	LC ADJUSTMENT	13.00CR
09	30	--			LATE CHARGES	8.00

CURRENT AMOUNT	30 DAYS	60 DAYS & OVER	BALANCE DUE
$1,693.91	$696.46		$2,390.37

K **KRAUSZ MANUFACTURING COMPANY**

ACCOUNTS PAYABLE

CASH REQUIREMENTS REGISTER

DATE APR 12 19

VENDOR	VENDOR NUMBER	DUE DATE	INVOICE AMOUNT	DISCOUNT	CHECK AMOUNT
SOLVAY GEN SUP	1016	4/16	$ 773.30	$ 15.47	$ 757.83
ROCHESTER PR CO	1021	4/16	1,620.18	32.40	1,587.78
CALABRIA CONT	1049	4/16	143.65	2.87	140.78
ONONDAGA STL CO	1077	4/16	5,982.82	119.66	5,863.16
BLACK & NICHOLS	1103	4/16	14.25	.71	13.54
AUSTERHOLZ INC	1240	4/16	624.77	12.50	612.27
AUSTERHOLZ INC	1240	4/16	1,833.19	36.66	1,796.53
CHRISTIE & CO	1366	4/16	745.54		745.54
WILSON & WILSON	2231	4/16	2,936.12	58.72	2,877.40
CLAR. HIGGINS	2590	4/16	1,000.00		1,000.00
HONOUR BROS	3101	4/16	97.36	1.95	95.41
BASTIANI & SON	3112	4/16	3,580.85	71.62	3,509.23
DRJ WIRE CO	3164	4/16	256.90	5.14	251.76
HASTING-WHITE	3258	4/16	1,144.42	22.89	1.121.53
DARONO ART MET	3427	4/16	32.75	.66	32.09
DARONO ART MET	3427	4/16	127.52	2.55	124.97
DARONO ART MET	3427	4/16	96.60	1.93	94.67

- ☐ It emphasizes the **management** orientation of information processing in business. The primary goal of computer-based information systems should be the support of *management decision making,* not merely the processing of data generated by business operations.
- ☐ It serves as a **systems** framework for organizing business computer applications. Business applications of computers should be viewed as interrelated and integrated *computer-based information systems* and not as independent data processing jobs.

MIS Subsystems

Management information systems are needed by all types of business managers because of the increased complexity and rate of change of today's business environment. For example, marketing managers need information about sales performance and trends. Financial managers need information concerning financing costs and investment returns. Production managers need information analyzing resource requirements and worker productivity. Personnel managers require information concerning employee compensation and professional development. Top managers need information to plan and control the strategic performance of their companies. Thus, effective management information systems must provide managers with a variety of marketing, financial, production, personnel, and strategic information products to support their decision-making responsibilities.

Providing information for management decision making by all levels of management is thus a complex task. Several major *MIS subsystems* are needed to provide information in a variety of forms for a variety of managerial levels, roles, styles, and responsibilities. These major subsystems include the four types of management information systems we introduced earlier. They are (1) management reporting systems, (2) decision support systems, (3) executive information systems, and (4) expert systems. We will discuss the roles of each of these MIS subsystems in this section.

MANAGEMENT REPORTING SYSTEMS

Figure 9–13 illustrates the concept of a management reporting system (MRS). It shows that hardware resources in the form of executive workstations, software resources of application packages, and people resources in the form of information specialists, all help managers get the information

Figure 9–13 The management reporting system concept. Notice that periodic, demand, and exception reports are produced as output.

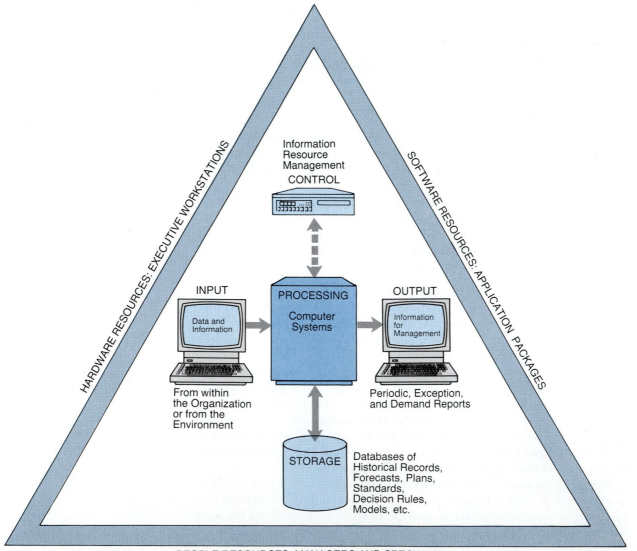

products they need from the data resources of the organization. Notice that the following system functions are included:

- ☐ **Input.** Collects data generated by operations information systems from the business firm and the business environment.

- ☐ **Processing.** Uses computer systems to transform data into information products for managers.

- ☐ **Storage.** Maintains databases containing data and information in the form of historical records, forecasts, plans, standards, decision rules, and models. Internal, external, and personal databases are used.

- ☐ **Output.** Provides a variety of information products needed to support the decision-making activities of managers. Displays, responses, and reports are provided (1) on demand, (2) according to a predetermined schedule, or (3) when exceptional conditions occur.

- ☐ **Control.** Depends on information resource management activities to control its performance. In this way, the MRS efficiently and effectively meets the information needs of managers. This management concept is explained in Chapter 15.

How do managers want and need their information? Do they prefer periodic scheduled reports or a quick response on demand? How about a prespecified report whenever an exceptional condition occurs? Or would an ad-hoc interactive modeling session with a computer be preferable? These are some of the choices facing system designers. They know that computer-based information systems can produce information to suit the timing and form preferences of most managers. For example, we saw in Chapter 5 that information can now be provided in the form of reports or video displays of *numeric data, text material,* or *graphics.* The major reporting alternatives for management information products are summarized below and illustrated in Figure 9–14.

Management Reporting Alternatives

Periodic Scheduled Reports

Examples of periodic scheduled reports are weekly sales analysis reports and monthly financial statements. This traditional form of providing information to managers uses a **prespecified** format designed to provide managers with information on a regular basis.

Exception Reports

Reports are produced only when exceptional conditions occur. Also, such reports usually contain information only about these exceptional conditions. For example, the credit manager is notified only if and when customers exceed their credit limits. Such exception reporting promotes *management by exception,* instead of overwhelming management with periodic detailed reports.

Figure 9–14 Types of management reports. Management reporting systems can produce periodic, demand, and exception reports for managers.

Periodic Report available each month giving information to managers about sales for each product.

```
                SALES BY PRODUCT REPORT
                MONTH ENDING 03/31/--


    PRODUCT         SOLD THIS    GROSS      PROFIT
                     MONTH       PROFIT     PERCENT
    ABRASIVES       2,720.19     271.36        10
    ACIDS AND
      CHEMICALS     1,216.27     170.27        14
    BRASS           6,220.83     435.45         7
    COPPER          9,337.18     664.73         7
```

Exception Report produced automatically whenever more than 20% of customers are delinquent in paying what they owe.

DELINQUENT ACCOUNTS REPORT

CUSTOMER NAME	BALANCE	CURRENT	OVER 30 DAYS	OVER 60 DAYS	90 DAYS & OVER	CREDIT LIMIT
ANDERSON CORP.	3704.35	1200.00	1121.50	850.00	532.85	3500.00
ARMSTRONG INTL.	3896.68	439.61	1911.25	499.00	1046.82	3000.00
FOXBORO CORP.	2222.18	1222.18	500.00	500.00		2000.00
SMYTHE CO.	1936.05	260.40	1100.00	575.65		1500.00
WELLS HARDWARE	3195.98	469.76	325.01	151.63	2249.58	3000.00

Demand Report produced whenever a manager wants to know information about the current status of purchases made from vendors.

PURCHASE ANALYSIS BY VENDOR

VENDOR'S NO.	VENDOR'S NAME	AMOUNT THIS MONTH	RETURNS YEAR TO DATE	NET AMOUNT YEAR TO DATE
27	ABBOT MACHINE CO.	1286.44		3194.26
58	ACE TOOL CO.			1975.15
66	ACME ABRASIVE CO.	342.86		1505.93
324	ALLAN ALLOYS CO.		95.10	4675.22
367	AMERICAN TOOL CO.			986.74
425	ANGUS METAL WORKS			842.89
475	APEX CORPORATION	2316.84	245.73	10476.79

Demand Reports and Responses

Information is provided whenever a manager demands it. For example, on-line video terminals and DBMS query languages and report generators allow managers to get immediate responses or reports as a result of their requests for information. They do not have to wait for periodic reports.

Decision support systems (DSS) are a natural progression from management reporting systems and earlier types of operations information systems. Decision support systems are interactive computer-based information systems that use *decision models* and *specialized databases* to provide information tailored to support specific decisions faced by individual managers. They are thus different from operations information systems, which focus on processing the data generated by business transactions and operations. They also differ from management reporting systems, which have primarily been focused on providing managers with *prespecified information* (reports) that could be used to help them make more effective, structured types of decisions.

Instead, decision support systems provide managers with *interactive responses* on an *ad-hoc* basis. Information is provided in an interactive session between a manager and a computer using an interactive modeling package. For example, using an electronic spreadsheet package results in a series of answers in response to alternative "what if?" questions from a manager. This differs from demand responses since managers are not demanding prespecified information. Rather, they are exploring possible alternatives and receiving tentative information based on a series of alternatives. Thus they do not have to specify their information needs in advance. Instead, the DDS interactively helps them find the information they need. See Figure 9–15.

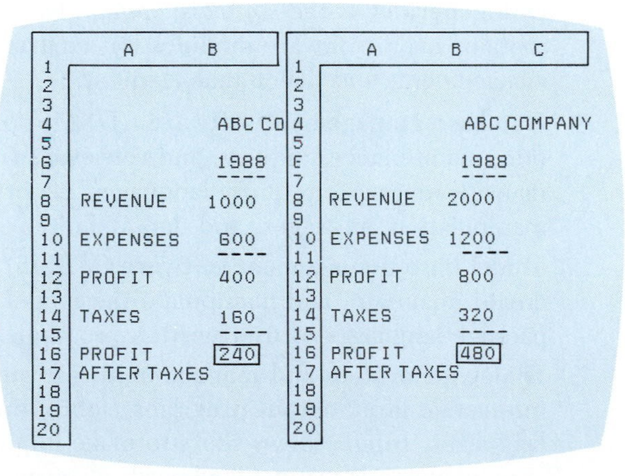

DECISION SUPPORT SYSTEMS

Figure 9–15 Using a spreadsheet program for decision support. A manager can interactively test the impact of various increases in sales revenue or other factors on the bottom line: profit after taxes. Notice what happened when revenue was increased to $2,000 in this example.

Figure 9–16 The decision support system concept. Notice that hardware, software, data, and model resources provide interactive decision support for managers.

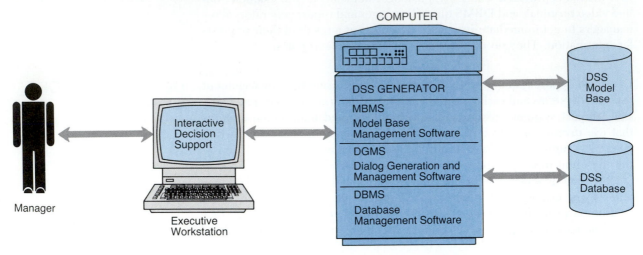

The Decision Support System Concept

Decision support systems help managers solve the *semistructured* and *unstructured* problems typically faced by decision makers in the real world. They are quick-response systems that are user-initiated and controlled and support the personal decision-making style of a manager. DSS are designed to use decision models and a decision maker's own insights and judgments in an interactive computer-based process leading up to a specific decision. Figure 9–16 illustrates the decision support system concept. Notice the following system components:

☐ An **executive workstation** is a personal computer or computer terminal that provides the DSS *hardware interface* for managers. A **DSS generator** is the *software engine* that drives the system. It contains major software modules for database management, model management, and dialog management.

☐ **Database management software.** (DBMS) provides database creation, maintenance, inquiry, and retrieval using typical database management system query languages, report generators, data manipulation languages, and data definition languages.

☐ **Model base management software** (MBMS) provides the ability to create, maintain, and manipulate the model base using modeling package languages or user-written programs.

☐ **Dialog generation and management software** (DGMS) consists of interactive input/output programs, subroutines, and nonprocedural languages. *Input*: allows users to make inquiries and responses or issue commands using a keyboard, electronic mouse, touch screen, voice input, and so on. *Output*: provides output in the form of numeric, text, and graphics visual displays or printed reports. Audio responses and menus, prompts, icons, and *help* displays may also be provided.

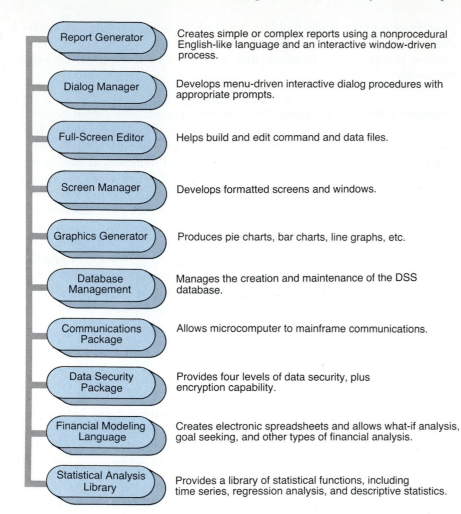

Report Generator	Creates simple or complex reports using a nonprocedural English-like language and an interactive window-driven process.
Dialog Manager	Develops menu-driven interactive dialog procedures with appropriate prompts.
Full-Screen Editor	Helps build and edit command and data files.
Screen Manager	Develops formatted screens and windows.
Graphics Generator	Produces pie charts, bar charts, line graphs, etc.
Database Management	Manages the creation and maintenance of the DSS database.
Communications Package	Allows microcomputer to mainframe communications.
Data Security Package	Provides four levels of data security, plus encryption capability.
Financial Modeling Language	Creates electronic spreadsheets and allows what-if analysis, goal seeking, and other types of financial analysis.
Statistical Analysis Library	Provides a library of statistical functions, including time series, regression analysis, and descriptive statistics.

Figure 9–17 The components and capabilities of a DSS generator: PC/FOCUS.

☐ A **database** of data and information is stored in a DSS database extracted from the databases of the organization, external databases, and a manager's personal database.

☐ A **model base** includes a library of models and analytical techniques stored as programs, subroutines, command files, and decision rules. The model base management software can combine these model components to create models for an individual manager needing support for a specific type of decision.

Figure 9–17 lists the components and capabilities of a popular DSS generator called FOCUS. Several other DSS software packages, such as IFPS, EXPRESS, MODEL, EMPIRE, and ENCORE, are available from independent consulting firms and computer manufacturers. Many are now available in microcomputer versions (e.g., PC/FOCUS or IFPS Personal). However, don't forget that even electronic spreadsheet packages (such as Lotus 1-2-3 and Multiplan) and especially integrated packages (such as Symphony, Enable, and Framework) are limited DSS generators. They provide some of the model building (spreadsheet models), model manipulation ("what if" analysis), database management and dialog management (menus, prompts, etc.) functions that are offered by more powerful DSS generators.

EXECUTIVE INFORMATION SYSTEMS

Executive information systems (EIS) are management information systems that are tailored to the strategic information needs of top management. Top executives get the information they need from many sources. This includes letters, memos, periodicals, and reports produced manually as well as by computer systems. Other sources of executive information are meetings, telephone calls, and social activities. Thus much of a top executive's information comes from noncomputer sources. Computer-generated information has not played a primary role in meeting many top executives' information needs.

The goal of computer-based executive information systems is to provide top management with immediate and easy access to information about key factors that are critical to accomplishing a firm's strategic objectives. Therefore, effective executive information systems should meet the following major critieria:

☐ EIS should be extremely easy to operate and understand. Response time should be immediate. Graphics displays should be used extensively. Realtime access to internal and external databases should be provided.

☐ EIS should provide information about the current status and projected trends in a company's critical success factors, as determined by their top executives. Information should be communicated in a form that is tailored to the preferences of the executives using the system.

Thus executive information systems are attempting to meet the special information needs of top management that are not being met by other forms of management information systems. Executives and information systems specialists in major corporations believe that advances in computer technology have made such systems feasible. Software packages that support EIS on mainframe, minicomputer, and microcomputer systems are now available. Figure 9–18 illustrates how an **EIS generator package** provides interactive graphics displays to top executives. It relies on other types of software to help access and transform data in internal, external, and special databases into information products for top management. The use of executive information systems is expected to grow rapidly as more top executives come to recognize their feasibility and benefits.

EXPERT SYSTEMS

The frontiers of information systems are being affected by developments in **artificial intelligence (AI).** Artificial intelligence is an area of computer science that is attempting to develop computers that can see, hear, walk, talk, feel, and think! Thus AI projects are developing natural programming languages, advanced industrial robots, and intelligent computers. A major

Figure 9–18 The executive information system concept. Notice that an EIS generator package relies on other major types of software to help access and transform data from internal, external, and special databases into interactive graphics displays for top executives.

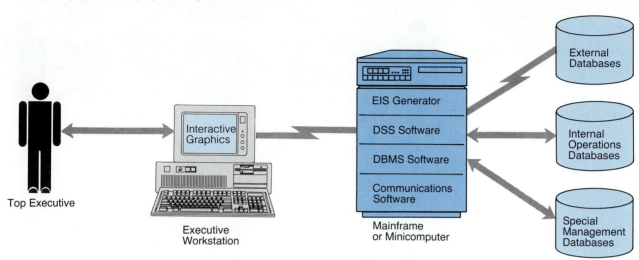

thrust is the development of computer functions normally associated with human intelligence, such as reasoning, inference, learning, and problem solving.

One of the most practical applications of this area of AI is the development of **expert systems.** An expert system is a computer-based information system that uses its knowledge about a specific complex application area to act as an expert consultant to users. The components of an expert system consist of a *knowledge base* and software modules that perform inferences on the knowledge and communicate answers to a user's questions. Figure 9–19 illustrates the interrelated components of an expert system.

An expert system's **knowledge base** typically consists of a *rule base* of IF–THEN rules and a *database* of facts and other information about a subject. The software modules usually consist of an **inference engine** and other programs for refining knowledge or communicating with users. The inference engine program processes the rules and data related to a specific problem. It then makes inferences resulting in recommended courses of action for a user. Inferences are made using *forward chaining* (reaching a conclusion by applying rules to facts), or *backward chaining* (justifying a proposed conclusion by determining if it results from applying rules to facts.)

Expert systems are also called **knowledge-based systems.** They are thus related to *knowledge-based DSS*, which add a knowledge base to the database and model base of traditional decision support systems. However, unlike decision support systems, expert systems usually provide answers to questions in a very specific problem area by making humanlike inferences about knowledge contained in a specialized knowledge base. They must also be able to explain their reasoning process and conclusions to a user. Figure 9–20 illustrates a dialog between an expert system package for bank loan loss analysis and a bank auditor.

Figure 9–19 Components of an expert system. The software modules perform inferences on a knowledge base built by an expert and/or knowledge engineer. This provides expert answers to a user's natural language questions in an interactive process.

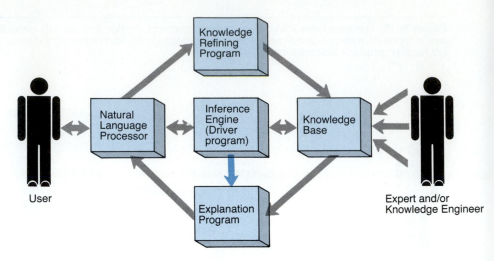

User

Expert and/or Knowledge Engineer

Figure 9–20 Using an expert system. Notice how this expert system package asks questions and explains its reasoning to a user.

```
Is the total of cash, accounts receivable and the current market
value of marketable securities equal to, or greater than, 75
percent of the current liabilities?

>> WHY?

    Your answer to this question will help determine whether the
    following rule is applicable in this consultation.

    rule 121:

    if  current-ratio = yes and
        current-ratio-industry = moderate and
        quick-ratio-industry = moderate and
        unused-line-of-credit = X2 and
        loan-officer-liquidity-evaluation = X3 and
        sell-noncurrent-assets = X4 and
        other-short-term-liabilities = X5

    then short-term-liquidity = moderate

Is the total of cash, accounts receivable and the current market
value of marketable securities equal to, or greater than, 75
percent of the current liabilities?

>> YES.
```

Expert systems are being applied to many specific application areas. Developing such large, complex expert systems typically requires the use of programming languages such as LISP or PROLOG and powerful special-purpose computers. However, there are relatively low-cost software packages available which help users develop their own smaller expert systems on microcomputers. These expert system *development tools* or **shells** consist of a generalized inference engine and a rule base manager program. They allow trained users to develop the specialized knowledge base and software modules for a specific application without starting from scratch. For example,

Medicine

Mycin diagnoses and prescribes treatments for meningitis and bacteremia infections. The Stanford University Medical Experimental Computer Facility developed the system.

Figure 9–21 Examples of expert systems. Notice the variety of applications that can be supported by such systems.

Training

Steamer teaches naval officers, through simluation, the techniques needed to run a steam propulsion plant similar to those used in many ships. The U.S. Navy Personal Research and Development Center developed it in cooperation with Bolt, Baranek and Newman, Inc.

Computer Systems

Xcon configures VAX computers on a daily basis for Digital Equipment Corp. DEC and Carnegie-Mellon University developed the system.

Chemistry

Dendral estimates the molecular structures of unknown compounds by analyzing mass spectrographic, nuclear magnetic resonance, and other data. Stanford University developed the system.

Engineering

Delta uses diagnostic strategies to identify and help maintenance workers correct malfunctions in diesel electric locomotives. The research and development center of General Electric Co. developed Delta.

Geology

Dipmeter Advisor estimates the subsurface geological structure of an area by analyzing dipmeter logs and other pertinent geological data. Schlumberger-Doll Research developed the program.

Business

Businessplan analyzes the financial performance of small businesses and produces recommendations in areas such as risk management, tax planning, employee benefits management, and pension planning. Developed by the Sterling Wentworth Corp. for use by financial planners on the IBM Personal Computer.

one shell uses a spreadsheet format to help users develop IF-THEN rules, while another automatically generates rules based on examples furnished by a user. Thus expert system shells are expected to accelerate the widespread use of expert systems. Figure 9–21 summarizes examples of several leading expert systems.

INTEGRATED INFORMATION SYSTEMS

Computer-based information systems in the real world are typically **integrated** combinations of management information systems and operations information systems. Thus most business information systems are designed to produce information and support decision making for various levels of management as well as do record-keeping and transaction processing chores.

For example, a payroll system that processes employee time cards and produces employee paychecks is an operations information system. An information system that uses payroll data to produce labor analysis reports, which shows variances and trends in labor cost and utilization, is a management information system. However, in most cases, these functions are combined in an integrated payroll/labor analysis system.

Another example involves sales order/transaction processing, which is an operations information system, and sales analysis, which is a management information system. However, both systems are typically integrated so that a sales order processing subsystem collects and records sales transaction data and provides input to a sales analysis subsystem, which produces management reports concerning sales activity. Figure 9–22 illustrates another typical example of integrated information systems in business.

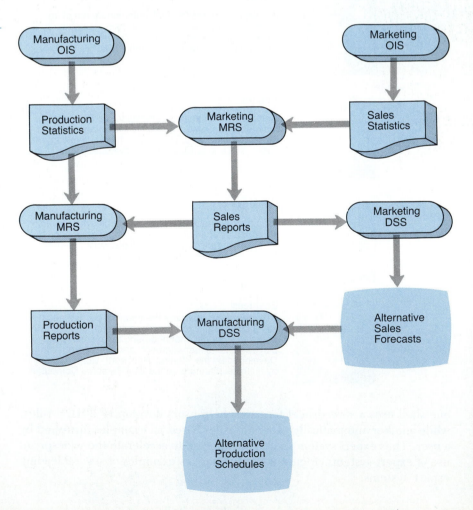

Figure 9–22 The interrelationships of business information systems. In this example, production and sales activity data are generated by manufacturing and marketing operations information systems. This data is used by marketing management reporting systems for sales reports and marketing DSS for sales forecasts. These are then used by production management reporting systems for production reports and production DSS for production scheduling.

REAL WORLD APPLICATION 9-2

E. I. du Pont de Nemours & Co., Inc.

According to conventional wisdom, an artificial intelligence (AI) project is a risky matter, requiring years of effort and millions of dollars. The entry price seemed too high for E. I. du Pont de Nemours & Co., Inc., according to Ed Mahler, manager of artificial intelligence at corporate headquarters in Wilmington, Delaware. "We decided, if that was the ante, we weren't going to play," Dr. Mahler said. Instead, Du Pont changed the rules of the game. Today, technical experts build their own expert systems, using application shells that eliminate the need for a programming language. Most of the development is done on PCs that are also used for other purposes, nearly eliminating capital costs.

Like the big-ticket projects that AI gurus oversee, Du Pont's payoff from a successful system is typically 10-to-1 or better, but the risks are minimal—a few days, a few thousand dollars. In less than a year, inspired and trained by Dr. Mahler's 12-member AI task force, employees have created more than 300 expert systems. By 1991, they expect to have 2,000 expert systems in use, yielding a 10 percent increase in net profits. At Du Pont, that means approximately $150 million.

The task force provides training courses ranging from management and supervisor awareness seminars to skill-building sessions in which participants learn to use the application shells. The group also does "jump starts"— joint rapid prototyping projects, taking between a couple of days and a week—that help the person with the expertise to start building a fully functional expert system.

Usually, Dr. Mahler said, using a shell speeds the writing of code by a factor of 10. He's baffled by the fuss people make over picking the right tool. "People make it a lot harder than it really is," he said. Shells are as different from each other as a word-processing package is from a spreadsheet, Dr. Mahler said. The structure of the knowledge dictates what kind of shell to use. "You ask yourself, 'How is the data? Is it in examples? Is it a backward chaining diagnostic? Does the expert reason in a forward direction?'"

After about eight months of operation, Dr. Mahler's AI group was logging a 90 percent success rate in the systems it helped develop. While the payoff from a single system may be small in terms of Du Pont's annual revenue, Dr. Mahler points out, "You make dollars out of pennies. A typical system may save between a half million and a million dollars in a year, after an investment of $20,000, counting personnel time and even a $5,000 PC."

Expert systems yield other, less tangible benefits, according to David Pensak, the task force technical overseer. Building an expert system forces people to set down rules of thumb and observations that have never been recorded. Further, he thinks that AI applications will make it easier for customers to do business with Du Pont. No sales representative can be knowledgeable in more than a small fraction of the thousands of products Du Pont makes, but an expert system could know them all. "If we have a salesman come in with his portable computer, and go through the entire product selection, I think that will get us a lot of business," he said. Expert systems, he added, can give Du Pont "such credibility for technical accuracy that people will always want to talk to us first."

Application Questions

☐ How is Du Pont using expert systems in its business? What is the role of expert system shells?

☐ What benefits result from the use of expert systems by Du Pont?

Source: Mickey Williamson, "At Du Pont, Expert Systems Are Key to AI Implementation," *PC Week*, January 13, 1987, pp. 35 and 57.

SUMMARY

☐ The business firm should be viewed as a system in which economic resources (input) are transformed by various organizational processes (processing) into goods and services (output). Information systems provide information on the operation of the business (feedback) to management for the direction and maintenance of the firm (control). The business firm is a subsystem of society and is surrounded by other systems of the business environment.

☐ Managers have to be provided with information that meets a variety of requirements. Information must be timely, accurate, complete, and concise. It must consist of both internal and external information, as well as information about the past and future. Finally, information must be tailored to the strategic, tactical, or operational level of the managers who need it.

☐ Major types of information systems include operations information systems such as transaction processing systems, process control systems, and automated office systems, and management information systems such as management reporting systems, decision support systems, executive information systems, and expert systems. These computer-based information systems make extensive use of hardware, software, and people resources to transform data resources into a variety of information products.

☐ Management information systems are systems that provide information needed for effective management decision making. The concept of management information systems was developed to provide a systems framework and management orientation for the development of efficient and effective computer applications in business. This includes management reporting systems, which provide prespecified information needed by managers on demand, according to a schedule, or on an exception basis.

☐ Decision support systems are interactive, computer-based information systems that use decision models and a management database to provide information tailored to support specific decisions faced by individual managers. They are designed to use a decision maker's own insights and judgments in an interactive computer-based process leading up to a specific decision.

☐ Executive information systems are easy to use and understand MIS for executives. They are management information systems that are tailored to the strategic information needs of top management. Expert systems are computer-based information systems that use a knowledge base about a specific complex application area and an inference engine program to act as an expert consultant to users.

☐ The concept of integrated information systems emphasizes that the management and operations information systems of an organization are usually combined into integrated business information systems. These systems provide information and decision support for several levels of management and also perform traditional data processing activities.

These are the key terms and concepts of this chapter. The page number of their first explanation is in parentheses.

1. A business as a system *(322)*
2. Artificial intelligence *(346)*
3. Automated office systems *(338)*
4. Business environment *(323)*
5. Critical success factors *(331)*
6. Decision-making activities *(331)*
7. Decision support systems *(343)*
8. DSS generator *(344)*
9. Executive information systems *(346)*
10. Expert systems *(346)*
11. Functions of business *(325)*
12. Functions of management *(329)*
13. Inference engine *(347)*
14. Information quality *(331)*
15. Information system *(335)*
16. Integrated information systems *(350)*
17. Internal versus external information *(332)*
18. Knowledge base *(347)*
19. Management information systems *(338)*
20. Management levels *(332)*
21. Management reporting alternatives *(341)*
    a. Periodic
    b. Exception
    c. Demand
22. Management reporting systems *(340)*
23. Managerial roles *(330)*
24. Operations information systems *(336)*
25. Past versus future information *(332)*
26. Process control systems *(337)*
27. Transaction processing systems *(337)*
28. Trends in business computer use *(326)*

Match one of the **key terms and concepts** listed above with one of the brief examples or definitions listed below. Try to find the "best fit" for answers that seem to fit more than one term or concept. Defend your choices.

_____ 1. Management is the control component of this system.

_____ 2. Is a feedback component of a business as a system.

_____ 3. Customers, competitors, suppliers, stockholders, government agencies, and so on.

_____ 4. Include transaction processing, process control, and automated office subsystems.

_____ 5. Handle routine information processing generated by business activities.

_____ 6. Include management reporting, decision support, executive information, and expert subsystems.

_____ 7. Provide information for managers in a variety of structured formats.

_____ 8. Provide interactive support for decision making.

_____   9. Serve as consultants to users.

_____   10. Controls and ongoing physical process.

_____   11. Provide electronic office communications.

_____   12. Perform traditional data processing and also provide information to managers.

_____   13. Marketing, production/operations, accounting, finance, personnel, and so on.

_____   14. Planning, organizing, staffing, directing, and controlling.

_____   15. Leader, liaison, monitor, entrepreneur, negotiator, and so on.

_____   16. Intelligence, design, choice, and review.

_____   17. Information is timely, accurate, complete, concise, and crucial.

_____   18. Key factors crucial to the success of the enterprise.

_____   19. Information providing forecasts of possible results.

_____   20. Information about competitors and economic developments.

_____   21. Information provided on a scheduled basis.

_____   22. Selected information on a selective basis.

_____   23. Information provided whenever you want it.

_____   24. Strategic, tactical, and operational management.

_____   25. Software containing modules for database management, model management, and dialog management.

_____   26. Hopes to develop computers that can see, hear, walk, talk, feel, and think.

_____   27. Software that applies rules to facts to reach conclusions.

_____   28. From record-keeping functions, to operations control functions, to strategic planning functions.

APPLICATION PROBLEMS

1. If you have not already done so, read and answer the questions after the two Real World Applications in this chapter.

2. Application A has the following characteristics: relatively little data input, numerous and complex computations, infrequently run. Application B has the following characteristics: voluminous files of data, relatively simple computations, periodic program runs. Which of these systems is most likely to be an operations information system? Which is probably a decision support system? Explain your choices.

3. The executives of ABC Department Stores currently receive some of the following types of information products: (*a*) monthly financial statements, (*b*) weekly sales analysis reports, and (*c*) weekly inventory status reports. The VP for information services is proud of how accurate and complete these reports are. But some ABC executives are complaining that these reports don't meet their information needs. Use the management information requirements summarized in Figure 9–7 and the examples shown in Figure 9–14 to analyze what the problem is, and to suggest and defend several possible solutions.

4. Have you used a personal computer (or mainframe computer terminal) and an electronic spreadsheet package or an integrated package yet? Analyze your experience in terms of the management reporting system model shown in Figure 9–13 and the DSS model shown in Figure 9–16. That is, list each system component of these models that you can identify when using these packages.

5. Use an electronic spreadsheet or integrated package. What features did it have that you feel would be helpful to a user in terms of decision-making support? Explain the reasons for your choices.

6. Use an electronic spreadsheet or integrated package. What features need to be added or improved to make these packages easier to use and more effective DSS generators? Explain how and why this should be done.

7. Assign one of the following types of systems to the examples below:
    a. Transaction processing   e. Decision support system.
        system.   f. Executive information system.
    b. Process control system.   g. Expert system.
    c. Automated office system.
    d. Management reporting
        system.

    _____ 1. Responds interactively to a series of "what-if" questions.
    _____ 2. Sensors capture data generated by a chemical process.
    _____ 3. Captures sales data and updates inventory files.
    _____ 4. Asks questions and suggests answers to a complex problem.
    _____ 5. Provides word processing and electronic mail services.
    _____ 6. Provides top management with graphics displays about organizational performance.
    _____ 7. Provides prespecified reports to management on a scheduled, exception, and demand basis.

8. In your day-to-day activities you probably receive information from a variety of computer-based sources. For example, banks, retail stores, schools, businesses, and government agencies may send you computer-generated forms and reports. Use Figure 9–7 to help you evaluate the quality of any two of these information products.

INFORMATION SYSTEMS DEVELOPMENT

Chapter Outline

Learning Objectives

The purpose of this chapter is to promote a basic understanding of the process by which computer-based information systems are developed. After reading and studying this chapter, you should be able to:

1. Explain what *the systems approach* means in terms of a systems viewpoint and process.

2. Discuss how methods of computer-assisted systems development are changing the traditional activities of information systems development.

3. Explain why and how users should be involved in systems analysis and design.

4. Outline the stages of the traditional information systems development cycle.

5. Describe the content of a feasibility study.

6. Outline some of the potential costs and benefits of a computer-based information system.

7. Explain the purpose and activities of systems analysis and systems design.

8. Identify the purpose and activities of systems implementation and maintenance.

9. Use several tools of systems analysis and design to help solve simple information processing problems.

10. Identify several input, processing, output, storage, and control considerations of systems analysis and design. Illustrate them with examples based on your own experience or on one of the information systems discussed in Chapters 12, 13, and 14.

Section I: Foundation Concepts

WHY LEARN SYSTEMS ANALYSIS AND DESIGN?

Suppose the manager of a firm where you worked asked you to find a better way to get information to the salespeople in your company. How would you start? What would you do? Would you just plunge ahead and hope you could come up with a reasonable solution? How would you know whether your solution was a good one for your company? Do you think that there might be a systematic way to help you develop a good solution to your manager's request? There is. It's a developmental process called **information systems development,** or, more popularly, **systems analysis and design.**

The computer-based information systems discussed in this text do not just happen. They must be conceived, designed, and implemented using a systems development process. Thus information systems development or systems analysis and design is a systematic process in which users and systems analysts **design** information systems based on an **analysis** of the information requirements of an organization.

Effective systems analysis and design is vital to the development of computer-based information systems. Ineffective and inefficient use of computers in business is frequently attributed to a failure to understand and apply basic systems concepts to the information requirements of a business. To a great extent, therefore, successful use of computers in business requires that every computer user should learn to accomplish or manage the basic activities of systems analysis and design.

THE SYSTEMS APPROACH

The **systems approach** is a term that describes the use of the systems concept in studying a problem and formulating a solution. The systems approach has two basic characteristics: (1) using a **systems viewpoint** and (2) using a **systems process.**

A Systems Viewpoint

When you use a **systems viewpoint,** you try to find systems, subsystems, and components of systems in any situation you are studying. This ensures that all important factors and their interrelationships are considered. This viewpoint encourages you to look for the components and relationships of a *system* as you analyze a specific problem and formulate its solution.

For example, we have used a systems viewpoint throughout this text as we analyzed information processing, computers, and business firms as **systems** of **input, processing, output, storage,** and **control** components. Systems analysis and design can thus be understood as a process where users and systems analysts determine how these basic information system functions *are* and *should be* accomplished for a particular business activity. Figure 10–1 illustrates this concept which can be applied to present or proposed information systems for an organization. Here are some basic questions systems analysis and design must answer:

☐ **Input.** How is data captured and prepared for processing? How should it be? What **data resources** are or should be captured?

☐ **Processing.** How is data manipulated and transformed into information? How should it be? What processing alternatives should be considered?

Figure 10–1 The system's approach as a systems viewpoint. Systems analysis and design must answer basic questions about present and proposed information system resources and activities.

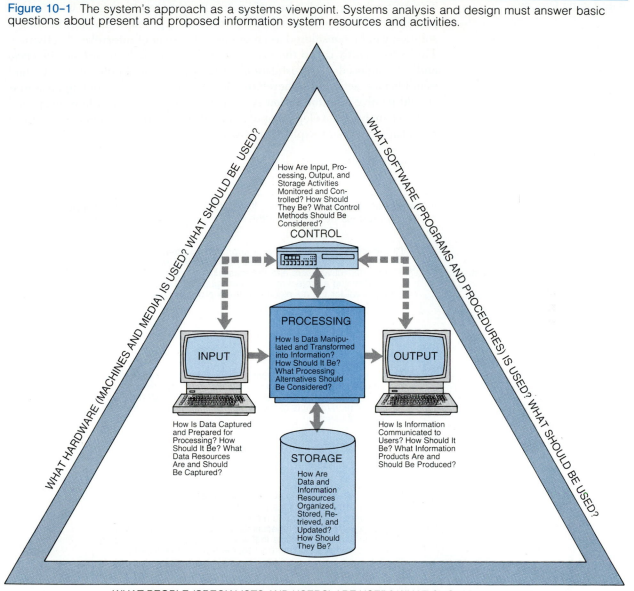

□ **Output.** How is information communicated to users? How should it be? What **information products** are and should be produced?

□ **Storage.** How are data and information resources organized, stored, updated, and retrieved? How should they be?

□ **Control.** How are input, processing, output, and storage activities monitored and controlled? How should they be? What control methods should be considered?

□ **Hardware, software, and people resources.** What hardware (machines and media), software (programs and procedures), and people (specialist and users) are or should be used to accomplish each of the information system activities of this system?

A Systems Process

The systems approach also refers to the **process** by which we study a problem and formulate a solution. Studying a problem and formulating a solution can be considered as an organized *system* of interrelated activities. This is frequently called the *systems development cycle* or *systems life cycle* and is composed of investigation, analysis, design, implementation, and maintenance activities. Therefore, developing new computer applications should involve an **information systems development cycle** where users and systems analysts develop computer-based information systems. The rest of this chapter is spent explaining how this is accomplished.

Figure 10–2 The traditional information systems development cycle. It emphasizes that developing a new user application should be a systematic multistep process consisting of the activities summarized below.

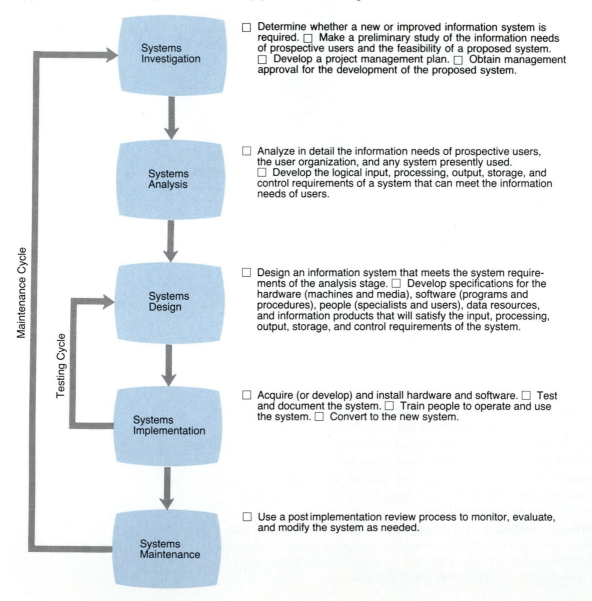

Systems Investigation

☐ Determine whether a new or improved information system is required. ☐ Make a preliminary study of the information needs of prospective users and the feasibility of a proposed system. ☐ Develop a project management plan. ☐ Obtain management approval for the development of the proposed system.

Systems Analysis

☐ Analyze in detail the information needs of prospective users, the user organization, and any system presently used. ☐ Develop the logical input, processing, output, storage, and control requirements of a system that can meet the information needs of users.

Systems Design

☐ Design an information system that meets the system requirements of the analysis stage. ☐ Develop specifications for the hardware (machines and media), software (programs and procedures), people (specialists and users), data resources, and information products that will satisfy the input, processing, output, storage, and control requirements of the system.

Systems Implementation

☐ Acquire (or develop) and install hardware and software. ☐ Test and document the system. ☐ Train people to operate and use the system. ☐ Convert to the new system.

Systems Maintenance

☐ Use a post implementation review process to monitor, evaluate, and modify the system as needed.

Maintenance Cycle

Testing Cycle

Figure 10–2 summarizes what goes on in each stage of the traditional information systems development cycle, which includes the stages of (1) **investigation,** (2) **analysis,** (3) **design,** (4) **implementation,** and (5) **maintenance.** It emphasizes that developing a new user application should be a systematic multistep process based on a systems development cycle concept.

You should realize however, that all of the activities involved are highly related and interdependent. Therefore, in actual practice, several developmental activities can be occurring at the same time. Also, different parts of a development project can be at different stages of the development cycle. For example, there may be a *testing cycle,* where a new system is tested and redesigned. Also typical is a *maintenance cycle,* where some of the activities of systems development are performed again to improve an established system.

THE SYSTEMS DEVELOPMENT CYCLE

The systems development process is changing. It is being automated by software packages such as systems development generators, application generators, screen generators, report generators, and so on. Figure 10–3 is an example of a systems development package. Other examples are shown in the next chapter. These packages allow users and systems analysts to use computers to perform some of the activities of the systems development process. Thus systems can be developed more quickly, with more user participation. Figure 10–4 outlines some of the changes caused by **computer-assisted systems development.** Let's look at its two main effects: **prototyping** and **user-developed systems.**

COMPUTER-ASSISTED SYSTEMS DEVELOPMENT

This is a "quick and dirty" type of systems development. It is widely used for the development of small applications. Typically, large systems still require using the traditional system development approach, but parts of such systems can frequently be prototyped. An *actual working model* (a **prototype**) of

Prototyping

Figure 10–3 An example of a systems development generator. The Excelerator package allows a systems analyst to interactively develop formal system specifications, data flow diagrams, a data dictionary, and the format of input screens and output reports.

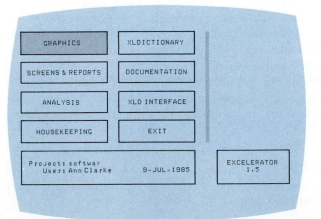
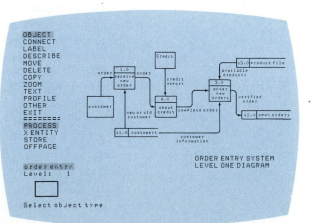

Figure 10-4 Differences in some of the activities of traditional and computer-assisted systems development. Notice the benefits in speed, cost, creativity, and level of difficulty when computers assist the process.

Systems Development Activities	Traditional Systems Development	Application Generator Used as a Prototyping Aid Followed by Programming	Computer-Assisted Systems Development
Requirements Analysis	A time-consuming, formal operation, often delayed by long application backlog.	The user's imagination is stimulated. Users may work at a screen with an analyst to develop requirements.	The user's imagination is stimulated. Users may develop their own requirements, or work with an analyst.
System Specifications	Lengthy document. Boring. Often inadequate.	Produced by prototyping aid. Precise and tested.	Disappears.
User Sign-Off	User is often not sure what he or she is signing off on. User cannot perceive all subtleties.	User sees the results and may modify them many times before signing off.	No formal sign-off. Adjustment and modification is an ongoing process.
Coding and Testing	Slow. Expensive. Often delayed because of backlog.	The prototype is converted to more efficient code. Relatively quick and error-free.	Quick. Inexpensive. Disappears to a large extent.
Documentation	Tedious. Time-consuming.	May be partly automated. Interactive training and HELP response may be created online.	Largely automatic. Interactive training and HELP responses are created online.
Maintenance	Slow. Expensive. Often late.	Often slow. Often expensive. Often late.	A continuing process with user and analyst making adjustments. Most of these adjustments can be made very quickly—in hours rather than months.

the information system needed by a user is developed quickly. Prototyping requires the use of application generator packages or other types of systems development packages. It involves an interactive process between a systems analyst and a user. The user can begin to use the prototype immediately. The prototype is usually modified several times by the systems analyst until the user finds it acceptable. Any program modules not directly developed by the application generator can then be coded using conventional programming languages. The final version of the system is then turned over to the user. See Figure 10–5.

User-Developed Systems

This is a "do-it-yourself" type of systems development. Many users do not need systems analysts and programmers to develop small applications. They can do it themselves with the help of the following resources:

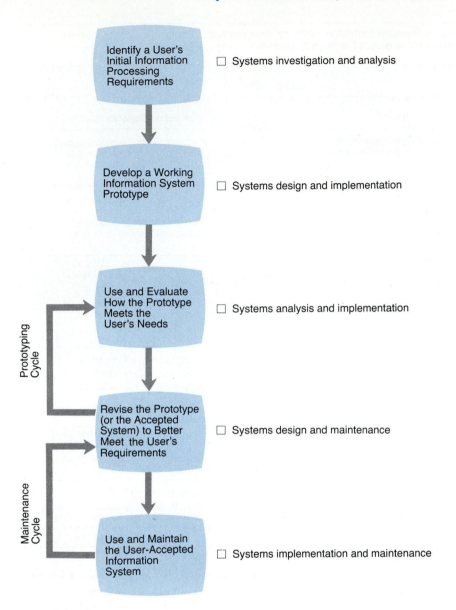

Identify a User's Initial Information Processing Requirements

☐ Systems investigation and analysis

Develop a Working Information System Prototype

☐ Systems design and implementation

Use and Evaluate How the Prototype Meets the User's Needs

☐ Systems analysis and implementation

Prototyping Cycle

Revise the Prototype (or the Accepted System) to Better Meet the User's Requirements

☐ Systems design and maintenance

Maintenance Cycle

Use and Maintain the User-Accepted Information System

☐ Systems implementation and maintenance

Figure 10–5 Information systems development with prototyping. Notice how prototyping overlaps the steps of the traditional systems development cycle.

☐ **Hardware resources.** Intelligent workstations provide both microcomputer power and mainframe power through data communications links to large computers.

☐ **Software resources.** Computer-assisted systems development packages can be used (such as application and systems development generators). General-purpose system and application packages (such as database management and electronic spreadsheet programs) can also help users develop their own applications.

☐ **Organizational resources.** Organizations establish *information centers* to provide users with hardware, software, and people support from systems analysts working as *consultants* to users. We will have more to say about this user support group in Chapter 15.

Figure 10–6 Responsibilities during traditional information systems development. Notice the extent of user involvement even when the information services staff is heavily involved.

	Responsibilities of	
Stages	Users	Information Services Staff
Investigation	Initiate study, suggest application, sketch information needs, describe existing processing procedures.	Listen to requirements, respond to questions, devise alternatives, assess using rough estimates, prepare preliminary survey.
Analysis	Help evaluate existing system and proposed alternatives, select alternative for design. Help describe existing system, collect and analyze data.	Evaluate alternatives using agreed-upon criteria. Conduct analysis, collect data, and document findings.
Design	Design, input, processing output, logic; plan for conversion and forecast impact on users, design manual procedures; remain aware of file structures and design. Review specifications, help develop specifications for manual procedures.	Present alternatives and trade-offs to users for their decisions. Combine user needs with technical requirements to develop specifications, develop technical conversion plan.
Implementation	Review the evaluation and acquisition of hardware and software. Generate test data and evaluate results. Develop materials, conduct training sessions. Phase conversion, provide resources.	Organize programming if required. Design modules, code programs. Evaluate and acquire hardware and software. Test software modules individually and in entire system. Aid in preparation of materials and train operations staff. Coordinate conversion, perform conversion processing tasks.
Maintenance	Conduct postimplementation audit. Provide data and use output, monitor system use and quality, suggest modifications and enhancements.	Help in postimplementation audit. Process data to produce output reliability, respond to enhancement requests, suggest improvements, monitor service.

USER INVOLVEMENT IN SYSTEMS DEVELOPMENT

Computer-assisted systems development methods make the job of information systems development easier, but they do not eliminate it. Such methods help you move more quickly through the stages of systems development by making it an automated, interactive process. There is less pressure to develop perfect systems the first time around. Hardware and software tools make it easier to go through several iterations of the systems development process until the system is refined to the point of acceptability.

However, users and systems analysts must still use **the systems approach** to build effective information systems. You cannot design a good system if you ignore how the system functions of input, processing, output, storage, and control will be performed. You cannot design a good system if you do not accomplish some of the major activities of systems development, such as determining feasibility, examining what user information needs really are, testing the system properly, and developing adequate documentation.

Figure 10–6 outlines in more detail the important responsibilities that users and systems development personnel should assume in each stage of the development of major computer-based information systems. Notice that

Figure 10–7 Systems development without user involvement. Effective information systems cannot be developed without involving users.

As Stated in the System Requirements

As Outlined in the System Specifications

As Designed by the Systems Analyst

As Implemented by Information Services

As Operated by the User

What the User Really Needed

users are deeply involved from inception to final installation and operation. In fact, users should be part of a *project team* along with systems development professionals such as systems analysts, programmers, auditors, and various technical specialists. In these ways, users are directly involved in systems development activity and decisions. A tongue-in-cheek reminder of what happens to a systems development project when users are not involved is illustrated in Figure 10–7.

User involvement has three major benefits:

☐ New systems should better reflect the true information requirements and capabilities of the users of the system.

☐ New systems will be more acceptable to users, since they are developed by a joint effort, rather than by "outsiders."

☐ User involvement helps ensure the cooperation of users in solving the problems that typically arise when any new system is installed and operated.

REAL WORLD APPLICATION 10–1

The Gap, Inc.

Jim Carolan looks like he plans to spend the day at the ballpark and not in the computer room. In his blue, short-sleeve polo shirt and jeans, Carolan's attire is atypical of the suited corporate systems planner or funky technical wizard. Clothing is an important part of business for the vice president of MIS at The Gap, Inc., San Bruno, California. In fact, selling casual clothing through its 641 stores is the company's business. "We're a shirt-sleeve organization," Carolan says, half jokingly. But his interest in The Gap's business has helped him create an MIS department that has cut turnover drastically and captured the respect of users, even as its budget has held steady for three years at about $9 million.

For its part, by getting analysts out of computer rooms and into the merchandising arena, Carolan's department is designing systems with a better understanding of The Gap's business and the bottom line. "We're not technology-driven, we're business-driven," Carolan says. New systems in the merchandising department, for example, allow the distribution group to review the sales of any item on a day-to-day basis, making it easier to isolate fast-moving or slow-selling goods. "We now have the ability to take reorders and make changes in the goods much faster," says Rick Eastwick, director of planning and distribution for the men's department.

Two years ago, the merchandising division threw out "98 percent of the application systems because they were too cumbersome for users to access," Eastwick says. "Today, those systems have been adapted to the selling process, and we now have the ability to react quicker to the retail business than we ever have before.

The systems are easier to use because [MIS staff members] have taken an active role in the business," He says. "MIS is aware of what's going on because they come to our floor, they go to The Gap stores, they wear Gap clothes and they stroll around asking what's new. It keeps their interest high. They even adopted our terminology. They're not just stereotypical computer heads," Eastwick says.

The Gap used to have "a standard data processing shop," says Jim Brownell, director of computer services. "We had all the classic symptoms where we'd go off to build the system thinking we knew what users wanted. The shop had some major failures because systems didn't deliver as planned," he said.

Now, MIS project leaders and programmers often are urged to spend as much as half their time out of the computer department learning about the way The Gap works, studying, for example, how goods are moved from warehouse to store. In a result that might spark envy among MIS managers elsewhere, programmer turnover is down to less than 10 percent, compared with 50 to 60 percent two years ago. Use of flextime and an optional four-day week have also helped.

Merchandising is one of the MIS department's largest and most important users, and also the one with which it enjoys the best relationship, Carolan says. Eastwick concurs. "There is more of a team environment here," he says. "We see them and they see us as a team that works to get the goods to the stores and sales to the bottom line."

Application Questions

□ What has The Gap done to involve analysts and users in systems development?

□ What benefits have occurred from making systems analysts part of the "business team"?

Source: Maura McEnaney, "Sales Drive DP at The Gap," *Computerworld,* September 29, 1986, pp. 65–66.

Section II: The Systems Development Process

Do we have an information problem? What is causing the problem? Would a new or improved information system help solve the problem? What would be a *feasible* information system solution to our problem?

These are the questions that have to be answered in the systems investigation stage—the first step in the systems development process. This stage results in the selection and preliminary study of a proposed system. Because the process of developing a major information system can be a costly one, this stage may require a preliminary study called a **feasibility study.** Systems investigation typically includes the steps shown in Figure 10–8 whenever a large information system is being proposed for development.

A **feasibility study** is a preliminary study that determines the information needs of prospective users and the objectives, constraints, basic resource requirements, cost/benefits, and feasibility of proposed projects. The findings of such a preliminary study are usually formalized in a written report, which is submitted to the management of the firm for approval before development work can begin.

SYSTEMS INVESTIGATION

Feasibility Studies

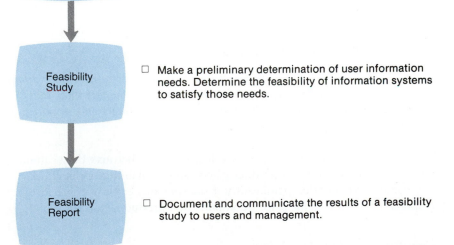

System Survey and Selection
☐ Survey the organization to screen and select potential systems development projects.

Feasibility Study
☐ Make a preliminary determination of user information needs. Determine the feasibility of information systems to satisfy those needs.

Feasibility Report
☐ Document and communicate the results of a feasibility study to users and management.

Figure 10–8 Activities of the systems investigation stage. These steps are involved whenever large information systems are being proposed.

Information-Gathering Methods

How do you get the information you need for a feasibility study and for the other stages of systems development? Information must be gathered from present and prospective users by:

- ☐ Personal interviews with users, operators, and managers.
- ☐ Questionnaires to appropriate individuals in the organization.
- ☐ Personal observation of business operations and any present system.
- ☐ Examination of documents, reports, data media, procedures manuals, and other methods of systems documentation.
- ☐ Inspecting accounting and management reports to collect operating statistics and cost data for information processing operations.

Now let's look at some of the basic factors that users and analysts need to identify in a feasibility study.

Determining System Objectives

Feasibility studies should begin by determining (1) what the objectives of the proposed information system are, and (2) how this fits into the organization's strategic plan for information systems. The proposed system must support the objectives for information systems specified in the organization's long-range strategic plan. If not, a reappraisal of the objectives of the proposed system or the strategic plan must be made. The specific objectives of the business activities involved (sales, purchasing, shipping, etc.) and the information systems that support those activities must be determined. Objectives should not be stated in vague terms. Compare the statement, "Improve efficiency," with a more specific statement:

Example.   Provide up-to-date production status information to the shipping department on a realtime basis.

Defining Problems and Opportunities

Problems and opportunities must be identified in a feasibility study. *Symptoms* must be separated from *problems*. For example, the fact that "sales are declining" is not a properly defined problem. Problem and opportunity statements that get closer to the facts are:

Example.   *Problem:* Salespersons are losing orders because they cannot get current information on product prices and availability. *Opportunity:* We could increase sales significantly if salespersons could receive instant responses to requests for price quotations and product availability.

Determining Information Needs

The feasibility study should make a preliminary determination of the *information needs* of prospective users. *Who* wants *what* information and *when*, *where*, *why*, and *how* they want it are the basic questions that must be answered. Users may express their information needs by describing a problem that has developed. For example, "We are not receiving production information early enough in our shipping department." Such statements are symptoms of an underlying information system problem that must be identified by further study. Information needs should also be stated specifically. For example, "Get me all the facts," or "Give me more information than I am getting now" are not specific statements of information needs. A better statement of information needs is:

Example. We need immediate notification concerning any products in inventory that have fallen below minimum inventory levels.

Identifying System Constraints

The feasibility study must identify the *constraints* of the proposed system, also known as the *restrictions* or *boundaries* of a system. Constraints are restrictions that limit the form and content of the system design. Constraints can be *external* to the business organization:

Example. Restrictions are typically required by law or industry agreement on the format and size of source documents or output documents, such as the checks of the banking industry and the forms required by the Internal Revenue Service.

Internal constraints may arise due to a scarcity of organizational resources or due to conflicting information needs and objectives of departments and personnel within an organization. For example, the objective of providing timely production status information to the shipping department may be restricted by this constraint:

Example. Operating costs of any new system must not exceed the costs of the present system, and no additional duties can be imposed on production personnel.

Determining System Criteria

An important step in systems investigation is defining the *criteria* to be used in evaluating the feasibility of the alternative systems being proposed. Criteria must also be ranked in order of their importance, because a criterion such as "low cost" may conflict with a criterion such as "instant response." Typical criteria categories to be specified include:

- ☐ Response time.
- ☐ Operating cost.
- ☐ Accuracy.
- ☐ Reliability.
- ☐ Capacity.
- ☐ Security.

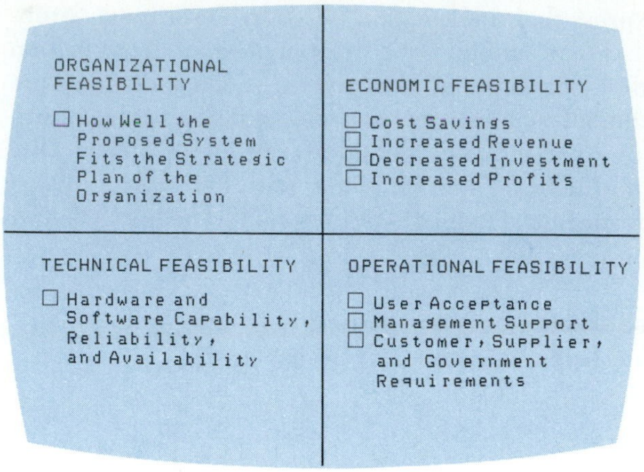

Figure 10–9 Organizational, economic, technical, and operational feasibility factors. This emphasizes that there is more to feasibility than cost savings or the availability of hardware and software.

ORGANIZATIONAL
FEASIBILITY

☐ How Well the
  Proposed System
  Fits the Strategic
  Plan of the
  Organization

ECONOMIC FEASIBILITY

☐ Cost Savings
☐ Increased Revenue
☐ Decreased Investment
☐ Increased Profits

TECHNICAL FEASIBILITY

☐ Hardware and
  Software Capability,
  Reliability,
  and Availability

OPERATIONAL FEASIBILITY

☐ User Acceptance
☐ Management Support
☐ Customer, Supplier,
  and Government
  Requirements

Figure 10–9 Organizational, economic, technical, and operational feasibility factors. This emphasizes that there is more to feasibility than cost savings or the availability of hardware and software.

The Feasibility of a System

The goal of feasibility studies is to evaluate alternative systems and to select the most feasible and desirable system for development. The feasibility of a proposed system can be evaluated in terms of four major categories, summarized below and illustrated in Figure 10–9.

☐ **Organizational feasibility**—how well the proposed information system supports the objectives of the organization's strategic plan for information systems.

☐ **Economic feasibility**—whether expected cost savings, increased profits, and other benefits exceed the costs of developing and operating the system.

☐ **Technical feasibility**—whether reliable hardware and software needed by a proposed system can be acquired or developed by the business firm in the required time.

☐ **Operational feasibility**—the willingness and ability of the management, employees, customers, suppliers, and so on of an organization to operate, use, and support a proposed system.

Cost/Benefit Analysis

Feasibility studies should include a **cost/benefit analysis** of the proposed system. Costs must include the costs of computer hardware and software, CPU time, systems analysis and design, programming, personnel, training, installation, and operations. Such **tangible costs** are comparatively easy to quantify, compared to the analysis of **intangible costs,** such as the loss of customer goodwill or employee morale caused by errors and disruptions arising from the installation of a new system.

  Tangible benefits are comparatively easy to estimate, such as the decrease in payroll costs caused by a reduction in personnel or a decrease in inventory carrying costs caused by a reduction in inventory of the proposed system. **Intangible benefits** are much harder to estimate. Such benefits as better customer service or faster and more accurate information for manage-

Figure 10–10 Possible benefits of computer-based information systems (with examples). The possible costs of computer-based information systems would be the opposite of each of these benefits.

Tangible Benefits

☐ Increase in sales or profits. (Improvement in product or service quality.)
☐ Decrease in information processing costs. (Elimination of unnecessary procedures and documents.)
☐ Decrease in operating costs. (Reduction in inventory carrying costs.)
☐ Decrease in required investment. (Decrease in inventory investment required.)
☐ Increased operational ability and efficiency. (Improvement in production ability and efficiency; for example, less spoilage, waste, and idle time.)

Intangible Benefits

☐ New or improved information availability. (More timely and accurate information, and new types and forms of information.)
☐ Improved abilities in computation and analysis. (Mathematical simulation.)
☐ Improved customer service. (More timely service.)
☐ Improved employee morale. (Elimination of burdensome and boring job tasks.)
☐ Improved management decision making. (Better information and decision analysis.)
☐ Improved competitive position. (Faster and better response to actions of competitors.)
☐ Improved business and community image. ("Progressive" image as perceived by customers, investors, other businesses, government, and the public.)

ment fall into this category. Figure 10–10 lists typical tangible and intangible benefits (with examples).

Return on Investment Analysis

Will investing in a new or improved system produce a satisfactory rate of return? This question is typically asked by management. One way to answer is to compute a percentage rate of **return on investment** for new or improved systems proposals.

$$\text{Return on Investment} = \frac{\text{Increased profits due to cost savings and/or increased revenue}}{\text{New investment required less any reductions in investment}}$$

The **return-on-investment** (**ROI**) concept emphasizes three potential methods of achieving **economic feasibility** for proposed systems:

☐ Cost reduction (such as lower operating costs).
☐ Increased revenue (such as an increase in sales).
☐ Decreased investment (such as a decrease in inventory requirements).

Project Planning

This activity involves the development of plans, procedures, and schedules for analysis, design, training, testing, acquisition, and installation. Such planning is an important part of a "project management" effort, which plans and controls the progress of systems development projects. This is necessary if a project is to be completed on time, within its proposed budget, and meet its design objectives. We will have more to say about this in Chapter 15.

The Feasibility Study Report

The results of systems investigation for a major application are recorded in written form in a **feasibility study report.** This report *documents* and *communicates* the findings of the feasibility study to management and other users. Management uses the information in the feasibility report as the basis for a decision to approve or not approve the proposal. The feasibility study report typically includes:

- ☐ Preliminary specifications of the proposed new or improved system, including systems criteria and constraints.
- ☐ An evaluation of the organizational, economic, technical, and operational feasibility of the proposed system.
- ☐ A plan for the development of the proposed system.

If management approves the recommendations of the feasibility study, the systems analysis stage can begin.

SYSTEMS ANALYSIS

What is **systems analysis?** Whether you want to develop a new application quickly or are involved in a massive long-term project, you still need to perform several basic activities of systems analysis. Many of these activities are an extension of those used in conducting a feasibility study. Some of the same information gathering methods (interviews, observations, etc.) are used, plus some new tools that we will discuss shortly. But systems analysis is not a preliminary study. It's the real thing.

Systems analysis traditionally involves a study of:

- ☐ The information needs of the organization and its users.
- ☐ The resources, products, and activities of any present information systems.
- ☐ The information system capabilities required to meet the information needs of users.

The final product of systems analysis is the **system requirements** for a proposed new or improved information system. (These are also called the *functional specifications* or the *functional requirements.*) For large development projects, this takes the form of a *system requirements report.* It specifies the capabilities needed to meet the information needs of users. Designing a system that meets these system requirements then becomes the goal of the **systems design** stage. See Figure 10–11.

Analysis of the User Organization

This activity can be quite complex for a systems analyst working on a big project who doesn't know much about a particular user organization. A long-time user will probably skip this step, as will systems analysts working on small projects. But **organization analysis** still is important. How can you

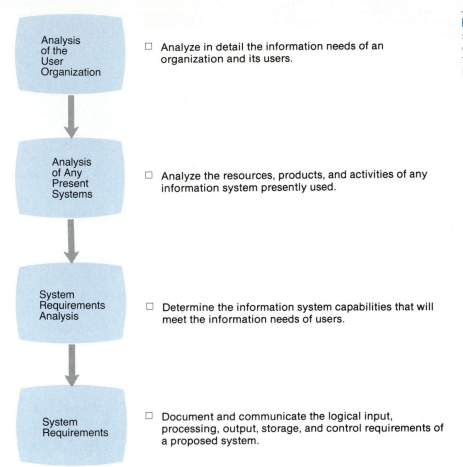

□ Analyze in detail the information needs of an organization and its users.

□ Analyze the resources, products, and activities of any information system presently used.

□ Determine the information system capabilities that will meet the information needs of users.

□ Document and communicate the logical input, processing, output, storage, and control requirements of a proposed system.

Figure 10–11 Activities of systems analysis. This stage determines the information system capabilities that meet the information needs of users.

improve an information system if you know very little about the *organizational environment* in which that system is located? You can't. That's why you have to know something about the organization, its management structure, its people, its business activities, and the information systems it has installed. You also have to know this in more detail for specific user departments that will be affected by the new or improved information system being proposed. For example, you cannot design a new inventory control system for a chain of department stores until you learn a lot about the company and the types of business activities that affect their inventory.

Before you design a new system, it is important to study the present system that will be improved or replaced (if there is one). You need to analyze how this system uses *hardware, software,* and *people resources* to transform the *data resources* of the organization into *information products* for users. You should analyze how these system resources are used to accomplish the information system activities of *input, processing, output, storage,* and *control.*

Analysis of the Present System

Figure 10–12 Analysis of the present system. Notice the generic system resources, products, and activities found in most computer-based information systems in business.

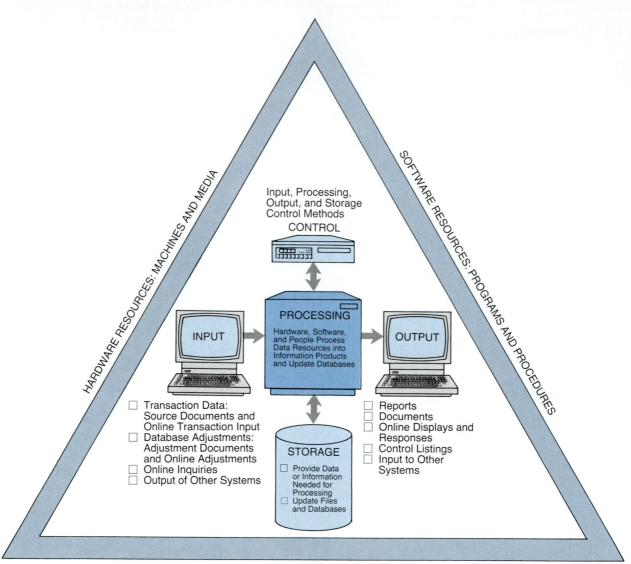

Look at Figure 10–12. It illustrates the generic system resources, products, and system activities found in most computer-based information systems in business. You should learn to look for these **generic system components** any time you study a business computer application. Let's look at some examples.

Input

Input is frequently collected from source documents (such as payroll time-cards) and converted to machine-sensible data by a data entry process (such as key-to-disk). Other input data may be generated by online terminals (such as POS terminals). Input into the system consists of:

☐ **Transactions data.** *Example:* Data describing sales transactions.

☐ **Database adjustments.** *Example:* Change a customer's credit limit using an online terminal in the credit department or by processing a "credit increase request form" mailed in by a customer.

☐ **Inquiries.** *Example:* What is the balance owed on a customer's account?

☐ **Output of other systems.** *Example:* The output of a sales transaction processing system includes data needed as input to an inventory control system to correctly reflect transactions that change the amount of inventory on hand.

Storage

In most applications additional data or information is supplied from the files and databases of the system. Most applications also *update* files and databases to reflect any new transaction input. For example, current credit balances of customers are supplied in response to inquiries from sales personnel. Also, credit sales transactions will increase customer credit balances.

Processing

Hardware, software, and people process data resources resulting in an updated database and output of information products. For example, the computer systems, programs, and specialists of a regional computer center connected to POS terminals in retail stores supply the processing power for a sales transaction processing system.

Output

Output can take the form of:

☐ **Reports.** *Example:* A sales analysis report outlining the sales made during a period by sales territory, product, and salesperson.

☐ **Documents.** *Example:* A paycheck or sales receipt.

☐ **Displays or responses.** *Example:* A video terminal displays the balance owed on a customer's account. Or the same information is transmitted to a telephone by a computer audio-response unit.

☐ **Control listings.** *Example:* Each time an employee paycheck is printed, a listing known as a *payroll register* is also printed and written on magnetic tape. This helps provide an *audit trail* for control purposes.

☐ **Input to other systems.** *Example:* Part of the output of a payroll system serves as input to a labor cost accounting system and the general ledger system of the firm.

Control

Input, processing, output, and storage **controls** are typically provided by the hardware, software, and people resources of the system. For example, computer hardware contains error checking circuitry. Software may include check point routines that automatically compute and check preliminary control totals. Control clerks and audit personnel should routinely check input and output control totals for accuracy. The absence of such controls would indicate a major failure of the systems development process, and a major potential for failure of the new information system.

System Requirements Analysis

This is the most difficult step of systems analysis. First, you must try to determine what your (or the users') specific information needs are (sometimes called *needs analysis* or *user-requirements analysis*). Second, you must try to determine the information processing capabilities needed for each system activity (input, processing, output, storage, control) to meet these information needs (sometimes called *functional requirements analysis*). Finally, you should try to develop **logical** system requirements. That means you should not tie your analysis to the **physical** resources of hardware, software, and people that might be used. That's a job for the systems design stage. The difficulty of the requirements analysis step is one of the major reasons for the development of alternative methods of systems development, such as packaged systems and prototyping. We'll discuss very shortly several tools to help you develop logical system requirements.

The focus of requirements analysis must be on the information requirements of the prospective users of the new system. Users must answer the question: "What information is really needed for decision making or other purposes?" Thus users and systems analysts must distinguish between the information *requirements* and the information *preferences* of the users of the proposed system; between *essential* information and *unwanted* or *unnecessary* information.

The development of management information and decision support systems requires that systems analysis focus on the information requirements of decisions that must be made within the organization. Several important characterisitics of information needed by managers were discussed in Chapter 9. Of course the information requirements of an organization cannot be limited to a decision-making focus. Organizations also require information for historical, legal, and operational purposes. For example, payroll tax information must be supplied to government agencies, financial information to stockholders, and sales information to customers.

System Requirements Report

For large systems projects, the system requirements are documented in a **system requirements report** that is the final product of systems analysis. This report provides a detailed description of the information needs of users and the logical input/output, processing, storage, and control requirements of a proposed system. Written descriptions, data flow diagrams, system flowcharts, input/output and storage layout formats, data dictionaries (and

Input Requirements
Source, content, format, organization, volume (average and peak), frequency, codes, and capture and conversion requirements for input.

Output Requirements
Format, organization, volume (average and peak), frequency, copies, user destinations, timing, and retention required for output.

Processing Requirements
Basic information processing activities required to transform input into output. Decision rules, models, and analytical techniques. Capacity, throughput, turnaround time, and response time needed for processing activities.

Storage Requirements
Organization, content, and size of the database, types and frequency of updating and inquiries, and the length and rationale for record retention or deletion.

Control Requirements
Accuracy, validity, safety, security, integrity, and adaptability requirements for system input, processing, output, and storage functions.

Figure 10–13 Examples of system requirements. They specify the information system capabilities required to meet the information needs of users.

other tools we will discuss shortly) are used to document these requirements. The kinds of input data available, the contents of necessary databases or files, and the control considerations required must be included. The types of information output needed, and processing requirements (such as volumes, frequencies, and turnaround times) must be described and illustrated. But what if a formal report is not issued? The systems analysis step should still consider and determine **system requirements** such as those outlined in Figure 10–13.

SYSTEMS DESIGN

Systems analysis describes *what* a system should do to meet the information needs of users. **Systems design** specifies *how* the system will accomplish this objective. Systems design involves developing both logical and physical design specifications that can satisfy the system requirements developed in the systems analysis stage. Designing efficient, economical, and effective systems for major information processing jobs is a challenging assignment. Of course for smaller individual user jobs, systems design frequently consists of the computer-assisted development and revision of prototype information systems. See Figure 10–14.

Logical System Design

Logical system design involves developing general specifications for how the basic information system activities of input, processing, output, storage, and control can meet user requirements. Early in the systems investigation stage, *logical design concepts* may have been developed in a feasibility study. These were a rough or general idea of the basic components and flows of the proposed information system. Several alternative logical design concepts may have been developed before a single basic concept was tentatively selected. In the systems design stage, these logical design concepts are refined and finalized.

Logical system design should also include the consideration of an *ideal system* and alternative *realistic systems*. Developing general specifications of

Figure 10–14 Activities of systems design. This stage develops logical and physical design specifications that can satisfy the system requirements developed in the systems analysis stage.

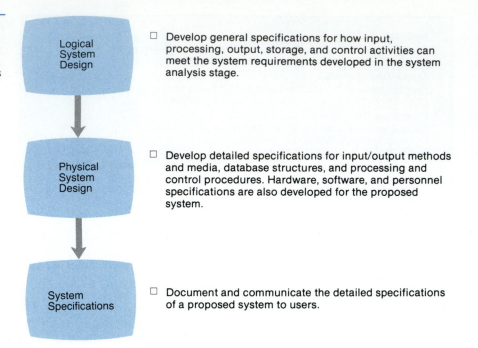

Logical System Design
☐ Develop general specifications for how input, processing, output, storage, and control activities can meet the system requirements developed in the system analysis stage.

Physical System Design
☐ Develop detailed specifications for input/output methods and media, database structures, and processing and control procedures. Hardware, software, and personnel specifications are also developed for the proposed system.

System Specifications
☐ Document and communicate the detailed specifications of a proposed system to users.

an ideal system encourages users and systems analysts to be creative. It emphasizes that meeting the information requirements of the organization is the primary goal of systems analysis and design. On the other hand, the development of alternative realistic systems encourages users and analysts to be flexible and realistic. It emphasizes that several ways must be found to meet system requirements. It also stresses the limited financial, personnel, and other resources of most organizations.

Trade-offs may have to be made between various system design criteria. For example, management may demand that inventory "stockouts" rarely occur, which might override the criterion of minimizing inventory costs. Some criteria, on the other hand, can be adjusted to accommodate the requirements of other criteria. For example, the criterion of low input/output costs may be adjusted to accommodate the criteria of user-friendly input/output interfaces, or effective data entry controls.

Physical System Design

Physical system design involves the detailed design of input/output methods and media, database structures, and processing and control procedures. Hardware, software, and personnel specifications are developed for the proposed system. Systems designers use their knowledge of business operations, information processing, and hardware and software to specify the **physical design** of an information system. Obviously, they must relate their design to the input, processing, output, storage, and control specifications developed in the previous logical design step. They must specify what types of hardware resources (machines and media), software resources (programs and procedures), and people resources (users and information systems staff)

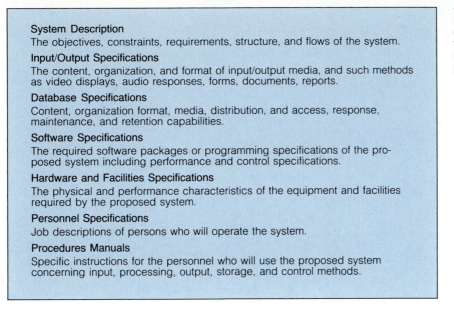

System Description
The objectives, constraints, requirements, structure, and flows of the system.

Input/Output Specifications
The content, organization, and format of input/output media, and such methods as video displays, audio responses, forms, documents, reports.

Database Specifications
Content, organization format, media, distribution, and access, response, maintenance, and retention capabilities.

Software Specifications
The required software packages or programming specifications of the proposed system including performance and control specifications.

Hardware and Facilities Specifications
The physical and performance characteristics of the equipment and facilities required by the proposed system.

Personnel Specifications
Job descriptions of persons who will operate the system.

Procedures Manuals
Specific instructions for the personnel who will use the proposed system concerning input, processing, output, storage, and control methods.

Figure 10–15 An outline of the contents of a system specifications report. Notice how it specifies the details of the proposed information system.

will be needed. They must specify how such resources will transform data resources (stored in files and databases they design) into information products (displays, responses, reports and documents). These specifications are the final product of the systems design stage. They are called the **system specifications.** For large systems, they are documented in a formal report. See Figure 10–15.

SYSTEMS IMPLEMENTATION

Once a proposed system has been designed, it must be implemented. **Systems implementation** involves development, acquisition, testing, documentation, and installation activities. It also involves the training of personnel to operate and use the system. See Figure 10–16.

Software Development

Software development is an optional stage. It develops any computer programs that must be written in-house (instead of purchased as software packages). This programming process can be difficult and time-consuming. The use of application generators and fourth-generation languages can simplify and automate this stage. We will discuss the programming process for software development in the next chapter.

Acquisition

The first step of the *acquisition* process is an evaluation of the proposals of manufacturers and other suppliers who furnish the hardware and software components required by the system specifications. The computer user must choose from among many different models and suppliers of hardware and software components. The evaluation and acquisition of such computer resources is discussed in Chapter 16.

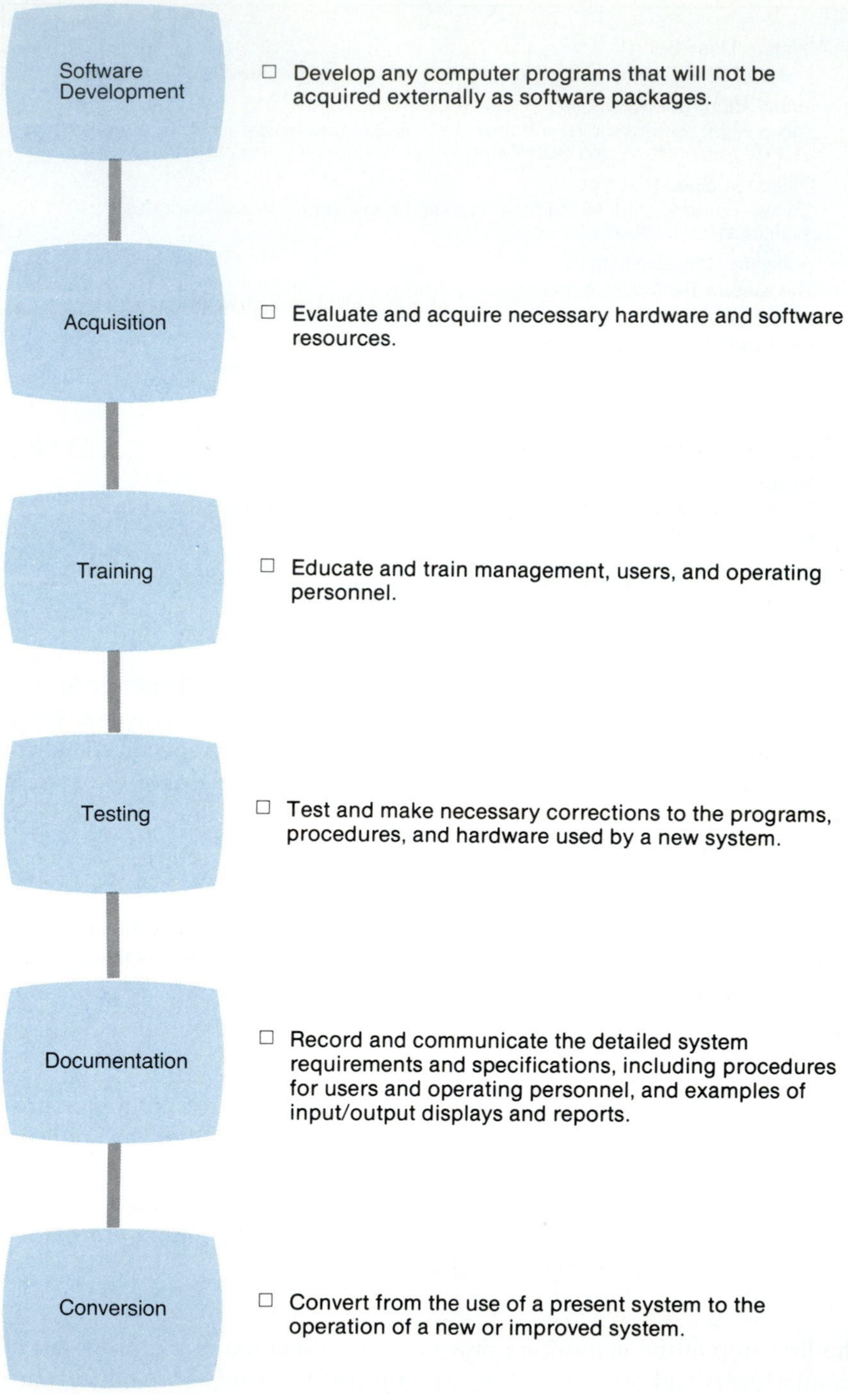

Figure 10-16 Activities of the systems implementation stage. A newly designed system becomes a reality in this stage of systems development.

Software Development
☐ Develop any computer programs that will not be acquired externally as software packages.

Acquisition
☐ Evaluate and acquire necessary hardware and software resources.

Training
☐ Educate and train management, users, and operating personnel.

Testing
☐ Test and make necessary corrections to the programs, procedures, and hardware used by a new system.

Documentation
☐ Record and communicate the detailed system requirements and specifications, including procedures for users and operating personnel, and examples of input/output displays and reports.

Conversion
☐ Convert from the use of a present system to the operation of a new or improved system.

Implementation of a new system involves *orientation* and *training* of management, users, and operating personnel, and the "selling" of the new system to each of these groups. Users and operating personnel must be trained in specific skills to operate and use the system. If an adequate job of management and user involvement in systems development has been accomplished, the "shock effect" of transferring to a new system should be minimized. If user representatives participated in the development of the system, the problems of installation, conversion, and training should be minimized.

Training

Systems implementation requires the *testing* of the newly designed and programmed system. This involves not only the testing and debugging of all computer programs but the testing of all other information processing procedures. This includes the production of test copies of reports and other output that should be reviewed by users of the proposed systems for possible errors. Testing not only occurs during the system's implementation stage, but throughout the system's development process. For example, input documents, screen displays, and processing procedures can be tested before their final form is determined. They should be examined and critiqued by users during the system's design stage. Immediate user testing is one of the benefits of a **prototyping** process.

Testing

Developing *system documentation* is an important process. It uses techniques of systems analysis and design to (1) *record* and (2) *communicate* the results of each stage of system development. For example, the contents of feasibility studies, system requirements reports, and system specifications reports are excellent sources of system documentation. In the **systems implementation** stage, a *system documentation manual* may be prepared to finalize the documentation of a large system. When computer-assisted development methods are used, documentation can be created and changed easily. It can be stored on magnetic disks and retrieved, displayed on a video screen, or printed on a printer. Figure 10–17 is an outline of system documentation contents.

Documentation

Proper documentation allows management to monitor the progress of a systems development project. It minimizes the problems that arise when changes are made in systems design. Documentation serves as a method of

System Documentation	
System Summary	Control Methods
System Specifications	Error Diagnostics
System Requirements	Computer Operations Summary
Data Dictionary	Manual Processing Procedures
Index of Computer Programs	Sample Screens, Forms, and Reports

Figure 10–17 An outline of the contents of system documentation. This records and communicates the results of the systems development process.

communication between the people that are responsible for a project. It is also vital for proper implementation and maintenance. Installing and operating a newly designed system or modifying an established system requires a detailed record of its systems design.

Conversion

The initial operation of a new computer-based system can be a difficult task. Such an operation is usually a *conversion process* in which the personnel, procedures, equipment, input/output forms, and database of an old information system must be converted to the requirements of a new system. However, conversion problems can be minimized if a proper job of project management for a systems development project is performed.

Conversion can be done on a *parallel* basis, whereby both the old and the new system are operated until the project development team and user-management agree to switch completely over to the new system. It is during this time that the operations and results of both systems are compared and evaluated. Errors can be identified and corrected, and the operating problems can be solved before the old system is abandoned. Installation can also be accomplished by a direct *cutover* or *plunge* to the newly developed system. It can also be done on a *phased* basis, where only a few departments, branch offices, or plant locations at a time are converted. A phased conversion allows a gradual implementation process to take place within an organization.

SYSTEMS MAINTENANCE

Systems maintenance is the monitoring, evaluating, and modifying of a system to make desirable or necessary improvements. This includes a *postimplementation review* process to insure that the newly implemented system meets the systems development objectives established for it. Errors in the development or use of the system must be corrected by the maintenance activity.

Installation of a new system usually results in the phenomenon known as the *learning curve*. Personnel who operate and use the system will make mistakes simply because they are not familiar with it. Such errors usually diminish as experience is gained with a new system. However, maintenance is necessary for other failures and problems that arise during the operation of a system. Systems maintenance personnel must then perform a *troubleshooting* function to determine the causes and solutions to a particular problem.

The systems maintenance activity requires a periodic review or *audit* of a system to ensure that it is operating properly and meeting its objectives. This activity is in addition to a continual monitoring of a new system. Systems maintenance also includes making modifications to a system due to changes within the business organization or in the business environment. For example, changes in the tax laws usually require changes to tax computations in payroll systems and tax accounting systems.

REAL WORLD APPLICATION 10–2

Pacific Northwest Bell

"Before we started using Excelerator," Ernie Lysen, systems analyst at Pacific Northwest Bell Telephone Co., Bellevue, Washington, explained, "we put user requirements on paper. As we went into the definition stage, we would have to retype or redo everything from one format to another. Now requirements go automatically into the application generator, onto a hard disk, and are immediately available to the coder, the designer, whoever wants to see and modify it. What we have is maintainable documentation."

Lysen and his colleagues at Pacific Northwest are in the first stages of redesigning the payroll system at U.S. West (a cooperative venture among Pacific Northwest, Northwestern Bell Telephone Co., and Mountain Bell Telephone Co.) using Excelerator, a microcomputer system development generator from Index Technology Corp.

Such systems development or application generators stress the importance of the user interface up front in the crucial application design and prototyping stages. By increasing user involvement in the design phase, vendors of micro-based application generators claim the finished, coded program will be much cleaner, requiring far less maintenance than many mainframe application generators.

Systems development using application generators does not stress design speed as much as design accuracy. By sitting at a user's microcomputer, a casual design atmosphere can be formed involving data processing analyst and user. Both can create and revise a program on a screen, sometimes in a matter of hours. A generator's built-in screen generation and screen flow abilities can direct both parties through a new application without disruptive breaks. Such immediacy can often provide a better sense of what the user wants.

At each stage of application development, many generator systems can capture and produce concise documentation automatically, a more difficult chore when handled manually. They can create files or databases and interact with a data dictionary to give substance to screen flowcharting. Included in the system are usually a number of utilities for generating reports and querying the database as well as online editing and testing facilities for taking applications through their final design stages before being coded or compiled.

However, not all products that vendors tout as application generators carry through every phase of an application life cycle. Many provide parts of the complete puzzle. Excelerator, for example, takes the cycle to the coding stage, where the design prototype can be programmed in either a third- or fourth-generation language. Thus, one of the primary reasons Pacific Northwest's Lysen chose Excelerator was because it still allowed the designed application to be programmed in COBOL, his company still being a COBOL shop. Chris Grejtak, Index Technology's vice president of research and marketing, explained, "There are times when fourth-generation languages are more appropriate than COBOL, PL/1, and Ada, but there is also a huge base of programmers whose expertise lies in the traditional languages. I don't think they should be locked into anything proprietary."

Application Questions

☐ Which stages of the systems development cycle are supported by tools such as Excelerator?

☐ What are the major benefits of such systems development generators?

Section III: Using Systems Development Tools—A Case Study

TOOLS OF ANALYSIS AND DESIGN

We have explained the basic concepts and activities of systems development. It is now time to discuss how to use several *tools* that will help you perform these activities. Information collected during the feasibility study and systems analysis stages describe the information requirements of users. It also describes the input, processing, output, storage, and control components of the system being studied. After this stage, such information must be "analyzed and synthesized," using several tools of systems analysis and design. We will give you examples of these tools in this section.

Remember that such tools are used in every stage of system development—as analytical tools, design tools, and as documentation methods. For example, **system flowcharts** and **data flow diagrams** can be used to (1) *analyze* an existing system, (2) express the *design* of a new system, and (3) provide the *documentation* method for a newly developed system.

Many tools and techniques can be used for systems analysis and design. Some tools are better than others, depending on the type of information processing activities that are being analyzed or designed. However, each tool has its advantages and disadvantages. We will discuss five tools in this section: (1) system flowcharts, (2) data flow diagrams, (3) system function diagrams, (4) grid charts, and (5) layout forms. Four other tools will be described in Chapter 11: (1) program flowcharts, (2) structure charts, (3) HIPO charts, and (4) decision tables.

Many other types of graphic, quantitative, and descriptive tools can be used for systems analysis and design. These include data dictionaries, entity diagrams, organization charts, position descriptions, mathematical models, statistical sampling, financial statements and reports, and work distribution charts. Also popular are a variety of forms that analyze the content and format of data records, data files, documents, and reports. Software packages for computer-assisted systems development have computerized many of the systems development tools mentioned. For example, some programs will automatically draw and revise system flowcharts or data flow diagrams based on a user's description of a system.

SALES PROCESSING AT ABC AUTO PARTS

Before we can show you how to use several tools of systems analysis and design, we need a business example to work on. Remember ABC Department Stores? We first described their sales processing system in Real World Application 1–2 in Chapter 1. We also used the information system model to analyze this system. We have also referred to ABC Department Stores in the application problems at the end of several chapters of this text. However, in this section let's look at the sales processing activity of the auto parts department at ABC Department Stores. This will give us a simple information processing example that we can analyze with the help of several tools of systems analysis. We can then use some of these same tools to help us design a new sales processing system.

At the present time, the auto parts department of ABC Department Stores has a manual sales processing system. The manager of the auto parts department and a systems analyst from the information services department conducted a feasibility study to determine the feasibility of computerizing this system. They found that this would be economically, technically, organizationally, and operationally feasible. Based on these findings, management gave its approval to this project. The systems analyst made personal observations of the sales processing system in action, and interviewed departmental employees. The following brief description of the present sales processing system is a summary of information gathered by the systems analyst.

The Present System

1. When a customer wants to buy an auto part, a sales clerk writes up a sales order form. Recorded on this form is customer data such as name, address, and account number, and product data such as name, product number, and price. A copy of the sales order form is given to the customer as a sales receipt.

2. Sales order forms are sent each day to the information services department where they are recorded on magnetic tape using key-to-tape data entry devices.

3. The file of sales transactions is now ready for computer processing. One of the important information processing jobs that needs to be done is the updating of the sales files and the preparation of sales analysis reports. One of the first jobs that the store's mainframe computer does is to sort the sales transactions by product number.

4. The sorted sales transaction file and a sales processing program are then used to update the sales master file to reflect the new sales that have been made. This results in the creation of a new sales master file on magnetic tape.

5. The sales file maintenance processing also produces a sales analysis file. This file contains historical data on previous sales as well as new sales data. The computer uses this file and a sales analysis program to perform sales analysis. Sales analysis reports are produced that tell store management the trends in sales performance of various products.

After performing the activities of systems design, the systems analyst proposed a new sales processing system. This system features online data entry using point-of-sale (POS) terminals and also relies on online database processing. A brief description of part of this proposed system follows:

The Proposed System

1. When a customer wishes to buy an auto part, the sales clerk enters the customer and product data using an online POS terminal. The POS terminal uses a keyboard for data entry and a video screen to display input data as well as data entry menus, prompts, and messages. POS terminals are online to the store's mainframe computer, which uses a comprehensive sales processing program.

2. The POS terminal prints out a sales receipt for the customer. It contains customer and product data and serves as a record of the sales transaction.

3. Errors in data entry may cause an error indication to be displayed by the POS terminal. The sales clerk must then follow various error procedures to correct the error.

4. The POS terminal then transmits sales transaction data to the store's mainframe computer. It immediately updates the sales records in the company's database, which is stored on magnetic disk units.

5. Each night the computer performs sales analysis processing using the updated sales records in the company database. Sales analysis reports are produced for department and store management.

6. Database management system software supports database inquiries by management, who can receive instant responses as sales analysis displays on their executive workstations. These are linked to the store's mainframe computer by data communications lines.

USING ANALYSIS AND DESIGN TOOLS

Many tools of analysis and design could have been used by the systems analyst in analyzing the present sales processing system and designing a new one. However, let's look at simple examples of five tools that the analyst might have used: (1) system flowcharts, (2) data flow diagrams, (3) system function diagrams, (4) grid charts, and (5) layout forms. This should help you understand the systems analysis and design concepts discussed in this chapter. It should also allow you to use some of these tools to help you solve simple information system problems.

System Flowcharts

A **system flowchart** helps you identify the flow of data media and the information processing procedures that take place in an information system. This is accomplished by using a variety of symbols connected by arrows to show the sequence of information processing activities. System flowcharts thus emphasize the media used and the processes that take place within an information system. Figure 10–18 illustrates some common system flowchart symbols.

Figure 10–19(a) shows how a system flowchart is used as a tool for the *analysis* of the existing *physical* sales processing and analysis system at ABC Auto Parts. It graphically portrays the flow of data media and the major information processing tasks that take place. Notice how the flowchart symbols indicate the physical equipment and media (hardware) used for input, output, and storage. For example, symbols and labels indicate the use of many paper documents and reports, a key-to-tape data entry device, and magnetic tape storage media.

Now look at Figure 10–19(b). It also is a system flowchart, but it is being used to illustrate the *physical design* of a new sales processing and analysis system. This proposed system will replace the system illustrated in Figure

Figure 10–18   Common system flowchart symbols.

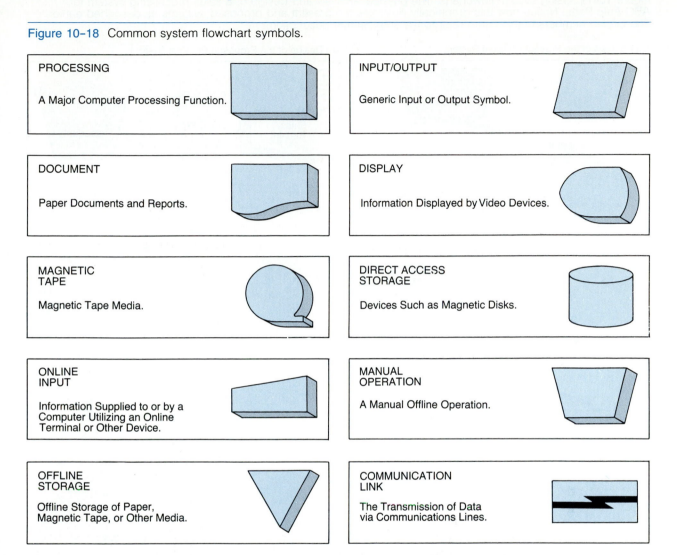

PROCESSING	INPUT/OUTPUT
A Major Computer Processing Function.	Generic Input or Output Symbol.
DOCUMENT	DISPLAY
Paper Documents and Reports.	Information Displayed by Video Devices.
MAGNETIC TAPE	DIRECT ACCESS STORAGE
Magnetic Tape Media.	Devices Such as Magnetic Disks.
ONLINE INPUT	MANUAL OPERATION
Information Supplied to or by a Computer Utilizing an Online Terminal or Other Device.	A Manual Offline Operation.
OFFLINE STORAGE	COMMUNICATION LINK
Offline Storage of Paper, Magnetic Tape, or Other Media.	The Transmission of Data via Communications Lines.

10–19(a). Notice how it shows an online data entry terminal, magnetic disk storage, and several printed reports. This is obviously a physical design, because the hardware devices and media that will be used in the new system are specified.

Data Flow Diagrams

A data flow diagram (DFD) helps you identify the logical flow of data in a system without specifying the media or hardware involved. Data flow diagrams use several unique symbols connected by arrows to represent such flows. Thus data flow diagrams illustrate the logical relationships among data, flows, sources, destinations, and stores. Figure 10–20 illustrates the four basic symbols used in data flow diagrams.

Figure 10–19 Using system flowcharts. The physical analysis and design of a sales processing system for ABC Auto Parts. Notice how this graphically illustrates the present and proposed systems as described earlier. The circled numbers in this figure refer to the steps in that description.

(a) Analysis of the Present Physical System

(b) Design of the Proposed Physical System

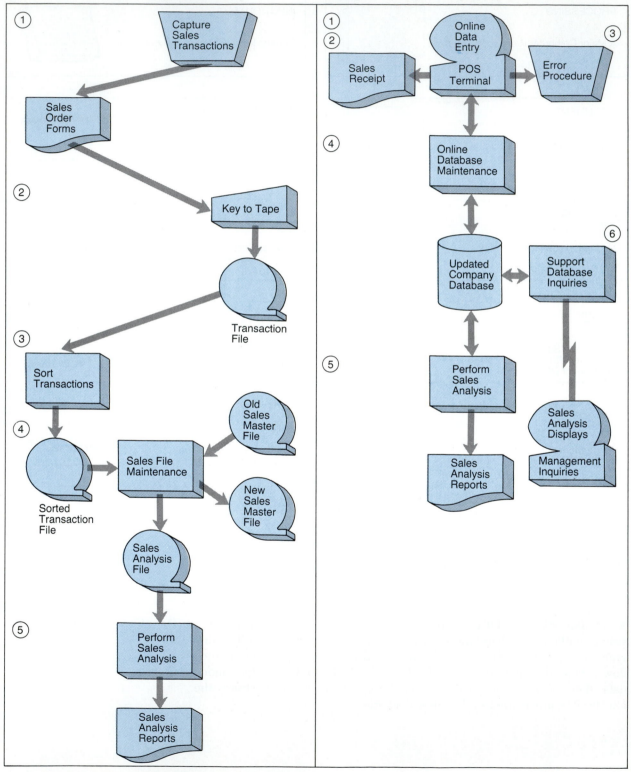

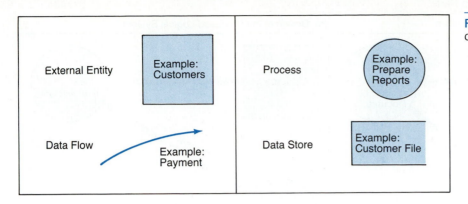

Figure 10-20 Basic data flow diagram symbols.

Figure 10–21 shows how a data flow diagram is used as a tool for both **logical analysis** and **logical design.** Notice that both portray the logical flow of data in both the present and proposed sales analysis and processing systems. That's because they do not specify the media and equipment involved. These DFDs only illustrate the *logical relationships* among the data, flows, sources, destinations, and stores in the sales processing and analysis system at ABC Auto Parts.

System Function Diagrams

A system function diagram helps you identify the input, processing, output, storage, and control features of an information system. It is based on the conceptual framework of the information systems model. Therefore it spotlights the hardware (machines and media), software (programs and procedures), people (specialists and users) and data resources used by the system, and the information products it produces. It thus uses the **systems viewpoint** for analysis and design that was illustrated in Figure 10–1. It helps document your answers to the basic questions of systems analysis and design asked in that figure. Figure 10–12 was another example of the use of this concept to identify the generic system components of most computer-based information systems in business.

Figure 10–22 shows examples of system function diagrams for both the present and proposed sales processing system of ABC Department Stores. Notice how these diagrams spotlight the resources and methods used to support the input, processing, output, storage, and control activities of these systems. These diagrams are incomplete since all we know about the present and proposed systems is the brief summary provided by the systems analyst. However, the diagrams still serve their purpose by helping us evaluate how the basic activities of information processing are accomplished.

Grid Charts

A grid chart helps you identify each type of data element and information product used in an information system. It identifies whether they are present in the form of input, output, or storage media. Grid charts are often used to identify redundant data elements and information products. This can result in the consolidation and elimination of forms, files, and reports.

Figure 10–21 Using data flow diagrams. This graphically illustrates the logical analysis and design of a sales processing system for ABC Auto Parts.

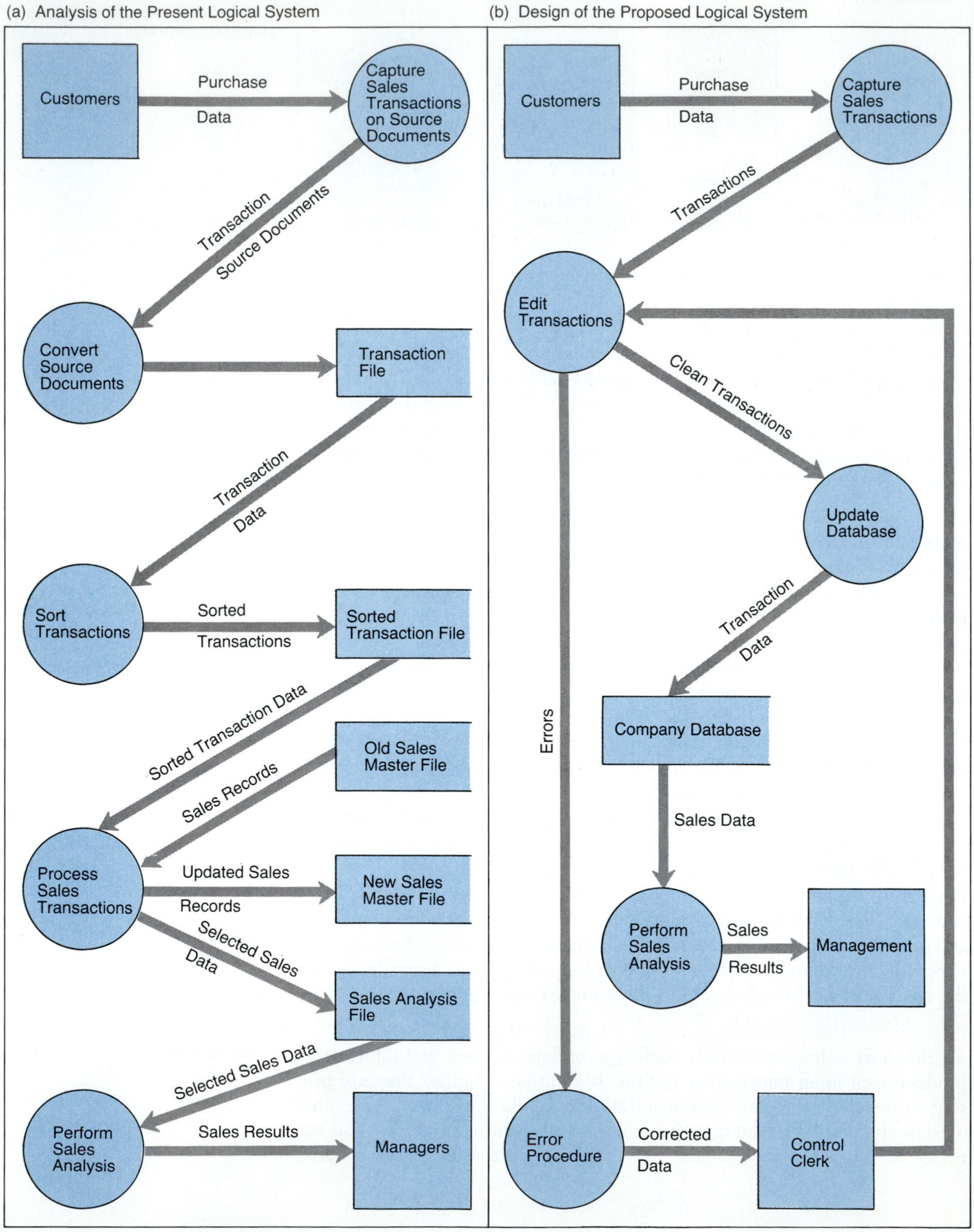

Figure 10–22 Using system function diagrams for the physical analysis and design of a sales processing system for ABC Auto Parts. Notice how they spotlight input, processing, output, storage, and control features of the present and proposed system.

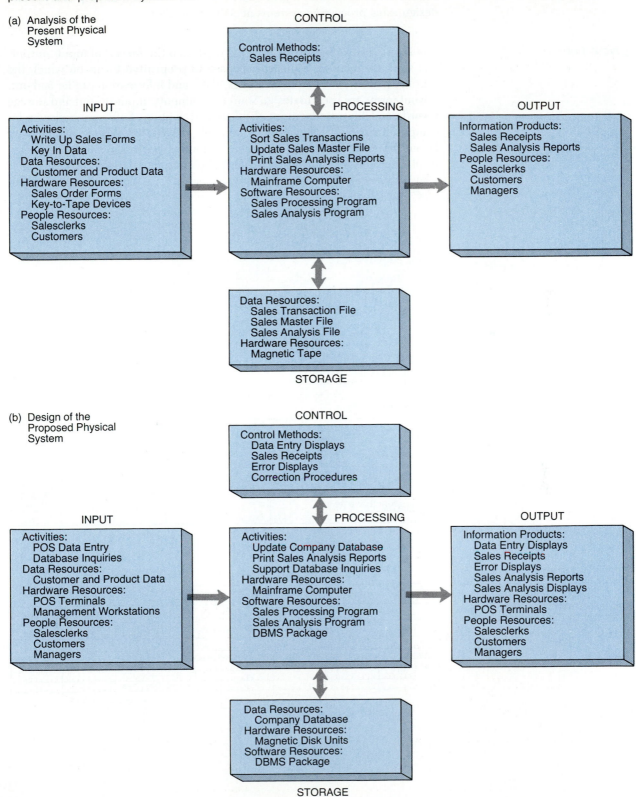

(a) Analysis of the Present Physical System

CONTROL

Control Methods:
  Sales Receipts

INPUT

Activities:
  Write Up Sales Forms
  Key In Data
Data Resources:
  Customer and Product Data
Hardware Resources:
  Sales Order Forms
  Key-to-Tape Devices
People Resources:
  Salesclerks
  Customers

PROCESSING

Activities:
  Sort Sales Transactions
  Update Sales Master File
  Print Sales Analysis Reports
Hardware Resources:
  Mainframe Computer
Software Resources:
  Sales Processing Program
  Sales Analysis Program

OUTPUT

Information Products:
  Sales Receipts
  Sales Analysis Reports
People Resources:
  Salesclerks
  Customers
  Managers

Data Resources:
  Sales Transaction File
  Sales Master File
  Sales Analysis File
Hardware Resources:
  Magnetic Tape

STORAGE

(b) Design of the Proposed Physical System

CONTROL

Control Methods:
  Data Entry Displays
  Sales Receipts
  Error Displays
  Correction Procedures

INPUT

Activities:
  POS Data Entry
  Database Inquiries
Data Resources:
  Customer and Product Data
Hardware Resources:
  POS Terminals
  Management Workstations
People Resources:
  Salesclerks
  Customers
  Managers

PROCESSING

Activities:
  Update Company Database
  Print Sales Analysis Reports
  Support Database Inquiries
Hardware Resources:
  Mainframe Computer
Software Resources:
  Sales Processing Program
  Sales Analysis Program
  DBMS Package

OUTPUT

Information Products:
  Data Entry Displays
  Sales Receipts
  Error Displays
  Sales Analysis Reports
  Sales Analysis Displays
Hardware Resources:
  POS Terminals
People Resources:
  Salesclerks
  Customers
  Managers

Data Resources:
  Company Database
Hardware Resources:
  Magnetic Disk Units
Software Resources:
  DBMS Package

STORAGE

Figure 10–23 illustrates a grid chart that could be used to help analyze and design sales processing systems at ABC Auto Parts.

Layout Forms

You should use **layout forms** to help you design the *format* of input, output, and storage media. They usually consist of preprinted forms on which the size and placement of titles, headings, data, and information can be laid out. Layout forms are used to design source documents, input/output and storage records and files, and output displays and reports. Software packages for computer-assisted systems development provide electronic versions of layout forms. For example, screen generator packages help you design display screens for data entry or information output. Figure 10–24 illustrates a layout form for the design of a display screen for a sales analysis report for ABC Auto Parts.

Figure 10–23 Using a grid chart. This identifies some of the data elements present in information products and data files of the sales processing system at ABC Auto Parts.

Fields \ Reports, Documents, and Files	Sales Order Form	Shipping Papers	Invoice	Sales by Customer Report	Customer Credit Report	Sales Master File
Customer Number	✓	✓	✓	✓	✓	✓
Customer Name	✓	✓	✓	✓	✓	✓
Customer Address	✓	✓	✓			✓
Discount Code			✓			✓
Credit Code				✓	✓	✓
Salesperson Name	✓			✓		✓

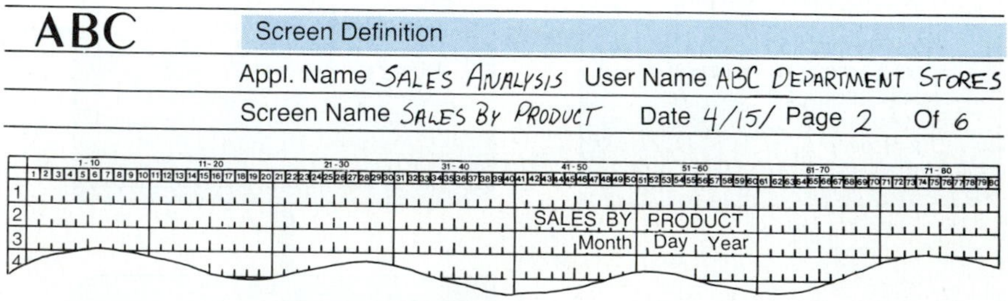

Figure 10–24 Layout form for display screen design of the Sales by Product report.

ABC   Screen Definition

Appl. Name *SALES ANALYSIS*   User Name *ABC DEPARTMENT STORES*

Screen Name *SALES BY PRODUCT*   Date *4/15/* Page *2*   Of *6*

SALES BY PRODUCT
Month Day Year

REAL WORLD APPLICATION 10–3

GTE Midwestern Telephone Operations

With the breakup of AT&T and the deregulation of the telecommunications industry, it has become even more critical for GTE Midwestern Telephone Operations (MTO) to be able to respond quickly to a dynamic market, introduce new services, and cut costs where possible. To such information challenges, MTO has applied the power of a systems development package called Ramis from On-Line Software of Fort Lee, N.J., to help people work smarter, according to Richard Wepfer, staff administrator for information resource management.

MTO is a leading provider of telecommunications products and services, providing more than three million lines to customers across the Midwest. "Deregulation led to short lead times. We needed to develop information systems quickly," Wepfer says. "In many cases, we did not know at the beginning of the development process what the ultimate requirements were going to be."

The situation called for a prototyping tool that would allow programmers or users to build models of applications before committing great amounts of resources to them. To meet the growing demands for realtime systems and increased access to corporate databases, MTO acquired Ramis.

Users in many MTO departments have applied Ramis to a variety of information problems. Human resources, for example, uses the tool to create, for the first time, an MTO-wide database of personnel information. In the past, MTO encountered problems when shifting personnel to meet emerging requirements, because pertinent information such as individual skills and training was not always available.

As a result, it was difficult for the department to monitor training, advancement, and executive-continuity policies. A central database application developed using Ramis provided all MTO human resources offices with instant password-controlled access to the same up-to-the-minute personnel files.

MTO's most sensitive application of Ramis was the development of a comparison billing system. The comparison bills show telephone customers their current flat rate contrasted with a usage-sensitive service rate based on their actual usage. Reports are being produced for selected cities in a four-state area and will be the basis for providing similar services to all MTO customers. By some estimates, developing the reports using COBOL would have required about 100 COBOL statements for each Ramis statement. Using Ramis, the comparison billing system required three weeks to complete.

The success of Ramis at MTO has been spurred by its popularity at the grass roots level. Wepfer says that although Ramis is also extensively used by programming professionals in information systems, "It is appropriate that, as a user tool, Ramis should base its success on what it has done for users as opposed to the DP professionals," he says. "It is an integral part of our multiuser tool chest."

Application Questions

☐ Why did MTO need a prototyping tool like Ramis?

☐ What benefits did Ramis provide to MTO's systems development process?

Source: "Integral Prototyping Tool," *Infosystems*, February 1987, pp. 21–22.

SUMMARY

☐ Users and systems analysts should use a systems approach to help them create or improve computer-based information systems. This means having a viewpoint that looks for systems, subsystems, and components of systems in any information processing situation. They should especially look for the basic system activities of input, processing, output, storage, and control.

☐ However, the systems approach also means using a systematic process to create computer-based information systems. This traditional information systems development cycle can be subdivided into stages of systems investigation, analysis, design, implementation, and maintenance.

☐ The process of developing computer-based information systems is changing due to problems with traditional systems development and the growth of user computing. Computer-assisted systems development methods, such as prototyping and user-developed systems, are changing many of the activities of the traditional systems development cycle.

☐ The investigation stage includes the conducting of a feasibility study to determine the organizational, economic, technical, and operational feasibility of a proposed information system. The determination of economic feasibility requires a cost/benefit analysis, which focuses on the tangible and intangible costs and benefits that would result from the implementation of a proposed system.

☐ Systems analysis involves an in-depth analysis of the information needs of users. Its objective is to determine the information requirements and other logical system requirements of a proposed information system. It also includes analyzing the information requirements of the organization and the functions of any present information system. Much of this can now be accomplished in an interactive computer-assisted prototyping process by users and systems analysts.

☐ Systems design involves the logical and physical design of an information system that meets the system requirements developed in the systems analysis stage. It develops specifications for a proposed system that specify the hardware, software, database, procedures, and personnel to be used by the system. Again, much of this can now be the result of a computer-assisted prototyping process.

☐ Once the steps of systems analysis and systems design are accomplished, a system is implemented by: (1) evaluating, acquiring, developing, and installing necessary hardware and software; (2) selecting and training required personnel; (3) testing the new system; (4) completing the documentation for the new system; and (5) converting to the new system. Finally, the systems maintenance activity assures the continual monitoring, evaluating, and improvement of established systems.

☐ In traditional systems development, information about present and proposed information systems is collected by personal interviews, questionnaires, personal observations, and examination of documents and reports. This information is then analyzed and synthesized, using various tools and techniques of systems analysis and design, such as system flowcharts, data flow diagrams, system function diagrams, layout forms, and grid charts.

These are the key terms and concepts of this chapter. The page number of their first explanation is in parenthesis.

1. Computer-assisted systems development *(361)*
2. Cost/benefit analysis *(370)*
3. Data flow diagram *(387)*
4. Economic feasibility *(370)*
5. Feasibility study *(367)*
6. Generic system components *(374)*
7. Grid chart *(389)*
8. Information systems development cycle *(360)*
9. Intangible
   a. Costs *(370)*
   b. Benefits *(370)*
10. Layout form *(392)*
11. Logical analysis and design *(376)*
12. Operational feasibility *(370)*
13. Organization analysis *(372)*
14. Organizational feasibility *(370)*
15. Physical analysis and design *(376)*
16. Prototyping *(361)*

17. Return on investment *(371)*
18. System flowchart *(386)*
19. System function diagram *(389)*
20. System requirements *(376)*
21. System specifications *(379)*
22. Systems analysis *(372)*
23. Systems approach
   a. Systems viewpoint *(358)*
   b. Systems process *(360)*
24. Systems design *(377)*
25. Systems implementation *(379)*
26. Systems investigation *(367)*
27. Systems maintenance *(382)*
28. Tangible
   a. Costs *(370)*
   b. Benefits *(370)*
29. Technical feasibility *(370)*
30. User-developed systems *(362)*
31. User involvement *(364)*

Match one of the **key terms and concepts** listed above with one of the brief examples or definitions listed below. Try to find the "best fit" for answers that seem to fit more than one term or concept. Defend your choices.

_____ 1. Recognizing the input, processing, output, storage, and control activities taking place when you use a computer.

_____ 2. Using an organized sequence of activities to study an information processing problem.

_____ 3. Consists of investigation, analysis, design, implementation, and maintenance activities.

_____ 4. Helps ensure the cooperation of users when a new system is implemented.

_____ 5. Using software packages that help you accomplish some of the activities of systems analysis and design.

_____ 6. Building a working model of a system and refining it into a finished product.

_____ 7. Users are provided with hardware, software, and systems consultants in an information center.

_____ 8. The first stage of the systems development cycle.

_____ 9. Helps you determine organizational, economic, technical, and operational feasibility.

_____ 10. A cost/benefit analysis shows that benefits outweigh costs for a proposed system.

_____ 11. Increased profits divided by net investment required for a new system.

_____ 12. The costs of acquiring computer hardware, software, and specialists.

_____ 13. Loss of customer goodwill caused by errors in a new system.

_____ 14. Increases in profits caused by a new system.

_____ 15. Improved employee morale caused by the efficiency and effectiveness of a new system.

_____ 16. Reliable hardware and software is available to implement a proposed system.

_____ 17. Customers will not have trouble using a proposed system.

_____ 18. The proposed system supports the strategic plan of the business.

_____ 19. Studying in detail the information needs of users and any information system presently used.

_____ 20. You had better know something about an organization, its people, and its business activities before you develop a new system for them.

_____ 21. Computer-based information systems in business typically have transaction data as input, and documents and reports as output.

_____ 22. A detailed description of user information needs and the input, processing, output, storage, and control capabilities required to meet those needs.

_____ 23. The process that results in specifications for the hardware, software, people, data resources, and information products needed by a proposed system.

_____ 24. A detailed description of the hardware, software, people, data resources, and information products required by a proposed system.

_____ 25. Acquiring hardware and software, testing and documenting a proposed system, and training people to use it.

_____ 26. Monitoring, evaluating, and modifying a system.

_____ 27. Shows you the flow of data media and information processing procedures in an information system.

_____ 28. Shows you the logical flow of data in an information system without specifying the media or equipment involved.

_____ 29. Shows you the input, processing, output, storage, and control features of an information system.

_____ 30. Shows you the data elements present in information products and data files.

_____ 31. Shows you the content and format of input, output, and storage media.

1. If you have not already done so, read and answer the questions after the three Real World Applications in this chapter.

2. Identify which statement below is most closely related to the concepts of
   a. The systems approach as a viewpoint.
   b. The systems approach as a process.
   c. Systems development with prototyping.
   d. User-developed systems.

   1. "We need intelligent workstations, systems development packages, and information centers to design our own systems."
   2. "Let's build a quick and dirty working model and try it out to see what changes are needed."
   3. "You had better show how we are going to handle the input, processing, output, storage, and control activities of this application."
   4. "You had better do a feasibility study, then determine the system requirements, develop the system specifications, then acquire hardware and software, and install and maintain the system."

3. Apply the systems approach as a systems viewpoint as expressed in Figure 10–1. That is, identify several input, processing, output, storage, and control considerations of systems analysis and design. Use examples drawn from the business computer applications discussed in Chapters 12, 13, and 14 to illustrate such considerations. For example, what do you think would be some input, processing, output, storage, and control considerations for a retail POS system, a manufacturing process control system, an automated bank teller machine system, a payroll system, and so on? Draw and label a system function diagram (like Figure 10–22) to organize and illustrate your answers.

4. Jim Shannon, systems analyst, was given the title of project manager to develop a new payroll system. He thought his first step should be to interview the head of the payroll department. When he met with Sara Henna, payroll manager, the first thing he asked for was an organization chart and current procedure manuals and user system documentation. Sara informed him that those items were not readily available, but she could have them for him in about a week. Not having reviewed the system documentation on the current system and now having no user documentation to discuss, Jim thought it best to reschedule another meeting with Sara in two weeks. Jim left Sara's office wondering how this two-week delay in his preliminary investigation would affect the total project. What could Jim have done to better prepare for his interview with Sara?

APPLICATION PROBLEMS

5. Assume a company currently has a payroll and labor analysis application as described in Chapter 14. You are a systems analyst and are assigned the task of developing a cost/benefit analysis for upgrading the current system to a Personnel Information System as was described in Chapter 13. Identify several tangible and intangible costs and benefits that will probably result from upgrading the current system. Do not assign dollar amounts.

6. Develop a system flowchart and a data flow diagram that express the flow of information processing activities as you see them in one or more of the following systems:
   a. The sales transaction processing system of ABC Department Stores described in Real World Application 1–2 of Chapter 1.
   b. The common business information systems described in Real World Application 14–2 of Chapter 14.
   c. One of the business information systems described in Chapters 12, 13, and 14. You will have to make several assumptions about how information processing activities are accomplished. Choose an application with which you are most familiar.

7. Construct a system function diagram similar to Figure 10–22 to analyze the information system resources and activities in one of the systems mentioned in Application Problem 6.

8. The conceptual framework of the information systems model used throughout this text can be expressed as an information system matrix as shown below. Use an information system matrix to analyze one of the systems mentioned in Application Problems 3, 6, or 7. Fill in as many cells as you can, using duplicate entries when necessary.

Information System Activities	Hardware Resources		Software Resources		People Resources		Data Resources	Information Products
	Machines	Media	Programs	Procedures	Specialists	Users		
Input								
Processing								
Output								
Storage								
Control								

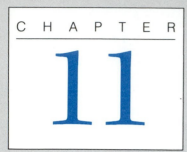

C H A P T E R

11

APPLICATION SOFTWARE DEVELOPMENT

Chapter Outline

Learning Objectives

The purpose of this chapter is to promote a basic understanding of application software development by analyzing (1) the activities of the five stages of the software development process, and (2) the use of several software development tools. After reading and studying this chapter, you should be able to:

1. Explain why users should have a basic knowledge of software development.
2. Summarize the functions of the five stages of software development.
3. Outline several ways that structured programming affects program design, coding, and debugging.
4. Identify the basic types of computer instructions.
5. Identify several types of programming errors and describe some checking and testing activities of program debugging.
6. Briefly explain the purpose of program flowcharts, pseudocode, structure and HIPO charts, and decision tables.
7. Prepare simple program flowcharts and pseudocode.
8. Identify major developments in computer-aided software engineering and explain how this affects both users and professional programmers.

Section I: The Software Development Process

WHY LEARN SOFTWARE DEVELOPMENT?

Understanding the fundamentals of computers and their hardware, software, and applications is an important achievement. However, it is equally important that you have a basic understanding of how computers are *programmed* to do what we want them to do (i.e., **computer programming** or **software development**). That is the purpose of this chapter.

However, an important fact of life of modern computer use is this: Most people who use computers don't develop their own software. Instead, they use software packages developed by external sources, or they use programs developed by the professional programming staff of their own organizations. So why learn software development? Because of these other facts of life:

☐ Businesspeople, managers, and other computer users must understand software development if they are to communicate effectively with programmers concerning computerized solutions to business problems.

☐ The development of microcomputers, time-sharing terminals, and simpler computer languages makes it possible for many computer users to be their own software developers.

☐ Software development no longer involves detailed coding of information processing instructions in a traditional programming language. Instead, users can develop an application program using a conversational *nonprocedural* language in an interactive "dialogue" with a computer.

Therefore, most people don't have to become expert *computer programmers*. However, they need to have a basic knowledge of computer software and its development to become *knowledgeable computer users*.

WHAT IS SOFTWARE DEVELOPMENT?

It is important for you to understand two major points about the software development process. First, the systems design stage of systems development (discussed in the previous chapter) usually results in a set of software specifications. It is at this point that a decision must be made. You must (1) buy a software package, or (2) develop a program in-house or hire outside programmers to do it for you. Until these decisions are made, software development cannot begin.

Secondly, you must understand that the software development process involves more than the writing of instructions in a programming language. The software development process may be subdivided into several stages: **program analysis, design, coding, verification,** and **maintenance.** Each stage of this process is summarized in Figure 11–1. We will discuss some of the tools and activities needed to accomplish these programming stages in this chapter.

Structured Programming

All of the stages of the software development process stress the concept of **structured programming.** Structured programming is a programming methodology that is part of a renewed emphasis on *software engineering*. This

Figure 11–1 The stages of the software development process. Notice the activities involved and the effect of computer-aided software engineering methods.

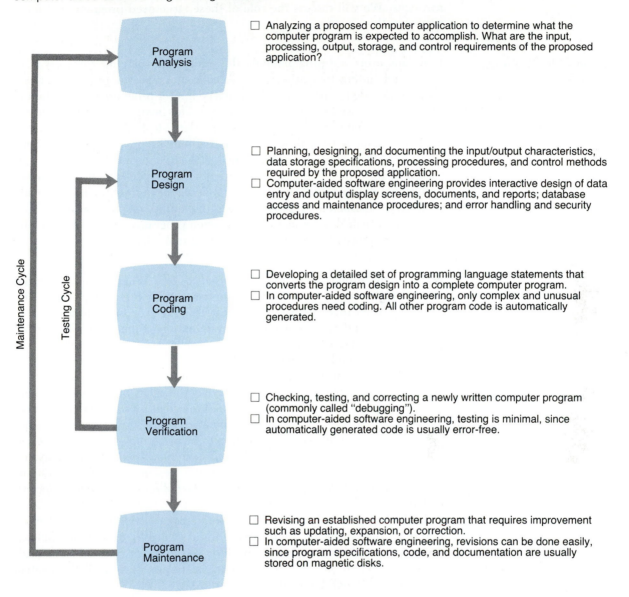

☐ Analyzing a proposed computer application to determine what the computer program is expected to accomplish. What are the input, processing, output, storage, and control requirements of the proposed application?

Program Analysis

☐ Planning, designing, and documenting the input/output characteristics, data storage specifications, processing procedures, and control methods required by the proposed application.
☐ Computer-aided software engineering provides interactive design of data entry and output display screens, documents, and reports; database access and maintenance procedures; and error handling and security procedures.

Program Design

☐ Developing a detailed set of programming language statements that converts the program design into a complete computer program.
☐ In computer-aided software engineering, only complex and unusual procedures need coding. All other program code is automatically generated.

Program Coding

☐ Checking, testing, and correcting a newly written computer program (commonly called "debugging").
☐ In computer-aided software engineering, testing is minimal, since automatically generated code is usually error-free.

Program Verification

☐ Revising an established computer program that requires improvement such as updating, expansion, or correction.
☐ In computer-aided software engineering, revisions can be done easily, since program specifications, code, and documentation are usually stored on magnetic disks.

Program Maintenance

Maintenance Cycle

Testing Cycle

involves the systematic design and development of software and the management of the software development process. Structured programming involves a *modular, top-down* program design. It stresses the use of a limited number of *control structures* to create structured *modules* of program code. Structured programming includes a variety of program design, coding, and testing techniques including *top-down design, modularity, stepwise refine-*

ment, and *chief programmer teams*. It also includes such tools as *structure* and *HIPO charts, structured coding, pseudocode,* and *structured walk-throughs*. We will discuss the role of these structured programming techniques in this chapter.

Computer-Aided Software Engineering

For many users and programmers, the software development process is an automated, interactive experience. A computer user or programmer can design and code the processing logic of a computer program with substantial realtime assistance from a computer system. This involves using a microcomputer or computer terminal to code, translate, test, debug, and develop alternatives for a new program in a realtime interactive process. Thus **computer-aided software engineering** (CASE) has become feasible. A major reason for these developments is the use of software packages that are part of **application development systems** (or *application generators*). They provide interactive assistance to programmers (including menus, prompts, and graphics) in their development of application programs. We will discuss the use of computer-aided software engineering tools shortly.

PROGRAM ANALYSIS

"What is the proposed program supposed to do?" Program analysis is the important first step in software development that answers that question. The amount of work involved is directly related to the type of application being programmed and to the amount of systems development work that has previously been accomplished. Program analysis is relatively simple for short problems and for many types of structured mathematical problems. Even complex problems and systems may not require extensive program analysis if a thorough job of systems development has been accomplished.

If the application to be programmed is viewed as a *problem* that requires a solution, then program analysis is really a process of *problem definition* and *problem specification*. If the application to be programmed is considered to be an information *system*, then program analysis should involve analyzing the *software specifications* produced by the design stage of the systems development cycle, or developing your own set of required *program specifications*.

In the program analysis stage, you should make a preliminary determination of (1) the **output** required, (2) the **input** available, (3) the data held in **storage** that will be provided or updated, (4) the **processing** (mathematical, logical, and other procedures) that may be required, and (5) the **control** procedures that will be needed. See Figure 11–2.

PROGRAM DESIGN

The **program design** stage of software development involves the planning and design of the specific input/output characteristics, processing procedures, data storage specifications, and control methods required by the proposed application. As in the case of the programming analysis stage, the amount of effort required in the program design stage depends on the complexity of the application and the amount of systems development work that has previously been performed.

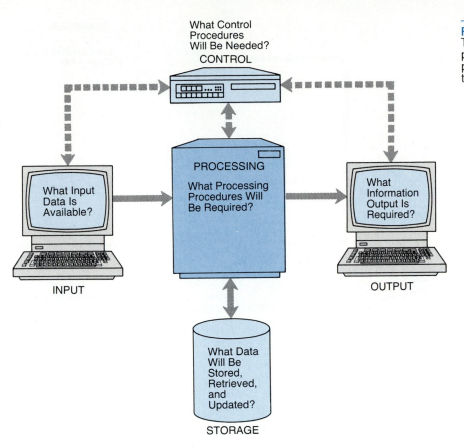

Figure 11–2 Program analysis. This is a system function approach to determining what a proposed program is supposed to do.

Traditional program design requires the development of a logical set of rules and instructions that specify the operations required to accomplish the proposed application. This aspect of program design is known in computer science as the development of an **algorithm,** which can be loosely defined as a set of rules or instructions that specify the operations required in the solution of a problem or in the accomplishment of a task. Of course, most algorithms are automatically generated when computer-aided software engineering methods are used.

In traditional programming design, the program is usually divided into several main subdivisions, or **program modules.** Programs may be subdivided into *generic program function modules* or into *application-specific modules.* For example, many programs use a beginning *initialization* module, *input, processing,* and *output* modules, as well as an ending *termination* module. Most programs also have *control* modules that deal with the testing and control of (1) the order of processing, (2) the repetition of processing steps *(looping),* (3) exceptional conditions, such as errors, and (4) other deviations from normal processing requirements. The use of *subroutines* or subprogram modules that may be used to perform common processing operations required by the program should also be considered during the design stage. See Figure 11–3.

Figure 11-3 Generic program function modules. Notice the examples of typical activities in each type of module.

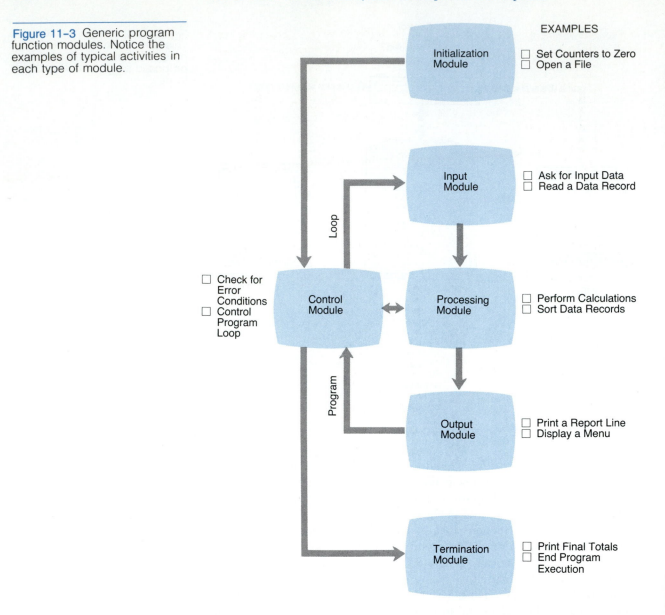

EXAMPLES

Initialization Module
☐ Set Counters to Zero
☐ Open a File

Input Module
☐ Ask for Input Data
☐ Read a Data Record

☐ Check for Error Conditions
☐ Control Program Loop

Control Module

Processing Module
☐ Perform Calculations
☐ Sort Data Records

Output Module
☐ Print a Report Line
☐ Display a Menu

Termination Module
☐ Print Final Totals
☐ End Program Execution

Loop

Program

Structured Design

Structured design is a method of *modular, top-down* design that is a major characteristic of structured programming. Let's take a look at the steps involved.

☐ The programmer must define the *output* that is to be produced, the *input* required, and the *major processing tasks* that are necessary to convert input into output.

☐ The major processing tasks are then *decomposed* into independent *functional modules*, which define the processing structure of the program. This is *modular* design.

☐ Finally, the processing *logic* or algorithm for each module is defined. The programmer designs the main module first, then the lower-level modules. This is *top-down design*.

Design tools, such as *structure charts*, *HIPO charts*, *flowcharts*, *pseudocode*, and *decision tables* are used to accomplish the design of each module. We will discuss these tools shortly. Each program module in a top-down design process is usually limited in its contents by the following restrictions:

☐ Each module should have only one entry and one exit point.

☐ Each module should represent only one program function; for example, "read master record."

☐ Each module should not require an excessive amount of program code. Some experts place this at no more than one page of program code, or about 50 lines of programming language instructions.

The purpose of these restrictions is to simplify and standardize the programming process by making programs easier to read, test, and correct. Dividing a lengthy program into modules facilitates not only the design process but also coding, testing, and documentation.

Program coding is the process that converts the logic designed during the program design stage into a set of programming language instructions. The term *programming* is frequently used to refer only to the program coding stage. However, as we have seen, four other important steps are also necessary. Coding is a rigorous logical process that requires programmers to strictly follow rules concerning the *syntax* (vocabulary, punctuation, and grammar) of the programming language being used.

PROGRAM CODING

Structured programming stresses that only three basic "control structures" should be used for program coding: (1) *sequence*, (2) *selection*, and (3) *repetition* (or loop). Using just these three basic control structures simplifies and standardizes program coding and makes the resulting programs easier to read and understand. Figure 11–4 illustrates the three basic control structures of structured programming in both traditional and *structured flowcharts*.

Using just these three structures simplifies the flow of program control and eliminates or minimizes *branching* forward and backward from the main flow of the program. Thus the main control module (also called the *mainline*) should clearly show that control flows from the top down (i.e., top to bottom without being transferred to earlier program modules). The cause of much unnecessary branching is blamed on "GO TO" instructions used in many programs. Therefore, this aspect of structured programming is sometimes called "GO TO–less" programming.

Program Control Structures

Sequence Structure

This structure expresses the fact that program instructions are usually executed in the order in which they are stored in the computer. In Figure 11–4 notice that program statements in function A will be executed before those for function B. Thus we say that "control" flows from function A to function B.

Selection Structure

This structure is also called the *decision* or IF–THEN–ELSE structure. It expresses a *choice* between two program control paths based on a *test* that results in either a true or false condition. In Figure 11–4 notice that, if the test is true, control will flow to function A and its statements will be executed. If the test is false, function B will be done.

Repetition (Loop) Structure

This structure is also called the DO–WHILE or DO–UNTIL structure. It expresses the performing of a program function *while* or *until* a condition is *true*. In Figure 11–4 notice the flow of program control that can be expressed as "do function A *while* the condition is true." The opposite control flow can be expressed by a variation of this structure, which would say "do function A *until* the condition is true."

Types of Instructions

The **types of instructions** available to a computer programmer for program coding depend on the program language used and the *instruction set* of the computer CPU. However, computer instructions can usually be subdivided into six categories: (1) specification, (2) input/output, (3) data movement, (4) arithmetic, (5) logical, and (6) control.

- ☐ *Specification instructions* are descriptive instructions that describe the data media to be used, the size and format of data records and files, the constants to be used, and the allocation of storage. Many of these instructions are based on the input/output and storage layout forms completed during the program design stage. The "FORMAT" statement of FORTRAN or the "PICTURE" statement of COBOL are examples of specification instruction statements.
- ☐ *Input/output instructions* transfer data and instructions between the CPU and input/output devices. "READ" or "PRINT" statements are examples of such instructions.
- ☐ *Data movement instructions* involve rearranging and reproducing data within primary storage. "MOVE," "SHIFT," or "STORE" instructions are examples.
- ☐ *Arithmetic instructions* are instructions that accomplish mathematical operations, for example, "ADD" and "SUBTRACT."
- ☐ *Logical instructions* perform comparisons and test conditions and control some branching processes, as illustrated in the decision symbol of program flowcharts. Examples are "IF–THEN" or "COMPARE" statements.

Figure 11-4 The three fundamental program control structures of structured programming. These structures are illustrated using traditional and structured flowchart symbols.

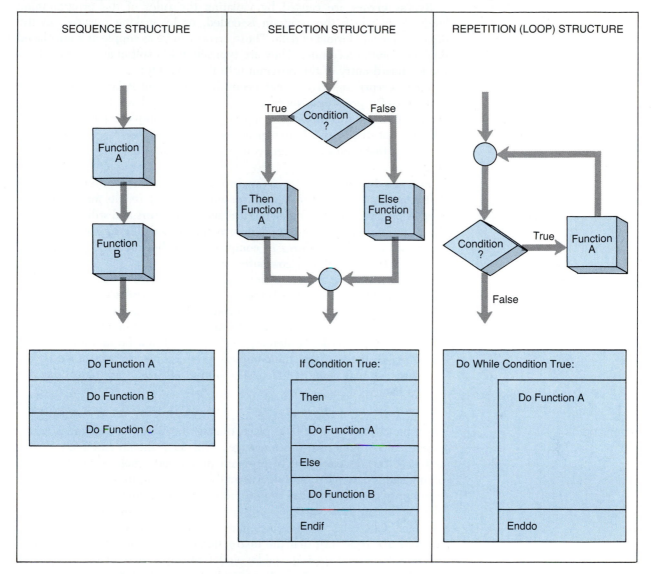

☐ *Control instructions* are used to stop and start a program, change the sequence of a program through some branching processes, and control the use of subroutines. "DO," "RETURN," and "STOP" statements are examples of control instructions.

Program verification, more commonly known as **debugging,** is a stage of software development that involves checking, testing, and correction processes. These activities are necessary because newly coded programs frequently contain errors *(bugs)* that must be identified and corrected by a debugging process.

PROGRAM VERIFICATION

Programming Errors

Programming errors are of three major types: **syntax, logic,** and **systems design errors.**

Syntax errors are caused by violating the rules of the programming language in which the program is coded, or by making mistakes in the organization and format of data. These errors can be as simple as a misplaced decimal point or a comma. They are typically the result of an error made in the keyboard entry of the program into the computer.

Logic errors are errors that occur because of mistakes in the logical structure of a program. Necessary procedures may have been omitted or incorrect procedures included in a program. For example, a payroll program that did not distinguish between hourly paid employees and salaried employees or that used an incorrect commission for salespersons would produce logic errors.

Systems design errors are errors in the design of a computer application that result in a program that produces unsatisfactory results for a computer user. A program may be free of clerical and logic errors and still not meet all the requirements of a proposed information processing application. Such errors are caused by failures in communication between the programmer and the systems analyst or computer user.

Syntax errors are easier to detect than logic errors, because they are usually identified during the language translation process when *diagnostic messages* identifying such errors are produced. Syntax errors may also cause the computer to reject a program during this process or later processing. Logic errors are harder to detect, since they will not be identified by the translator diagnostics, and the complete program may be processed by the computer without being rejected. The output of such a program, however, will be incorrect.

Checking

Program checking must take place during the program design, program coding, and program verification stages. Checking should take place during and after the development of program design aids such as HIPO charts, pseudocode, flowcharts, and decision tables. The purpose of this procedure is to verify that all program requirements are being met and to determine that the design aids correctly represent the processing logic required by the program. Checking should take place at the completion of the program coding stage to ensure that the instructions correctly translate the logic of the flowcharts and decision tables and that any syntax errors have been identified. This process is made easier if structured programming methods have been used. They can significantly simplify and standardize program logic and coding, thus making programs easier to read and correct.

The final checking process involves attempting to have the program or program module translated into a machine language program that is acceptable to the computer. An assembler, compiler, or interpreter (language translator program) is used to accomplish this process. (Refer back to Figure 3–9 in Chapter 3.) During or after such a translation process, diagnostic messages will be printed, identifying any syntax errors in the program. You should make necessary corrections to the program and then make another attempt. This process must be repeated until an error-free "pass" is accomplished. Then the resulting machine language program is ready for a test period.

Structured Walkthroughs

Structured walkthroughs are an aid to good programming design, coding, and debugging, and are one of the tools of structured programming. They require a *peer* review (by other programmers) of program design and coding to minimize and reveal errors in the early stages of programming. Their aim is to promote errorless and *egoless* programming by having other programmers involved in any programming process. Thus structured walkthroughs may involve the *team programming* concept, where several programmers are assigned to develop the same program under the direction of a *chief programmer*. Team members review each other's design and coding at regular intervals as each program module is designed and then coded. Structured walkthroughs are an attempt to minimize the cost of program verification by catching errors in the early stages of programming. Waiting until the program has reached the testing stage makes corrections more difficult and costly to make.

You should *test* a properly checked program to demonstrate whether it can produce correct results using *test data*. This testing should attempt to simulate all conditions that may arise during processing. Therefore, test data must include unusual and incorrect data as well as the typical types of data that will usually occur. Such test data is needed to test the ability of the program to handle exceptions and errors, as well as more normal forms of data. You should prepare the test data by manually calculating and determining correct results. After the object program has processed the test data, the output is compared to the expected results. If correct results are produced, the program or program module is considered properly tested and ready for use.

Testing

In structured programming, the higher-level modules of a program are supposed to be coded and tested first. Since the lower-level modules are not ready for testing, "dummy modules" are created in their place so each higher-level module can be tested. As lower-level modules are tested, higher-level modules are tested again. This allows coding and testing modules separately and from the "top down." This process simplifies finding errors, because errors can be isolated in specific modules. Then, when even the lowest-level program modules are successfully tested, the program is considered fully tested as an individual program. However, one final *systems test* step remains. The program must be tested together with other programs that are part of the same information system. Only when these programs show that they can properly work together are they considered fully tested.

The final phase of program verification is a temporary period, in which actual data is used to test a computer program. If the program has been designed to replace an older program, this procedure is known as "parallel processing." The parallel run allows the results of the new program to be compared to the results produced by the old program it is to replace.

PROGRAM MAINTENANCE

The final stage of software development begins after a program has been accepted as an operational program. **Program maintenance** refers to the revision of programs that is needed if they are to be improved, updated, expanded, or corrected. The requirements of information processing applications are subject to continual revisions due to changes in company policies, business operations, government regulations, and so on. Also, changes in the capabilities of newly acquired computer hardware and the continual development of new versions or "releases" of system or application software by vendors are a major cause of programming maintenance. Program maintenance is, therefore, an important stage of software development—involving the analysis, design, coding, and verification of changes to operational computer programs.

Recent studies have shown that programming maintenance uses a major part of the budget of the information processing departments of many computer-using organizations. Much more time, effort, and money is spent by these organizations in maintaining present programs than in developing new ones! Solving this problem is another major reason for the trend toward structured programming and computer-aided software engineering.

Program Documentation

Program documentation is a process that should occur throughout all stages of software development. Program documentation is the detailed description of the design and the instruction content of a computer program. Program documentation is extremely important in diagnosing program errors, making programming changes, or reassembling a lost program, especially if its original programmer is no longer available. Descriptive material produced in each stage of software development should be collected and refined, and new material developed. A *program documentation manual* is usually assembled for large programs. This might include contents as shown in Figure 11–5.

Large computer users frequently have a separate category of application programmers, called maintenance programmers, whose sole responsibility is program maintenance. Theirs is a difficult assignment, since they must

Figure 11–5 The contents of program documentation. This records and communicates the design and content of a program.

Program Specifications
Describe what the program is supposed to do.

Program Description
Consists of structure charts, HIPO charts, pseudocode, input/output and storage layout sheets, program flowcharts, decision labels, program listing, and a narrative description of what the program does.

Verification Documentation
Includes listings of test data and results, memory dumps, and other test documents.

Operations Documentation
Consists of operating instructions that describe the actions required of the computer operator during the processing of the computer program.

Maintenance Documentation
A detailed description of all changes made to the program after it was accepted as an operational program.

REAL WORLD APPLICATION 11–1

Romano Bros. Beverage Co.

Romano Bros. Beverage Co., a large independent wine and spirits distributor in Chicago, annually ships 3.5 million cases of wine and spirits to 9,500 retailers in northern Illinois. Two IBM 4331 mainframe computer systems do their billing, inventory control, warehouse picking, truck routing, and accounts receivable.

The company installed the SQL/DS database management system running under the DOS/VSE operating system in October 1984. At the time, IBM recommended against this, saying that a larger mainframe was needed. In spite of IBM's misgivings, SQL (Structured Query Language) has proven invaluable to Romano Bros., even in this underpowered configuration.

Joseph Schmitt, former administrative vice president at Romano Bros., says, "We have been using SQL for 25 months and never had to think at all about another language except in two instances when we wanted to copy data from external files into our database. We spent about three man-days writing those programs in PL/1. For the remainder of the 24 months, SQL has stood alone very well, thank you.

"The payoff from using SQL is in real dollars. Beverage sales managers often need vast amounts of selected-detail sales history to prepare unanticipated analyses to meet competitive situations. Before 1985, each special request from one of our managers typically took one to three weeks to fulfill. We had to write a batch program for each particular report. Many of the requests, of course, were never fulfilled at all.

"By the middle of the year, we had learned to use SQL well enough so that I could sit with a sales manager at an interactive terminal and explore data and discuss results. Often, the manager's request would be continually reshaped as we explored. In many instances, 20 to 40 minutes in front of the terminal gave the manager all the answers he needed. No printed reports, no programming.

"More complicated requests might take one to four hours to answer with SQL. Nevertheless, the sales manager usually had the formatted printout from SQL, with calculated percentages and subtotals, on his desk the same day. Still no programming.

"By the end of the year, we had eliminated the backlog of requests for special sales reports because we had eliminated all programming of them. Our programming staff was able to concentrate on the programming of system controls, data validation, accounting controls, etc. Our whole electronic data processing operation reached a new level of sophistication."

Application Questions

☐ Mr. Schmitt says using SQL eliminates programming. What stages of the software development process are really eliminated?

☐ What benefits have resulted from the use of a DBMS query language like SQL when users want information?

Source: Joseph W. Schmitt, "SQL Pays Off in Real Dollars," *Computerworld*, October 27, 1986, pp. 19–20.

revise programs they did not develop. This should emphasize the importance of the structured programming and computer-aided software engineering approaches, since they provide simplified, standardized, and structured documentation that is easy to read and understand. Such documentation is essential for proper program maintenance. Inadequate documentation may make program maintenance impossible and require the rewriting of an entire program.

Section II: Using Software Development Tools

We have stressed in this chapter that there are several tools available to help you during the software development process. They help you in the program design stage, and in the coding, verification, documentation, and maintenance stages as well. For example, *program flowcharts* or *pseudocode* can help you design the logic of a program. However, they also serve as documentation methods that help you in coding, testing, and modifying programs. Programming tools include structure charts, HIPO charts, flowcharts, pseudocode, and decision tables. Systems development tools such as system flowcharts, data flow diagrams, system function diagrams, and layout forms were explained in Chapter 10. Let's take a look at examples of each **programming tool.** Finally, we will examine several examples of the *software development tools* that provide support for computer-aided software development.

PROGRAM FLOWCHARTS

Program flowcharts were one of the first programming tools and are still widely used. A program flowchart illustrates the detailed sequence of steps required by a computer program. You should learn to use tools such as program flowcharts or pseudocode to:

☐ Visualize the logic and sequence of steps in an operation.

☐ Experiment with various programming approaches.

☐ Keep track of all processing steps, including procedures for alternatives and exceptions.

Once final versions of program flowcharts are completed, they serve as a guide during the program coding, testing, documentation, and maintenance stages. Program flowcharts can vary in their complexity, ranging from general flowcharts to detailed program flowcharts. Figure 11–6 illustrates the symbols used in program flowcharts.

Figure 11–7 is a general program flowchart of a salesperson payroll report program, which is a simplified example of one of the computer programs that might be required in a payroll system. It outlines the steps that result in the printing of the Salesperson Payroll Report. This process would ordinarily be just a segment of a larger payroll program but has been modified to illustrate the use of program flowcharting symbols.

In the example of Figure 11–7, salesperson payroll data records are read as input. Commissions and gross pay are calculated and included in a printed report. Each symbol in the flowchart has been numbered so that we can explain the function of each symbol and show the flow of processing and control activities in this program.

A **program loop** (see function 11 in Figure 11–7) allows any computer program to repeat automatically a series of operations. In this example, the main program loop of input, processing, and output operations is repeated until the last payroll record is read. When the last record is read, the

	**PROCESSING** A group of program instructions which perform a processing function of the program.
	**INPUT/OUTPUT** Any function of an input/output device (making information available for processing or recording processed information).
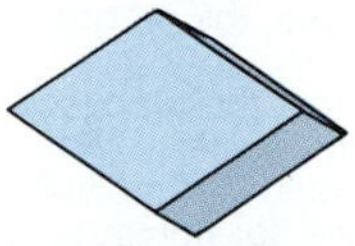	**DECISION** The decision function used to document points in the program where a branch to alternate paths is possible based upon variable conditions.
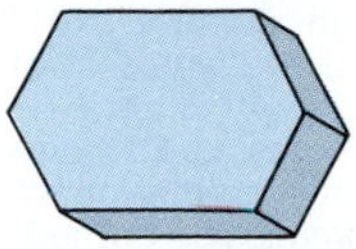	**PREPARATION** An instruction or group of instructions which changes the program.
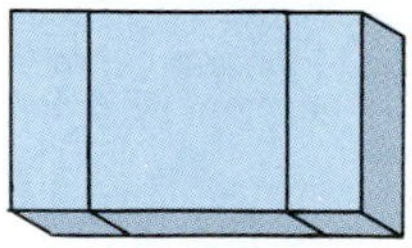	**PREDEFINED PROCESS** A group of operations not detailed in the particular set of flowcharts.
	**TERMINAL** The beginning, end, or a point of interruption in a program.
	**CONNECTOR** An entry from, or an exit to, another part of the program flowchart.
	**OFFPAGE CONNECTOR** A connector used instead of the connector symbol to designate entry to or exit from a page.
	**FLOW DIRECTION** The direction of processing or data flow.
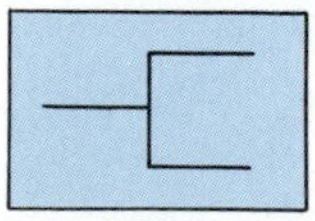	**ANNOTATION** The addition of descriptive comments or explanatory notes as clarification.

Figure 11-6 Common program flowchart symbols.

Figure 11–7 An example of a program flowchart for a program that produces a salesperson payroll report.

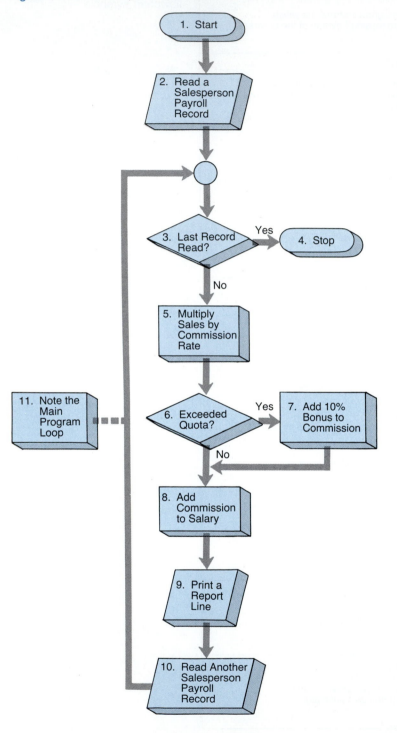

1. This is the start of the program.
2. The first salesperson payroll record is read as illustrated by the input/output symbol. It should contain data "fields" like the name, monthly salary, commission rate, and sales quota of each salesperson. The data record could be stored on magnetic tape or disk.
3. This is the "last record" decision point. Has the last data record been read?
4. If the answer is yes, the program comes to a stop.
5. If the answer is no, the processing symbol indicates that the sales amount on this data record should be multiplied by the commission rate to compute the sales commission earned.
6. Another decision point. Have the sales made exceeded the sales quota set for this salesperson?
7. If the answer is yes, a 10 percent bonus (10 percent of the normal commission) is added to the commission earned.
8. If the answer is no (and also whenever completing step 7) the sales commission earned is added to the regular monthly salary to compute the monthly *gross pay* for the salesperson.
9. A line on the Salesperson Payroll Report is printed. This would probably include the name, quota, sales, commission, salary, and gross pay for each salesperson.
10. Another salesperson payroll record is read, and the program "loops" back to a connector symbol that marks the beginning of the main program loop.
11. This *comment* symbol points out the main *loop* of the program.

program *branches* to a stop. The *looping* process is shown in this flowchart by an arrow that connects the beginning and ending symbols of the loop, though two connector symbols (see Figure 11–6) could have also been used.

Structured flowcharts are a tool of structured programming. They illustrate the steps in a computer program using the three **basic program control structures.** They use a "box-within-a-box" format to show what is to be done and in what order. Many people find them easier to understand than regular flowcharts. Use of structured flowcharts emphasizes the structured process within a computer program. Figure 11–8 is a compact, structured flowchart revision of the traditional flowchart shown in Figure 11–7.

STRUCTURED FLOWCHARTS

Another popular tool of structured program design that is part of structured programming is **pseudocode,** also called *structured English.* Pseudocode is the expression of the processing logic of a program module in ordinary

PSEUDOCODE

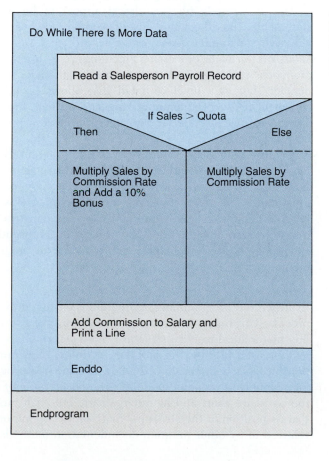

Figure 11–8 An example of a structured program flowchart for salesperson payroll report processing.

Figure 11–9 An example of the pseudocode for salesperson payroll report processing.

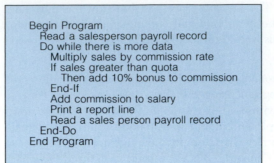

```
Begin Program
   Read a salesperson payroll record
   Do while there is more data
      Multiply sales by commission rate
      If sales greater than quota
         Then add 10% bonus to commission
      End-If
      Add commission to salary
      Print a report line
      Read a sales person payroll record
   End-Do
End Program
```

English language phrases. Pseudocode was developed as an alternative to flowcharts. In many programming assignments, flowcharts were found to be an unsatisfactory way of expressing the structure, flow, and logic of a program. Pseudocode allows you to express your thoughts in regular English phrases, with each phrase representing a programming process that must be accomplished in a specific program module.

The pseudocode phrases almost appear to be programming language statements; thus the name "pseudocode." However, unlike programming language statements, pseudocode has no rigid rules; only a few optional *keywords* for major processing functions are recommended. Therefore, programmers can express their thoughts in an easy, natural, straightforward manner, but at a level of detail that allows pseudocode to be directly convertible into programming language coding. Figure 11–9 provides an example of pseudocode for the same salesperson payroll program that we have flowcharted earlier.

Figure 11–10 is an example of a simple program that accomplishes salesperson payroll report processing. It uses the logic outlined in the program flowchart, structured flowchart, and pseudocode examples we have just illustrated. The instructions in this program are written in the BASIC programming language. Notice how close these instructions are to the labels in the program flowchart and the phrases in the pseudocode example. This should emphasize how helpful such tools are for program design and documentation.

STRUCTURE CHARTS

In structured programming, a program is designed by a modular, top-down process. This results in a program that consists of a series of modules related in a hierarchical treelike structure. A **structure chart** or *hierarchical chart* may be used to show the program modules, their purpose, and their relationships. Such charts show the flow of logic in a program using a "tree" of interconnected program modules. The *visual table of contents* is related to the structure chart and hierarchy chart, but each module is numbered so that its position in the structure chart and its operations can be more easily referred to by other program documentation methods. See Figure 11–11.

Figure 11-10 An example of
a simple BASIC program for
salesperson payroll report
processing. It uses the logic
outlined in the previous
flowchart and pseudocode
examples.

```
100   REM PAYROLL PROGRAM USING BASIC
110   READ SALESMAN.ID, SALES, SALARY
120   WHILE SALESMAN.ID <> 9999
130       COMMISSION = SALES * .05
140       IF SALES > 10000 THEN COMMISSION = COMMISSION * 1.1
150       GROSS.PAY = SALARY + COMMISSION
160       PRINT SALESMAN.ID, GROSS.PAY
170       READ SALESMAN.ID, SALES, SALARY
180   WEND
190   DATA 1234, 4500, 200
200   DATA 2345, 7200, 300
210   DATA 9999, 0, 0
220   END
```

Figure 11-11 An example of a visual table of contents for a payroll program.

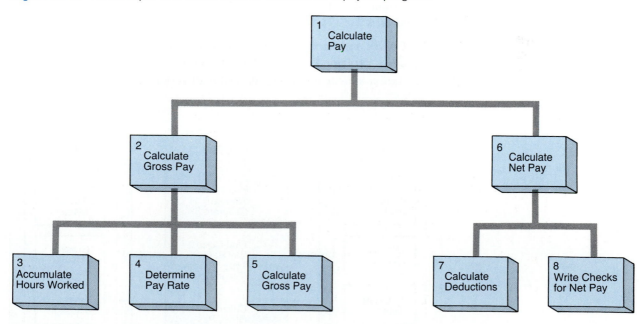

HIPO CHARTS

Another aid in structured design is the **HIPO chart** or *HIPO diagram* (hierarchy + input/processing/output). It is used to record the input/processing/output details of the hierarchical program modules. The HIPO chart aids the programmer in determining:

☐ The *output* required—its format, media, organization, volume, frequency, and destination.

☐ The *input* available—its source, format, media, organization, volume, and frequency.

☐ The *processing* needed—the mathematical, logical, and other procedures required to transform input into output.

A HIPO chart for the *main program module* (also called the *main control module*) is done first and gives an overall view of the input/processing/output of the program. The HIPO charts or diagrams can then be constructed for the other lower-level modules in the program. Figure 11–12 is an example of a HIPO chart for a gross pay calculation. (Note that it is part of module 2 in the visual table of contents of Figure 11–11.)

DECISION TABLES

Decision tables are another important tool of the systems analyst and computer programmer and are used in conjunction with, or in place of, flowcharts. Using flowcharts for the analysis and design of complex programs involving many specified conditions and decision paths becomes an extremely difficult process. The flow of data and the logical sequence of the program is hard to follow, and errors or omissions may result. Therefore, decision tables may be used in such cases as a tool for the design of programs involving complex conditional decision logic. A decision table is a tabular presentation of system or program logic. There are four basic parts to a decision table:

☐ *Condition statements*, which are conditions or questions similar to those contained in a flowchart decision symbol.

☐ *Action statements*, which describe all actions that can be taken.

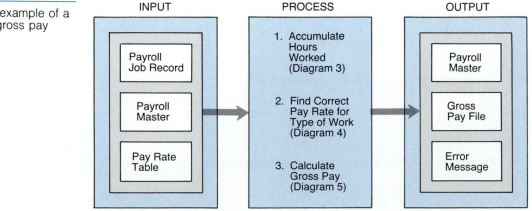

Figure 11–12 An example of a HIPO chart for a gross pay calculation.

INPUT	PROCESS	OUTPUT
Payroll Job Record	1. Accumulate Hours Worked (Diagram 3)	Payroll Master
Payroll Master	2. Find Correct Pay Rate for Type of Work (Diagram 4)	Gross Pay File
Pay Rate Table	3. Calculate Gross Pay (Diagram 5)	Error Message

☐ *Condition entries*, which indicate what conditions are being met or answers the questions in the condition statements.

☐ *Action entries*, which indicate the actions to be taken.

The columns in a decision table illustrate various **decision rules.** They specify that **if** certain conditions exist, **then** certain actions must be taken. Depending on the complexity of the decision logic, condition entries are indicated by a *Y* (yes), or an *N* (no), or comparison symbols *(relational operators)* such as $<\leq=\geq>$. Quantities and codes may also be used, or entries may be left blank to show that a condition does not apply. Action entries are usually indicated by an *X*. When a decision table is completed, each rule indicates a different set of conditions and actions.

A simple example should help clarify the construction and use of a decision table. Figure 11–13 illustrates a decision table based on the payroll system and program examples flowcharted in the preceding pages. The decision logic has been made more complex than in the previous example to illustrate the usefulness of decision tables for the analysis of decision logic. Examine Figure 11–13 to see what actions are taken when various possible conditions occur.

Payroll Table No. 1		Decision Rule Numbers						
		1	2	3	4	5	6	7
Conditions	Hourly paid employee	Y						
	Salaried employee		Y					
	Executive employee			Y				
	Unclassified employee				Y			
	Salesperson					Y	Y	Y
	Made sales?					N	Y	Y
	Exceeded quota?					N	N	Y
Actions	Compute wages	X						
	Compute salary		X					
	Compute sales salary					X	X	X
	Compute commission						X	X
	Compute bonus							X
	Salesperson gross pay processing					X	X	X
	Net pay processing	X	X			X	X	X
	Go to payroll table number:			2	3			

Figure 11–13 An example of a decision table for employee payroll processing.

Example.   Decision rule number 6 concerns the case of a salesperson who has made sales for the month but has not exceeded his or her sales quota. Given these conditions, the payroll processing actions that must be taken are to compute his or her salary and commission (but not a bonus), perform other salesperson payroll processing, and perform net pay processing common to all employees. The information in column 6 of the decision table can therefore be expressed in words by the following decision rule statement.

> **If** an employee is a salesperson who has had sales for the month but has not exceeded his or her sales quota, **then** compute his or her salary and commissions, and complete salesperson payroll processing and all-employee net pay processing.

TOOLS FOR COMPUTER–AIDED SOFTWARE ENGINEERING

Application development system packages are used for computer-aided software engineering. They contain a variety of programs called **software development tools.** These tools support interactive and automated program logic design, editing, coding, testing, debugging, and maintenance. They include diagramming tools, program specifications tools, design analyzers, screen generators, and code generators. Of course, you should realize that many of the programs in an application development system can be acquired separately or in other combinations. Thus such software development tools as *program generators*, *report generators*, and *screen generators* are being used to automate parts of the programming process.

Another major development in computer-aided software engineering is the emergence of fourth-generation languages (4GL), as discussed in Chapter 3. They include nonprocedural languages that encourage users and programmers to specify the *results* they want. The computer then determines the *sequence of instructions* that will accomplish those results. This differs from traditional programming languages, which require users and programmers to develop the sequence of instructions the computer must follow to achieve a result. Thus, fourth-generation languages greatly simplify and accelerate the programming process. These languages are typically provided by database management system packages and application development system packages. They provide easy database access and interactive program development support.

In computer-aided software engineering, application development software supports the interactive design of input/output and storage components first, automatically generating the necessary code. Then the processing and control components may be designed (and coded), using a very high-level programming language. Figure 11–14 illustrates the variety of software development tools in three application development systems: NATURAL by Software AG, MANTIS by Cincom, and IDEAL by Applied Data Research. Look at the names of each program in NATURAL and each function in the MANTIS menu. Notice how the IDEAL application development system accomplishes the application development process. This should give you a good idea of the many different types of automated assistance these software packages can provide to users and programmers.

Computer-aided software engineering emphasizes the concept of the *programmer workstation* (or *workbench*). This provides users and profes-

Figure 11–14 Examples of the software development tools in three major application development systems. Notice the names of the programs in NATURAL, the activities in MANTIS, and the process in using IDEAL.

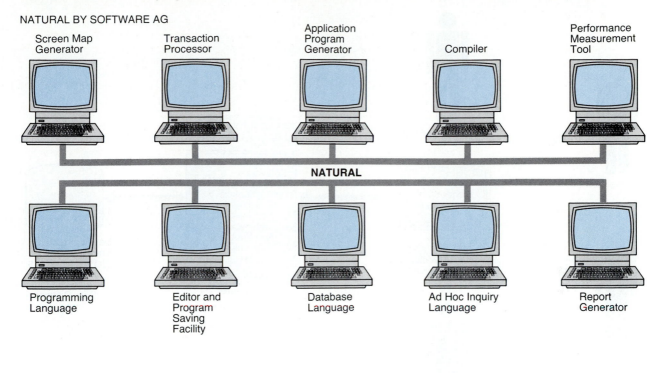

NATURAL BY SOFTWARE AG

Screen Map Generator · Transaction Processor · Application Program Generator · Compiler · Performance Measurement Tool

NATURAL

Programming Language · Editor and Program Saving Facility · Database Language · Ad Hoc Inquiry Language · Report Generator

MANTIS BY CINCOM

```
                    MANTIS

            FACILITY   SELECTION

RUN A PROGRAM BY NAME . . . . . . . . . . .    1
DISPLAY A PROMPTER . . . . . . . . . . . .     2
DESIGN A  PROGRAM  . . . . . . . . . . . .     3
    "      SCREEN . . . . . . . . . . . . .    4
    "      FILE  . . . . . . . . . . . . .     5
    "      PROMPTER . . . . . . . . . . . .    6
    "      INTERFACE  . . . . . . . . . . .    7
    "      TOTAL FILE VIEW . . . . . . . .     8
    "      EXTERNAL FILE VIEW . . . . . . .    9
RUN A PROGRAM BY MENU . . . . . . . . . . .   10
SIGN ON AS ANOTHER USER . . . . . . . . . .   11
DIRECTORY OF  PROGRAMS  . . . . . . . . . .   12
    "         SCREENS  . . . . . . . . . .    13
    "         FILES  . . . . . . . . . . .    14
    "         PROMPTERS  . . . . . . . . .    15
    "         INTERFACES  . . . . . . . . .   16
    "         TOTAL VIEWS  . . . . . . . .    17
    "         FILE VIEWS  . . . . . . . . .   18

TERMINATE . . . . . . . . . . . . . . . .   PA2
```

IDEAL BY APPLIED DATA RESEARCH

■ Input/output and storage definitions. Developed by filling out special-purpose, fill-in-the-blank screen formats, or "panels."
□ A declaration of the application and its inputs and outputs.
□ The logical database definition (or traditional file record layout for applications that use conventional file access methods).
□ Possible report definitions.
□ Screen panel layouts and definitions for online screen-oriented applications.
□ Input and output parameters.
■ Processing logic developed by use of a very high-level language: IDEAL/PPL.
□ The definition of working data (data local to the program).
□ The logic, computations, terminal interaction and database maintenance rules, procedures, and actions.

sional programmers with programming support, as illustrated in Figure 11–15. This concept includes:

☐ **Hardware support**—an intelligent terminal with advanced display and graphics capabilities.

☐ **Software development tools**—programming software such as the programs found in application development systems and database management systems. They provide automated assistance in the development of software.

Figure 11-15 An example of the support provided for computer-aided software engineering. Notice the hardware, software, and people resources provided.

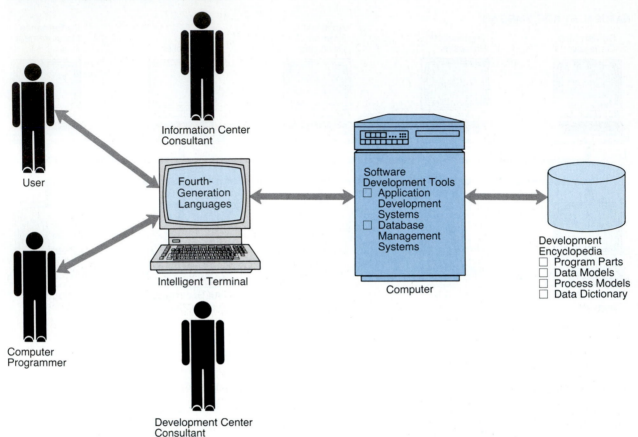

☐ **Fourth-generation languages**—nonprocedural programming languages that simplify and accelerate program development.

☐ **Development encyclopedia**—an automated library of standard program modules, data models, process models, a data dictionary, and other standard structures and procedures. This controls and facilitates the automatic generation of correct and consistent programs.

☐ **Development centers**—provide expert organization support to professional programming staff, as well as to advanced user-programmers. The members of the development center serve as consultants to the application development group of the firm. Their role is similar to that of an industrial engineering group in a manufacturing company. Thus they analyze programming productivity and quality, recommend better methods or resources, and help implement recommendations.

☐ **Information centers**—Support facilities for the computer users of an organization. They provide *hardware support* for users who need it by providing the use of microcomputers, intelligent terminals, advanced graphics terminals, high-speed printers, plot-

REAL WORLD APPLICATION 11–2

IDS/American Express

If the use of expert systems for assistance on the front end of software development—the analysis specification and design phase—can be combined with more traditional development methods, the result will be a step forward for computer-aided software engineering (CASE). Automated front-end packages could, for example, be combined with rapid prototyping, which incorporates user feedback as the application is developed. Application generators could then generate the program code to complete the cycle.

Several well-muscled CASE systems exist to provide assistance in automating much of this process in the mainframe world, such as Pacbase from CGI Systems, Inc., Telon from Pansophic Systems, Inc., APS from Sage Software, Inc., Transform by Transform Logic Corp., and Gamma from the former Tarkenton Software. In the mainframe world, "pieces of the development process have been automated, but no one has a coherent system," Charles W. Bachman observes. Bachman Information Systems is attempting to develop an integrated development system using expert system modules.

Many organizations are not waiting for this new generation of development systems. They are proceeding with the biggest and best mainframe development systems available, although the expense of these systems, which cost from $150,000 to $300,000, represents a major commitment to a particular technology and does not encourage experimentation. One example is IDS/American Express in Minneapolis.

When IDS, a personal financial services company, was taken over three years ago, its new parent, American Express, directed it to rewrite all of its financial systems and organize them on a customer basis rather than spreading each account across several unrelated applications, recalls Alan F. Bignall, vice president of corporate systems. The unit was going to have to undertake the process while experiencing a 20 percent annual growth rate and while managing the assets of $29 billion of its customers' investments, he adds.

Bignall's unit chose CGI Systems' Pacbase to launch a data-driven development process controlled by a data dictionary and exploiting stored modules of reusable code. IDS generated its first major application, client administration and management, in six months. Pacbase generates about 88 percent of the COBOL needed for each application, with the rest provided by custom COBOL programming. Furthermore, Bignall finds he can devote an unusually high percentage of his 400 programmers—more than half—to new development, although he says it still takes a lengthy two to three months to learn Pacbase's fourth-generation language and system procedures.

Application Questions

☐ Why did IDS decide to use a CASE tool such as Pacbase?

☐ What advantages are there to this method of software development?

☐ How will future CASE tools be improved?

Source: Charles Babcock, "Program Power," *Computerworld,* January 5, 1987, pp. 51–52.

---

ters, and so on. *Software support* is provided with advanced software packages such as application development systems, nonprocedural languages, database management systems, and a variety of application software packages. *People support* is provided by a staff of user consultants.

SUMMARY

☐ Application software development is a process that results in the development of a detailed set of information processing instructions for computers. Software development may be subdivided into the five stages summarized in Figure 11–1.

☐ Structured programming is a programming methodology that involves the use of a modular, top-down program design. It uses a limited number of control structures to create structured modules of program code. Structured programming includes program design and verification techniques such as structure and HIPO charts, pseudocode, and structured walkthroughs.

☐ Programming tools such as program flowcharts, pseudocode, structure charts, HIPO charts, and decision tables are important techniques used not only in program design but also to assist in program coding, debugging, documentation, and maintenance.

☐ Computer-aided software engineering involves the use of such software tools as application development systems and other hardware, software, and organizational resources to make computer programming an automated, interactive process.

KEY TERMS AND CONCEPTS

These are the key terms and concepts of this chapter. The page number of their first explanation is in parentheses.

1. Algorithm *(405)*
2. Application development system *(422)*
3. Basic control structures *(407)*
4. Computer-aided software engineering *(404)*
5. Debugging *(409)*
6. Decision tables *(420)*
7. Development center *(424)*
8. HIPO charts *(420)*
9. Information center *(424)*
10. Logic error *(410)*
11. Program analysis *(404)*
12. Program coding *(407)*
13. Program design *(404)*
14. Program documentation *(412)*
15. Program flowcharts *(414)*
16. Program loops *(414)*
17. Program maintenance *(412)*
18. Program module *(405)*
19. Programming tools *(414)*
20. Pseudocode *(417)*
21. Software development tools *(422)*
22. Stages of software development *(402)*
23. Structure charts *(418)*
24. Structured design *(406)*
25. Structured flowcharts *(417)*
26. Structured programming *(402)*
27. Structured walkthroughs *(411)*
28. Syntax error *(410)*
29. System design error *(410)*
30. Types of instructions *(408)*

Match one of the **key terms and concepts** listed above with one of the brief examples or definitions listed below. Try to find the "best fit" for answers that seem to fit more than one term or concept. Defend your choices.

_____ 1. Program analysis, design, coding, verification, and maintenance.

_____ 2. A programming methodology that creates structured modules of program instructions.

_____ 3. Using a modular, top-down program design.

_____ 4. Software development becomes an automated, interactive process.

_____ 5. A major software package for computer-aided software engineering.

_____ 6. Determining what a proposed program is supposed to do.

_____ 7. Developing the processing logic of a program.

_____ 8. Converting program logic into computer instructions.

_____ 9. Sequence, selection, and repetition instruction sets.

_____ 10. Input/output and arithmetic instructions are examples.

_____ 11. Checking, testing, and correcting a program.

_____ 12. You leave out a comma in a program instruction.

_____ 13. You forget to compute overtime pay in a payroll program.

_____ 14. You do not provide adequate headings in a report.

_____ 15. Requires a review of program design by other programmers.

_____ 16. A description of the design and instruction content of a program.

_____ 17. Revising programs that need to be improved or changed.

_____ 18. Examples are program flowcharts, pseudocode, and structure charts.

_____ 19. Examples are design analyzers, screen generators, diagramming tools, and code generators.

_____ 20. A set of instructions that specify the operations required to accomplish a task.

_____ 21. A set of instructions that represents only one program function.

_____ 22. Uses symbols connected by arrows to illustrate the detailed sequence of steps in a program.

_____ 23. Expresses program logic in ordinary English phrases.

_____ 24. Shows the purpose and relationships of the modules in a program.

_____ 25. Emphasizes the input, processing, and output details of a program module.

_____ 26. Uses a box-within-a-box format to show the steps in a program.

_____ 27. Used to design programs involving complex conditional decision logic.

APPLICATION PROBLEMS

1. If you have not already done so, read and answer the questions after the two Real World Applications in this chapter.

2. Match each of the following stages of the software development process with one of the examples listed below.

   a. Program analysis.
   b. Program design.
   c. Program coding.
   d. Program verification.
   e. Program maintenance.

   1. Changing a payroll program to reflect changes in income tax rates.
   2. Using pseudocode to help you develop the logic of a program.
   3. Determining what input data is available for a proposed information processing assignment.
   4. Writing program instructions in the BASIC programming language.
   5. Checking a program for possible errors.

3. Construct a simple program flowchart that illustrates the flow of data and some of the processing steps required to accomplish an information processing task. Use an information processing task of your choice, such as the processing of payroll records, student grades, sales transactions, or mathematical computations.

4. Figure 11–16 is a program flowchart for a COBOL program. The program produces a report, listing each individual sale and the total sales for a restaurant. In addition, any sale over $100 is flagged with an exception message. Each record contains the dollar amount of the sale and whether the sale was for breakfast, lunch, or dinner. Structured program coding allows three structures: sequence structure, selection structure, and repetition or loop structure. In Figure 11–16, the letter next to parts of the flowchart represents one of these structures. For each letter identify the appropriate structure.

5. In order to develop a structured program, you could produce a structure chart before you developed a program flowchart. The structure chart breaks the program into functional modules and shows their hierarchical relationship. For the program flowchart in Figure 11–16, one could identify the following modules:

   a. Produce sales report.
   b. Open files.
   c. Write title of report.
   d. Get first record.
   e. Process record.
   f. Format exception message.
   g. Accumulate total sales.
   h. Format detail output line.
   i. Write detail output line.
   j. Get next record.
   k. Format total sales output line.
   l. Write total sales output line.
   m. Close files.

   Produce a structure chart using these modules, using the flowchart and the letter of the modules to help you.

6. Develop the pseudocode for the program expressed as a flowchart in Figure 11–16.

7. Construct a decision table for a customer billing program given the following requirements:

   a. If the balance due is less than or equal to zero, do not send a bill.
   b. If the balance due is greater than zero, send a bill.
   c. If the balance due exceeds the credit limit, print customer exception report.

Figure 11-16 A COBOL program flowchart for sales report.

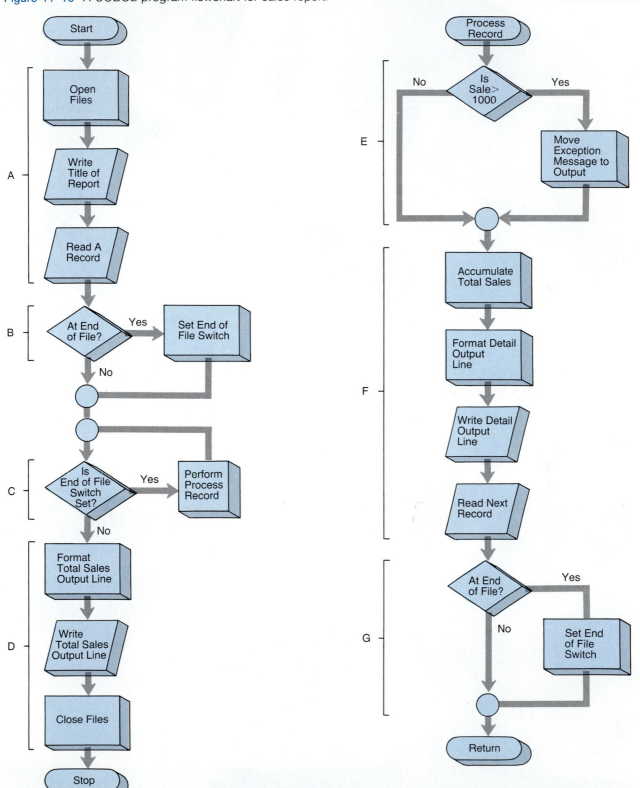

INFORMATION SYSTEMS APPLICATIONS

AUTOMATED OFFICE INFORMATION SYSTEMS

Chapter Outline

Learning Objectives

The purpose of this chapter is to promote a basic understanding of the role played by computers in office automation. After reading and studying this chapter, you should be able to:

1. Discuss the purposes of the major types of automated office systems.
2. Identify the system functions of automated office systems.
3. Explain the role of word processing in automated offices.
4. Identify several types of electronic office communications and their benefits to knowledge workers.
5. Discuss the advantages and disadvantages of automated office systems.

OVERVIEW

Most of us would not like to work in an office where all information processing activities were done manually. Office machines such as electric typewriters, copying machines, and dictation machines have made office work a lot easier and productive. But the *mechanized office* is giving way to the *automated office*. Computers are changing the equipment and work habits of today's office workers. Investment in computer-based workstations and other automated equipment is transforming traditional manual office methods and paper communications media. This has resulted in the development of automated systems that rely on word processing, data processing, telecommunications, and other information systems technologies.

Automated office systems are computer-based information systems that collect, process, store, and transmit data and information in the form of electronic office communications. Such systems can increase the productivity of executives and other **knowledge workers** by significantly reducing the time and effort needed to produce, access, and receive office communications. (Knowledge workers include executives, managers, supervisors, and professionals such as planners, engineers, analysts, scientists, and other staff personnel.)

Studies made of how knowledge workers spend their time have determined that **office automation** (OA) can save a significant amount of a knowledge worker's time (15 percent is one estimate). The major areas that could be improved include less productive office activities such as seeking information, waiting, organizing work, scheduling, and filing. More productive office activities, such as meetings, telephone calls, and creating documents, can also be improved by automated office systems. Studies have also shown that office workers have less plant and equipment invested per worker ($2,000/worker) than factory workers ($25,000/worker) or agricultural workers ($50,000/worker). Thus increased investment in automated office systems would probably result in increased productivity by office workers.

Figure 12–1 outlines the major automated office systems, while Figure 12–2 summarizes their many capabilities. We will discuss such systems in this chapter, concentrating our attention on word processing and office communications applications.

AUTOMATED OFFICE SYSTEM ACTIVITIES

You should think of automated office systems as *computer-based information systems*. This is illustrated in the *automated office system model* in Figure 12–3. Notice that *hardware resources* (intelligent workstations and media), *software resources*, (automated office programs and procedures), and *people resources* (knowledge workers and other users) are required. These three system resources transform *text data resources* into finished *information products* using the information system activities of *input, processing, output, storage,* and *control*. Let's look at some typical examples of these activities.

Figure 12–1 An overview of automated office systems. These computer-based information systems collect, process, store, and transmit data and information in the form of electronic office communications.

AUTOMATED OFFICE SYSTEMS

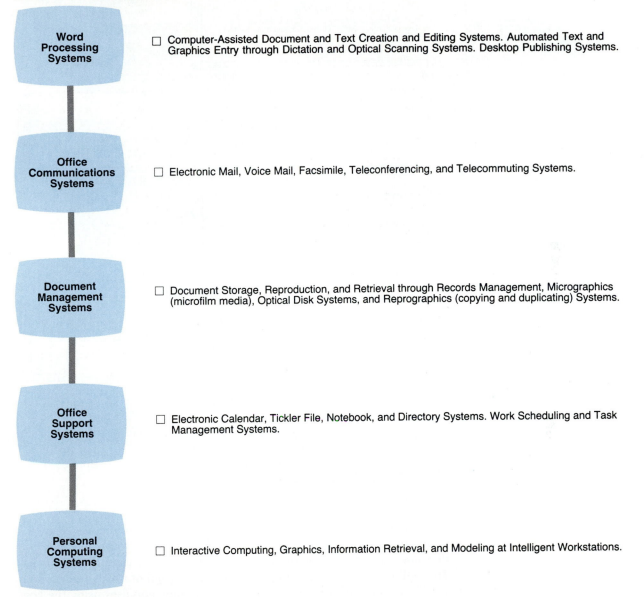

Word Processing Systems
☐ Computer-Assisted Document and Text Creation and Editing Systems. Automated Text and Graphics Entry through Dictation and Optical Scanning Systems. Desktop Publishing Systems.

Office Communications Systems
☐ Electronic Mail, Voice Mail, Facsimile, Teleconferencing, and Telecommuting Systems.

Document Management Systems
☐ Document Storage, Reproduction, and Retrieval through Records Management, Micrographics (microfilm media), Optical Disk Systems, and Reprographics (copying and duplicating) Systems.

Office Support Systems
☐ Electronic Calendar, Tickler File, Notebook, and Directory Systems. Work Scheduling and Task Management Systems.

Personal Computing Systems
☐ Interactive Computing, Graphics, Information Retrieval, and Modeling at Intelligent Workstations.

Input activities include the creation or origination of ideas, facts, or messages expressed in words. This typically involves the entry of text using the keyboard of a microcomputer or terminal. This *keyboarding* activity converts words into electronic impulses in the storage circuitry of the computer. Then it may record them on a magnetic disk and simultaneously display

Input Activities

Figure 12–2 Example of the capabilities of automated office systems. Notice how such capabilities automate many traditional office functions.

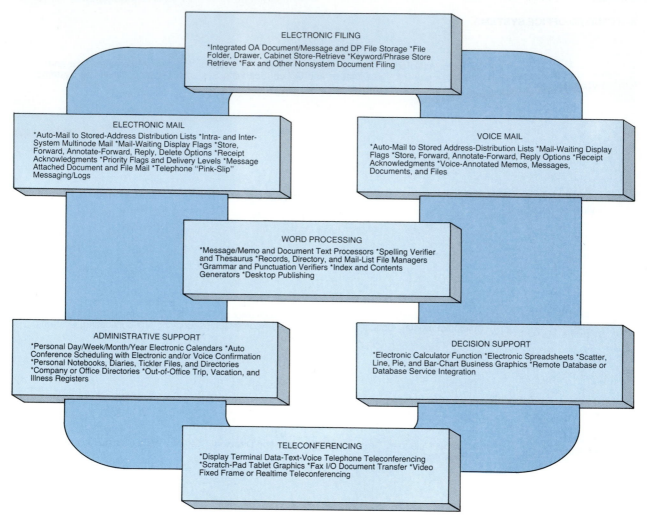

ELECTRONIC FILING

*Integrated OA Document/Message and DP File Storage *File Folder, Drawer, Cabinet Store-Retrieve *Keyword/Phrase Store Retrieve *Fax and Other Nonsystem Document Filing

ELECTRONIC MAIL

*Auto-Mail to Stored-Address Distribution Lists *Intra- and Inter-System Multinode Mail *Mail-Waiting Display Flags *Store, Forward, Annotate-Forward, Reply, Delete Options *Receipt Acknowledgments *Priority Flags and Delivery Levels *Message Attached Document and File Mail *Telephone "Pink-Slip" Messaging/Logs

VOICE MAIL

*Auto-Mail to Stored Address-Distribution Lists *Mail-Waiting Display Flags *Store, Forward, Annotate-Forward, Reply Options *Receipt Acknowledgments *Voice-Annotated Memos, Messages, Documents, and Files

WORD PROCESSING

*Message/Memo and Document Text Processors *Spelling Verifier and Thesaurus *Records, Directory, and Mail-List File Managers *Grammar and Punctuation Verifiers *Index and Contents Generators *Desktop Publishing

ADMINISTRATIVE SUPPORT

*Personal Day/Week/Month/Year Electronic Calendars *Auto Conference Scheduling with Electronic and/or Voice Confirmation *Personal Notebooks, Diaries, Tickler Files, and Directories *Company or Office Directories *Out-of-Office Trip, Vacation, and Illness Registers

DECISION SUPPORT

*Electronic Calculator Function *Electronic Spreadsheets *Scatter, Line, Pie, and Bar-Chart Business Graphics *Remote Database or Database Service Integration

TELECONFERENCING

*Display Terminal Data-Text-Voice Telephone Teleconferencing *Scratch-Pad Tablet Graphics *Fax I/O Document Transfer *Video Fixed Frame or Realtime Teleconferencing

them on a video screen. One may also write on paper or dictate ideas to a secretary who records them in shorthand coding. Or you could talk into dictation equipment that records spoken words on magnetic tape media. This will then require the *transcription* (conversion) of words recorded on written material or magnetic media into electronic impulses using the keyboard of a microcomputer or terminal.

Some systems use remote, pooled dictation in which users dial a central transcription service and dictate by telephone into magnetic tape recorders. Another technology that is automating word processing and desktop publishing is the use of optical scanning devices. They read printed text and graphics and convert them into electronic input for computers. Thus printed paper documents have become another source of input for automated office systems. Finally, the use of telephones for *voice mail* and the use of *voice input devices* allow direct entry of spoken words into computer systems.

Figure 12-3 An automated office information system model. Automated office systems use hardware, software, and people resources to perform information system activities that transform text data resources into information products such as documents and messages.

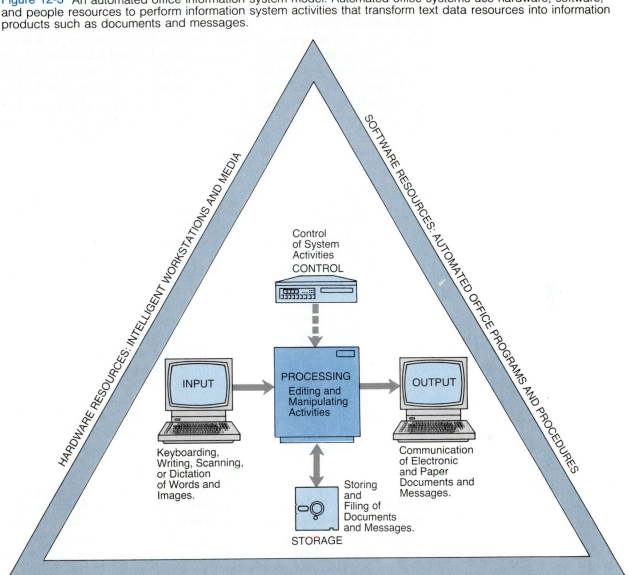

Processing activities typically include *editing* activities in which displayed material is visually proofed by the operator and electronically proofed by word processing and other software. Corrections and other changes can then be made electronically. Characters, words, sentences, paragraphs, and pages can be inserted, moved, deleted, or changed in a variety of ways. Word processing may involve use of options such as an online *spelling dictionary* and *thesaurus*. These automatically correct the spelling or provide alternatives for the words in a document. Grammar and punctuation verifiers, idea processors, and style checkers are other options that can be used.

Processing Activities

Text processing activities include the automatic typing of letters and documents according to a predetermined format. The computer stops at predetermined places for the manual or electronic insertion of variable information such as names and addresses on a form letter sent to a firm's customers. Standard phrases and paragraphs (nicknamed *boilerplate*) stored on magnetic disks are retrieved and automatically typed. The operator then inserts names, dates, and other information at appropriate points in the text to produce form letters, legal documents, and all types of reports. **List processing** allows long mailing lists of names and addresses (and other lists) to be automatically merged with previously created standard text (such as form letters). (This is frequently called *mail merge.*)

Output Activities

Output activities involve using electronic or paper communications to appropriate persons. Electronic communications can be in the form of video displays or digitized voice messages. Printers are used to print paper documents. Multiple copy forms may be used or copies can be made with office copying machines.

Intelligent copiers and other **reprographics** equipment (such as copying and duplicating machines) provide advanced copying features. Document images can be transmitted in electronic digital form over telecommunications channels to intelligent copiers and other devices and converted back to paper documents. This is known as **facsimile.** Electronic messages sent between intelligent workstations over **electronic mail** networks are another important form of output in automated office systems.

Finally, **desktop publishing** systems are a major advanced output function. Organizations can now use microcomputers, laser printers, and advanced text processing and graphics software to produce their own newsletters, brochures, printed reports, manuals, and books. We will have more to say about these applications in the next section of this chapter.

Storage Activities

Storage activities include (1) *storing* documents or messages on magnetic disks for temporary storage before printing, and (2) *filing*, which involves storing material in a structured and organized manner so that it can be retrieved easily when needed. Documents are usually stored as files on magnetic disks. A document can be stored and retrieved under several different categories, though only one copy may exist on a magnetic disk. A finished document might be given a document number or file number that describes it by subject matter, title, author, document category, or other descriptive or identifying characteristic. **Text management** systems are used to index and manage the documents stored in large text databases.

Some automated office systems use **micrographics** equipment that can store a microfilm (or microfiche) copy of a document, display a full-size image on a screen, prepare a full-size paper copy, and transmit an electronic image to another terminal in the automated office system. Micrographic media and optical disks are frequently used for such long-term *archival* storage. The use of optical disk devices has resulted in the development of *image bases* for the storage of digitized document and graphics images.

Control of automated office activities is accomplished by computer programs and by manual procedures. Some functions can be *hardwired* in the electronic circuitry of the computer, or stored as *firmware* in ROM modules. Most programs are stored on secondary storage media such as magnetic disks until needed. A wide variety of software packages are available to control automated office system activities.

Automated office systems began with the automation of the office typewriter. One of the first major developments was the introduction of the IBM magnetic tape Selectric typewriter (MTST) in 1964. It had electronic circuitry and used magnetic tape to store what was being typed. Changes could be made electronically without retyping, and the finished copy could be typed automatically on paper. Other automatic typewriter systems began to appear, including some that used CRT units to display keyed-in material so it could be visually edited before typing a final copy. Finally, *electronic typewriters* with video displays and computerized features were developed. Today, most automated office activities are done on microcomputers or on computer terminals connected to mini or mainframe computers. However, there is still a big market for "dumb" *electric* typewriters and "smart" *electronic* typewriters.

AUTOMATED OFFICE WORKSTATIONS

Microcomputers and computer terminals have become **intelligent workstations.** People in the office use them for word processing, data processing, electronic mail, graphics, and many other personal computing applications. They are frequently tied together in local area networks. Data communications links to host mainframe computers and databases in wide area networks are common. There are four major categories of computerized workstations for automated offices.

- ☐ **Stand-alone workstations** consist of a microcomputer with a keyboard, video monitor, floppy disk or hard disk storage, and a printer.
- ☐ **Shared logic systems** consist of video terminals that share the processing power and storage capacity of a minicomputer. These minicomputer systems include printers for hard copy output and magnetic disk units for secondary storage.
- ☐ **Shared resource systems** use intelligent terminals as word processing workstations. They usually are part of a distributed local area network (LAN) in a large building or other large worksite. These workstations are essentially microcomputers that share expensive *system resources,* such as large-capacity disk drives (*file servers*) and high-speed printers that are part of the network.
- ☐ **Time-sharing systems** consist of computer terminals connected by telecommunications lines to a central computer. Automated office software as well as programs for other applications are stored on this *host* computer. Many users can share the computer at the same time. Thus any computer system with data communications and time-sharing capabilities can provide automated office services.

Figure 12–4 illustrates automated office workstations in a large office building that combine the features of shared logic, shared resource, and time-sharing systems.

Figure 12–4 Automated office workstations using a shared logic and shared resource local area network and time-sharing features.

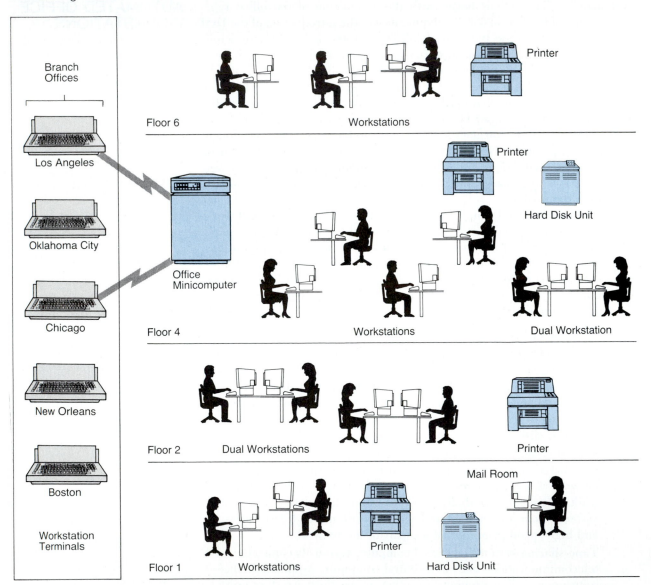

REAL WORLD APPLICATION 12–1

United Telephone Company

One of the strongest integrated office automation products on the market, particularly on the networking side, is Digital Equipment Corp.'s All-In-1. All-In-1 comes with electronic mail, calendar management, basic word processing, and desk management. It also supports DEC's Business Operations Support System, which links spreadsheet, report generation, and graphics functions. Additional software options, which most users choose, include Decalc, WPS Plus, Decgraph, Decslide, and Datatrieve. Users can also purchase a videotex package. All-In-1 also provides consistent user interfaces and an interrupt function that allows easy movement between applications.

DEC's ability to connect with other systems and provide integrated applications were key reasons why United Telephone Co. in Florida chose All-In-1 and a VAX-11/785 minicomputer when it decided to acquire an integrated office system. The company needed a system that could connect with IBM mainframes and minicomputers and Hewlett-Packard systems on both corporatewide and departmental networks, according to DP manager William Gainey. United Telephone evaluated systems from IBM, DEC, Wang, Data General, and HP based on price, performance, functionality and network capability. "We found that there was less than a 10 percent variation in cost between the systems," Gainey says. "So it boiled down to a couple of key issues: Can the vendor provide the support required? And which one could do the job for our company? All-In-1 came out on top, and DG's Comprehensive Electronic Office was a close second," he recalls. "The other three vendors were quite a ways back."

Since deciding on the DEC system, United Telephone has implemented it in a network of more than 300 users at 12 locations. The firm runs two departmental Microvax IIs to take some of the processing load off the VAX.

Altogether, the OA system encompasses 120 Decmate word processors, 73 VT240 graphics terminals, and 23 Rainbow PCs. Through the host computer, these DEC machines communicate with each other and with 19 IBM micros, including Personal Computer XTs and 3270 Personal Computers, which can emulate VT100 terminals.

Users can also access the system via phone lines. When users dial in, Dectalk software converts electronic messages to voice messages. Ultimately, United Telephone plans to install Version 2.0 of DEC's Videotex software, which will allow users to hear a Dectalk recitation of requested videotex pages.

Gainey says he is satisfied with United Telephone's choice of OA systems but feels that DEC and other vendors should be more willing to connect with each other's systems.

Currently, for example, IBM PC users can only communicate with a DEC host computer in the limited role of networked terminals, which is a problem because it does not tap the full processing power of the PCs. Gainey says he would like to see enhancements that will allow PCs to communicate with the system as casual users. "As a buyer of equipment, we would like to see the walls broken down between vendors to allow bidirectional communication. The vendors have to meet this need so that we are not trapped in one set of equipment," he says. Nevertheless, Gainey says his company is committed to All-In-1 for the foreseeable future. "The decision we made was correct at the time, and I would make the same decision today. The market principals are IBM and DEC, and they will continue to be."

Application Questions

☐ What automated office capabilities are produced by DEC's All-In-1 package?

☐ Why did United Telephone choose All-In-1? What are its benefits and limitations?

Source: Michael Sullivan-Trainor, "Integrated OA Systems," *Computerworld*, June 30, 1986, p. 34.

Section II: Automated Office Applications

In this section we will analyze the major types of automated office systems and how they are used in today's office environment.

WORD PROCESSING

Word processing is the automated transformation of ideas into a readable form of communication. Word processing involves the manipulation of **text data** (characters, words, sentences, and paragraphs) by a computer system. It produces information products in the form of **documents** (letters, memos, forms, and reports). Word processing was the first, and is still the most common automated office system.

You can do word processing on a personal computer with the help of a word processing software package or an integrated package with a word processing module. We briefly described such packages in Chapter 3. Word processing programs have become the most popular type of application software package available for use with personal computers. Word processing makes writing and printing documents dramatically easier. Also, it can increase the quality of your writing because editing, correcting, and revising text material becomes much easier to do.

Section II, "Doing Word Processing," in Appendix A at the end of this book provides you with an introductory tutorial on how to use a word processing package to create your own documents.

Figure 12–5 illustrates word processing activities that take place in a large office. These figures show how a personnel department responds to inquiries concerning employment opportunities with a personal letter composed of variable information and standard paragraphs.

DESKTOP PUBLISHING

One of the fastest-growing application areas in automated office systems is **desktop publishing.** Organizations large and small are using desktop publishing systems to produce their own printed materials. They can design and print their own newsletters, brochures, manuals, and books with several type styles, graphics, and colors on each page. What constitutes a desktop publishing system? Here's the minimum needed:

☐ A personal computer with a hard disk.
☐ A laser printer.
☐ Software: a word processing program, graphics package, and page makeup package.

If you want higher-quality printing, you should invest in a more powerful computer with advanced graphic capabilities, a more expensive graphics and page makeup package with more extensive features, and a laser printer with a greater variety of capabilities.

How does desktop publishing work? Here's the process:

1. Prepare your text and illustrations with a word processing program and a graphics package. Use an optical scanner to input text and graphics from other sources.

Figure 12–5 Steps in an office word processing application. Notice the use of standard paragraphs to produce a personalized letter for the personnel department.

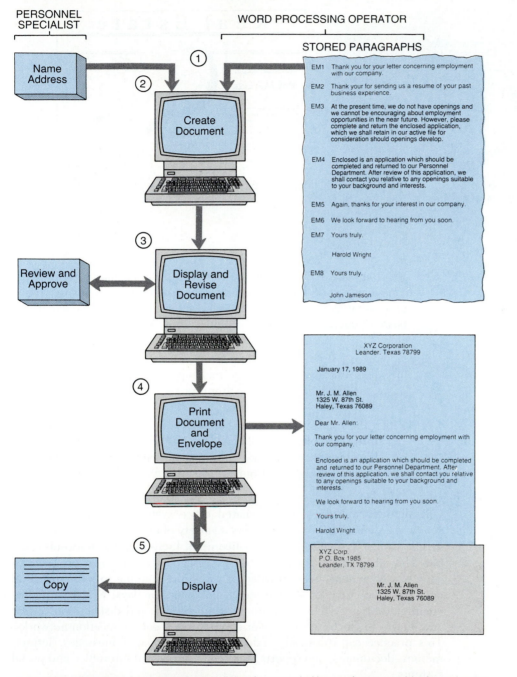

1. A member of the personnel department dictates a listing of names and addresses of persons applying for employment and also indicates the appropriate standard paragraphs which should be selected from those stored in the system.
2. A word processing *operator* creates a *document* (letter) from the variable information and the chosen standard paragraphs using an office workstation (a personal computer or a computer terminal).
3. If this were a more complex document, the operator could visually and electronically proof the letter, print out a *draft copy* for the personnel specialist to review and approve, and make all necessary revisions electronically.
4. A personalized letter and an envelope are printed for each applicant.
5. A copy of each letter is transmitted to a workstation terminal at the personnel department. It can electronically store the letter on a magnetic disk file, or print a paper copy if requested. Electronic mail systems could also electronically store and display a short message that tells the personnel specialist that these particular letters were sent.

Figure 12–6 Desktop publishing in action. The video display shows the use of page makeup software to produce a newsletter on a laser printer.

2. Use the page makeup program to develop the format of each page. This is where desktop publishing departs from standard word processing and graphics. Your video screen becomes an *electronic pasteup board* with rulers, column guides, and other page design aids.

3. Now merge the text and illustrations you developed into the page format you designed. The page makeup software will automatically move excess text to another column or page, and help you size and place illustrations and headings.

4. When the pages look the way you want them on the screen, you can store them electronically on your hard disk. Then print them on a laser printer to produce the finished printed material. That's desktop publishing! See Figure 12–6.

OFFICE COMMUNICATIONS SYSTEMS

One of the major areas of automated office systems is *electronic office communications*. This concept covers a variety of electronic communication services, such as **electronic mail, voice mail, facsimile,** and **teleconferencing.** They allow organizations to send a message in text or voice form, send a copy of a document, or send video pictures of a meeting to participants all over the globe, and do it in seconds, not hours or days! Electronic office communications systems support the transmission and distribution of text and images in electronic form over computerized communication networks. This practice can drastically reduce the flow of paper messages, letters, memos, documents, and reports that flood our present interoffice and postal systems.

Such services have been developed to meet two basic objectives: (1) more *cost-effective* communications and (2) more *time-effective* communications than traditional written and telephone communications methods. Electronic communications systems are designed to minimize *information float* and *telephone tag.* **Information float** is the time (at least several days) when a written letter or other document is in transit between the sender and receiver, and thus unavailable for any action or response to occur. **Telephone tag** is the process of (1) repeatedly calling people, (2) finding them unavailable, (3) leaving messages, and (4) finding out later that you were unavailable when they finally returned your call!

Electronic office communications systems can also eliminate the effects of mail that is lost in transit, or phone lines that are frequently busy. They can also reduce the cost of labor, materials, and postage of office communications (from more than $5 for a written message to less than 50 cents for an electronic message is one estimate). Also, the amount of time wasted in regular phone calls can be reduced (by one third is another estimate). Let's take a brief look at the communications methods that promise such results.

ELECTRONIC MAIL AND VOICE MAIL

We have used various forms of **electronic mail** for a long time. Western Union's telegram and mailgram services are examples. So are their TWX, Telex, and Teletype services, which have provided long-distance communications (using printing terminals) for news media services and large organizations for many years. Another long-standing form of electronic mail is **facsimile.** It is a remote copying process in which copies of photographs, documents, and reports can be transmitted and received in hard copy from anywhere in the world. Also, we have been able for many years to use computer terminals, word processors, and data communications channels to transmit and print reports and documents at remote sites.

So what is new about electronic mail? New, easy to use, and lower-cost systems have been developed. Computer manufacturers and software suppliers have taken advantage of advances in computer technology (such as low cost and more powerful personal computers and video terminals) and advances in digital communications technology (such as local networks and intelligent communications interface devices).

Today, you can send an electronic message to one or more individuals in an organization for storage in their *electronic mailboxes* on magnetic disk devices. Whenever they are ready, they can read their electronic mail by displaying it on the video screen of their terminals, personal computers, or *intelligent workstations.* So with only a few minutes of effort (and a few microseconds of transmission) a message to one or many individuals can be composed, sent, and received. Many large computer-using business firms and government agencies are using electronic mail. Communications companies such as GTE, TELENET, and MCI also offer such services. Personal computer networks like CompuServe and The Source offer electronic mail services. This includes an **electronic bulletin board** service where electronic messages can be posted for other subscribers to read. Figure 12–7 shows you video displays provided by the MCI electronic mail service.

Voice Mail

Another variation of electronic mail is **voice mail** (also called *voice store-and-forward*) where *digitized voice messages*, rather than electronic text, are used. In this method you first dial the number of the voice mail service and enter your identification code. Once you are accepted, you dial the voice

Figure 12-7 Using electronic mail. The main menu and electronic mail being created using the MCI Mail Service.

MCI MAIL MAIN MENU

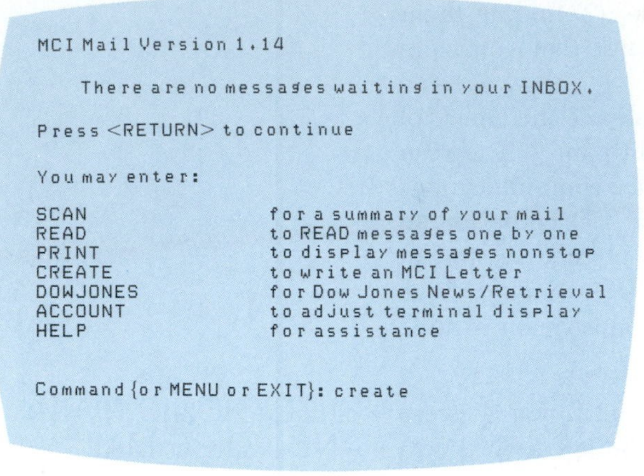

ELECTRONIC MAIL EXAMPLE

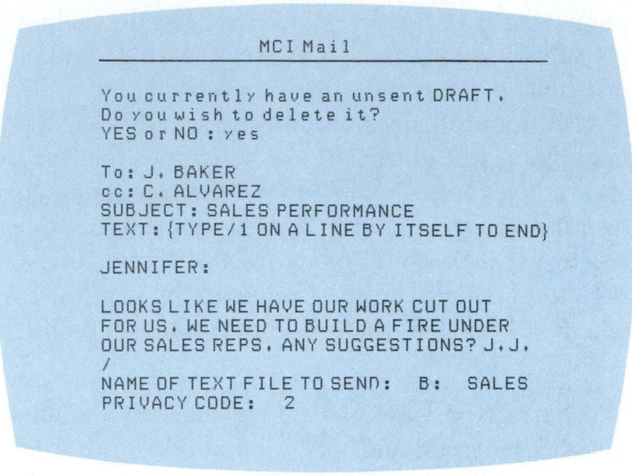

```
MCI Mail Version 1.14

    There are no messages waiting in your INBOX.

Press <RETURN> to continue

You may enter:

SCAN              for a summary of your mail
READ              to READ messages one by one
PRINT             to display messages nonstop
CREATE            to write an MCI Letter
DOWJONES          for Dow Jones News/Retrieval
ACCOUNT           to adjust terminal display
HELP              for assistance


Command {or MENU or EXIT}: create
```

```
                 MCI Mail

You currently have an unsent DRAFT.
Do you wish to delete it?
YES or NO : yes

To: J. BAKER
cc: C. ALVAREZ
SUBJECT: SALES PERFORMANCE
TEXT: {TYPE/1 ON A LINE BY ITSELF TO END}

JENNIFER:

LOOKS LIKE WE HAVE OUR WORK CUT OUT
FOR US. WE NEED TO BUILD A FIRE UNDER
OUR SALES REPS. ANY SUGGESTIONS? J.J.
/
NAME OF TEXT FILE TO SEND:   B:   SALES
PRIVACY CODE:   2
```

mail number of the people you wish to contact and speak your message. Your analog message is digitized and stored on the magnetic disk devices of the voice mail computer system. Whenever anyone wants to hear their voice mail, they simply dial their mailbox number and listen to the stored messages, which the computer converts back into analog voice form.

TELECONFERENCING AND TELECOMMUTING

Why do people have to spend travel time and money to attend meetings away from their normal work locations? They don't have to if they use **teleconferencing,** a growing type of electronic office communications. Teleconferencing is the use of video and audio communications to allow conferences and meetings to be held with participants who may be scattered across a country, a continent, or the globe. Teleconferencing is being promoted as a way to save employee time and thus increase productivity. Less travel to and from meetings should also reduce travel expenses and energy consumption. However, some corporations have found that teleconferencing is not as effective as face-to-face meetings, especially when important participants are not trained in how to communicate using these media.

There are several variations of teleconferencing. In some versions, participants key in their presentations and responses whenever convenient from online terminals connected to a central conference computer. Since all participants don't have to do this at the same time, this form of teleconferencing (called *computer conferencing*) is closer to the electronic mail methodology. In the other variation of teleconferencing (sometimes called *video conferencing*), sessions are held in realtime, with major participants being televised, while other participants may take part with voice input of questions and responses. Several major communications carriers and hotel chains now offer teleconferencing services for such events as sales meetings, new product announcements, and employee education and training. See Figure 12-8.

Figure 12-8 Teleconferencing in action. In this example, Martin Marietta Data Systems uses teleconferencing to hold a meeting at their corporate headquarters in Bethesda, Maryland, with their aerospace facility in Denver, Colorado.

Telecommuting

Why can't we take electronic mail and teleconferencing one step further and set up an automated office at home? We can, with **telecommuting.** This term describes the use of telecommunications to replace commuting to work from our homes. It is also used to describe the use of telecommunications to carry on work activities from temporary locations other than your office or home. Some people refer to this as the creation of *virtual offices.*

Telecommuting requires that workers have intelligent workstations at home. Other workers may use a computer terminal or microcomputer with data communications capability to access their company's computer network and databanks. These workers and their superiors and colleagues use electronic mail and voice mail to communicate with each other about job assignments.

Telecommuting is being tried by several major corporations and many independent professionals. It seems to be most popular for jobs that involve a lot of individual work such as programmers, systems analysts, writers, consultants, and so on. It is especially helpful for handicapped persons and working mothers of young children. However, studies have shown that telecommuting is not appropriate for many jobs and people. Productivity and job satisfaction seem to suffer unless workers spend several days each week at the office or other work site with their colleagues. So telecommuting should be considered as only a temporary or partial work alternative in automated office systems.

OFFICE SUPPORT SYSTEMS

One major category of automated office systems is **office support systems.** These include electronic calendar, tickler file, electronic mail directory, scheduling, and task management systems. They provide computer-based support services to managers and other office professionals to help organize their work activities. These services computerize manual methods of planning such as paper calendars, appointment books, directories, file folders, memos, and notes.

Typically, you use an intelligent workstation and support service software to display one of these services on your video monitor. For example, you could enter the date and time of a meeting into an electronic calendar. An *electronic tickler file* will automatically remind you of important events. Electronic schedulers use the electronic calendars of several people to help you schedule meetings and other activities with them. Electronic mail directories help you contact people easily. Finally, electronic task management packages help you plan a series of related activities so that scheduled results are accomplished on time. See Figure 12–9.

Desktop Organizers

Microcomputer users can get some of the benefits of office support systems by the use of **desktop organizer** software packages. Desktop organizers are low-cost integrated packages that help computer users organize routine office tasks. A typical desktop organizer might include programs that provide a calculator, calendar, appointment book, note pad, address book, phone list, alarm clock, and other features. Thus they provide an electronic replacement for many common office devices. They are typically "memory resident" programs that stay in the background until a computer user issues a command. Then they pop up in one or more display windows on your video screen. See Figure 12–10.

ADVANTAGES AND DISADVANTAGES

Automated office systems can significantly improve office communication processes. Automated office systems can:

- Increase the productivity of secretarial personnel and reduce the costs of creating, reviewing, revising, and distributing written office communications.
- Shorten the turnaround time between the preparation and receipt of a document by moving information quickly and efficiently to the people who need it.
- Reduce the frustration, expense, and errors involved in revising variable or standard text material.
- Store, retrieve, and transmit electronic documents and messages quickly and efficiently.
- Increase the productivity of executives, professionals, and other *knowledge workers* who are heavy users of office communications. For example, most of the managerial roles discussed in Chapter 9 involve extensive information transfer activities which can be effectively supported by automated office systems.

Of course, all of these advantages are not acquired without some negative effects. First, the cost of automated office hardware is significantly higher than the equipment it replaces. Another limitation is less obvious. Auto-

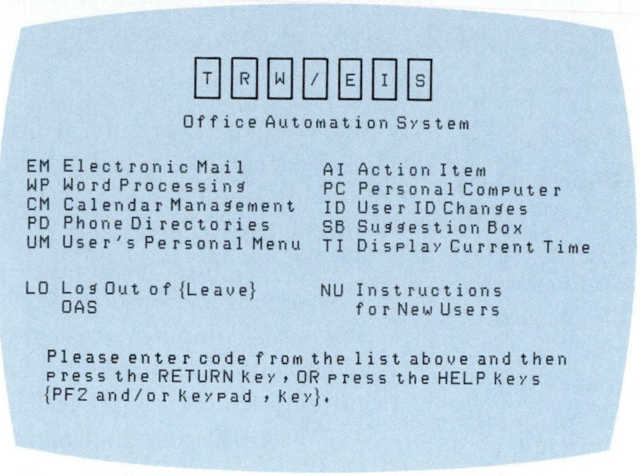

Figure 12-9 The main menu display of an office automation system for the TRW Corporation. Notice the office support services listed.

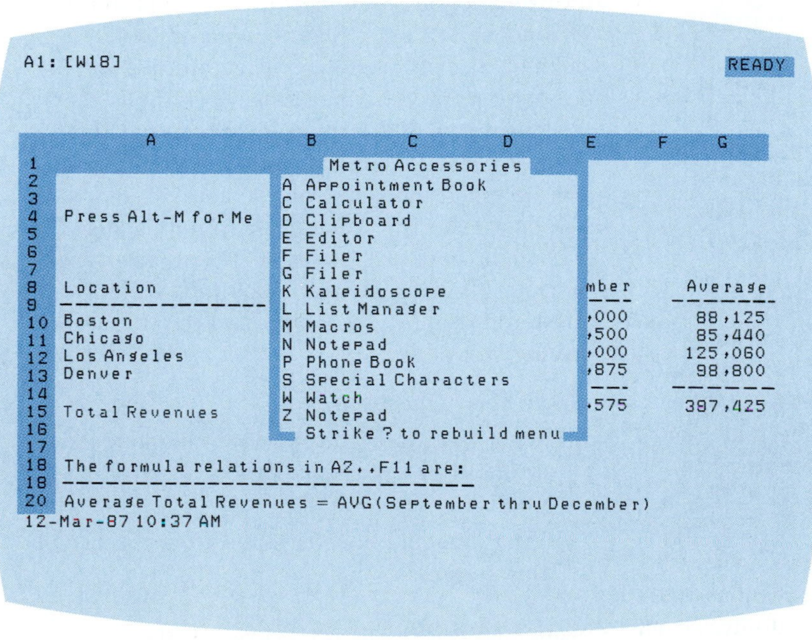

Figure 12-10 Using a desktop organizer. Notice how this Lotus 1-2-3 spreadsheet user has brought up a menu window of desktop accessories provided by the Metro desktop organizer package.

mated office systems can disrupt traditional office work roles and work environments. For example, some word processing systems have caused employee dissatisfaction by giving some secretaries nothing but typing to do, and isolating them from other employees. Such problems must be solved before employees will accept and cooperate with a technology that significantly changes their work roles, processes, and environment. Only then will the promises of increased productivity and job satisfaction be fulfilled.

REAL WORLD APPLICATION 12–2

Coca-Cola Foods

Manufacturers and industry analysts may be enthusiastic about the growth potential of the desktop publishing market, but early users involved with the technology are mostly delighted with the range of benefits they are already accruing.

At Coca-Cola Foods in Houston, Cheryl Currid, manager of sales systems, planning, and information, uses desktop publishing for manuals, sales-presentation materials, and other documents. While her department hasn't yet settled on a single desktop package, Ms. Currid said she is very happy with the results of their experimentation. "We have kind of eased our way into desktop publishing." she said, "and we aren't 100 percent where I would like to be, but we are excited about the potential. It is worth learning new products, because we always pick up something new and usually save 10 times the cost of the software at the same time," Ms. Currid added.

As an example, she mentioned a 40-page document that was recently formatted using scLaserplus, a desktop publishing software package from Software Channels Inc., of Kingwood, Texas. "Last year we spent $3,600 for typesetting on that document," she said, "and this year it only cost us the price of the software—which was about $200."

Ms. Currid is also using WordPerfect, from WordPerfect Corp., of Orem, Utah, which she said "is excellent for writing long manuals and supports the LaserJet output beautifully," even though it isn't a page makeup package like scLaserplus. Using the word processor for a lot of tasks is also consistent with her definition of desktop publishing as "the ability to turn out good-looking documents with local control," she added. Most of the documents at Coca-Cola Foods are produced on one of about 50 Personal Computers that are networked, driving about 40 LaserJet and LaserJet Plus printers from Hewlett-Packard.

"We made a commitment early on to lasers, and we haven't bought anything else," Ms. Currid remarked. "The lasers have more than paid for themselves when you look at what we save by not sending typesetting jobs out." Previously, jobs that were sent for typesetting cost about $125 per page, compared to a current cost of 3 cents per page on the LaserJet printers. Almost as important as the dollar savings is the reduced turnaround time, Ms. Currid said. She has found that her group can be much more responsive and get jobs out the door faster by using desktop publishing. Although there are jobs that still require typesetting, Ms. Currid said, many jobs are now mastered using the LaserJet and desktop publishing software.

Application Questions

☐ What hardware and software components are used in Coca-Cola Food's desktop publishing system?

☐ What benefits have resulted from the use of this system?

Source: Jon Pepper, "Early Users Voice Enthusiasm over Publishing Results," *PC Week*, January 6, 1987, p. 111.

□ Automated office systems combine word processing, data processing, telecommunications, and information systems technologies to develop computerized administrative and management workstations in the office and other workplaces. Automated office systems include advanced word processing systems, desktop publishing systems, electronic mail and message systems, teleconferencing and telecommuting systems, and advanced office support systems.

□ Automated office systems can be viewed as systems of input, processing, output, storage, and control components. Ideas are expressed in words and entered into a computer (input); edited and manipulated electronically (processing); stored and filed electronically, or on magnetic, optical, micrographic, or paper media (storage); under the direction of automated office programs (control); and communicated electronically or on paper to a recipient (output).

□ Word processing is the automation of the transformation of ideas into a readable form of communication. Word processing involves the manipulation of text data (characters, words, sentences, and paragraphs) by a computer system. It produces information products in the form of documents (letters, memos, forms, manuscripts, and reports).

□ Automated office systems increase the productivity of office personnel and reduce the costs of office communications. They shorten the turnaround time between the preparation and receipt of documents and messages, reduce the expense and errors involved in producing documents, and increase the productivity of executives and professionals who are heavy users of office communications. However, the cost of automated office hardware is higher than the equipment it replaces, and office automation may disrupt traditional office work roles and work environments.

SUMMARY

These are the key terms and concepts of this chapter. The page number of their first explanation is in parenthesis.

KEY TERMS AND CONCEPTS

1. Automated office system activities *(434)*
2. Automated office systems *(434)*
3. Desktop organizer *(448)*
4. Desktop publishing *(442)*
5. Document *(442)*
6. Electronic bulletin board *(445)*
7. Electronic mail *(445)*
8. Facsimile *(445)*
9. Information float *(445)*
10. Intelligent workstations *(439)*
11. Knowledge worker *(434)*
12. List processing *(438)*
13. Office support systems *(447)*
14. Reprographics *(438)*
15. Shared logic systems *(439)*
16. Shared resource systems *(439)*
17. Telecommuting *(447)*
18. Teleconferencing *(446)*
19. Telephone tag *(445)*
20. Text data *(442)*
21. Voice mail *(445)*
22. Word processing *(448)*
23. Word processing package *(448)*

REVIEW AND
APPLICATION QUIZ

Match one of the **key terms and concepts** listed above with one of the brief examples or definitions listed below. Try to find the "best fit" for answers that seem to fit more than one term or concept. Defend your choices.

_____   1. Automate most forms of office communications.

_____   2. Examples are input by optical scanning and output by voice mail.

_____   3. Text data is manipulated and documents are produced.

_____   4. Characters, words, sentences, and paragraphs.

_____   5. Letters, memos, forms, and reports.

_____   6. Merging names and addresses with form letters.

_____   7. They can be stand-alone units, shared-logic, shared resource, or time-sharing systems.

_____   8. Turns a microcomputer into a word processor.

_____   9. Producing multiple copies of documents.

_____   10. Terminals sharing the processing power of a minicomputer.

_____   11. Microcomputers sharing magnetic disk drives and printers.

_____   12. Users can produce their own brochures and manuals.

_____   13. Use your workstation to send and receive messages.

_____   14. Use your telephone as an electronic message terminal.

_____   15. The time a document is in transit between sender and receiver.

_____   16. You and the person you want to contact repeatedly miss each others phone calls.

_____   17. Transmitting images of documents electronically.

_____   18. Saves travel time and money spent on meetings.

_____   19. Using telecommunications so you can work at home.

_____   20. Integrates calculator, calendar, address book, notepad, and other functions.

_____   21. Electronic calendar, tickler file, and meeting scheduling services for automated offices.

_____   22. Managerial and professional personnel.

APPLICATION
PROBLEMS

1. If you have not already done so, read and answer the questions after the two Real World Applications in this chapter.

2. Have you used a personal computer (or mainframe computer terminal) and a word processing package to create and edit a document yet? The section on using word processing packages in Appendix A at the end of this book is available to help you if necessary. Analyze your word processing experience, using the automated office system model of Figure 12–3. Explain how each system function was accomplished, using the features provided by your word processing package.

3. Match one of the following automated office systems with the examples listed below.
   a. Desktop publishing.   d. Teleconferencing.
   b. Electronic mail.   e. Voice mail.
   c. Office support systems.   f. Word processing.

   _____ 1. Composing, editing, and printing a letter to a customer.
   _____ 2. Producing a company newsletter with text and graphics.
   _____ 3. Being prompted that you have scheduled a meeting.
   _____ 4. Visually displaying messages that have been sent to you.
   _____ 5. Listening to a computer-generated message from an associate.
   _____ 6. Participating in a company-sponsored TV workshop.

4. What word processing features and benefits do you like most? Use the automated office system model to help you suggest several ways that any two of the system functions (input, processing, output, storage, and control) could be improved to help users like yourself do a better job of word processing.

5. Which of the automated office systems (other than word processing) mentioned in this chapter would you find most useful? Explain why.

6. Compare the experiences of United Telephone with voice mail and Coca-Cola Foods with desktop publishing in Real World Applications 12–1 and 12–2. Do you agree or disagree with their conclusions? Explain.

7. The executives of ABC Department Stores are dissatisfied with their present telephone system. They want to purchase a new digital system with advanced features such as call forwarding, which automatically switches a call to another number where an executive might be reached. Your job is to try to convince them to install an electronic mail and message system. Explain your position. Use the concepts of **information float** and **telephone tag** in your presentation.

8. Play devil's advocate: List three things you can think of that could go wrong with various automated office systems. (Hint: for example, top executives could get stage fright and perform poorly in teleconferencing.) Now come up with a solution to each of the problems you generated. Be prepared to defend your solutions.

C H A P T E R

13

INFORMATION SYSTEMS IN MARKETING, PRODUCTION/OPERATIONS, AND PERSONNEL

Chapter Outline

Learning Objectives

The purpose of this chapter is to promote a basic understanding of how computers are used in business by analyzing computer applications in marketing, production/operations, and personnel. After reading and studying this chapter you should be able to:

1. Identify how computer-based information systems support the marketing, production/operations, and personnel functions.
2. Identify how computer-based information systems support manufacturing, retailing, and other industries.

Section I: Information Systems in Marketing

The business function of **marketing** is concerned with the planning, promotion, and sale of existing products in existing markets and the development of new products and new markets to better serve present and potential customers. Thus marketing performs a vital function in the operation of a business enterprise. Performing the marketing function in business has become a much more difficult assignment because of the dynamic environment of today, which includes:

☐ Rapidly changing market demands.

☐ Steadily increasing consumer pressures.

☐ Shortened product life spans.

☐ Proliferation of new products.

☐ Intensified competition.

☐ Growing government regulations.

Business firms have increasingly turned to the computer to help them perform the vital marketing function in the face of the rapid changes of today's environment. The computer has been the catalyst in the development of *marketing information systems*, which integrate the information flows required by many marketing activities. We shall now briefly analyze marketing information systems and several computer applications in marketing. This should provide you with a basic understanding of how computers help business firms perform their marketing activities.

MARKETING INFORMATION SYSTEMS

Marketing information systems provide information for the planning and control of the marketing function. *Marketing planning information* assists marketing management in product planning, pricing decisions, planning advertising and sales promotion strategy and expenditures, forecasting the market potential for new and present products, and determining channels of distribution. *Marketing control information* supports the efforts of management to control the efficiency and effectiveness of the selling and distribution of products and services.

The major types of marketing information systems are illustrated in Figure 13–1, and summarized below. Notice that these subsystems provide information needed by marketing management and other business information systems. This includes accounting and production/operations information systems. Figure 13–2 summarizes some of the major benefits of marketing information systems.

Sales Order Processing

A basic form of this system will be analyzed in the next chapter. It captures and processes customer orders and produces invoices for customers and data

Figure 13-1 Marketing information systems provide information for the planning and control of major components of the marketing function. Notice that they also provide information to accounting and production/operations information systems.

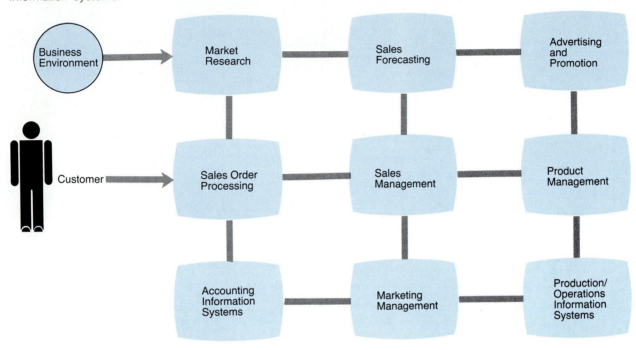

needed for sales analysis and inventory control. In many firms, it also keeps track of the status of customer orders until goods are delivered.

Sales Management

This system provides information to help sales managers plan and monitor the performance of the sales organization. The sales analysis application described in the next chapter is a basic form of this system.

Product Management

Management needs information to plan and control the performance of specific products, product lines, or brands. Computers can help provide price, revenue, cost, and growth information for existing products and new product development. Information and analysis for pricing decisions is a major function of this system. Information is also needed on the manufacturing and distribution resources that proposed products will require. Computer-based models may be used to evaluate the performance of current products and the prospects for success of proposed products.

Figure 13-2 Benefits of computer-based marketing information systems. Notice the specific examples of benefits generated by major types of marketing applications.

	Typical Applications	Benefits	Examples
CONTROL SYSTEMS	Control of marketing costs.	More timely computerized reports.	Undesirable cost trends are spotted more quickly so that corrective action may be taken sooner.
	Diagnosis of poor sales performance.	Flexible online retrieval of data.	Executives can ask supplementary questions of the computer to help pinpoint reasons for a sales decline and reach an action decision more quickly.
	Management of fashion goods.	Automatic spotting of problems and opportunities.	Fast-moving fashion items are reported daily for quick reorder, and slow-moving items are also reported for fast price reductions.
	Flexible promotion strategy.	Cheaper, more detailed, and more frequent reports.	Ongoing evaluation of a promotional campaign permits reallocation of funds to areas behind target.
PLANNING SYSTEMS	Forecasting.	Automatic translation of terms and classifications between departments.	Survey-based forecasts of demand complex industrial goods can be automatically translated into parts requirements and production schedules.
	Promotional planning and corporate long-range planning.	Systematic testing of alternative promotional plans and compatibility testing of various divisional plans.	Complex simulation models operated with the help of data bank information can be used for promotional planning by product managers and for strategic planning by top management.
	Credit management.	Programmed decision rules can operate on data bank information.	Credit decisions are automatically made as each order is processed.
	Purchasing.	Detailed sales reporting permits automation of management decisions.	Computer automatically repurchases standard items on the basis of correlation of sales data with programmed decision rules.
RESEARCH SYSTEMS	Advertising strategy.	Additional manipulation of data is possible when stored for computers in an unaggregated database.	Sales analysis is possible by new market segment breakdowns.
	Pricing strategy.	Improved storage and retrieval capability allows new types of data to be collected and used.	Systematic recording of information about past R&D contract-bidding situations allows improved biding strategies.
	Evaluation of advertising expenditures.	Well-designed data banks permit integration and comparison of different sets of data.	Advertising expenditures are compared to shipments by county to provide information about advertising effectiveness.
	Continuous experiments.	Comprehensive monitoring of input and performance variables yields information when changes are made.	Changes in promotional strategy by type of customer are matched against sales results on a continuous basis.

Advertising and Promotion

Management needs information to help it achieve sales objectives at the lowest possible costs for advertising and promotion. Computers use market research information and promotion models to help (1) select media and promotional methods, (2) allocate financial resources, and (3) control and evaluate results.

Sales Forecasting

The basic functions of sales forecasting can be grouped into the two categories of short-range forecasting and long-range forecasting. Short-range forecasting deals with forecasts of sales for periods up to one year, while long-range forecasting is concerned with sales forecasts for a year or more into the future. Computers use market research data, historical sales data, promotion plans, and statistical forecasting models to generate short-run and long-run sales forecasts.

Market Research

The market research information subsystem provides *marketing intelligence* to help management make more effective marketing decisions. It also provides marketing management with information to help plan and control the market research projects of the firm. Computers help the market research activity collect, analyze, and maintain an enormous amount of information on a wide variety of market variables that are subject to continual change. This includes information on customers, prospects, consumers, and competitors. Market, economic, and demographic trends are also analyzed. Data can be purchased in computer-readable form from external sources, or the computer can help gather data through *computer-assisted telephone interviewing* techniques. Finally, statistical analysis software packages help computers analyze market research data and spot important marketing trends.

Marketing Management

Computers assist marketing management in developing short- and long-range plans outlining product sales, profit, and growth objectives. They also provide feedback and analysis concerning performance-versus-plan for each area of marketing. Computer-based marketing models in decision support systems and expert systems are also being used to investigate the effects of alternative marketing plans.

Computers have traditionally been used by many retailers for such basic applications as customer billing, inventory control, and accounting. These retailing applications will be analyzed in the next chapter and will not be repeated here. However, computers are also being used for more advanced applications, such as management information systems and point-of-sale systems. For example, Figure 13–3 illustrates basic components of a retail

COMPUTER APPLICATIONS IN RETAILING

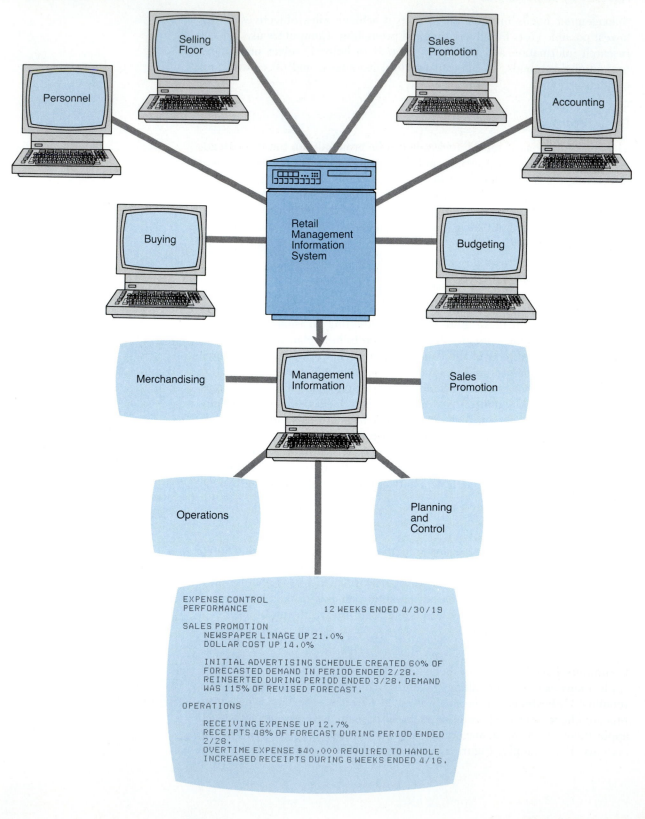

Figure 13–3 A retail management information system. Notice how various aspects of retail operations provide input that results in information to retail management. Also note the specific example of the type of information that can be provided.

management information system. It also depicts the kind of customized management report that can be provided on demand to the online terminals of retail executives.

Online *point-of-sale terminals* in retail outlets are a major computer application in retailing. Most **POS systems** consist of several cash register–like terminals that are online to a data controller located somewhere in the store. The data controller can be a minicomputer with peripherals, or it can merely be a unit for storing transactions from the POS registers on magnetic tape and transmitting data over communication lines to a regional computer center. Thus, POS terminals, in-store computers, and central computer facilities provide retailers with computer-based *retail information systems*.

In many POS systems, the "cash register" is an *intelligent terminal* that can guide the operator through each transaction, step by step. Many terminals are programmed to allow clerks to enter price and other data by merely pressing a single key for each type of product sold. POS terminals can also perform necessary arithmetic operations, such as tax, discount, and total calculations. Some terminals also permit online credit verification for credit transactions.

Most POS terminals can automatically read information from tags or merchandise labels. Hand-held **wands** or other optical reading devices are used with some terminals to scan the merchandise label and capture price and stock data. Data may be printed on the merchandise labels and tags in OCR characters or may use various optical bar coding methods. For example, the grocery industry uses the *Universal Product Code* (UPC) and bar coding on merchandise labels. Products can then be scanned by optical reading devices at automated checkout counters. (Refer back to pages 10 and 21 in the color pictorial section of Chapter 1) and to the optical scanning segment in Chapter 5 for photographs and explanations of these devices.

Obviously, POS terminals, in-store computers, data controllers, and other data communications hardware are expensive devices. Are they worth it?

One major benefit of such systems is their ability to produce advanced types of *sales and advertising impact analysis* by quickly providing a detailed analysis of sales by store and product, as well as such vital merchandising facts as shelf life, shelf position, displays, and the promotions and displays of competitors.

Another major benefit is the realtime inventory management provided by POS systems. This is vital to retail stores that have a high proportion of their assets in inventory. POS systems help keep inventory costs low by identifying and tracking inventory from suppliers to store to customer. They provide instant merchandise information to store personnel. They also let store managers control promotional and other changes to merchandise prices on a continual basis. Figure 13–4 summarizes the results experienced by large retail chains when they compared POS systems to traditional cash register systems.

Figure 13-4 A comparison of POS systems and traditional cash-register systems. Notice the benefits of POS systems.

☐ POS terminals cost about 20 percent more than the cash registers they replaced.

☐ It takes only one fourth the time to complete a sales transaction on a POS terminal, compared to a conventional cash register.

☐ The number of checkout registers can be significantly reduced with a POS system. Checkout personnel requirements can also be reduced.

☐ The POS terminal can perform functions either impossible or uneconomical on the conventional cash register (such as credit verification). Also, most of the input data required by retail information systems can be captured by POS terminals.

☐ Use of a minicomputer as a communications controller allows store managers to make online inquiries concerning merchandise availability and customer credit and to receive much faster reports on sales activity, merchandise replenishment, customer billing, clerk productivity, and store traffic.

☐ POS terminals demonstrate greater accuracy, increased customer service, and a significant reduction in personnel training time.

Advanced Retailing Systems

Major retail chains are attempting to gain a competitive advantage over their competitors with more advanced applications of computers. Let's take a look at a few of them.

☐ Personal computers are entering retail stores by the thousands. The PC with a cash drawer device and communications capability is replacing traditional cash registers and POS terminals. The PC with a cash drawer acts like a POS terminal during store hours. However, it can also provide specialized information on specific customers to store personnel to help increase sales or improve credit management. After store hours, the PC can be put to work to do more traditional information processing chores.

☐ Expert systems are being developed to help retailers in key areas. This includes trying to capture the expertise of buyers to improve merchandise planning and acquisition. What to buy, what sizes to buy, what is moving, what is not? These are questions such systems are trying to answer. The computer-assisted design of store layouts is another example. Most stores continually revise their store layouts to keep a "fresh look" that promotes sales. Computers and expert systems can easily help with this assignment.

☐ Computers are being used to promote a **just-in-time** inventory policy to drastically lower investment in merchandise inventories while still maintaining adequate stock levels. Computer systems of both retailers and their suppliers are being linked by electronic ordering, invoicing, and receiving applications. Electronic mail systems among stores, administrative offices, and suppliers are also being used to promote this policy as well as providing improved office communications.

Dominick's Finer Foods, Inc.

Dominick's Finer Foods, Inc. can best be described as a "late bloomer" when it comes to using personal computers. Less than two years ago, the Northlake, Illinois, grocery chain had virtually no PCs. Today, the company uses more than 350 IBM Personal Computer ATs in strategic applications designed to aid Dominick's in its fight to become the dominant grocery chain in the Chicago area.

Already the privately held retailer has seen its share of the more than $6 billion market surge from 13 percent in 1984 to 22 percent in 1986, making it the second-largest chain in the six-county area comprising Chicago and its suburbs. Although Dominick's doesn't report revenue or earnings, 1986 sales are estimated at $1.5 billion. And observers say Dominick's is on course to maintain a 30 percent growth rate in 1987, when the company will add up to 7 new stores to its existing chain of 88.

Much of Dominick's dramatic growth can be tied to the innovative use of PCs within each of its grocery stores. IBM Personal Computer AT–based systems automatically issue store coupons at the check-out counters, record employees' time and attendance data, and manage the growing number of specialty departments, including movie video rentals. One example of their innovative use of PCs for marketing centers on the store coupons issued by many grocery chains.

In an effort to upstage the competition, Dominick's Finer Foods, Inc., of Chicago, uses IBM Personal Computer ATs to issue store coupons. Each of Dominick's 88 stores has an AT linked by loop cables to the stores' IBM point-of-sale (POS) terminals. As a customer's groceries are scanned at the check-out counter, the AT enters the POS data loop and, in essence, makes note of every item that is purchased. The AT can then issue a coupon based on what a customer purchases. If, for example, the AT is programmed to issue a coupon for Coke to everyone who buys Pepsi,

the system automatically issues a Coke coupon to each Pepsi buyer. The system, called The Coupon Solution, is marketed by Catalina Marketing Corp., of Los Angeles.

As the only grocery chain in the Chicago area with The Coupon Solution, Dominick's uses the system as a powerful marketing tool. Managers can target customers for marketing campaigns based on purchasing habits. If managers want to improve sales in their seafood department, for example, they can program the AT to issue all customers a 10 percent–off certificate for fish.

The system was designed to work on an IBM Personal Computer XT, but Mr. Broadwell convinced Catalina Marketing to modify its system to run on an AT. And keeping in line with its PC strategy, which calls for implementing PC applications as quickly as possible, Dominick's installed, tested, and had coupon systems running in every store in less than six months.

Dominick's dramatic infusion of ATs into its business operations is not without problems. With more ATs being used at each store, the need for data communications between stores and corporate headquarters has greatly increased. As it stands now, communications is via phone lines and 2,400-bps modems. But increased data communications traffic seems a small stumbling block in Dominick's PC strategy. And it's apparent that the PC will continue to be one of Dominick's trump cards as it plays for the top spot in the Chicago grocery market.

Application Questions

☐ How does Dominick's use Personal Computers to support marketing activities? Other store functions?

☐ What are the benefits of computer use for Dominick's? Could other types of retail stores also benefit in similar ways?

Source: Craig Zarley, "Grocery Chain Adopts Major PC Policy," *PC Week*, January 6, 1987, pp. 55–68.

Section II: Information Systems in Production/Operations

The **production/operations** function includes all activities concerned with the planning, monitoring, and control of the processes that produce goods or services. Thus, the production/operations function is concerned with the management of the operational systems of all business firms. Computers are used for such **operations management** functions not only by manufacturing companies but also by all other firms that must plan, monitor, and control inventories, purchases, and the flow of goods and services. Therefore, firms such as transportation companies, wholesalers, retailers, financial institutions, and service companies must use production/operations information systems to plan and control their operations. In this section, we will concentrate on manufacturing and physical distribution to illustrate the application of computers to the production/operations function.

MANUFACTURING INFORMATION SYSTEMS

Computer-based **manufacturing information systems** use several major techniques in order to support **computer integrated manufacturing** (CIM). CIM is an overall concept that stresses that computer use in *factory automation* must be an integrated system of technologies. That's because computers are automating many of the activities needed to produce products of all kinds. For example, computers are used to help engineers design products, which is called **computer-aided design** (CAD). Then they are used to help plan the types of material needed in the production process, which is called **material requirements planning** (MRP). Finally, **computer-aided manufacturing** (CAM) may be used to help manufacture products. This may be accomplished by monitoring and controlling the production process in a factory *(shop floor control)*, directly controlling a physical process *(process control)*, a machine tool *(machine control)*, or a machine with some human-like capabilities *(robots)*.

Some of the benefits of computer-based manufacturing information systems are:

☐ Increased efficiency due to better production schedule planning and better balancing of production workload to production capacity.

☐ Improved utilization of production facilities, higher productivity, and better quality control resulting from continuous monitoring, feedback, and control of plant operations.

☐ Reduced investment in production inventories through better planning and control of production and finished goods requirements.

☐ Improved customer service by reducing out-of-stock situations and producing products that better meet customer requirements.

Figure 13–5 illustrates major types of manufacturing information systems. Let's take a brief look at each of them.

Figure 13–5 Manufacturing information systems are heavily dependent on the use of computers in each of the major systems shown. Computers are used for planning and control of products, resources, facilities, and the production process itself.

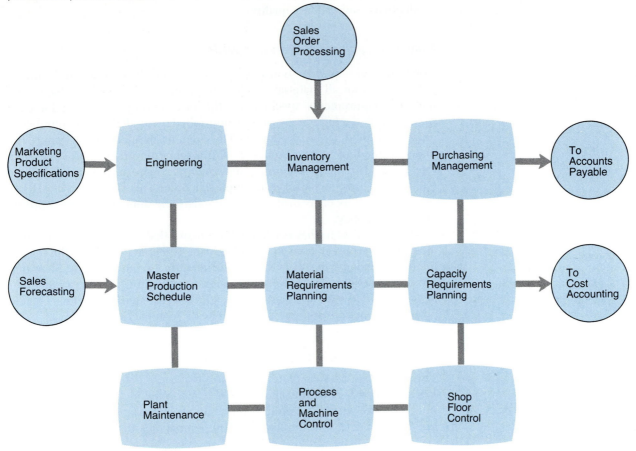

Master Production Schedule (MPS)

Computers assist in the development of a master production schedule for a manufacturing firm. The schedule is based on many factors, including sales forecasts (from the marketing information system) and forecasts of other production resources, such as manufacturing facilities and materials. The computer provides information required for the detailed scheduling of production. This consists of assigning production starting dates, making short-range capacity adjustments, allocating materials from production inventories, and "releasing" production orders to the plant floor.

The use of computers in production scheduling has become even more important due to recent developments in manufacturing. Master production schedules are being greatly affected by the development of **just-in-time** (JIT) production policies. Instead of mass production of large quantities, JIT schedules small quantities of production, with raw materials arriving "just in time" for each stage of production. This minimizes inventory costs. Subdividing the production process into small segments also seems to improve productivity and product quality.

Material Requirements Planning (MRP)

Computers are used to translate the master production schedule into a detailed plan for all material required to produce scheduled products. The material requirements specified by the engineering subsystem for each product (called a *bill of materials*) is multiplied *(exploded)* by the number of units scheduled to be produced. The amount of material on hand, the material needing to be purchased, and a schedule of purchases are then calculated. This helps minimize investment in material inventories while still adhering to the master production schedule. This last aspect of MRP is being adjusted by many firms to accommodate the demands of a just-in-time production policy.

The MRP concept has become so successful that it has been extended to include all resources used in manufacturing (such as people, facilities, and finances). Called MRP II and renamed **manufacturing resource planning,** this new concept is an attempt to link all manufacturing subsystems together in an integrated system. It also involves links to the marketing, finance, and personnel functions to forge a companywide manufacturing system.

Capacity Requirements Planning (CRP)

This subsystem uses computers to ensure that there is sufficient manufacturing capacity to meet the master production schedule. Capacity is determined by the amount of production facilities such as equipment, supplies, buildings, and, of course, manufacturing employees that are available.

Engineering

This subsystem uses **computer-aided engineering** (CAE) and **computer-aided-design** (CAD) methods to analyze and design products and manufacturing facilities. Products are designed according to product specifications determined in cooperation with the product management subsystem of the marketing information system. One of the final outputs of this design process is the bill of materials for a product that is used by the MRP subsystem. The engineering subsystem is also frequently responsible for determining standards for product quality (i.e., *quality control*).

Computer-aided design packages and supermicrocomputers have teamed up to give engineers their own *engineering workstations*. Engineers use these high-powered computing and advanced graphics workstations for product design and testing. Input is by light pen, joystick, or keyboard, with the CAD package refining an engineer's initial drawings. Output is in two- or three-dimension graphics that can be rotated to display all sides of the object being designed. The engineer can zoom in for close-up views of a specific part, and even make parts of the product appear to move as they would in normal operation. The design can then be converted into a finished mathematical model of the product. This is used as the basis for production specifications and numerical control programs. See pages 20 and 21 of the pictorial section of Chapter 1 for photographs of CAD in action.

Shop Floor Control

Computers are used to monitor and control events on the shop floor during the production process. Thus this subsystem is a major focus of **computer-aided manufacturing** (CAM) activity. Computers track the status of all work in progress through a variety of data collection terminals used by production employees, and specialized devices (sensors, counters, OCR scanners, etc.). Information gathered and processed includes production counts, material usage, labor used, and machine downtime. Personal computers are playing an increasing role as intelligent factory terminals in local area networks, dedicated to shop floor control. See page 8 in the pictorial section in Chapter 1 for a photograph of a typical scene showing computer use on the shop floor.

Plant Maintenance

This subsystem provides management with information for maintenance planning, work order dispatching, maintenance costing, and preventive maintenance scheduling.

Other Subsystems

The remaining subsystems are discussed in more detail in the next few pages. Purchasing management and inventory management are obviously concerned with the purchase, receipt, and storage of materials and the shipping of finished products. Process and machine control involve the use of computers to accomplish the actual production process.

COMPUTER–AIDED MANUFACTURING

As we mentioned earlier, computer-aided manufacturing is the use of computers to directly assist the manufacturing process. This includes the use of computers for shop floor control, process control, machine control, and robotics. Let's now take a look at the last three of these technologies.

Process Control

Process control is the use of computers to control an ongoing physical process. Process control computers are used to control physical processes in petroleum refineries, cement plants, steel mills, chemical plants, food product manufacturing plants, pulp and paper mills, electric power plants, and so on. Many process control computers are special-purpose or dedicated general-purpose minicomputer systems. A process control computer system requires the use of special sensing devices that measure physical phenomena such as temperature or pressure changes. These continuous physical measurements are converted to digital form by analog-to-digital converters and relayed to computers for processing. Process control computer programs use

Figure 13–6 A process control computer system. Computers are used to directly control an ongoing physical process in many industries. Examples are the production of petroleum, steel, chemicals, food products, paper, and electric power.

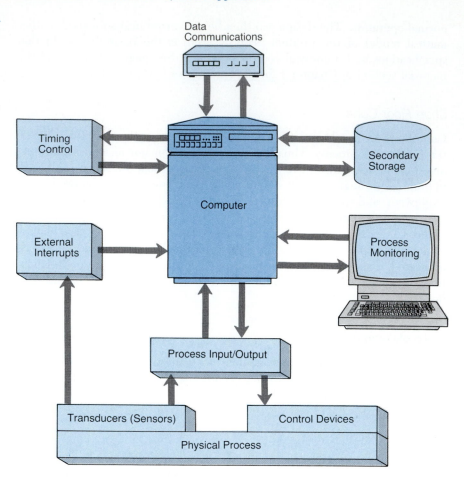

mathematical models to analyze the data generated by the ongoing process and compare it to standards or forecasts of required results. Output of a process control system can take three forms:

☐ Periodic and on-demand reports analyzing the performance of the production process. Personal computers have become a popular method of analyzing and reporting process control data.

☐ Messages and displays about the status of the process. A human operator can then take appropriate measures to control the process.

☐ Direct control of the process by the use of control devices that control the process by adjusting thermostats, valves, switches, and so on. See Figure 13–6.

Machine Control

Machine control is the use of a computer to control the actions of a machine. This is also popularly called **numerical control.** The control of machine tools in factories is a typical numerical control application, though it also refers to the control of typesetting machines, weaving machines, and other industrial machinery.

Figure 13–7 From computer-aided design to direct machine control. Computers can be involved from the design stage to the actual production process of a product.

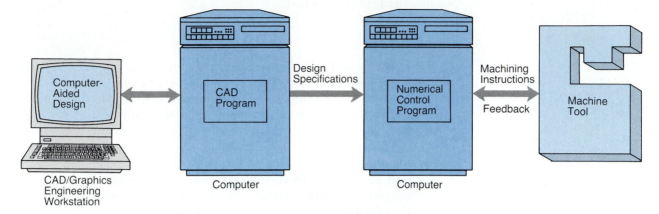

Numerical control computer programs for machine tools convert geometric data from engineering drawings and machining instructions from process planning into a numerical code of commands, which controls the actions of a machine tool. Machine control can be accomplished offline by using special paper tape or magnetic tape units, which use the output of a computer to direct a machine. *Direct numerical control* (DNC) involves the online control of machines by a computer.

Machine control may involve the use of special-purpose microcomputers called *programmable logic controllers* (PLCs). These devices operate one or more machines according to the directions of a numerical control program. Specially equipped personal computers that can withstand a factory environment are being used to develop and install numerical control programs in PLCs. They are also used to analyze production data furnished by the PLCs. This helps engineers fine-tune machine performance. See Figure 13–7.

An important development in machine control and computer-aided manufacturing is the creation of a new breed of *smart machines* and *robots*. These devices directly control their own activities with the aid of built-in microcomputers. **Robotics** is the technology of building and using machines with *computer intelligence* and computer-controlled *humanlike physical capabilities* (dexterity, movement, vision, and so on). That's what robots are. Robotics has become a major thrust of research and development efforts in the field of *artificial intelligence* (AI).

Robots are used to increase productivity and cut costs, particularly in hazardous areas or activities. Robots follow programs loaded into their onboard special-purpose microcomputers. Input is received from visual and/or tactile sensors, processed by the microcomputer, and then translated into movements of the robot. This typically involves moving its "arms" and "hands" to pick up and load items or perform some other work assignment such as painting, drilling, or welding. Robotics developments are expected

Robotics

to make robots more "intelligent" and improve their visual and tactile capabilities. See page 9 in the pictorial section of Chapter 1 for a photograph of industrial robots in action.

PHYSICAL DISTRIBUTION INFORMATION SYSTEMS

A major activity of the production/operations function is known as **physical distribution.** Physical distribution is concerned with moving raw materials to the factory and moving products from the production floor to the ultimate consumer. Physical distribution involves a "distribution network" that connects raw material sources, manufacturing plants, warehouses, wholesale and retail outlets, and customers. It also involves the storage, transfer, and transportation of goods from manufacturer to customer.

Physical distribution information systems are frequently computerized. The major physical distribution information systems are illustrated in Figure 13–8. They include:

Physical Distribution Planning

This information subsystem provides information for the planning of the physical distribution system of a business firm. Mathematical models may be used to analyze alternative distribution networks by considering such factors as customer characteristics, manufacturing locations and capabilities, the number and location of warehouses, processing and inventory management policies, and alternative transportation arrangements.

Inventory Control

This important system processes inventory data and provides information to assist management in minimizing inventory costs and improving customer service. For example, after receiving notice of customer orders, it prepares shipping documents and records changes of items in inventory. Then it may notify management of items needing reordering and provide them with inventory status reports. A basic form of this system will be analyzed in the next chapter.

Distribution Center Management

This system supports the management and operations of "distribution centers," which consist of warehouses, shipping and receiving terminals, and other distribution support facilities. Its objective is to process data and provide information to assist management in the effective use of warehousing, shipping, and receiving personnel, facilities, and equipment, while maintaining a high level of customer service. See page 9 of the pictorial section in Chapter 1.

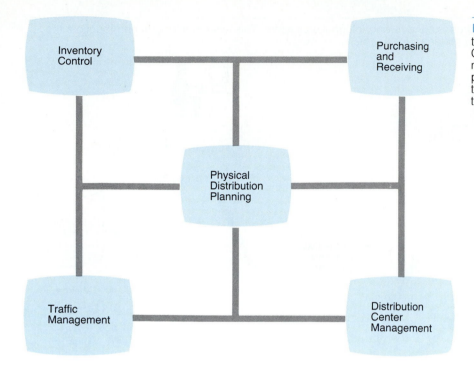

Figure 13–8 Physical distribution information systems. Computers help move raw material to the factory and products from the factory floor to distribution centers and to the ultimate consumer.

Traffic Management

This system supports the daily planning and control of the movement of products within the distribution network of a firm. It must provide information required for the scheduling of transportation requirements, the tracking of freight movement, the audit of freight bills, and the determination of efficient and economical methods of transportation.

Purchasing and Receiving

This system provides information to ensure availability of the correct quantity and quality of the required materials at the lowest possible price. The purchasing system assists in the selection of suppliers, placement of orders, and the follow-up activities to ensure on-time delivery of materials. The receiving system identifies and validates the receipt of materials and routes the received material to its proper destination in storage or on the production floor. Figure 13–9 illustrates a purchasing/receiving information system.

Figure 13–9 An example of a purchasing/receiving information system. This system supports and monitors the purchase, receipt, and storage of materials for a firm.

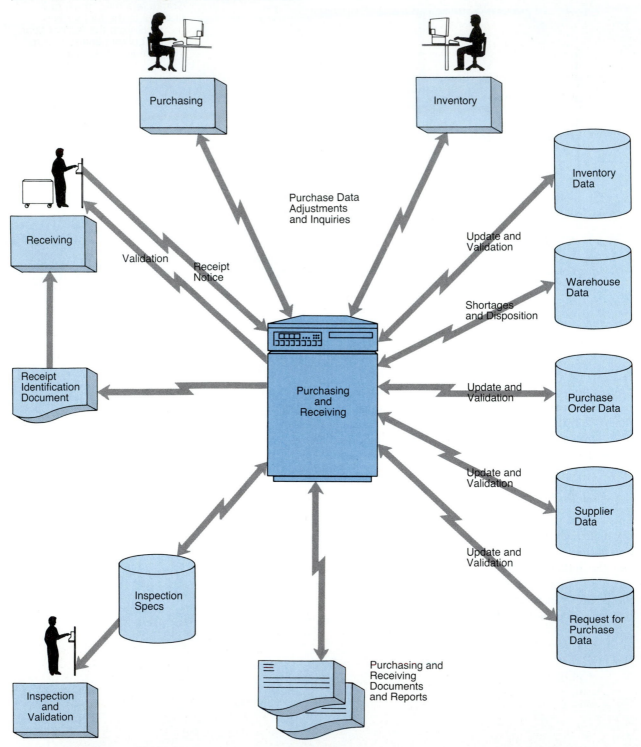

REAL WORLD APPLICATION 13–2

Ex-Cell-O Corporation

In Detroit, home of the U.S. automobile industry, the word around town is CIM. It's the word around Schenectady, New York; Greenville, South Carolina; and Wausau, Wisconsin, too. Users and vendors alike are pointing to computer-integrated manufacturing (CIM) as the answer to America's smokestack industries' woes. But CIM is a highly challenging issue that entails the automation and integration of an entire manufacturing enterprise. Its complexity has generated plenty of confusion from which only a handful of manufacturers have emerged as successful CIM implementers. One of them is the Cone Drive division of Ex-Cell-O Corporation.

Cone Drive's CIM system is based on an IBM Mapics system, a manufacturing resource planning system running on an IBM System/38, and an IBM Cadam system for engineering design work running on an IBM 4341, according to Paul Brauninger, director of MIS. Both systems, he says, have helped streamline operations. Mapics has helped reduce inventory by 25 percent and reduce quoted lead times by 50 percent, according to Brauninger. It has also enabled Cone Drive to cut the number of employees in the materials control department in half. Meanwhile, the Cadam system has reduced drawing time by 60 percent, getting part drawings to the shop floor at a quicker rate, Brauninger says.

Yet he is quick to add that the two systems would have been useless had it not been for the management and planning portions of CIM that were concurrently implemented. Back in 1980, Cone Drive was faced with "increasing pressure from our customers to do a better job of supplying the product to them on a timely basis with shorter lead times," Brauninger explains. The need to respond was critical. Customers could turn to Cone Drive competitors that were new to the scene from Japan, West Germany, and Asia, Brauninger adds. The original intent was not to automate but simply to find a better way to do business, he emphasizes. The computer systems were of secondary importance.

Cone Drive mapped out a strategy to automate the manufacturing and engineering end of the business, the first phase of which focused on establishing more control of products and processes—for instance, reducing inventory and shortening lead time. The second step, begun last year and expected to be the focus of this year's efforts, is a more advanced level of automation—flexible manufacturing cells. Since it is a small company, integration has been a manageable issue. IBM Personal Computers are set up on the shop floor as well as in office areas throughout Cone Drive to support the computing needs of each small manufacturing group or cell.

PCs are linked to the host computers depending on the job function of their operators. This direct host-computer-to-workstation cabling allows an operator on the shop floor to view a Cadam drawing file or to request shipping information from the Mapics program.

The first flexible manufacturing cell, which incorporates just-in-time principles, will be completed this year. The company is also scheduled to review bar code technology and Brauninger says he hopes to incorporate a bar coding system this year to keep track of products on the factory floor. To Brauninger, the flexible cells and bar coding add to the ammunition Cone Drive has been stocking up for six years against its competitors. "If you can't do a good job of supplying a product at a low cost, your life expectancy is very short," he comments.

Application Questions

☐ In what ways is the Cone Drive Division implementing computer-integrated manufacturing?

☐ What benefits have resulted from such activities?

Source: Rosemary Hamilton, "Smokestack Revival," *Computerworld,* January 5, 1987, pp. 61–62.

Section III: Personnel and Other Information Systems

In this section we will briefly explore information systems in personnel and several other computer-applications that should contribute to a well-rounded understanding of the use of computers in business.

HUMAN RESOURCE INFORMATION SYSTEMS

The *personnel* function involves the recruitment, placement, evaluation, compensation, and development of the employees of an organization. **Personnel information systems** are traditionally used by business firms to (1) produce paychecks and payroll reports, (2) maintain personnel records, and (3) analyze the amounts, types, and costs of labor used in business operations. Many firms have gone beyond these traditional functions and have developed **human resource information systems** (HRIS), which also support (1) recruitment, selection, and hiring, (2) job placement, (3) performance appraisals, (4) employee benefits analysis, (5) training and development, and (6) health, safety, and security.

Such information systems support the concept of *human resource management*, which emphasizes (1) *planning* to meet the personnel needs of the business, (2) development of employees to their full potential, and (3) *control* of all personnel policies and programs. The goal of human resource management is the effective and efficient use of the *human resources* of a company. The major computer applications in personnel are summarized below and illustrated in Figure 13–10.

Payroll and Labor Analysis

Computers process data concerning employee compensation and work activity and produce paychecks, payroll reports, and labor analysis reports. This application is discussed in the next chapter.

Personnel Record-Keeping

This application is concerned with additions, deletions, and other changes to the records in the personnel database. Changes in job assignments and compensation, or hirings and terminations, are examples of information that would be used to update the personnel database.

Employee Skills Inventory

The computer is used to locate specific human resources within a company and to maximize their use. The employee skills inventory system uses the employee skills data from the personnel database to locate employees within a company who have the skills required for specific assignments and projects. See Figure 13–11.

Training and Development Analysis

Computers help personnel management plan and control employee recruitment, training, and development programs by analyzing the success history

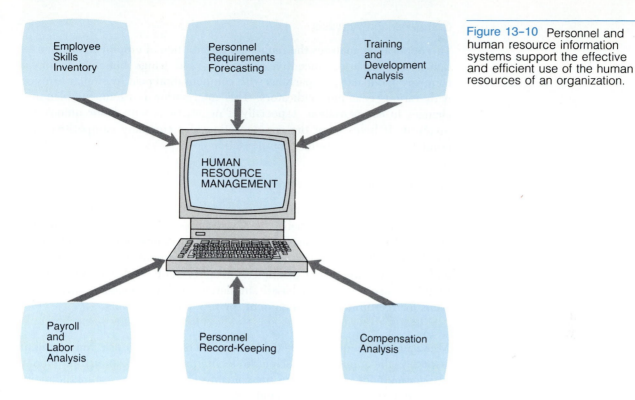

Figure 13–10 Personnel and human resource information systems support the effective and efficient use of the human resources of an organization.

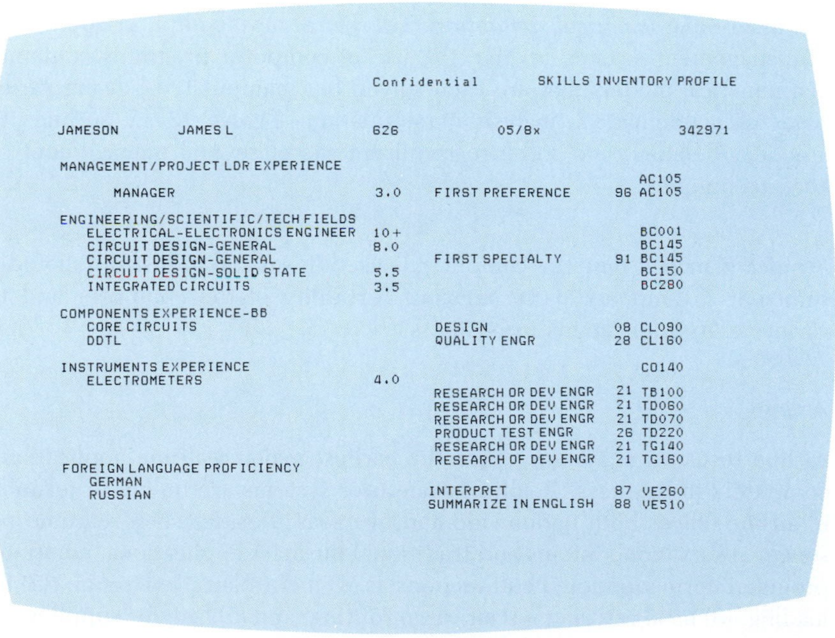

Figure 13–11 An example of a skills inventory profile report. This information helps match employee skills with specific job needs.

of present programs. They also analyze the career development status of each employee to determine whether development methods such as training programs or performance appraisals should be recommended.

Compensation Analysis

This application analyzes the range and distribution of employee compensation (wages, salaries, incentive payments, and fringe benefits) within a company and makes comparisons with compensation paid by similar firms or with various economic indicators. This information is useful for planning changes in compensation, especially if negotiations with labor unions are involved. It helps keep the compensation of a company competitive and equitable, while controlling compensation costs.

Personnel Requirements Forecasting

Short- and long-range planning is required to assure a business firm of an adequate supply of high-quality human resources. This application provides information required for forecasts of personnel requirements in each major employment category for various company departments or for new projects and other ventures being planned by management. Such long-range planning may use a computer-based simulation model to evaluate alternative plans for recruitment, reassignment, or retraining programs.

MANAGEMENT SCIENCE APPLICATIONS

Management science represents a major area of computer use. Management science is the application of scientific technique to organizational problems, using a methodology based on the concepts and techniques of mathematics and other sciences. Management science techniques usually involve the formulation of *mathematical models* of the system being investigated. Mathematical models can be used for problem solving, using either *mathematical analysis* or *mathematical simulation*. Therefore, most computer applications in management science involve the use of computer programs containing mathematical models that are then solved or "manipulated," using various types of mathematical analysis or simulation. Figure 13–12 outlines the function, benefits, and software requirements of several management science techniques.

OTHER BUSINESS APPLICATIONS

A quick glance at how the computer is used in several industries should be sufficient to emphasize the amazing versatility of the computer and the variety of its applications in business.

Airlines

Airline reservation systems were the earliest major realtime application of computers in business. Realtime computer systems are online to terminals in airline offices both nationwide and overseas. Besides such realtime passenger reservation systems and traditional business applications, computers provide information for such functions as (1) flight plan preparation, (2) fuel loading, (3) meal catering, (4) air cargo routing, and (5) freight, supplies, and spare parts inventory control.

Figure 13-12 Examples of selected management science applications. Notice how dependent these applications are on computer software resources.

Management Science Technique	Application	Benefits	Software Tools Available
Mathematical Analysis	Uses complex mathematics for solving engineering/research problems.	Computational processing is peformed at electronic speeds. Special languages and subroutines facilitate expression and solution of problems.	Math library-precoded routines (e.g., numerical analysis, interpolation, exponential and log functions, and matrix analysis).
Statistical Analysis	Analysis of quantitative and statistical data for such applications as market research, sales forecasting, inventory control, research, and quality control.	Improves accuracy and validity of decision making by providing more sophisticated analysis.	Statistics library (e.g., variance, T-ratio, standard deviation, binomial distribution, random number generator, regression analysis, and so on).
Linear Programming	Mathematical technique for solving problems of competing demands for limited resources where there are a great number of interacting variables.	Resolves complex problems that can only be approximated or guesstimated by conventional means. Increases accuracy and improves decision making in broad classes of decisions.	Linear programming (LP) packages assist in problem structuring and formulation and then provide high-speed computing power to efficiently produce solutions based on alternate decision rules.
Network Analysis	Scheduling, costing, and status reporting of major projects.	Improves planning, scheduling, and implementing of complex projects comprised of multiple events and activities. Permits continuous evaluation of projects' progress to increase probabilities of on-time, on-cost performance.	PERT (program evaluation and review technique) and CPM (critical path method) software systems for processing large networks of events and activities producing a variety of computer reports to pinpoint schedule slippages, critical events, and action needed to get back on schedule.
Queueing Theory	Solving problems where it is desirable to minimize the costs and/or time associated with waiting lines or queues.	Improves management ability to improve operations like checkout counters, receiving docks, machine centers, or turn-toll stations.	General-purpose simulators aid the construction and development of complex simulation models. The simulator has the ability to produce random numbers to test various activity patterns and optimize the use of resources.
Simulation	Determines the impact of decisions using hypothetical or historical data in lieu of incurring the expense and risk of trying out decisions in actual operations.	Business managers can test and project the effects of decisions on a wide variety of operational areas, thus ensuring optimal results when the decisions and policies are put into practice.	General-purpose simulators, decision support system generators, modeling packages, and electronic spreadsheet packages.

Agribusiness

Agriculture has become a big business—"agribusiness." Many corporate and family farms and ranches are now using the power of the computer. Major applications include (1) farm and crop record-keeping and analysis, (2) financial and tax accounting, and (3) optimal feed-blending, fertilizing, and crop-rotation programs. Computer services are provided by government agricultural extension agencies, commercial banks, computer service bureaus, and farm cooperatives. Microcomputer-based devices to automatically control farm machinery for planting, fertilizing, irrigating, and harvesting are a more recent development.

Construction

Large construction companies have been using computers for many years for traditional business applications such as payroll and general accounting. Scientific applications requiring mathematical computations for design engineering analysis have also been used. Techniques like PERT (Program Evaluation and Review Technique) and CPM (Critical Path Method) are used for construction planning and scheduling. The computer can use such techniques to produce plans and schedules for each stage of complex construction projects.

Insurance

Like the banking industry, the insurance industry was an early user of computers. Insurance companies have a huge data processing job because of the large number of insurance policies, claims, premium notices, and dividends that must continually be processed. Large numbers of customers and complex insurance policy provisions require the maintenance of large databases. Complex actuarial computations (such as life expectancy statistics) must also be performed. Realtime inquiry systems allow branch offices to interrogate the central database for customer policy information. Another application is the use of the computer to perform part of the *underwriting* function by preparing detailed insurance coverage proposals for presentation to prospective customers.

Real Estate

Real estate applications fall into several major categories. Real estate investment applications analyze financial, tax, marketing, and physical requirements data to compute rate-of-return alternatives for proposed real estate projects. Property management applications assist the management of rental property by processing rental statements, rental payments, and maintenance and utility disbursement, and by providing various management reports. Property listing applications (also called a multiple listing service) maintain up-to-date listings of all properties registered for sale with participating real estate agents.

REAL WORLD APPLICATION 13–3

Canadian Broadcasting Company

The Canadian Broadcasting Company is Canada's national broadcasting service. It recently began implementing a more integrated Human Resources Management System to provide vital information about CBC's employees. The CBC spends more than $750 million annually on payroll. It employs 11,600 permanent employees, more than 5,000 casual or temporary employees, and up to 50,000 contract people, and generates more than 12,000 payroll checks per week. "Without an integrated system, it's hard to get reliable information to top management," Michael Nekechuk, database administrator, says. "That's one of the major needs that the Human Resources Information System is bound to satisfy."

Existing human resource systems within CBC were fragmented. The broadcasting organization sought a more integrated approach to give management needed information about the workforce. The result is the Human Resources Information System, a massive project made up of eight subsystems, the most critical of which are the Employee Demographics and the Leave & Attendance subsytems.

The Employee Demographics subsystem is the foundation for the Human Resources Information System. Seven other subsystems sample this database to satisfy any information needs that they have. The Leave & Attendance subsystem, for example, relies on the Employee Demographics database to validate such information as to what union employees belong to and whether or not they are eligible for overtime. The system also generates appropriate transactions to feed the Payroll subsystem.

Dealing with 23 different bargaining agents to negotiate 29 separate agreements is a complex matter for any organization. The Leave & Attendance subsystem helps keep track of the various bargaining agreements on behalf of its many classifications of employees.

"We were after a fully integrated database and productivity tool that would consolidate information and give us increased productivity in our systems development process," Nekechuk says. Nor did CBC give much credence to buying a human resources software package. "We recognized the fact that in the best case a package would have satisfied only 50 percent of the actual application requirements." The decision was made to develop a Human Resource Information System from the ground up using a 4GL programmer productivity tool to satisfy their requirements.

In early discussions, the company concluded that, at a minimum, the new framework would have to be integrated with a relational DBMS driven by a data dictionary. The overall objective of the task force was to identify a system that would improve the productivity of systems development—both at the design phase and in future maintenance. "After considerable analysis we selected the IDEAL fourth-generation language and the DATACOM/DB database management system as the tools to address our particular concerns," Nekechuk says.

By moving to a database solution, CBC expects to manage its human resources better, reduce the application backlog, enhance the integrity of the corporate database, promote security, and improve the quality and timeliness of information for top management. When fully completed, the Human Resources Information System will give the CBC a consolidated and integrated information system with which it will gain better understanding and control over its growing work force and the finances that support it.

Application Questions

☐ How does CBC use computers for human resource management?

☐ What benefits do they expect from the completed system?

Source: "ADR/IDEAL a Big Hit at Canadian Broadcasting Co.," *ADRware News* 3, no. 2, 1986, pp. 10–15.

SUMMARY

☐ Marketing information systems provide information for the planning and control of the marketing function. Marketing planning information assists marketing management in product planning, pricing decisions, planning advertising, and sales promotion strategy and expenditures, forecasting the market potential for new and present products, and determining channels of distribution. Marketing control information supports the efforts of management to control the efficiency and effectiveness of the selling and distribution of products and services. The major types of marketing information systems are sales order processing, sales management, product management, advertising and promotion, sales forecasting, market research, and market management.

☐ Computer-based manufacturing information systems use several major subsystems to achieve computer-aided manufacturing (CAM). Computers are automating many of the activities needed to produce products of all kinds. For example, computers are used to help engineers design products, which is called computer-aided design (CAD). Then they are used to help plan the types of material needed in the production process, which is called material requirements planning (MRP). Finally, they may be used to directly manufacture the products on the factory floor, by directly controlling a physical process (process control), a machine tool (numerical control), or a machine with some humanlike capabilities (robots)! The major subsystems in a manufacturing information system are (1) master production schedule, (2) material requirements planning, (3) capacity requirements planning, (4) engineering, (5) shop floor control, (6) plant maintenance, and (7) other subsystems.

☐ This chapter analyzed computer applications in personnel, such as human resource information systems, and applications in the retailing industry, such as POS systems and retail expert systems. Management science application and applications in a variety of industries were also discussed.

KEY TERMS AND CONCEPTS

These are the key terms and concepts of this chapter. The page number of their first explanation is in parentheses.

1. Computer-aided design *(466)*
2. Computer-aided engineering *(466)*
3. Computer-aided manufacturing *(467)*
4. Computer integrated manufacturing *(464)*
5. Human resource information systems *(474)*
6. Just-in-time systems *(465)*
7. Management science applications *(476)*
8. Manufacturing information systems *(464)*
9. Manufacturing resource planning *(466)*

10. Marketing information systems *(456)*

11. Material requirements planning *(466)*

12. Numerical control *(468)*

13. Personnel information systems *(474)*

14. Physical distribution applications *(470)*

15. Point-of-sale systems *(461)*

16. Process control *(467)*

17. Retailing applications *(459)*

18. Robotics *(469)*

Match one of the **key terms and concepts** listed above with one of the brief examples or definitions listed below. Try to find the "best fit" for answers that seem to fit more than one term or concept. Defend your choices.

REVIEW AND APPLICATION QUIZ

_____ 1. Includes subsystems for sales management, product management, and promotion management.

_____ 2. Point-of-sales systems are an example.

_____ 3. Turn the cash register into a data entry terminal.

_____ 4. Includes subsystems for material requirements planning, engineering, and shop floor control.

_____ 5. Helps the design process using advanced graphics, terminals, and software.

_____ 6. Helps engineers analyze the design of products.

_____ 7. Terminals on the shop floor track the progress of work.

_____ 8. A conceptual framework for factory automation.

_____ 9. Using computers to control a petroleum refinery.

_____ 10. Using computers to control machine tools.

_____ 11. Computerized devices that can take over some production activities from human workers.

_____ 12. Includes subsystems for purchasing and receiving, warehouse management, and traffic management.

_____ 13. Schedule small quantities of production and order only the raw materials needed for each stage.

_____ 14. An integration of the planning and control of resources used in manufacturing.

_____ 15. Translates the production schedule into a detailed plan for all materials required.

_____ 16. Have traditionally used computers for payroll, personnel record-keeping, and labor analysis.

_____ 17. Use computers to support employee recruitment, placement, evaluation, compensation, and development.

APPLICATION PROBLEMS

1. If you have not already done so, read and answer the questions after the three Real World Applications in this chapter.

2. Match one of the following marketing information systems with one of the examples listed below.
   a. Advertising and promotion.
   b. Market research.
   c. Product management.
   d. Sales forecasting.
   e. Sales management.
   f. Sales order processing.

   _____ 1. Processes sales and produces invoices.
   _____ 2. Helps in new product development and pricing decisions.
   _____ 3. Produces short- and long-range sales projections.
   _____ 4. Provides information on sales performance.
   _____ 5. Helps select promotional methods and media.
   _____ 6. Provides marketing intelligence to management.

3. Match one of the following manufacturing information systems with one of the examples listed below.
   a. Capacity requirements planning.
   b. Engineering.
   c. Master production schedule.
   d. Material requirements planning.
   e. Plant maintenance.
   f. Shop floor control.

   _____ 1. Analyzes and designs products and facilities.
   _____ 2. Assigns production starting dates.
   _____ 3. Determines the availability of equipment and facilities.
   _____ 4. Prepares preventive maintenance schedules.
   _____ 5. Explodes a bill of materials.
   _____ 6. Tracks the status of all work in production.

4. Match one of the following applications in personnel and human resource management with one of the examples listed below.
   a. Compensation analysis.
   b. Employee skills inventory.
   c. Payroll and labor analysis.
   d. Personnel record-keeping.
   e. Personnel requirements forecasting.
   f. Training and development analysis.

   _____ 1. Produces employee paychecks and earnings statements.
   _____ 2. Provides short- and long-range projections of personnel requirements.
   _____ 3. Analyzes employee wages, salaries, incentive payments, and fringe benefits.
   _____ 4. Helps plan employee recruitment and career development.
   _____ 5. Tracks employee capabilities for job assignments.
   _____ 6. Maintains the personnel database of the organization.

5. The marketing manager of ABC Department Stores has been told by several store managers that the company's advertising and promotion budget is too low and is not being spent to promote the right products at the right times. How should the marketing information systems shown in Figure 13–1 be used to determine if there is a problem, and the solution to that problem?

6. What has been your experience with POS terminals? Give your reaction to each of the benefits of POS terminals shown in Figure 13–4. Can you add any to that list? Can you think of any other disadvantages than higher hardware cost? Explain any of these additional benefits or disadvantages.

7. Do any of the computer-based information systems in production/operations apply to nonmanufacturing companies like ABC Department Stores? Use the information systems illustrated in Figures 13–5 and 13–8 to support your answer.

8. Explain how you might use computer-based human resource information systems to determine:
    a. The cost to the company of a proposal for an increase in fringe benefits.
    b. The amount of labor costs for a particular product line.
    c. The degree of compliance with equal opportunity and work safety laws.

C H A P T E R

14

INFORMATION SYSTEMS IN ACCOUNTING AND FINANCE

Chapter Outline

Learning Objectives

The purpose of this chapter is to promote a basic understanding of how the computer is used in business by analyzing computer-based information systems in accounting and finance and seven common computer applications in business. After reading and studying this chapter, you should be able to:

1. Identify several computer applications in accounting and finance.
2. Summarize the objectives, input, database, and output of several common business information systems.

ACCOUNTING INFORMATION SYSTEMS

Accounting information systems are the oldest and most widely used business information systems. They record and report business transactions and other economic events. Accounting information systems are based on the double-entry bookkeeping concept, which is hundreds of years old, and other more recent accounting concepts such as responsibility accounting and profitability accounting. Computer-based accounting systems record and report the flow of funds through the organization on a historical basis and produce financial statements such as the balance sheet and income statement. Such systems also produce forecasts of future conditions such as projected financial statements and financial budgets. A firm's financial performance is then measured against such forecasts by other analytical accounting reports. Figure 14–1 provides an overview of the relationships of various accounting information systems.

Operational accounting systems emphasize legal and historical record-keeping and the production of accurate financial statements. *Management accounting systems* focus on the planning and control of business operations. They emphasize cost accounting reports, the development of financial budgets and projected financial statements, and analytical reports comparing actual to forecasted performance. In the next section we will analyze several operational accounting applications such as accounts receivable, accounts payable, and general ledger. Other major computer applications in accounting include the following:

Fixed Asset Accounting

Fixed asset accounting involves the physical control and the financial record-keeping caused by the use and depreciation of fixed assets. Land, production and distribution facilities, office buildings, equipment of all kinds, and furniture and furnishings must be accounted for.

Cost Accounting

Cost accounting involves the accumulation and apportionment of costs within a business firm. For example, operating costs must be grouped into specific cost categories and attributed to specific products, projects, departments, and so on.

Tax Accounting

Tax accounting involves the recording and payment of business taxes such as income taxes, sales taxes, and inventory taxes to local, state, federal, and foreign governments.

Figure 14-1 Accounting information systems are integrated systems of accounting applications. Notice how these applications all contribute to produce the important financial data, statements, and reports of a firm.

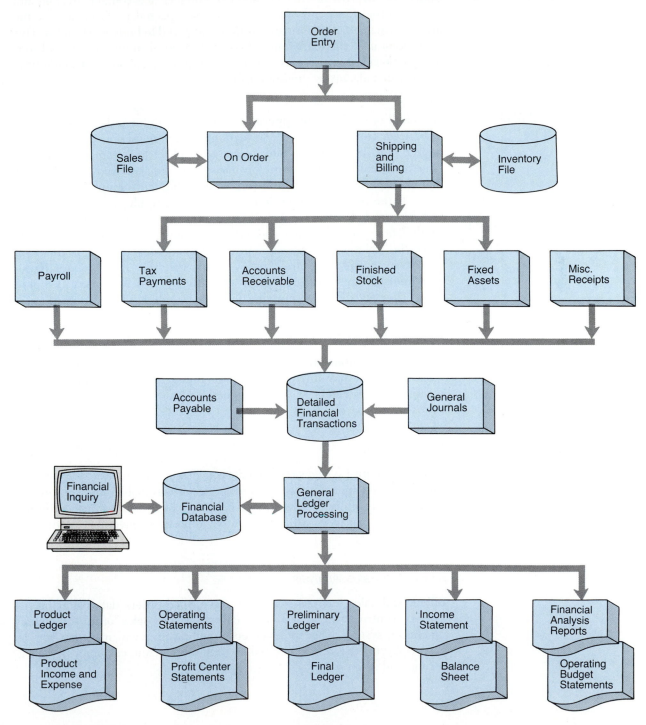

Budgeting

Budgeting involves the development of budgets that contain revenue and expense projections and other estimates of expected performance for the firm. A firm's actual performance is then compared to budget estimates. This application makes extensive use of computerized planning models and software packages. Input is received from the planning models of marketing, finance, manufacturing, and other functions.

COMMON BUSINESS INFORMATION SYSTEMS

Out of all of the possible applications of the computer in business, several basic accounting and related information systems stand out. They are common to most business computer users. Most of these systems exist in both large and small computer-using business firms. You can find them in firms that are experienced computer users or are using the computer for the first time. Three of these applications (accounts receivable, accounts payable, and general ledger) are *accounting* information systems. The others are combinations of accounting and related business information systems in *marketing* (sales order/transaction processing and sales analysis), *production/ operations* (inventory control), and *personnel* (payroll). These **common business information systems** are summarized below and illustrated in Figure 14–2. They are discussed in more detail in Section II of this chapter.

Sales Order/Transaction Processing

Sales order/transaction processing systems process sales orders received from customers and other types of sales transactions. They produce sales receipts for customers and data needed for sales analysis and inventory control.

Inventory Control

Inventory control systems receive data concerning customer orders, prepare shipping documents if the ordered items are available, and record all changes in inventory. They notify management of items needing reordering and provide managers with comparative reports on inventory status, activity, and costs.

Billing and Sales Analysis

Billing and sales analysis systems receive filled-orders data from the inventory control system and sales data from the sales order/transaction processing system. They produce customer invoices and management reports analyzing the sales generated by each salesperson, customer, product, region, and so on.

Accounts Receivable

Accounts receivable systems keep records of amounts owed by customers from data generated by customer invoices and payments. They produce monthly customer statements and credit management reports.

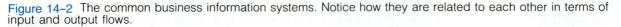

Figure 14-2 The common business information systems. Notice how they are related to each other in terms of input and output flows.

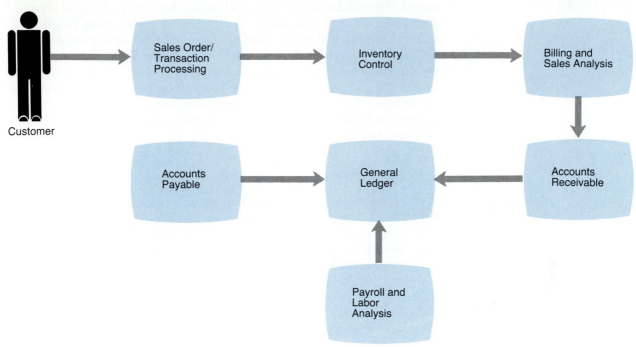

Accounts Payable

Accounts payable systems keep track of data concerning purchases from and payments made to suppliers. They prepare checks in payment of outstanding invoices and produce cash management reports.

Payroll and Labor Analysis

Payroll and labor analysis systems receive and maintain data from employee time cards and other work records. They produce paychecks and other documents such as earning statements, payroll reports, and labor analysis reports. Other reports are also prepared for management and government agencies.

General Ledger

General ledger systems process data received from accounts receivable, accounts payable, payroll and labor analysis, and many other business information subsystems. They produce the general ledger trial balance, the income statement and balance sheet of the firm, and various income and expense reports for management.

FINANCIAL INFORMATION SYSTEMS

Computer-based **financial information systems** support management in decisions concerning (1) the financing of a business and (2) the allocation and control of financial resources within a business firm. Major financial information systems include cash management, portfolio management, credit management, capital budgeting, financial forecasting, financing requirements analysis, and financial performance analysis. *Accounting information systems* are also frequently included as a major group of financial information systems. Figure 14–3 illustrates that the financial performance analysis system ties together the other financial information systems to produce financial planning and control information. The characteristics and functions of these computer-based systems are summarized below.

Cash Management

The computer collects information on all cash receipts and disbursements throughout a company on a realtime or periodic basis. Such information allows business firms to deposit or invest excess funds more quickly, and thus increase the income generated by deposited or invested funds. The computer also produces daily, weekly, or monthly forecasts of cash receipts or disbursements (cash flow forecasts), which are used to spot future cash deficits or cash surpluses. Mathematical models may be used to determine optimum cash collection programs and to determine alternative financing or investment strategies for dealing with forecasted cash deficits or surpluses.

Portfolio Management

Many business firms invest their excess cash in short-term marketable securities (such as U.S. Treasury bills, commercial paper, or certificates of deposit) so investment income may be earned until the funds are required. The "portfolio" of such securities must be managed by buying, selling, or holding each type of security so an optimum "mix" of securities is developed that minimizes risk and maximizes investment income.

Credit Management

Computerized credit management information systems plan and control the extension of credit to the customers of a firm. Information is used to control credit policies to minimize bad-debt losses and investment in accounts receivable, while maximizing sales and profitability. Systems of this type use the computer to automate the screening of credit applications and the decision to accept or reject a credit application.

Capital Budgeting

The computer is used to evaluate the profitability and financial impact of proposed capital expenditures. Long-term expenditure proposals for plant and equipment can be analyzed using a variety of techniques such as present value analysis and probability analysis.

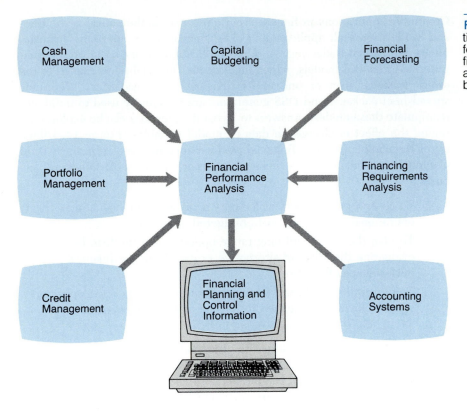

Figure 14-3 Financial information systems provide information for decisions concerning the financing of a business and allocation of funds within a business firm.

Financial Forecasting

This application provides information and analytical techniques that result in such economic or financial forecasts as national and local economic conditions, wage levels, price levels, and interest rates. It is heavily dependent on data gathered from the external environment and on the use of various mathematical models and forecasting techniques.

Financing Requirements Analysis

The computer supports the analysis of alternative methods of financing the business. Information concerning the economic situation, business operations, the types of financing available, interest rates, and stock and bond prices are used to develop an optimum financing plan for the business.

Financial Performance Analysis

This application uses data provided by other financial information systems. It uses *financial performance models* to evaluate present financial performance and formulates plans based on their effect on projected financial performance.

FINANCIAL PERFORMANCE MODELS

Computer applications in finance frequently use mathematical techniques and models for such applications as cash management, portfolio management, and capital budgeting. Another application involves the use of computerized financial models, which analyze the financial performance of the entire business firm or one of its divisions or subsidiaries. Electronic spreadsheet packages and DSS generators are frequently used to build and manipulate these models. Answers to "what if" questions can be explored by seeing the effect of changes in data or model variables. Figure 14–4 illustrates the components of a **financial performance model** of a business firm. Computerized financial performance models are used for the following purposes:

☐ To control present performance by analyzing and evaluating current operations, in comparison to budgeted objectives.

☐ To plan the short- and long-range operations of the firm by evaluating the effect of alternative proposals on the financial performance of the firm.

☐ To determine the future financing requirements and the optimum types of financing required to finance alternative proposals.

APPLICATIONS IN BANKING

Computers have had a major impact on the **banking industry.** The computer has not only affected the accounting and reporting operations required by traditional bank services but has influenced the form and extent of all such services and made possible a variety of new computer services. The com-

---

Figure 14–4 An example of a financial performance model. Notice how the model allows managers to evaluate the effects of possible changes in many factors on the financial performance of a firm.

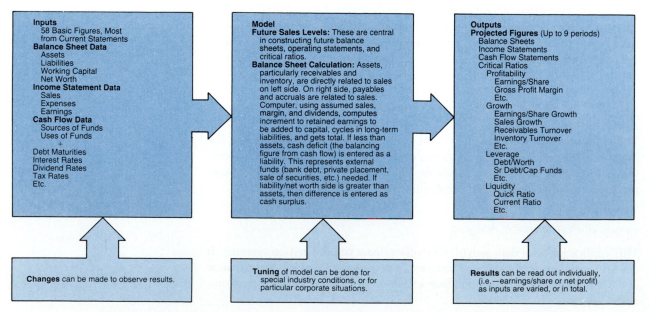

Inputs
58 Basic Figures, Most from Current Statements
Balance Sheet Data
  Assets
  Liabilities
  Working Capital
  Net Worth
Income Statement Data
  Sales
  Expenses
  Earnings
Cash Flow Data
  Sources of Funds
  Uses of Funds
    +
Debt Maturities
Interest Rates
Dividend Rates
Tax Rates
Etc.

Changes can be made to observe results.

Model
Future Sales Levels: These are central in constructing future balance sheets, operating statements, and critical ratios.
Balance Sheet Calculation: Assets, particularly receivables and inventory, are directly related to sales on left side. On right side, payables and accruals are related to sales. Computer, using assumed sales, margin, and dividends, computes increment to retained earnings to be added to capital, cycles in long-term liabilities, and gets total. If less than assets, cash deficit (the balancing figure from cash flow) is entered as a liability. This represents external funds (bank debt, private placement, sale of securities, etc.) needed. If liability/net worth side is greater than assets, then difference is entered as cash surplus.

Tuning of model can be done for special industry conditions, or for particular corporate situations.

Outputs
Projected Figures (Up to 9 periods)
  Balance Sheets
  Income Statements
  Cash Flow Statements
  Critical Ratios
    Profitability
      Earnings/Share
      Gross Profit Margin
      Etc.
    Growth
      Earnings/Share Growth
      Sales Growth
      Receivables Turnover
      Inventory Turnover
      Etc.
    Leverage
      Debt/Worth
      Sr Debt/Cap Funds
      Etc.
    Liquidity
      Quick Ratio
      Current Ratio
      Etc.

Results can be read out individually, (i.e.—earnings/share or net profit) as inputs are varied, or in total.

puter is playing an even more decisive role in the operation of many banks through its use in financial models and other management science applications. Some traditional and new bank services that are computerized follow.

Demand Deposit Accounting

Demand deposit accounting involves the automation of checking account processing. This was the first and most widely used computer application in banking. It depends heavily on the magnetic ink recognition character technology explained in Chapter 5. MICR-coded checks and deposit slips and MICR reader-sorters are used to automate the capture of input data. Output of this system includes special reports concerning checking account activity and monthly customer statements.

Realtime Banking

Most banks use *transaction terminals* at teller windows and automated teller machines (ATMs or "cash machines") that are electronically linked to the computers in the bank. Such machines are really special-purpose *intelligent terminals*, which automatically update a customer's checking and savings account balances on the computer and perform various banking services for bank customers. Mutual savings banks and savings and loan associations are other major users of computers for realtime banking applications.

Consumer, Commercial, and Mortgage Loans

Banks have computerized many aspects of the data processing required by their lending activities to consumers and business firms. The widespread development of bank credit card plans has greatly increased the use of computers to process the multitude of transactions generated by millions of bank credit card holders. Output of this application includes monthly customer statements, interest and tax reports, and various loan analysis reports.

Trust Applications

The trust function of banks involves the management of corporate trusts, personal trusts, pension funds, and health and welfare funds. The computer is used to handle a variety of accounting chores and to produce management reports and legal documents. Advanced trust applications involve the use of computerized security analysis and portfolio selection.

Computer Services

Many banks are offering computer services to other banks and financial institutions, business and professional firms, government and public organizations, and individuals. Some banks have "spun off" their information services departments into subsidiaries that compete with computer service bureaus.

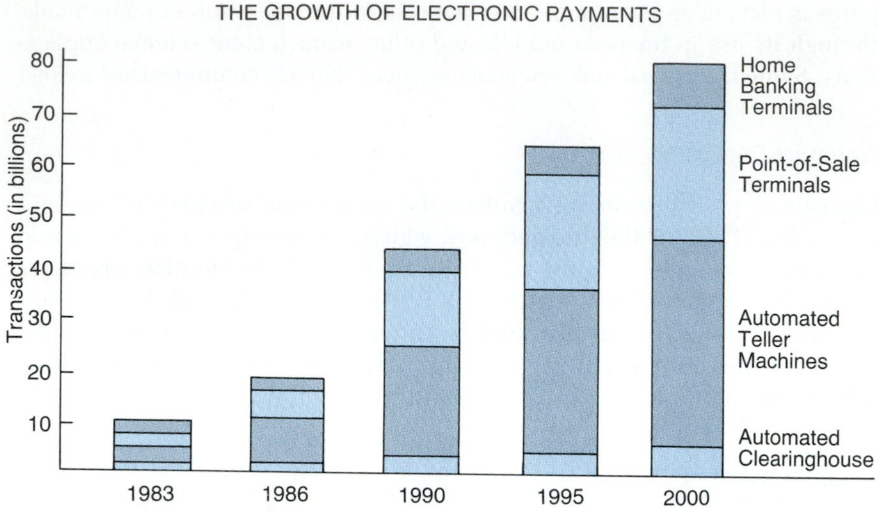

Figure 14–5 Forecasted growth
in electronic funds transfer systems use. Notice the growth
expected in these four major
applications of EFT technology.

Figure 14–5 Forecasted growth in electronic funds transfer systems use. Notice the growth expected in these four major applications of EFT technology.

THE GROWTH OF ELECTRONIC PAYMENTS

Electronic Funds Transfer Systems

The computer is the primary component of **electronic funds transfer (EFT)** systems that will one day replace cash and checks as the primary method of payment. The banking industry is in the forefront of efforts to develop and install EFT systems. Automated teller machines (ATMs), automated clearinghouse (ACH) arrangements, POS terminals, computerized pay-by-phone systems, and other home banking devices are evidences of this development. See Figure 14–5.

APPLICATIONS IN INVESTMENTS

Computers have been used by firms in the *investment industry* for many years to perform "back office operations," that is, recording transactions, billing customers, and preparing monthly statements. More recent applications of the computer in the investment industry are summarized below.

The Stock Market

Under the prodding of the SEC (Securities and Exchange Commission), the stock exchanges and other organizations in the investment industry are developing a computerized "central market" that will automate and centralize securities trading. Realtime computer-based information networks are currently used to facilitate the exchange of information between securities brokers, dealers, and large institutional investors. For example, the National Association of Securities Dealers (NASD) operates a nationwide realtime computer-based information network for over-the-counter (OTC) stocks, called NASDAQ.

Financial Information Retrieval

Investment advisory service companies now provide the investment industry with computerized data banks, computer developed reports, and specialized time-sharing services. Figure 14–6 summarizes the information provided by the widely used Dow Jones Information Service.

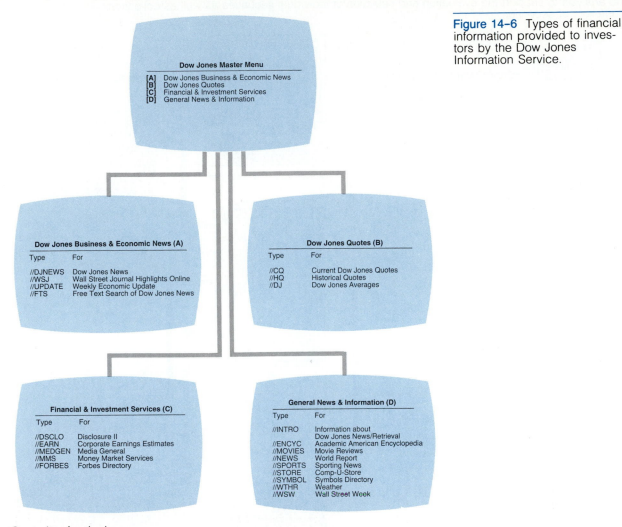

Figure 14–6 Types of financial information provided to investors by the Dow Jones Information Service.

Security Analysis

This type of analysis focuses on the financial position and prospects of a corporation to forecast the market price of its securities. Computerized security analysis uses data provided by financial advisory services and time-sharing companies. Various types of financial, economic, and market analyses are then made to forecast alternative values for a security.

Portfolio Management

Portfolio management involves the management of a combination of securities by holding, selling, or buying selected securities to minimize the risk and to maximize the return of the entire "portfolio" of investments. Computerized portfolio management relies on software containing mathematical models that can select one or more portfolios that minimize risk for specific levels of investment return while satisfying various investment constraints. In most cases, the portfolio selection process produces a list of acceptable portfolios, which are reviewed by a portfolio manager, who then makes the final hold, buy, and sell decisions for each portfolio managed. See Figures 14–7 and 14–8.

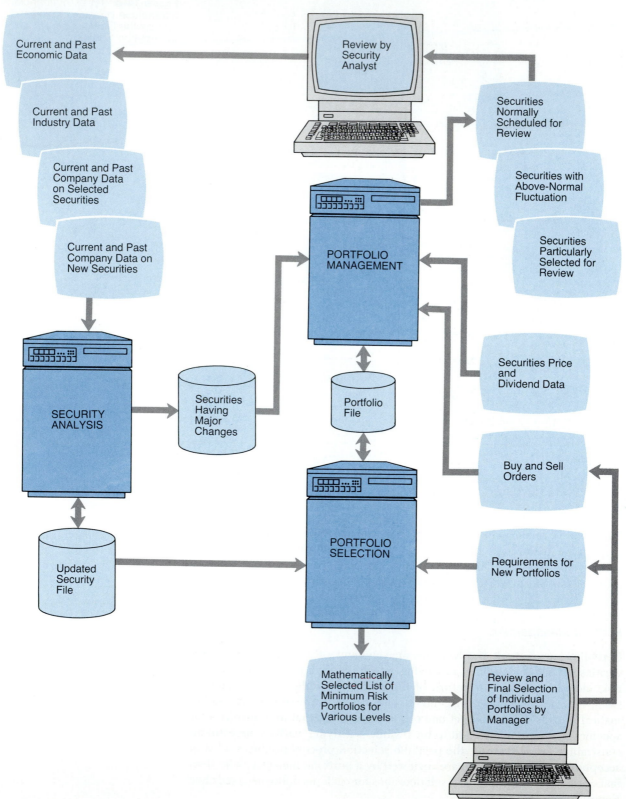

Figure 14–7 An integrated portfolio management system. Notice that this system includes information and analysis to support the evaluation and selection of individual securities as well as collections (portfolios) of securities.

Current and Past Economic Data

Review by Security Analyst

Securities Normally Scheduled for Review

Current and Past Industry Data

Securities with Above-Normal Fluctuation

Current and Past Company Data on Selected Securities

Securities Particularly Selected for Review

Current and Past Company Data on New Securities

PORTFOLIO MANAGEMENT

SECURITY ANALYSIS

Securities Having Major Changes

Portfolio File

Securities Price and Dividend Data

Updated Security File

PORTFOLIO SELECTION

Buy and Sell Orders

Requirements for New Portfolios

Mathematically Selected List of Minimum Risk Portfolios for Various Levels

Review and Final Selection of Individual Portfolios by Manager

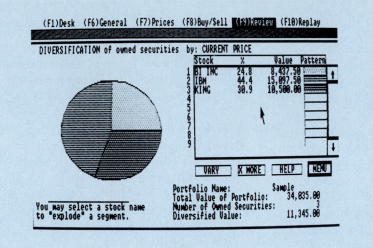

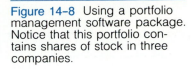
Figure 14-8 Using a portfolio management software package. Notice that this portfolio contains shares of stock in three companies.

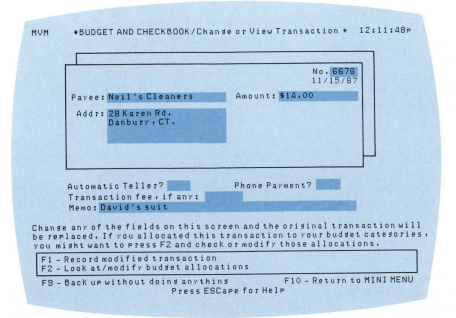

Figure 14-9 Using a personal finance software package. This is a display from the popular Managing Your Money package. Notice how you can write and record checks and view their impact on your personal budget.

PERSONAL FINANCIAL MANAGEMENT

Personal finance packages allow microcomputers to be used for financial record-keeping analysis, and planning. Financial data, such as budgets, taxes, mortgage and other installment payments, transportation and other expenses, and investments, can be organized and stored for later retrieval and analysis. The personal computer, therefore, can help with personal and family budgets, income tax preparation, bank checking and savings account balancing, medical and other insurance claims processing, tracking the stock market, evaluating various investment opportunities, and other forms of financial analysis and planning. Figure 14-9 shows a display of a popular personal finance software package.

REAL WORLD APPLICATION 14–1

The Market Pro

Market Pro is a stock market program that combines the three main functions of other stock market programs—technical analysis, fundamental analysis, and portfolio management—in one package, for $395. Market information on stocks and bonds comes from the I. P. Sharp remote database in Vancouver, British Columbia, and the Market Pro program has its own built-in communications routine for automatic linkup and downloading. You have to have a modem, of course. The program also has a menu selection for automatic linking to the Dow Jones database service.

What do such programs really do for you? In other words, is this a total waste of time and money? I don't think so, and, in fact, I believe that the personal computer is an ideal tool for analyzing the stock market. It is a lightning-fast number cruncher thrust into a problem that is nothing but numbers. Mine told me the market was about to drop two days before the Dow Jones averages fell more than 60 points in one day. It doesn't know how much the market will drop, of course; only that it is very likely to. And it can't make you do anything; it only rings the bell.

For those of you completely unfamiliar with what such programs do, here is a very quick summary of the three major components of the Market Pro program:

☐ Technical Analysis does market timing. Its efficacy rests on a series of mathematical formulas that analyze the changes in the number of advancing and declining stocks and the amount of volume that is going into these changes. There are other factors as well, but those are the biggies. The results of those calculations are displayed on your video screen. They indicate the direction the market, or an individual stock, is likely to take. The formulas can be "tuned" for selectivity over short swings—as brief as five min-

utes or any time frame up to long swings of a decade or more. As with any predictive indicator, they are sometimes wrong.

☐ Fundamental Analysis looks at things that most people believe matter about a company: sales, earnings, debt, assets, and so on. Using a computer for fundamental analysis compresses the labor of weeks into minutes. The most common approach is to create what's called a "screen" to sift through thousands of stocks and pass only those that meet certain criteria. For example, you can tell the machine to look for stocks that sell for less than 10 times earnings, have paid a dividend for more than 10 years, and have very low debt in relation to assets and steadily growing sales. And the machine will search whatever database it is connected to and come up with a display of dozens of stocks that meet your limits. This is the way major mutual funds and investment managers normally select their buys.

☐ Portfolio Management is record-keeping. A sophisticated portfolio-management program will also calculate rates of return and adjust them for tax liability. It will even permit "what if" scenarios, in which you can make theoretical changes in the portfolio's makeup and see immediately what effect that would have on its yield and tax position.

Application Questions

☐ What three types of investment applications are accomplished by software like the Market Pro?

☐ What is the advantage of using personal computers for each of these applications?

Source: Bob Schwabach, "Program for Macs Analyzes Market," Copyright, Universal Press, 1986.

Section II: Common Business Information Systems

This section discusses in more detail the **common business information systems** introduced in Section I of this chapter. These are (1) sales order/transaction processing, (2) inventory control, (3) billing and sales analysis, (4) accounts receivable, (5) accounts payable, (6) payroll and labor analysis, and (7) general ledger. The description of each common business information system that follows has been simplified, since our purpose is to understand computer applications from the viewpoint of business computer users, rather than that of accountants or computer specialists. Therefore, no attempt is made to describe all of the variations that are possible for each common computer application.

The particular form of these applications will vary depending on the type of business firm involved. For example, the sales order processing system that will be described is most often used by business firms whose customers are other business firms, rather than consumers. Another example is the inventory control system that we will describe. It is most widely used to control the inventory of wholesale or retail firms or the finished goods inventory of manufacturing firms. However, in all cases the applications we describe represent a basic form that should be understood by all business computer users.

The objectives of the **sales order/transaction processing** system are:

☐ To provide a fast, accurate, and efficient method of recording and screening customer orders and sales transactions.

☐ To provide the inventory control system with information on accepted orders so they can be filled as quickly as possible.

Figure 14–10 is a general systems flowchart that summarizes the components of the sales order/transaction processing system that should be understood by computer users.

Sales transactions and sales orders from customers or salespersons are received by mail, telephone, or are made in person. They can be recorded on sales receipt or sales order forms and then converted into other media unless OCR documents are used. Alternatively, *point-of-sale terminals* and other types of remote terminals may be used to enter sales order and sales transaction data directly into the computer system. The keyboards of such terminals or optical scanning *wands* might be used for such direct entry. Though sales data are the primary form of input into the system, other types of input data must also be captured. Data from "miscellaneous transactions," such as returned items and credits for damaged goods, are also entered into the system.

The sales order/transaction processing system uses a *customer master file* as its database. The customer master file contains data on each customer such as (1) name, number, address, and phone number; (2) codes indicating sales tax liability, eligibility for discounts, and so on; and (3) other information, for

THE SALES ORDER/ TRANSACTION PROCESSING SYSTEM

Objectives

Input

Database

Figure 14–10 A sales order/
transaction processing system.
This system processes sales
orders and other sales transactions made by customers.

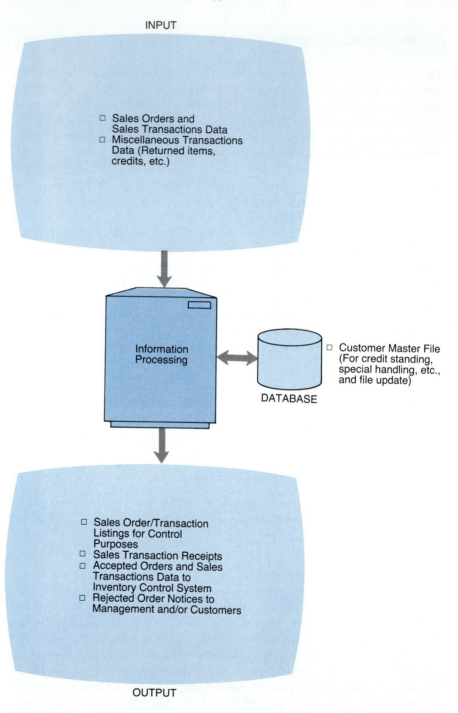

Figure 14–10 A sales order/transaction processing system. This system processes sales orders and other sales transactions made by customers.

example, location, line of business, credit limits, and assigned salespersons. This file provides information on the credit standing of customers, special handling requirements, and other information that is used to decide which orders should be accepted. The file can also be updated to reflect changes in credit standing, new customers, address changes, and so on.

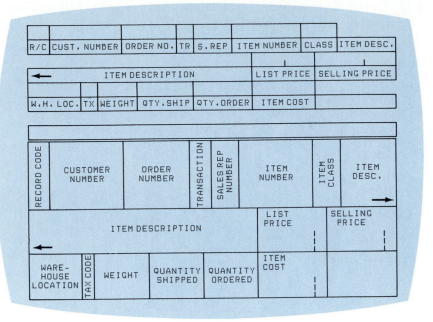

Figure 14–11 An example of a sales transaction record display. This formatted screen illustrates the variety of data that might have to be captured to describe a single sales transaction.

Output

Like most business computer applications, the output of the sales order/ transaction processing system includes listing (also called logs or registers) of each sales order transaction. These control listings document each transaction and allow control totals to be established. The purpose of such controls is to guard against errors or fraud in the input or processing of the data. They also provide an "audit trail" to facilitate the auditing of the system. One of the primary outputs of the system consists of data describing accepted sales orders and completed sales transactions. This data becomes input for the inventory control system. Figure 14–11 illustrates the types of data required to describe a single sales transaction.

The output of many sales order/transaction processing systems also includes notices or receipts to customers acknowledging completed sales transactions or receipt of their orders. In most nonretail business firms, sales invoices (bills) describing filled and shipped sales orders are produced by a billing system, which will be described shortly. Orders not accepted by the system because of inaccurate information are corrected after consultation with salespersons or customers and reentered into the system. Orders rejected for exceeding credit limits or other reasons are usually referred to operating management (such as credit managers or sales managers) for corrective action or may be returned to the customer.

THE INVENTORY CONTROL SYSTEM

The objectives of the **inventory control** system are:

Objectives

☐ To provide high-quality service to customers by using a fast, accurate, and efficient method of filling customer orders and avoiding "stock-outs."

☐ To minimize the amount of money invested in inventory and required to cover inventory "carrying costs."

☐ To provide management with information needed to help achieve the two preceding objectives.

Figure 14–12 is a general systems flowchart that summarizes the major components of the inventory control system.

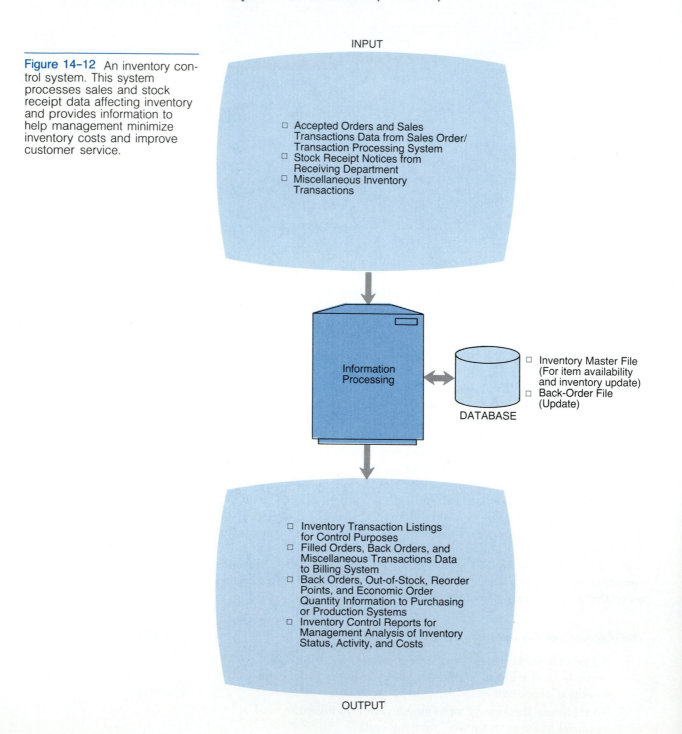

Figure 14–12 An inventory control system. This system processes sales and stock receipt data affecting inventory and provides information to help management minimize inventory costs and improve customer service.

INPUT

☐ Accepted Orders and Sales Transactions Data from Sales Order/Transaction Processing System
☐ Stock Receipt Notices from Receiving Department
☐ Miscellaneous Inventory Transactions

Information Processing

☐ Inventory Master File (For item availability and inventory update)
☐ Back-Order File (Update)

DATABASE

☐ Inventory Transaction Listings for Control Purposes
☐ Filled Orders, Back Orders, and Miscellaneous Transactions Data to Billing System
☐ Back Orders, Out-of-Stock, Reorder Points, and Economic Order Quantity Information to Purchasing or Production Systems
☐ Inventory Control Reports for Management Analysis of Inventory Status, Activity, and Costs

OUTPUT

Input into the inventory control system consists of accepted order data, sales transaction data, as well as data describing stock received by the receiving department of the business firm. Input may also include *miscellaneous inventory transactions* such as adjustments for lost or damaged stock.

Input

The database of this application consists of an *inventory master file*, which is checked for item availability and updated to reflect changes in inventory caused by filling sales orders or receipt of new stock. A *back-order file* is also updated for sales orders that cannot be filled because of stock-outs. Some customers are willing to wait until new stock is received. The back-order file provides data on outstanding back orders that must be filled when stock receipt notices are received for back-ordered items.

Database

The output of the inventory control system includes inventory transactions listings for control purposes. Data describing filled orders, back orders, and miscellaneous sales order transactions are a major system output and become the primary input into the billing and sales analysis system. Information concerning back orders, out-of-stock items, reorder points, and economic order quantities is sent to the purchasing or production departments for entry into their information subsystems. The purchasing department will use such information to procure more inventory, while a manufacturing firm would use this information to schedule the production of additional finished goods inventory.

Output

A final major category of output consists of inventory control reports for management. These reports analyze inventory status, activity, and costs. Management must determine (1) whether the items being reordered and the amounts being reordered require adjustment, (2) the amount of unfilled orders that are occurring, (3) whether any items are becoming obsolete, (4) unusual variations in inventory activity, and (5) the items that account for the majority of the inventory costs and sales of the business. Figure 14–13 illustrates several inventory control reports.

Fixed order points and order quantities may be arbitrarily set by management and used by the inventory control system. However, the computer can be programmed to use mathematical techniques to calculate optimum order points and economic order quantities for use by the inventory control system. Such calculations take into account the cost of an item, its carrying cost, its annual sales, the cost of placing an order, and the length of time it takes to process, procure, and receive an item. In any case, effective inventory control can bring major benefits. Too little stock on hand may mean lost sales or excessive rush orders for stock replenishment. Too much stock may mean increased carrying costs, higher interest on invested capital, additional warehousing expenses, and greater loss due to obsolescence. In many cases, carrying costs of inventory can run as high as 25 percent per year of the investment in inventory!

Figure 14–13 Examples of inventory control reports for management. Notice how they analyze inventory status, activity, and costs.

Stock No.	Description	Opening Balance	+ Receipts	– Issue	= On Hand	PLANNING			
						+ On Order	= Available	Order Point	OP
11398	TRANSFORMER	210			210	300	510	400	
11402	MOTOR ASM 50	1205	500		1705	1500	3205	2000	
11610	CAM	10341		1423	8918		8918	9000	*
11682	LEVER	433	3500	1255	2678	500	3178	2750	

Item No.	Cumulative Count		Annual Units	Unit Cost	Annual $ Sales	Cumulative Sales	
	Number	%				$	%
T 7061	1	.01	51,533	3.077	158,629	158,629	.5
–	–	–	–	–	–	–	–
S 6832	13	.12	243,224	.317	77,102	1,652,385	5.0
K 5322	110	1.0	8,680	3.286	28,522	5,882,489	17.8
S 5678	549	5.0	244,690	.045	11,011	13,252,124	40.1
S 6121	2,198	20.0	7,239	.490	3,547	23,662,146	71.6
–	–	–	–	–	–	–	–
–	–	–	–	–	–	–	–
S 6219	6,593	60.0	15,360	.050	768	31,395,306	95.0
–	–	–	–	–	–	–	–
–	–	–	–	–	–	–	–
M 3742	10,988	100.0	0	.073	0	33,047,690	100.0

THE BILLING AND SALES ANALYSIS SYSTEM

Objectives

The objectives of the **billing and sales analysis** system are:

☐ To prepare customer invoices (bills) quickly and accurately and thus maintain customer satisfaction and improved cash flow into the business.

☐ To provide management with sales analysis reports, which provide information concerning sales activity and trends that is required for effective marketing management.

Figure 14–14 summarizes the important components of the billing and sales analysis system.

Input

The input into the billing and sales analysis system consists of data from the inventory control system that describes the filled orders, back orders, and miscellaneous transactions.

Figure 14-14   A billing and
sales analysis system. This
system bills customers and
analyzes sales performance for
management.

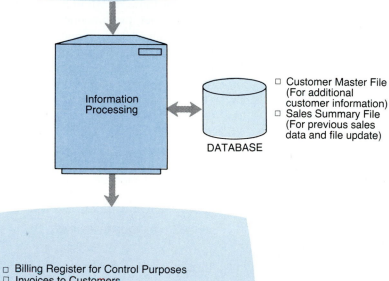

INPUT

□ Filled Orders, Back Orders, and
  Miscellaneous Transactions Data
  from the Inventory Control System

Information
Processing

□ Customer Master File
  (For additional
  customer information)
□ Sales Summary File
  (For previous sales
  data and file update)

DATABASE

□ Billing Register for Control Purposes
□ Invoices to Customers
□ Shipping Documents for Shipping
  Department
□ Invoice Summary Data to Accounts
  Receivable System
□ Sales Analysis Reports for Management
  by Product, Customer, Salesperson,
  Sales Territory, Etc.

OUTPUT

The database for this system consists of the *customer master file*, which is   Database
used to provide additional information about a customer that is required by a
billing operation. Examples are customer "ship-to" addresses, shipping instructions, and special handling. A *sales summary file* is updated with

current sales order data and provides information concerning previous sales for the sales analysis reports.

Output

The output of the billing and sales analysis system includes a *billing register*, which is a summary listing of all invoices that is used for control purposes. A major output of the system is the customer invoice such as that shown in Figure 14–15. (The computer calculates all required invoice amounts.) Other outputs of the system includes shipping documents such as "picking slips," shipping labels, bills of lading, and delivery receipts. The computer frequently lists the items on the invoice in a warehouse-location sequence so a copy of the invoice can be used as a *picking slip* by warehouse personnel when assembling an order for shipment. Summarized data for each invoice is entered into the accounts receivable system.

The final major output of the billing and sales analysis system is sales analysis reports for management such as those shown in Figure 14–16. Sales analysis reports can analyze sales by product, product line, customer, type of customer, salesperson, and sales territory. Such reports help marketing management determine the sales performance of products, customers, and salespeople. They can determine whether a firm is expending too much sales effort on low-volume customers or low-profit products. For example, one business found that it had over 1,000 accounts, representing one third of all

Figure 14–15 An example of a customer invoice. This document is an important information product for customers that is generated by a billing system.

LAURENTIAN INDUSTRIES, INC.

SOLD TO	SHIP TO	CUSTOMER NO.
S. W. STAPLES 498 RIVERVIEW STREET SAN JOSE, CALIF. 94067	RODRIGUEZ DESIGN HOMES DIVISION OF S. W. STAPLES 8363 OLIVE STREET SUNNYVALE, CALIF. 95117	430875

DATE 09/15/––	INV. NO. 138265	ORDER NO. 717690	SHIPPING INSTRUCTIONS VIA SMITH TRANSPORT	STATED TERMS 2% 15 DAYS NET 30	SALESPERSON G. PEREZ

QUANTITY ORDERED	QUANTITY SHIPPED	QUANTITY B/O	DESCRIPTION	UNIT PRICE	EXTENDED AMOUNT	DISCOUNT AMOUNT	NET AMOUNT	TAX-ABLE
40	40		B500 TWINLITE SOCKET B	.60	24.00	1.20	22.80	
350	100	250	B506 SOCKET ADAPTER BRN	.32	32.00	3.20	28.80	
200	150	50	C151C SILENT SWITCH IVORY	1.20	180.00	9.00	171.00	*
175	175		A210 PULL CORD GOLD	.42	73.50		73.50	*
60		60	1436 LAMP ENTRANCE	.50				
175	105	70	A200 FIXTURE 5 LIGHT	20.13	2113.65	211.37	1,902.28	
			FREIGHT CHARGE				18.95	
			PACKING CHARGE				45.00	

TAXABLE	TAX	FREIGHT	MISC. SPECIAL CHARGE		INVOICE AMOUNT
244.50	12.23	18.95	45.00		2,274.56

customers, who purchased less than 1 percent of their total sales volume. The firm also found that it had almost 2,000 accounts that bought at least $1,000 annually and accounted for 95 percent of their sales volume!

```
                    LAURENTIAN INDUSTRIES, INC.

                       SALES BY ITEM CLASS

                    MONTH ENDING 03/31/--

      ITEM                            SOLD THIS      GROSS      PROFIT
     CLASS    CLASS DESCRIPTION         MONTH        PROFIT     PERCENT

       1      ABRASIVES               2,720.19      271.36        10

       2      ACIDS AND CHEMICALS     1,216.27      170.27        14

       3      BRASS                   6,220.83      435.45         7
```

```
                    LAURENTIAN INDUSTRIES, INC.

                COMPARATIVE SALES ANALYSIS BY CUSTOMER

                      FOR EACH SALESPERSON

                    PERIOD ENDING 07/31/--

   SLP.   CUST.   SALESPERSON/CUSTOMER    THIS PERIOD    THIS PERIOD
   NO.    NO.            NAME              THIS YEAR      LAST YEAR

    10             A R WESTON
          1426     HYDRO CYCLES INC         3,210.26       4,312.06
          2632     RUPP AQUA CYCLES         7,800.02       2,301.98
          3217     SEA PORT WEST CO            90.00CR       421.06

                   SALESPERSON TOTALS      10,920.28       7,035.10

    12             H T BRAVEMAN
          0301     BOLLINGER ASSOCIATES       100.96           0.00
```

Figure 14–16 Examples of sales analysis reports for management. Notice how they analyze sales performance by product, profitability, time period, salesperson, and customer.

THE ACCOUNTS RECEIVABLE SYSTEM

Accounts receivable represents the amounts of money owed to a company by its customers (accounts). The objectives of the accounts receivable system are:

Objectives

☐ To stimulate prompt customer payments by preparing accurate and timely monthly statements to credit customers.

☐ To provide management with the information required to control the amount of credit extended and the collection of money owed, in order to maximize profitable credit sales while minimizing losses from bad debts. Figure 14–17 illustrates a typical accounts receivable system.

Input

Input into the system consists of invoice summary data from the billing system and source documents showing payments received from customers. The usual customer payment document is the return portion of an invoice or statement, which the customer returns by mail along with a check in payment of the account. Another type of input into this system are "miscellaneous adjustments," which are prepared by the accounting department to adjust customer accounts for mistakes in billing, the return of goods, bad debt write-offs, and so on.

Database

The database for the accounts receivable application includes the *accounts receivable file*, which provides current balances for each customer account, and which is also updated by the new billing, payments, and adjustments input data. The *customer master file* is used to provide data needed for customer statement preparation. The customer credit-standing information in this file is also updated as a result of changes in accounts receivable balances.

Output

Proper information systems control requires that listings and control totals be prepared for all cash received and for each customer account in the accounts receivable file. Thus the output of the accounts receivable system includes an accounts receivable register and a cash receipts register. Monthly statements are also prepared for each customer that show recent charges and credits, as well as the present balance owed. See Figure 14–18. Notice that this customer statement also indicates amounts that are overdue.

The accounts receivable system can also be programmed to automatically produce delinquency notices that are sent to customers whose accounts are seriously overdue. Management reports produced by the system include a delinquent account report and an *aged trial balance* report (also called an *aged accounts receivable report*). Figure 14–19 illustrates an aged trial balance that helps the credit manager identify accounts seriously overdue and requiring special collection efforts. The final output of the accounts receivable system consists of accounts receivable summary data, which is used as input by the general ledger system.

INPUT

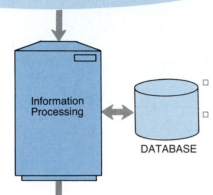

□ Invoice Summary Data from
   Billing and Sales Analysis
   System
□ Payments from Customers
□ Miscellaneous Adjustments Data
   from Accounting Department

Figure 14–17   An accounts receivable system. This system
provides monthly customer
statements as well as credit
management documents and
reports.

Information
Processing

DATABASE

□ Accounts Receivable File
   (For current balances and
   file update)
□ Customer Master File
   (For customer data and
   file update)

□ Accounts Receivable and Cash
   Receipts Registers for Control
   Purposes
□ Monthly Statements to Customers
□ Aged Trial Balance and Delinquent
   Account Report for Credit
   Management
□ Delinquency Notices to Delinquent
   Customers
□ Accounts Receivable Summary
   Data for General Ledger System

OUTPUT

Figure 14–18 An example of a monthly customer statement. Since this is such an important information product for customers, it had better be correct!

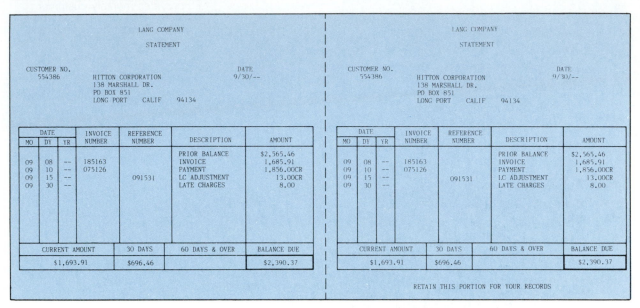

Figure 14–19 An example of an accounts receivable aged trial balance. Notice how this credit management report spotlights customers whose accounts are overdue.

ACCOUNTS RECEIVABLE AGED TRIAL BALANCE

DATE _____ 6/30/ _____

CUSTOMER NUMBER	CUSTOMER NAME	BALANCE	CURRENT	OVER 30 DAYS	OVER 60 DAYS	90 DAYS & OVER	CREDIT LIMIT	EXCEEDS CREDIT LIMIT
13985	ANDERSON CORP.	1324 35	1200 00	121 50		2 85	3500 00	
14007	ARMSTRONG INTL.	3896 68	439 61	1911 25	499 00	1046 82	3000 00	*
37243	CONTI RENTAL	379 80	379 80				500 00	
48277	DELTA LIGHTING	241 28	65 98	175 30			500 00	
63365	FOXBORO CORP.	222 18	222 18				2000 00	
72466	HINDS ELECTRIC	2767 15	1632 09	1135 06			15000 00	
78144	INNSBRUCK ELEC.	861 70	27 50	54 40	127 23	652 57	1000 00	
85433	MILLER SUPPLY	457 90	202 60	50 70	120 70	83 90	500 00	
87542	PALMER APPL.	40 24	40 24				500 00	
93421	SMYTHE CO.	336 05	260 40		75 65		1500 00	
95642	WELLS HARDWARE	3195 98	469 76	325 01	151 63	2249 58	3000 00	*

Accounts payable refers to the amounts of money that a business firm owes its suppliers. The primary objectives of the accounts payable system are:

□ Prompt and accurate payment of suppliers to maintain good relationships, insure a good credit standing, and secure any discounts offered for prompt payment.

□ Provide tight financial control over all cash disbursements of the business.

□ Provide management with information needed for the analysis of payments, expenses, purchases, and cash requirements.

Figure 14–20 illustrates the accounts payable application.

Input into the accounts payable system consists of invoices (bills) from suppliers and others who have furnished goods or services to the business firm. Input also may be in the form of expense vouchers for various business expenses and miscellaneous payments and adjustments from the accounting department. (A *voucher* is an accounting form that records the details of a transaction and authorizes its entry into the accounting system of a firm.) For example, expense vouchers may be prepared to reimburse employees for authorized expenditures. Typically, salespersons and managerial personnel request reimbursement by completing an "expense account" statement and submitting it to the accounting department.

Payments from "petty cash" or adjustments from suppliers for billing errors are other types of miscellaneous input. Receiving reports from the receiving department acknowledge the receipt of goods from suppliers and are required before payment can be authorized. A copy of purchase orders from the purchasing department provides data describing purchase orders that have been sent to suppliers. This data is used to record "pending payables" and to help determine whether the business firm has been accurately billed by its suppliers.

The database for the accounts payable application is the *accounts payable file*, which provides current balances for all accounts and is updated by the new input data.

As in previous applications, information systems control requires that an *accounts payable transaction register* be produced. This output document lists all system transactions and computes various control totals. A major form of output of the system are checks in payment of authorized invoices and expense vouchers. A *cash disbursements report* provides a detailed record of all checks written and contributes to proper financial control of the cash disbursements of the firm.

An important output of the system for management is the *cash requirements report*, which lists or summarizes all unpaid invoices and expense vouchers. It identifies all invoices eligible for cash payment discounts during the current period. The computer also can be programmed to analyze unpaid invoices and expense vouchers. Forecasts of the cash requirements for several future periods can thus be included in the cash requirements report. The accounts payable system can also produce *purchase analysis reports* for management, which summarize the purchases and payments

Figure 14–20 An accounts payable system. This system processes and pays vendor invoices and employee expense vouchers. It also produces reports for management on cash disbursements, cash requirements, and purchasing activity.

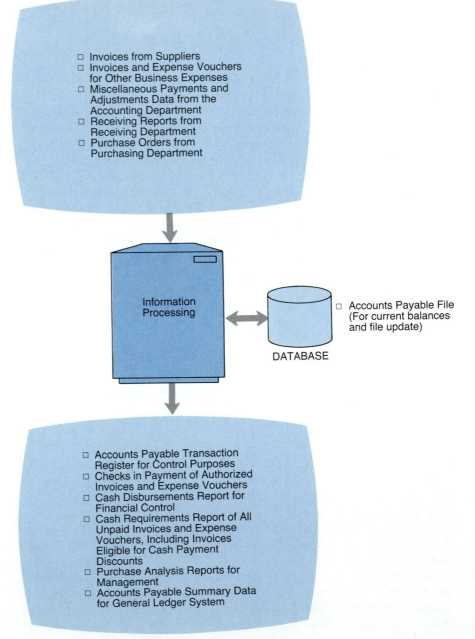

INPUT

□ Invoices from Suppliers
□ Invoices and Expense Vouchers for Other Business Expenses
□ Miscellaneous Payments and Adjustments Data from the Accounting Department
□ Receiving Reports from Receiving Department
□ Purchase Orders from Purchasing Department

Information Processing

□ Accounts Payable File (For current balances and file update)

DATABASE

□ Accounts Payable Transaction Register for Control Purposes
□ Checks in Payment of Authorized Invoices and Expense Vouchers
□ Cash Disbursements Report for Financial Control
□ Cash Requirements Report of All Unpaid Invoices and Expense Vouchers, Including Invoices Eligible for Cash Payment Discounts
□ Purchase Analysis Reports for Management
□ Accounts Payable Summary Data for General Ledger System

OUTPUT

made to each supplier of the firm. (This report is sometimes produced by a separate *purchasing* system.) The final category of output consists of summarized accounts payable transaction data, which becomes input data for the general ledger system. See Figure 14–21.

Figure 14–21 Examples of purchase analysis and cash requirements reports. Notice how these reports analyze purchasing activity and required cash payments to vendors.

PURCHASE ANALYSIS BY VENDOR

VENDOR'S NO.	VENDOR'S NAME	AMOUNT THIS MONTH	RETURNS YEAR TO DATE	NET AMOUNT YEAR TO DATE	NET AMOUNT LAST YEAR TO DATE	INCREASE OR DECREASE	
27	ABBOT MACHINE CO	1286 44		3194 26	3010 42	183 84	
58	ACE TOOL CO			1975 15	1859 76	115 39	
66	ACME ABRASIVE CO	342 86		1505 93	1482 50	23 43	
324	ALLAN ALLOYS CO		95 10	4675 22	4410 15	265 07	
367	AMERICAN TOOL CO			986 74	1293 84	307 10	CR
425	ANGUS METAL WORKS			842 89	795 22	47 67	
475	APEX CORPORATION	2316 84	245 73	10476 79	9473 65	1003 14	
502	ARCO STATIONERY CO			319 42	445 93	126 51	CR

KRAUSZ MANUFACTURING COMPANY
ACCOUNTS PAYABLE

CASH REQUIREMENTS STATEMENT

VENDOR	VENDOR NUMBER	DUE DATE	INVOICE AMOUNT	DISCOUNT	CHECK AMOUNT
SOLVAY GEN SUP	1016	4/16	$ 773.30	$ 15.47	$ 757.83
ROCHESTER PR CO	1021	4/16	1,620.18	32.40	1,587.78
CALABRIA CONT	1049	4/16	143.65	2.87	140.78
ONONDAGA STL CO	1077	4/16	5,982.82	119.66	5,863.16
BLACK & NICHOLS	1103	4/16	14.25	.71	13.54
AUSTERHOLZ INC	1240	4/16	624.77	12.50	612.27
AUSTERHOLZ INC	1240	4/16	1,833.19	36.66	1,796.53
CHRISTIE & CO	1366	4/16	745.54		745.54
WILSON & WILSON	2231	4/16	2,936.12	58.72	2,877.40
CLAR. HIGGINS	2590	4/16	1,000.00		1,000.00
HONOUR BROS	3101	4/16	97.36	1.95	95.41
BASTIANI & SON	3112	4/16	3,580.85	71.62	3,509.23
DRJ WIRE CO	3164	4/16	256.90	5.14	251.76
HASTING-WHITE	3258	4/16	1,144.42	22.89	1,121.53
DARONO ART MET	3427	4/16	32.75	.66	32.09
DARONO ART MET	3427	4/16	127.52	2.55	124.97
DARONO ART MET	3427	4/16	96.60	1.93	94.67

THE PAYROLL AND LABOR ANALYSIS SYSTEM

Objectives

The primary objectives of the **payroll and labor analysis** system are:

☐ Prompt and accurate payment of employees.

☐ Prompt and accurate reporting to management, employees, and appropriate agencies concerning earnings, taxes, and other deductions.

☐ Providing management with reports analyzing labor costs and productivity.

The payroll and labor analysis application is widely computerized. It involves many complex calculations and the production of many types of reports and documents, many of which are required by government agencies. Besides earnings calculations, many types of taxes and fringe benefit deductions must be calculated. Payroll processing is also complicated because many business firms employ both hourly paid employees and salaried personnel, and may have several kinds of incentive compensation plans. Figure 14–22 illustrates the payroll and labor analysis application.

Input

The input into the payroll and labor analysis system consists of employee time cards or other records of time worked or attendance. Time cards are normally used by hourly paid employees, while some type of attendance record is usually kept for salaried personnel. Additional input includes records of employee incentive compensation such as factory piecework or salesperson commissions. Input may also be in the form of miscellaneous payroll adjustments from the personnel or accounting departments such as changes in wage rates, job classifications, and deductions.

Database

The database for the payroll and labor analysis application includes a *payroll master file*, which provides additional payroll data needed for payroll calculations and reports. This file is updated by the new input data. A *labor analysis summary file* provides previous labor analysis data and is also updated each time new input data are processed.

Output

All payroll transactions, all paychecks written, and all deductions made are listed and totaled on control registers. Of course, the primary output of the system consists of payroll checks and earning statements for employees of the firm. See Figure 14–23. In addition, tax and other deductions reports are prepared periodically for management, employees, and appropriate agencies. For example, quarterly tax reports must be sent to the U.S. Internal Revenue Service, and forms summarizing income and taxes withheld must be sent to employees before January 31 of each year. Reports listing and summarizing other tax and deduction information are prepared for management and various agencies such as school districts, city, county, and state agencies, labor unions, insurance companies, charitable organizations, and credit unions.

Labor analysis reports for management are another major form of output of the payroll and labor analysis system. See Figure 14–24. These reports analyze the time, cost, and personnel required by departments of the firm or

INPUT

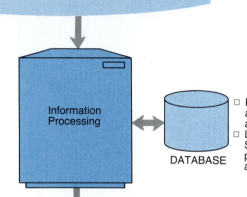

□ Employee Time Cards or Other
  Records of Time Worked or
  Attendance
□ Employee Incentive Compensation
  Records
□ Miscellaneous Payroll Adjustments
  from Personnel or Accounting
  Departments

Information
Processing

DATABASE

□ Payroll Master File (For
  additional payroll data
  and file update)
□ Labor Analysis
  Summary File (For
  previous labor data
  and file update)

□ Payroll, Paycheck, and Deductions
  Registers for Control Purposes
□ Payroll Checks and Earnings
  Statements to Employees
□ Tax and Other Deductions Reports
  to Management, Employees, and
  Appropriate Agencies
□ Payroll Summary Data for
  General Ledger System
□ Labor Analysis Reports for
  Management by Department,
  Job, Project, Etc.

OUTPUT

Figure 14–22 A payroll and
labor analysis system. This system processes employee work
activity data and produces
paychecks and earnings statements. It also produces various
reports for management and
government agencies concerning taxes, deductions, and
labor costs.

by jobs and projects being undertaken. They assist management in planning
labor requirements and controlling the labor cost and productivity of ongoing projects. The final output of the payroll and labor analysis system is
payroll summary data, which is used as input by the general ledger system.

Figure 14–23 An example of a paycheck and earnings statement. For many people, these documents are the most important information products produced by an information system!

	90–1211
	0519
CHECK DATE 1/16/––	
J.R. SMITH & CO.	
	CHECK NUMBER
	1303
PAY 393 DOLLARS AND 80 CENTS	** 393.80
TO THE ORDER OF A H ANKSTER	
	SPECIMEN
COMMERCIAL TRUST BANK	
⑃0210⑃0987⑃ 4121 00360⑃	

EMPLOYEE NUMBER	EMPLOYEE NAME	DEPT.	PAY PERIOD	PAY PERIOD ENDED	CHECK NO.	CHECK DATE
0123	A H ANKSTER	03	3	1/16/––	**1303**	1/16/––

EARNINGS AND STATUTORY DEDUCTIONS

HOURS	RATE	REGULAR PAY	OVERTIME PAY	OTHER PAY	GROSS PAY	FED. W/TAX	F.I.C.A. TAX	STATE TAX
50.0	10.00	400.00	150.00	50.00	600.00	90.00	43.20	18.00

VOLUNTARY DEDUCTIONS

MEDICAL INS.	LIFE INS.	CREDIT UNION	UNION DUES	CHARITY	SAVINGS BONDS	ALL OTHERS	NET PAY
12.00	8.00	20.00	10.00	5.00			393.80

SOCIAL SECURITY AND W–2 INFORMATION

SOCIAL SECURITY NO.	EXEMPT	Y.T.D. GROSS	Y.T.D. FED. W/TAX	Y.T.D. FICA	Y.T.D. STATE TAX	
312–32–1337	X	1,400.00	210.00	100.80	42.00	*NOT NEGOTIABLE*

THE GENERAL LEDGER SYSTEM

The **general ledger** system consolidates financial data from all of the other accounting subsystems and produces the monthly and annual financial statements of the firm. The many financial transactions of a business are first recorded in chronological order in *journals*, then transferred ("posted") to *subsidiary ledgers*, where they are organized into "accounts" such as cash, accounts receivable, and inventory. The summary of all accounts and their balances is known as the *general ledger*.

At the end of each accounting period (at the end of each month or fiscal year) the balance of each account in the general ledger must be computed, the profit or loss of the firm during the period must be calculated, and the financial statements of the firm (the balance sheet and income statement) must be prepared. This is known as "closing the books" of the business. The *income statement* of the firm presents its income, expenses, and profit or loss for a period. The *balance sheet* shows the assets, liabilities, and net worth of the business as of the end of the accounting period.

```
DATE 8/08/--                    WORK IN PROGRESS REPORT
                                     FOR JULY 19--

        FINISH  PROGRESS  WORK           EST JOB  ACT JOB  % HRS  EST JOB   ACT JOB   % $
JOBNO   DATE    DATE      DEPT   EMPNO   HOURS    HOURS    USED   DOLLARS   DOLLARS   USED

11111   10/30   6/30/--                  120.0    30.0     25.0   635.00    190.00-   30.0
                7/05/--   360    00508                8.0                    40.00
                7/10/--   360    00508                8.0                    40.00
                7/11/--   360    00604                6.0                    24.00
                7/30/--   360    00501               10.0                    60.00

        TO DATE STATUS                   120.0    62.0     51.7   635.00    354.00    55.7

23468   9/30    4/30/--                  100.0    80.0     80.0  1000.00    700.00    70.0
                7/06/--   400    10105                8.0                    80.00
                7/28/--   506    36350                4.0                    80.00
                7/29/--   506    36350                4.0                    80.00
                7/30/--   506    36350                5.0                   100.00

        TO DATE STATUS                   100.0   101.0    101.0  1000.00   1040.00   104.0

33335   7/15    6/30/--                   40.0    42.0    105.0   160.00    200.00   125.0
                7/14/--   500    40608                4.0                     8.00
                7/18/--   360    00508                8.0                    40.00

        TO DATE STATUS                    40.0    54.0    135.0   160.00    248.00   155.0
```

Figure 14–24 An example of a labor analysis report. This work in progress report compares estimated to actual labor hours and costs for each job or project.

Objectives

The primary objective of the general ledger system is to accomplish the accounting tasks mentioned in the preceding paragraph in an accurate and timely manner. Using computers for the general ledger application can result in greater accuracy, earlier closings, and more timely and meaningful financial reports for management. This can frequently be accomplished with less personnel and costs than manual accounting methods. Figure 14–25 is a general systems flowchart of the general ledger application.

Input

Input into the general ledger system consists of summary data from the accounts receivable, accounts payable, and payroll systems, as well as financial data from other information systems (such as production control, purchasing, and engineering) that we described in the previous chapter. Another form of input is "miscellaneous accounting entries" from the accounting department that record changes to such accounts as cash, marketable securities, and plant and equipment.

Database

The database of the general ledger application is the *general ledger file*, which is updated by the new input data and provides information on past, current, and budgeted balances for each general ledger account.

Output

The output of the general ledger system includes a listing of all transactions for control purposes and a *general ledger trial balance report*, which provides accounting control by summarizing and balancing all general ledger accounts. The *income statement* and *balance sheet* of the firm for an accounting period are major outputs of the system and are of primary importance to

Figure 14–25 A general ledger system. This system processes summary data from other accounting information systems. It produces important statements and reports that document a firm's financial status and performance.

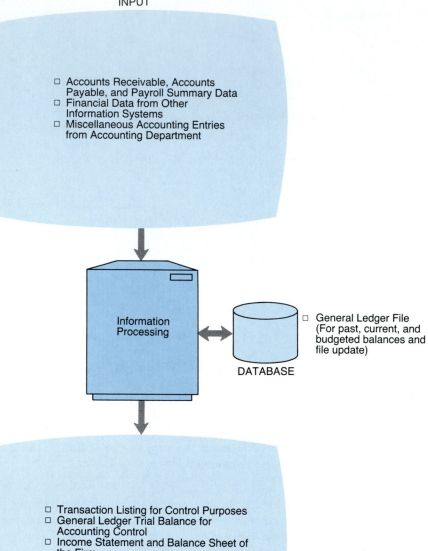

INPUT

☐ Accounts Receivable, Accounts
  Payable, and Payroll Summary Data
☐ Financial Data from Other
  Information Systems
☐ Miscellaneous Accounting Entries
  from Accounting Department

Information
Processing

☐ General Ledger File
  (For past, current, and
  budgeted balances and
  file update)

DATABASE

☐ Transaction Listing for Control Purposes
☐ General Ledger Trial Balance for
  Accounting Control
☐ Income Statement and Balance Sheet of
  the Firm
☐ Income and Expense Analysis Reports
  for Management

OUTPUT

financial management and the top management of the firm. A final important output of the system is *income and expense analysis reports.* Such reports analyze the financial performance of a department or the business firm by comparing current performance to past and forecasted (budgeted) figures. The difference ("variance") between actual and budgeted amounts shows managers in what area their performance is falling short or surpassing their financial objectives for a period. See Figures 14–26, 14–27, and 14–28.

Figure 14-26 Examples of a comparative income statement and balance sheet. The balance sheet reports the current status of a firm's assets, liabilities, and owners investments. The income statement reports a firm's income, expenses, and profit for a period.

HASTING-WHITE TOOL COMPANY
COMPARATIVE BALANCE SHEET

PERIOD ENDING JUNE 30, 19–

MAJOR ACCOUNT	DESCRIPTION		PREVIOUS PERIOD THIS YEAR	CURRENT PERIOD THIS YEAR	CURRENT PERIOD LAST YEAR	OVER* OR UNDER-	% OVER* OR UNDER-
	ASSETS						
	CASH AND RECEIVABLES						
111	CASH		$ 15,673.38	$ 16,739.73	$ 15,248.61	$ 1,491.12 *	9.8*
112	ACCOUNTS RECEIVABLE		32,967.21	33,291.18	32,968.32	322.86 *	.9*
113	RESERVE FOR BAD DEBTS		329.67 –	332.91 –	329.68 –	3.23 *	.9*
114	NOTES RECEIVABLE		1,000.00		1,500.00	1,500.00 –	100.0*
115	MARKETABLE SECURITIES		2,164.30	5,898.13	3,673.21	2,224.92 *	60.6*
		TOT	$ 51,475.22 *	$ 55,596.13 *	$ 53,060.46 *	$ 2,535.67 *	
	INVENTORIES						
116	INVENTORIES		$ 183,621.83	$ 161,298.67	$ 149,238.61	$ 12,060.06 *	8.1*
		TOT	$ 183,621.83 *	$ 161,298.67 *	$ 149,238.61 *	$ 12,060.06 *	
	LAND AND BUILDINGS						
121	LAND						
122	BUILDINGS			$ 50,238.96		$ 50,238.96 *	*
123	RES. FOR DEPREC.		2,116.45 –	2,363.74 –	1,767.88 –	595.86 –	33.7*
		TOT	$ 2,116.45 –	$ 47,875.22 *	$ 1,767.88 –	$ 49,643.10 *	
	EQUIP. AND MACHINERY						
124	EQUIP. AND MACHINERY		$ 10,873.98	$ 8,339.61	$ 16,298.38	$ 7,958.77 –	48.8–
125	RES. FOR DEPREC.		3,245.67 –	3,469.22 –	2,975.12 –	494.10 *	16.6*
		TOT	$ 7,628.31 *	$ 4,870.39 *	$ 13,323.26 *	$ 8,452.87 *	

SOUTH LAKE SAND COMPANY
COMPARATIVE INCOME STATEMENT

PERIOD ENDING MAY 31, 19–

ACCOUNT NUMBER	DESCRIPTION	CURRENT PERIOD THIS YEAR	CURRENT PERIOD LAST YEAR	YEAR-TO-DATE THIS YEAR	YEAR-TO-DATE LAST YEAR	INCREASE* OR DECREASE-
411	SALES					
411-100	GROSS SALES	$1,223,195.85	$1,083,474.02	$4,739,999.14	$3,415,174.67	$1,324,824.47 *
411-200	LESS RETURNS & ALLOW	1,726.40	1,912.71	3,245.97	3,464.22	218.25 –
	NET SALES	$1,221,469.45	$1,081,561.31	$4,736,753.17	$3,411,710.45	$1,325,042.72 *
412-100	LESS COST OF SALES	581,786.15	541,950.16	2,852,146.73	2,008,762.23	843,384.50 *
	GROSS PROFIT	$ 639,683.30*	$ 539,611.15*	$1,884,606.44*	$1,402,948.22*	$ 481,658.22 *
421	SELLING EXPENSES					
421-100	SALARIES & COMMISSIONS	$ 184,373.27	$ 179,264.48	$ 705,623.06	$ 541,579.46	$ 164,043.60 *
421-200	TRAVELING EXPENSE	14,425.15	13,790.80	53,726.92	42,968.21	10,758.71 *
421-300	DELIVERY EXPENSE	6,140.20	5,956.00	28,364.15	16,428.19	11,935.96 *
421-400	ADVERTISING EXPENSE	1,582.00	1,450.25	18,250.00	5,225.75	13,024.25 *
421-500	OFFICE SALARIES	27,684.35	25,829.15	94,342.18	79,415.14	14,927.04 *
421-600	STATIONERY & SUPPLIES	1,380.60	1,295.00	4,982.76	3,576.82	1,405.94 *
421-700	TELEPHONE	1,315.85	1,305.62	4,148.15	3,381.26	766.89 *
421-800	BUILDING	6,725.00	6,215.10	25,175.00	18,634.55	6,540.45 *
421-900	MISCELLANEOUS	1,460.38	1,385.75	4,965.48	3,519.47	1,446.01 *
	TOTAL SELLING EXPENSE	$ 245,086.80*	$ 236,492.15*	$ 939,577.70*	$ 714,728.85*	$ 224,848.85 *

Figure 14-27 An example of a general ledger summary report. This report summarizes all balance sheet and income statement accounts and their balances.

A B C COMPANY

SUMMARY LEDGER REPORT

03/31/--   PAGE 01

ACCOUNT NO. MAJ. MIN.		ACCOUNT DESCRIPTION	ACCOUNT BALANCES YEAR TO DATE THIS YEAR	LAST YEAR
111	000	CASH ON HAND AND IN BANKS	36,710.23	25,893.26
112	000	ACCOUNTS RECEIVABLE - NET	122,273.47	117,762.80
114	000	NOTES RECEIVABLE	8,000.00	4,000.00
116	000	INVENTORIES	703,402.65	590,808.40
121	000	LAND	500,000.00	500,000.00
122	000	BUILDINGS	1,850,000.00	1,800,000.00
123	000	ACCUMULATED DEPRECIATION ON BUILDINGS	49,000.00	48,000.00
124	000	EQUIPMENT AND MACHINERY	450,850.00	425,465.00
125	000	DEPREC RESERVE FOR EQUIP AND MACH	79,456.00	76,305.00
221	000	NOTES PAYABLE	40,000.00	35,000.00
321	000	SURPLUS	75,203.76	50,397.73
411	000	SALES	1,075,113.85	950,675.33
412	000	COST OF GOODS SOLD	375,819.10	255,839.19
421	000	SELLING EXPENSE	185,615.25	195,267.48

Figure 14-28 An example of an income and expense analysis report for management. Notice how this highly summarized report compares actual to planned income, expenses, and profit.

ABC DEPARTMENT STORES

PRESIDENTIAL LEVEL

EARNINGS SUMMARY

4 WEEKS ENDED   AUGUST 2, 19-

	ACTUAL	PLANNED	VARIANCE
SALES	2,475.0	2,300.0	+ 7.6%
GROSS MARGIN	993.0	900.0	EVEN
CONTROLLABLE EXPENSE	388.0	350.0	OK
OPERATING PROFIT	605.0	550.0	+10.0%
FIXED EXPENSE	310.0	300.0	+ 3.3%
NET PROFIT	295.0	250.0	
PROVISION FOR TAX	129.8	110.0	
NET PROFIT AFTER TAXES	165.2	140.0	+18.0%

COMMENTS: EACH STORE MET PLANNED GOALS WITHIN PRESCRIBED TOLERANCES.

YEAR TO DATE: SALES   17.5 MILLION   +5.1 OVER PLAN
NET AFTER TAXES: 1.1 MILLION   +9.7 OVER PLAN

REAL WORLD APPLICATION 14–2

Dac-Easy Accounting

After a meaningful relationship lasting nearly two years, I'm leaving my accounting system for a new one. I'm not the fickle type, and the thought of setting up a new chart of accounts, designing financial statements all over again, and keying in two years' worth of historical data is not something I take lightly. I really intended to be faithful when I shelled out several hundred dollars for the system I currently use, but the lure of Dac-Easy Accounting is just too much to resist.

Here's the bad news first: Dac-Easy does everything a high-priced multimodule accounting system does except for one thing: there is no payroll system. Also, if your annual gross revenues are a billion dollars or more, then Dac-Easy is not for you. The largest number it can handle is $999,999,999.

Now the good news: Dac-Easy integrates modules for general ledger, accounts payable, accounts receivable, purchase orders, billing, inventory, and forecasting—all on a single floppy disk at a list price of $69.95. The integrated accounting system that is most similar to Dac-Easy costs $650 per module and omits the forecasting feature.

Dac-Easy is, above all, a fully integrated system. Entries made in one part of the system are automatically posted to the other relevant parts. For example, sales invoices are posted automatically to accounts receivable and the general ledger; items listed on the invoice are deducted automatically from inventory. The system automatically enters back-order information if there are not enough units in inventory to fill the order. That's integration.

Dac-Easy also does other wonderful things with inventory information: It forecasts requirements based on past sales and issues inventory alerts when stock levels fall below specified minimums. Inventory reports can be sorted by profit per unit, by gross return on investment or by any of nine other criteria.

Tracking accounts receivables can be done

by the open-invoice or balance-forward methods. Open invoice keeps each invoice on record until its balance is zero; balance forward deletes individual customer transactions at the end of the month and carries only the account balance into the new month. If your company uses one system and the new accounting package insists on the other, you either give in or file for divorce on the basis of irreconcilable differences. Dac-Easy gives you the choice.

Best of all is the fact that you don't have to close out one month before starting another. You can post transactions to any month, simply by entering the correct date at data-entry time and then by choosing the correct month at posting time. This feature is what stole me away from my current accounting system. Without it, I must wait until all invoices from the previous month have been received, entered, and posted before I can start entering transactions for the present month.

The forecasting module is a real gem, and another reason why I'm switching over. Forecasting can be done with every module, and you can choose from several methods for computing the forecast. Before you develop your budget, you can try out each method and see what difference results.

There are other features as well: the ability to add custom messages to invoices and past-due statements; the ability to produce more reports than any one business could possibly need, sorted and ranked in an enormous variety of ways, and aging reports—both for accounts receivable and for accounts payable.

Application Questions

☐ What common business information systems are supported by the Dac-Easy Accounting Package?

☐ What are some of the benefits of this package for a small business user?

Source: Mickey Williamson, "Dac Software's Dac-Easy Accounting," *PC Week*, August 27, 1985, p. 70.

SUMMARY

☐ Important computer-based information systems in accounting, finance, banking, and investments were discussed in this chapter. Figures 14–1, 14–2, and 14–3 summarize many of these systems.

☐ Several common business information systems exist in both large and small computer-using business firms, whether they are experienced computer users or are using the computer for the first time. The objectives, input, database, and output of the following seven common business applications were described in this chapter: (1) sales order/transaction processing, (2) inventory control, (3) billing and sales analysis, (4) accounts receivable, (5) accounts payable, (6) payroll and labor analysis, and (7) general ledger.

KEY TERMS AND CONCEPTS

These are the key terms and concepts of this chapter. The page number of their first explanation is in parentheses.

1. Accounting information systems *(486)*
2. Accounts payable *(511)*
3. Accounts receivable *(508)*
4. Applications in banking *(492)*
5. Applications in investments *(494)*
6. Billing and sales analysis *(504)*
7. Common business information systems *(488)*
8. Electronic funds transfer *(494)*
9. Financial performance models *(492)*
10. Financial information systems *(490)*
11. General ledger *(516)*
12. Inventory control *(501)*
13. Payroll and labor analysis *(514)*
14. Personal financial management *(497)*
15. Sales order/transaction processing *(499)*

REVIEW AND APPLICATION QUIZ

Match one of the **key terms and concepts** listed above with one of the brief examples or definitions listed below. Try to find the "best fit" for answers that seem to fit more than one term or concept. Defend your choices.

_____ 1. Accomplish legal and historical record-keeping and gather information for the planning and control of business operations.

_____ 2. Includes systems like inventory control, accounts payable, payroll, and general ledger.

_____ 3. Processes orders received from customers.

_____ 4. Records changes in inventory.

_____ 5. Produces customer invoices.

_____ 6. Keeps track of amounts owed by customers.

_____ 7. Keeps track of purchases from suppliers.

_____ 8. Produces employee paychecks.

_____ 9. Produces the financial statements of the firm.

_____ 10. Includes systems for cash management, capital budgeting, and financing requirements analysis.

———— 11. Provides a DSS capability for financial analysis.

———— 12. Includes checking account, loan, and credit card processing.

———— 13. Using automated teller machines and POS terminals.

———— 14. Includes security analysis and portfolio management.

———— 15. Includes financial planning and record-keeping for individuals.

1. If you have not already done so, read and answer the questions after the two Real World Applications in this chapter.

APPLICATION PROBLEMS

2. Match one of the following accounting information systems with one of the examples listed below.
   a. Budgeting.   c. Fixed asset accounting.
   b. Cost accounting.   d. Tax accounting.

   ———— 1. Includes record-keeping for the use and depreciation of equipment.
   ———— 2. Involves revenue and expense projections.
   ———— 3. Records the liability and payment of business taxes.
   ———— 4. Records and apportions costs within a business.

3. Match one of the following financial information systems with one of the examples listed below.
   a. Capital budgeting.   d. Portfolio management.
   b. Cash management.   e. Financial forcasting.
   c. Credit management.   f. Financing requirements analysis.

   ———— 1. Helps businesses deposit or invest excess funds quickly.
   ———— 2. Supports the analysis of alternate financing methods.
   ———— 3. Evaluates the profitability of proposed long-term expenditures.
   ———— 4. Develops projections for future wage, price, and interest levels.
   ———— 5. Manages for an optimum mix of securities.
   ———— 6. Helps minimize bad debt losses.

4. Five examples of information processing are given below. Identify the common business information system that would include these activities:
   a. Checks are printed for all employees on sick leave.
   b. A detailed listing of all products in stock is produced.
   c. Payments from customers being entered via a VDT are checked for the presence of all required fields.
   d. Out-of-date customer addresses are replaced with current addresses.
   e. A trend analysis report of overhead expenses for five years is produced.

5. The controller (chief accounting officer) of ABC Department Stores wants the firm to purchase a large integrated software package, which would significantly change the input and output methods for all of the

common business information systems of the firm. The marketing VP objects to the changes that would result to the sales order/transaction processing system and to the sales analysis application. The director of personnel objects to the changes that would occur in the payroll and labor analysis application. The controller feels that, since these are accounting applications, she should have the final say in this decision. Why do you think the marketing VP and personnel director are concerned? What would you recommend? Defend your recommendation.

6. Which common business information system should be improved if the following complaints were brought to your attention?
   a. "Month-end closings are always late."
   b. "We are never sure how much of a certain product we have on the shelves."
   c. "Many of us didn't get a W-2 form this year."
   d. "We're tired of manually writing up a receipt every time a customer buys something."
   e. "Our suppliers are complaining that they are not being paid on time."
   f. "Our customers resent being sent notices demanding payment when they have already paid what they owe."
   g. "Nobody is sure which of our sales reps is our top producer."

7. List three of the computer applications in banking that you have personally experienced due to your use of specific banking services. What do you like about how each of these is computerized? What would you recommend to improve each of these services, in terms of computer hardware (machines and media), software (programs and procedures), and people (specialists and users)?

8. The VP for finance of ABC Department Stores is pleased with its computer-based information systems in accounting. But he says its applications in finance are inadequate. What are some of the computer-based systems he might be dissatisfied with? Which of these financial applications would you select as the most important for a department store? Why?

MODULE

V

MANAGEMENT
OF
INFORMATION
SYSTEMS

C H A P T E R

15

MANAGING INFORMATION SYSTEM RESOURCES

Chapter Outline

Learning Objectives

The purpose of this chapter is to promote a basic understanding of the major challenges that computer-based information systems present to business managers by analyzing (1) the information resource management concept and (2) the management of information services. After reading and studying this chapter, you should be able to:

1. Identify two major ways that computers have affected managers.

2. Explain how the computer can support either the centralization or decentralization of information systems, management, and business operations.

3. Identify the five major dimensions of the information resource management concept and explain their implications for the management of information system resources.

4. Explain how the problem of poor computer performance can be solved by management involvement in planning and control.

5. Identify several reasons for user resistance to computerization.

6. Discuss how and why solving the problems of user resistance requires meaningful user involvement.

7. Identify several activities that are involved, and outline the job responsibilities of several types of careers in each of the five basic functions of an information services organization: systems development, user services, data administration, operations, and administration.

8. Identify several methods for managing the system development function, including the concept of project management.

9. Identify some of the planning and control activities of the computer operations management function.

Section I: Information Resource Management

Who should manage MIS? Managers or technicians? Users or specialists? Somebody has to. Inadequate management of information services by many business firms is well documented. Thus there is a real need for you to understand how to manage this vital organizational function. In this section we will stress the **information resource management** concept, which emphasizes that managing the information system resources of a business firm has become a major responsibility of business managers. In the next section we will analyze the basic functions performed by information services groups within a computer-using firm, and discuss methods of managing these functions. Finally, we will discuss some of the career opportunities available in the information systems field.

THE IMPACT OF COMPUTERS ON MANAGEMENT

When computers were introduced into business, predictions were made that there would be significant changes in management. The information processing power and programmed decision-making capability of computers would cause drastic reductions in employees, including middle management and supervisory personnel. A centralized computer system would process all of the data for an organization, control most of its operations, and make most of its decisions. This has not proven to be the case.

Changes in organizational structure and types of personnel have occurred, but they have not been as dramatic as predicted. Naturally, highly automated systems do not require as many people as manual methods. Therefore, there have been significant reductions in the amount of people required to perform manual tasks in certain organizations. However, this has been countered to some extent by the need for increased information processing personnel and computer professionals to run the computer-based systems of the organization.

Centralization or Decentralization of Operations and Management

Have computers caused centralization or decentralization of business operations and management? Modern computer systems can support either the **centralization** (with a large central computer) or **decentralization** (with a distributed processing network) of **information systems** within an organization. The same observation can be applied to the centralization and decentralization of **operations** and **management** within computer-using organizations.

- ☐ **Centralization.** Large central computer systems allow top management to centralize decision making formerly done at lower levels of the organization. Centralization of operations can reduce the number of branch offices, manufacturing plants, and warehouses needed by the firm.
- ☐ **Decentralization.** Distributed systems of computers tied together by data communications networks allow top management to delegate more responsibility to middle managers. They can also decentralize operations by increasing the number of branch offices (or other company units) while still having the ability to control the organization.

Thus whether the computer encourages centralization or decentralization of business operations and management depends on the philosophy of top management and the nature of the operations of a specific business firm.

Management Impact

The **impact of computers on management** seems to be concentrated into two main areas. First, computers have dramatically increased the information base and information processing capacity available to managers. Computing power and information resources are now more readily available to most managers. Advances in personal computing, hardware and software packages, distributed processing, database processing, office automation, and decision support systems have been responsible for this development. Thus computer use has spread from lower and middle managers to top management. Figure 15–1 illustrates the results of a study of computer use among senior executives in 1,000 U.S.-based companies.

Secondly, computers have presented managers with a major *managing* challenge. Managing the information system resources of a business firm has become a major management responsibility. Data, information, and computer hardware, software, and personnel are valuable resources that must be managed by all levels of management for the good of the entire organization. This activity is no longer the sole province of information systems managers and specialists. Thus the concept of **information resource management** has arisen as a major new responsibility of management. Managers must now be involved in managing information system resources to ensure effective use of information for the operational and strategic benefit of the firm.

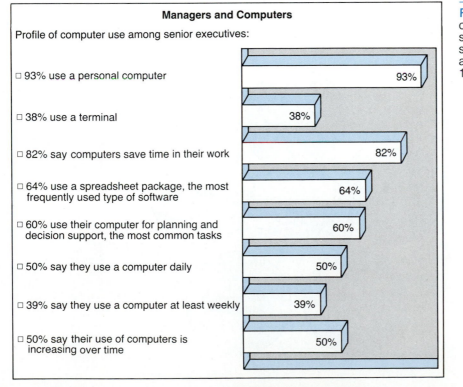

Figure 15–1 Managers' use of computers. Notice that even senior executives are making significant use of computers according to a recent study of 1,000 corporations.

INFORMATION RESOURCE MANAGEMENT

What is **information resource management** (IRM)? It is a concept that has become a popular way to emphasize a major change in the role and mission of the information services function in many organizations. IRM has the following five major dimensions, as illustrated in Figure 15–2.

Resource Management

IRM views data, information, and computer hardware, software, and personnel as valuable resources that should be effectively and efficiently managed for the benefit of the entire organization. If plant and equipment, money, and people are considered valuable organizational resources, so should its data and information resources!

Integrated Technologies

IRM emphasizes that all technologies that process and deliver data and information must be managed as an integrated system of organizational resources. This includes telecommunications and office systems, as well as computer-based information processing. These "islands of technology" are bridged by the IRM concept, and are a major responsibility of the executive in charge of all information services, the **chief information officer** (CIO) of the organization.

Management Responsibility

IRM emphasizes that managing information system resources has become a major responsibility of the management of the organization at all levels. It is not just the responsibility of the organization's chief information officer. If you're a manager, IRM is one of your responsibilities!

Figure 15–2 The information resource management (IRM) concept. Notice that there are five major dimensions to the job of managing information system resources.

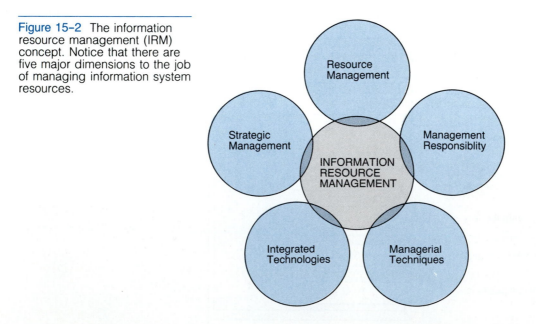

Managerial Techniques

The IRM concept stresses that the management of an organization must apply managerial concepts and techniques to the management of information resources. They must use managerial techniques (like planning models, management by objectives, financial budgets, etc.) just as they do with other major resources and activities of the business.

Strategic Management

Finally, the IRM concept stresses that the information services function in the firm must be more than a provider of computer services. It must also make major contributions to the profitability and strategic objectives of the firm. Information services must move from being an *information utility* to being a *producer of information products* that earn profits for the firm and give it a *comparative advantage* over its competitors. Figure 15–3 summa-

Figure 15–3 Examples of ways companies can gain a competitive edge with their information systems resources.

Customer Service
By letting customers tap into your database to track their orders and shipments, you build loyalty and smooth relations.

New Businesses
Information technologies make whole new products and services possible. Hardware, software, and information resources can be imbedded in new customer services or products.

Product Development
By providing a toll-free number for consumer questions and complaints, your computers can capture ideas for product improvement and new products.

Locking in Customers
By creating exclusive computer communications with customers for order entry and exchange of product and service data, you can help thwart competitors.

Market Intelligence
By assembling and manipulating data on demographics and competitors, your computers can help you spot untapped niches, develop new products, and avoid inventory crunches.

Financial Management
By setting up computer links between the treasurer's office and your banks, you can obtain financial information faster—and that means better cash management.

Telemarketing
Testing cold leads by telephone first—using computer runs to ferret out the best prospects—helps slash sales-force expenses and boost productivity.

Sales Productivity
Giving salespeople portable computers so they can get messages faster and enter orders directly adds up to quicker deliveries, better cash flow, and less paperwork.

Selling Extra Processing Power
You can use off-peak processing power to develop completely new services for outsiders. That way, you can transfer some of the high costs of building your information network

rizes several ways that companies can use information system resources to gain a competitive edge.

Information resource management is a vital concept in today's computer environment because of three major developments:

☐ Information systems technology and its application to users' needs is growing and changing rapidly. Hardware and software resources can now better support a wide variety of traditional and new business uses.

☐ Inadequate performance and unsatisfactory use of information systems and resources is a major problem in many organizations. Top management is unwilling to accept this state of affairs, and is demanding new approaches to managing information services.

☐ Information systems can now give a firm a major strategic advantage over its competitors in the market place. Top management wants to find new and creative ways to use information resources in pursuing the strategic objectives of the firm.

Several major advances in information systems technology have made implementing the IRM concept both feasible and necessary. These include advances in database processing, data communications, distributed processing, and application development. Therefore, information resource management relies on information systems technologies to provide the organization with:

☐ *Distributed systems* of user department and headquarters computer facilities for dispersing computing power throughout the organization.

☐ *Interconnected* by data communications networks for sharing computing resources.

☐ *Integrated* by a common database systems approach for sharing data resources.

☐ *Developed* by user-driven and computer-assisted applications development facilities for responsive user applications.

☐ *Coordinated* by an organizationwide information systems plan for effective information resource management.

Information Systems Planning

A growing number of business firms are developing a "master information systems plan" for managing the information system resources of their organizations. This plan involves a study of how the information services function can contribute to the stratetic objectives contained in the long-range master plan for the entire organization. The emphasis is on planning a **portfolio** of computer-based information systems that will improve the firm's performance and competitive position. Assessment is made of information systems problems and opportunities, and of hardware, software, and people capabilities.

The master plan formulates policies, objectives, and strategies for delivering information services and allocating information system resources. It also contains a description of the information systems development projects that

Figure 15-4 Information systems planning. Notice the many activities, considerations, and outputs in both strategic and annual planning.

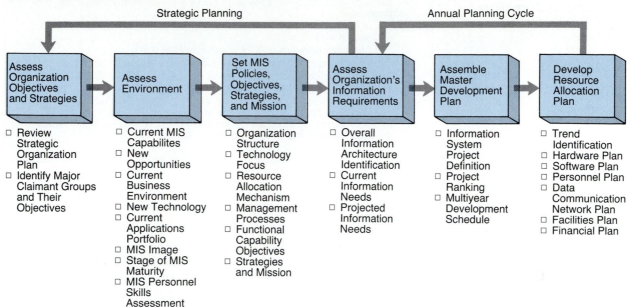

	Strategic Planning			Annual Planning Cycle	
Assess Organization Objectives and Strategies	Assess Environment	Set MIS Policies, Objectives, Strategies, and Mission	Assess Organization's Information Requirements	Assemble Master Development Plan	Develop Resource Allocation Plan
□ Review Strategic Organization Plan □ Identify Major Claimant Groups and Their Objectives	□ Current MIS Capabilites □ New Opportunities □ Current Business Environment □ New Technology □ Current Applications Portfolio □ MIS Image □ Stage of MIS Maturity □ MIS Personnel Skills Assessment	□ Organization Structure □ Technology Focus □ Resource Allocation Mechanism □ Management Processes □ Functional Capability Objectives □ Strategies and Mission	□ Overall Information Architecture Identification □ Current Information Needs □ Projected Information Needs	□ Information System Project Definition □ Project Ranking □ Multiyear Development Schedule	□ Trend Identification □ Hardware Plan □ Software Plan □ Personnel Plan □ Data Communication Network Plan □ Facilities Plan □ Financial Plan

the business firm intends to accomplish in the future (i.e., in the next two to five years). The plan indicates a tentative timetable for the projects and provides "ball park" estimates of the resources required and the benefits to be obtained. In some large firms, long-range planning groups at the corporate level or in the information systems division gather data and formulate the alternatives required in the planning process. These alternatives are presented to top management for review and final decision making. Figure 15-4 illustrates the major activities and outputs in long-range and annual MIS planning.

POOR COMPUTER PERFORMANCE

Computers are used by business firms to reduce costs, increase profits, provide better service to customers, and provide better information to management. Computers should reduce the cost of doing business by automating the processing of data and the control of operations. Better customer service and improved management information are supposed to result from the speed and accuracy of the computer. Thus computers should improve the competitive position and profit performance of business firms.

However, these promised benefits have not occurred in many documented cases. Studies by management consulting firms, computer-user groups, and others have shown that many business firms moved too far and too fast into computer processing without adequate management involvement. It is obvious that the management of these computer-using firms have not been successful in managing their own computers and information services departments. Valuable information system resources are not being

Figure 15–5 Examples of performance problems in computing. Such problems occur in both large and small firms.

☐ Users cannot obtain applications when they want them. There is often a delay of years because of the large backlog of systems development projects.

☐ It is difficult or impossible to obtain changes that managers need in a reasonable amount of time.

☐ The programs have errors in them or sometimes don't work.

☐ Systems delivered often do not match the true user requirements.

☐ Specifications, on which users have to sign off, are difficult to check and are usually full of inconsistencies, omissions, and errors.

☐ Systems cost much more to develop and to maintain than anticipated.

☐ Because of the long time required to obtain results, the most important decision support systems are never implemented. The support is needed more quickly than the time needed to create the programs.

effectively, efficiently, and economically used by such business firms. For example:

☐ Computers are not being used *effectively* by companies that use them primarily for record-keeping applications, instead of decision making and strategic applications.

☐ Computers are not being used *efficiently* by information service departments that provide inadequate service to users while failing to properly utilize their computing capacity.

☐ Many computer systems are also not being used *economically*. Information processing costs have risen faster than other costs in many business firms, even though the cost of processing each unit of data is decreasing due to improvements in hardware and software technology.

Poor computer performance can take many forms, as illustrated by the list of problems in computing gathered from users and management and shown in Figure 15–5. Further, poor computer performance is not limited to small business firms with limited financial and human resources. Many large business firms have openly admitted their failure to manage computers effectively.

What is the solution to the problem of poor computer performance? There are no quick and easy solutions to this problem. However, the experiences of successful computer users reveal that the basic ingredient of high-quality computer performance is extensive and meaningful **management** and **user involvement** in the development and operation of computer-based information systems. This should be the key ingredient in shaping the response of management to the challenge of improving the quality of computer services.

MANAGEMENT INVOLVEMENT

Proper management involvement requires the knowledgeable and active participation of managers in the planning and control of computer-based information system resources. Managers must practice information resource management: the management of hardware, software, people, data, and

information resources. Being an involved manager means knowing the answers to such questions as:

☐ How do our information system resources contribute to the short-
and long-term profitability of this company? To helping us meet the
strategic objectives of this company?

☐ Have we invested too little or too much in information system
resources?

☐ Do we have realistic long-range plans for information systems
development and for acquisition of computer resources that will
improve the efficiency of business operations and the quality of
management decisions?

☐ Are information systems development projects and our computer
operations being properly managed?

Without a high degree of management involvement, managers will not
know the answers to such questions and thus will not be able to control the
quality of computer performance.

Several studies have shown that companies successfully using computers
view the development and management of computer-based information
systems as a responsibility of both top management and operating management. For example, these companies have come to understand that systems
analysts cannot design information systems that effectively support the decision needs of management without management involvement in the systems
design process. Systems development projects will not "manage themselves." They need the planning and control activities of management personnel. The information services department needs the active support of top
management and user management to improve and maintain the quality of
computer services. Figure 15–6 illustrates the following levels of management involvement.

☐ Many business firms use an *executive information services* committee of top management to develop long-range plans and to
coordinate the development of information systems. This committee
includes the senior management of the major divisions of the firm,
as well as the vice president of the information services organization.

☐ A *steering committee* of middle managers, operating managers, and
management personnel from the information services department
may be created to oversee the progress of project teams. The
committee meets on a regular basis during the existence of systems
projects to review progress made, to settle disputes, and to change
priorities, if necessary.

☐ Development of major strategic information systems requires
management involvement. This is accomplished through active
participation by individual managers in systems development projects. Managers must also provide constructive feedback concerning
the quality of computer services provided to their units by the
information services department.

Figure 15–6 Examples of management involvement. Successful information services performance requires several levels of management involvement.

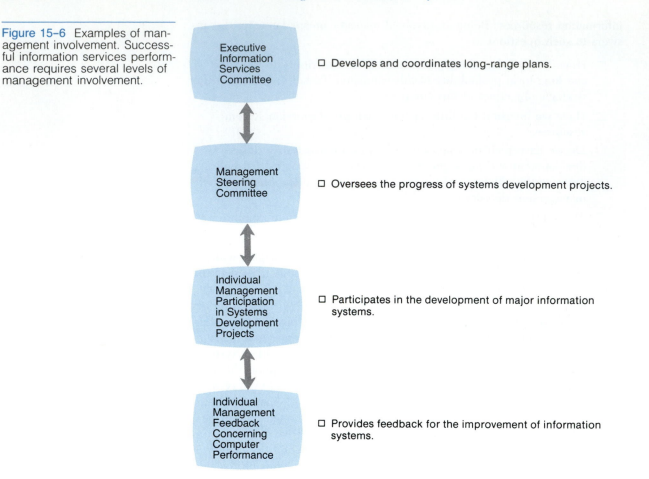

Executive Information Services Committee
□ Develops and coordinates long-range plans.

Management Steering Committee
□ Oversees the progress of systems development projects.

Individual Management Participation in Systems Development Projects
□ Participates in the development of major information systems.

Individual Management Feedback Concerning Computer Performance
□ Provides feedback for the improvement of information systems.

USER INVOLVEMENT

Any "new way of doing things" generates some resistance by the people affected. However, computer-based information systems can generate a significant amount of fear and reluctance to change. There are many reasons for this state of affairs, some of which we will explore in a discussion concerning the impact of computers on society in Chapter 17. Whatever the reasons for **user resistance,** it is the responsibility of business managers and computer professionals to find ways of reducing the conflict and resistance that arises from the use of computers. A brief summary of several reasons for user resistance is outlined in Figure 15–7.

Solving the problems of user resistance requires meaningful **user involvement** based on formal methods of (1) *education,* (2) *communication,* and (3) *participation.* Like management, user personnel must be educated in the fundamentals of computer technology and its application to business information systems. This basic knowledge should be supplemented by programs of orientation, education, and training concerning specific computer-based information systems.

Ignorance. Computer users do not have a sufficient knowledge of information processing, while computer professionals do not have a sufficient knowledge of the operations and problems of the business. Users may lack awareness of a computer's capabilities and limits.

Performance. Poor computer performance, resulting in broken promises and inadequate service. Users may be getting either too little or too much information.

Participation. Users have not been made active participants in systems development and systems maintenance.

Ergonomics. Hardware and software are not designed for ease of use, safety, and comfort of end users; not "user friendly."

Communication. Computer users may not understand the technical jargon of computer professionals, and information systems personnel may not understand the unique terminology of each group of computer users.

Personnel Problems. Some computer users resent the influence of computer professionals on their work activities. Information services personnel are viewed as "technical types," with different work assignments, different working conditions, and different promotion and other personnel policies.

Organizational Conflict. The information services department is viewed as trying to gain too much influence and control within the organization, getting involved in too many operations of the company, and receiving a disproportionate share of the financial resources of the company. Users may feel their job security is threatened by computers.

Figure 15–7 Reasons for user resistance.

We have discussed several methods of increasing user participation and communication in previous chapters. We have emphasized, in particular, the necessity of (1) providing resources such as information centers, which allow users to develop their own systems and (2) including user representatives on project teams charged with the development of major information systems. We stressed that direct user participation should provide the type of user involvement required to improve the quality of information services and to reduce the potential for user resistance. Such user involvement helps assure that computer-based information systems are "user oriented" in their design. Systems that tend to inconvenience or to frustrate their users cannot be effective systems, no matter how efficiently they process data.

Several methods of user involvement are employed by successful organizations. The manager of the information services department may meet frequently with the heads of user departments on an individual basis to discuss the status of new and existing systems. In addition, some firms have created *user liaison* positions. Computer-user departments are assigned representatives from the information services department, who perform a vital role by "troubleshooting" problems, gathering and communicating information, and coordinating educational efforts. These activities improve communication and coordination between the user and the information services department. This avoids the "runaround" effect that can frustrate computer users and is an important reminder of the user orientation of the information services department. Finally, the creation of information centers that provide hardware, software, and people resources to users is a major development in user involvement.

Pillsbury Company

Squeezing in a meeting during breakfast in his hotel suite, genial yet intent in sizing up the focus of an interview, John Hammitt exhibits the businesslike demeanor suited to the concept of chief information officer. Indeed Hammitt, who started his career as a chemical engineer and who holds an MBA from the University of Chicago, describes his role at Pillsbury Co. as guiding information systems strategy and investments, with no day-to-day responsibilities.

But, unlike some others in such a position, Hammitt eschews the title of chief information officer, taking instead vice president for information management. In fact, he thinks the title of CIO is a little presumptuous. "I think we do ourselves more harm than good by trying to propose a title like that, that maybe inflates the position without necessarily having substance behind it," he said during an interview while visiting Dallas.

But Hammitt, 42, who reports to Pillsbury's executive vice president and chief financial officer, Roger Headrick, says he firmly believes in the value of a corporate information strategist. That has been his role since joining Minneapolis-based Pillsbury in 1983 after serving as director of information systems for Morton Thiokol, Inc. Hammitt arrived at Pillsbury after the company had experienced a 10-year hiatus in substantial spending on information systems. "It was more and more difficult to know what was going on on a timely basis," he says. Different people had been in charge of various pieces of the information operation.

Hammitt moved in with a three-pronged strategy: to create a culture tying information systems investments more closely to bottom-line considerations; to bring on managers who are well grounded in general business; and to tighten management through more stringent accounting, planning, and personnel development.

Now, with an information technology blueprint in hand, Hammitt's department is on a track of 20 percent per year spending growth, a rate that about equals Pillsbury's gain in sales for the past fiscal year. It is introducing systems integrating IBM, Honeywell, Inc., and Hewlett-Packard Co. computers for planning, production, and distribution for Pillsbury's packaged food and for Burger King Corp. and other restaurant operations. The aim is to provide customers with the lowest possible delivered cost, Hammitt says.

Hammitt's planning has resulted in a corporatewide information systems architecture incorporating data management, communications, hardware, software, and users. Hammitt says he believes the most important attribute of an information systems strategist is an ability to regard the systems with a long-term, companywide perspective in order to anticipate problems and opportunities.

"I see an awful lot of people in our profession today who, because they have operated so closely to the technology, lose sight of what value that has to the company at large," he says. The key is to help top managers appreciate where investments in technology could make a difference, regardless of the details of the investment. "We're in a business climate now that requires that we distinguish ourselves from our competition in whatever way we can. I think that that comes through the creativity of finding some talented people and putting them together and getting out of the way, supporting them in their success."

Application Questions

☐ Is John Hammitt practicing information resource management? Explain.

☐ Is he acting like a chief information officer? Explain.

Source: David A. Ludlum, "MBA's Recipe for Success Has Dough Raising at Pillsbury MIS," *Computerworld,* October 13, 1986, pp. 1 and 6.

Section II: Managing Information Services

How do computer-using firms manage the delivery of information services to their users? In this section we will analyze how information services groups are (1) organized into functional areas, (2) staffed by information systems specialists, and (3) managed by a variety of managerial techniques. This should give you a good idea of the managerial responsibilities involved in providing information services to users. Figure 15–8 illustrates the challenge of managing information services as seen by the information systems managers of the 1,000 largest corporations in the United States.

ORGANIZING INFORMATION SERVICES

How are information services organized? In larger organizations, information services are usually provided by departmental or divisional units. We will use the name *information services department* for these groups, though such other names as information systems, information processing, computer services, data processing, EDP, or MIS department are also used. However, no matter what name is used, information services departments perform several basic functions and activities. These can be grouped into five basic functional categories: (1) **systems development**, (2) **user services**, (3) **data administration**, (4) **operations**, and (5) **administration**. Figure 15–9 illustrates this grouping of **information services functions** and activities into a functional organizational structure.

The internal organizational structure of an information services organization must reflect its major functions and activities. However, the particular structure used depends on many factors, including organizational location, centralization or decentralization of information processing activities, and the size of the information services organization. Figure 15–10 illustrates the organizational structure of a medium-scale information services organization, including job titles commonly used in such organizations.

Organizational Location

The location of the information services function within the structure of a business firm depends on (1) the type and size of computer operations, and (2) the emphasis given to computer services by management. Large-scale operations usually become independent departments or divisions whose managers may have vice presidential status in the firm. The use of large computers with centralized databases and many remote data communications terminals support such **centralization** of information services. However, the use of microcomputers, minicomputers, and intelligent terminals, connected by data communications networks, supports **decentralization** of information services. Computer power is dispersed among the user departments of an organization in such distributed processing systems.

The extent to which business firms should centralize or decentralize information services depends on many factors. *Centralized* computer facilities may be *more economical* and *efficient* in terms of hardware, software, and personnel cost and use. This is especially true of firms with a high volume of repetitive business data processing. In addition, centralization fosters integration and standardization of information systems within an organization. However, *decentralized* computer services are usually *more responsive* to user needs, encourage greater use of computers, and reduce

Figure 15–8 This illustrates the challenge of managing information services as seen by the information systems managers of the 1,000 largest corporations in the United States.

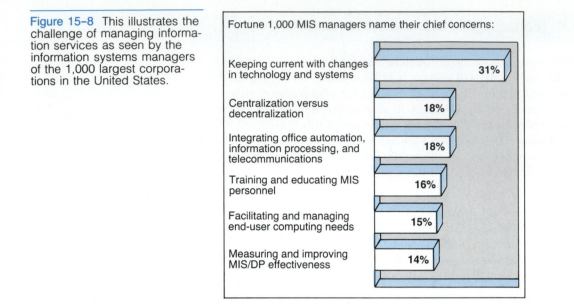

Fortune 1,000 MIS managers name their chief concerns:

Keeping current with changes in technology and systems	31%
Centralization versus decentralization	18%
Integrating office automation, information processing, and telecommunications	18%
Training and educating MIS personnel	16%
Facilitating and managing end-user computing needs	15%
Measuring and improving MIS/DP effectiveness	14%

Figure 15–9 A functional organizational structure for an information services department. Notice the activities that take place in each of the five major functions of information services.

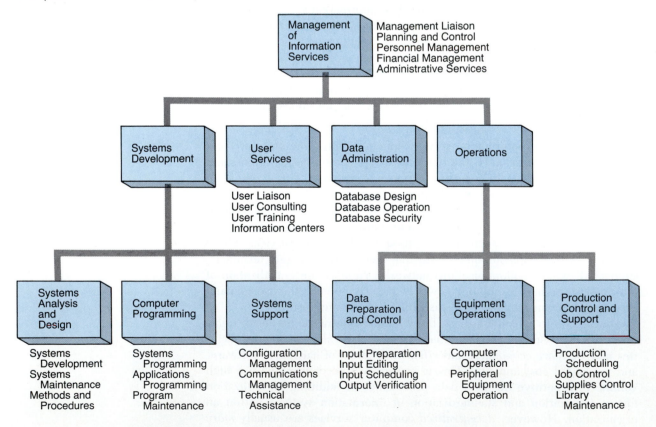

Management of Information Services

Management Liaison
Planning and Control
Personnel Management
Financial Management
Administrative Services

Systems Development

User Services

User Liaison
User Consulting
User Training
Information Centers

Data Administration

Database Design
Database Operation
Database Security

Operations

Systems Analysis and Design

Systems Development
Systems Maintenance
Methods and Procedures

Computer Programming

Systems Programming
Applications Programming
Program Maintenance

Systems Support

Configuration Management
Communications Management
Technical Assistance

Data Preparation and Control

Input Preparation
Input Editing
Input Scheduling
Output Verification

Equipment Operations

Computer Operation
Peripheral Equipment Operation

Production Control and Support

Production Scheduling
Job Control
Supplies Control
Library Maintenance

Figure 15–10 An example of a medium-scale organizational structure. Notice the job titles of personnel in the information services organization.

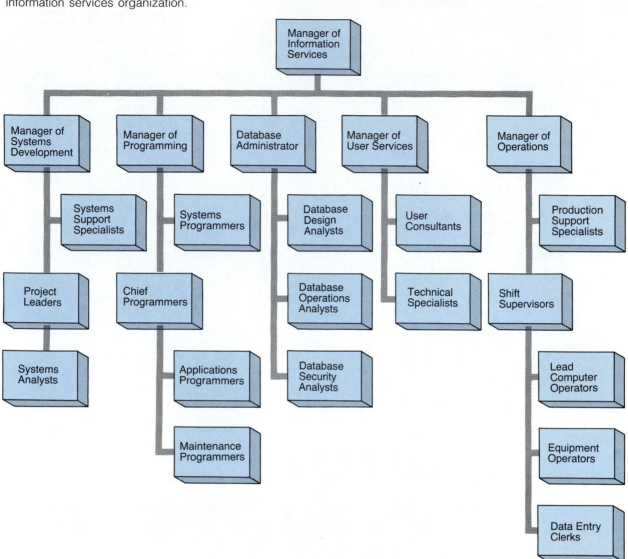

the risks of computer errors and malfunctions. Therefore, many firms are turning to *information centers* as one way to get the benefits of centralized computing resources, yet make them available for end-user computing close to the users' worksites.

The success or failure of an information services organization rests primarily on the quality of its people. Many computer-using firms consider recruiting, training, and retaining qualified personnel as their greatest single problem. Millions of persons are employed in the information services organizations of computer users. National employment surveys continually forecast short-

PEOPLE IN INFORMATION SERVICES

Figure 15-11 Examples of annual salaries for information services personnel in 1987. Notice the variety of job types and the wide range in reported salaries.

Job Title	Salaries		
	Low	Average	High
Vice President of MIS	$51,500	$61,505	$99,999
Director of DP or MIS	37,900	49,754	72,500
Manager of Systems Analysis	36,333	44,505	75,000
Senior Systems Analyst	33,000	38,502	49,250
Systems Analyst	29,667	32,107	38,600
Manager of Applications Programming	37,500	43,753	62,000
Senior Applications Programmer	26,400	31,856	39,333
Applications Programmer	22,750	25,926	34,250
Systems Analysis/Programming Manager	32,618	44,229	65,000
Senior Systems Analyst/Programmer	31,620	33,514	43,500
Systems Analyst/Programmer	25,505	29,854	36,120
Manager of Systems Programming	40,000	48,453	62,500
Senior Systems Programmer	32,000	40,773	51,000
Manager of Database Administration	33,100	47,255	65,000
Database Administrator	25,200	37,357	51,000
Data Communications Manager	40,000	45,417	60,000
Data Communications Analyst	26,500	33,087	41,600
Information Center Manager	31,384	41,029	51,857
User Services Specialist	18,833	27,578	38,000
Manager of Computer Operations	28,750	32,958	48,000
Shift Supervisor	22,500	26,236	33,500
Lead Computer Operator	19,251	20,563	26,333
Computer Operator	15,831	17,699	24,000
Control Clerk	15,120	16,359	22,581
Data Entry Supervisor	16,737	20,720	30,000
Data Entry Operator	13,995	14,958	19,000
Word Processing Supervisor	19,500	24,144	35,000
Word Processing Operator	13,250	15,495	25,000

ages of qualified information services personnel. Employment opportunities in the computer field are excellent, since business firms are expected to continue to expand their use of computers. Therefore, it is important to analyze the types of jobs and the managerial problems associated with information services personnel.

Figure 15-11 gives valuable insight into the variety of job types and the high salaries commanded by many computer services personnel. Of course, these figures are national averages for 1987. Actual salaries can range higher and lower, depending on such factors as the size and geographic location of the information services organization.

Managing Information Services Personnel

Managing information services involves the management of managerial, technical, and clerical personnel. One of the most important jobs of information service managers is to recruit qualified personnel and to develop, organize, and direct the capabilities of the existing personnel. Employees must be continually trained to keep up with the latest developments in a fast-moving and highly technical field. Employee job performance must be continually evaluated and outstanding performance rewarded with salary increases or promotions. Salary and wage levels must be set, and career paths must be designed so individuals can move to new jobs through promotion and transfer as they gain in seniority and expertise.

The management and development of information services personnel poses some unique problems for management. For example, systems analysts and computer programmers are creative, professional personnel. Many firms have found that such professionals cannot be managed with traditional work rules or evaluated by traditional performance criteria. How do you measure how well a systems analyst or programmer is doing? This question has plagued the management of many computer-using business firms.

However, it should be emphasized that this question is not unique to computer professionals but is common to the management of many professional personnel. This is especially true of the scientists and engineers employed in the research and development activities of many organizations. For example effective project planning, controlling, and reporting techniques (especially the modular and team approach of structured programming, analysis, and design) can be used. This helps provide information needed for the evaluation of systems development and programming personnel.

Another personnel management problem area is the professional loyalty of information services personnel. Like other professionals, computer specialists may have a greater loyalty to the information systems profession than to the organization that employs them. For example, computer programmers may consider themselves programmers first and employees second. When this attitude is coupled with the shortages of many types of computer specialists, a serious problem in retaining qualified personnel may arise.

This problem can be solved by effective personnel management. For example, many firms provide information services personnel with opportunities for merit salary increases, project leadership opportunities, and attendance at professional meetings and educational seminars. This helps provide the flexible job environment needed to retain competent personnel. Challenging technological and intellectual assignments, and a congenial atmosphere of fellow professionals are other major factors frequently cited in helping to retain information services personnel. Figure 15–12 gives some examples of what motivates information systems personnel.

Let's begin our study of the basic functions of an information services department with an analysis of the administrative positions and responsibilities involved. The administration of information services requires the performance of several managerial activities. These activities include planning, controlling, managerial liaison, personnel management, financial management, and administrative services. The content of these activities is summarized in Figure 15–13.

ADMINISTRATION OF INFORMATION SERVICES

Figure 15–12 Keys to motivation of information services personnel from a recent survey of information systems professionals.

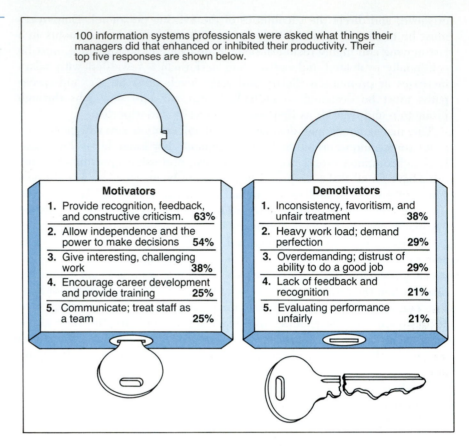

100 information systems professionals were asked what things their managers did that enhanced or inhibited their productivity. Their top five responses are shown below.

Motivators

1. Provide recognition, feedback, and constructive criticism.   **63%**
2. Allow independence and the power to make decisions   **54%**
3. Give interesting, challenging work   **38%**
4. Encourage career development and provide training   **25%**
5. Communicate; treat staff as a team   **25%**

Demotivators

1. Inconsistency, favoritism, and unfair treatment   **38%**
2. Heavy work load; demand perfection   **29%**
3. Overdemanding; distrust of ability to do a good job   **29%**
4. Lack of feedback and recognition   **21%**
5. Evaluating performance unfairly   **21%**

Figure 15–13 Managerial responsibilities in the administration of information services.

Planning. Long- and short-range planning of computer operations, systems development projects, hardware, software, and facilities acquisitions.

Controlling. Monitoring and evaluating of computer operations, systems development projects, and the utilization of hardware, software, facilities, and personnel. Reporting systems are developed to compare performance with plans.

Managerial Liaison. Communicating and reporting to management concerning the plans and performance of the information services department. Managerial liaison also includes meeting and maintaining proper relationships with hardware and software vendors and suppliers.

Personnel Management. Defining personnel requirements, recruiting, and selection of personnel, employee training and development, performance evaluation, and personnel record-keeping.

Financial Management. Developing and maintaining methods of financial record-keeping and financial analysis so that the cost of computer operations and systems development projects can be analyzed and controlled. This activity also includes billing computer users for information services costs, providing cost estimates for planning purposes, and purchasing required hardware, software, and services.

Administrative Services. The supply of services, such as secretarial and clerical assistance, hardware maintenance scheduling, and custodial services.

People in administrative positions direct and supervise the activities of the computer services organization. They include administrative staff positions that support the manager of information services in planning and control activities.

However, a major new senior management position is appearing that transcends traditional information services management. The position of **chief information officer (CIO)** oversees all information technology for a firm, not just traditional computer-based information services. Thus all telecommunications services, automated office systems, and other administrative support services are the responsibility of this executive. Also, the CIO does not direct day-to-day information services activities but concentrates on long-term planning and strategy. See Figure 15–14.

Other administrative positions include the managers of systems analysis and design, programming, systems support, production support, and shift supervisors who supervise equipment operations during each shift of a working day. Additional classifications exist in many computer services organizations due to the recognition of seniority and the assignment of supervisory responsibilities. Thus such titles as lead systems analyst, lead programmer, and lead computer operator recognize the assignment of supervisory responsibilities to these positions. Another widely used administrative job type is the position of project manager or team leader. This person is frequently a senior systems analyst or programmer who supervises the activities of a systems development project team.

The systems development function is responsible for the investigation, analysis, design, implementation, and maintenance of information systems within the computer-using organization. These activities were discussed in Chapter 10. In addition, the systems development function includes activities such as systems and applications programming, configuration management, and communications management.

SYSTEMS DEVELOPMENT

Chief Information Officer. Oversees all the information technology for a firm, including information processing, telecommunications, and office systems. Concentrates on long-term planning and strategy.

Manager of Information Services. Plans and directs the activities of the entire information services organization.

Manager of Systems Development. Directs the activities of systems development personnel and projects.

Operations Manager. Directs the operation of all information processing equipment and the production of all information processing jobs.

Training Coordinator. Develops and administers training programs for information services personnel and computer users.

Budget and Costing Specialist. Develops budgets for the information services organization and evaluates performance against the budget. Develops and administers a system for allocating the cost of computer services to computer users.

Figure 15–14 Job descriptions in administration of information services.

The most common types of jobs in this category are *systems analysts*, *programmers*, and *programmer/analysts*. Larger computer service operations expand this job operation into several specialized job types. Descriptions for some jobs in this category are summarized in Figure 15–15. Figure 15–16 shows traditional and new career paths in systems development.

Planning, organizing, and controlling the systems development function of an information services department is a major managerial responsibility. Typically, several methods of **project management** are used to manage systems development.

Project Management

Project management involves the management of the development work required by large information system projects. The concept of project management requires that each major information system be developed by a *project team* according to a specific *project plan* that is formulated during the systems investigation stage. Assigning systems analysts and programmers to specific projects headed by a project leader allows better control of the progress of systems development. The alternative is to assign personnel to work on projects on a "when available" basis. This method usually results in a lack of project control and a waste of human and financial resources.

The Project Plan

Descriptions of the tasks involved and the assignment of responsibility for each task are included in the project plan. Estimated start-up and completion dates for the entire project, as well as for major checkpoints or "milestones" in the development of the project, are also included. Specified

Figure 15–15 Systems development job descriptions.

Systems Analyst. Gathers and analyzes information from users needed for the development or modification of information systems. Develops a statement of system requirements and prepares detailed system specifications. Supervises installation of new systems and evaluates existing systems for possible improvements.

Systems Designer. Translates system requirements prepared by the systems analyst into alternative systems designs. Develops detailed system specifications for the system being developed.

Communications Analyst. Plans, design, and installs data communications networks, including the specification and selection of software, terminals, and communications control equipment.

Programmer. Develops program logic and codes; tests and documents computer programs.

Applications Programmer. Develops programs required for specific applications of computer users.

Maintenance Programmer. Modifies and improves existing programs.

Systems Programmer. Develops, modifies, and maintains the operating system and other system software used by an information services organization.

Analyst Programmer. A systems analyst who does his or her own applications programming, or vice versa; an applications programmer who does his or her own systems analysis and design.

amounts of time, money, and staff are allocated to each segment of the project. The project plan includes provisions for handling suggested changes to the proposed system. This typically includes a "design freeze" policy, which prohibits major changes in systems design after specified project deadlines unless the change is formally approved by management. Provisions are usually made for revision of the project schedule due to unforeseen developments. Record-keeping forms that report the progress of individual members of a systems development project are also used in many project management systems. Good project management also requires that each phase of systems development be properly documented before new stages are begun.

Project Management Techniques

Major information systems development projects are typically planned and controlled by several types of project management techniques. For example, many firms use special reporting forms to ensure that all systems development projects are properly authorized and controlled. The use of financial and operating budgets is another method of managing systems development projects. Budgets serve as a short-range planning device as well as a method of control. Deviations from budgeted amounts identify projects that need closer management attention.

Several types of charts are used to plan and control projects. One is the Gantt chart, which specifies the times allowed for the various activities required in information systems development. Another is the PERT system (Program Evaluation and Review Technique), which involves developing a network diagram of required events and activities. See Figure 15–17. Computer-assisted systems development includes the use of project management software packages that help users and systems managers accomplish these project management techniques.

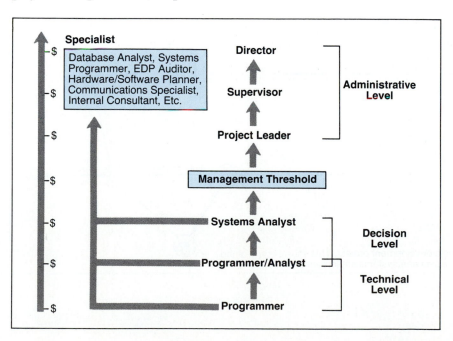

Figure 15–16 Career paths for systems development personnel. Notice the traditional upward path into management and the newer path into various specialist positions.

Figure 15–17 Two project management techniques: The Gantt chart and the PERT network.

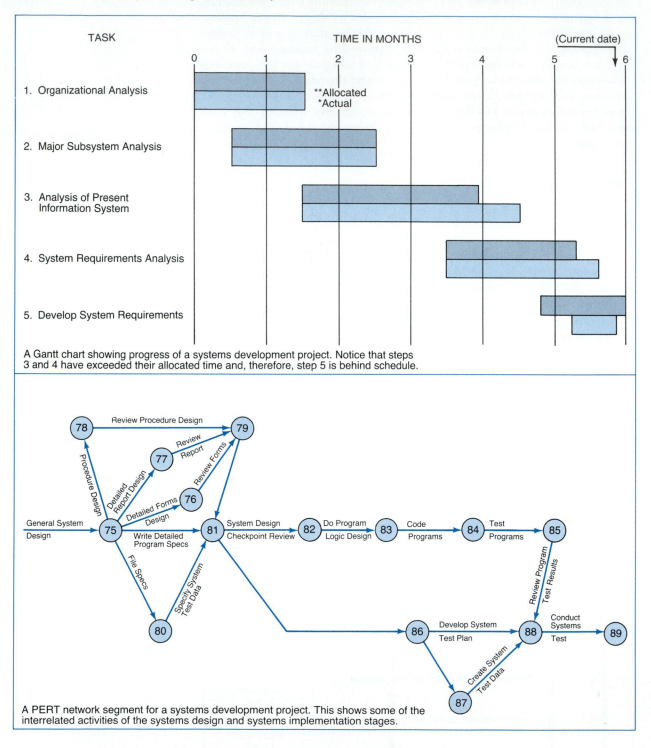

A Gantt chart showing progress of a systems development project. Notice that steps 3 and 4 have exceeded their allocated time and, therefore, step 5 is behind schedule.

A PERT network segment for a systems development project. This shows some of the interrelated activities of the systems design and systems implementation stages.

The number of people in organizations who use or want to use computers to help them do their jobs has outstripped the capacity of many information services departments. Therefore, new ways of providing hardware, software, and people support to users are being developed. The most important is the **information center.** These centrally located support facilities provide:

☐ **Hardware support** for users who need it by providing the use of microcomputers, intelligent terminals, advanced graphics terminals, high-speed printers, plotters, and so on.

☐ **Software support** is provided with advanced software packages such as application development systems, nonprocedural languages, database management systems, and a variety of application software packages.

☐ **People support** is provided by a staff of user consultants—systems analysts/programmers who are trained to educate and help users take advantage of the hardware and software resources of the information center.

USER SERVICES

This major new information services function has created three new job categories in the information centers of large computer-using organizations. They are being filled right now with "people who like to work with people," including former systems analysts and programmers, but also with former computer users. Figure 15–18 summarizes these job descriptions.

Careers in User Services

The widespread use of database processing for business information systems has made managing data and information a major information service function. Since the databases of an organization are used by many different applications, they need to be centrally coordinated and controlled by a data administration function. This usually includes the use of a *database administrator* (DBA), or a database administration department. The functions of data administration include:

DATA ADMINISTRATION

☐ **Data standards.** Designing and defining the standards for data used in the organization and its databases. Development and maintenance of a central data dictionary.

Information Center Manager. Manages the information center and works with the manager of information services in planning the supply of computing services to end users.

Systems Consultant. Assists computer users in the development, prototyping, and maintenance of application systems. Trains users in the use of application development tools and application packages. Frequently serves as a liaison between computer users and the computer services department.

Technical Specialist. Evaluates, selects, installs, and maintains the hardware and software resources of the information center. Provides technical assistance to systems consultants and users.

Figure 15–18 Job descriptions in user services.

☐ **Database design.** Designing the structure and organization of databases. Defining and standardizing the data in the databases. Database software and hardware evaluation and selection.

☐ **Database operations.** Day-to-day control and liaison with users. Maintenance of the databases. Coordination with information centers' use of databases.

☐ **Database security.** Designing, monitoring, and maintaining controls for the security of databases.

Careers in Data Administration

This is another relatively new category of information services careers in large computer-using organizations. Figure 15–19 summarizes four major job types that have been created to implement the database administration function.

OPERATIONS

The operations function of the information services department is concerned with the performance of information processing activities through the use of hardware, software, and personnel resources. The operations function includes major activities such as data preparation, equipment operation, production control, and production support. The content of these activities is summarized below.

☐ **Data preparation and control.** Includes converting input source documents into machine-sensible form such as key-to-disk operations, using a variety of data entry equipment. The data control aspect of this activity refers to the continual checking and monitoring of input data and output reports to insure their accuracy, completeness, and timeliness.

☐ **Equipment operation.** Includes the operation of computer systems, including online peripheral equipment and data communications terminals and control equipment. It also includes the operation of

Figure 15–19 Job descriptions in data administration.

Database Administrator. Designs and maintains the databases of the organization. Prepares and enforces standards for the use and security of information in databases. Develops and maintains a central data dictionary. For large computer-using organizations, this becomes a management position, with duties delegated to other specialists.

Database Design Analyst. Designs the structure and defines the data elements in organizational databases. Evaluates database hardware and software.

Database Operations Analyst. Coordinates day-to-day use of databases with users and other information services staff. Enforces database standards. Maintains the database.

Database Security Analyst. Designs and maintains controls for the security and integrity of databases. Monitors databases to ensure proper use.

offline equipment, such as offline magnetic tape units and printers, and other types of offline data conversion or output support equipment.

☐ **Production control.** Includes the scheduling, monitoring, and control of facilities and processing jobs. It includes the scheduling of equipment, data files, and necessary information processing supplies, scheduling and logging job input and output, and communicating with users on scheduling requirements and the status of specific jobs.

☐ **Production support.** Activities that support information processing operations include acquisition and maintenance of supplies, maintaining a library of data files on magnetic tape or magnetic disks, maintaining a library of operations documentation, providing for the physical security of the computer facilities, and distribution of computer output.

Operations personnel are responsible for the operation of information processing equipment, especially computers and data entry devices. They are also responsible for monitoring and controlling the production status of information processing jobs. See Figure 15–20.

Careers in Computer Operations

Planning and controlling the operations of the information services department is a major management responsibility. Production planning methods result in forecasts of information processing job loads and hardware and software usage. Production control methods monitor computer operations to gather information concerning:

Managing Computer Operations

☐ Job-processing times, hardware and software utilization, time spent by operating personnel, and the production status of each job.

Computer Operator. Monitors and controls the computer by operating the central console. Adjusts the configuration of the computer system in response to messages from the operating system or to instructions contained in the operations documentation. Operates peripheral equipment in smaller installations.

Peripheral Equipment Operator. Assists the computer operator by setting up and operating tape drives, magnetic disk drives, printers, and so on. Also operates offline input/output equipment.

Data Entry Operator. Converts data on source documents into machine-sensible form by use of a keyboard-driven machine such as a key-to-disk, key-to-tape, or video terminal.

Production Coordinator. Coordinates and controls the mix of data processing jobs to achieve optimum equipment utilization and service to users. Prepares and maintains schedules for data processing jobs and maintains records of job and equipment performance.

Figure 15–20 Job descriptions in computer operations.

REAL WORLD APPLICATION 15–2

Ocean Spray Cranberry, Inc.

Plymouth, Massachusetts. The view from the MIS department extends from the Pilgrims' 1620 landing place across sand dunes to a bluefish-filled harbor. The setting tells the casual observer that Ocean Spray Cranberry, Inc. is a tiny regional juice bottler hiding in a quiet New England tourist town where storms spatter sea water on office windows. Ocean Spray's contemporary-style offices—complete with exposed wood beams—seem to support the misconception that the company does not belong in the button-down ranks of big business. Exposed beams even show up in place of the normal suspended ceilings in the computer room, where an IBM 3083 Model EX mainframe computer sits just eight feet above Plymouth Harbor's high-water mark.

Ocean Spray once was but is no longer a "sleepy little regional company." It has gone national, which means its MIS department has to cope with and plan for steady growth and the changing nature of the firm's business, reports MIS director Thomas Modestino. Growth has meant moving up from a minicomputer to an IBM 3090 mainframe.

The company's projected MIS strategy includes the installation of a 3090 Model 150 and periodic updates of a capacity-planning model that Modestino uses to forecast CPU requirements for major applications on a six-month basis through 1990. In addition, the company has gone from a centralized strategy to a decentralized one and back again. In five years, Ocean Spray has added and expanded an information center to support personal computers, developed an electronic order and bill processing system and manufacturing software, and installed a decision support system. All of these moves are intended to support the company's revenue growth while keeping its employment ranks lean. For example, automated order processing can save several jobs at each field location.

In connection with centralization and moving personal computers into field locations, Ocean Spray established an information center and is providing mainframe-based decision support tools to sales and logistics personnel. In addition, the firm has installed and is modifying a manufacturing software system and is emphasizing electronic ordering, invoicing, and

☐ Computer malfunctions, the number and type of reruns, processing delays and errors, and other evidences of unsatisfactory or unusual conditions.

Such information is used to evaluate computer system utilization, costs, and performance. This provides information for both production planning and control of computer system performance. It is also used as the basis of **chargeback** systems which allocate costs to users based on the information services rendered. Finally, such information is used in **quality assurance**

bill payment. Within five years, electronic orders are expected to jump from 5 percent of all Ocean Spray orders to between 70 percent and 80 percent. The Ocean Spray information center provides training to users and tests new technology, particularly microcomputer products. Ocean Spray has about 110 personal computers in headquarters and remote field locations and has approximately 150 employees using IBM 3270 or other terminals.

Modestino says that while decentralization was the popular philosophy industrywide in 1981, and the minicomputer-based solution worked for a time, Ocean Spray outgrew the decentralized system. He notes that it became difficult to keep a common version of an application on multiple remote systems.

Ocean Spray found that its order processing system was redundant with the three levels of processing and that order processing often took 24 hours from receipt at a remote location until a shipment order was returned to that location. With centralization, the order can be processed at headquarters and printed out within minutes on the PC at the remote plant that will fill the order.

Asked whether it is unusual for a company to reverse itself and return to a mainframe-intensive environment, Modestino says, "I'm not sure we are bucking a trend. As you get down into minicomputers, you have to ask yourself what you are doing with the minicomputer that you can't do with a PC. You also won't hear too many people disagree that it is better to have all of your data stored in one place. What we said was, 'Let's store it once, accurately, in one place.'"

Application Questions

☐ Is Ocean Spray really centralizing their information services function? Explain.

☐ How has Thomas Modestino changed the delivery and types of information services provided at Ocean Spray?

Source: James Connolly, "Capacity Plan: Ocean Spray MIS Prepares to Meet 1990," *Computerworld*, September 22, 1986, pp. 1 and 143.

programs which stress quality control of service to computer users.

Software packages known as **system performance monitors** are available. They monitor the processing of computer jobs and help develop a planned schedule of computer operations that can optimize the use of a computer system. Advanced operating systems use performance monitors to monitor computer system performance and produce detailed statistics that are invaluable for effective production planning and control. For example, a system performance monitor could automatically generate the reports shown in Figure 15–21.

Figure 15–21 A computer system performance monitor in action. Notice the activities and files involved and the reports produced.

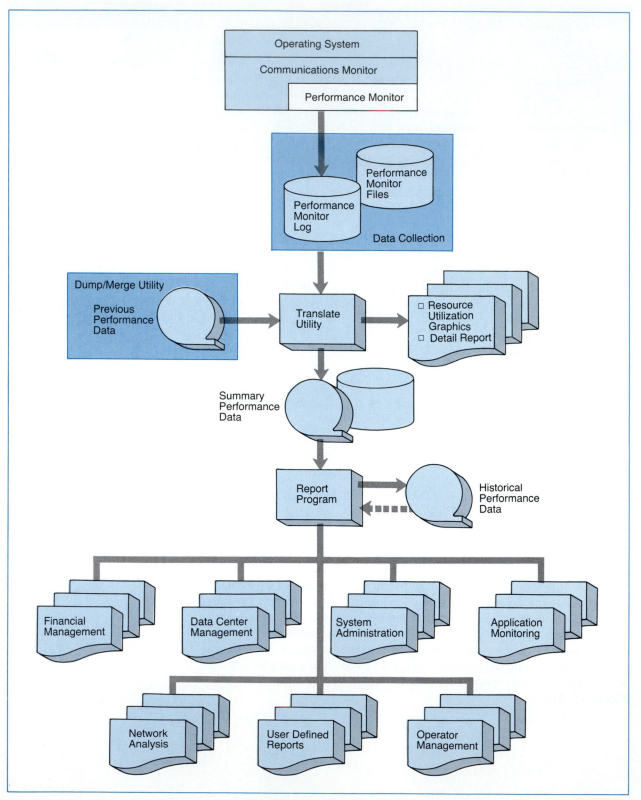

□ Managing the information system resources of a business firm has become a major new responsibility of business management, known as information resources management (IRM). Business computer users must learn how to manage the hardware, software, people, data, and information resources of their firms for the strategic benefit of the entire organization.

□ Poor computer performance in many business firms is well documented and reveals that many computer users and computer professionals have not learned how to manage this vital but expensive business resource. The computer is not being used effectively, efficiently, and economically by many business firms.

□ The experiences of successful computer users reveal that the basic ingredient of high-quality computer performance is extensive and meaningful management and user involvement in the development and operation of computer-based information systems. This should be the key ingredient in shaping the response of management to the challenge of improving the quality of computer services.

□ The major activities of information services organizations can be grouped into five basic functional categories: (1) systems development, (2) user services, (3) data administration, (4) operations, and (5) administration.

□ The organizational structure, location, and staffing of an information services department must reflect these five basic functions and activities. However, many variations exist, which reflect the attempts of business computer users to tailor their organizational and staffing arrangements to their particular business activities and management philosophy, as well as to the capabilities of centralized or distributed information processing.

□ There is a wide variety of career choices and job types in many computer-using organizations. However, computer services personnel can be grouped into five occupational categories that coincide with the basic functional categories of systems development, user services, data administration, operations, and administration. Managing the technical personnel in an information services department is a major personnel management assignment.

□ Another major managerial responsibility in computer-using business firms is the management of their systems development projects. This requires a variety of project management techniques. Managing computer operations requires many applications of operations management, including various production planning and control techniques.

SUMMARY

KEY TERMS AND CONCEPTS

These are the **key terms and concepts** of this chapter. The page number of their first explanation is in parentheses.

1. Careers in information services
   a. Applications programmer (548)
   b. Computer operator (553)
   c. Database administrator (552)
   d. Data entry operator (553)
   e. Systems analyst (548)
   f. Systems consultant (551)
2. Centralization of
   a. information services (541)
   b. operations and management (530)
3. Chief information officer (547)
4. Computer's impact on management (531)
5. Decentralization of
   a. information services (541)
   b. operations and management (530)
6. Information resource management (532)

7. Information services functions
   a. Administration (545)
   b. Data administration (551)
   c. Operations (552)
   d. Systems development (547)
   e. User services (551)
8. Information systems planning (534)
9. Management involvement (536)
10. Managing information services personnel (544)
11. Operations management (553)
12. Poor computer performance (535)
13. Project management (548)
14. User involvement (538)
15. User resistance (539)

REVIEW AND APPLICATION QUIZ

Match one of the **key terms and concepts** listed above with one of the brief examples or definitions listed below. Try to find the "best fit" for answers that seem to fit more than one term or concept. Defend your choices.

_____ 1. Managers have a lot of information and information processing power.

_____ 2. Computers have not been used efficiently, effectively, and economically.

_____ 3. A management steering committee is an example.

_____ 4. The management of data, information, and computer hardware, software, and personnel for the strategic benefit of the entire organization.

_____ 5. Information services proposals must fit into the long-range plans of the organization.

_____ 6. Computers can help management increase the number of regional and branch offices.

_____ 7. Computers can help managers consolidate operations.

_____ 8. Some of the causes are ignorance, performance problems, and lack of participation and communication.

_____ 9. User representatives on systems development teams and information centers are examples.

_____ 10. Systems analysis and design, computer programming, and systems maintenance activities.

_____ 11. User liaison, consulting, and training activities.

_____ 12. Database design, operation, and security.

_____ 13. Data preparation and control and equipment operations.

_____ 14. Planning, controlling, liaison, personnel, and financial management of information services.

_____ 15. Develops programs for information processing jobs of users.

_____ 16. Analyzes users' information needs and develops specifications for new information systems.

_____ 17. Assists users in the use of application packages and application development tools.

_____ 18. Designs and maintains the databases of an organization.

_____ 19. Operates computers and peripheral devices.

_____ 20. Inputs data from source documents into a computer system.

_____ 21. Oversees all of the information services technology of the firm including telecommunications and administrative services.

_____ 22. Management of the development work for proposed information systems.

_____ 23. Planning and control of information processing operations.

_____ 24. Recruiting and developing information services employees.

_____ 25. The use of microcomputers and minicomputers at user sites connected by data communications networks.

1. If you have not already done so, read and answer the questions after the two Real World Applications in this chapter.

2. Match one of the following five dimensions of information resource management with one of the examples listed below.
   a. Integrated technologies.
   b. Management responsibility.
   c. Managerial techniques.
   d. Resource management.
   e. Strategic management.

   _____ 1. Data, information, and computer hardware, software, and people are valuable organizational resources.

   _____ 2. If you're a manager, IRM is one of your responsibilities.

   _____ 3. Telecommunications, automated office systems, and computer-based processing must be managed together.

   _____ 4. Use planning models and financial budgets in managing information systems.

   _____ 5. Using information systems to gain a competitive edge.

APPLICATION PROBLEMS

3. Match one of the following five basic functions of information services departments with one of the examples listed below.
   a. Administration of information services.
   b. Data administration.
   c. Operations.
   d. Systems development.
   e. User services.

   _____ 1. Managing data entry and computer processing.
   _____ 2. Designing new user applications.
   _____ 3. Developing database structures for the organization.
   _____ 4. Running information centers.
   _____ 5. Planning, control, liaison, and administrative services.

4. Match one of the following job titles in the information services industry with one of the examples listed below.
   a. Applications programmer.
   b. Chief information officer.
   c. Computer operator.
   d. Database administrator.
   e. Systems analyst.
   f. Systems consultant.

   _____ 1. Developing a central data dictionary.
   _____ 2. Operates computer systems and peripheral equipment.
   _____ 3. Develops software for users.
   _____ 4. Managing all of the information services of an organization.
   _____ 5. Helping users use computer hardware and software.
   _____ 6. Developing prototypes of new user applications.

5. The information services department at ABC Department Stores was recently studied by a management consulting firm brought in by top management. One of its recommendations was the need for more management involvement in the information systems function. It recommended that this include both corporate management and store managers. Jim Klugman, the VP for MIS, says that he can't see how this will work in practice. Help Jim by outlining several ways this recommendation can be implemented. (Hint: See Figure 15–6.)

6. The management consulting team also recommended more user involvement in systems development and information system operations at ABC Department Stores. The VP for MIS says he won't be able to serve users' information needs if they are so involved that they get in the way of his professional MIS staff. Make several recommendations to the VP for MIS on how user involvement could be implemented.

7. Jim Klugman, the VP for MIS at ABC Department Stores, says that IRM is just another buzzword like MIS. He says that any organization has information processing jobs to do, and his job is to see that they get done efficiently. Do you agree with Jim? What would Jim's attitude be if he believed in the IRM concept? Finish the following sentence for him: "Since I believe in the IRM concept, I feel that the job of the MIS department is to . . ."

8. ABC Department Stores has a large mainframe computer and a 40-person MIS department at corporate headquarters. POS terminals at each department store as well as video display terminals for store managers and buyers are connected in a data communications network to the host computer. Also, a few store managers use personal computers at work. Several store managers feel that ABC should move to a more decentralized information services organization. The VP for MIS says that a distributed processing approach would not work for a department store chain. What do you think? How would you decentralize information services? What problems can you foresee?

9. There is a two-year backlog of user systems development requests at ABC Department Stores. The VP for MIS wants to hire more programmers and systems analysts to reduce this backlog. Top management is resisting this proposal, saying that new ways should be found to solve this problem. Jim Klugman, the VP for MIS, says that concepts like information centers and distributed processing wouldn't work at ABC because each department store is too small to support its own computer facilities and information centers. What do you think? What solution do you have?

10. There has been a rash of resignations of programmers and systems analysts from the MIS department at ABC Department Stores in recent months. One analyst says she is leaving because computing at ABC isn't challenging enough. Another says he feels isolated from developments taking place in the computer industry. A third analyst says she doesn't have enough contact with computer users at ABC. What are these analysts revealing about what motivates information services personnel? How would you solve some of these problems?

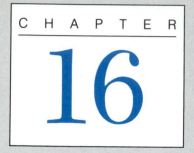

ACQUIRING INFORMATION SYSTEM RESOURCES

Chapter Outline

Learning Objectives

The purpose of this chapter is to promote a basic understanding of how computer resources should be acquired by analyzing (1) the role of the computer industry, (2) the financing and cost of computer resources, (3) the evaluation of computer resources, and (4) factors in microcomputer selection. After reading and studying this chapter you should be able to:

1. Identify several types of firms in the computer industry and the products or services they supply.
2. Identify several benefits and limitations of using external information processing services.
3. Discuss several evaluation factors that should be considered in evaluating hardware, software, and vendor support.
4. Summarize the benefits and limitations of the rental, leasing, and purchase of computer resources.
5. Describe several major categories of information systems costs and identify several specific costs in each category.
6. Identify several methods of controlling the cost of systems development and computer operations.
7. Explain the major factors that must be considered in selecting a microcomputer system.

Section I: Sources and Costs of Information System Resources

THE COMPUTER INDUSTRY: HARDWARE, SOFTWARE, AND SERVICES

Who needs the computer industry? Computer users do. They must acquire **information system resources** (hardware, software, and personnel) and **external services** from many sources in the computer industry. Therefore, you should have a basic understanding and appreciation of the role of the computer industry. You should view the computer industry as a vital source of computer hardware, software, and services. Your effective and efficient use of computers requires the continual support of firms within the computer industry. Figure 16–1 groups the major types of firms within the computer industry into the three major categories of hardware suppliers, software suppliers, and service suppliers.

Though the computer industry consists of over 5,000 companies, only a few firms manufacture *mainframe* computers. The International Business Machines Corporation (IBM), has a major share of the market for such computers. Other mainframe manufacturers include the Unisys Corporation, Control Data Corporation (CDC), and the NCR Corporation.

Of course, the development of *minicomputers* and *microcomputers* has greatly increased the number of companies manufacturing computers. Minicomputers are manufactured by several of the major computer manufacturers such as IBM and the Digital Equipment Corporation (DEC). Other companies, such as Hewlett-Packard, AT&T, Data General, Wang Laboratories, and Prime Computer, specialize in minicomputer manufacturing. Important manufacturers in the microcomputer system and personal computer market include the IBM, Apple Computer, the Tandy Corporation, Commodore International, Hewlett-Packard, and a host of other domestic and foreign firms.

Figure 16–2 lists the top 10 mainframe, microcomputer, minicomputer, and computer software manufacturers in 1986. Of course, there are many other firms in the computer industry that supply hardware, software, and services. For example, large companies such as Intel, Motorola, and National Semiconductor produce microprocessors, memory chips, and other devices. Companies like TRW, General Motors, ADP, Computer Sciences, and McDonnel Douglas are major suppliers of computer services.

Hardware Suppliers

The primary sources of computer hardware are the major computer manufacturers, who manufacture many sizes of computer systems, as well as peripheral equipment and media. Other computer manufacturers may produce microcomputers, minicomputers, small computer systems, special-purpose computers, and a few types of peripheral devices. Other hardware suppliers can be classified as *independent peripheral manufacturers*. These firms confine themselves to the production of peripheral input, output, and storage equipment such as video terminals or magnetic disk drives.

Two other categories of computer hardware manufacturers are the *original equipment manufacturer* (OEM) and the *plug compatible manufacturer* (PCM). OEMs manufacture and sell computers by assembling components

Figure 16–1 The computer industry is a vital source of hardware, software, and services for computer users. Notice that computer manufacturers and retailers can provide hardware and software as well as services.

HARDWARE SUPPLIERS
Computer Manufacturers.
Independent Peripheral Manufacturers.
Original Equipment Manufacturers.
Data Processing Supplies Companies.
Computer Retailers.
Computer Leasing Companies.
Used-Computer Equipment Companies.

SOFTWARE SUPPLIERS
Computer Manufacturers.
Computer Retailers.
Independent Software Companies.
User-Developed Software Suppliers.

SERVICE SUPPLIERS
Computer Manufacturers.
Computer Service Centers.
Computer Retailers.
Time-Sharing Service Companies.
Telecommunications Service Suppliers.
Data Bank Service Suppliers.
Facilities Management Companies.
Independent Consultants.
Other Service Suppliers:
    Computer Time Rental, Systems Design,
    Contract Programming, Education,
    Hardware Maintenance, Turnkey Systems.

produced by other hardware suppliers. PCMs manufacture computer mainframes and peripheral devices that are specifically designed to be compatible (by just "plugging in") with the mainframes or peripherals of major computer manufacturers, especially IBM. Such firms claim that their hardware is similar to that produced by IBM or other major manufacturers but provides better performance at lower cost. For example, the Amdahl Corporation and the National Advanced Systems Company produce large mainframe computers that are marketed as lower-priced versions of IBM mainframes.

Computer retailers sell microcomputers and peripherals to individuals and small businesses. They are an important type of hardware supplier resulting from the development of microcomputer systems used as personal computers and small business computers. Thousands of retail computer stores include independent retailers, national chains such as Computerland and The Computer Store, and some outlets owned by computer manufacturers, such as the Radio Shack stores of the Tandy Corporation.

Figure 16–2 The top 10 mainframe, mini, micro, and computer software companies in the computer industry. Notice (1) the major presence of IBM and international corporations, (2) some of the relatively young firms in the microcomputer industry, and (3) the low ranking of microcomputer software companies.

MAINFRAME SYSTEMS

Rank	Company	Revenues ($ millions)
1	IBM	$14,450.0
2	Fujitsu Ltd.	2,469.7
3	NEC Corp.	2,274.9
4	Unisys Corp.	2,200.0
5	Hitachi Ltd.	1,371.4
6	Groupe Bull	821.9
7	Honeywell Bull	740.0
8	Siemens AG	582.9
9	Cray Research Inc.	525.5
10	Amdahl Corp.	497.6

MICROCOMPUTER SYSTEMS

Rank	Company	Revenues ($ millions)
1	IBM	$5,650.0
2	Apple Computer Inc.	1,781.0
3	Olivetti SpA	1,267.6
4	Tandy Corp.	997.0
5	Unisys Corp.	800.0
6	NEC Corp.	697.3
7	COMPAQ Computer Corp.	625.2
8	AT&T	600.0
9	Toshiba Corp.	581.5
10	Zenith Electronics Corp.	548.0

MINICOMPUTER SYSTEMS

Rank	Company	Revenues ($ millions)
1	IBM	$ 3,000.0
2	Digital Equipment Corp.	2,000.0
3	Hewlett-Packard Co.	1,100.0
4	Wang Laboratories Inc.	804.7
5	Toshiba Corp.	765.5
6	Fujitsu Ltd.	620.2
7	Unisys Corp.	600.0
8	Olivetti SpA	429.5
9	Mitsubishi Electric Corp.	474.7
10	Data General Corp.	450.1

COMPUTER SOFTWARE

Rank	Company	Revenues ($ millions)
1	IBM	$5,514.0
2	Unisys Corp.	861.0
3	Digital Equipment Corp.	560.0
4	NEC Corp.	507.1
5	Fujitsu Ltd.	389.2
6	Siemens AG	387.1
7	Hewlett-Packard Co.	375.0
8	Hitachi Ltd.	331.0
9	Nixdorf Computer AG	299.5
10	Lotus Dev. Corp.	283.0
11	Microsoft Corp.	260.2

Another important source of computer hardware is computer leasing companies, which purchase computers from computer manufacturers and lease them to computer users at rates that may be 10 to 20 percent lower than manufacturers' rental price. Leasing companies are able to offer lower prices because they are willing to gamble that they can recover their costs and make a profit at the lower rates before their computers become obsolete. A final source of computer hardware is used-computer-equipment companies, which purchase used computers and peripheral equipment from computer users and sell them at substantial discounts.

Software Suppliers

System software and *application software* can be obtained from several sources if computer users do not wish to develop their own programs. Computer manufacturers are the largest source of software in the computer industry. They supply most of the system software (such as operating systems and other control programs and service programs) for computer users and are the major source of application packages. However, independent software companies, which specialize in the development of software packages, have become major software suppliers. Microsoft Corporation and Lotus Development Corporation are major examples. You can also get software from computer retailers, mail-order companies, and from other computer users. "User-developed software suppliers" are computer users who have developed application programs or service programs that are marketed to other computer users.

The five major sources of external information processing services are computer manufacturers, computer service centers, computer retailers, time-sharing companies, facilities management companies, and independent consultants. These and other types of firms in the computer industry offer a variety of services. For example, off-premise computer processing of customer jobs, time-sharing services, computer-time rental, systems design services, contract programming, consulting, "turnkey" systems, education, and hardware maintenance are offered. Many companies, especially computer manufacturers, supply several or almost all of these services. The following is a summary of three of these services.

External Service Suppliers

☐ **Computer service centers** (or service bureaus) provide a variety of information processing services. They process the jobs of many small firms that do not wish to acquire their own computer systems. Larger computer users also use service bureaus to handle specialized applications (such as computer-output microfilm) or when problem situations occur such as peak volume periods or during periods of computer down time.

☐ **Time-sharing service companies** provide realtime processing services to many subscribers using remote terminals and a central computer system. Time-sharing service companies are used by many computer users who have specialized data processing needs that require realtime processing and a large computer system.

☐ **Facilities management companies** are firms that take complete responsibility for a computer user's operation. Thus a business firm may "subcontract" all information processing service needs to an outside contractor. The facilities management firm might take over all computer facilities at the user's site, using its own hardware, software, and personnel.

External services are most popular with small firms and firms that are using computer processing for the first time. However, the majority of computers in the United States are purchased or leased by organizations for their own use. The advent of economical and easy-to-use micro- and minicomputer systems has accelerated this development. To counteract this trend, computer service centers and consultants sell computer hardware, software, and systems development services to their customers. This includes the offering of **turnkey** systems, where all of the hardware, software, and systems development needed by a user are provided by the service supplier. Ideally, the user should merely have to "turn the key" to begin operating and using the system.

Reasons for External Services

The major benefit of using external service suppliers is that you pay only for the information processing services that you need. Purchasing or leasing computer hardware or software and employing a staff of information services professionals creates fixed costs such as minimum machine rental payments, depreciation charges, and the salaries of professional and managerial information processing personnel. The use of external services also eliminates the personnel and management problems caused by the employment of a group of highly paid technical professionals in a rapidly changing and highly technical field such as computers and information processing.

The managements of many organizations use external services to avoid the problems that arise from having to manage computer hardware, software, or personnel. They may also turn to external services to avoid the problems of obsolescence caused by major changes in computer technology, or user needs. In some cases the cost of external services may be lower than if the computer-using firm performed its own information processing services. This may be due to economies of scale, since a large information processing service company may use larger and more efficient computer hardware and software to serve its many customers.

External services do have several limitations. The loss of control over information processing procedures and confidential information is one limitation. Off-premise computer processing may be inconvenient. The cost of external services may be significantly higher in some cases, because the external service company must not only meet expenses but must include a profit in its fee to computer users. Many firms are unwilling to depend on an outsider to provide vital information processing services. They want to have more control over processing procedures, report deadlines, and changes in hardware, software, and processing schedules.

FINANCING COMPUTER RESOURCES

Computer hardware can be rented, purchased, or leased. Software is purchased, leased, or is sometimes made available without charge by hardware manufacturers. Computer manufacturers offer all three methods of financing, while peripheral equipment manufacturers usually offer purchase or lease arrangements. Independent computer-leasing companies use long-term lease arrangements, while used-computer-equipment companies offer used equipment for purchase. The benefits and limitations of each method of financing computer acquisitions are analyzed below.

Rental

Computer users may favor the *rental* arrangement for several reasons. For example, the rental price includes the cost of maintenance, and the rental agreement can be canceled without penalty by the user with only a few months' notice. Thus, computer users do not have to arrange for the maintenance of the equipment and do not have to commit to a long series of lease payments or to the financing of a large purchase price. Renting computer hardware provides greater flexibility in changing equipment configurations and greatly reduces the risk of technological obsolescence, since users are not locked in to a purchased computer that has become obsolete due to major technological developments.

The monthly rental price is commonly based on 176 hours of use per month (8 hours per day for 22 working days in an average month). Use of rented computers for second and third shifts results in additional charges, which are much lower than the rate for the first 176 hours. The major disadvantage of equipment rental is the higher total cost incurred if equipment is rented for more than four or five years. Hardware manufacturers usually base their rental prices on a two- to four-year life, during which they will recover the cost of the equipment as well as substantial profit. Therefore, if computer hardware is going to be used for a longer period, especially if it is going to be used for more than 176 hours per month, the cost of rental is higher than the cost of purchase.

Purchase

The number of computer users *purchasing* their equipment has grown in recent years for several reasons. First, the prices of microcomputers, minicomputers, and small computers are low enough to make outright purchase affordable for many computer users. Second, computer users feel that the increased capabilities and cost savings of fourth-generation computer equipment is worth the risk of technological obsolescence. Also, more computer users are using their computers for more than one shift per working day. If they purchase their computers, they do not have to pay additional charges for such overtime use.

One of the major disadvantages of the purchasing arrangement is that equipment maintenance is not included in the purchase price and, therefore, must be arranged separately with the computer manufacturer, an independent computer maintenance company, or be maintained by the computer user's own personnel. Two other major disadvantages have been previously mentioned: (1) the risk of technological obsolescence and (2) the necessity to finance a large purchase price.

Leasing

Leasing computer hardware from independent computer-leasing companies was a major development of the third generation of computers. So successful did such third-party leasing become that computer manufacturers themselves now offer long-term lease arrangements. Leasing companies typically purchase specific equipment desired by a user and then lease it to the user for a long-term period such as five years. Leasing arrangements include a maintenance contract, purchase and trade-in options, no charges for extra shift operation, and a reduction in lease charges after a minimum time period. However, a cancellation charge is assessed if a lease is terminated before the end of the minimum lease period.

The leasing method combines some of the advantages and disadvantages of rental and purchase. Leasing does not require the financing of a large purchase price and is less expensive than renting equipment for the same period. The decline of lease charges after a minimum period, the inclusion of maintenance in the lease charges, and the absence of additional charges for overtime usage are other benefits. The major disadvantage is the long-term period of the lease contract that cannot be terminated without the payment of a substantial cancellation charge.

Figure 16–3 The cost of computer resources and services. The typical budget of computer-using organizations shows the predominance of hardware and personnel costs in a 1987 *Datamation* survey.

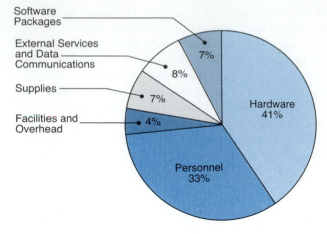

Figure 16–3 The cost of computer resources and services. The typical budget of computer-using organizations shows the predominance of hardware and personnel costs in a 1987 *Datamation* survey.

THE COSTS OF COMPUTER RESOURCES

Acquiring computer resources may involve substantial expenditures. **Hardware costs** have always been a major part of information processing costs but have been steadily decreasing. **Software costs** have been growing. Software costs include the salary costs of systems and programming personnel who develop in-house programs, plus the cost of external software packages. Another way to look at the costs of computer resources spotlights the size of **personnel costs.** This includes salaries of systems analysts, programmers, operations personnel, and administrative staff. Figure 16–3 illustrates that personnel costs are also a major cost category in providing computer services.

The growth in software and personnel costs is related to a growth in the cost of developing and maintaining new computer applications. That's because the salaries of systems analysts and programmers who develop and maintain application and systems software make up a sizable portion of the costs of computer services. The size of such costs is one of the chief reasons for the trend toward the purchase of software packages and the automation of the systems development and programming process.

Another way to analyze the cost of providing computer services is to group costs into three major functional categories. These are (1) systems development, (2) operations, and (3) administration. A summary of costs based on these categories is shown in Figure 16–4.

Controlling Computer Costs

The cost of providing computer services has become a major operating expense of computer-using business firms. Therefore, an extensive **cost control** program is necessary if computer costs are to be controlled. Some of the major cost control techniques that are used are summarized below.

Figure 16-4 Providing computer-based information services results in systems development, operations, and administrative costs.

SYSTEMS DEVELOPMENT COSTS	OPERATIONS COSTS	ADMINISTRATIVE COSTS
Systems Development Personnel. Systems Development Hardware, Software, and Supplies. Facilities Preparation and Furnishing. Personnel Training. Other Installation and Conversion Costs.	Hardware, Software, and Supplies for Operations. Program Maintenance. Operations Personnel. Occupancy and Utilities. Communications and External Services.	Management Personnel. Administrative Staff. Secretarial and Clerical Personnel. Miscellaneous Costs. Organizational Overhead.

Systems Development

The costs of systems development must be controlled by a formal *project management* program, in which a combination of plans, budgets, schedules, and reporting techniques is used to control the cost and direction of a systems development project. Some computer users also find it cheaper to use contract programming or systems design services from external sources, rather than hire the additional personnel required for such systems development efforts. Other firms find that buying or leasing software packages provides a cheaper method of systems development for many applications. Of course, the use of computer-assisted programming and systems development methods and information centers is a popular solution for the control of systems development costs.

Computer Operations

Several techniques are used to control computer operations costs. A formal *cost accounting* system is a major control technique. All costs incurred must be recorded, reported, allocated, and *charged back* to specific computer users. Under this arrangement the computer services department becomes a "service center" whose costs are charged directly to computer users, rather than being lumped with other administrative and service costs and treated as an overhead cost.

The use of *financial budgets* is another method of managing computer costs. Financial budgets should be required for computer operations as well as for systems development. Cost control is exercised by identifying and investigating the reasons for deviations from the budget. Finally, **external services,** such as facilities management and computer service bureaus, have been found to be a cheaper method of computer operations for some computer-using firms. Some computer users have found such services to be a decisive method of identifying and reducing the cost of computer operations.

REAL WORLD APPLICATION 16–1

The IBM Corporation

IBM, or "Big Blue" if you're in the computer industry, has been the dominant player in the national and world computer markets for decades. Its DP revenues are larger than the combined revenues of its closest 10 competitors. It is a major force in the mainframe, minicomputer, microcomputer, and software markets. However, after ending one of its worst sales years in a particularly dismal fashion, IBM faces major challenges to restore profit growth according to analysts. While many predict a rebound based on reduced costs and new products such as the 9370 mid-range computer system, others suggest that IBM's traditional approach to the computer industry has created fundamental barriers to future success.

"The company's strategy and cost structure was built on an expected 30 percent to 40 percent annual increase in mainframe processing demand," said analyst Thomas Rooney of Donaldson, Lufkin & Jenrette, Inc. "More and more large users are pulling applications off the mainframe onto departmental and smaller systems, and that trend will continue. It is a fundamental change in the nature of demand, indicating IBM's problems are deeper than people are willing to recognize."

IBM's well-publicized mid-range systems' shortcomings were apparently acknowledged by Chairman John F. Akers, who cited "unsatisfactory levels of demand for parts of our product line" as one reason for Big Blue's performance. All indications are that the 9370, dubbed the "VAX killer" in reference to Digital Equipment Corp.'s highly successful mid-range computers, could be IBM's make-or-break product this year.

"Since sales of PCs were flat and large mainframe sales were up, the problem was obviously in the mid-range," said Michael Geran of E.F. Hutton & Co., Inc. Salomon Brothers, Inc., analyst Marc Schulman esti-mated that IBM has received 30,000 orders in the United States and 15,000 orders overseas for the 9370 mid-range mainframe. He predicted that IBM will ramp up the volume of 9370 production in the second quarter, producing significant revenue just as Big Blue sees the positive benefits of last year's work force reductions and plant closings.

"By mid-year, all the people coming off the payroll will be off, costs will be down and shipments will be up," Schulman said. "And as the use of IBM's connectivity software and DB2 database management system proliferates, that will consume considerable machine cycles (requiring more processing power). I expect a recovery, but by no means a return to the glory days of 1983 and 1984."

Schulman predicted that IBM will gear up a new product cycle including a 15 percent price/performance enhancement of the 3090 large mainframe computer system, a six-processor version of the 3090, and successors to the industry standard IBM Personal Computer family.

Note: IBM introduced a new line of microcomputers in April of 1987. The Personal System/2 line includes a low-end Model 30 which uses an Intel 8086 microprocessor, Models 50 and 60 based on the 80286 microprocessor, and a high-performance Model 80 which uses the advanced 32-bit Intel 80386 microprocessor.

Application Questions

☐ What are some of the changes taking place in the computer industry that have hurt IBM?

☐ How is IBM responding to these challenges? Do you think they will succeed? How is IBM doing now?

Source: Adapted from Clinton Wilder, "Rebound at IBM Seen Hampered by CPU Trends," *Computerworld,* January 26, 1987, pp. 1 and 91.

Section II: Evaluating and Selecting Information System Resources

How do computer-using organizations evaluate and select hardware and software? Typically, they require suppliers to present bids and proposals based on *system specifications* developed during the design stage of systems development. Minimum acceptable physical and performance characteristics for all hardware and software requirements are established. Most large business firms and all government agencies formalize these requirements by listing them in a document called an RFP (request for proposal) or RFQ (request for quotation). The RFQ is then sent to appropriate vendors, who use it as the basis for preparing a proposed purchase agreement. See Figure 16–5.

A formal evaluation process reduces the possibility of buying inadequate or unnecessary computer hardware or software. This sometimes happens because computer users or computer specialists want to keep up with their competitors and with the latest developments in computing. Badly organized computer operations, inadequate systems development, and poor purchasing practices may also cause inadequate or unnecessary acquisitions. Therefore it is necessary to use various methods of evaluation to measure several key factors for computer hardware, software, and services.

Whatever the claims of hardware manufacturers and software suppliers, the *performance* of hardware and software must be demonstrated and evaluated. Independent hardware and software information services (such as *Datapro Reports*) should be used to gain detailed specification information and evaluations. Hardware and software should be demonstrated and evaluated. This can be done on the premises of the computer user or by visiting the operations of other computer users who have similar types of hardware or software. Other users are frequently the best source of information needed to evaluate the claims of manufacturers and suppliers. Vendors should be willing to provide the names of such users.

Large computer users frequently evaluate proposed hardware and software by requiring the processing of special "benchmark" test programs and test data. Users can then evaluate test results to determine which hardware device or software package displayed the best performance characteristics. Special simulators have also been developed that simulate the processing of typical jobs on several computers and evaluate their performances.

Computer users may use a scoring system of evaluation when there are several competing proposals for a hardware or software acquisition. Each evaluation factor is given a certain number of maximum possible points. Then each competing proposal is assigned points for each factor, depending on how well it meets the specifications of the computer user. Scoring each evaluation factor for several proposals helps organize and document the evaluation process. It also spotlights the strengths and weaknesses of each proposal. See Figure 16–6.

When you evaluate computer *hardware*, you should investigate specific *physical* and *performance characteristics* for each hardware component to be acquired. This is true whether evaluating mainframes, microcomputers,

EVALUATING HARDWARE, SOFTWARE, AND SUPPORT

Hardware Evaluation Factors

Figure 16-5 Example of a request for quotation (RFQ). Notice how it specifies the capabilities that must be met in the supplier's bid for 10 dot matrix printers.

ABC DEPARTMENT STORES INC.

PHONE (602)323-4557   BOX 5124   PHOENIX, ARIZONA 86581-0058

REQUEST FOR QUOTATION

0001	1	1
REQUEST NO	PAGE	OF

1 ACME COMPUTER SUPPLY CO.
   2704 E. MCDOWELL ROAD
   PHOENIX, ARIZONA 85283

2

3

TERMS: (1) YOU ARE INVITED TO BID ON GOODS AND/OR SERVICES ITEMIZED BELOW.
(2) THIS REQUEST FOR QUOTATION IS NOT INTENDED TO BE RESTRICTIVE. BRAND NAME OR MANUFACTURER'S NAME MAY BE USED FOR PURPOSE OF DESCRIPTION AND/OR TO ESTABLISH THE QUALITY DESIRED. BIDS ARE NOT RESTRICTED TO SUCH BRAND OR MANUFACTURER.
(3) THE ATTENTION OF THE BIDDER IS DIRECTED TO THE TERMS AND CONDITIONS ON THE REVERSE SIDE WHICH ARE INCORPORATED HEREIN.

WE RESERVE THE RIGHT TO REJECT ANY AND ALL BIDS.

RETURN THIS QUOTATION TO PURCHASING DEPT. AT ABOVE ADDRESS

DATE	BUYER	REQUISITION NO.	
6/24/8X	G. WILLIAMS	0001	**QUOTATION DUE DATE** 7/24/8X

LINE	OBJECT CODE	QUANTITY	UNIT	PART NUMBER AND DESCRIPTION	UNIT PRICE	AMOUNT
1	08561	10	1	IMPACT DOT MATRIX PRINTER		

MINIMUM SPECIFICATIONS:

FULLY COMPATIBLE WITH IBM PERSONAL COMPUTER, PC-XT, PORTABLE PC, COMPAQ PORTABLE COMPUTER, TEXAS INSTRUMENTS PROFESSIONAL COMPUTER AND HEWLETT PACKARD HP 150 TOUCHSCREEN PERSONAL COMPUTER

PRINTING SPEED: 100 CHARACTERS PER SECOND

PAPER FEED SPEED: 200 MILLISECONDS PER LINE

PRINTING DIRECTION: BIDIRECTIONAL, LOGIC SEEKING

CHARACTER MATRICES: (298 TOTAL)
   96 ROMAN CHARACTERS
   96 ITALIC CHARACTERS
   32 ROMAN INTERNATIONAL CHARACTERS
   32 ITALIC INTERNATIONAL CHARACTERS
   32 GRAPHICS CHARACTERS

PICA CHARACTER WIDTH AND HEIGHT: 2.1 x 3.1 mm

COLUMN WIDTH: 80 COLUMNS PICA

PAPER WIDTH: 4 INCHES TO 10 INCHES ADJUSTABLE

PAPER FEED: ADJUSTABLE SPROCKET FEED

PRINT HEAD: DISPOSABLE IMPACT DOT MATRIX

RIBBON TYPE: CARTRIDGE RIBBON

FORMS HANDLING: HORIZONTAL AND VERTICAL TABS, MARGINS, FORM LENGTH, SKIP-OVER-PERFORATION, AND VARIABLE LINE FEEDS.

GRAPHICS CAPABILITY: HIGH-RESOLUTION GRAPHICS. SIX DENSITIES AND A GRAPHICS CHARACTER SET.

IMPORTANT → SHOW ARIZONA AND LOCAL SALES TAX WHEN APPLICABLE. IF NOT SHOWN AS SEPARATE ITEM, IT WILL BE ASSUMED TO BE INCLUDED IN UNIT AND TOTAL PRICES.

	SALES TAX	

THIS IS NOT AN ORDER

	TOTAL	

SHIPMENT WILL BE MADE	TERMS	F.O.B. POINT
_____ Days after Receipt of Order		ABC DEPARTMENT STORES PHOENIX, ARIZONA

We quote as shown, except as otherwise noted. The undersigned agrees that this quotation is a firm offer which shall be irrevocable and open for acceptance for _____ calendar days (60 calendar days unless otherwise specified) from the date set for submission of quotes.

SIGNATURE   DATE

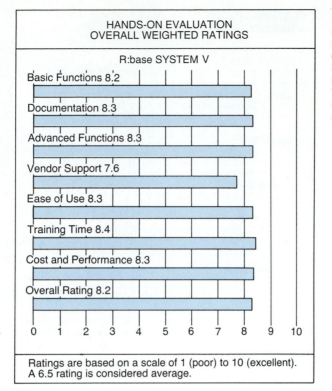

HANDS-ON EVALUATION
OVERALL WEIGHTED RATINGS

R:base SYSTEM V

Basic Functions 8.2

Documentation 8.3

Advanced Functions 8.3

Vendor Support 7.6

Ease of Use 8.3

Training Time 8.4

Cost and Performance 8.3

Overall Rating 8.2

0   1   2   3   4   5   6   7   8   9   10

Ratings are based on a scale of 1 (poor) to 10 (excellent).
A 6.5 rating is considered average.

Figure 16–6 An example of a scoring system for evaluating software packages. This is an overall evaluation of the R:base System V database management system package. This was the highest rated DBMS package in 1986 in the *Datapro Reports* on microcomputers.

or peripheral devices. Specific questions must be answered concerning many important factors. These **hardware evaluation factors** and questions are summarized in Figure 16–7.

You should evaluate *software* according to many factors that are similar to those used for hardware evaluation. Thus the factors of *performance, cost, reliability, availability, compatibility, modularity, technology, ergonomics,* and *support* should also be used to evaluate proposed software acquisitions. In addition, however, the **software evaluation factors** summarized in Figure 16–8 must also be considered. You should answer the questions they generate in order to properly evaluate software purchases.

Software Evaluation Factors

Vendor support services that assist you during the installation and operation of hardware and software must be evaluated. Assistance during installation or conversion of hardware and software, employee training, and hardware maintenance are examples of such services. Some of these services are provided without cost by hardware manufacturers and software suppliers. Other types of services can be contracted for at a negotiated price. **Evaluation factors** and questions for **vendor support services** are summarized in Figure 16–9.

Evaluation of Vendor Support

Figure 16–7 A summary of major hardware evaluation factors. Notice how you could use this to evaluate a computer system or peripheral device.

HARDWARE EVALUATION FACTORS	RATING
Performance What is its speed, capacity, and throughput?	
Cost What is its lease or purchase price? What will be its cost of operation and maintenance?	
Reliability What is the risk of malfunction and its maintenance requirements? What are its error control and diagnostic features?	
Availability When is the firm delivery date?	
Compatibility Is it compatible with existing hardware and software? Is it compatible with hardware provided by competing suppliers?	
Modularity Can it be expanded and upgraded by acquiring modular "add on" units?	
Technology In what year of its product life cycle is it? Is it "ahead of its time" or does it run the risk of obsolescence? Has it been recently developed or is it due to be replaced by a new technology?	
Ergonomics Has it been "human factors engineered" with the user in mind? Is it "user friendly," designed to be safe, comfortable, and easy to use?	
Connectivity Can it be easily connected to wide area and local area networks of different types of computers and peripherals?	
Environmental Requirements What are its electrical power, air conditioning, and other environmental requirements?	
Software Is system and application software available that can best use this hardware?	
Support Are the services required to support and maintain it available?	
OVERALL RATING	

SELECTING A MICROCOMPUTER SYSTEM

Which microcomputer system should you buy? That's a question you will be faced with sooner or later. It's a difficult question to answer quickly, but it can be answered after a reasonable amount of research and analysis. Let's briefly hit the high points of what you should consider. Figure 16–10 summarizes six basic questions that you must answer satisfactorily in order to make a proper selection decision.

SOFTWARE EVALUATION FACTORS	RATING
Efficiency Is the software a well-written system of computer instructions that does not use much storage space or CPU time?	
Flexibility Can it handle its processing assignments easily without major modification?	
Security Does it provide control procedures for errors, malfunctions, and improper use?	
Language Is it written in a programming language that is used by our computer programmers and users?	
Documentation Is the software well documented? Does it include helpful user instructions?	
Hardware Does existing hardware have the features required to best use this software?	
Other Factors What are its performance, cost, reliability, availability, compatibility, modularity, technology, ergonomics, and support characteristics? (Use the hardware evaluation factor questions in Figure 16–7.)	
OVERALL RATING	

Figure 16–8 A summary of selected software evaluation factors. Notice that most of the hardware evaluation factors in Figure 16–7 can also be used to evaluate software packages.

Applications

Do you need a microcomputer? What do you want to do with a microcomputer? Since there are so many things that microcomputers can do, you have to answer these questions first. How you answer will then determine the microcomputer software and hardware you should buy. For example, do you want to do word processing? Games? Financial spreadsheet analysis? Common business applications? Home management? Graphics? Database management? Or a combination of these uses? For example, if you want a computer to play video games, plus do a few simple home management tasks, then you can get by with the lower-priced microcomputer systems (about $200 to $700). If, on the other hand, you want to do word processing, spreadsheet analysis, database management, and graphics, you will probably have to move up to a medium-priced system (about $1,000 to $2,000). So what you really have to do is a *needs analysis*, just as in any systems development process.

Software

Once you have narrowed the applications you are interested in doing, you can then investigate the software that will allow your microcomputer to accomplish these tasks. You should ask yourself two basic questions: What types of *system software* (operating systems, programming language trans-

Figure 16–9 Vendor support evaluation factors. These factors focus on the quality of support services computer users may need.

VENDOR SUPPORT EVALUATION FACTORS	RATING
Performance What has been their past performance in terms of their past promises?	
Systems Development Are systems analysts and programming consultants available? What are their quality and cost?	
Maintenance Is equipment maintenance provided? What is its quality and cost?	
Conversion What systems development, programming, and hardware installation services will they provide during the conversion period?	
Training Is the necessary training of personnel provided? What is its quality and cost?	
Backup Are several similar computer facilities available for emergency backup purposes?	
Proximity Does the vendor have a local office? Are sales, systems development, programming, and hardware maintenance services provided from this office?	
Business Position Is the vendor financially strong, with good industry market prospects?	
Hardware Do they have a wide selection of compatible hardware and accessories?	
Software Do they have a wide variety of useful system software and application packages?	
OVERALL RATING	

lators, communications control programs, etc.) are needed? What types of *application software* (word processing package, electronic spreadsheet package, database management package, game programs, home management package, graphics package, common business applications packages, and so on) will I need? How you answer these questions will play a major role in determining the hardware you will need.

Hardware

Once you have narrowed your applications and software alternatives, you can determine your basic hardware requirements. You have to answer two basic hardware questions:

☐ What *microprocessor* and *primary memory* capacity is needed?

☐ What *peripheral devices* are required?

MICROCOMPUTER SELECTION QUESTIONS	ANSWERS
Applications What do I want to do with my microcomputer?	
Software What types of systems and application software packages will I need?	
Hardware What microprocessor, memory capacity, and peripheral devices are needed?	
Capabilities What specific capabilities are essential in the hardware devices and software packages I need?	
Costs How much can I afford to pay?	
Sources Where should I purchase the hardware, software, and services I need?	
SELECTION DECISION	

Figure 16–10 Six basic microcomputer selection questions. You must answer these questions satisfactorily to make a good selection decision.

For example, the software needed for some applications will only work with specific microprocessors, a minimum memory capacity, and minimum peripheral requirements. More specifically, many business application packages for microcomputers will only work with the Microsoft DOS operating system, the Intel 8088 microprocessor, at least 256K of main memory, one floppy disk drive, a video monitor, and a printer if you want printed output. Why? Because those were the minimum specifications for the widely used IBM Personal Computer and its many compatible cousins.

By the way, be sure to demand proof that a microcomputer is *compatible* with another microcomputer's software (i.e., that programs written for one microcomputer can run without modification on another). For example, there are several supposed IBM PC compatibles or *clones* that have difficulty using some of the software packages designed for the IBM PC. This compatibility problem is growing as more high performance microcomputers are developed. Examples are the IBM Personal System/2 Model 80 or the COMPAQ Deskpro 386 which use the 32-bit Intel 80386 microprocessor. Development of the Personal System/2 line of microcomputers with proprietary designs by IBM makes the compatibility question even more important.

Capabilities

Once you have listed the *types* of hardware and software you will probably need, you must determine the specific hardware and software *capabilities* that are required for your applications. There is such a variety of possible features and capabilities that this should be considered a separate step in the selection process. You should find answers to questions that deal with specific hardware and software capabilities. This includes such features as power, clarity, print quality, ease-of-use, expandability, and so on that may vary among different hardware and software products.

Some examples: Should you settle for a microcomputer model that just meets your needs or one that can expand its capabilities as your needs grow? Will you need a *graphics high-resolution color* video monitor or will a *low-resolution monochrome* monitor work well enough? Will you need a *correspondence*-quality printer, or will a *draft*-quality printer be OK? Should you buy a powerful *command-driven* word processing software package, or settle for a less-powerful but more *user friendly, menu-driven* package? Will you need a simple file management package or a more powerful DBMS package that can handle your business records as your needs grow? Note that these hardware and software questions deal with specific capabilities (power, clarity, print quality, ease-of-use, expandibility, and so on) that may vary among different hardware and software products.

Costs

Before you finally select the types and capabilities of hardware and software you will need, you had better look at the costs involved. You will quickly see that every hardware or software capability has its price, and that the price of a computer system that does all that you want can escalate out of sight! At this point, you will probably have to lower your expectations, tighten your belt, and settle for less than you originally wanted.

One of the first things you will discover is that the microprocessor is one of the cheapest parts of a microcomputer system. By itself, it may cost less than $20! Even the cost of the main system unit with all of its circuitry can be surpassed by the cost of peripheral devices such as high-resolution color graphics video monitors and correspondence-quality printers. And don't forget software. Many popular software packages cost hundreds of dollars each! Of course, some computer systems come with specific hardware and software *bundled* together in one package. For example, you can get a system with a built-in video monitor and disk drive, plus spreadsheet and word processing software packages included in one price. Only you can determine whether this combination of products and features meets your needs.

Sources

Microcomputer hardware and software are available from many sources. You can deal directly with some hardware manufacturers and software suppliers, though you will probably do most of your shopping at one of the thousands of retail computer stores (like Computerland and The Computer Store). They sell many different brands of microcomputers, peripheral devices, and software packages. They also frequently provide educational and maintenance services. The Tandy Corporation has a chain of thousands of Radio Shack stores selling its computers. Sears and other department stores, as well as discount stores, also carry microcomputer products. Many corporations and other organizations encourage microcomputer purchases by their employees. They sell hardware and software products at substantial discounts through their information centers, or by special arrangements made with manufacturers or retailers. Most hardware and software products are also available by mail order, usually at lower prices than at computer retail stores. That also goes for used equipment you can pick up at retailers or from other computer users.

Of course, the saying "you get what you pay for" has a lot of truth to it. Buying a less-expensive, off-brand microcomputer, peripheral device, or software package may lead to performance, reliability, or maintenance problems. Also, though *full-service* computer retail outlets may have higher prices, they sell products from the more reputable hardware and software suppliers, have on-site education and repair services, and thus provide you with more reliable service and support. However, once you become an experienced and knowledgeable microcomputer user, you can probably deal safely with reputable mail-order, discount, and specialized hardware and software suppliers.

You can become a more knowledgeable microcomputer user by more education and hands-on experience, and by reading books about computers and various computer industry and consumer periodicals. A flood of computer books and periodicals is being published, some of them of questionable value. However, among the many excellent periodicals are *Personal Computing, Infoworld, Byte*, and magazines for specific types of computers, like *PC Magazine* for owners of the IBM Personal Computers and compatibles, and *A+* for Apple Computer users. In addition, there are many hardware and software catalogs and buyers guides that are good sources of comparative product information. Finally, visiting computer stores, joining computer clubs and users groups, and attending national and regional computer shows are good ways to get inside information, product literature, and see equipment demonstrations. Figure 16–11 illustrates important points about retail, mail-order, used, and corporate plan sources. Figure 16–12 summarizes important tips for smart microcomputer shopping.

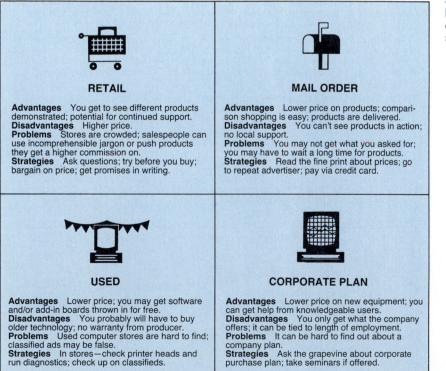

Figure 16–11 Sources of microcomputer hardware and software.

RETAIL

Advantages   You get to see different products demonstrated; potential for continued support.
Disadvantages   Higher price.
Problems   Stores are crowded; salespeople can use incomprehensible jargon or push products they get a higher commission on.
Strategies   Ask questions; try before you buy; bargain on price; get promises in writing.

MAIL ORDER

Advantages   Lower price on products; comparison shopping is easy; products are delivered.
Disadvantages   You can't see products in action; no local support.
Problems   You may not get what you asked for; you may have to wait a long time for products.
Strategies   Read the fine print about prices; go to repeat advertiser; pay via credit card.

USED

Advantages   Lower price; you may get software and/or add-in boards thrown in for free.
Disadvantages   You probably will have to buy older technology; no warranty from producer.
Problems   Used computer stores are hard to find; classified ads may be false.
Strategies   In stores—check printer heads and run diagnostics; check up on classifieds.

CORPORATE PLAN

Advantages   Lower price on new equipment; you can get help from knowledgeable users.
Disadvantages   You only get what the company offers; it can be tied to length of employment.
Problems   It can be hard to find out about a company plan.
Strategies   Ask the grapevine about corporate purchase plan; take seminars if offered.

Figure 16–12 Tips for smart microcomputer shopping. Notice the importance of being prepared before you shop.

SMART SHOPPING TIPS

Know What You Want. Before you walk into a computer store, you should have done some advanced investigation by reading product reviews in magazines, looking through the feature descriptions in ads, and/or talking to someone in your company's data processing department. This will make it easier for you to narrow down your selection.

Don't Shop on Price Alone. Sometimes the least expensive price translates into the shoddiest service, or worse, some unscrupulous practices. If you need the support, be prepared to spend 5 or 10 percent more.

Be Informed. If you keep up with what's new, there's no chance you'll end up making a purchase that is better for the dealer than for you. A product that is—or is about to become—out-of-date is the best sale for the dealer because it clears his shelf, but it's the worst sale for you because you miss the latest in technology.

Evaluate the Computer Store. Before you ask for help, look around and listen. Are other people being helped promptly by intelligent sales professionals? Are customers coming in with complaints? The quality of the store will reflect the quality of the purchase.

Try Before You Buy. Because dealers sometimes have limited stock, they may ask you to test a different model of computer than the one you'll be buying. Be wary. A hard disk model, for instance, is much faster than a floppy system, so you might expect performance you won't get with the product you purchase.

Get Any Promises in Writing. If the dealer promises to come to your office or house to set up the computer, make sure it says so in the sales contract or the bill of sale. Otherwise, there is nothing to bind the dealer to his or her promises made in the heat of the sale.

Consider Mail Order. If you know exactly what you need and want to shave a few dollars off the price, a reputable mail-order firm may be the right place for you to shop. What you give up in support, you'll save in cash. But, order by credit card—if anything goes wrong, you'll have better leverage. Don't buy from a mail-order house that is advertising for the first time. And don't buy from a company that doesn't list a street address and phone number.

Don't Rely on One Source. Take cues from the way the mail-order house treats you. If it takes 10 phone calls to find out if they have what you want and to take the order, then you should use another mail-order company. If they are out of the product you want, don't wait for them to get stock.

Beware of No-Name Products. Whether you're buying retail or mail order you should generally avoid outdated models or products from companies that are no longer in business—even if there are specials on them. You can, of course, save money this way, but only if you are aware of the warranty limitations and other drawbacks.

Consider a Used Product. Newspaper ads and a few used-computer dealers can outfit you with hardware nearly as good as new, but at half the price. Remember, however, that you're likely to be at least one step behind current product cycles when you buy used hardware. And, be aware that electromechanical devices such as disk drives and printers may be the worst products to buy used.

Look for a Corporate Buying Plan. Before you pay full price or shop by mail order, check to see if your company has an employee purchase plan that offers computer products at a discount. Be persistent, since a lot of corporate buying plans are not well publicized.

REAL WORLD APPLICATION 16–2

Tales of Four PC Buyers

Elaine Ratner

Most buyers of personal computers turn to a computer retail store first. At least there you can get a chance to see how a particular computer works and compare software alternatives firsthand. Elaine Ratner knew that she needed this kind of support. She was buying a computer for the first time and wanted to have a salesperson show her how to get started. But she did some preliminary investigation by reading magazines and talking to friends. "I started by looking for the right software," says the Oakland, California, writer, who is currently coauthoring a cookbook called *Dessert at the Stanford Court.* "I decided I needed Xywrite II Plus because it could index and that's important when you're doing a cookbook."

Next, Ratner scoured the newspapers for the best price she could find on a MS-DOS computer because Xywrite only runs on MS-DOS machines. She ended up at a Berkeley store that had the lowest price on a Leading Edge Model D. Ratner was interested in the Model D because its lower price meant she could also afford a hard disk. By the time Ratner's shopping spree was over, she had an Amdek monitor, a Diablo printer, and a Model D with a 10-megabyte hard disk.

Lyle Johnson

When Lyle Johnson took responsibility for buying personal computers for his law firm, McNamee, Allen & Johnson, he didn't simply run off to the local computer store and buy what the salesperson suggested. The first thing he did was evaluate the San Jose, California, law firm's needs. Since document handling and correspondence were the primary duties of the staff, he looked into word processing software at the same time he compared computers.

Knowing what he wanted, Johnson looked for the best deals he could get. He found them at an auction at a Silicon Valley company, a neighborhood used-computer store, and through a friend's employee purchase plan. He ended up buying three Morrow computers, with either WordStar or Newword (a program much like WordStar) included; a Bondwell 14 computer; a Hewlett-Packard Laserjet printer; and an assortment of other peripherals. "We have saved anywhere from 20 to 25 percent buying personal computers this way," he says.

Merrill Cobb

Merrill Cobb, president of Seismic Exploration Corp., in Huffman, Texas, not only supplied his own company with mail-order equipment, but has made a business out of buying mail-order products and then reselling beefed-up computers to local businesses. "I buy the computer from a dealer and then buy the guts of the thing through mail order," Cobb says. "With the discounts given through mail order, I still beat the retailers' prices and make a profit."

In his main occupation, Cobb helps drilling companies by using seismic equipment to search for oil and gas. He uses an Apple IIe computer for word processing and a Panasonic Senior Partner for Lotus 1-2-3 spreadsheets. Buying mail order for his company is the simplest and quickest approach, he says. "It's a whole lot easier to pick up the phone than drive 5 to 50 miles for the best price. I know all about installing cards and cables, so I don't need to pay extra for support."

Continued on page 584

REAL WORLD APPLICATION 16–2

Continued from page 583

Margo Levine

Margo Levine's strategy revolved around her company's buying plan. In fact, she probably wouldn't have purchased a computer if it weren't for the plan. As a principle partner at the management consulting firm of Temple, Barker & Sloan in Lexington, Mass., Levine wanted a computer she could use at home to cut down on late hours at the office. She also wanted a computer that was transportable enough to take with her for weekends in New Hampshire.

Levine bought a COMPAQ portable with a hard disk through her company's purchasing agent who, by buying in large quantities,

received a 25 percent discount off retail prices. To further encourage Levine, her company kicked in a full 50 percent of the remaining cost, as long as she stayed at the company for a year or more. "I shopped around just enough to know that I was getting a good price," Levine says. "I didn't have to do any of the legwork; the company did it for me."

Application Questions

☐ What four ways of buying microcomputers are found in these examples? Which would you prefer? Why?

☐ Which of the six basic selection questions in Figure 16–10 are being considered by these microcomputer buyers?

Source: Jim Bartino, "Buying Smarter," *Personal Computing,* April 1986, pp. 60–65.

SUMMARY

☐ Computer users should have a basic understanding of the computer industry, since it is a vital source of computer hardware, software, and services. The computer industry consists of a few major computer manufacturers and many smaller suppliers of hardware, software, and services. Effective and efficient use of computers requires the continual support of many firms within the computer industry.

☐ Information systems development and processing services can be acquired from sources outside the business firm instead of developing such capabilities within an organization. Many business firms use the external services provided by computer service centers, time-sharing companies, facilities management companies, and so on. The major benefit of using external services is that computer users pay only for the specific services needed and do not have to acquire or manage hardware, software, and personnel. Loss of control over the information processing function, inconvenience, and higher costs are possible limitations of external services.

☐ A major concern of computer users is the control of the cost of computer resources. Acquiring computer resources usually involves substantial expenditures for hardware, software, services, supplies, and personnel compensation. Major cost control programs are necessary to control the cost of systems development, computer operations, and administration.

☐ Computer users should have a basic understanding of how to evaluate the acquisition of computer resources. Manufacturers and suppliers should be required to present bids and proposals based on system specifications developed during the design stage of systems development. A formal evaluation process reduces the possibility of incorrect or unnecessary purchases of computer hardware or software. Several major evaluation factors, such as performance, cost, and reliability, should be used to evaluate computer hardware, software, and vendor support. The use of rental, purchase, or lease arrangements in financing computer acquisitions must also be evaluated.

☐ Selecting a microcomputer system is an important decision requiring research and analysis. Major factors that you should consider are the applications for which the microcomputer is to be used, the hardware and software required, the specific capabilities required, the costs involved, and the best sources to deal with.

These are the key terms and concepts of this chapter. The page number of their first explanation is in parentheses.

KEY TERMS AND CONCEPTS

1. Computer cost categories *(570)*
2. Computer cost control *(570)*
3. Computer industry *(564)*
4. Computer retailers *(565)*
5. Computer service center *(567)*
6. External services *(567)*
7. Facilities management *(567)*
8. Financing computer resources *(568)*
9. Hardware evaluation factors *(573)*
10. Hardware suppliers *(564)*
11. Microcomputer selection factors *(576)*
    a. Applications
    b. Software
    c. Hardware
    d. Capabilities
    e. Costs
    f. Sources
12. Software evaluation factors *(575)*
13. Software suppliers *(566)*
14. Vendor support evaluation factors *(573)*

Match one of the **key terms and concepts** listed above with one of the brief examples or definitions listed below. Try to find the "best fit" for answers that seem to fit more than one term or concept. Defend your choices.

REVIEW AND APPLICATION QUIZ

_____ 1. The source of hardware, software, and services for users.

_____ 2. Contracting with outside firms for computer processing, education, maintenance, and so on.

_____ 3. An outside firm that does some of your firm's computer processing for you.

_____ 4. An outside firm that takes over your firm's on-site computer center.

_____ 5. Performance, cost, reliability, technology, and ergonomics.

_____ 6. Performance, cost, reliability, technology, ergonomics, efficiency, language, and documentation.

_____ 7. Maintenance, conversion, training, and business position.

_____ 8. Rental, leasing, and purchase of hardware and software.

_____ 9. Hardware, software, and personnel costs versus systems development, operations, and administrative costs.

_____ 10. What do I want to do with my microcomputer?

_____ 11. What system and application software packages will I need for my microcomputer?

_____ 12. What microprocessor, memory capacity, and peripheral devices do I need for my microcomputer?

_____ 13. What specific microcomputer software and hardware capabilities do I need?

_____ 14. How much can I afford to pay for a microcomputer system?

_____ 15. Where should I purchase the microcomputer hardware, software, and other services I need?

APPLICATION PROBLEMS

1. If you have not already done so, read and answer the questions after the two Real World Applications in this chapter.

2. Match one of the following evaluation factors with the most appropriate example listed below.

    a. Business position.   *d.* Efficiency.
    b. Compatibility.   *e.* Ergonomics.
    c. Connectivity.   *f.* Technology.

    _____ *1.* An easy-to-use hardware device or software package.

    _____ *2.* A software package that is very fast and uses minimal memory space.

    _____ *3.* A state-of-the-art computer system that uses an advanced microprocessor.

    _____ *4.* A computer company that has a large market share and is well financed.

    _____ *5.* A software package written for the Macintosh computer won't work on the IBM Personal Computer.

    _____ *6.* A computer system that can easily communicate with other computer systems in a network.

3. Assume you are going to buy a personal computer system. List all of the types of firms in the computer industry that you would have to depend on directly or indirectly for hardware, software, and services. (Hint: Use Figure 16–1.)

4. Assume you are going to buy a personal computer system. Make a "wish list" of the hardware, software, and vendor support features you want this system to have. (Hint: Refer to Figures 16–7, 16–8, and 16–9, but get more specific.)

5. Assume you are going to buy a personal computer system. Go to a local computer retailer and see how much it will cost you to implement the "wish list" you developed in problem 3. Are any features you wanted impossible to achieve?

6. Joan Alvarez, a store manager for ABC Department Stores, is considering buying a new personal computer and an integrated applications package that does spreadsheet analysis, graphics, database management, word processing, and communications. Her two main evaluation criteria are (1) ergonomics and (2) technology. List several features she should consider in evaluating both hardware and software by those two criteria. (Hint: Use Figure 16–7 to help you get started.)

7. If you had to buy a microcomputer today, which one would you buy? Explain why in terms of the selection criteria of: (1) applications, (2) software, (3) hardware, (4) capabilities, (5) costs, and (6) sources. Make a list of your reasons for each of these criteria.

8. The VP for information systems of ABC Department Stores is trying to justify a large increase in his department's budget in the coming year. He is having trouble explaining to the VP of finance why software costs and personnel costs are related. Help him out with your own explanation.

CHAPTER

17

CONTROLLING INFORMATION SYSTEM RESOURCES

Chapter Outline

Learning Objectives

The purpose of this chapter is to promote a basic understanding of how business firms must control their information system resources by analyzing (1) control techniques for information systems and (2) the control implications of computer crime and ethics. After reading and studying this text, you should be able to:

1. Outline several types of information system controls, procedural controls, and physical facility controls that can be used to provide information system security.

2. Discuss the impact of computers in terms of their major beneficial and adverse effects on society.

3. Identify major types of computer crime and explain their effect on the development of information system controls.

4. Identify several ethical considerations arising from the use of computers by end users and information systems professionals.

Section I: Control of Information Systems

INFORMATION SYSTEM SECURITY

Do computer-based information systems increase or decrease the probability of errors, fraud, and destruction of information processing facilities? Computers have proven that they can process huge volumes of data and perform complex calculations more accurately than manual or mechanical information systems. However, we know that (1) errors do occur in computer-based systems, (2) computers have been used for fraudulent purposes, and (3) computers and their data files have been accidentally or maliciously destroyed.

There is no question that computers have had some detrimental effect on the detection of errors and fraud. Manual and mechanical information processing systems use paper documents and other media that can be visually checked by information processing personnel. Several persons are usually involved in such systems and, therefore, cross-checking procedures are easily performed. These characteristics of manual and mechanical information processing systems facilitate the detection of errors and fraud.

Computer-based information systems, on the other hand, use machine-sensible media such as magnetic disks and tape. They accomplish processing manipulations within the electronic circuitry of a computer system. The ability to check visually the progress of information processing activities and the contents of data files is significantly reduced. In addition, a relatively small number of personnel may effectively control all of the processing activities of the entire organization. Therefore, the ability to detect errors and fraud can be reduced by computerization. This makes the development of *information system controls* mandatory.

Controls are needed to ensure information system security, that is, the *accuracy*, *integrity*, and *safety* of information system activities and resources. Controls can minimize *errors*, *fraud*, and *destruction* in an information services organization. Effective controls provide **quality assurance** for information systems. They can make a computer-based information system more free of errors and fraud than manual types of information processing. There are three major types of controls needed to achieve information system security as illustrated in Figure 17–1 and listed as follows:

- ☐ Information system controls.
- ☐ Procedural controls.
- ☐ Physical facility controls.

INFORMATION SYSTEM CONTROLS

Information system controls are methods and devices that attempt to ensure the accuracy, validity, and propriety of information system activities. Controls must be developed to ensure proper data entry, processing techniques, storage methods, and information output. Thus information system controls can be organized according to the input, processing, output, and storage activities of any information system. See Figure 17–2.

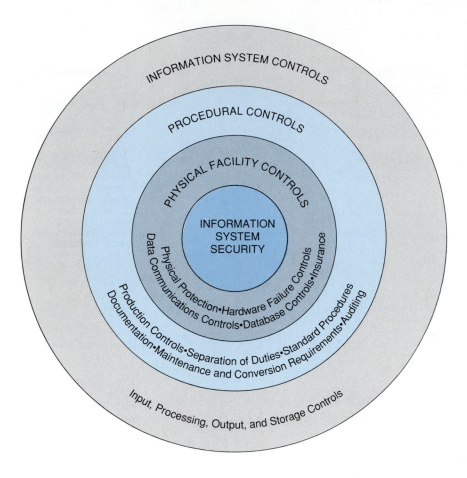

Figure 17–1 The controls needed for information system security. Specific types of controls can be grouped into three major categories: information system, procedural, and physical facility controls.

Remember the phrase "garbage in, garbage out" (GIGO)? That's why controls are needed for proper entry of data and instructions into an information system. Examples of input controls that are frequently used are summarized below.

Input Controls

Recording Controls

Input recording aids help reduce the chance for error. Examples include formatted data entry screens, machine-readable media, templates over the keys of key-driven input devices, and prerecorded and prenumbered forms.

Registration Controls

Source documents can be registered by recording them in a logbook when they are received by data entry personnel. External labels attached to the outside of magnetic tapes or disks are another method of registering the contents and disposition of input data. Realtime systems that use direct access files frequently record all inputs into the system on magnetic tape

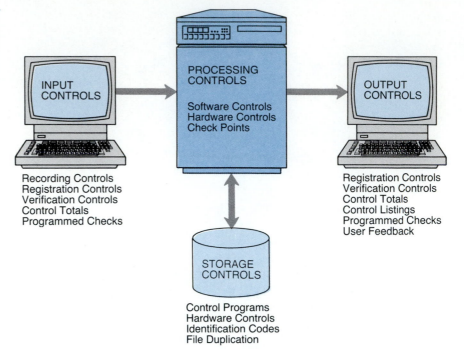

control logs. Such logs preserve evidence of all system inputs. They also include *control totals* that can be compared to control totals generated during processing.

Verification Controls

Verification controls include visual verification of source documents, input media, and data entry displays by clerical personnel. Machine verification as performed by intelligent data entry terminals is another example.

Control Totals

A *record count* is a control total that consists of counting the total of source documents or other input records and comparing this total to the number of records counted at other stages of input preparation. If the totals do not match, a mistake has been made. *Batch totals* and *hash totals* are other forms of control totals. A *batch total* is the sum of a specific item of data within a batch of transactions, such as the sales amount in a batch of sales transactions. *Hash totals* are the sum of data fields that are added together only for control comparisons. For example, employee social security numbers could be added to produce a control total in the input preparation of payroll documents.

Programmed Checks

Computer programs can include instructions to identify incorrect, invalid, or improper input data as it enters the computer system. For example, computers can check for invalid codes, data fields, and transactions. Also, the computer may be programmed to conduct "reasonableness checks" to determine if input data exceeds certain specified limits or is out of sequence.

Once data is entered correctly into a computer system it must be processed properly. Processing controls are developed to identify errors in arithmetic calculations and logical operations. They are also used to ensure that data are not lost or do not go unprocessed.

Processing controls can be categorized as *software controls* and *hardware controls* and are summarized below.

Processing Controls

Software Controls

Validity checks, reasonableness checks, sequence checks, and control total checks similar to the programmed checks on input, mentioned above, are also used during the processing stage. The computer can also be programmed to check the internal file labels at the beginning and end of magnetic tape and disk files. These labels contain information identifying the file as well as providing control totals for the data in the file. These internal file labels allow the computer to ensure that the proper storage file is being used and that the proper data in the file has been processed.

Another major software control is the establishment of *checkpoints* during the processing of a program. Checkpoints are intermediate points within a program being processed where intermediate totals, listings, or "dumps" of data are written on magnetic tape or disk or listed on a printer. Checkpoints minimize the effect of processing errors or failures since processing can be restarted from the last checkpoint, rather than from the beginning of the program. They also help build an **audit trail,** which allows transactions being processed to be traced through all of the steps of processing. These and many other input, processing, output, and storage controls may be provided by specialized system software packages known as *system security monitors*. See Figure 17–3.

Hardware Controls

Hardware controls are special checks built into the hardware to verify the accuracy of computer processing. Examples of hardware checks include:

- ☐ Multiple read-write heads on magnetic tape and disk devices.
- ☐ Parity checks (described in Chapter 2) and echo checks, which require that a signal be returned from a device or circuit to verify that it was properly activated.
- ☐ Malfunction detection circuitry within the computer. This may include a microprocessor that is used to support remote diagnostics and maintenance.
- ☐ Switches and other devices. Switches can be set that prohibit writing on magnetic tapes or disks. On magnetic tape reels, a removable plastic or metal ring can be removed to prevent writing on a tape. The write/protect notch on floppy disks has a similar function.

☐ Miscellaneous hardware controls. There are many other kinds of hardware controls, such as redundant circuitry checks, overflow checks, arithmetic sign checks, and CPU timing and voltage checks.

Figure 17–3 An overview of the features of a major software package for computer security. This is IBM's Resource Access Control Facility (RACF), a system security monitor.

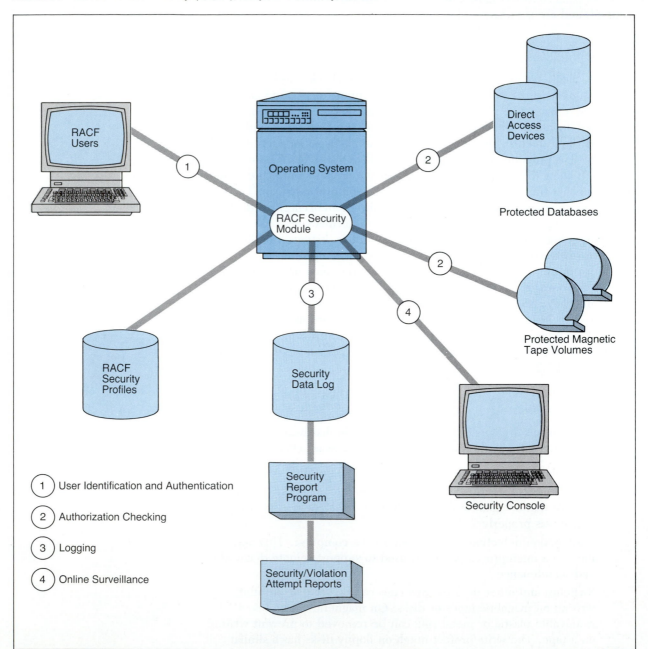

How can we control the quality of the information products produced by an information system? Output controls are developed to ensure that information products are correct and complete and are transmitted to authorized users in a timely manner. Several types of output controls are similar to input control methods. For example, output is frequently logged, identified with route slips, and visually verified by input/output control personnel. Control totals on output are usually compared with control totals generated during the input and processing stages. Control listings can be produced that provide hard copy evidence of all output produced.

Prenumbered output forms can be used to control the loss of important output documents such as stock certificates or payroll check forms. Distribution lists help input/output control personnel ensure that only authorized users receive output. Access to the output of realtime processing systems is typically controlled by security software that identifies who can receive output and the type of output they are authorized to receive. Finally, persons who receive output should be contacted for feedback on the quality of output. This is an important function of systems maintenance and quality assurance activities.

Output Controls

How can we protect our data resources? Many databases and files are protected from unauthorized or accidental use by security programs that require proper identification before they can be used. Hardware devices and software routines are used to protect the databases of realtime processing systems from unauthorized use or processing accidents. Account codes, passwords, and other identification codes are frequently used to restrict access to authorized users. A catalog of authorized users enables the computer system to identify eligible users and determine which types of information they are authorized to receive. Many database management packages can help provide such control features.

Control over files of computer programs and data may be maintained by a librarian or database administrator. These employees are responsible for maintaining and controlling access to the libraries and databases of the organization. Many firms also use backup files, which are duplicate files of data or programs. Such files may be stored off premise, that is, in a location away from the computer center, sometimes in special storage vaults in remote locations.

Many realtime processing systems use duplicate files that are updated by data communication links. Files are also protected by *file retention* measures, which involve storing copies of master files and transaction files from previous periods. If current files are destroyed, the files from previous periods are used to reconstruct new current files. Usually, several *generations* of files are kept for control purposes. Thus master files from several recent periods of processing (known as *child, parent, grandparent* files, and so on) may be kept for backup purposes.

Storage Controls

Procedural controls are methods that specify how the information services organization should be operated for maximum security. They facilitate the accuracy and integrity of computer operations and systems development activities. Some of these controls are discussed below.

PROCEDURAL CONTROLS

Production Control

A production control section should monitor the progress of information processing jobs, data entry activities, and the quality of input/output data. This is an important *quality assurance* function.

Separation of Duties

A basic principle of procedural control is to assign the duties of systems development, computer operations, and control of data and program files to separate groups. For example, systems analysts and computer programmers may not be allowed to operate the computer console or make changes to data or programs being processed. In addition, the responsibility for maintaining a library of data files and program files is assigned to a librarian or database administrator.

Standard Procedures

Manuals of standard procedures for the operation of information systems should be developed and maintained. Following standard procedures promotes uniformity and minimizes the chances of errors and fraud. It helps employees know what is expected of them in operating procedures and output quality. It is important that procedures be developed for both normal and unusual operation conditions. For example, procedures should tell employees what to do differently when their computers are not working.

Documentation

System, program, and operations documentation must be developed and kept up-to-date to ensure the correct processing of each computer application. Documentation is also invaluable in the maintenance of a system as needed improvements are made.

Authorization Requirements

Requests for systems development, program changes, or computer processing must be subject to a formal process of review before authorization is given. For example, program changes generated by maintenance programmers should be approved by the manager of programming after consultation with the manager of computer operations and the manager of the affected user department.

Conversion Scheduling

Conversion to new hardware and software, installation of newly developed information systems, and changes to existing programs should be subjected to a formal notification and scheduling procedure to minimize their detrimental effects on the accuracy and integrity of information services.

Auditing of Information Services

The information services organization and its activities must undergo periodic examinations or *audits* to determine the accuracy, integrity, and safety of all computer-based information systems. We will discuss this important aspect of procedural control shortly.

Physical facility controls are methods that protect physical facilities and their contents from loss or destruction. Computer centers are subject to such hazards as accidents, natural disasters, sabotage, vandalism, industrial espionage, and theft. Therefore, physical safeguards and various control procedures are necessary to protect the hardware, software, and, most importantly, the vital data resources of computer-using organizations. Several important physical facility controls are described below.

PHYSICAL FACILITY CONTROLS

Physical Protection Controls

Providing maximum security and disaster protection for a computer installation requires many types of controls. Only authorized personnel are allowed access to the computer center through such techniques as identification badges for information services personnel, electrical door locks, burglar alarms, security police, closed-circuit TV, and other detection systems. The computer center should be protected from disaster by such safeguards as fire detection and extinguishing systems; fireproof storage vaults for protection of files; emergency power systems; electromagnetic shielding; and temperature, humidity, and dust control.

Data Communications Controls

The communications control hardware and software described in Chapter 8 play a vital role in the control of data communications activity. In addition, data can be transmitted in "scrambled" form and unscrambled by the computer system only for authorized users. This process is called **encryption.** It transforms digital data into a scrambled code before it is transmitted and then decodes the data when it is received. Special hardware and software must be used for the encryption process. Other control methods are typically used, such as the automatic disconnect and call-back system illustrated in Figure 17–4.

Computer Failure Controls

A variety of controls are needed to prevent computer failure or minimize its effects. Computers fail or "go down" for several reasons—power failure, electronic circuitry malfunctions, mechanical malfunctions of peripheral equipment, hidden programming errors, and computer operator errors. Therefore, the information services department must take steps to prevent equipment failure and to minimize its detrimental effects.

Computers with automatic and remote maintenance capabilities should be acquired. A program of *preventive maintenance* of hardware must be developed. Adequate electrical supply, air conditioning, humidity control, and fire prevention standards must be set. A *backup computer system* capability should be arranged with other computer-using organizations.

Major hardware or software changes should be carefully scheduled and implemented. Computer operators must have adequate training and supervision.

Many firms are acquiring **fault-tolerant** computer systems to ensure against computer failure. These systems have multiple central processors,

Figure 17–4 A data communications access control system. Notice how the disconnect and call-back feature works for authorized and nonauthorized users.

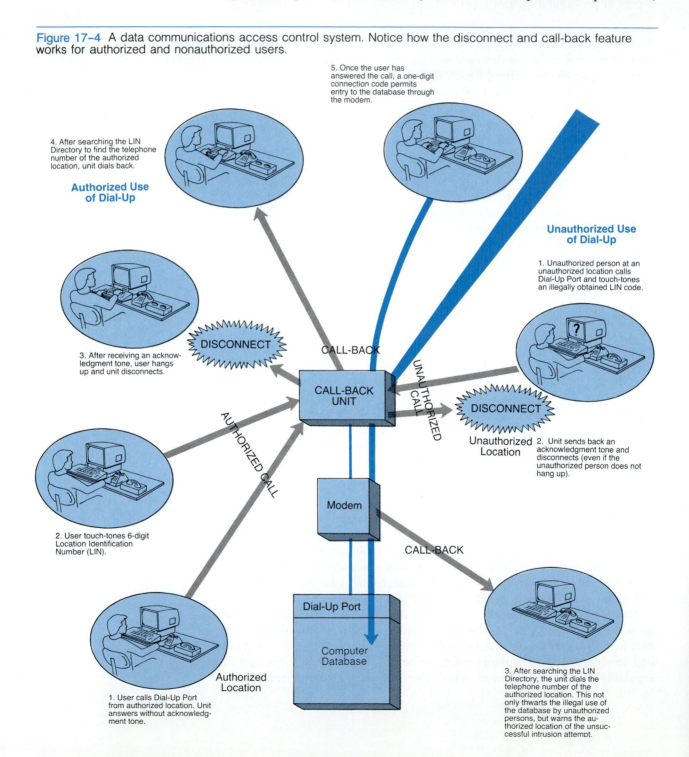

5. Once the user has answered the call, a one-digit connection code permits entry to the database through the modem.

4. After searching the LIN Directory to find the telephone number of the authorized location, unit dials back.

Authorized Use of Dial-Up

Unauthorized Use of Dial-Up

1. Unauthorized person at an unauthorized location calls Dial-Up Port and touch-tones an illegally obtained LIN code.

3. After receiving an acknowledgment tone, user hangs up and unit disconnects.

DISCONNECT

CALL-BACK

UNAUTHORIZED CALL

CALL-BACK UNIT

DISCONNECT

Unauthorized Location

2. Unit sends back an acknowledgment tone and disconnects (even if the unauthorized person does not hang up).

AUTHORIZED CALL

2. User touch-tones 6-digit Location Identification Number (LIN).

Modem

CALL-BACK

Dial-Up Port

Computer Database

Authorized Location

1. User calls Dial-Up Port from authorized location. Unit answers without acknowledgment tone.

3. After searching the LIN Directory, the unit dials the telephone number of the authorized location. This not only thwarts the illegal use of the database by unauthorized persons, but warns the authorized location of the unsuccessful intrusion attempt.

peripherals, and system software. This may provide a *fail-safe* capability where the computer system continues to operate at the same level even if there is a major hardware or software failure. Some fault-tolerant computer systems offer a *fail-soft* capability where the computer system can continue to operate at a reduced but acceptable level in the event of a major system failure.

Adequate insurance coverage should be secured to protect the computer-using business firm. Financial losses can be substantial in the event of accidents, disasters, fraud, and other risks. Many insurance companies offer special computer security policies. These include insurance against fire, natural disasters, vandalism and theft, liability insurance for data processing errors or omissions, fidelity insurance for the bonding of information services personnel as a protection against fraud, and so on. The amount of such insurance should be large enough to replace computer equipment and facilities. Insurance is also available to cover the cost of reconstructing data and program files.

Insurance

An information services department should be periodically examined or *audited* by internal auditing personnel of the business firm. In addition, periodic audits by external auditors from professional accounting firms are a good business practice. Such audits should review and evaluate whether proper and adequate *information system controls*, *procedural controls*, and *physical facility controls* have been developed and implemented. There are two basic approaches for auditing the information processing activities of computer-based information systems. They are known as (1) "auditing around the computer" and (2) "auditing through the computer."

AUDITING INFORMATION SYSTEMS

Auditing around a computer involves verifying the accuracy and propriety of computer input and output without evaluating the computer programs used to process the data. This is a simpler and easier method that does not require auditors with programming experience. However, this auditing method does not trace a transaction through all of its stages of processing and does not test the accuracy and integrity of computer programs. Therefore, it is recommended only as a supplement to other auditing methods.

Auditing through the computer involves verifying the accuracy and integrity of the computer programs that process the data, as well as the input and output of the computer system. Auditing through the computer requires a knowledge of computer operations and programming. Some firms employ special *EDP auditors* for this assignment. Special *test data* may be used to test processing accuracy and the control procedures built into the computer program. The auditors may develop special *test programs* or use *audit software packages*.

EDP auditors use such programs to process their test data. They then compare the results produced by their audit programs with the results generated by the computer user's own programs. One of the objectives of such testing is to detect the presence of unauthorized changes or *patches* to computer programs. Unauthorized program patches may be the cause of "unexplainable" errors or may be used by an unscrupulous programmer for fraudulent purposes. See Figure 17–5.

Auditing through the computer may be too costly for some computer applications. Therefore a combination of both auditing approaches is usually employed. However, both auditing approaches must effectively contend with the changes caused by computer-based information systems to the audit trail.

The **audit trail** can be defined as the presence of documentation that allows a transaction to be traced through all stages of its information processing. This begins with a transaction's appearance on a source document and ends with its transformation into information on a final output document. The audit trail of manual information systems was quite visible and easy to trace. However, computer-based information systems have changed the form of the audit trail. Information formerly available to the auditor in the form of visual records is no longer available or is recorded on media that can be interpreted only by machines. Realtime processing systems have increased the invisibility of the traditional audit trail. Paper documents and historical files are frequently eliminated when remote terminals and direct access files are used.

Such developments make the auditing of such systems a complex but vital assignment. Therefore, auditing personnel should be included on the project team of all major systems development projects and consulted before smaller systems projects are implemented. In addition, auditing personnel should be notified of changes to computer programs caused by the program maintenance activity. Such procedures give the auditor the opportunity to suggest methods of preserving the audit trail. The auditor can also ensure that adequate information system controls are designed into systems that are being developed or modified.

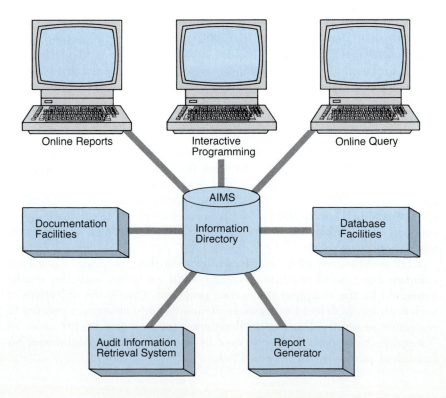

Figure 17–5 An example of the capabilities of an audit software package. This is Cullinet's Audit Information Management System (AIMS).

REAL WORLD APPLICATION 17–1

The EDP Audit

Honestly, now. When an electronic data processing (EDP) auditor walks into your office, you: (1) panic and dash for the exit, (2) grin and bear it, (3) welcome the visit, (4) don't know—never happens in your organization.

Anyone who checked (3) can turn the page. Unfortunately, I imagine most of you are still reading. If you checked (1), you can turn the page, too. In fact, you can close the whole paper. You've got bigger things to worry about. Like the name of a good lawyer. Now we've got the "grin and bear its" and the "don't knows." A "don't know" answer isn't your problem. It's your management's. Unless they're asleep, you won't be able to say "never happens here" for long. That leaves the "grin and bear its." You are the majority. Most MIS managers rank an EDP audit with a bad case of hives or having a tooth pulled. That's too bad, because it doesn't have to be that way.

An audit is a review with a fancy name. The focus of an EDP audit is on control of information systems. Can management be certain they are under control? Do applications work the way the business should run? Is access to sensitive data restricted? Is information seen by different managers consistent? Surely no MIS manager can object to any of these. If an audit helps reach these ends, it should be welcome.

"EDP audits should be of value, both to the MIS manager and to the business unit the system serves," says Polaroid Corp. assistant manufacturing controller Peg Gavenonis of her own experience as an auditor. She continues: "The time dedicated to an EDP audit must have profitable results that yield a more efficient and effective system and one that will provide information fit for management's use."

MIS managers are human, though. Nobody likes good advice, no matter how useful it ought to be. Hence, much of the resentment of the audit. Sure, it's good for you. So is cod liver oil. But being good for you doesn't make

it taste good. To make an audit more palatable, Phelps Dodge Corp.'s vice president for MIS Michael Cangemi suggests looking at the example of accountants. Accountants know their work will be audited because it has been for the better part of a century, he points out. They know what auditors want. They set up their systems to be auditable and to pass audits.

Cangemi, who is a past president of the EDP Auditors Association and previously headed EDP auditing for Phelps Dodge, says MIS personnel must take on the conceptual responsibilities that accountants have assumed for decades. "DP management has to realize that they are responsible for computer controls," he says. "If they accept that, they will welcome the auditor as the second best way to see if their systems are well controlled. The best way is for them to do it themselves."

Once MIS managers accept this responsibility, an audit will be a chance to exchange thoughts, show off a little, and pick up new ideas. No doubt everyone has a wish list of what they would like to see happen on the way to this nirvana:

☐ All auditors must be able to carry out a basic test of EDP operations, which will free the more specialized EDP auditors to function in a more consultative role.

☐ EDP auditors, in turn, must think like managers and apply their skill to management problems.

☐ MIS managers must get up to speed on control, security, and quality assurance.

Application Questions

☐ What is the objective of an EDP audit? What control issues are evaluated?

☐ What are the benefits of an EDP audit to information systems managers?

Source: Efrem Mallach, "Learning How to Profit from the EDP Audit Experience," *Computerworld*, January 19, 1987, p. 17.

Section II: Computer Crime, Ethics, and Society

THE IMPACT OF COMPUTERS ON SOCIETY

We are in the midst of an "information revolution." As we have seen in this text, the widespread use of computers has significantly magnified our ability to analyze, compute, and communicate. What should our attitude be toward the use of computers in business and society? To answer this question, we should analyze some of the major social and economic effects of computers. **Social applications** of computers include their use in solving human and social problems such as crime and pollution. **Socioeconomic effects** of computers refer to the impact on society of the use of computers. For example, computerizing a production process may have the *adverse* effect of a decrease in employment opportunities and the *beneficial* effect of providing consumers with products of better quality at lower cost. Business managers must understand the beneficial and adverse effects of computer usage on society. Such an understanding will help them plan and control the development and operation of computer-based information systems within their organizations. Figure 17–6 illustrates several major aspects of the impact of computers on society that we will now briefly explain. Then we will go into more depth on the issues of computer crime and ethics.

Social Applications

Computers can have many direct beneficial effects on society when they are used to solve human and social problems through social applications such as medical diagnosis, computer-assisted instruction, governmental program planning, environmental quality control, and law enforcement. Computers can be used to help diagnose an illness, prescribe necessary treatment, and monitor the progress of hospital patients. Computer-assisted instruction (CAI) allows a computer to serve as a "tutor," since it uses conversational computing to tailor instruction to the needs of a particular student. This is a tremendous benefit to students, especially those with learning disabilities.

Computers can be used for crime control through various law enforcement applications that allow police to identify and respond quickly to evidences of criminal activity. Computers have been used to monitor the level of pollution in the air and in bodies of water; to detect the sources of pollution and to issue early warnings when dangerous levels are reached. Computers are also used for the program planning of many government agencies in such areas as urban planning, population density and land use studies, highway planning, and urban transit studies. Computers are being used in job placement systems to help match unemployed persons with available jobs. These and other applications illustrate that the computer can be used to help solve the problems of society.

Impact on Employment and Productivity

The impact of computers on **employment** and **productivity** is directly related to the use of computers to achieve automation. There can be no doubt that the use of computers has created new jobs and increased productivity, while also causing a significant reduction in some types of job opportunities. Computers used for office information processing or for the numerical control of machine tools are accomplishing tasks formerly performed by many

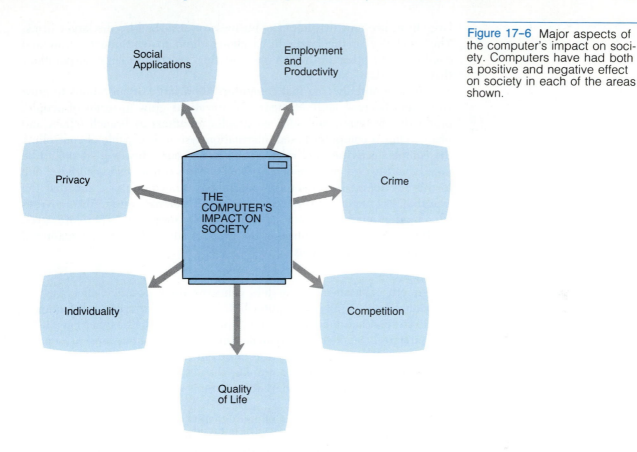

Figure 17–6 Major aspects of the computer's impact on society. Computers have had both a positive and negative effect on society in each of the areas shown.

clerks and machinists. Also, jobs created by computers within a computer-using organization require different types of skills and education than do the jobs eliminated by computers. Therefore, individuals within an organization may become unemployed unless they can be retrained for new positions or new responsibilities.

However, there can be no doubt that the computer industry has created a host of new job opportunities for the manufacture, sale, and maintenance of computer hardware, software, and for other services. Many new jobs, such as systems analysts, computer programmers, and computer operators, have been created in computer-using organizations. Many new jobs have been created in service industries which provide services to the computer industry and to computer-using firms. Additional jobs have been created because computers make possible the production of complex industrial and technical goods and services that would otherwise be impossible to produce. Thus jobs have been created by activities that are heavily dependent on computers in such fields as space exploration, microelectronic technology, and scientific research.

The impact of computers on **competition** concerns the effect that computer systems have on the size of business organizations. Computers allow large firms to become more efficient. This can have several anticompetitive effects. Small business firms that could exist because of the inefficiencies of

Impact on Competition

large firms are now driven out of business or absorbed by the larger firms. The efficiency of the larger firms allows them to continue to grow and combine with other business firms and thus create the large corporations that exist today.

It is undoubtedly true that computers allow large organizations to grow larger and become more efficient. Organizations grow in terms of people, productive facilities, and such geographic locations as branch offices and plants. Only a computer-based information system is capable of controlling the complex activities and relationships that occur. However, it should be noted that the cost and size of computer systems continues to *decrease*, due to the development of microcomputers and minicomputers, and that the availability of computer services continues to *increase*, due to the activities of computer service bureaus and time-sharing companies. Therefore, even small firms can take advantage of the productivity and efficiency generated by computer-based systems.

Impact on Individuality

A frequent criticism of computers concerns their negative effect on the **individuality** of people. Computer-based systems are criticized as impersonal systems that dehumanize and depersonalize activities that have been computerized, since they eliminate the human relationships present in noncomputer systems. Because it is more efficient for an information system to deal with an individual as a number than as a name, many people feel a loss of identity that seems inherent in systems where they seem to be "just another number."

Another aspect of the loss of individuality is the regimentation of the individual that seems to be required by some computer-based systems. These systems do not seem to possess any flexibility. They demand strict adherence to detailed procedures if the system is to work. The negative impact of computers on individuality is reinforced by "horror stories" that describe how inflexible and uncaring computer-based systems are when it comes to rectifying their own mistakes. Many of us are familiar with stories of how computerized customer billing and accounting systems have continued to demand payment and send warning notices to a customer whose account has already been paid, despite repeated attempts by the customer to have the error corrected.

However, computer-based systems can be designed to minimize depersonalization and regimentation. "People oriented" and "user friendly" information systems can be developed. The computer hardware, software, and systems design capabilities that make such systems possible are increasing rather than decreasing. The use of microcomputers promises to dramatically improve the development of people-oriented information systems (through personal computing and distributed processing) and even of everyday products and services (through microprocessor-powered "smart" products).

Impact on the Quality of Life

Since computerized business systems increase productivity, they allow the production of better-quality goods and services at lower costs, with less effort and time. Thus the computer is partially responsible for the high standard of living and increased leisure time we enjoy. In addition, the computer has eliminated monotonous or obnoxious tasks in the office and the factory that formerly had to be performed by people. In many instances, this allows people to concentrate on more challenging and interesting assignments, has upgraded the skill level of the work to be performed, and created challenging jobs requiring highly developed skills in the computer industry and within computer-using organizations. Thus computers can be said to upgrade the **quality of life** because they can upgrade the quality of working conditions and the content of work activities.

Of course, it must be remembered that some jobs created by the computer—data entry, for example—are quite repetitive and routine. Also, to the extent that computers are utilized in some types of automation, they must take some responsibility for the criticism of assembly-line operations that require the continual repetition of elementary tasks, thus forcing a worker to "work like a machine" instead of like a skilled craftsperson. Many automated operations are also criticized for relegating people to a "do nothing" standby role, where workers spend most of their time waiting for infrequent opportunities to "push some buttons." Such effects do have a detrimental effect on the quality of life, but they are more than offset by the less burdensome and more creative jobs created by the computer.

Modern computer systems make it technically and economically feasible to collect, store, integrate, interchange, and retrieve data and information quickly and easily. This characteristic has an important beneficial effect on the efficiency and effectiveness of computer-based information systems. However, the power of the computer to store and retrieve information can have a negative effect on the **right to privacy** of every individual. Confidential information on individuals contained in centralized computer databases by credit bureaus, government agencies, and private business firms could be misused and result in the invasion of privacy and other injustices. Unauthorized use of such information would seriously invade the privacy of individuals. Errors in such data files could seriously hurt the credit standing or reputation of an individual.

Impact on Privacy

Such developments were possible before the advent of computers. However, the speed and power of large computers with centralized direct access databases and remote terminals greatly increases the potential for such injustices. The trend towards nationwide information systems with integrated databases by business firms and government agencies substantially increases the *potential* for misuse of computer-stored information.

The Federal Privacy Act strictly regulates the collection and use of personal data by governmental agencies (except for law enforcement investigative files, classified files, and civil service files). The law specifies that individuals have the right to inspect their personal records, make copies, and correct or remove erroneous or misleading information. It also specifies that federal agencies (1) must annually disclose the types of personal data files they maintain, (2) cannot disclose personal information on an individual to any other individual or agency except under certain strict conditions, (3) must inform individuals of the reasons for requesting personal information from them, (4) must retain personal data records only if it is "relevant and necessary to accomplish" an agency's legal purpose, and (5) must "establish appropriate *administrative*, *technical*, and *physical safeguards* to ensure the security and confidentiality of records."

In 1986, the Electronic Communications Privacy Act and the Computer Fraud and Abuse Act were enacted. These federal laws are the latest attempt to enforce the privacy of computer-based files and communications. These laws prohibit intercepting data communications messages, stealing or destroying data, or trespassing in federal-related computer systems. Such legislation should emphasize and accelerate the efforts of systems designers to use hardware, software, and procedural controls to maintain the accuracy and confidentiality of computerized databases.

COMPUTER CRIME

What is computer crime? Who commits computer crimes? Who are the victims of such crimes? What are some solutions to the problems of computer crime? Informed computer users should know the answers to these questions. Computer crime is a growing threat caused by the widespread use of computers in our society. It thus presents a major challenge to the development of effective controls for computer-based information systems.[1]

Computer Crime Laws

One way to understand computer crime is to see how current legislation defines it. The best example of this is the Computer Fraud and Abuse Act of 1986. In a nutshell, this law says that computer crime involves access of "federal interest" computers (used by the federal government), or operating in interstate or foreign commerce (1) with intent to defraud, (2) resulting in more than a $1,000 loss, and (3) access to certain medical computer systems. Trafficking in computer access passwords is also prohibited. Penalties for violations of this law are severe. They include 1 to 5 years in prison for a first offense, 10 years for a second offense, and 20 years for three or more offenses. Fines could range up to $250,000, or twice the value of stolen data. Figure 17–7 summarizes the criminal acts prohibited by this law.

Examples of Computer Crime

Another way to understand computer crime is to examine examples of major types of criminal activity involving computers. This typically involves (1) money theft, (2) service theft, (3) program and data theft, (4) program copying, (5) data alteration, (6) program damage, (7) data destruction, (8) malicious access, and (9) violation of privacy. These examples also reveal the types of people who become computer criminals and the institutions and individuals who are victims of computer crime. Figure 17–8 illustrates the results of a survey to identify computer criminals and victims.

Money Theft

Many computer crimes involve theft of money. These range from complex bank frauds like the $21 million Wells Fargo Bank theft or the $10.2 million

---

[1] Parts of this section are adapted from J. J. Bloombecker, "New Federal Law Bolsters Computer Security Efforts," *Computerworld*, October 27, 1986, pp. 55–59.

CRIMINAL ACTIONS WITH COMPUTERS

☐ "Knowingly . . . obtains information that has been determined by the U.S. Government . . . to require protection against unauthorized disclosure for reasons of national defense or foreign relations . . . or any restricted data."

☐ "Intentionally . . . obtains information contained in a financial record of a financial institution . . . or contained in a file of a consumer reporting agency on a consumer, as such terms are defined in the Fair Credit Reporting Act."

☐ "Intentionally accesses a computer without authorization if such computer is exclusively for the use of the Government of the United States or, in the case of a computer not exclusively for such use, if such computer is used by or for the Government of the United States and such conduct affects such use."

☐ "Knowingly and with intent to defraud, accesses a federal interest computer without authorization, or exceeds authorized access, and by means of such conduct furthers the intended fraud and obtains anything of value, unless the object of the fraud and the thing obtained consists only of the use of the computer."

☐ "Intentionally accesses a federal interest computer without authorization, and by means of one or more instances of such conduct alters information in that computer, or prevents authorized use of that computer, and thereby causes loss to one or more others of a value aggregating $1,000 or more during any one-year period, or modifies or impairs . . . the medical examination . . . diagnosis . . . treatment . . . or care of one or more individuals."

☐ "Knowingly and with intent to defraud trafficks . . . in any password or similar information through which a computer may be accessed without authorization if (a) such trafficking affects interstate or foreign commerce; or (b) such computer is used by or for the Government of the United States."

Figure 17-7 Computer crime and the law. The Computer Fraud and Abuse Act specifies the following as criminal acts involving computers.

Security Pacific Bank theft to simple, even trivial falsifications of records that allow money to be misappropriated.

Service Theft

Use of computer hardware and software for one's own benefit may be for commercial or noncommercial purposes. One example is the case of a programmer who kept private files on the New York City Board of Education computer. In Indiana, a county employee was convicted of theft under the state's criminal code for using less than $10 worth of the memory of a county computer system. Another case involved a Long Island, New York, university computer system. In this case, the manager of the computer center and his assistant used the school's computer to service commercial accounts for their own enrichment. They received at least $53,000 in revenue from one of their clients.

Program and Data Theft

Data and programs are themselves valuable property and thus are the subject of theft from computer systems. Employees have been charged with computer crime or trade secret theft on several occasions involving disputes between employee and employer as to what the employee is entitled to take

Figure 17–8 Computer criminals and victims. Notice the types of people who commit computer crime and the institutions and individuals who are their victims.

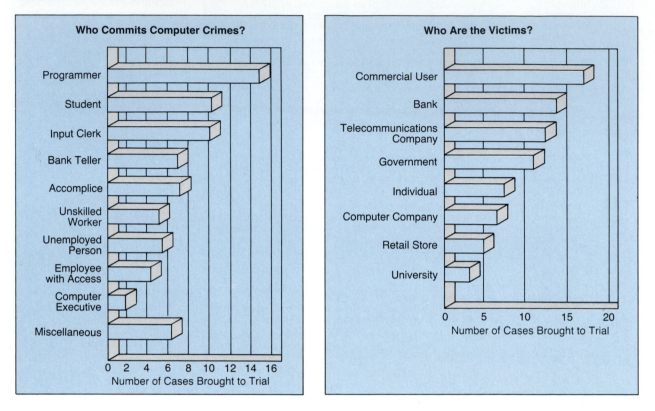

upon leaving the company. Thus computer crime is adding a new twist to acts of industrial espionage between competing firms.

Program Copying

This is another major form of program theft. Several major cases involving unauthorized copying of software by users or competing software companies have been widely reported. This includes lawsuits by software companies like Lotus Development Corporation or Ashton-Tate against major corporations allowing unauthorized copying of their programs, as well as lawsuits against competitors marketing supposed copies or "clones" that copy the "look and feel" of their popular software packages.

Data Alteration

Some changes in data allow criminals to derive significant gains, tangible or intangible. A recent prosecution in Los Angeles resulted in a guilty plea by an employee of the University of Southern California who had been taking payments from students and changing their grades in return. Other reported schemes involved changes in credit information and changes in department of motor vehicles records that facilitated the theft of the cars to which the records referred.

Program Damage

Programmers familiar with a system can do considerable harm by erasing or replacing parts of major programs. A recent case involved a plan to erase the operating systems of two computers maintained by a Los Angeles corporation that operated several restaurants and fast-food outlets. In another case, a "logic bomb" was used to interfere with operations at the Department of Water and Power in Los Angeles. A logic bomb is a program that causes a computer system not to operate as it should.

Data Destruction

Mostly as acts of mischief, contents of files have been destroyed. In San Francisco, United States Leasing International, Inc. found that several people replaced words in their files with curse words, friends' names, and similar material. In other cases, a hidden program routine or "worm" has been used to maliciously erase the data or program contents of magnetic disks.

Malicious Access

"Hacking" is the unauthorized access and use of computer systems. One of the leading issues in reaction to hacking is the problem of what to do when a hacker gets access to a computer system, reads some files, but neither steals nor damages anything. This situation is becoming increasingly common in the computer crime cases that are prosecuted. In California, a court found that the typical computer crime statute language prohibiting "malicious" access to a computer system did apply to users gaining access to others' computer systems.

Violation of Privacy

A consistent fear relating to computers is that the computer will facilitate invasions of privacy. With the growing awareness of the dangers that computer crime poses to average citizens, it can be anticipated that invasions of privacy will increasingly be punished through the use of computer crime law. This includes laws like the Federal Privacy Act, and the Electronic Communications Privacy Act.

Information Systems and Computer Crime

It should now be obvious that computer-based information systems are vulnerable to many types of computer crime. The increased use of computers and the widespread distribution of computer power through interconnected networks of computers has significantly increased the potential for computer crime. Even the proliferation of microcomputers in business, government, education, and the rest of society provides new opportunities for computer crime. (See Figure 17–9.) Thus computer crime presents a major challenge to information systems developers. Designing effective information system controls has now become a vitally important assignment. Users, systems developers, and systems auditors must utilize and require many of the control methods discussed in the previous section. Only then will information systems security be a realizable goal.

Figure 17–9 Microcomputers and the potential for computer crime. Notice the many ways that a microcomputer system is vulnerable to computer crime.

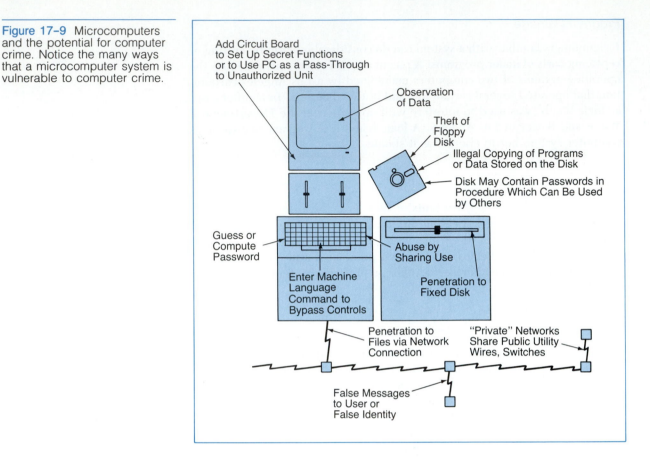

COMPUTER ETHICS

What should computer users do about computer crime and other abuses of computer power? That's where **computer ethics** comes in. Computer professionals and users must accept their responsibilities as part of the people resources required in any computer-based information system. But what are these responsibilities?

One way to answer that question is to examine the responsibilities contained in a code of professional conduct for computer professionals. A good example is the code of professional conduct of the Association for Computing Machinery (ACM). It is the largest national organization of professionals in the computing field. Its code of conduct outlines the ethical considerations inherent in the major responsibilities of a professional in the computer industry. Figure 17–10 is a summary of the ACM code.

The ACM code provides general guidelines for ethical conduct in the development and operation of computer-based information systems. Users and computer professionals could follow such guidelines by (1) acting with integrity, (2) increasing their competence, (3) setting high standards, (4) accepting responsibility for their work, and (5) advancing the health, pri-

ACM CODE OF PROFESSIONAL CONDUCT

CANON 1

An ACM member shall act at all times with integrity.

Ethical Considerations

An ACM member shall properly qualify himself when expressing an opinion outside his areas of competence. A member is encouraged to express his opinion on subjects within his area of competence.

An ACM member shall preface any partisan statements about information processing by indicating clearly on whose behalf they are made.

An ACM member shall act faithfully on behalf of his employers and clients.

CANON 2

An ACM member should strive to increase his competence and the competence and prestige of the profession.

Ethical Considerations

An ACM member is encouraged to extend public knowledge, understanding, and appreciation of information processing, and to oppose any false or deceptive statements relating to information processing of which he is aware.

An ACM member shall not use his professional credentials to misrepresent his competence.

An ACM member shall undertake only those professional assignments and commitments for which he is qualified.

An ACM member shall strive to design and develop systems that adequately perform the intended functions and that satisfy his employer's or client's operational needs.

An ACM member should maintain and increase his competence through a program of continuing education encompassing the techniques, technical standards, and practices in his fields of professional activity.

An ACM member should provide opportunity and encouragement for professional development and advancement of both professionals and those aspiring to become professionals.

CANON 3

An ACM member shall accept responsibility for his work.

Ethical Considerations

An ACM member shall accept only those assignments for which there is reasonable expectancy of meeting requirements or specifications, and shall perform his assignments in a professional manner.

CANON 4

An ACM member shall act with professional responsibility.

Ethical Considerations

An ACM member shall not use his membership in ACM improperly for professional advantage or to misrepresent the authority of his statements.

An ACM member shall conduct professional activities on a high plane.

An ACM member is encouraged to uphold and improve the professional standards of the Association through participation in their formulation, establishment, and enforcement.

CANON 5

An ACM member should use his special knowledge and skills for the advancement of human welfare.

Ethical Considerations

An ACM member should consider the health, privacy, and general welfare of the public in the performance of his work.

An ACM member, whenever dealing with data concerning individuals, shall always consider the principle of the individual's privacy and seek the following:

—To minimize the data collected.
—To limit authorized access to the data.
—To provide proper security for the data.
—To determine the required retention period of the data.
—To ensure proper disposal of the data.

Figure 17–10 The Code of Ethics of the Association for Computing Machinery (ACM). Notice how it stresses integrity, competence, high standards, responsibility, and concern for human welfare.

REAL WORLD APPLICATION 17-2

First Chicago Bank

"We strive for security balance," declares Arthur J. Bilek, as he thrusts his arms forward and brings both extended, palms-down hands into a parallel plane. Bilek is vice president and director of security risk management at First Chicago, one of the nation's largest banks, where extensive computerization manages the flow of billions of dollars every day. The balance Bilek and his security risk management operation strive for is one that matches each security risk with appropriate protection against the risk. The aim is to thwart computer crime and other security threats without undue expense and with minimum disruption of normal business procedure.

Appropriate protection for First Security begins with a clear and detailed understanding of all the bank's asset—personnel, cash and securities, facilities and equipment, operations and activities, information resources, and so on. "A threat to any of these assets is considered a security risk," he explains. Thus, step one in the security risk management program is to identify the assets, assigning an identification code to each item within an asset group.

In the data processing area, assets include mainframes and peripherals in the computer centers; data networks and distributed processing systems; personal computers; related office automation devices; operational and application software; bank-owned personal computers used at home by bank personnel; and, of course, all databases.

Once identified, each asset is valued. This takes into consideration both damage and replacement costs and the negative impact on the business of any security breach involving the asset. Asset identification and evaluation data become part of the central database of the bank security risk management's exclusive computer system.

Step two in the program considers the security threat to the asset—burglary, theft, vandalism, terrorism, fire, electronic break-in, and other risks. In this threat evaluation, security risk management personnel work closely with managers in the user departments. The severity of the threat, the probability of occurrence, and the exposure of the asset are examined. A risk analysis ranking—from low to high—is applied to each asset and added to the security risk management's computer

vacy, and general welfare of the public. This would help both users and specialists avoid computer crime and increase the security of information systems.

Of course, codes of conduct are guidelines, not laws. Thus a more obvious guide to ethical conduct in computing would be the computer crime laws discussed earlier. This includes the Fair Credit Act, the Federal Privacy Act, the Electronic Communications Privacy Act, the Computer Fraud and Abuse Act, and other federal and state computer crime laws. Users and computer professionals should take such laws seriously. Truly ethical behavior would involve following the *spirit*, not just the *letter* of the provisions in these laws. Thus, organizations should establish policies and individuals should act in a cooperative and mutually beneficial spirit of ethical responsibility in computing.

database. Bilek believes that the threat from hackers and electronic break-ins will increase with the proliferation of personal computer use. Safeguards against this threat already are in place and, Bilek says, will be regularly reviewed and upgraded as this threat becomes more serious.

Step three uses the asset threat evaluation and risk analysis data to develop the all-important security risk management plan for the asset. This phase involves clear communication and close cooperation between security risk management staff and the user department's manager. And here, too, the concept of appropriate protection comes into sharp focus. "The risk management plan for the asset, which also is entered in detail into our computerized asset database, spells out the protective measures to be applied, the controls and procedures to be maintained," Bilek points out. "We seek total acceptance of the security measures and full agreement with the controls and procedures from the manager. This acceptance is absolutely vital to successful implementation," he adds.

The final step in First Chicago's security program is monitoring and review of the asset

risk management plan implementation and performance. Every loss, every departure from proscribed procedure, and every breach of control policy is reported and investigated. Security auditors and managers of user departments regularly check and test security measures. Security risk management staffers keep abreast of external security environments and situations such as a reported growth in hacker and electronic break-in attempts. Periodically, but at least annually, the risk rankings of each asset are subject to thorough review, and the risk management plan for the asset is adjusted as current circumstances warrant.

Application Questions

☐ What four security risk management steps does First Chicago take to protect itself from computer crime?

☐ What information system resources are protected? Does First Chicago's security program seem capable of protecting such resources from computer crime? Explain.

Source: "Security at First Chicago: A Strategy for Matching Each Risk with Protection," *Information Processing,* Fall 1985, pp. 15–16.

It should now be obvious that managers should insist that the societal and personal impact of using computers must be considered when a computer-based information system is being developed. A major management objective should be to develop systems that can be easily and effectively used by people. The objectives of the system must also include the protection of the privacy of the individuals and the defense of the system against computer crime. Control hardware, software, and procedures must be included in the systems design. The potential for misuse and malfunction of a proposed system must be analyzed with respect to the impact on computer-using organizations, individuals, and society as a whole.

Many of the potential negative effects of computer usage mentioned previously have or would result from errors in information systems development. Increased emphasis on the control capabilities of computer-based

Controls and Personal and Social Responsibility

information systems would protect us from many of these potential effects. Computer-based systems can be designed to prevent their own misuse and remedy their own malfunctions. Computers make it possible for us to monitor the activities of computer-based systems and thus prevent computerized crime and correct systems malfunctions. Managers must recognize that the *design and maintenance of system controls* is the key to minimizing the negative effects of computer misuse and malfunction.

It should also be obvious that many detrimental effects of the computer on society are caused by individuals and organizations who are not willing to accept the social responsibility for their actions. Like other powerful tools, computers possess the potential for great good or evil. Managers, computer users, and computer professionals must accept the responsibility for their proper and beneficial use.

SUMMARY

☐ One of the most important responsibilities of the management of computer-using business firms is the security and control of its information services activities. Controls are needed that ensure the accuracy, integrity, and safety of the information processing activities and resources of computer users. Such controls attempt to minimize errors, fraud, and destruction in the information services department. These controls can be grouped into three major categories: (1) information system controls, (2) procedural controls, and (3) physical facility controls.

☐ The information services department should be periodically audited to review and evaluate whether proper and adequate information system, procedural, and facility controls have been developed and implemented. Information systems auditing, therefore, plays a vital role in ensuring proper managerial control of computer resources and information system activities.

☐ Computers have had a major impact on society and thus impose serious responsibilities upon the management of computer-using business firms. Social applications of computers provide a direct beneficial effect to society when they are used to solve human and social problems. Computers have had a major effect on employment, productivity, and competition in the business world. Computers have had both beneficial and detrimental effects on individuality, the quality of life, and privacy.

☐ Computer crime poses a growing threat to society. Such crimes typically involve the theft, destruction, or unauthorized use of hardware, software, or data. Several major laws have been enacted to counter computer crime.

☐ Managers must accept the responsibility for the proper and beneficial use of computers in their business firms. Managers must insist that effective measures be taken to ensure that the social and economic effects of computer usage are considered during the development and operation of computer-based information systems.

These are the key terms and concepts of this chapter. The page number of their first explanation is in parentheses.

1. Auditing information systems *(599)*
2. Audit trail *(600)*
3. Controls and social responsibility *(613)*
4. Computer crime *(606)*
5. Computer ethics *(610)*
6. Information system controls *(590)*
7. Information system security *(590)*
8. Physical facility controls *(597)*
9. Procedural controls *(595)*
10. Social applications of computers *(602)*
11. Socioeconomic effects of computers
   a. Competition *(603)*
   b. Employment *(602)*
   c. Individuality *(604)*
   d. Privacy *(605)*
   e. Productivity *(602)*
   f. Quality of life *(604)*

Match one of the **key terms and concepts** listed above with one of the brief examples or definitions listed below. Try to find the "best fit" for answers that seem to fit more than one term or concept. Defend your choices.

_____ 1. Ensures the accuracy, integrity, and safety of information system activities and resources.

_____ 2. Control totals are an example.

_____ 3. The separation of the duties of computer programmers and computer operators is an example.

_____ 4. Fire and access detection systems are examples.

_____ 5. Periodically examining the accuracy and integrity of computer processing.

_____ 6. The presence of documentation that allows a transaction to be traced through all stages of information processing.

_____ 7. Computerized monitoring of environmental quality is an example.

_____ 8. Employees may have to retrain or transfer.

_____ 9. We can produce more goods per worker.

_____ 10. Helps big firms get bigger and small firms survive.

_____ 11. Tedious jobs are decreased and leisure time increased.

_____ 12. Personal information in computer-accessible files.

_____ 13. You are more than just a number.

_____ 14. Fraudulent transfer of funds is an example.

_____ 15. Computer professionals must act with integrity and competence in their work.

_____ 16. Managers must insist on proper controls in the development of computer-based information systems.

APPLICATION PROBLEMS

1. If you have not already done so, answer the questions after the two Real World Applications in this chapter.

2. Match one of the following types of controls with one of the examples listed below.

   a. Input controls.
   b. Processing controls.
   c. Output controls.
   d. Storage controls.
   e. Procedural controls.
   f. Physical facility controls.

   _____ 1. Proper documentation is required for all applications.
   _____ 2. Duplicate files are kept for backup purposes.
   _____ 3. Control totals are computed for entry of transactions data.
   _____ 4. Checkpoints are established and monitored.
   _____ 5. Fault-tolerant computer systems are used.
   _____ 6. Prenumbered forms are used for important computer-produced documents.

3. Match one of the following impact areas of computers on society with one of the examples listed below.

   a. Competition.
   b. Employment.
   c. Individuality.
   d. Privacy.
   e. Productivity.
   f. Quality of life.

   _____ 1. Computer-based systems can depersonalize and regimentize activities in society.
   _____ 2. Computers can help keep large organizations under control.
   _____ 3. Computers can take over tedious jobs.
   _____ 4. Computers can make it easier to access personal information.
   _____ 5. Computers have created new types of jobs.
   _____ 6. Computers make possible the manufacture of complex products.

4. Match one of the following methods of computer crime with one of the examples listed below.

   a. Malicious access.
   b. Money theft.
   c. Program and data theft.
   d. Program and data damage.
   e. Program copying.
   f. Violation of privacy.

   _____ 1. Planting a "logic bomb" or "worm" in a program.
   _____ 2. Falsifying records to cover fraud.
   _____ 3. Taking software or data when leaving a company.
   _____ 4. Unauthorized duplication of software packages.
   _____ 5. Copying personal data files.
   _____ 6. Unauthorized entry or "hacking."

5. An information systems auditor has written a report criticizing the
    controls ABC Department Stores has implemented in its payroll and
    accounts payable applications. His report states that these two
    applications should have more stringent controls than other common
    business applications. Why? What risks are involved? What controls
    can you suggest to minimize such risks?

6. Look at Figure 17–6. Can you give one positive and one negative
    example of the impact of computers on society for each of the seven
    impact areas shown in that figure? Give it a try.

7. A customer of ABC Department Stores was repeatedly billed for items
    she had already paid for. The credit department blamed the com-
    puter. The MIS department blamed an error in a program. The
    programmer blamed data entry personnel. Explain how each of these
    could have caused the error, and how the error could have been
    avoided.

8. An employee of ABC Department Stores made copies of a software
    package for several friends in violation of the purchase agreement for
    the program. Is this a computer crime? Is this behavior ethical?
    Explain.

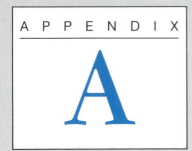

APPENDIX

A

PERSONAL COMPUTER APPLICATIONS

Appendix Outline

Learning Objectives

The purpose of this appendix is to provide you with a brief, simple, step-by-step introduction to the use of the most popular types of application software packages for microcomputers and many larger computers. They are (1) operating system programs, (2) word processing programs, (3) electronic spreadsheet programs with graphics capabilities, (4) database management programs, and (5) integrated packages that combine all of these functions into one package. Reading this appendix and completing its hands-on exercises and assignments should allow you to achieve the *appreciation*, *knowledge*, and *experience* needed to effectively use such programs.

More specifically, your goal should be to accomplish these basic functions:

1. How to use a microcomputer and its operating system.
2. How to create, edit, store, and print a document using word processing functions.
3. How to build, modify, store, print, and use an electronic spreadsheet.
4. How to create and use a database and retrieve, display, and report information.
5. How to use graphics displays to analyze data and communicate information.

After you attain these objectives, you will still need further knowledge and experience before you can be an advanced business or professional user. You can gain more knowledge by consulting the manuals and books available for most software packages. They provide you with information describing in detail how to use the full capabilities of these packages. With such knowledge, and more hands-on experience, you can begin to accomplish many valuable professional assignments with these popular software packages.

Section I: Using the PC and DOS

Outline

Introduction to the PC
Introduction to DOS
Getting Started
Using Other Software
Managing Disks
Managing Files

INTRODUCTION TO THE PC

This section is an introduction to the use of personal computers (PCs) and their operating systems. It assumes you have access to:

☐ A PC with at least 256K (about 256,000 bytes) of main memory, two floppy diskette drives (or one floppy and one hard disk drive), a one-color display, and a printer.

☐ A copy of DOS (the main system control program) for the PC. Either the IBM version (called PC-DOS) or the generic version (called MS-DOS) will do. This appendix assumes you use DOS Version 2.0 or higher.

The PC is the most common kind of microcomputer in the business world. The first version was made by International Business Machines Corp. (IBM). However, many manufacturers of computers have made their own versions. IBM Personal Computers were regarded as a standard. Other PCs usually act like an IBM PC, so they are called "IBM compatibles" or "clones." Such compatibles are not always perfect imitations of IBM micro-computers, so you will sometimes find a program that runs well on an IBM PC, but not on a compatible.

What you will read here are the features and uses of PCs that are widely found. Descriptions should be valid for most PCs, including IBM's Personal System/2 line. What is not covered here is a set of microcomputers that are not compatible with IBM equipment. These include all Apple computers, most Commodore, Atari, and older Radio Shack computers, and any computer running the CP/M operating system.

What makes a PC a PC? It is not the physical appearance of the microcomputer. Basically, it is a combination of the internal circuitry and the operating system that is unique. Most important is the use of microprocessor chips by the Intel Corporation—the 8088, 8086, 80286, and 80386. The 8088 microprocessor is the most common of the four chips. The others are more recent and more powerful versions. The four chips are fairly compatible. For example, an 80286 will execute any instruction that an 8088 will execute (but not vice versa).

PCs use either the PC-DOS or MS-DOS operating system. It is the combination of DOS with the 8088 (or similar) chip that makes the computer a PC. This combination is now the single most common computing system in the world, by far the most common in business applications.

Physical Setup

Personal computers may vary quite a bit in their components, but still have a lot in common. If you have a "desk" model, you will have at least the following four separate major components shown in Figure A1–1:

A typical PC setup. Common variations include the use of a hard disk, half-height drives placed one above the other, or 3.5-inch floppy disk drives.

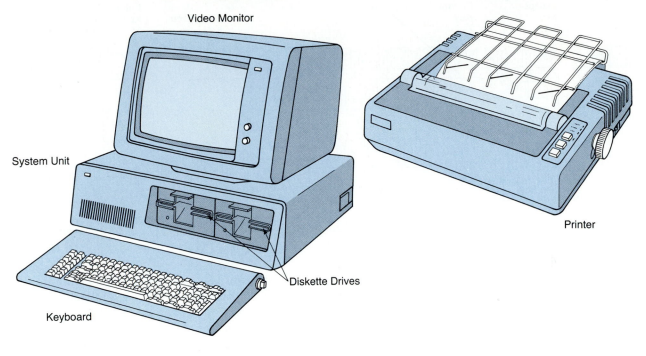

1. **A system unit.** Inside this unit are the circuit boards, a power supply, a cooling fan, and possibly a hard disk drive. The circuit boards contain many microelectronic memory, logic, and control chips, including the main **microprocessor.** At the back of the unit are several outlets of various kinds. These allow the computer to use peripherals such as a visual-display screen, printer, keyboard, and perhaps a modem for communicating with other computers. At the front of the system unit you will usually see the **floppy disk** drives and a **hard disk** drive if you have one. These *secondary storage* devices are used to store data and programs until they must be transferred into the *primary storage* chips (memory) of the computer.

2. **A video monitor,** usually resting on top of the system unit. This visual display unit normally looks like a television set; it may have either a color or monochrome display. Most of the visual display units you are likely to see for the next few years make use of the cathode-ray tube technology, so they are frequently called CRTs. An important concept when working with computers that use visual display devices is the **cursor,** which indicates where on the display the next character will appear. Usually the cursor looks like a flashing line or rectangle. When your computer is turned on, if you type a few spaces (using the space bar at the bottom of the keyboard), you should be able to see the cursor move to the right.

Figure A1–2 A typical PC keyboard. There are many variations of this popular keyboard layout.

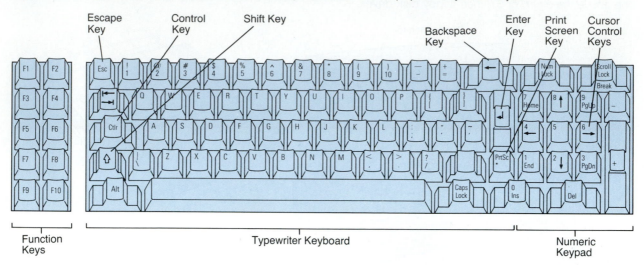

3. **A keyboard.** The keyboard is usually connected to the computer's system unit by a long, coiled cable somewhat like a telephone receiver cable. This allows you to move the keyboard around to suit yourself. If you have never seen one of these keyboards before, you should take a moment to familiarize yourself with its general layout before going on. Look at Figure A1–2. Notice that there are many more keys than on a typical typewriter keyboard. The arrangement of the keys is usually different from that of a typewriter. Figure A1–3 summarizes the functions of several important PC keys.

4. **A printer.** The printer is usually connected to the PC by means of a "parallel" connection. This basically means that it receives one whole line of output from the computer at a time. The most common kind of printer for personal computers uses a dot matrix mechanism to form printed characters. However, other technologies, such as the daisy wheel print mechanism and the laser printer, are also used.

Besides these devices, you may have other equipment; for example, you might have a data communication **modem** or cables to connect your computer to a network of some kind. If your computer is running in a network, you may be able to share data or programs with other computers. You may also find that you have to transfer programs to your microcomputer from a central computer that acts as a "server" to other computers networked around it. Again, this should not greatly affect what you read here.

INTRODUCTION TO DOS

DOS is the **operating system** or main system control program that PCs need to operate. When supplied by IBM for IBM microcomputers it is called PC-DOS; when supplied by Microsoft Corporation for compatibles it is called MS-DOS. The two kinds of DOS have certain technical differences, and are not completely alike in all respects, but they are enough alike to let us treat them both as if they were the same thing.

ENTER (also called RETURN). Usually placed where the carriage return key would be on an electric typewriter. Sometimes the ENTER key is marked with an arrow pointing down and to the left.

SHIFT. Located at the lower left and lower right of the alphanumeric part of the keyboard. This key works by pressing it together with other keys; usually the action is to capitalize a letter, but sometimes there may be other effects.

CAPS LOCK. Usually located at the left of the alphanumeric part of the keyboard, except on IBM computers, where it may be at the lower right corner of the alphanumeric portion. This key is not like the shift-lock key on a typewriter; its action applies only to the alphabetic keys. Numerals and punctuation keys are not affected by CAPS LOCK.

CONTROL. Usually placed on the left side of the alphanumeric (main) part of the keyboard. This key functions like a typewriter's shift key—you push it at the same time you press another key. This key is typically marked ''Ctrl'' or something similar.

ALT. Usually placed near the lower left side of the alphanumeric (main) part of the keyboard. This key is like the CONTROL and SHIFT keys—it works in combination with other keys; you push both ALT and the other key at the same time.

ESCAPE (probably marked Esc). Usually at the top left of the alphanumeric portion. This key is usually pressed by itself. It often has the function of interrupting or stopping a program.

BACKSPACE. Usually at the top right of the alphanumeric portion. This key usually erases characters to the left of the cursor. It is not the same as the LEFT arrow key, located on the numeric/cursor keypad, although both keys are often marked with an arrow pointing to the left.

NUM LOCK. Located at the top of the numeric keypad. This key is a ''toggle'' (on-off) switch, which changes the action of the numeric keypad keys from cursor movement to numbers, and back again.

BREAK. Located at the top of the numeric keypad (on most machines). On IBM keyboards, this key may say SCROLL LOCK on its top, with BREAK written on the face of the key. BREAK is normally meant to be used in combination with the CONTROL key; pressing CONTROL + BREAK will usually halt a program or command.

Cursor movement keys. These are marked on the numeric keypad. When the keypad is in cursor mode (set by NUM LOCK), the arrow keys and other keys function to move the cursor around the CRT screen.

Function keys. Usually located either at the extreme left of the keyboard or across the top. These keys have special functions that vary from program to program or even inside a program; to know what they do you must read the manual for the program that you are using. The function keys can be used in combination with the ALT, SHIFT, and CONTROL keys.

Figure A1–3 A summary of important PC keys.

There are several different versions of DOS; usually, a program that runs under an older version (with a lower version number such as 1.0 or 1.1) will also run under a newer version (with a higher version number such as 3.0 or 3.1). The opposite is not true. Many current programs now require a DOS version of 2.0 or later. In addition, disks that were written under older versions of DOS are usually readable by computers running later versions, but the reverse is not true.

What DOS Does

The most important software package for any computer is its operating system. An operating system is an integrated system of programs that supervises the operations of the CPU, controls the input/output and storage functions of the computer system, and provides various support services as the computer executes your application programs. Therefore, if you want to use a PC, you must load and use its operating system (DOS) before you can accomplish any other task.

DOS performs many functions for the user. For example, it allows you to make use of the computer's main and secondary memory devices (especially disks) to store programs and data. DOS also manages input and output to and from such devices as keyboards, CRTs, and printers. DOS works on **files,** which are either specific collections of data or individual programs located on storage devices such as floppy disks. Data and programs normally cannot be accessed except in files.

DOS uses various programs. These are computer programs like any others, but they are special in that they do such jobs as copy files, format disks, and show lists of file names in use. The special DOS programs are known as **DOS commands.** Some of these programs are used so often that they are copied ("loaded") into the computer's main memory, where they can be accessed very quickly. These programs are called "resident." Other DOS commands (programs) are used less often, so they are left on a disk, ready to be called up when you need them.

This means that to use some DOS commands, you must have a diskette containing those commands in one of the computer's diskette drives. If you try to use a nonresident DOS command when your computer can't find it on a diskette, you will get an error message such as "bad command or file name." The consequences of this are not too bad. You simply can't use the command until you put a diskette containing it into one of the disk drives.

When you turn the computer on, you usually will put a floppy disk containing the operating system (DOS) into one of the computer's diskette drives (the procedure is described in detail shortly). As the computer's power comes on, a simple program located on a chip (specifically, a ROM "read only memory" chip) inside the system unit is activated. This program's main function is to copy the resident parts of the operating system into main memory. When the copying or **loading** process is complete, the computer has been "booted up" and is ready for use.

If you try to start the computer and do not have a "system disk" in the right diskette drive, what happens varies depending on what kind of computer you have. IBM Personal Computers will activate a ROM-stored BASIC language interpreter display. Other computers may simply print a message on the video screen telling you to put a system disk in one of the diskette drives. No damage is done by not having a system disk in the diskette drive; you just haven't loaded the operating system (on most PCs). Because you haven't loaded the operating system, you will find it impossible to run most programs.

GETTING STARTED

Here is how to start up your computer. You will use the floppy disk drives. Remember that they and their disks are the units of your computer system that are the most vulnerable to damage. Treat drives and disks with care.

1. Insert System Disk

If it is not already open, gently open the disk-retaining door or latch on diskette drive A. On most PCs, this drive will be either the top of two drives or the one on the left. The computer will look in Drive A for a system disk. Insert the diskette in the disk drive with its label facing toward the top of the drive and the long, narrow opening that shows the surface of the diskette

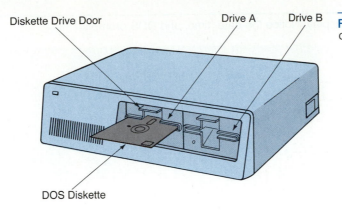

Diskette Drive Door   Drive A   Drive B

DOS Diskette

Figure A1–4 Inserting a floppy disk into a disk drive.

itself facing into the disk drive (see Figure A1–4). Be careful not to fold or bend the disk while inserting it! Gently close the disk-retaining door or latch.

2. Turn On the Computer

Turn on the computer's video monitor, printer (if one is attached), and any other accessories. Now reach toward the rear of the system unit's right side and turn on the computer itself. If you listen closely, you should be able to hear the fan come on.

3. Greetings

If you correctly inserted a DOS diskette in Drive A, a greeting message will appear on the CRT screen. This usually takes about 10 to 60 seconds, depending partly on how much main memory there is. The time is used for system diagnostics that do such things as check the quality of the main memory chips. You may be asked to type in the date and time. Type them in, following the form shown on the screen. Press the ENTER (or RETURN) key after each entry. Figure A1–5 shows what a typical screen looks like after the start-up process has been completed.

Note: Some diskettes have an "autostart" file on them. This automatically causes certain DOS commands to be executed and other programs to be started when the computer boots up. If you have such a diskette, some of the start-up procedures mentioned here (such as entry of the date and time) will not be necessary.

HANDS–ON EXERCISE A1–1

Starting the Computer

Obtain a system disk and follow the instructions above to start up your computer. Don't forget to fill in the date and time.

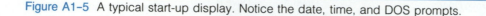

Figure A1–5 A typical start-up display. Notice the date, time, and DOS prompts.

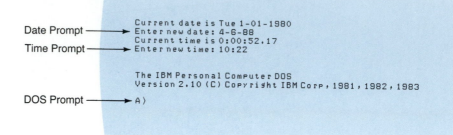

Date Prompt ⟶

Time Prompt ⟶

DOS Prompt ⟶

```
Current date is Tue 1-01-1980
Enter new date: 4-6-88
Current time is 0:00:52.17
Enter new time: 10:22


The IBM Personal Computer DOS
Version 2.10 (C) Copyright IBM Corp. 1981, 1982, 1983

A>
```

4. The DOS Prompt

When the start-up routine has ended, the DOS "command processor" will be loaded and ready to execute commands. The **DOS prompt,** a letter and a "greater than" symbol followed by a flashing cursor, will appear, probably fairly near the top of the screen. For example, **A>** is typically displayed. The computer will now treat anything that you type in from the keyboard as a DOS command.

The letter before the greater-than symbol indicates the "default disk drive." This is the disk drive to which the computer will look for files if you don't specify a disk drive. Normally, when the system has just booted up, Drive A will be the default drive, but this can be changed. For example, you can make Drive B the default drive by typing B: after the DOS prompt and pressing ENTER. B> is then displayed.

5. Giving Commands

The usual way to give a command to DOS is to type the command's name, then press ENTER. You can use either capital or small letters. For example, the command CLS clears the screen. You can type either:

     cls

or

     CLS

and get the same result. If the command was a resident part of DOS, it will be executed as soon as you press ENTER; if the command is stored as a file on a diskette, the computer will look on the disk, copy the command into main memory, then execute it. For these nonresident commands, if you don't specify a disk drive, the computer will look on the default drive. You can specify the disk drive by putting its name before the name of the command. For example, if your command is FORMAT, you could type:

     FORMAT

(followed by pressing ENTER). The computer would look on the default disk drive for a copy of FORMAT. However, if you typed:

`B:FORMAT`

(again, followed by ENTER), the computer would try to find the command on Drive B.

HANDS–ON EXERCISE A1–2

Giving Commands

You can always give the commands DATE and TIME to the DOS prompt if you want to change the date and time. Alternatively, if you just want to see the date or time, you can just give the command DATE or TIME, then press ENTER when prompted to enter a new date or time. Try this now.

Figure A1–6 summarizes the functions of special keys that work while DOS is active.

DOS Keystroke Functions

Figure A1–6 Common DOS keystroke functions.

INTERRUPT

ESCAPE. Cancels the current line of commands that you are typing.
CONTROL + BREAK. Usually stops a command or program.
CONTROL + NUM LOCK. Usually causes output from a program to pause until you press another key.
CONTROL + ALT + DEL. Interrupts a command or program and reloads DOS.

RETYPING

F1. Retypes the last command given, one letter at a time. You can retype as much of the last command as you want, then make changes to the end of it.
F3. Retypes the entire last command given, lets you edit it (using BACK-SPACE, etc.), then press ENTER.

UPPER- OR LOWERCASE

CAPS LOCK or SHIFT. Switches you between upper- and lowercase. It makes no difference whether you give commands to DOS in capital or lowercase letters.

AUTOMATIC REPETITION

Most keys on the keyboard will repeat automatically if you hold them down.

CORRECTING MISTAKES

If the mistake is only one or two letters, use the backspace key to erase back to the point of the mistake, and type over.
If the mistake is several letters, before pressing ENTER, press ESCAPE, which cancels the whole line, and type the line over.
If the mistake occurs after pressing ENTER, DOS will try to execute what you typed. Use CONTROL + BREAK if necessary to stop what you started. In other words, it is important to look at what you have typed before pressing ENTER.

PRINTER OUTPUT

Continuous printout: If you want everything you do to be sent not just to the CRT screen but also to the printer, press CONTROL + PRTSC. After you press CONTROL + PRTSC, everything that appears on the screen will also appear on the printer until you press CONTROL + PRTSC again.
Screen dump: Pressing SHIFT + PRTSC will copy the contents of the screen to the printer. This can be a quick and convenient way to get short printouts.

HANDS–ON EXERCISE A1–3

Handling Errors

Try typing DATF instead of DATE, then press ENTER. Note what happens. Now try typing DBTE, and correct it before you press ENTER.

USING OTHER SOFTWARE

How do other software packages work with DOS? For example, you will have to load the software packages mentioned in this appendix into your computer using DOS. Almost all programs written for the PC assume the following routine:

1. You load DOS into memory from the DOS system disk.
2. The DOS prompt (probably A>) is displayed on your screen.
3. You remove the DOS system disk from Drive A and insert the program disk for the software package you want to use.
4. You key in a brief program name that will cause the program to be executed by loading it from your disk into main memory, then starting execution. For example: BASIC, LOTUS, DBASE, and so on.
5. The screen may show prompts or messages that tell you how to begin using the program you have just loaded.

HANDS–ON EXERCISE A1–4

Using Programs

Follow the above routine to load a program provided by your instructor. Then use the program if you can. If not, exit to DOS as indicated by the program displays, or press CONTROL + ALT + DEL to reload DOS.

Floppy diskettes for PCs are usually of the 5¼-inch size. However, IBM Personal System/2 microcomputers use the 3½-inch size. The diskette consists of a thin, circular piece of plastic coated with a magnetic surface. The diskette itself is permanently enclosed in a plastic case. The diskette actually turns inside its case.

A floppy diskette must be **formatted** before you can use it. That is, it must have a standard pattern of bits magnetized (or "written") on its surface. This organizes the disk into a number of recording "tracks" and "sectors." Most PCs use both sides of the diskette, but some older models may have single-sided disk drives.

PCs normally use "soft-sectored" diskettes, which can be formatted by your computer's diskette drives. For most purposes and for most PCs, you should obtain "double-sided, double density" (DS/DD) diskettes.

Warning: The following paragraphs describe the formatting procedure. This procedure is destructive. It will remove any data or programs you might have had stored on a diskette, and leave in their place a "blank" disk. Don't format disks without being sure you really mean to!

To prepare a diskette for use, you format it using the FORMAT command. Usually, you will have your system disk in Drive A (the default drive), and will be formatting a blank diskette that is in Drive B. Give the command:

    FORMAT B:

The command will be retrieved from your system disk in Drive A and will tell you to put your blank disk to be formatted in Drive B. Do this (don't forget to close the drive door or latch), then press any key. Formatting takes a while—about a minute. Don't remove your diskette from drive B until FORMAT asks if you want to format another diskette.

If you want to format several diskettes, keep answering "Y" to the question about formatting another diskette, and follow the directions on the screen. If you are finished formatting, answer "N" to the question. You will be returned to the DOS command processor and the DOS prompt will be displayed.

If you want to put a copy of the operating system on the diskette that you are formatting, give the command:

    FORMAT B:/S

If you don't add the "/S" part when giving the command, the diskette in Drive B will be formatted without leaving space for the operating system, and it will be impossible to add the operating system later without reformatting the disk. On the other hand, the operating system takes quite a bit of space (more than ¹⁄₁₀ of the disk on most systems), so you probably won't want it on every diskette you use.

MANAGING DISKS

Preparing Disks for Use

HANDS–ON EXERCISE A1–5

Formatting a Disk

Obtain a diskette that does not contain data or programs you want to save. Format it, following the instructions above. Try formatting it both with and without the operating system. At the end of the format operation, the program FORMAT will report the number of free bytes on the disk. Compare the results with and without the operating system on the disk, so that you can see how much space the operating system takes.

Taking Care of Disks

Diskettes are remarkably sturdy, but are not immune to damage. Don't bend or fold them. Keep them clean—if dust or smoke gets on the surface, the particles can remove the magnetic coating as the diskette turns. Finally, keep your diskettes out of heat and direct sunlight; heat can warp the diskette's case, and sunlight can destroy the magnetic patterns that are used to store bits of information on the disk. If your diskette gets damaged, you probably will lose some or even all of the information on it, and it may not be possible to reformat the disk.

A Command that Checks Disks

The command CHKDSK will verify the condition of your disk. If you encounter errors in reading or writing a disk, it is wise to use the DOS command CHKDSK to examine the status of your disk. The syntax is CHKDSK (disk). For example, you could type:

CHKDSK B:

to validate the disk in Drive B.

Write Protection and Copy Protection

A 5¼-inch disk has a small, square notch in its upper right corner. If this notch is uncovered, the diskette can be written to by the disk drive. If the notch is covered, the diskette is "write-protected," and cannot be written on. If you want to write-protect your diskette, you can use a special sticker supplied by the diskette manufacturer for the purpose, or an ordinary piece of tape to cover the write-protection notch. Some diskettes are "copy protected" to prevent you from making a copy of them. Usually (but not always) the copy protection takes the form of a special pattern of bits written somewhere on the diskette. When you try to copy a copy-protected diskette you will usually get an error message indicating that something has gone wrong. However, a copy-protected diskette can usually be used in the same way that an unprotected diskette can, so long as you do not try to copy it.

Copying Diskettes: The Law

It is generally illegal to copy any copyrighted software without the permission of the copyright holder. Some software comes with the permission; some does not. The one kind of copy you can freely make is a backup copy for your own use; you may not sell or give the backup to anyone else. You can freely copy uncopyrighted programs or data.

Copying Diskettes: The Procedure

The nonresident DISKCOPY command in DOS will make copies of diskettes for you if the diskettes are not copy protected. Usually you will operate with the source (original) disk in Drive A and the target disk in Drive B. To copy a disk from Drive A to Drive B, put your system disk in Drive A, and give the command:

    DISKCOPY A: B:

Note that the source drive comes first, and the target drive comes second. DISKCOPY will be loaded from your system disk, then will tell you to put the source disk in Drive A and your target disk in Drive B. When you have done this, press any key and copying will begin. The target disk does not have to be formatted before copying. Like FORMAT, DISKCOPY will ask you if you want to repeat the process when it is finished with one copy. When the copy is finished, the target disk will be an exact duplicate of the source; if the operating system was on the source, it will also be on the target.

HANDS–ON EXERCISE A1–6

Copying a Disk

Try making a copy of an unprotected disk. Make sure that the disk to which you are copying does not contain data or programs that you might want to save. To see what happens, you might also obtain a disk that is copy-protected, and try copying it.

You can use the nonresident command DISKCOMP to compare two disks to
find out if they are identical. The form of the command is:

    DISKCOMP A: B:

which compares the diskettes in Drives A and B.

> HANDS–ON EXERCISE A1–7
>
> ## Comparing Disks
>
> Use the disk of which you just made a copy in the example above, and run DISKCOMP to compare it to its original. Then compare two different disks.

MANAGING FILES

As we have said, a file is a collection of data or a program stored on a storage device such as a floppy diskette. Under virtually all circumstances, the contents of a file can be accessed only if you know the file's name. How are files created? They are always created by specific commands or programs. Once created, however, files can be copied, renamed, or erased.

File Names

In DOS, a **file name** has two parts: the name proper, and the extension. The name proper can be up to eight characters long, and cannot have any spaces, periods, commas, or the characters ^, *, +, =, [,], :, ;, ", <, >, ?, /, !, or \ in it. The extension is from one to three characters long (with the same characters allowed). The two parts of the file's full name are written with a period between them. The following are examples of legal file names:

    LETTER
    LETTER.1
    LETTER.OLD

To give a full specification for the computer to find your file, you often must indicate the disk drive where the file is to be found. For example, you must type B:LETTER.OLD if that file is stored on a disk in Drive B. If you leave off the drive specification, the computer will look on the default drive (often Drive A).

File extensions are often used to indicate the type of file. For example, BAS indicates a file containing a BASIC program, PAS indicates one containing a Pascal program, WKS indicates a Lotus 1-2-3 worksheet, and so on. The extension BAK often indicates a backup or spare copy of a file, made before beginning work on the file. The extension $$$ is often used to indicate a temporary file that is to be erased when processing finishes.

Wild Card File Names

Sometimes you would like to write a name that refers to a whole group of files. You can do this by using the so-called wild card characters * and ?. The asterisk (*) stands for any legal string of characters; the question mark (?) stands for any single legal character. Examples:

.
Matches all files.
LET*.*
Matches all files whose names begin with LET.

*.BAS
Matches all files with the extension .BAS.
LETTER?.1
Matches LETTERA.1, LETTERB.1, LETTERC.1, and so on.

You can find out what files you have on your disk by using the DIR command to list the files. The files, their names, sizes (in bytes), and date and time of creation will be shown. Examples: The File Directory

DIR
Gives a directory of all files on the default disk drive.
DIR B:
Gives a directory of all files on Drive B.
DIR *.BAK
Gives a directory of all files on the default drive with extensions of BAK.

You can also list the directory in a "wide" format, which only shows file names. Do this by adding the parameter /W to the DIR command. For example:

DIR B:*.WKS/W
Will list all files on Drive B with the extension WKS.

HANDS–ON EXERCISE A1–8

File Directories

Try the command DIR by itself, and see what it gives you. Next, make sure you have a formatted disk in Drive B, and try the command DIR B: Now try the command DIR *.COM on the system disk when it is in Drive A. Experiment with other DIR command forms to see what results they give.

Files can be **copied** from one location to another and from one name to another. The original file is not affected by the copying. The command to do this is COPY, which has the form: Copying Files

COPY (source) (target)

Examples are:

COPY LETTER.NEW LETTER.OLD
Copies LETTER.NEW to LETTER.OLD on the same disk.
COPY A:LETTER.NEW B:LETTER.OLD
Copies LETTER.NEW on Drive A to LETTER.OLD on Drive B.
COPY *.NEW *.OLD
Copies all files with extension NEW to files with the same name but extension OLD; the originals are still around, still have the extension NEW.

COPY A:*.* B:
Copies all files on Drive A to Drive B, where the new files will have the same name as the originals on A.

COPY B:*.* A:
Copies all files on Drive B to Drive A; make sure you see the difference between this and the preceding example!

COPY B:*.*
Copies all files on Drive B to the default drive, which is often, but not always, Drive A.

Notice that if you have a file named VALUABLE and you copy another file named TRASH over it, the former contents of VALUABLE are replaced with a duplicate of the contents of TRASH. The former contents of VALU-ABLE are permanently lost.

HANDS–ON EXERCISE A1–9

Copying Files

Use the system disk in Drive A and your own disk in Drive B for this example. First, give the comand DIR B: to see what is on your disk in Drive B. Next, copy COMMAND.COM from Drive A to Drive B (command: COPY COMMAND.COM B:). Give the DIR B: command again to see what the result was. Now give the command COPY B:COMMAND.COM B:FILE.X. Give the DIR:B command again to see the result.

Renaming Files

The command RENAME will change a file's name. The contents are not affected. The syntax (or form) is the same as for the COPY command:

RENAME A:VERSION.1 VERSION.2
Renames VERSION.1 to VERSION.2; the file remains on Drive A.

RENAME *.TXT *.BAK
Renames all files on the default drive with extension TXT to the same name, but extension BAK.

HANDS–ON EXERCISE A1–10

Renaming Files

Use the command RENAME B:COMMAND.COM FILE.Y to rename a file on your own disk. Then use the DIR command to see the new file name listed in the directory.

The ERASE command will remove a file from your disk. You may type **Erasing Files** either ERASE or the short form DEL (for "delete"). Its syntax is like that of the DIR command. For instance:

ERASE LEFT.OVR
Removes file LEFT.OVR from your disk.

ERASE WRONG.*
Removes all files with name WRONG from your disk.

ERASE B:*.*
Erases all files from Drive B; you will be asked if you really mean this before the erasure takes place.

Although erasing a file is basically a permanent and irreversible operation, sometimes erasure can be undone by the use of special programs called *utilities*. An expert on the DOS operating system may thus be able to help if you accidentally erase a file.

HANDS–ON EXERCISE A1–11

Erasing Files

Try ERASE on one or two files on your own disk. Then use the DIR command to note that the file(s) is (are) no longer listed in the file directory.

Sometimes it is nice to know if two files are the same. The command COMP **Comparing Files** will find out for you. The syntax is essentially the same as for COPY:

```
COMP A:VERSION.1 B:VERSION.2
```

HANDS–ON EXERCISE A1–12

Comparing Files

Copy COMMAND.COM from the system disk to your disk. Now copy COMMAND.COM on your disk to COMMAND.X. Give the command COMP B:COMMAND.COM B:COMMAND.X. This shows you what comparison of two identical files should look like. Next, copy some other file from the system disk to your disk. Now compare it with COMMAND.COM. This shows you what happens when you compare two distinct files.

Displaying a File's Contents

You can see what's in a file by "dumping" its contents to your video screen with the command TYPE. This works fine if the contents are mostly letters and numbers. If the file contains program code or encoded data, you may get some surprising results from TYPE—the screen may fill up with funny symbols and the computer may beep. No harm is usually done, but often the result makes no sense. The syntax is the same as for ERASE:

```
TYPE B:WHATSIN.IT
```

HANDS–ON EXERCISE A1–13

Typing Files

Use DIR to find out if there is a file named AUTOEXEC.BAT or CONFIG.SYS on your system disk. These files should respond to TYPE by showing you a short, human-readable display on your screen. Try TYPE on COMMAND.COM; this should generate unintelligible symbols on your screen, although you may occasionally be able to pick out sequences of characters that make some sense.

Printing a File's Contents

The command PRINT works just like TYPE, except that the output goes to the system printer instead of the video screen.

HANDS–ON EXERCISE A1–14

Printing

Try PRINT on human-readable files such as AUTOEXEC.BAT. Do not try PRINT on files like COMMAND.COM! If you try to PRINT these files, nonprinting "control" characters will probably be sent to your printer. Some of these characters can cause things like ejection of a page, or may turn off the printer.

SUMMARY

You have now learned the components of a personal computer and how you can use its operating system (DOS). This should give you a good introductory understanding of the capabilities and uses of microcomputer operating systems. Consult the DOS manual if you need more information. Refer to the DOS Action Summary in Figure A1–7 for a helpful summary of DOS commands.

Action	Keystrokes
KEYSTROKE ACTIONS	
Delete previous character	BACKSPACE
Cancel current line	ESCAPE
Enter a command	ENTER
Halt a command or program	CONTROL + BREAK
Pause output	CONTROL + NUM LOCK (any other key to resume)
Toggle printer trace on/off	CONTROL + PRT SC
Print screen	SHIFT + PRT SC
Copy last line 1 character at a time	F1
Copy last line	F3
Reload DOS ("reboot")	CONTROL + ALT + DEL
DISK COMMANDS	
Prepare a disk for use	FORMAT {disk}:
Prepare a system disk for use	FORMAT {disk}:/S
Copy a disk	DISKCOPY {source}: {target}:
Compare two disks	DISKCOMP {disk}: {disk}:
Check a disk's integrity	CHKDSK {disk}:
FILE COMMANDS	
A file name consists of two parts: up to 8 for a character name, up to 3 for a letter extension.	
In reference to files, * stands for any string of characters, ? for any one character.	
Get a directory of files	DIR {file}
Get a directory of a disk	DIR {disk}:
Copy one file to another	COPY {source file} {target file}
Rename a file	RENAME {old name} {new name}
Erase a file	ERASE {file}
Compare two files	COMP {file} {file}
Display a file on monitor screen	TYPE {file}
Print a file on printer	PRINT {file}
SYSTEM COMMANDS	
Set system date	DATE
Set system time	TIME
Clear screen	CLS

Figure A1–7 DOS Action Summary. This presents a helpful summary of DOS commands for quick reference.

These are the key terms and concepts of this section. The page number of their first explanation is in parentheses.

KEY TERMS AND CONCEPTS

1. Copying disks *(A–13)*
2. Copying files *(A–15)*
3. Cursor *(A–3)*
4. Disk drive *(A–3)*
5. Displaying a file *(A–18)*
6. DOS *(A–4)*
7. DOS commands *(A–6)*
8. DOS prompt *(A–8)*
9. Erasing files *(A–17)*
10. File directory *(A–15)*
11. File name *(A–14)*
12. Floppy disk *(A–11)*
13. Formatting disks *(A–11)*
14. Function keys *(A–5)*

15. Keyboard *(A–4)*   20. Printer *(A–4)*
16. Loading DOS *(A–6)*   21. Printing a file *(A–18)*
17. Microprocessor *(A–3)*   22. System unit *(A–3)*
18. Operating system *(A–5)*   23. Using other software *(A–10)*
19. PC *(A–2)*   24. Video monitor *(A–3)*

REVIEW AND APPLICATION QUIZ

Match one of the **key terms and concepts** listed above with one of the brief examples or definitions listed below. Try to find the "best fit" for answers that seem to fit more than one term or concept. Defend your choices.

_____ 1. An IBM microcomputer or compatible.

_____ 2. The operating system for PCs.

_____ 3. The main processing chip of a microcomputer.

_____ 4. The main system control program of a computer.

_____ 5. The main input device of a microcomputer.

_____ 6. A visual display device for a microcomputer.

_____ 7. Produces printed paper output.

_____ 8. Houses the microprocessor memory chips, circuit boards, and disk drives.

_____ 9. A flexible magnetic disk for storing data and programs.

_____ 10. The device that reads and records on magnetic disks.

_____ 11. Transferring the operating system from a disk into the computer's memory.

_____ 12. A small flashing rectangle on the video screen.

_____ 13. Keys that perform special functions depending on the software being used.

_____ 14. Tells you that DOS is loaded and is ready to execute DOS commands.

_____ 15. Placing a standard pattern of magnetized bits on a disk, which organizes it into tracks and sectors.

_____ 16. Copying the complete contents of one disk to another.

_____ 17. Copying selected files from one disk to another.

_____ 18. A listing of the files on a disk.

_____ 19. Each data file or program file on a disk has a unique name.

_____ 20. Deleting files from a disk.

_____ 21. Showing the contents of a file on your video monitor.

_____ 22. Listing the contents of a file on your printer.

_____ 23. Many of them help you manage files and disks.

_____ 24. First you load DOS, then you enter a brief program name.

HANDS–ON ASSIGNMENTS

Now it's time for you to use DOS on your own to manage your personal computer. Good luck!

A1.1 If you have not already done so, complete the 14 HANDS–ON EXERCISES contained in this section, which give you practice in using DOS commands.

A1.2   Load DOS and then use one of the programs provided with DOS. They are either on the DOS system disk or on the DOS supplementary disk. Do a directory (DIR) of files on the disks to find the names of such programs.

For example, you probably have the program MORTGAGE.BAS (a program written in BASIC) on the supplementary DOS disk. This simple business application program is usually included with several other demonstration programs on a supplementary disk that is packaged with the main DOS system disk.

Put the DOS disk (with BASIC on it) in Drive A. Place the disk that contains MORTGAGE.BAS in Drive B, then give the command BASIC B:MORTGAGE. Follow the prompts and menus that tell you how to use this simple program. Use MORTGAGE to find mortgage payment comparisons and a mortgage amortization analysis for a mortgage loan whose amount, interest rate, and number of years you select. For example, you might try a mortgage amount of $75,000, an interest rate of 10 percent, and a 15-year time period. Print out the results using the SHIFT and PRTSC keys.

A1.3   Use one of the other programs packaged with DOS. A good example is EDLIN, a line editor program. You can use this program to build a file of data records (such as student names and test scores) and save it on your data disk. Then you can retrieve the file from the disk, and add, delete, or change (edit) the records in the file, and print a hard copy. You can use the left and right arrow keys, BACKSPACE, INS, and DEL to help you edit each line of the file. Here are some basic EDLIN commands:

EDLIN {File}	Start editing named file.
m	Edit line m.
mI	Insert a line at line m.
m,nD	Delete lines m through n.
m,nL	List lines m through n.
m,n,pM	Move lines m through n to line p.
m,n,p,qC	Copy lines m through n to lines starting at p, q times.
nA	Append n lines of text from a file to memory.
E	End edit, saving file.
Q	Quit edit, not saving file.

A1.4   There are many additional DOS commands that are useful for specialized purposes. Obtain a DOS manual for your system and write a brief description of the function of the following commands. Then try out these commands to see what they do. (Some commands may work only with certain types of hardware.)

ASSIGN	SYS
GRAPHICS	TREE
MODE	VOL
PATH	

Section II: Doing Word Processing

Outline

Introduction
Organization of Word Processing Packages
Getting Started
Creating a Document
Editing a Document
Correcting Errors
Getting Help
Saving and Printing Documents
Terminating and Restarting
Advanced Word Processing Functions

INTRODUCTION

The concept of **word processing** and its role in office automation is discussed in Chapter 12. Word processing packages and the word processing modules of integrated packages can turn your microcomputer into a top-flight word processing machine. Word processing programs have become the most popular type of application software package available for use with personal computers.

For our purposes, word processing consists of two basic levels of activity:

1. The processing of **text data** (words, phrases, sentences, and paragraphs).
2. The creation, editing, and printing of **documents** (letters, memos, business forms, reports, and so on).

Thus word processing programs allow you to use a microcomputer or other computer to create, edit, format, store, retrieve, and print documents of all kinds. Word processing makes writing and printing documents dramatically easier. Also, it can increase the quality of your writing because editing, correcting, and revising text material is so much easier to do.

Computers and word processing packages allow you to:

☐ Use a keyboard to enter text data into your computer and edit the resulting document.

☐ See your document displayed on the video screen.

☐ Move to any point in a document, and add, delete, or change words, sentences, or paragraphs.

☐ Move a block of text from one part of the document to another.

☐ Insert standard information from another document file.

☐ Selectively change all occurrences of a particular word or phrase.

☐ Check your document for spelling or grammatical errors.

☐ Store your document as a document file on a magnetic disk and retrieve it any time.

☐ Print the contents of a document file according to a variety of predesigned formats.

We can think of word processing packages as having three major levels of organization:

1. Program level—the types of programs and subprograms that make up the word processing package. For example, a typical package may consist of an integrated set of programs, including an editor program, a formatting program, a print program, and dictionary, thesaurus, and mailing list programs.

2. Menu level—most popular word processing packages provide menus to help the user select commands, or are menu-driven (i.e., much of their operation comes from you selecting from a list of choices provided by a series of menus). The menu organization of the WordStar Professional Word Processing Package is shown in Figure A2–1.

3. Screen level—the video screen display of most word processing packages is organized into several specialized areas, including the display of special characters and symbols. The WordStar screen organization is shown in Figure A2–2.

ORGANIZATION OF WORD PROCESSING PACKAGES

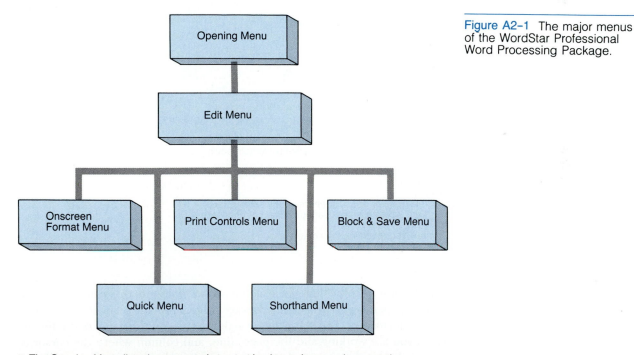

Figure A2–1 The major menus of the WordStar Professional Word Processing Package.

□ The Opening Menu lists the commands to start basic word processing operations.
□ The Edit Menu lists basic editing commands.
□ The Onscreen Format Menu contains formatting commands.
□ The Print Controls Menu lists commands for printing variations.
□ The Block and Save Menu contains commands for operations on "blocks" of text or files.
□ The Quick Menu lists commands for quick versions of editing and other commands.
□ The Shorthand Menu allows you to use short versions of command sequences.

Figure A2–2 An example of the screen organization of the WordStar Professional Word Processing Package.

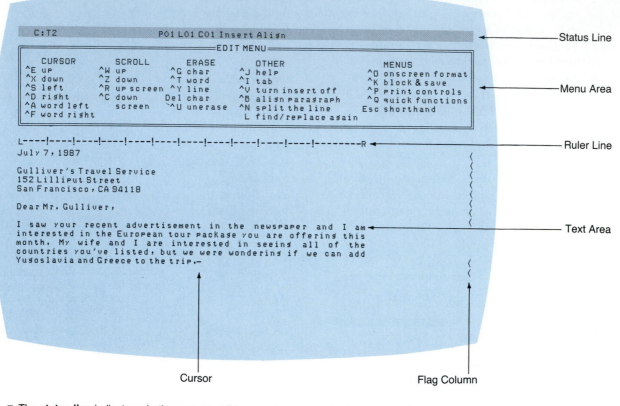

- The **status line** indicates whether you are editing or printing and whether certain editing features are in operation.
- The **menu area** displays lists of commands (menus), help screens, messages, or questions (prompts).
- The **ruler line** indicates margins and tabs.
- The **text area**, which can be moved (scrolled) up or down, is where your work appears.
- The **flag column** displays a character "flag" which specifies various editing or printing alternatives for each line.
- The **cursor**, a small block of light, indicates your place on the screen as you type.

Let's describe the functions of the *status line* and the *ruler line* as it applies to many word processing packages. They provide you with some very useful information. The **status line** usually shows you the name of the file on which you are working and the page, line, and column where the cursor is located. It also shows you whether the *insert* mode is on or off. See Figure A2–3. In most word processing packages, pressing an INSERT key will toggle the insert mode on and off. If it is *off*, anything you type will replace anything previously on the screen. If it is *on*, what you type will cause other material on the screen to move over to make room for what you are typing. As you can see, turning the insert mode on or off is one of the most important actions you must take when you begin to use a word processing package! You

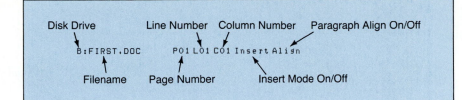

The status line display of WordStar. Notice how it helps you keep track of your word processing activity.

will probably want to type your material with insert mode off. Then toggle it on or off depending on whether you wish to insert or replace material that you have typed.

The **ruler line,** which appears just above the screen space available for typing in text, shows where the margin and tab stops are set. Most word processing packages allow you great flexibility in setting tabs and margins. The location of the margins is typically marked with an L for the left margin and an R for the right margin. Tab stops may be marked with an exclamation point (!) for normal tab stops, or the cross-hatch symbol or pound sign (#) for a decimal tab stop. A decimal tab stop lines up what you type, based on the location of decimal points in numbers that may be part of your text material.

GETTING STARTED

Let's find out how to do word processing. We will work through a few simple examples of the use of a microcomputer word processing program to write a simple business letter. We will use the WordStar Professional Word Processing Package (Release 4.00), which has commands and functions that are common to many word processing and integrated packages. So read this tutorial to get a feel for the basic functions you can accomplish with the word processing package or module you will use. Let's now create, edit, store, retrieve, and print a business letter.

☐ You begin by inserting your word processing program into the A disk drive of the computer. *Note:* See the first section of this appendix if you need additional information on starting a microcomputer, using floppy disks, or loading the DOS operating system.

☐ You then load the word processing program by typing in a brief program name after the operating system prompt and pressing the ENTER key. For example, you would enter the command WS if you were using WordStar.

☐ After some initial copyright information is shown, you should then see an OPENING MENU display. Figure A2–4 shows the Word-Star opening menu. You are now ready to begin creating a document.

CREATING A DOCUMENT

Suppose you want to write a short business letter. First you need to open a **document file.** Use the D command key indicated on the opening menu. An explanation of this command, the rules for naming files, and some of the control characters you can use will then be displayed.

Figure A2-4 The OPENING
MENU of the WordStar Professional Word Processing
Package. Notice the variety of
actions you can accomplish besides starting a document.

```
=============================== OPENING MENU ===============================

    D    open a document              L    change logged drive/directory
    N    open a nondocument           C    protect a file
    P    print a file                 E    rename a file
    M    merge print a file           O    copy a file
    I    index a document             Y    delete a file
    T    table of contents            F    turn directory off
    X    exit WordStar              Esc    shorthand
    J    help                         R    run a DOS command
```

You are then prompted to name the file you want to edit. Let's call this file LETTER1 because it is our first letter. However, in many cases, you may want to store this letter and other documents on a separate **file disk.** This is typically a floppy disk in Drive B of your microcomputer. If this is the case, you should name this document file B:LETTER1. See Figure A2-5. *Note:* If you want to, WordStar allows you to change the default or "logged" disk drive to B by selecting the L option from the opening menu. Then all your documents will be saved on the B drive without your having to specify B: every time you use the name of a file.

A file name for a document typically contains eight characters, including letters, numbers, and some special characters. No distinction is made between uppercase and lowercase letters. If you want your file name to provide additional identifying information, you can add an *extension* to your file name. Simply add a period and three more characters to the end of the file name. For example, you might add .TXT (for text) or .DOC (for document) to your file names. Thus you could name a report you were writing RE-PORT.TXT.

After you enter your file name, an EDIT MENU will be displayed on the screen. You are now using the *editor program* of WordStar. As in many word processing packages, this edit menu is really a *help* display. It explains the functions of various keys to be used in the creation and editing of your letter. The rest of the screen is available for you to type your letter. You can now create and edit your document by typing it in, using appropriate keys to help you in the editing process. See Figure A2-6.

Notice that, as you type in words, the editor constantly reformats and modifies the appearance of the screen. Notice that you do not have to press ENTER at the end of every line. You just keep typing, since the editor does the "carriage returns" for you. Due to this **word wrap** feature, text material that would extend past the right margin is automatically "wrapped around" to the left margin of the next line. Of course, whenever you want to force the starting of a new line or paragraph, you can do so by pressing the ENTER key.

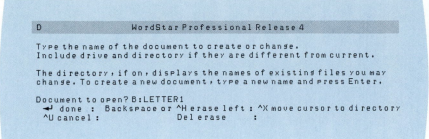

```
 D                         WordStar Professional Release 4

 Type the name of the document to create or change.
 Include drive and directory if they are different from current.

 The directory, if on, displays the names of existing files you may
 change. To create a new document, type a new name and press Enter.

 Document to open? B:LETTER1
   ↵  done  :  Backspace or ^H erase left : ^X move cursor to directory
   ^U cancel :             Del erase      :
```

Figure A2–5 Creating a document file named LETTER1. Notice the helpful prompts and options.

Figure A2–6 The EDIT MENU of WordStar. Notice that it is really a help display of editing actions.

```
═══════════════════════════════EDIT MENU═══════════════════════════════
   CURSOR          SCROLL         ERASE        OTHER              MENUS

 ^E  up          ^W  up         ^G  char      ^J help          ^O onscreen format
 ^X  down        ^Z  down       ^T  word      ^I tab           ^K block & save
 ^S  left        ^R  up screen  ^Y  line      ^V turn insert off  ^P print controls
 ^D  right       ^C  down       Del char      ^B align paragraph  ^Q quick functions
 ^A  word left       screen     ^U unerase    ^N split the line   Esc shorthand
 ^F  word right                               ^L find/replace again
```

Editing a simple document requires several fundamental editing operations. For example, you need to move the cursor around the screen and delete or insert text material. If your computer has special *function* keys, a listing of keys and the functions they accomplish may be shown at the bottom of your screen. Also if your computer has *cursor control* (arrow) keys, you will use them to move the cursor around on your video monitor screen.

Many editing commands can also be given by pressing the CONTROL, ALT, or SHIFT keys and holding them down while pressing another key. These *key combinations* may be represented on the screen by the *caret symbol* (^) for the CONTROL key, and the appropriate letter of the key that needs to be pressed. For example, the main menu example tells you that pressing the CONTROL and Y keys will delete an entire line. Thus to delete a line, you should move the cursor to that line, then press the CONTROL key and the Y key together. Figure A2–7 summarizes fundamental editing functions of WordStar. Most word processing packages will use a variety of function keys and key combinations to accomplish such editing functions.

EDITING A DOCUMENT

Figure A2–7 Fundamental
WordStar editing functions.
Notice the key combinations
that accomplish various editing
actions.

Control Keys	Alternate Keys	Explanation
		CURSOR MOVEMENT
CTRL–S	←	Moves cursor one character to the left
CTRL–D	→	Moves cursor one character to the right
CTRL–A	CTRL←	Moves cursor one word to the left
CTRL–F	CTRL→	Moves cursor one word to the right
CTRL–E	↑	Moves cursor up one line
CTRL–X	↓	Moves cursor down one line
CTRL–QE	HOME	Moves cursor to first line on screen
CTRL–QX	END	Moves cursor to last line on screen
CTRL–I	TAB	Moves cursor to next tab mark
		SCROLLING
CTRL–W	CTRL–PAGE UP	Moves screen view up one line
CTRL–Z	CTRL–PAGE DOWN	Moves screen view down one line
CTRL–R	PAGE UP	Moves up one whole screen
CTRL–C	PAGE DOWN	Moves down one whole screen
		DELETING
CTRL–G	DEL	Deletes character at the cursor
CTRL–H	BACKSPACE	Deletes character to the left of the cursor
CTRL–T	F6	Deletes one word to the right of the cursor
CTRL–Y	F5	Deletes the line the cursor is on
		MISCELLANEOUS
CTRL–M	RETURN	Starts a new line
CTRL–V	INS	Toggles insert mode ON and OFF
CTRL–U	F2	Unerases the last erased text
CTRL–OC	SHIFT–F2	Centers line the cursor is on
CTRL–B	F7	Aligns text in paragraphs

HANDS–ON EXERCISE A2–1

Creating and Editing a Business Letter

Figure A2–8 shows you a simple business letter you should type in your first exercise.

☐ Load your word processing program, and change the logged drive to Drive B if you want to store your letter on a file disk in that drive.

☐ Select the document creation option from the opening menu, and give the file name of LETTER1 to the document file you wish to create.

☐ When the main menu appears, you know you're ready to type and edit your letter using the word processing editor. Refer to previous figures for displays that may appear on your video screen. Refer to Figure A2–7 for the editing functions you may have to accomplish.

☐ Type the letter shown in Figure A2–8. Try to reproduce the spacing and layout of the letter as exactly as possible. Set the left margin to column 10, the right margin to column 75, and begin the address in column 55.

```
                                              ABC Corporation
                                              123 Aardvark Avenue
                                              Somewhere, XX 12345
                                              January 31, 1989

Mr. Rupert R. Rubout
456 Zebra Street
Nowhere, XX 12345


Dear Mr. Rubout:

    In regard to your letter of January 6, 1989, our Mark IV three-prong, two-slot
blivit is available only in the colors magenta, chartreuse, and tangerine. We regret
that we cannot accept your order for a grey blivit.
    At present, delivery on Mark IV blivits is running about two months from the place-
ment of an order. If we can be of service, please let us know.

                                              Sincerely yours,


                                              Diane D. Delete
                                              Sales Manager
```

Figure A2–8 An example of a business letter: document file LETTER1.

CORRECTING ERRORS

Don't worry about any mistakes you make while trying to type the simple letter required in the previous exercise. The beauty of a word processing package is that it makes correcting and revising text material easy to do. Let's briefly review some of the ways you can correct any errors you make.

Suppose you choose the wrong command from the opening menu. In many word processing packages you can immediately get back to that menu by pressing the ESCAPE key or an "UNDO" key combination. In Word-Star, press the CTRL-U keys or the F2 key to cancel a command or operation. However, if you have responded to prompts within a command function, you may first have to press other "interrupt" keys. The screen may display a message such as "***Press ESC key to continue." You can then press the ESCAPE key to get back to the opening menu.

If you open a document or other file and realize it isn't the file you want, you have to press a specified key combination to get back to the opening menu. In WordStar, press the CTRL-KQ keys. If you have done any typing or made any changes to the file, you will be asked whether you want to abandon the file without saving it. You will have to answer with a Y or N before you can get back to the opening menu. Then you can open another file or perform another function.

Once you begin to type a document, you can use the BACKSPACE, TAB, and cursor control keys to move your document around on the screen and just type over any mistakes that you make. However, you will also want to use editing keys for deleting and inserting characters, words, and lines. These keys simplify corrections and changes because they minimize having to retype incorrect material.

GETTING HELP

When using most word processing programs, you can get help on a variety of topics by pressing specified help keys. Most word processing packages provide **help displays** to users. Use this feature whenever you want an explanation of a word processing operation. Help commands usually allow you to select topic areas that you want explained. A WordStar help message is displayed by pressing CTRL-J or F1, and is shown in Figure A2–9. It explains the keys you can press to get help on a variety of topics when editing your document.

Figure A2–9 An example of a WordStar help message. It tells you how to get explanations of the edit menu commands.

```
To get help with the Edit Menu above, press one of the keys that are
shown to the left of each description in the menu at the top of the
screen. (Remember that "^" means you should use the control key.)

For a general explanation of the screen, press question mark (?).
For help with dot commands, press dot (.).
For help with saving your work, press ^KD.

If you would like to change the help level, press ^J again.
```

After you have created and edited a document, you will want to save a copy of the document on a magnetic disk and produce a printed copy on your system printer. Pressing specified SAVE command keys will store your document on the logged disk. Some SAVE keys will cause you to save and resume editing, save and send you back to the opening menu, or save and return you to the operating system. In WordStar, pressing F9 or CTRL–KS will save your document and allow you to resume editing it. Pressing F10 or CTRL–KD will save and close your document file and return you to the opening menu. Pressing CTRL–KX will save your document and return you to the operating system.

Important note: You should make a habit of continually storing parts of a long document that you are creating on your magnetic disk. Pressing the F9 or CTRL–KS keys every few minutes will allow you to "save as you go" without exiting from the editor program. The display of your document remains on the screen. This action minimizes the amount of your document that you would lose due to an accidental erasure of the contents of main memory. Most of your document will have been safely stored on your magnetic disk.

SAVING AND PRINTING DOCUMENTS

You can **print** your document by using the P (print) option from the opening menu. After you have pressed the P key, you must enter the file name of the document you wish to print (LETTER1 for example). If you press the ENTER key, you will be presented with a list of print options. As a beginning user, you can usually ignore these options by pressing the EN-TER key after each option prompt until the actual printing process begins. See Figure A2–10.

Printing Your Document

After storing or printing your completed document, you will usually return to the opening menu. You can exit completely from the word processing program by giving an EXIT command at this point. In WordStar, you would

TERMINATING AND RESTARTING

Figure A2–10 A print command display. Notice the helpful prompts and the various printing options.

```
P                    WordStar Professional Release 4

To skip further questions, press the Esc key at any point. Press ↵
at any question to use the default answer.

Document to print? LETTER1
  ↵ done  : Backspace or ^H erase left : ^X move cursor to directory
^U cancel :              Del erase      :

            Number of copies?
Pause between pages (Y/N)?
    Use form feeds (Y/N)?
            Starting page?
              Ending page?
    Nondocument (Y/N)?
        Name of printer?
```

press the CTRL–KX keys. You will then be back under the control of the operating system, so the operating system prompt will appear.

If you want to return to the word processing program, enter the same WS command you used the first time you loaded the program. After you are presented with the opening menu, select the D (document) option to **re-trieve** a copy of the document you saved previously. Enter the name of that document file in response to a file name request. An electronic copy of your document is then retrieved from the disk and displayed on the screen below the edit menu display. You can then begin to work with that document, as you did previously, making additional corrections and revisions as needed.

If you want to keep the original version intact, you must not use its file name when saving a revised document. You should give the revised document a new file name. Use the E option command shown in the opening menu to rename a revised document. Then that document can be stored under its new file name.

HANDS–ON EXERCISE A2–2

Storing and Printing Documents

Make any additional corrections needed to the letter you typed in the previous exercise. Save this letter on your system disk as the document file: LETTER1. Then have a copy printed on your system printer. Now exit from the word processing program.

ADVANCED WORD PROCESSING FUNCTIONS

You have now created, edited, saved, retrieved, and printed a document. Let's look at some advanced word processing capabilities that we can use to easily make additional changes to a document.

Search and Replace

After you have typed a letter, report, or other document, you may wish to find out where and how many times you use a certain word or phrase. You may also wish to replace this word or phrase with alternative text. This is called a **search and replace** operation. It is a powerful feature of word processing packages. You could use the cursor control and scroll control keys to visually examine the entire document, but this would be time-consuming and difficult. Instead, you can speed up your search by using commands that help you move around your document more quickly, as well as automatically finding and replacing text material.

Figure A2–11 shows a supplementary edit menu called the QUICK MENU that displays search and replace commands and additional edit command options. Three search and replace commands of greatest interest to beginning users are summarized below.

```
======================= QUICK MENU =======================
      CURSOR              FIND              OTHER                SPELL
E upper left      P previous     F find text      U align paragraphs L check rest
X lower right     V last find    A find/replace   M math      Q repeat  M check word
S left side       B beg block    G char forward      ERASE                O enter word
D right side      K end block    H char back      Y line to right        SCROLL
R beg doc         0-9 marker     I find page      Del line to left   W up, repeat
C end doc         ? char count   (or line)        T to character     Z down
```

Figure A2–11 The QUICK MENU is a supplementary edit menu of WordStar. Notice its additional editing actions.

☐ CTRL–F1 or CTRL–QF will find any "string" of characters (words or phrases, including blanks) in the document. When you give this command, WordStar will ask you what you want to find. Just type it in. There are several options you can select from.

☐ CTRL–F2 or CTRL–QA will allow you to find and replace words or phrases in the entire text. You can select the word or phrase you want changed. Then enter the word or phrase you want to change it to. The changes can be performed automatically, or semi-automatically with pauses for confirmation. Several options are allowed.

☐ CTRL–F3 or CTRL–L is used after doing a find or a replace action. It will allow you to move directly to the next string to be found or replaced.

Spelling Checking

Another powerful and useful feature of many word processing packages is spelling checking. It is similar to the search and replace operations, but uses a dictionary. SHIFT–F3 or CTRL–QL will highlight the first word (after the cursor) that does not agree with the spelling of a similar word in the spelling dictionary. This assumes you have loaded the spelling dictionary that comes on a separate disk. WordStar will then suggest several correct versions. However, it is up to you to make any changes to the word in question, including substituting one of the spellings suggested by WordStar. If you just want to check the spelling of one particular word, use the CTRL-QN or SHIFT-F4 keys. This will just check the spelling of the word at the cursor. Figure A2–12 shows some of the options provided in the SPELLING CHECK MENU of WordStar.

Changing the Format of Documents

Word processing packages make it easy to control how a document will look when printed. Several common page-formatting options are provided that allow you to have a choice of several formats and styles for whatever type of document you are using. **Formatting** commands allow you to change the format of what appears on the screen and will eventually be printed. Figure A2–13 shows you the WordStar ONSCREEN FORMAT MENU that displays some of the options provided for this purpose. The beginning user does

Figure A2–12 The options in the SPELLING CHECK MENU of WordStar. Note the spelling suggestions for a misspelled word.

```
════════════════════ SPELLING CHECK MENU ════════════════════
  I  ignore, check next word       E  enter correction         ^U quit
  A  add to personal dictionary    T  turn auto-align off
  B  bypass this time only         G  global replacement is off

        Word:   "ferward"
  Suggestions:  1 forward  2 foreword
```

Figure A2–13 The ONSCREEN FORMAT MENU displays a variety of options for changing the appearance of a document.

```
═══════════════════════ ONSCREEN FORMAT MENU ═══════════════════════
  MARGINS               TYPING                    DISPLAY
  L set left            W turn word wrap off      D turn print controls off
  R set right           J turn right justify off  H turn hyphen help on
  X release             E enter soft hyphen       P turn preview on
  T turn ruler off      G temporary indent        TABS
  F ruler from text     S set line spacing        I set tab stop
  O ruler to text       C center line             M clear tab stop
```

not need to bother with most of these, since most word processing packages take care of simple formatting. The ones you are most likely to use are the commands that set margins and tab stops, center lines, and set line spacing. These commands begin by pressing the CTRL–O keys, which bring up the **ONSCREEN FORMAT MENU.**

For example, you can change the preset margins that WordStar provides. These are set at column 1 on the left and column 65 on the right. Thus to change the right margin, press CTRL–OR and specify the new column value you want.

Another example is centering text. It is easy to center a title or heading in a document after you have typed it. Move the cursor anywhere on the title you want centered. Then press SHIFT–F2 or CTRL–OC. Presto, the title is centered!

Changing the format of documents may require you to *align* or *reformat* the paragraphs in your document. This is called *paragraph reformatting.* Many word processing packages automatically reformat paragraphs for you. Reformatting consists of adjusting the spaces within each line of a paragraph. If you change margins or change the words in a paragraph, the spacing will normally need to be changed, too. To reformat a paragraph, move the cursor in front of the first line of the paragraph, then press CTRL–B or F7. To reformat an entire document, press CTRL-QU. This will reformat all paragraphs from the cursor position to the end of the document.

```
╔══════════════════ BLOCK & SAVE MENU ══════════════════╗
║          SAVE                 BLOCK                FILE         ║
║  S save & resume edit  B mark begin    C copy  O copy     P print   ║
║  D save document       K mark end      V move   E rename          ║
║  X save & exit WordStar H turn display on Y delete J erase         ║
║  Q quit without saving W write to disk M math   L logged drive/dir ║
║          CURSOR        M turn column mode on    R insert a document║
║  0-9 set/hide marker   I turn column replace on F run a DOS command║
╚═══════════════════════════════════════════════════════╝
```

Figure A2–14 The BLOCK AND SAVE MENU displays commands to store documents on disks and to manipulate document sections (blocks).

Manipulating Document Sections: Blocks

One of the major capabilities of word processing packages is that they allow you to do "cut and paste" operations to your document. This means that you can move sentences, paragraphs, or pages around within the document, rather than having to retype them. The section of your document that is to be manipulated is called a **block.** A block is a section of your document that has been marked with special commands. Once a block has been marked, you can move it, delete it, copy it, or write it out to its own file.

Figure A2–14 shows you a BLOCK AND SAVE MENU, which displays the many document-manipulating options available. Other options having to do with file management are also shown in this menu. You can display this menu by pressing CTRL–K. The important block commands for a beginning user are briefly explained below.

☐ MARK the beginning and end of a block. Use CTRL–KB or SHIFT–F9 to mark the beginning of a block. Use CTRL–KK or SHIFT–F10 to mark the end of the block.

☐ MOVE the block. The procedure is this: first you mark the beginning and end of the block. Then you move the cursor to the place where you would like to have the block located. Then press CTRL–KV or SHIFT–F7.

☐ COPY a block. First, mark the beginning and end of the block. Then move the cursor to the place where you want the copy to be inserted and press CTRL–KC or SHIFT–F8. The original block will be untouched, and a duplicate of it will be placed where you want it.

☐ DELETE a block. Mark the beginning and end of a block. Then press CTRL–KY or SHIFT–F5. The block will disappear.

☐ WRITE a block. You can store a marked block by writing it on your disk with this command, which is handy if you are creating files of "boilerplate" (i.e., standardized paragraphs). Press CTRL–KW.

☐ READ a block. You can insert a file from your disk into your document with this command which is handy for the insertion of boilerplate material. Press CTRL–KR.

Special Printing Effects

Most word processing packages provide you with special printing effects to emphasize words in your document. Most useful to the beginning user would be the underlining of words or the printing of words in **boldface.** Special printing effects commands are displayed in the PRINT CONTROLS MENU shown in Figure A2–15. In WordStar and many word processing packages these commands do not change the words on the display screen. Instead, special characters are inserted in the text, which cause special print effects during the actual printing process.

Note: Beginning users should be reminded that most special printing effects commands must be applied to both the beginning and end of the word or phrase you wish to affect. If you don't, you may end up with a line or document that is completely underlined or boldfaced!

Boldface Printing

The printer may print words in **boldface** by overstriking characters several times. The way in which you use this command is to place a boldface character at the beginning and end of what you want to appear in boldface print. The screen display will show the presence of these characters. For example, if you want to boldface the word **attention,** you would move the cursor to the beginning of the word and press CTRL–PB or the F4 key. Then move the cursor to the end of the word and press these keys again. The boldface effect for that word will appear when you print your document.

Underlining

Underlining works the same way as boldfacing. That is, you need an underlining character inserted at the beginning and end of whatever you want underlined. Press CTRL–PS or the F3 key in both cases.

Figure A2–15 The PRINT CONTROLS MENU displays commands for a variety of special printing effects.

```
══════════════════ PRINT CONTROLS MENU ══════════════════
         BEGIN & END                        OTHER
B bold        X strikeout        H overprint char  O binding space
S underline   D double strike    ↵ overprint line  C print pause
V subscript   Y italics/color    F phantom space   I column tab
T superscript K indexing         G phantom rubout  @ fixed position
                              QWER custom          M normal pitch
                                 L form feed        A alternate pitch
```

HANDS–ON EXERCISE A2–3

Additional Document Revision

Retrieve the file containing the letter that you typed and saved in Exercises A2–1 and A2–2 and change it as follows:

1. The letter should inform Mr. Rubout that the color grey is available on special order at an extra cost of $300 per unit.

2. The margins should be reset to 15 on the left and 65 on the right. You will have to rearrange the address of ABC Corporation. Do this by centering it on screen. Make sure you reformat the letter so the body of the letter fits inside the new margins. Move the closing salutation and signature section to the left margin.

3. Use a REPLACE command to change the spelling of every occurrence of "blivit" to "blivvit."

4. Save and print this revised letter. (First, rename it document file LETTER1A.) See Figure A2–16.

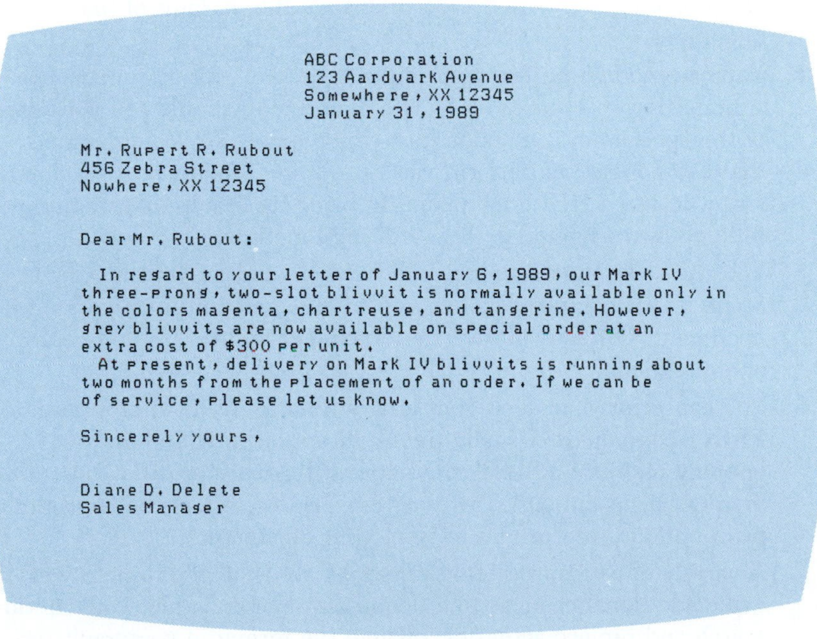

ABC Corporation
123 Aardvark Avenue
Somewhere, XX 12345
January 31, 1989

Mr. Rupert R. Rubout
456 Zebra Street
Nowhere, XX 12345

Dear Mr. Rubout:

   In regard to your letter of January 6, 1989, our Mark IV three-prong, two-slot blivvit is normally available only in the colors magenta, chartreuse, and tangerine. However, grey blivvits are now available on special order at an extra cost of $300 per unit.
   At present, delivery on Mark IV blivvits is running about two months from the placement of an order. If we can be of service, please let us know.

Sincerely yours,

Diane D. Delete
Sales Manager

Figure A2–16 The revised business letter: document file LETTER1A. Notice the changes made in this version of the letter.

SUMMARY

We have now explained and practiced the creation and editing of a simple letter (a document file) using the WordStar Professional Word Processing Package. As an example, we have also stored, printed, retrieved, and revised this file. This should have given you a good introductory understanding of the capabilities and uses of microcomputer word processing. Figure A2–17 is a summary of important WordStar commands for your reference. Consult the manual for the package you are using if you need more information.

Let's summarize the basic activities you accomplish when you do word processing, no matter what word processing package you use.

1. You load the word processing package or module from the magnetic disk on which it is stored into the main memory of the computer. This should result in an opening menu display on your video monitor.

2. Now create or open a document file. Use the appropriate command indicated on the opening menu display. Give the document you are creating a file name. Remember that you may want to store this document on a separate file disk in Drive B of your microcomputer. If this is the case, you should include the B: prefix in your document file name.

3. Once you enter your document file name, a main editing menu will probably be displayed. You can now begin to enter text by typing it on the screen using the keyboard as you would use a typewriter. The word processor will automatically format each line for you. Use the ENTER key to force the starting of a new line or paragraph. Other commands can be used to change the margins of the document.

4. You can modify the text by using a variety of editing functions as summarized in Figure A2–7. The main menu should tell you some of the special keys, function keys, and control key combinations that can be used to perform various editing functions. Also, don't forget to use a HELP command to bring up a help display that will tell you how to perform these editing functions.

5. You can store the document you have created on your file disk. Some SAVE commands allow you to save and continue working in a document. Others will save the document and return you to the opening menu.

6. You can print your document at any time by using appropriate PRINT commands. Usually this is an option provided on the opening menu. A PRINT command will usually provide you with a menu of print options. Turn on your printer, select the appropriate print options, and print a copy of your document.

7. A variety of word processing functions are available to help you make additional changes to a document. For example, you can do search and replace activities, change the format of paragraphs or your entire document, manipulate sections of your document (blocks), and cause special print effects to take place during the printing process.

Figure A2–17 Summary of important WordStar Professional Word Processing Package Commands.

Function	Control Keys	Other Keys
MOVE CURSOR		
Right one character	^D	→
Left one character	^S	←
Up one line	^E	↑
Down one line	^X	↓
Right one word	^F	^→
Left one word	^A	^←
To tab right	^I	Tab
To top of screen	^QE	Home
To right end of last onscreen line	^QX	End
To beginning of document	^QR	^Home
To end of document	^QC	^End
To right end of line	^QD	^F10
To left end of line	^QS	^F9
To beginning block marker	^QB	
To end block marker	^QK	
To marker 0–9	^Q0–9	
To specified page (document)	^QI	^F4
To specified line (nondocument)	^QI	
To previous cursor position	^QP	
To last find/replace or block	^QV	
Forward to specified character	^QG	
Back to specified character	^QH	
SCROLL (MOVE SCREEN)		
Up one line	^W	^PgUp
Down one line	^Z	^PgDn
Up one screen	^R	PgUp
Down one screen	^C	PgDn
Up screen continuously	^QW	
Down screen continuously	^QZ	
(Use 0–9 to control speed; 0 is fastest)		

Function	Control Keys	Other Keys
DELETE AND INSERT		
Delete character at cursor	^G	Del
Delete character left	^H	Backspace
Delete word at cursor	^T	F6
Delete line	^Y	F5
Delete line to right	^QY	
Delete line to left	^Q Del	
Delete to next specified character	^QT	
Delete a block	^KY	
Erase a file	^KJ	
Insert on/off	^V	Ins
Insert carriage return (split line)	^N	
Unerase (restore deleted text)	^U	F2
HELP		
Get help with specified command	^J	F1
Change help level	^J^J	F1F1
Help with screen layout	^J?	F1?
Help with dot commands	^J.	F1.
BLOCK OPERATIONS		
Mark block beginning	^KB	Shift F9
Mark block end	^KK	Shift F10
Hide/display marked block	^KH	Shift F6
Column mode	^KN	
Column replace mode	^KI	
Copy block	^KC	Shift F8
Delete block	^KY	Shift F5
Move block	^KV	Shift F7
Block math	^KM	
Convert block to lower-case	^K'	
Convert block to upper-case	^K''	
Write block to disk	^KW	
Set/remove marker 0–9	^K0–9	

8. An **EXIT** command is used to exit from the word processing program you are using. This returns you to the operating system prompt or the main menu of the integrated package you may be using. Or you may prefer to create a new document file or retrieve a document you had previously saved. Then you would use the appropriate command to open a document file and begin the word processing activities listed here again.

Figure A2-17　Continued

Function	Control Keys	Other Keys
SAVE FILES		
Save and resume edit	^KS	F9
Save, return to Opening Menu	^KD	F10
Save and exit WordStar	^KX	
Quit without saving	^KQ	
Save and print	^KDP^R	^PrtSc
FIND AND REPLACE		
Find text	^QF	^F1
Find/replace text	^QA	^F2
Strings:		
^P　Enter Ctrl sequence that follows		
?　Wild card		
Options:		
W　Whole words		
B　Look backwards		
G　Start from beginning or end		
U　Ignore case		
?　Use ? as wild card		
A　Align paragraph after replacement		
N　Replace without asking approval		
R　Replace for rest of document		
Find/replace text again	^L	^F3
Forward to specified character	^QG	
Back to specified character	^QH	
Cursor to last find/replace	^QV	
COMMANDS TO USE AT PROMPTS		
Safely cancel a command or operation	^U	F2
Delete answer	^Y	F5
Repeat previous answer	^R	
SPELLING		
Check rest of document	^QL	Shift F3
Check word at cursor	^QN	Shift F4
Enter word to check	^QO	
Options:		
I　Ignore, check next word		
A　Add to personal dictionary		
B　Bypass this time only		
E　Enter correction		
T　Auto-alignment		
G　Global replace		
^U　Quit spelling check		

Function	Control Keys	Other Keys
FILE OPERATIONS		
Insert a file from disk	^KR	
Copy a file	^KO	
Rename a file	^KE	
Print or merge print a file	^KP	
Erase a file	^KJ	
Run a program/DOS command	^KF	
Change logged drive/ directory	^KL	
ALIGNMENT OF TEXT		
Alignment/word wrap	.AW	
Justification	.OJ	
Microjustification	.UJ	
Proportional spacing	.PS	
Print time formatting	.PF	
Word wrap	^OW	
Align paragraph	^B	F7
Align rest of paragraphs (document)	^QU	
Align text at column number	^P@	
Hyphen help	^OH	
Enter soft hyphen	^OE	
DESIGN THE PRINTED PAGE		
Bold	^PB*	F4
Double strike	^PD*	
Underline	^PS*	F3
Strikeout	^PX*	
Subscript	^PV*	
Superscript	^PT*	
Italics/color	^PY*	
* = use command at beginning and end of text to be included		
Overprint character	^PH	
Overprint line	^P↵	
Binding space	^PO	
Phantom space	^PF	
Phantom rubout	^PG	
Alternate pitch	^PA	
Normal pitch	^PN	
Print pause	^PC	
Line feed without carriage return	^PJ	
Form feed	^PL	
Custom print functions	^PQ,^PW,^PE,^PR	

Figure A2–17 Concluded

Function	Control Keys	Other Keys
TABS AND MARGINS		
Change left margin	.LM	^F5
Change right margin	.RM	^F6
Use a new ruler line	.RR	
Ruler line characters:		
L left margin		
R right margin		
P paragraph margin		
! tab stop		
# decimal tab stop		
- space		
Margin at top of page	.MT	
Margin at bottom of page	.MB	
Paragraph margin	.PM	^F7
Set left margin	^OL	
Set right margin	^OR	
Release margins	^OX	
Set ruler from text	^OF	
Embed current ruler line as a .RR	^OO	F8
Set tab stop	^OI	
Clear tab stop	^ON	
Temporary indent	^OG	
Set tab interval (non-document)	^O	
Eight-column tab	^PI	

Function	Control Keys	Other Keys
PAGE LAYOUT/FORMAT		
Conditional page	.CP	
Page break	.PA	^F8
Line height	.LH	
Change page number	.PN	
Page length	.PL	
Page offset	.PO	
Line spacing	.LS	
Omit page number	.OP	
Restore default page numbers	.PG	
Page number column	.PC	
Center line	^OC	Shift F2
Set line spacing	^OS	
Justification	^OJ	
DISPLAY OF TEXT WHILE EDITING		
Print control display	^OD	Shift F1
Preview mode	^OP	
Ruler display	^OT	
Display block markers	^KH	
Soft-space display	^OB	

KEY TERMS AND CONCEPTS

These are the key terms and concepts of this chapter. The page number of their first explanation is in parentheses.

1. Block *(A–35)*
2. Boldface *(A–36)*
3. Creating a document *(A–25)*
4. Document file *(A–25)*
5. Documents *(A–22)*
6. Editing a document *(A–27)*
7. File disk *(A–26)*
8. Formatting a document *(A–33)*
9. Help display *(A–30)*
10. Insert mode *(A–24)*
11. Printing a document *(A–31)*
12. Retrieving a document *(A–32)*
13. Ruler line *(A–24)*
14. Saving a document *(A–31)*
15. Search and replace *(A–32)*
16. Spelling checking *(A–33)*
17. Status line *(A–24)*
18. Text data *(A–22)*
19. Word processing *(A–22)*
20. Word wrap *(A–26)*

REVIEW AND APPLICATION QUIZ

Match one of the **key terms and concepts** above with one of the brief examples or definitions listed below. Try to find the "best fit" for answers that seem to fit more than one term or concept. Defend your choices.

_____ 1. The processing of text data for the creation of documents.

_____ 2. Words, phrases, sentences, and paragraphs.

_____ 3. Letters, memos, business forms, reports, and so on.

_____ 4. A letter or memo is created, stored, and retrieved in this unique type of data element.

_____ 5. Indicates the file name of a document and whether certain editing features are in operation.

_____ 6. Indicates margins and tabs.

_____ 7. Text past the right margin is automatically transferred to the left margin of the next line.

_____ 8. If this is operative, previously typed text will move over to make room for what you are typing.

_____ 9. Use this feature when you want an explanation of a word processing operation.

_____ 10. Use this magnetic medium to save copies of your documents.

_____ 11. Assigning a file name to a document and then beginning to enter text.

_____ 12. Making changes and corrections to text material.

_____ 13. Making changes to the appearance of a document.

_____ 14. Storing a document file on a magnetic disk.

_____ 15. Transferring a document file from a magnetic disk to the main memory of the computer.

_____ 16. Using a printer to produce a paper copy of a document.

_____ 17. Searches for spelling errors.

_____ 18. Find a word or phrase and change it automatically.

_____ 19. A specially marked section of a document.

_____ 20. Darkens and thickens printed text that you want emphasized.

HANDS–ON ASSIGNMENTS

It's time for you to create and edit some documents and data files of your own, using a word processing package or module. Good luck!

A2.1 If you have not already done so, create, edit, and revise the simple business letter as explained in HANDS–ON EXERCISES A2–1, A2–2, and A2–3.

A2.2 Retrieve the letter (LETTER1A) you modified in HANDS–ON EXERCISE A2–3. Address it to a new person and make appropriate changes in its form and content, using several block, global search and replace, reformatting, and special printing effects commands.

For example, use your name and address, the current date, and indicate that grey blivvets are now in stock at low sale prices for immediate delivery. Change blivvet back to blivet. Boldface or underline the sentence telling of the low sale prices. Move it so it is the first sentence of the letter. Save the letter as LETTER2 and print a copy.

A2.3   Write and edit a short letter or memo. For example, make an announcement to your employees or inquire about a new job opening. Save and print this letter.

A2.4   Retrieve the letter you created in the preceding assignment (A2.3). Change it so it is addressed to someone else. Change some facts or figures in the letter, using several block, global search and replace, and reformatting commands. Save and print this revised letter.

A2.5   You may already realize that one of the most difficult kinds of typing is typing statistical or accounting reports. To help you see the value of a word processor in doing this kind of work, let's type a short statistical table.

Edit the ruler line to install decimal tabs at columns 40, 50, 60, and 70. Take all other tabs out of the ruler line, except for an ordinary tab at position 10. Now type the following table using the tab key:

SALES BY TERRITORY, 1984—1987

Territory	1984	1985	1986	1987
Northern	$25,237	$47,888	$23,377	$34,002
Western	26,478	26,202	25,991	25,404
Southern	46,550	49,863	56,512	66,904
Central	43,200	41,835	43,676	48,200
Eastern	4,789	8,127	12,438	15,003

A2.6   Some kinds of documents occur frequently in a standard form. Standardized forms or paragraphs are often called boilerplate. For example, memos usually begin something like this:

```
DATE:      4/17/89
TO:        Mary Smith, Sales
FROM:      John Doe, Accounting

SUBJECT:   Your travel vouchers
```

Prepare a simple, standard memo header, including places for date, a recipient's name (TO), a sender's name (FROM), and a subject. Then save this as a file named MEMO.HED. Now create a memorandum, beginning it by inserting the standard memorandum header that you just created. Use the commands provided by your word processor to write and read blocks of text to and from a file disk. For example, in WordStar, use CTRL-KW to store the memo header on your file disk and CTRL-KR to retrieve it and insert it in your document.

Section III: Doing Electronic Spreadsheets and Graphics

Outline

INTRODUCTION TO ELECTRONIC SPREADSHEETS

What is an *electronic spreadsheet?* How does one use *graphics programs?* This section will provide answers to these questions and get you started in the use of spreadsheets and graphics. We briefly reviewed software packages for these applications in Chapter 3. These include electronic spreadsheet packages, graphics packages, and integrated packages with spreadsheet and graphics capabilities.

An **electronic spreadsheet** is a *worksheet* of rows and columns that is stored in the computer's memory and is displayed on its video screen. The computer's keyboard or other devices, such as an electronic mouse or touch screen, are used to enter data and to manipulate the data in the worksheet. Users can build a **model** by entering the data and relationships (formulas) of a problem into an electronic spreadsheet, make a variety of changes, and visually evaluate the results of such changes. Once an electronic spreadsheet has been developed, it can be stored on a magnetic disk for later use or be printed as a paper report on a printer.

An **electronic spreadsheet program** is a valuable tool for accounting, finance, marketing, and business planning. It can be used for the solution of any problem that requires comparisons, projections, or the evaluation of alternatives. Therefore, electronic spreadsheets are used for many applications. Typical business uses include sales forecasting, profit and loss analysis, product pricing, investment analysis, development of budgets, cash flow analysis, financial statement preparation, construction bidding, real estate investment, bank loan analysis, and many other applications for individuals, business firms, and other organizations.

Special-purpose spreadsheet models called **templates** are also available to help you solve specific business problems. Templates are electronic spreadsheet forms that have been developed for specific occupations, operations, or classes of problems. Column and row headings are already set up, and formulas and special functions defining mathematical and logical relationships between the elements in the spreadsheet are already included. These worksheet models have been developed for specific business applications such as accounting, real estate, banking, engineering, and the like.

They are available as separate programs or are included in advanced spreadsheet packages. For example, you can buy electronic spreadsheet programs designed for tax accounting, financial analysis, or real estate investment applications. Users only need to enter data to produce results (for example, a completed tax return).

The electronic spreadsheet's **"what if"** capability makes an electronic spreadsheet program a simple but important type of *decision support system* (DSS) package. It allows managers to interact with a computerized model by comparing the effects of alternative proposed decisions. This interactive evaluation process significantly assists managers in the making of many business decisions. After setting up a spreadsheet model, managers can ask "what if" questions to quickly and easily discover the effect any change will have on the "bottom line" of their model. For example, what if we give employees an increase in salary? What if shipping costs increase? What if interest rates go up? What if we purchase, rather than lease, a new piece of equipment? What if we cut the recruiting budget? What if we add additional production capacity? Such questions should give you an idea of the variety of uses, the computational power, the modeling capability, and the decision-making support provided by electronic spreadsheets.

How are spreadsheets organized? The typical electronic spreadsheet is a matrix or grid of many rows and columns. For example, the spreadsheets of many packages have 63 columns and 254 rows, or 256 columns and 2,048 rows. The spaces formed by the intersection of rows and columns are called **cells.** Thus a spreadsheet may contain over 520,000 cells! Cells are identified by their column-row coordinate, (i.e., the number or letter of the column and row in which the cell is located.) In most spreadsheets, rows are numbered and columns are specified by letters, with the column of a cell mentioned first, then its row. For example, cell C12 identifies a cell at the intersection of the 3rd column and the 12th row of the spreadsheet. Thus in a 63-column by 254-row spreadsheet, the rows would be numbered from 1 to 254; the 63 columns would be specified by the letters A through Z, AA through AZ, and BA through BK. However, some spreadsheet programs use numbers to designate both rows and columns.

SPREADSHEET FORMAT AND ORGANIZATION

Finally a group of cells is called a **range.** A range is a cell, column, row, or a rectangular grouping of cells, columns, and/or rows. A range is identified by the cells in two of its diagonally opposite corners. Thus a range can have an address of B5 to F12 or F12 to B5, and so on.

Since an electronic spreadsheet is so large, only a section is displayed on the video screen at any one time. The display screen is a **window** that lets you see a portion of the larger worksheet in memory. The section of the spreadsheet you can see through a window is sometimes called a **page.** Each page is usually 8 columns wide and 20 rows long, unless you change the width of the columns or split the screen into two or more windows. Thus a window can be moved around for you to see and work on any part of the spreadsheet that you wish. See Figure A3–1.

A *cursor* (called a **cell pointer**) is located at all times in one of the cells of the worksheet. Data are entered into this cell by using the keyboard of the computer. This cursor typically is a *reverse video* rectangle of light, or a

Figure A3–1 The window of an electronic spreadsheet. Your video screen is a window that allows you to see part of a much larger worksheet stored in memory.

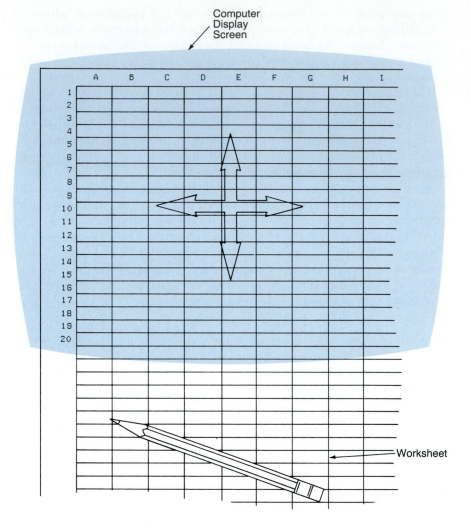

color bar, that fills one or more spreadsheet cells. The cell pointer is moved from cell to cell within the spreadsheet by the use of *cursor control keys* (or combinations of other keys, an electronic mouse, or a touch-screen). The cursor control keys are labeled with either an up, down, left, or right arrow, and move the cursor in those directions. To view other parts of the spreadsheet, you move the cell pointer across the worksheet with the cursor control key. When the cell pointer reaches the edge of the current window (top, bottom, left, or right edges), the window begins to shift or **scroll** across the spreadsheet in the direction the cell pointer is moving.

Most electronic spreadsheet programs display column or row numbers and letters along the top and left-hand margin of the spreadsheet window, as well as additional information at the top or bottom of the screen. Figure A3–2 illustrates the display screen format of a Lotus 1-2-3 electronic spreadsheet. Notice that this display is a window that allows you to see only

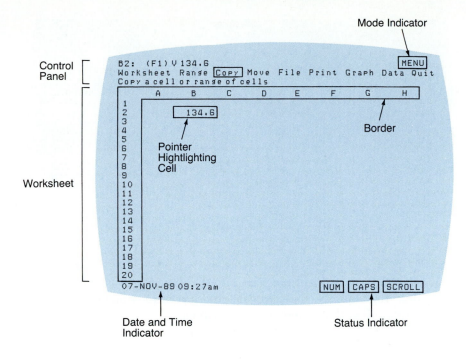

Figure A3–2 The display screen format of Lotus 1-2-3.

20 rows and 8 columns of the larger spreadsheet stored in the memory of the computer. Notice also that the rectangular cursor is at cell B2, which is at the intersection of the second column and second row of the spreadsheet. This cell contains the number 134.6.

Most spreadsheet packages display a **control panel** above or below the worksheet. It usually consists of three lines of information, as shown in Figure A3–2.

☐ **First line.** Shows the cell address where the cursor or cell pointer is presently located on the worksheet, the display format, protection status, and the actual contents of the cell in which the cursor is located.

☐ **Second line.** Shows a menu of command options when you are in the command mode. Or it shows the characters being entered into a cell, or edited, along with appropriate prompts or comments.

☐ **Third line.** Shows a submenu of command options or short comments explaining what menu item the cursor is highlighting.

Before we get into the details of developing an electronic spreadsheet, let's look at a brief overview of the entire process. Look closely at Figure A3–3. It is a display of a simple financial spreadsheet developed with an electronic spreadsheet program. A financial analyst for the ABC Company developed this simple spreadsheet of the company's recent financial performance. If you were the analyst, you could build and use this spreadsheet in the following manner:

OVERVIEW OF SPREADSHEET DEVELOPMENT

Figure A3–3 An example of a simple financial spreadsheet developed to analyze the financial performance of the ABC Company.

SPREADSHEET EXAMPLE

ABC COMPANY: FINANCIAL PERFORMANCE

	1987	1988	1989	TOTAL	AVERAGE
REVENUE	1000	1100	1200	3300	1100
EXPENSES	600	660	720	1980	660
PROFIT	400	440	480	1320	440
TAXES	160	176	192	528	176
PROFIT AFTER TAXES	240	264	288	792	264

1. Load the **spreadsheet program** into the computer from a floppy disk. Immediately, the spreadsheet format of rows and columns is displayed on the computer's video screen.

2. Enter the **titles and headings** of this spreadsheet, using the keyboard of the computer.

3. Enter **data** (dollar amounts) into the cells of categories where you already know the values that should be displayed. For example, revenue for 1987 was $1,000.

4. Begin entering **formulas** into the remaining cells that express the relationships between each category of values on the spreadsheet. For example, if you know that expenses are 60 percent of sales, you would enter the formula +B8*.6 into cell B10. (Note that 1987 revenue is in cell B8, and 1987 expenses are in cell B10.) The computer immediately calculates $600 as the value for 1987 expenses ($1,000 × .6) and displays it in cell B10. You would continue this process until all cells contain appropriate formulas and display values calculated by the computer.

5. You could then **save** the spreadsheet you created on a floppy disk for use at another time and **print** out a copy for your records.

6. This process is not as burdensome as it sounds. The spreadsheet program provides special built-in **functions** for calculations like the total and average amounts. It also automatically fills in cells (at your command) with similar data and formula relationships with its **replication** ability.

7. You could then make "**what if**" assumptions, and the spreadsheet program would automatically perform calculations based on these assumptions and display the results. For example, you could change 1987 sales to $2,000 and the computer would instantly calculate and display $480 as the profit after taxes for 1987 based on that assumption. In this way you could analyze the effect of various changes on the past, present, and future financial performance of the ABC Company.

GETTING STARTED

At this point you should have a basic idea of what electronic spreadsheets are, as well as their many benefits and uses. You should also have a good idea of the format and organization of an electronic spreadsheet, both in memory and as it appears on the video screen. Now it's time to work through a simple example of the use of an electronic spreadsheet package. A version similar to Lotus 1-2-3 (or its many clones like VP-Planner) will be used in our examples. Many other spreadsheet packages are quite similar to Lotus 1-2-3, which is the most widely used and imitated electronic spreadsheet package. The spreadsheet we will build as we go along will be the ABC Company: Financial Performance spreadsheet example shown in Figure A3–3.

See the first section of this appendix if you need additional information on using a microcomputer and loading DOS. Here's how to get started:

1. Insert your electronic spreadsheet program disk into disk drive A. You may want to also insert a **file disk** in drive B for later storage of your spreadsheets.

2. Type in a brief program name after the operating system prompt. (for example: A>LOTUS) and press the ENTER key. Or select the spreadsheet option on the main menu of an integrated package.

3. Once the program is loaded from the disk, you can erase a copyright notice by pressing any key. A blank spreadsheet form will then appear on the screen.

4. Notice that the cursor is at the first cell (A1). At this point, you should use the cursor control keys to explore the entire spreadsheet.

HANDS–ON EXERCISE A3–1

Viewing the Spreadsheet

Before we continue, you should become familiar with the electronic spreadsheet by using the cursor control keys to move the screen window around the entire worksheet in memory. (This is called **scrolling** the window.) See how many columns and rows there are by looking at the column letters and row numbers as they scroll by. Then use the PAGE UP and PAGE DOWN keys (Pg Up and Pg Dn) to move up or down a page at a time. Then use the TAB key to move a page at a time to the right of the spreadsheet. To move a page at a time to the left, press the SHIFT key as well as the TAB key. If you want to go directly to a certain cell in the worksheet, press the F5 function key (the GOTO key) and enter its cell address (such as H23) in response to the GoTo prompt. Finally, use the HOME key to return you to the first cell (A1) of the spreadsheet.

USING COMMANDS

Electronic spreadsheets use **commands** to manipulate the worksheet and its contents in various ways. For example, you can use a BLANK command to erase the contents of a cell. You could use a COPY command to copy the contents of cells, rows, and columns throughout the spreadsheet. Or you can insert or delete a column or row by using INSERT or DELETE commands.

In many spreadsheets, commands are activated by pressing the slash (/) key. This displays a **main menu** of commands above or below the spreadsheet. Selecting any of these main menu commands will provide you with a **command menu** or comment that specifies the options available to accomplish that command. Selecting an option from a command menu will provide you with a comment, prompt, or **submenu** of additional options! Thus several levels of menus may be provided to accomplish major spreadsheet functions. This is what is meant by a **menu-driven** program. Figure A3–4 gives you an overview of the command options provided by the major menus of Lotus 1-2-3.

In many microcomputer packages, you can select an option or command from a menu by moving the cursor to it and pressing the ENTER key. Or you can use the keyboard to type and enter the first character of a command displayed on a menu. One other typical feature should be mentioned at this

---

Figure A3–4 An overview of the menus and commands of Lotus 1-2-3. Notice the variety of command options provided.

Lotus Access System Menu
1-2-3, PrintGraph, Translate, Install, View, Exit
Lotus 1-2-3 Main Menu
Worksheet, Range, Copy, Move, File, Print, Graph, Data, System, Quit
Worksheet Command Menu
Global, Insert, Delete, Column, Erase, Titles, Window, Status, Page
Range Command Menu
Format, Label, Erase, Name, Justify, Protect, Unprotect, Input, Value, Transpose
Copy Command Comment
Copy a cell or range of cells
Move Command Comment
Move a cell or range of cells
File Command Menu
Retrieve, Save, Combine, Xtract, Erase, List, Import, Directory
Print Command Comment
Output a range to the printer or a print file
Graph Command Menu
Type, X, A, B, C, D, E, F, Reset, View, Save, Options, Name, Quit
Data Command Menu
Fill, Table, Sort, Query, Distribution, Matrix, Regression, Parse
System Command Comment
Invoke the DOS Command Interpreter
Quit Command Comment
End 1-2-3 session (Have you saved your work?)

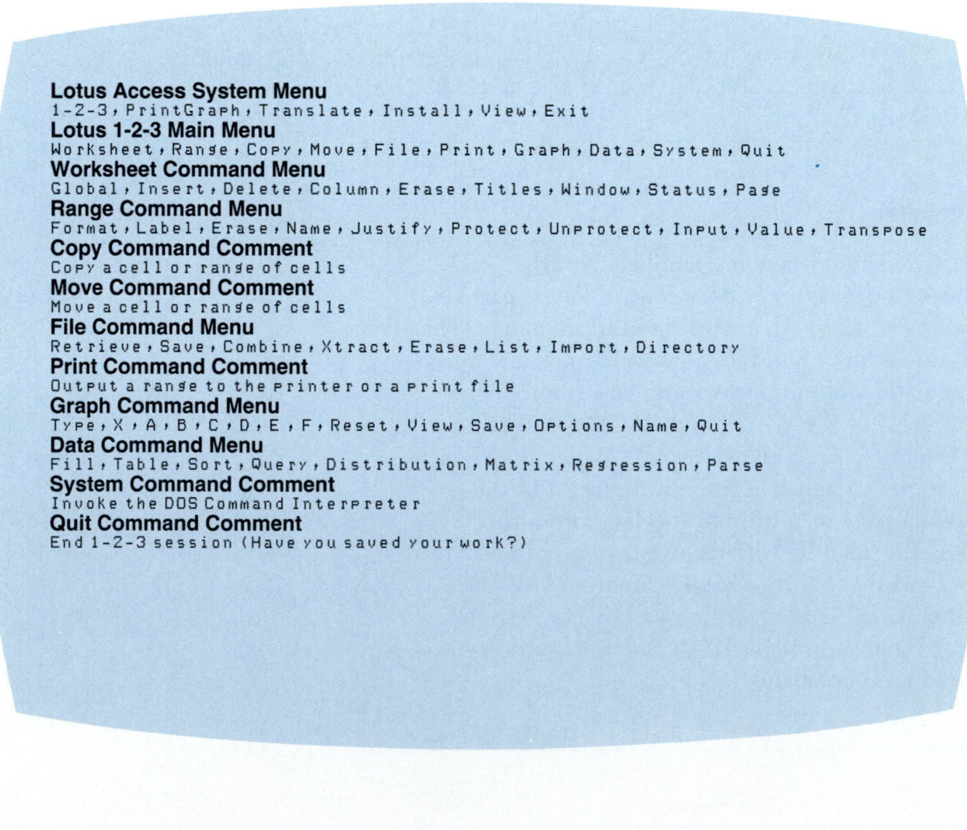

time. Like many microcomputer packages, electronic spreadsheet programs make extensive use of the **function keys** found on many microcomputers. Figure A3–5 outlines how you might use the 10 function keys on many PC keyboards.

ENTERING DATA

Data is entered at the cell location where the cursor is placed by simply typing it in and either depressing the ENTER key, or one of the cursor control keys. If you use the ENTER key, the cursor remains at the same cell location. If you use one of the cursor control keys, the data are entered at the cell location where the cursor was located and the cursor moves to another cell. You can usually enter many characters of data into a cell. For example, many spreadsheets allow up to 125 characters in each cell. However, only eight numbers or nine letters will be displayed on the screen unless you change the standard column width of your spreadsheet.

Each cell in an electronic spreadsheet can be filled with one of three possible types of information: numbers, words, and formulas. More specifically, a cell can contain:

☐ **Text data,** such as titles and other text material.
☐ **Numeric data** or numbers.
☐ **Mathematical formulas,** which perform standard arithmetic functions (add, subtract, multiply, etc.) as well as special **functions** (sum, average, net present value, etc.) provided by the spreadsheet program.

CORRECTING ERRORS

You are now ready to select a specific command or to enter items in the worksheet and perform various functions on the data it contains. But what if you make a mistake or need help? Here are some examples of what you do in most packages.

☐ If you make a mistake while typing and recognize it before you press the ENTER key, press the BACKSPACE key to erase one character at a time, or the ESCAPE key to erase all of the characters at once.

```
  Function Keys       The ten function keys on the IBM keyboard are used by
                      1-2-3 as follows:

  F1:   [HELP]        Displays Help screen
  F2:   [EDIT]        Switches to/from EDIT mode for current entry
  F3:   [NAME]        Displays menu of range names
  F4:   [ABS]         Makes/Unmakes cell address absolute
  F5:   [GOTO]        Moves cell pointer to a particular cell
  F6:   [WINDOW]      Moves cell pointer to other window (split-screen only)
  F7:   [QUERY]       Repeats most recent /Data Query operation
  F8:   [TABLE]       Repeats most recent /Data Table operation
  F9:   [CALC]        Recalculates all formulas (READY mode only)
                      Converts formula to its value (VALUE and EDIT modes)
  F10:  [GRAPH]       Draws graph using current graph settings
```

Figure A3–5 What the function keys do in Lotus 1-2-3. This is also an example of a help display provided by 1-2-3.

☐ Once you have entered something into a cell, you can change its contents by moving the cursor to that cell. Then enter new data into that cell, or use a RANGE ERASE command to erase the contents of that cell. In either case, you must use the ENTER key to complete each of these procedures.

☐ Sometimes the spreadsheet will give you a "beep" and display the word EDIT on the mode indicator after you make an entry. This means you have made an error and have been placed into the edit mode. The edit mode allows you to change selected characters in a cell entry by using several keys to move the cursor and add or delete characters. Use the right and left cursor control keys to move the cursor one character to the right or left, the HOME key to move to the first character, and the END key to move the cursor to the last character of the entry you are editing. The DELETE key will delete the character at the cursor; the BACKSPACE key will delete the character to the left of the cursor. Then insert a new character by simply typing it in.

☐ If you have selected a command and don't want to complete it, just keep pressing the ESCAPE key until you return to a menu or submenu you prefer, or to the worksheet display.

☐ If you want to erase the entire spreadsheet and start over again, use an ERASE spreadsheet command. Then press a Y to confirm this serious decision!

Getting Help

One of the best features of Lotus 1-2-3 and many other electronic spreadsheet programs are **help screens.** Here's what you do if you need help at any time. Press the F1 function key (the HELP key). This will cause the display of a help screen that contains explanations of the command or function that you were working on just before you pressed the HELP key. (This is called a *context-sensitive* help facility.) You can select additional levels of help by moving the cursor to a specific topic on the help screen and pressing the ENTER key. When you are done with the help screen, press the ESCAPE key. This will return the program to where you were before you asked for help. Figure A3–4 was an example of a help screen on a specific topic. Figure A3–6 shows an index of help screens in Lotus 1-2-3.

ENTERING NUMBERS AND TEXT

Electronic spreadsheet programs use simple rules to distinguish between numeric, text, and formula entries, depending on the first character typed. The following rules are common to many spreadsheet programs.

☐ An entry beginning with a letter is assumed to be a text entry (such as a row or column heading) and is identified as a **label.**

☐ An entry beginning with a number is assumed to be a numeric entry and is identified as a **value.**

☐ If the first character you enter is a plus ($+$), minus ($-$), or an opening parenthesis, your entry will be treated as a formula or as a number. This rule also holds true for the $, @, and # characters. A formula or a function is also identified as a **value.**

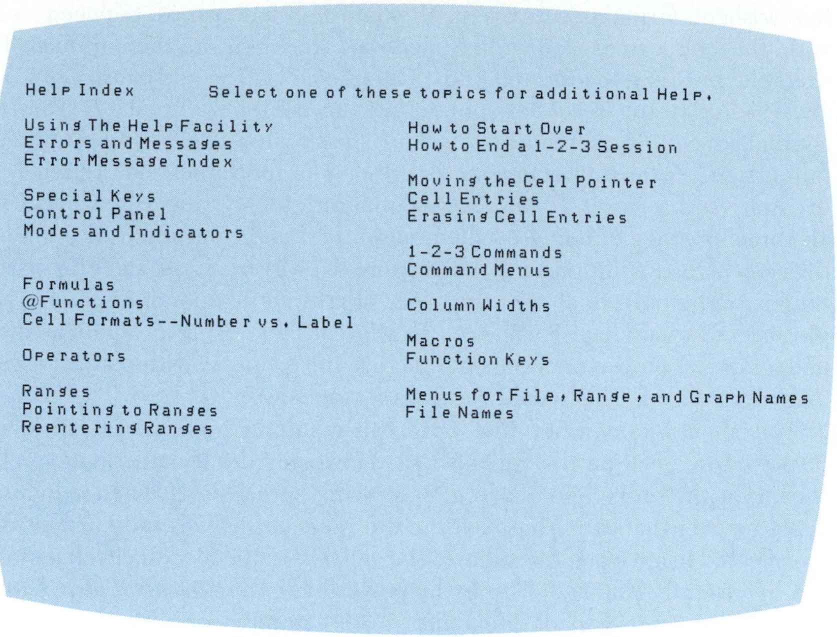

Figure A3–6 The help index display of Lotus 1-2-3. Helpful explanations are provided on these topics.

Help Index   Select one of these topics for additional Help.

Using The Help Facility   How to Start Over
Errors and Messages   How to End a 1-2-3 Session
Error Message Index
                                 Moving the Cell Pointer
Special Keys   Cell Entries
Control Panel   Erasing Cell Entries
Modes and Indicators
                                 1-2-3 Commands
                                 Command Menus
Formulas
@Functions   Column Widths
Cell Formats--Number vs. Label
                                 Macros
Operators   Function Keys

Ranges   Menus for File, Range, and Graph Names
Pointing to Ranges   File Names
Reentering Ranges

☐   A text entry (a label) can begin with blanks or a number (such as the date 1988) if you first press the apostrophe or the double quote key (for example, '1988 or "1988).

A spreadsheet will usually identify a label entry by displaying the letter L or an apostrophe (') on the entry line of the control panel. A numeric or formula entry is identified by the letter V in some spreadsheets. If you mix numbers, letters, and special characters improperly, a spreadsheet program may refuse to accept your entry. It will give you a "beep" and put you into an edit mode so you can correct your entry.

The distinction between numeric and label entries is important, because cells containing numeric entries can be manipulated by formulas and functions, whereas cells containing text material cannot (with a few exceptions). Many spreadsheets also allow labels to go beyond the boundaries of a cell (helpful for title and other text material), whereas numeric data and formulas cannot. Also, a formula must be differentiated from numeric and text entries, because only the value of the formula, not the formula itself, is usually displayed in a cell.

Labels are automatically left justified in their cells; numbers and formulas are automatically right justified. Numbers are usually not allowed to use the last position at the right of a cell. It is reserved for a decimal point, even if there is none. If you want to change this automatic justification, you usually must start your entries with special characters, such as:

'   to left justify your cell entry.
"   to right justify your cell entry.
^   to center your cell entry.
\   to repeat your next character in the rest of the cell.

ENTERING AND USING FORMULAS

Spreadsheet formulas express mathematical relationships between cells, with the cell names acting like algebraic variables in the formula. For example, entering the formula (B5 − C2) into cell D7 would cause cell D7 to always display the result of subtracting the contents of cell C2 from the contents of cell B5. Spreadsheet formulas use a plus sign (+) for addition, a minus sign (−) for subtraction, an asterisk (*) for multiplication, a slash (/) for division, and a caret (^) for exponentiation. Most spreadsheets use the algebraic practice of doing exponentiation first and then multiplication and division before addition and subtraction. However, as in algebra, parentheses can be used to change the order of arithmetic operations. For example, 1 + 2*3 would have a value of 7 in a spreadsheet using an algebraic order of operations. However, you could modify the formulas with parentheses as follows: (1 + 2)*3. This would result in a value of 9.

You should remember that only the result or value of a formula is displayed in a cell on the spreadsheet. However, the formula in any cell is shown on the entry line above or below the spreadsheet when the cursor is placed over that cell. Thus anytime the value of the cells used in a formula are affected in any way, the value of the cell where the formula itself is stored can be instantly changed. This is the powerful *automatic calculation* feature of electronic spreadsheet programs. For example, consider the formula, (D7 = +B5 − C2). Whenever the value of either cell B5 or cell C2 changes, the value of cell D7 will instantly change to display a new result.

Do you realize that the entire example spreadsheet shown in Figure A3–3 is based on the entry of only one numeric data element: 1987 sales of $1,000? All other numbers in the spreadsheet are generated by formulas!

But let's get back to the simple spreadsheet you have just built as displayed in Figure A3–7. What do the formulas you have entered mean? Nothing very complicated. You have just specified that (1) EXPENSES are 60 percent of REVENUE, (2) PROFIT equals REVENUE minus EXPENSES, (3) TAXES are 40 percent of PROFIT, and (4) PROFIT AFTER TAXES equals PROFIT minus TAXES.

Now let's see a simple demonstration of the powerful automatic recalculation and "what if" capability of an electronic spreadsheet. **What** would

---

HANDS–ON EXERCISE A3–2

Starting and Using a Simple Spreadsheet

Enter the titles and headings of the spreadsheet example shown in Figure A3–3, and data for REVENUE in 1987 of $1,000. Then enter the formulas for EXPENSES +B8*0.6, PROFIT +B8 − B10, TAXES +B12*0.4, and PROFIT AFTER TAXES +B12 − B14. What happens as you enter each formula? Notice that the formula for a cell is shown only on the first line of the control panel. The cell itself displays the *value* or *result* of the computation of the formula.

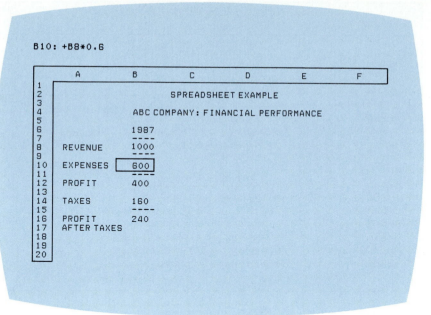

B10: +B8*0.6

	A	B	C	D	E	F
1						
2		SPREADSHEET EXAMPLE				
3						
4		ABC COMPANY: FINANCIAL PERFORMANCE				
5						
6		1987				
7		----				
8	REVENUE	1000				
9		----				
10	EXPENSES	600				
11		----				
12	PROFIT	400				
13						
14	TAXES	160				
15		----				
16	PROFIT	240				
17	AFTER TAXES					
18						
19						
20						

Figure A3–7 Starting an electronic spreadsheet. Start by entering titles and headings. Then begin entering data or formulas in appropriate cells. Notice that the formula for 1987 expenses, which was entered in cell B10, is displayed above the spreadsheet.

PROFIT AFTER TAXES have been **if** revenue for 1987 had increased to $1,500? $1,800? $2,000? Try it and see, instantly.

USING FUNCTIONS

All electronic spreadsheet programs contain many built-in mathematical formulas and computational routines called **functions.** Functions give us a much easier way of performing computations and other tasks than building a formula ourselves with a long string of mathematical symbols and cell names. Most electronic spreadsheets have **mathematical** functions (like SUM), **statistical** functions (like AVERAGE), **financial** functions (like Net Present Value), and **logical** functions (like IF . . . THEN). All function entries usually begin with the @ symbol before typing the name of the function. Most functions have **arguments** (usually contained within parentheses), which specify the cells or other values that will be used in computations. A listing of the spreadsheet functions in Lotus 1-2-3 is shown in Figure A3–8.

As an example, let's look at the following function:

@SUM(A7 . . . A12)

In this example, @ signals that this entry is a function; SUM is the name of the function, and (A7 . . . A12) is the argument. When this function is entered into a cell, it immediately displays the results of adding together the values in cells A7, A8, A9, A10, A11, and A12.

It should be noted here that the entry of cell coordinates in formulas and functions in most electronic spreadsheets can be accomplished in two ways. First, you can type in the cell coordinates when needed. Or, you can use the cursor movement keys to move the cursor over to a cell. This automatically inserts that cell's coordinates into the formula.

Function	Result
	General Computational Functions
@AVG(list)	Arithmetic mean of the values in a list.
@COUNT(list)	Number of nonblank entries in a list.
@MAX(list)	Largest value in a list.
@MIN(list)	Smallest value in a list.
@SUM(list)	Sum of each value in a list.
@NPV	Calculates the net present value of future cash flows.
@NA	Avoids error messages when cells with labels or blanks are evaluated arithmetically.
	Arithmetic Functions
@ABS(v)	Absolute value of an argument.
@EXP(v)	e (2.71828 . . .) to the power specified by an argument.
@INT(v)	Integer portion of an argument.
@LN(v)	Natural log (base e) of an argument.
@LOG10(v)	Logarithm (base 10) of an argument.
@SQRT(v)	Square root of an argument.

COPYING SPREADSHEET ENTRIES

Do you want to key in repetitive data, text, formulas, and functions, in column after column, row after row of a worksheet? Of course not. Most electronic spreadsheet packages can save you a lot of time and effort in constructing a worksheet. They allow you to **copy** the contents of any part of a spreadsheet to any other part of the spreadsheet. Thus cells, columns, rows, and other ranges can be copied or *replicated*.

One feature of Lotus 1-2-3 and similar programs that is very helpful in the copying process (as well as in many other commands) is an **expanding cursor.** You are usually prompted to supply the coordinates of a range during the execution of many commands. For example, during the execution of a COPY command you are asked to:

☐ Enter range to copy from:

☐ Enter range to copy to:

You can, of course, just key in the column and row coordinates of the ranges involved. (Some spreadsheets call them the *source* and *target* ranges.) Or you could use the expanding cursor to "paint a picture" of the parts of the worksheet involved. This involves the following process:

1. Move the cursor to a corner cell of the range you want to copy.
2. Enter COPY.
3. Use the cursor keys (or electronic mouse or touch-screen) to indicate the range you want to copy. Notice how the cursor expands to "paint" the range in reverse video. Then press the ENTER key.
4. Move the cursor to a corner of the range you want to copy material into. Then *anchor* the cursor to this corner by pressing the period (.) key. Now use the cursor control keys to expand the cursor until it highlights the entire range. Then press the ENTER key. (You can usually remove an anchored cursor by pressing the ESCAPE key.)

HANDS–ON EXERCISE A3–3

Completing a Spreadsheet

Finish the spreadsheet shown in Figure A3–3. You don't have to key in all of the numbers and formulas. Instead, do the following:

1. Key in the column headings for 1988 (in C6) and 1989 (in D6), TOTAL (in E6) and AVERAGE (in F6). Key in or copy the dotted line below these figures if you want to.

2. Key in formulas for the revenues for 1988 and 1989, assuming that 1988 revenues will be 110 percent of 1987 (+ B8*1.1 in cell C8) and that 1989 revenue will be 120 percent of 1987 (+ B8*1.2 in cell D8). Notice how the revenue amounts for those years are instantly calculated and displayed.

3. Now copy the range that includes the formulas for 1987 EXPENSES, PROFIT, and PROFIT AFTER TAXES (B10 . . . B16) to the range that will include those same figures for 1988 and 1989 (C10 . . . D16). Again notice how the appropriate amounts are instantly calculated and displayed. (Even the dotted lines between amounts have been copied!) Move the cursor to the cells with number values and see for yourself, from the control panel display, that they now contain formulas adjusted to reflect their new cell addresses.

4. Enter the formulas for TOTAL REVENUE and AVERAGE REVENUE. But use the SUM and AVERAGE functions to save yourself some work. Thus enter @ SUM (B8 . . . D8) into cell E8, and @AVG (B8 . . . D8) into cell F8. Now copy the formulas in these two cells into the remaining cells of columns E and F of your spreadsheet. Then, copy range E8 . . . F8 to range E10 . . . F16. Then erase any zeros or error messages appearing between your spreadsheet values, using an ERASE command. (Use the backward slash (\) and the minus key to enter dotted lines in your spreadsheet if you wish.) Now your spreadsheet should look just like Figure A3–3. Congratulations!

There is a major difference in how spreadsheets copy formulas. Some spreadsheets (like VisiCalc and PC-Calc) ask you to specify whether a formula should be copied (1) without changing its cell references (an *absolute* copy) or (2) whether the formula should be copied with its cell references changed to indicate its new column and row address (a *relative* or *adjusted* copy). Spreadsheets like Lotus 1-2-3 and Multiplan assume that the *absolute* value of labels and numbers, and the *relative* value of formulas and functions are what you want copied.

Example.   Suppose you wanted to copy the formula (B8*0.5 + B20) from cell B2 to G2. If you made a *relative* copy, the formula copied into cell G2 would be (G8*0.5 + G20). If you wanted an *absolute* copy, you would have to add dollar signs to the cell references in the formula. Thus the formula (B8*.05 + B20) would be copied into cell G2 as (B8*0.5 + B20).

SAVING AND RETRIEVING A SPREADSHEET

Spreadsheets can be saved on a magnetic disk and retrieved later for additional use. A /FILE SAVE command sequence is used to store a spreadsheet on the disk. However, the spreadsheet prompt first asks for the name of the file in which the spreadsheet will be saved. You must then supply a file name, usually up to eight characters. For example, BUDGET, CHECK, INCOME, and so on.

Note: If your computer has only one disk drive, you may wish to remove the spreadsheet program diskette from the disk drive and replace it with a file disk of your own on which you can store the spreadsheets and other files that you develop. If your system has two disk drives, the program disk should remain in the first drive and your file disk should be in the second drive.

A spreadsheet stored on a magnetic disk can be easily retrieved. You should use a /FILE RETRIEVE command sequence that loads a spreadsheet from the disk into the computer's memory. During the execution of this command, the spreadsheet prompt will ask you for the name of the specific spreadsheet file you wish to load. Once you enter the name that was used to store the file, the spreadsheet is retrieved from the disk, stored in memory, and displayed on the screen.

HANDS–ON EXERCISE A3–4

Saving and Retrieving a Spreadsheet

☐ Use a /FILE SAVE command sequence to save your spreadsheet. This includes giving your spreadsheet a name (of up to eight characters). How about EXAMPLE1?

☐ Use a /FILE RETRIEVE command sequence to retrieve the EXAMPLE1 spreadsheet, even though it is still displayed on your screen. The screen will go blank and then your spreadsheet will reappear. This proves that you have correctly stored and retrieved your spreadsheet.

Once you have completed the spreadsheet and used it to analyze a particular business problem or opportunity, you will probably want to print a paper copy of the spreadsheet on the printer of your computer system. A PRINT command is used to obtain a printout in Lotus 1-2-3 and most spreadsheets. This will cause the printing of a rectangular area of the worksheet whose upper left corner is the cell in which the cursor was located at the time the PRINT command was given. The lower right corner of the spreadsheet to be printed must be specified by entering the name of the cell at that corner in response to a spreadsheet prompt.

When you select a PRINT command from the Lotus 1-2-3 main menu, the spreadsheet prompt asks whether you wish to send your output to a printer or to a file on your diskette for later printing. If you select the PRINTER option in response to this prompt, you will be asked to enter the cell coordinates at the lower right corner of the spreadsheet you wish to print. As soon as this is done, the computer will begin printing your spreadsheet.

If you want to store a *printfile* of your spreadsheet on your disk for later printing, you should select the PRINTFILE option. The spreadsheet prompt will then ask you to supply a file name for this printfile (which should be different than the file name you used to store the spreadsheet itself). Once you enter the printfile name and the coordinates of the spreadsheet, the printfile is stored on your disk.

PRINTING SPREADSHEETS

HANDS–ON EXERCISE A3–5

Printing Your Spreadsheet

Print the spreadsheet you completed in Exercise A3–4. First, retrieve it from the disk if you have not done so. Then use the PRINT command. Enter the cell coordinates of the range you want printed or of the entire spreadsheet in response to a spreadsheet prompt. Select any other options offered that you want, such as page size, spacing, and so on. Printing will begin when you give a GO command, or press the ENTER key after the last option.

Notice that this produces a copy of the spreadsheet as in Figure A3–3. The row numbers, column letters, and control panel display that are shown on your screen are not printed. These can be printed for that part of the spreadsheet shown on your video monitor if you press the SHIFT and the PRINT-SCREEN keys.

HANDS–ON EXERCISE A3–6

Using Your Spreadsheet

You have now built, saved, and printed your first spreadsheet. Now you can use it as a decision support tool by playing "what if" games as you did earlier. For example, retrieve the spreadsheet from the diskette and change revenue figures or change the tax rate and see what happens to your "bottom line." Figure A3–9 is a display of the spreadsheet that results from changing 1987 revenue to $2,000. Notice how quickly and completely this changes the values in your spreadsheet! Save or print any of these spreadsheet variations, if you wish. However, this is not necessary. The original EXAMPLE1 spreadsheet is stored safely on your disk.

CHANGING A SPREADSHEET

Most electronic spreadsheets provide a variety of commands that allow you to change the organization and appearance of the spreadsheet. Let's discuss a few commands that are useful even when developing a simple spreadsheet. Figure A3–10 outlines typical commands that change the format or appearance of a worksheet.

Changing Column Width

Most spreadsheet programs allow you to change the width of all or individual columns. Using a WORKSHEET GLOBAL COLUMN command sequence will allow you to change the width of all columns in the spreadsheet to a new standard width. You can change the width of individual columns with a COLUMN command. First you move the cell pointer to the column you want changed. Then you invoke the COLUMN command, specify the new width, and press ENTER. The width of that column is immediately changed.

Figure A3–9 An example of "what if" analysis. This is the spreadsheet that results from changing 1987 revenue to $2,000.

```
                        SPREADSHEET EXAMPLE

                   ABC COMPANY: FINANCIAL PERFORMANCE

                     1987      1988      1989     TOTAL    AVERAGE
                    ----------------------------------------------
        REVENUE      2000      2200      2400      6600      2200

        EXPENSES     1200      1320      1440      3960      1320
                    ----------------------------------------------
        PROFIT        800       880       960      2640       880

        TAXES         320       352       384      1056       352
                    ----------------------------------------------
        PROFIT        480       528       576      1584       528
        AFTER TAXES
```

Columns and rows can be easily added to or removed from an existing electronic spreadsheet, using the WORKSHEET INSERT or DELETE command sequences. To insert a row, move the cursor to a row above the position where you want a new row to be created and enter the INSERT ROW command. All rows below the cursor will be moved down to make room for the new row. To insert a column, move the cursor to a column to the left of the position where you want a new column to be created and enter the INSERT COLUMN command. The column in which the cursor had been located and all columns to its right will be moved to the right to make room for the new column. All formulas contained in the spreadsheet are automatically adjusted to compensate for the new cell locations that result from these movements.

To delete a row, the cursor is moved somewhere in the row or column you want to delete. Then, enter a DELETE ROW or DELETE COLUMN command. Deleting rows or columns can cause errors in other parts of the spreadsheet that might have referred to a cell in a deleted row or column. Therefore, check your spreadsheet for this possible side effect after deleting a row or column.

Inserting and Deleting Rows and Columns

The FORMAT command allows you to alter the way information is displayed in a cell. For example, you might want all of the money values in a column to display a dollar sign and two decimal places. This command usually allows you to select from several format options and to choose to have up to 15 decimal places displayed. Thus if you wanted two decimal places shown, a number like 12.30 could appear as:

Changing Formats

Format Option	Cell Display
General	12.3
Fixed	12.30
Currency	$12.30
Percent	1230.00%
Scientific	1.23E + 01

Enter / **Worksheet** and one of the following commands:
  Global   Establish formats for the entire worksheet.
  Delete   Delete columns or rows.
  Column-Width   Change the width of individual columns.
  Erase   Erase the worksheet in memory.
  Titles   Lock horizontal and vertical titles.
  Window   Split the screen into horizontal or vertical windows.

Enter / **Range** and one of the following commands:
  Format   Alter the display format of a cell or range.
  Label-Prefix   Align labels in a cell or range.
  Name   Assign a name to a cell or range.
  Protect   Protect the contents of a cell or range from alteration.

Figure A3–10 Commands that modify the 1-2-3 worksheet format.

To change display formats, move the cursor to a cell or range, give the /RANGE FORMAT command sequence, and then select the format option you wish to use. To change the format of the entire spreadsheet, you must use a /WORKSHEET GLOBAL FORMAT command sequence. *Note:* The fixed and currency format command options are useful because so many spreadsheets contain financial data expressed as dollars and cents.

Locking Titles

Most spreadsheets use titles to identify the data in the rows and columns of the spreadsheet. Most electronic spreadsheet packages allow row and title columns to be "locked in place" so the titles can remain on the screen as the cursor moves the screen window to other parts of the spreadsheet stored in memory. This feature also makes it impossible to move the cursor into a title area of the worksheet when using the cursor control key. Titles can be locked using a /WORKSHEET TITLES command sequence. You then enter the coordinates of the cell where the lowest row or right-most column of the title is located. The spreadsheet prompt then gives you the option of locking horizontal or vertical titles.

Multiple Windows

Most electronic spreadsheet programs allow you to subdivide the video screen into two or more windows from which you can view different parts of the spreadsheet stored in memory. This capability is important because it is frequently impossible to keep the important parts of a spreadsheet that a user wants to see together in one window. Therefore, most spreadsheets have a /WORKSHEET WINDOW command sequence, which allows you to split the screen horizontally or vertically into several windows. You can

---

HAND–ON EXERCISE A3–7

Changing the Spreadsheet's Appearance

Explore the worksheet commands shown in Figure A3–10 to modify the appearance and format of the spreadsheet. Select each command. Then move the control panel cursor to each of the options in its submenu, noticing each explanation given. Notice the wealth of alternatives you have to change the format and appearance of the spreadsheet. We don't have room to explain all of them in this appendix. You will have to explore them on your own with the help of a user's manual and help menus. But you should try a few of them. Remember: Use the ESCAPE key to get yourself out of any command sequence you don't want to continue with.

For example, you should try changing column widths individually or for the entire spreadsheet (a global change); insert and delete rows or columns; lock titles and split the screen into two windows and then clear it back to a single window. Try formatting a column so numeric entries display a dollar sign, or protect it so its values can't be changed.

choose to have the windows move independently or together around the spreadsheet.

One of the outstanding features of some graphics packages and the graphics modules of integrated packages is their ability to graph parts of your spreadsheets or files easily and immediately. Once you enter a simple graphics command sequence, your results are displayed instantly. Graphics displays thus become just another method of manipulating and displaying parts of your spreadsheets or files. Let's close this section by graphing parts of the ABC Company: Financial Performance spreadsheet. It will give you a taste of how easy graphics are when using a microcomputer and a package with graphics capabilities such as Lotus 1-2-3.

USING GRAPHICS DISPLAYS

HANDS–ON EXERCISE A3–8

Graphing Your Spreadsheets and Files

1. First, let's graph part of the Financial Performance spreadsheet. Retrieve the EXAMPLE1 spreadsheet file from your disk. Now enter the GRAPH command. Select a TYPE option from the graph command menu. Now you should choose one of several types of graphs from a TYPE option submenu such as:

   a. Line.   *d*. Stacked-Bar.
   b. Bar.   *e*. Pie.
   c. XY.

2. After you enter your choice, select an X-AXIS option from the graphics command menu. You are then prompted to enter the X-axis range coordinates. Let's decide right now to graph PROFITS AFTER TAXES from 1987, 1988, and 1989. Therefore, enter the range coordinates (B6 . . . D6). These are the cell coordinates for the range that includes the headings for each year.

3. Now select a FIRST DATA RANGE option from the graphics command menu. You are asked to enter the coordinates of the first data range. Enter B16 . . . D16, which are the coordinates of the range that includes the PROFIT AFTER TAXES for each year.

4. Now enter a VIEW command and your graph appears instantly on the screen. See Figure A3–11.

5. Which type of graph did you display? Do you want to try another? It's easy. Just press the ESCAPE key, select a TYPE option, choose another type of graph, and enter a VIEW command. Presto! You have another type of graphic display. Figure A3–12 shows what would be displayed if you had chosen a pie graph.

Continued on page A–64

Figure A3–11 A bar graph of the annual profits after taxes of the ABC Company.

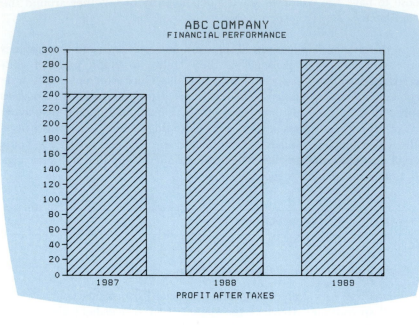

Continued from page A–63

6. Do you want to add a few subtitles to your graph to explain what it illustrates? Select a TITLES option and key in graph and axis titles.

7. How about using graphics to help you answer "what if" questions? It's easy. Press the ESCAPE key until you are back to the worksheet display. Change the example spreadsheet any way you want. For example, what if EX-PENSES were 70 percent of REVENUE? Change the formula in cell B10 and see how this affects your bottom line (PROFIT AFTER TAXES). However, instead of just looking at numbers on a spreadsheet, why not see the change graphically? Just press a GRAPH function key. Instantly, a graph of the new bottom line appears. Thus, graphics makes it easy to evaluate repetitive "what if" analysis.

8. If you want to save your EXAMPLE1 spreadsheet file with its current graphics settings, use a **FILE SAVE** command sequence. However, if you want to prepare a printed copy of your graph, use a **GRAPH SAVE** command sequence. You will need to use a special PrintGraph program disk that is included in the Lotus 1-2-3 package. It will allow you to print a copy of your graphs on a dot matrix, laser, or other printer that has graphics capabilities.

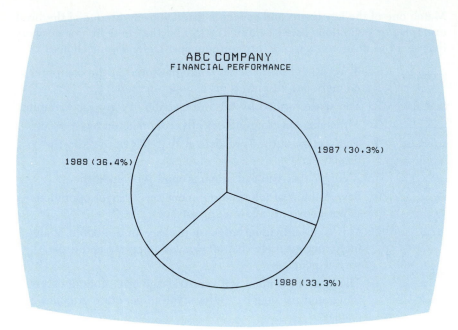

Figure A3–12 A pie graph of the annual profits after taxes of the ABC Company. Notice that Lotus 1-2-3 automatically calculated the percentages shown.

SUMMARY

We have now run through a complete example of the creation and manipulation of a simple spreadsheet and the generation of graphics displays. This should have helped you tie together the features of electronic spreadsheet and graphic packages that we have covered in this section. Consult the manual for the package you are using if you need more specific information. For example, you will need to find out the specific commands used to get help screens, copy entries, and store, retrieve, print, and graph spreadsheets. To help you get started, take another look at "Overview of Spreadsheet Development" near the beginning of this section.

KEY TERMS AND CONCEPTS

These are the key terms and concepts of this chapter. The page number of their first explanation is in parentheses.

1. Cell (A–45)
2. Cell pointer (A–45)
3. Command (A–50)
4. Control panel (A–47)
5. Copy (A–56)
6. Electronic spreadsheet (A–44)
7. Format commands (A–60)
8. Functions (A–55)
9. Graphics program (A–63)
10. Graph types (A–63)
11. Help screen (A–52)
12. Label (A–52)
13. Print (A–59)
14. Range (A–45)
15. Retrieve (A–58)
16. Save (A–58)
17. Scrolling (A–46)
18. Spreadsheet program (A–44)
19. Template (A–44)
20. Value (A–52)
21. "What if" analysis (A–45)
22. Window (A–45)

REVIEW AND APPLICATION QUIZ

Match one of the **key terms and concepts** listed above with one of the brief examples or definitions listed below. Try to find the "best fit" for answers that seem to fit more than one term or concept. Defend your choices.

_____ 1. A worksheet of rows and columns stored in the computer's memory and displayed on its video screen.

_____ 2. The space formed by the intersection of a row and column.

_____ 3. A rectangular grouping of cells, columns, or rows.

_____ 4. The section of the spreadsheet that you can see on the display screen.

_____ 5. A cursor that you can move around the spreadsheet.

_____ 6. Several lines of information about spreadsheet operations either above or below a spreadsheet.

_____ 7. This is an individual software package or a module of an integrated package that allows you to create and use spreadsheets.

_____ 8. This is an individual software package or a module of an integrated package that allows you to generate graphics displays.

_____ 9. How you instruct a spreadsheet to carry out an operation for you.

_____ 10. Text data such as a title.

_____ 11. A number or a formula.

_____ 12. Mathematical formulas and computational routines built in to the spreadsheet program.

_____ 13. Moving the display screen window across the spreadsheet in memory.

_____ 14. Making alternative changes to spreadsheet data or formula values in order to evaluate the results of such alternatives.

_____ 15. Use this feature instead of keying in repetitive spreadsheet entries.

_____ 16. Store your spreadsheet on a magnetic disk.

_____ 17. Transfer your spreadsheet from a magnetic disk into the memory of the computer.

_____ 18. Produce a paper copy of your spreadsheet on a computer printer.

_____ 19. Helps you change the organization and appearance of the spreadsheet.

_____ 20. Contains explanations of spreadsheet commands and operations.

_____ 21. Includes line, bar, and pie alternatives.

_____ 22. Predeveloped spreadsheet models available for specific applications.

It's time for you to create some simple spreadsheets and graphics displays of your own. That is the purpose of the following assignments. Good luck!

A3.1 If you have not already done so, create, manipulate, store, print, and graph the ABC Company: Financial Performance spreadsheet as explained in the eight HANDS–ON EXERCISES of this section.

A3.2 Build the simple Checkbook Example spreadsheet shown in Figure A3–13. All values for checks, deposits, and the opening balance have to be entered. However, the remaining BALANCE values are computed by formulas you must insert in each cell where a balance is shown. Store and print this spreadsheet.

A3.3 Build the Home Budget Example spreadsheet shown in Figure A3–14. Insert the values for January but use a SUM function to create a formula that computes the total expenses for that month. Then use COPY commands to create the values for February and March. Use the SUM and AVERAGE functions and COPY commands to develop the TOTAL and AVERAGE columns. Compute the PERCENT column by dividing the total for an expense category by the grand total for three months. For example, the percentage for food is $600 divided by $2,190. That could be expressed as a formula like +E8/E18. Use a FORMAT command and a PERCENT option to round your percent calculations to two decimal places. Store and print this spreadsheet.

CHECKBOOK EXAMPLE SPREADSHEET

DATE	DESCRIPTION	CHECK	DEPOSIT	BALANCE
9-15				1234.56
9-16	EXXON	20.55		1214.01
9-17	DEPOSIT		200.25	1414.26
9-18	K-MART	17.98		1396.28
9-19	PIZZA HUT	10.43		1385.85

Figure A3–13 Checkbook example spreadsheet.

HOME BUDGET EXAMPLE SPREADSHEET

ACCOUNT	JAN	FEB	MAR	TOTAL	PERCENT	AVERAGE
FOOD	200	200	200	600	27.40	200
RENT	300	300	300	900	41.10	300
GAS	100	100	100	300	13.70	100
FUN	80	80	80	240	10.96	80
MISC	50	50	50	150	6.85	50
TOTAL	730	730	730	2190	100	730

Figure A3–14 Home budget example spreadsheet.

Figure A3–15 Payroll example
spreadsheet.

```
                        PAYROLL SPREADSHEET EXAMPLE

            NAME              SSNO             RATE      TOTAL HOURS      OT HOURS

        ALVAREZ J.S.      632403718           14.00        44.00           4.00
        KLUGMAN K.L.      435182906           12.00        35.00           0.00
        OBRIEN J.A.       576434572           12.50        45.50           5.50
        PORTER M.L.       342877915           12.50        40.00           0.00
```

A3.4 Build the Payroll File spreadsheet shown in Figure A3–15. Key in employee names, social security numbers, hourly pay rates, total hours worked, and overtime hours worked. However, employee gross pay needs to be calculated by a formula that should be replicated in the rest of that column. Hints: (1) Before entering employee social security numbers, press the apostrophe or the double quote key so the number is entered as a label, not as a floating point number; (2) if you want to see more of the employees' names on the spreadsheet display, use a GLOBAL COLUMN command sequence to increase the width of all columns; (3) gross pay should equal hourly rate times hours worked plus overtime pay. Overtime pay should equal 0.5 times the hourly rate times overtime hours worked.

A3.5 Use the spreadsheets you create in these assignments to perform "what if" analyses. For example, change revenue, expense, or tax values and formulas in the ABC Company's financial spreadsheet. What happens to the company's profits? What might this mean to the company's management? Next, change checks or deposits in the Checkbook spreadsheet, expenses values in the Home Budget spreadsheet, or pay rates in the Payroll File spreadsheet. Print the results of these changes. Write a short explanation of what happens and its implications for a computer user.

A3.6 Create graphics displays of parts of the spreadsheets you developed in previous assignments. For examples, develop a pie chart of home budget expense items or a bar graph of employee hours worked. Make changes to entries in these spreadsheets and use graphics to help you perform "what if" analysis. Figure A3–16 is an example of how you could generate a bar graph of the hours worked by employees from the payroll file spreadsheet of Figure A3–15.

A3.7 One of the most valuable uses of spreadsheets is analysis of financial statements. One common kind of analysis is to study each expense as a percentage of sales. To do this, prepare a spreadsheet that presents a simple income statement. In the next assignment we will perform an actual analysis of this spreadsheet. Figure A3–17 is an example of a simple income statement:

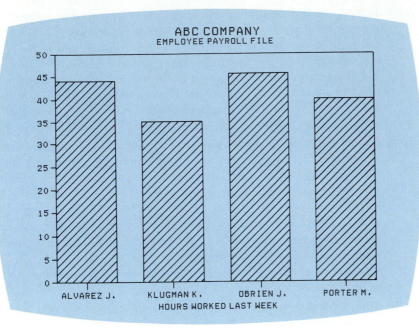

Figure A3–16 Bar graph of hours worked by employees.

Figure A3–17 An example of a simple income statement.

XYZ Company
Income Statement
For the Year Ended December 31, 1987

Sales		$300,000
Returns and allowances		−5,000
Net sales		295,000
Cost of goods sold		150,000
Gross profit on sales		145,000
Expenses:		
Advertising	4,000	
Administrative	25,000	
Utilities	20,000	
Miscellaneous	1,000	
Total expenses		50,000
Net profit		$ 95,000

Prepare this income statement as a spreadsheet. You will need to format the figures, to supress decimal zeros, and include dollar signs. Use formulas for net sales, cost of goods sold, gross profit on sales, total expenses, and net profit, instead of entering the values shown above. To test your spreadsheet, change Sales to $400,000, and check to see that the Net Profit increases to $145,000. Print your spreadsheet and save it for use as part of the next assignment.

A3.8 In this exercise we analyze the spreadsheet prepared in assignment A3.7. To perform the analysis, add a percentage column to the right of the income statement. In each column, and in the appropriate rows, put the percentage that each figure is of Sales. Let the percentage be expressed to the nearest whole percent, so that .13 appears as 13, and so on. Thus this column allows you to analyze each amount in the income statement as a percentage of sales.

A3.9 Spreadsheets can sometimes be used as simple file managers. As an example, let's build a list of club members. In column A, put the club members' names (last name first). In column B, put their street addresses. In column C, put their cities, and in columns D and E their states and zip codes. You will have to adjust column widths to get satisfactory results. Now enter about a dozen names of club members, together with their residence information, and print a report. If necessary, sort the spreadsheet so that the database is in alphabetical order. To show how file maintenance would be done, delete one or two members and add a new one.

A3.10 Auditors and corporate executives are often very concerned about the uses to which spreadsheets are put, and whether the spreadsheets are valid. An invalid spreadsheet can result in erroneous calculations costing a company millions of dollars. One way to validate a spreadsheet is to examine the formulas used in it. Print out one of the spreadsheets you have constructed in previous assignments. However, use the PRINT command's CELL FORMULAS option to print out the formulas in each cell instead of their values. Such printouts are a vital part of spreadsheet documentation. Explain how an auditor could use the contents of the printout to detect a spreadsheet that is faulty.

Section IV: Doing Database Management and Report Generation

Outline

In previous sections of Appendix A we saw that word processing programs manage data that is organized into text expressions such as sentences and paragraphs. We also saw that electronic spreadsheet programs manage data that can be organized into rows, columns, and formulas relating cells to each other. In this section we will see how file management programs, database management system programs, or the database management modules of integrated packages help you manage and use data. Such programs have become one of the most popular types of software for use with personal computers.

INTRODUCTION TO DATABASE MANAGEMENT

Before we can explain the use of such packages, we need to review the meaning of several important concepts.

Basic Concepts

- A **character** consists of a single alphabetic, numeric, or other symbol. Examples are the letters of the alphabet, numbers, and special symbols such as dollar signs and decimal points.

- A **field** is a grouping of characters that represent a characteristic of a person, place, thing, or event. For example, your *name field* would consist of the alphabetic characters of your name, while your *address field* would consist of the numbers and letters of your home address.

- A **record** is a collection of interrelated fields describing a single *entity* in the real world. For example, the payroll record of an employee might consist of a name field, a social security number field, a department field, a salary field, and other similar fields.

- A **file** is a collection of interrelated records. For example, a payroll file might consist of the records of the employees of a firm.

- A **database** is a collection of interrelated files and records. For example, the database of a business might contain such files as payroll, inventory, customer, and so on.

- A **database management system** (**DBMS**) is a set of computer programs that control the creation, maintenance, and use of a database. We will explain the use of microcomputer DBMS packages similar to dBASE III Plus in this section.

Database Software

Microcomputer data management packages come in several different forms. Some are **file management** programs that use "flat file" or "filing card" structures. These programs maintain data in single files whose fields are permanently fixed. Flat-file systems are good for certain limited tasks such as membership lists and mailing lists.

Microcomputer **database management system** packages typically use a more flexible kind of database structure—the "relational" model. Though the relational database structure has its limitations, relational database management systems are easy to understand and use. A relational DBMS allows a user to think of data as arranged in tables, with the records as rows and the fields as columns. This simple tabular structure is a major benefit of the relational database model.

A database management program allows you to set up a database of files and records on your personal computer system. With such computerized files, you can store and retrieve information much faster and more efficiently than with a manual filing system using paper files. Most DBMS microcomputer packages allow you to perform three primary jobs:

Database creation. Helps you define and organize the content, relationships, and structure of the data needed to build a database.

Database interrogation. Helps you access the data in a database to support various information processing assignments. This typically involves information retrieval and report generation. Thus you can selectively retrieve and display information, and produce printed reports and documents.

Database maintenance. Helps you add, delete, update, correct, and protect the data in a database.

GETTING STARTED

Let's find out how to use this important software tool. We will work through simple examples, using typical database management program features. We will use dBASE III Plus, which is widely recognized as a standard for microcomputer database management software packages. Let's do the following tasks:

☐ Create a database. This is where you define the fields used by the records in your database.

☐ Enter and edit data in your database.

☐ Retrieve and display data in a variety of formats.

☐ Change the database. You can add, delete, sort, or modify records.

☐ Generate printed reports from your database.

Let's imagine that we want to create a *personnel database* for a small company. The information that we will want to store will be workers' names, social security numbers, gender, department, pay rate, number of hours worked in the most recent pay period, and total pay. Figure A4–1 displays the file we will create and manipulate in this section. It is a simplified **payroll file** containing information about a few employees of a hypothetical company. Creating and manipulating this file will give you a good introduction to the use of microcomputer database management programs.

Figure A4–1 An example of an employee payroll file. Notice that it consists of five employee records, each containing seven data fields.

Record#	NAME	SSNO	GENDER	DEPT	RATE	HOURS	PAY
1	ALVAREZ J.S.	632403718	F	PRODUCTION	14.00	44.0	644.00
2	PORTER M.L.	342877915	F	ACCOUNTING	12.50	40.0	500.00
3	OBRIEN J.A.	576434572	M	INFO SYSTEMS	12.50	45.5	603.12
4	KLUGMAN K.L.	435182906	M	FINANCE	12.00	35.0	420.00
5	WILSON J.H.	644809371	M	MARKETING	10.00	40.0	400.00

The procedure to start using a database management program such as dBASE III Plus is as follows:

1. Load DOS into your computer as explained in Section I of Appendix A, "Using the PC and DOS."

2. Put your first dBASE III Plus program disk (System Disk #1) in drive A and your own file disk in drive B.

3. Now type DBASE after the DOS prompt (for example: A>DBASE). Then press the ENTER key to load the program and bring up the opening display. Press ENTER to continue.

4. When the message "Insert System Disk 2 and Press ENTER" appears, you should remove System Disk #1, put System Disk #2 in drive A, and press ENTER. This will bring up the menu display of the dBASE III Plus "Assistant" mode.

5. If you want to, you could switch to the *command driven mode* of dBASE III Plus by pressing the ESCAPE key at this point. This will replace the Assistant display with a single dot and a flashing cursor. You can switch back to the Assistant display by pressing the F2 function key.

Database Management Commands

dBASE III Plus and many database management packages can use commands to carry out their operations. These commands resemble common English verbs, and can be modified to further specify the action desired. dBASE III Plus has a **command-driven** mode called the "dot prompt" mode. You can type in the words of a command such as CREATE when a dot and a flashing cursor are displayed. Pressing the ENTER key will execute the command.

Commands have a *general form* or correct syntax. Let's look at a typical example.

Syntax	DISPLAY [<scope>] [<expression list>] [FOR <condition>] [WHILE <condition>] [OFF] [TO PRINT]
Description	Lists the current record. Use DISPLAY with a scope and an expression list to see selected fields or a combination of fields. Use the FOR and WHILE

conditions to display specific contents of the records. Use TO PRINT to get a hard copy of the list, and use OFF to suppress the record numbers. DISPLAY lists with periodic pauses.

Example   DISPLAY ALL NAMES FOR GENDER = 'M'

Explanation   Display the names of all males in a file.

A sample of typical dBASE III Plus commands is shown in Figure A4–2.

Database Management Menus

dBASE III Plus and other database management programs allow you to use menus instead of commands to carry out their operations. In this **menu-driven** approach, the opening or main menu offers a selection of alternative database management operations. Selecting one of the main menu choices leads you to submenus of database operations, data entry screens, instructions, prompts, and so on. This makes the menu-driven approach easier to use than the command-driven alternative, especially for beginning users. However, the menu-driven approach usually involves more steps and thus is slower than the direct entry of database management commands. Therefore, experienced users may prefer the command-driven approach.

Notice the variety of menu options provided by the Assistant mode of dBASE III Plus in Figure A4–3. This is the menu-driven mode of the widely used dBASE III Plus database management package. Figure A4–4 illustrates the organization of a typical Assistant screen display. You can use your cursor control keys to move a highlighted rectangle to the option you want performed and press the ENTER key. Thus you can use selections from a series of "pull-down" menus to create a database, enter data, retrieve data, and produce reports. The action line of the Assistant display even shows you the dBASE III Plus command generated by the use of the Assistant's menus.

Getting Help

Many command-driven database management programs include a HELP command that provides you with on-screen explanations of database management operations. In the command-driven mode of dBASE III Plus, you can press the F1 function key (the HELP key) to get a main help menu. In

---

Figure A4–2 A sample of dBASE III Plus commands. Notice some of the things you can do with a DBMS package.

☐ BROWSE—provides full-screen window viewing and editing.
☐ COPY—makes a copy of an existing database file.
☐ CREATE—creates new database files.
☐ DISPLAY—displays records, fields, and expressions.
☐ EDIT—Alters specific data fields in a database.
☐ INDEX—creates an index file.
☐ INSERT—inserts data into a file.
☐ JOIN—creates a new file from two other files.
☐ LIST—lists the records in a file.
☐ LOCATE—finds a record that fits a condition.
☐ REPORT—formats and displays a report of data.
☐ SORT—sorts the records in a file on one data field.
☐ USE—specifies the database file to be used.

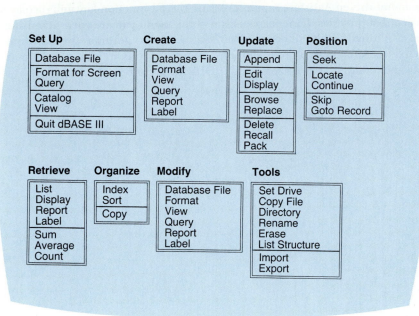

Set Up
Database File
Format for Screen Query
Catalog View
Quit dBASE III

Create
Database File Format View Query Report Label

Update
Append Edit Display
Browse Replace
Delete Recall Pack

Position
Seek Locate Continue
Skip Goto Record

Retrieve
List Display Report Label
Sum Average Count

Organize
Index Sort
Copy

Modify
Database File Format View Query Report Label

Tools
Set Drive Copy File Directory Rename Erase List Structure
Import Export

Figure A4–3 An overview of the menus of dBASE III Plus Assistant. Notice that each main menu option generates a pull-down menu of additional options.

Figure A4–4 An explanation of the menu and screen layout of the dBASE III Plus Assistant. This screen shows the pull-down menus of the RETRIEVE option.

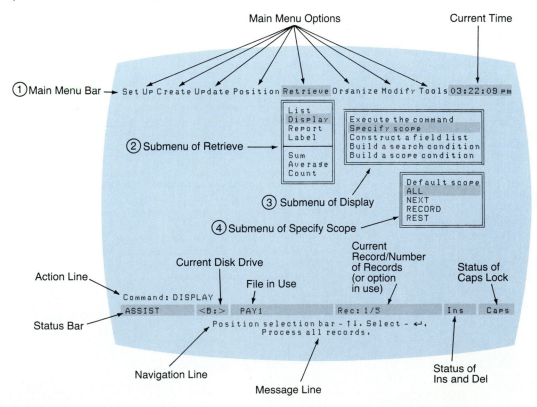

the menu-driven Assistant mode, pressing the F1 function key will display a screen that provides a brief explanation of the menu you are currently using. You can usually make selections from this screen to get more explanations, or help screens about other operations. Figure A4–5 is an example of a main help menu and a help screen for the DISPLAY command.

Figure A4–5 Examples of help screens. The first screen is the main help menu. The second screen explains the DISPLAY option and gives its command format.

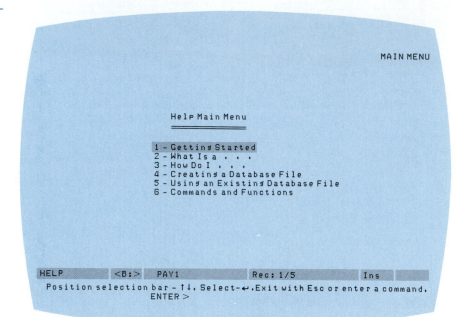

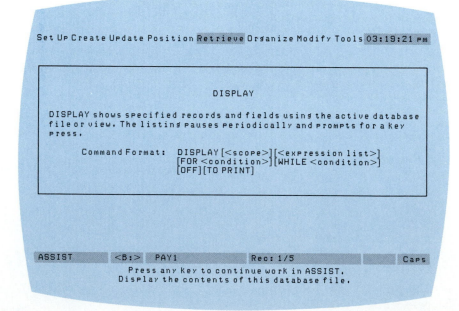

HANDS–ON EXERCISE A4–1

Getting Started

Load the dBASE III Plus program into your microcomputer as described earlier in the "Getting Started" part of this section. The main Assistant display should appear. Refer back to Figure A4–4 while you examine the Assistant display. Use the cursor control keys to move the highlighted rectangle to each option on the main menu bar. Notice the pull-down menus that appear. Press the F1 HELP key after you select each main menu option. A help screen explaining each option should appear. Press any key to get back to the main Assistant display. Press the ESCAPE key to get to the dot prompt mode, and the F1 key to get a main help menu. Select explanations from one of the options in this menu. Return to the dot prompt by pressing the ESCAPE key, and then to the main Assistant display by pressing the F2 key.

CREATING A DATABASE

The first thing you do when using dBASE III Plus or any database management program is to **create** the files you want in your database. What this means is that you are going to specify the characteristics of the **fields** that make up each **record** in a particular **file.** This procedure is also called *defining* the file or database. It is also known as creating the *data dictionary,* since you are defining the characteristics and structure of the records and files in your database, which is the function of a data dictionary.

Before we create a file, we'd better have a pretty good idea of the *design* or *structure* of the records in that file. Let's agree that we want our database to include a **payroll file** for the employees of our company. This payroll file will contain the records of our employees (i.e., information about each employee that might be needed to properly pay them). For demonstration purposes, let's limit each record to six fields as follows:

1. Employee name (NAME), 15 character positions.
2. Social security number (SSNO), 9 character positions.
3. Gender (GENDER), 1 character position.
4. Department (DEPT), 14 character positions.
5. Hourly rate of pay (RATE), 5 numeric positions, 2 decimal places.
6. Number of hours worked (HOURS), 4 numeric positions, 1 decimal place.

Figure A4–6 illustrates the menu choices and entries you make in creating the record format for a simple payroll file. Let's take a look at what happens when you create a file.

Figure A4–6 Creating the payroll file. In the first screen, we use the CREATE option to create a file named PAY1. In the second screen, we specify the characteristics of the fields that will be contained in each record in this file.

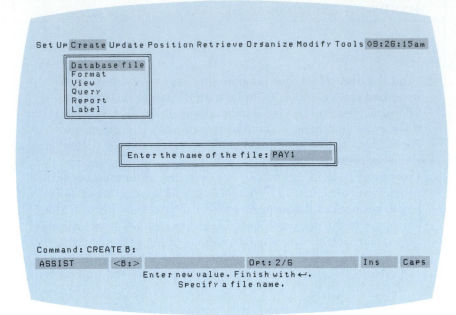

☐ First you select the CREATE option by using the cursor control key. Then select the DATABASE FILE option from the pull-down menu by pressing the ENTER key. Then select the B: drive from a small pull-down menu that appears by using the cursor control keys and the ENTER key. This will store any files you create on the file disk in drive B.

□ Then enter the name of the file you want to create in the highlighted rectangle as shown in Figure A4–6. Let's call our file PAY1.

□ A *field-definition* screen then appears. You must now specify the structure of each record as shown by the second screen of Figure A4–6. This involves specifying the name, type, width, and decimal places of each of the fields that make up the records that will be stored in this file. As we said previously, we are limiting each record in our payroll file to six fields. We give each of these fields a name and indicate whether they consist of CHARACTER data or NUMERIC data. Also specified is the maximum number of characters each field might contain and the number of decimal places needed for our numeric data fields. Note: a decimal point takes up one character position in a numeric field.

□ Each time you key in information specifying a field, you press the ENTER key. The program responds with a field number for the next field and a flashing cursor.

□ After you finish specifying all six fields, the prompt will ask for the specification for a seventh field. At this point, press the ENTER key twice to end the file creation process.

□ The file structure you have created is then saved on your file disk. The program immediately asks if you want to enter data into the file. You respond with a Y if you want to begin the data entry process.

HANDS–ON EXERCISE A4–2

Creating a Database

Create the PAY1 file in your database, using the CREATE option. Specify the structure of the records in the file by specifying the name, type, width, and decimal places for each of the six fields in a payroll record as shown in Figure A4–6. This includes employee name, social security number, gender, department, hourly rate of pay, and number of hours worked.

Once you have created a file, your next step is to **enter data** into that file. Let's assume you answered with a Y to the prompt that asked if you wanted to enter data into the file.

□ A data entry screen appears (see Figure A4–7) and you can begin to type in data. The file name and the record number of the first record to be entered is in the status bar at the bottom of the screen. The name of each field in that record is also displayed. So is a highlighted area that indicates the minimum length established for each field.

ENTERING DATA INTO A DATABASE

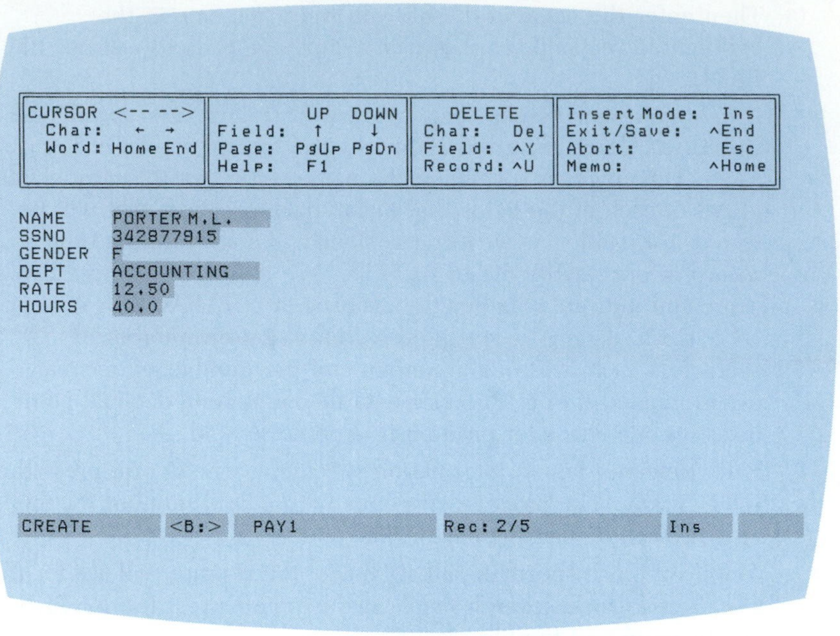

Figure A4-7 Entering an employee's data record into the payroll file using a data entry screen.

```
CURSOR  <-- -->              UP  DOWN  ||  DELETE       ||  Insert Mode:  Ins
  Char:   ←   →    Field:    ↑    ↓   ||  Char:   Del  ||  Exit/Save:  ^End
  Word: Home End   Page:  PgUp PgDn   ||  Field:   ^Y  ||  Abort:       Esc
                   Help:    F1        ||  Record:  ^U  ||  Memo:      ^Home


NAME     PORTER M.L.
SSNO     342877915
GENDER   F
DEPT     ACCOUNTING
RATE     12.50
HOURS    40.0




CREATE          <B:>    PAY1               Rec: 2/5              Ins
```

☐ You can then begin to type data into the highlighted area for each field of the record. Figure A4–7 shows what the data entry screen looks like while you are entering data for an employee into the fields of a record in the payroll file.

☐ When a field is filled or when you press the ENTER key, the cursor jumps down to the next field. When the last field of the first record is completed, it is stored on your file disk. Then the field definition screen for the next record is automatically displayed.

☐ When you have completed adding records to this file, press the ENTER key when the cursor is at the beginning of the first field of the next record. You will then leave the data entry mode and once again be presented with the main Assistant display.

HANDS–ON EXERCISE A4–3

Entering Data into a Database

Enter data into the fields of several employee records in the PAY1 payroll file. Use the same data as shown in Figure A4–1. When you are finished, press the ENTER key instead of filling the fields of another record.

Adding Data to a Database

You may frequently wish to add more data records to a previously created file. However, whenever you want to work on an established file for any

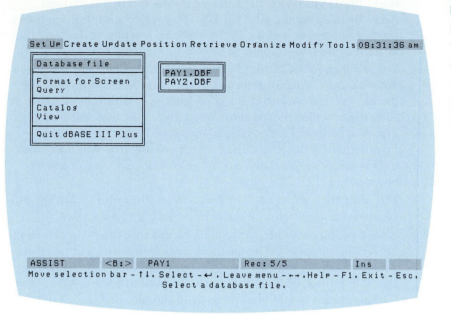

Figure A4–8 Figure A4–8 Opening and adding records to a file. The first screen shows the use of the Set Up option to open a previously created file (PAY1). The second screen shows how you would use the Update and Append options to begin the process of adding additional employee data records to the PAY1 file.

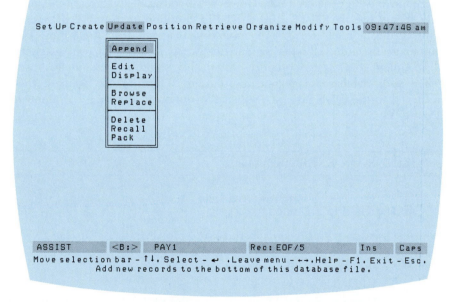

purpose, you must first ask the program to transfer it from your magnetic disk into main memory. This makes it an *active* file, and its name will be displayed in the status bar at the bottom of the main Assistant display. You should do this as follows:

☐ First you should select the SET UP option from the main Assistant display. As the first screen in Figure A4–8 shows, you must then select the DATABASE FILE file option in the first pull-down menu by pressing the ENTER key. Then select the B: drive from another submenu, and the PAY1 file from a listing of database files in another pull-down menu as shown in Figure A4–8.

☐ You are then asked if this file is indexed. If you indicate that it is not with an N, you are returned to the main Assistant menu, and the file you have selected is loaded from your disk into memory. If you answer with a Y, you must select the index that will be used from a submenu of index names, by pressing the ENTER key. Pressing either the left or right cursor control keys will then cause the file and its related indexes to be loaded from your disk into memory.

☐ You must then select the APPEND option from the UPDATE pull-down menu as shown in the second screen of Figure A4–8.

☐ A field-definition screen of the next record that can be added to the file will be displayed. This includes field names and widths in the same format as it did when you first entered records into the file after using the CREATE option. (Refer back to Figure A4–7). You can then begin to add more records to the file, just as you did then.

Leaving the Database Management Program

You can now use a variety of menu options to manipulate the data you have stored in the PAY1 payroll file. However, if you want to stop at this point, you should use the QUIT dBASE III PLUS option in the SET UP menu. This should be done every time you end your use of dBASE III Plus. This automatically closes all open file and stores any changes on your magnetic disk. Unless your files are properly closed, they could be accidentally erased when your database management program is terminated. You are then returned to the DOS prompt. Notice this option in the SET UP menu in Figure A4–8.

HANDS–ON EXERCISE A4–4

Adding Data to a Database

☐ Add several records to the PAY1 file. First open the file with the SET UP DATABASE FILE option. Then add a record to the file with the APPEND option of the UPDATE menu.

☐ Now use the QUIT option from the SET UP menu to exit from the program. At the DOS prompt, reload the dBASE III Plus program as previously outlined in the "Getting Started" part of this section.

Database management programs such as dBASE III Plus allow **full-screen editing** of the data you enter into a file. Errors can be corrected during and after data entry in a variety of ways. During data entry, errors can be corrected by backspacing and writing over them. You can also use the cursor control keys to move the cursor around to make corrections until the last field is completed and the record is stored. Other keys you can use are shown in special boxes in the display screens of the data entry, edit, and other screens. Refer back to Figure A4–7.

If you wish to correct or revise previously entered records, you can use the EDIT or BROWSE options in the UPDATE menu of the main Assistant display. Using the EDIT option allows you to edit a single record. It causes a data entry screen of the last record that had been accessed (called the current record) to be displayed. This includes the name and contents of each data field. The cursor control keys can then be used to move the cursor around and make changes. The PAGE UP and PAGE DOWN keys can be used to select other records for editing.

The BROWSE option allows you to display and edit a screenful of records from a file. See Figure A4–9. BROWSE displays up to 17 records and as many fields as will fit on the screen. Thus the display screen is a *window* that you can scroll across the file stored in memory. You should use cursor control keys and other keys (shown in boxes at the top of the BROWSE screen) to scroll through the database. You should then move the cursor on the screen so you can edit any field of any record in the file. Pressing the CONTROL and END keys saves any changes made using the EDIT or BROWSE options and returns you to the main menu.

EDITING AND
CORRECTING
ERRORS

HANDS–ON EXERCISE A4–5

Editing a Database

Edit several records in the PAY1 file. Use an EDIT command to make changes to one of the records. Use a BROWSE command to make changes to several records. For example, change the pay rate or hours worked of several employees. Store the changes on your file disk.

Figure A4–9 Using the BROWSE option to edit the payroll file. The first screen shows how the UPDATE and BROWSE options are selected. The second screen displays the field names and contents of the records in the PAY1 file.

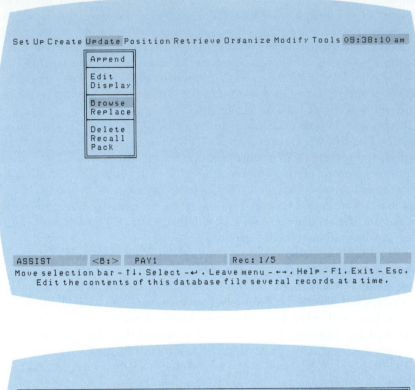

RETRIEVING DATA FROM A DATABASE

You now know how to create, enter, and edit data in a database file. It's time to learn how to **retrieve** data from your database. Database management programs provide several options and commands to assist in the retrieval of data. This allows you to be selective in both the format and contents of data you wish to see displayed or printed. Let's examine two fundamental retrieval options: DISPLAY and LIST.

Figure A4–10 Using the DISPLAY option to display all of the records in a file. The first screen shows how the appropriate RETRIEVE options are selected from pull-down menus. The second screen displays all the records in the file.

```
Set Up Create Update Position Retrieve Organize Modify Tools 09:12:04 am

                    List
                    Display      Execute the command
                    Report       Specify scope
                    Label        Construct a field list
                                 Build a search condition
                    Sum          Build a scope condition
                    Average
                    Count
                                          Default scope
                                          ALL
                                          NEXT
                                          RECORD
                                          REST




Command: DISPLAY
ASSIST        <B:>   PAY1              Rec: 1/5
                  Position selection bar - ↑↓. Select - ↵.
                         Process all records.
```

```
Set Up Create Update Position Retrieve Organize Modify Tools 09:16:18 am




Record #  NAME          SSNO       GENDER  DEPT          RATE  HOURS
       1  ALVAREZ J.S.  632403718  F       PRODUCTION   14.00   44.0
       2  PORTER M.L.   342877915  F       ACCOUNTING   12.50   40.0
       3  OBRIEN J.A.   576434572  M       INFO SYSTEMS 12.50   45.5
       4  KLUGMAN K.L.  435182906  M       FINANCE      12.00   35.0
       5  WILSON J.H.   644809371  M       MARKETING    10.00   40.0




ASSIST        <B:>   PAY1              Rec: 1/5
              Press any key to continue work in ASSIST.
```

Figure A4–10 shows how you can use the DISPLAY option in the RE-
TRIEVE pull-down menu to display all of the records in a file. Notice that
you select the SPECIFIED SCOPE and ALL options from two submenus.
You can then select the EXECUTE COMMAND option in the first submenu and a listing of all the records in the file is displayed as shown by the
second screen in Figure A4–10.

Displaying Records

The DISPLAY ALL option will show you only one screenful of records from a file at a time. Pressing any key displays the next group of records in the file. But what if you want to display only selected fields or selected records from a file? You can do so by variations of the DISPLAY option. If you execute the DISPLAY option without any modifications, it will display only the current record. This is called the DEFAULT scope. Or you could use the RECORD option in the SPECIFIED SCOPE submenu to display a record by specifying its record number.

Figure A4–11 shows how you can use the DISPLAY option to display specified fields from selected records in a file. Here are the steps involved:

☐ First, specify the scope as ALL. Then construct a field list by selecting fields from a submenu that displays the fields in your records. In this case, we selected the name, department, and hours fields.

☐ Then select the BUILD A SEARCH CONDITION option and select fields from a FIELDS submenu that specifies the characteristics of the records you wish to be displayed. In this case, we wish to display the records of employees who earn $12.50 per hour and who worked 40 or more hours. Notice from Figure A4–11 that you can combine such search conditions with either an AND or OR relationship.

The second screen of Figure A4–11 shows the resulting display of information about two employees. Also notice the form of the DISPLAY command that appears on the command line of the first screen in Figure A4–11. This is the command you could enter in the dot prompt mode to perform the same display operations as were accomplished using the menus of the Assistant mode. *Note:* On the IBM Personal Computer and similar computers you can press the SHIFT and PRINT SCREEN keys to print what is on the video screen. For continuous printing, toggle the CONTROL and PRINT SCREEN keys to start and stop printing.

Listing Records

The LIST option is similar to the DISPLAY option, but will display or print all of the data records in a file, unless it is modified so that only records that meet certain criteria are selected. All of the records in the file will be printed or will scroll by the screen. You can stop this scrolling by pressing the CONTROL and S keys together. To list records, just select the LIST option from the RETRIEVE submenu, and continue as you would using the DISPLAY option. However, you will be asked "Direct The Output To The Printer? [Y/N]". If you type Y, the records in the file will be printed on your printer, as well as being displayed on your video screen.

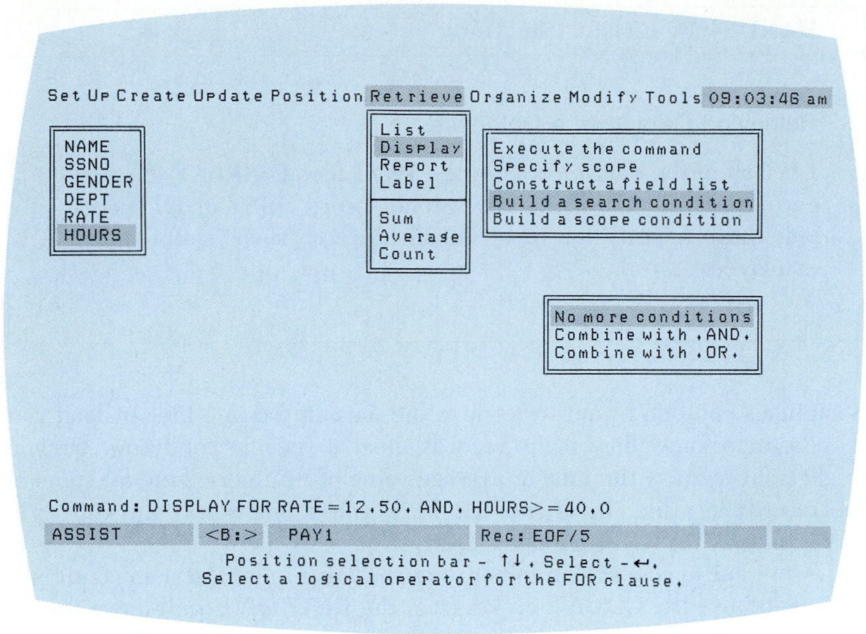

```
Set Up Create Update Position Retrieve Organize Modify Tools 09:03:46 am

  ┌──────────┐          ┌──────────┐  ┌──────────────────────────────┐
  │ NAME     │          │ List     │  │ Execute the command          │
  │ SSNO     │          │ Display  │  │ Specify scope                │
  │ GENDER   │          │ Report   │  │ Construct a field list       │
  │ DEPT     │          │ Label    │  │ Build a search condition     │
  │ RATE     │          │          │  │ Build a scope condition      │
  │ HOURS    │          │ Sum      │  └──────────────────────────────┘
  └──────────┘          │ Average  │
                        │ Count    │
                        └──────────┘
                                         ┌──────────────────────────┐
                                         │ No more conditions       │
                                         │ Combine with .AND.        │
                                         │ Combine with .OR.         │
                                         └──────────────────────────┘



  Command: DISPLAY FOR RATE=12.50 .AND. HOURS>=40.0
  ASSIST        <B:>    PAY1              Rec: EOF/5
                  Position selection bar - ↑↓. Select -↵.
                Select a logical operator for the FOR clause.
```

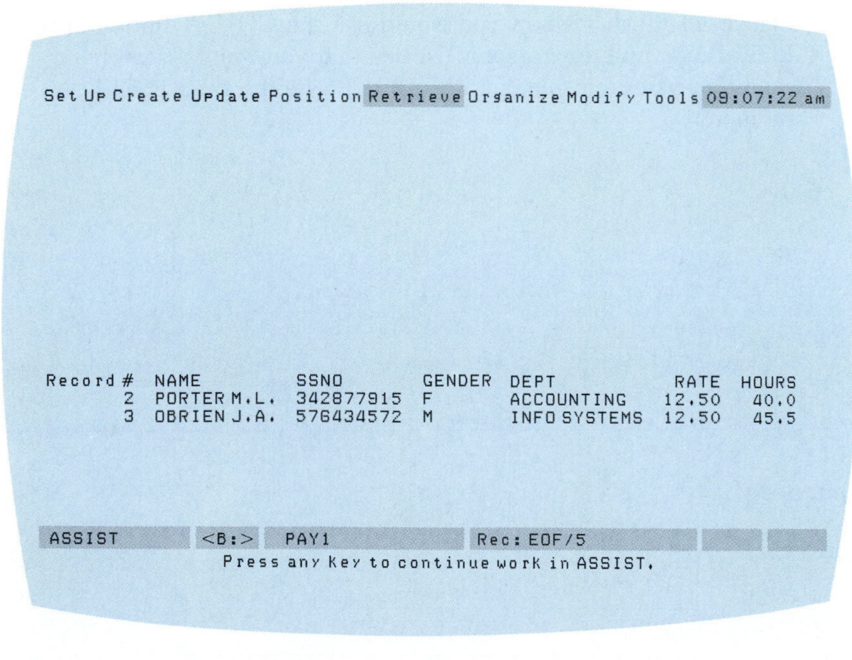

Figure A4–11 Using the DISPLAY option to display specified fields from selected records in a file. The first screen is a composite display that shows how the appropriate RETRIEVE options are selected from pull-down menus. Notice the DISPLAY command that appears above the status bar. The second screen displays the records of two employees who earn $12.50 per hour and who worked 40 or more hours.

```
Set Up Create Update Position Retrieve Organize Modify Tools 09:07:22 am











  Record #  NAME         SSNO         GENDER  DEPT          RATE   HOURS
        2   PORTER M.L.  342877915    F       ACCOUNTING    12.50   40.0
        3   OBRIEN J.A.  576434572    M       INFO SYSTEMS  12.50   45.5






  ASSIST        <B:>    PAY1              Rec: EOF/5
                Press any key to continue work in ASSIST.
```

HANDS–ON EXERCISE A4–6

Retrieving Data from a Database

LIST all of the data records in the PAY1 file. DISPLAY the current record. DISPLAY the second record. LIST or DISPLAY only those records that meet specific criteria, such as all female employees.

Retrieving Other Information

Sometimes you don't want to retrieve the data stored in a file. Instead you may want to know how many records meet a specific condition. Or you might want to know the total or average value of a numeric field for some of the records in a file. In dBASE III Plus, you would select the COUNT, SUM, and AVERAGE options.

If you want to *count* the number of records that meet a certain condition, you should use the COUNT option from the RETRIEVE pull-down menu. For example, you may want to count the employees who worked over 40 hours.

☐ Figure A4–12 shows how you would use the COUNT option in the RETRIEVE pull-down menu. Notice that you build a search condition based on selecting the HOURS field from a FIELD submenu.

Figure A4–12 Using the COUNT option. This screen shows the use of the COUNT option in the RETRIEVE pull-down menu to count the number of employees who worked more than 40 hours. The SUM and AVERAGE options can be used in a similar way.

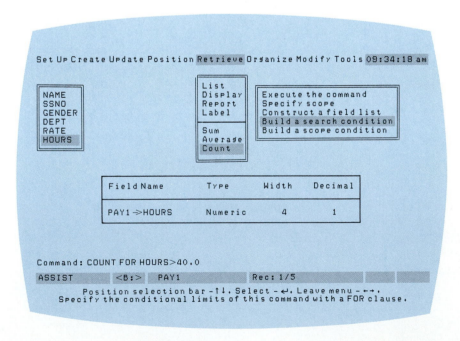

☐ You must then select the *greater than* condition from a CONDI-
TIONS submenu that appears and enter 40.0 in response to an
"Enter a Numeric Value:" prompt.

☐ You then select a NO MORE CONDITIONS option in another
submenu, and the EXECUTE THE COMMAND option from the
first submenu. The number of records that meet the conditions
specified (in this case two records) is then displayed.

☐ If you want the *total value* of a certain field for records that meet a
specified condition, then you should use the SUM option from the
RETRIEVE pull-down menu in a similar fashion.

☐ If you want the *average value* of a certain field for all or some of
the records in a file, then you should use the AVERAGE option
from the RETRIEVE pull-down menu just as we used the COUNT
option.

HANDS–ON EXERCISE A4–7

Retrieving Information about Your Records

Count the number of employees earning $12.50 per hour and
total the amount of hours they have worked. Use the COUNT
and SUM options. Then find out the average hourly rate of all
employees using the AVERAGE option.

CHANGING THE DATABASE

After you have used your database for a while, you may decide that some
changes are needed. Changing a database usually has one of the following
four dimensions:

☐ Changing the *order* of records in a file and deleting unwanted
records.

☐ Changing the *data* in specific fields for selected records in a file.

☐ Generating *new files* that are variations of the files already in the
database and deleting unwanted files.

☐ Changing the *structure* (characteristics of specified fields) of the
records in a file.

Sorting Data

One way that you might want to change your database is to *sort* the records
in a file into a different order, or to create an *index* for a file that is organized
differently than the file itself. Figure A4–13 shows you how this is done.
Suppose you wish to sort the records in the PAY1 file into social security
number order.

☐ First you would select the SORT option from the ORGANIZED
pull-down menu. Then you would select the social security number
field from a field submenu as shown in the first screen of Figure

Figure A4-13 Sorting the PAY1 file. The first screen shows how the SORT option is selected from the ORGANIZE menu. The social security number field (SSNO) is then selected as the sorting key. The second screen shows how a new file is created (PAY2) that will contain the employee data records sorted into social security number order.

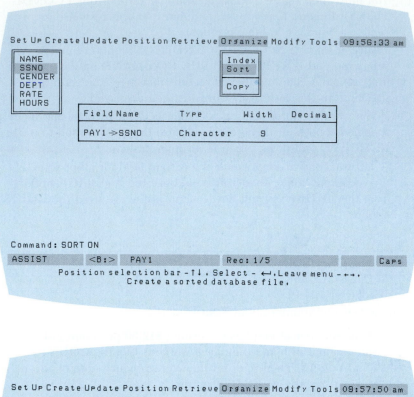

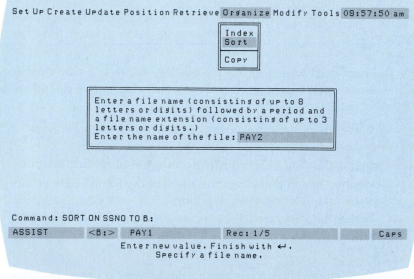

A4-13. (Leave this menu by pressing a right or left cursor control key.)

☐ Then select the B: drive and enter a file name for the new file that will be created to contain the employee data records sorted into social security number order. See the second screen of Figure A4-13.

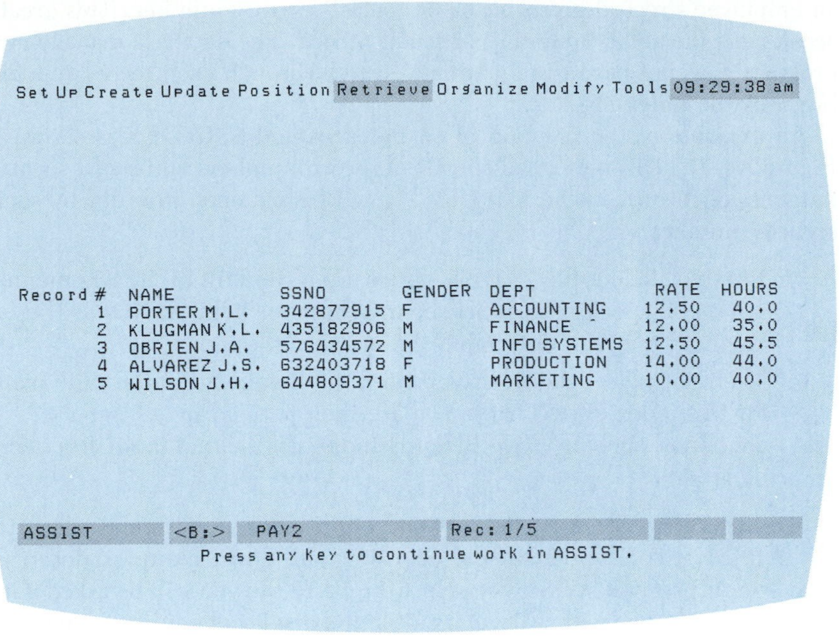

Figure A4–14 A listing of the
PAY2 file. Notice that it is sorted
into social security number
order.

```
Set Up Create Update Position Retrieve Organize Modify Tools 09:29:38 am




Record #   NAME           SSNO        GENDER  DEPT          RATE   HOURS
       1   PORTER M.L.    342877915   F       ACCOUNTING    12.50   40.0
       2   KLUGMAN K.L.   435182906   M       FINANCE       12.00   35.0
       3   OBRIEN J.A.    576434572   M       INFO SYSTEMS  12.50   45.5
       4   ALVAREZ J.S.   632403718   F       PRODUCTION    14.00   44.0
       5   WILSON J.H.    644809371   M       MARKETING     10.00   40.0




ASSIST         <B:>    PAY2                Rec: 1/5
              Press any key to continue work in ASSIST.
```

☐ Then you could use the LIST option of the RETRIEVE pull-down
menu to display the records in the new PAY2 file. Figure A4–14
shows that we have succeeded in sorting them into social security
number order.

HANDS–ON EXERCISE A4–8

Sorting a File

Sort the PAY1 file into numerical order, using employee social
security numbers. Use the SORT option in the ORGANIZE
menu to create a PAY2 file sorted into social security number
order. Use the LIST option of the RETRIEVE menu to display
this file's contents.

Sorting a file can be a slow and involved process if a lot of data has to be
sorted using several sorting keys. Also, the sorting process creates a new file
of the same information sorted in a different order. This takes up more disk
storage space. An alternative is to create an **index** to a file. This index is
organized in the order that you wish to access the data in the file. An index is
a special file that contains a listing of record numbers and related field
values. It is sorted in ascending order according to key fields you specify.
For example, an index could consist of record numbers and social security
numbers taken from a payroll file. This index could be used to quickly find

Using an Index

an employee's record given his or her social security number. This greatly accelerates the ability to find a particular record. The database management program does not have to sequentially search through each record in a file, but uses the index instead.

An example of the creation of an index named SSINDEX is shown in Figure A4–15. This index will consist of record numbers and social security numbers of records in the PAY1 file. It will be arranged in order by social security number.

☐ First you select the INDEX option from the ORGANIZED menu. Then you specify the social security number field (SSNO) as the key field that will determine the order of the index.

☐ Then you select the B: drive from a submenu and enter a file name for this index (SSINDEX). You are then notified by a brief comment, such as "Five Records Indexed," that an index has been created.

If you want to check on the creation of an index, you should select the DATABASE FILE option in the SET UP pull-down menu as described earlier in this section. When you select the PAY1 file you will be asked if it is indexed. Answering with a Y will result in the display of a submenu with the name of any indexes (such as SSINDEX) that have been created for that file. You can then select a specific index for use with the PAY1 file. For instance, suppose you select SSINDEX. Using the LIST or DISPLAY options in the RETRIEVE pull-down menu will display the PAY1 file as if it were organized into social security number order.

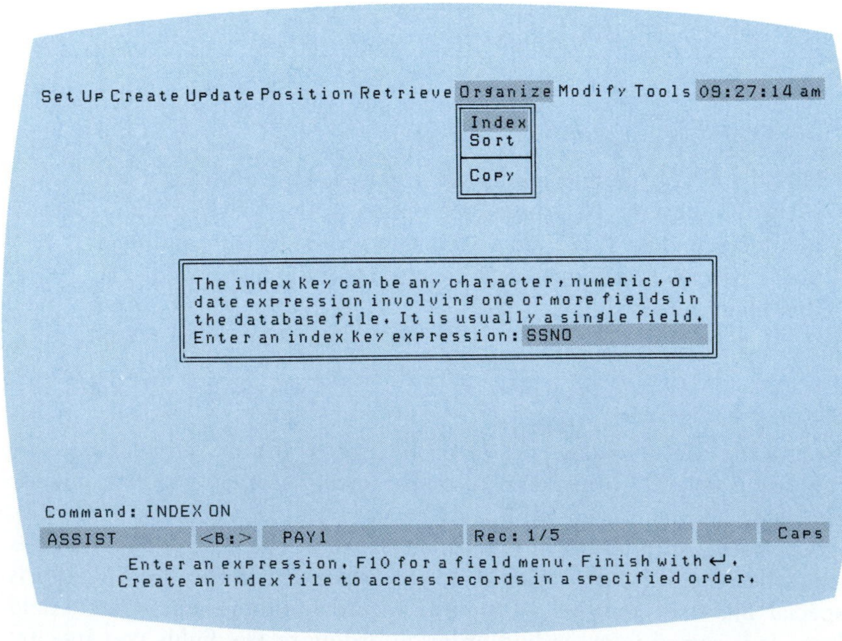

Figure A4–15 Creating an index for the PAY1 file. This screen shows how you select the INDEX option from the ORGANIZE menu. Then you specify the social security number field (SSNO) as the key field which will determine the order of the index. An index is created after you specify a file name for it (SSINDEX) in a subsequent screen.

HANDS–ON EXERCISE A4–9

Creating and Using an Index

Use the INDEX option of the ORGANIZE menu to create an index of employee social security numbers and employee record numbers for the PAY1 file. Then use the SET UP DATABASE FILE options and the LIST option to display the records in the PAY1 file in social security number order.

Most database management programs allow you to change the data in your files. If you want to change the contents of one or more fields in many records at one time, you should use a REPLACE command. For example, suppose you wanted to give all employees in the accounting department a 10 percent hourly rate increase.

Changing Data

☐ Figure A4–16 shows how you would select the REPLACE option from the UPDATE pull-down menu and then select the RATE field from a FIELDS submenu.

☐ You would then enter the expression RATE*1.1 when prompted to enter a number or numeric expression. This means that you want to increase the rate of selected records by 10 percent.

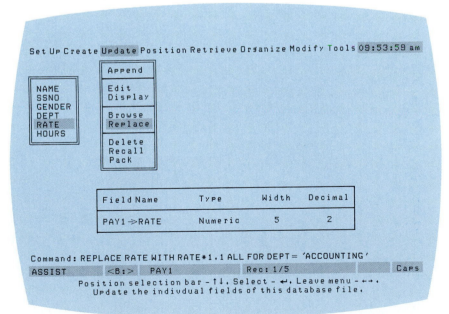

Figure A4–16 Replacing the contents of records in a file. This screen shows how you could automatically change the contents of data fields in selected records. In this example, the entire REPLACE command is shown on the command line. This emphasizes how you would select options from several submenus to give all accounting department employees a 10 percent increase in their hourly rate.

□ Then use the right or left cursor control key to specify that you do not want to change any other field. You should also select a scope of ALL from the submenu that appears on your screen.

□ Then select BUILD A SEARCH CONDITION, the DEPT field, and the EQUAL TO options from various pop-up submenus.

□ You should enter the term ACCOUNTING when you are prompted to "Enter a character string."

□ Finally, select NO MORE CONDITIONS from a submenu, and EXECUTE THE COMMAND from the REPLACE pull-down menu.

A message such as "1 record replaced" will then appear to indicate that the one accounting employee in the PAY1 file (M.L. Porter) has been given a 10 percent increase in her hourly rate. You can now use the LIST or DISPLAY options in the RETRIEVE menu to see for yourself that this has occurred.

Deleting Records

Most database management packages allow you to delete records from your database. This is accomplished by the use of the DELETE option. Figure A4–17 shows how the DELETE option of the UPDATE menu can be used to delete records by specifying a record number. In this example, here's how the fourth record in the file is deleted:

□ The SPECIFY SCOPE and RECORD options are selected from two submenus and the number 4 is entered as a numeric value.

Figure A4–17 Deleting records from a file. This screen shows the use of the DELETE option in the UPDATE menu and options in other submenus to delete record number 4 from the PAY1 file.

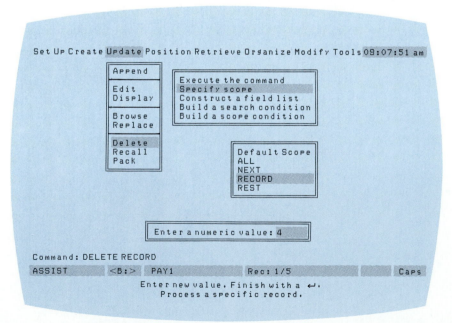

☐ When you select EXECUTE THE COMMAND, a message is displayed that tells you "1 Record Deleted."

☐ Notice by using the LIST option from the RETRIEVE menu that the DELETE command does not immediately remove records physically from a file. Instead, it marks them with an asterisk. These records will be ignored and not used in processing.

☐ If you change your mind and wish to activate a deleted record, you can do so with the RECALL option in the UPDATE menu. The process you use is similar to the DELETE option.

☐ If you wish to physically erase deleted records from a file, you can do so with the PACK option in the UPDATE menu. Choosing that option executes it immediately and provides a message indicating that such records have been removed.

Performing File Operations

You can perform a variety of operations on files by using the options in the TOOLS pull-down menu in the Assistant display. Figure A4–18 shows that this menu allows you to copy, rename, and erase files, and perform other file operations. For example, if you select the COPY file option, you can copy the contents of the PAY1 file into another newly created file. You must specify the disk drive and filename of the file you want copied and the name of the new file that will be created. When the copying is complete a message is displayed specifying the number of bytes that have been copied into the new file. *Note:* Before you can copy a file, it must be closed. You can do this by selecting another file, or by using a CLOSE DATABASES command in the dot prompt mode.

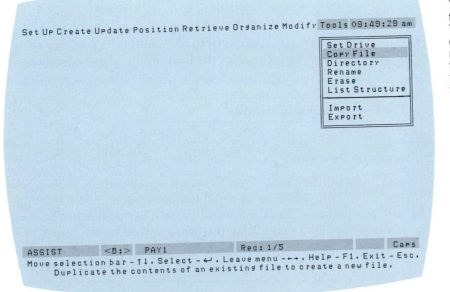

Figure A4–18 Copying a file. This screen shows the use of the COPY file option from the TOOLS menu. This copies the contents of a file into another newly created file. Also notice the RENAME, ERASE, and other file options you can select from the TOOLS menu.

HANDS–ON EXERCISE A4–10

Deleting Records and Files

Copy the PAY1 file to a temporary file called TEMP.DBF.
Delete two records from that file. List the file. Then recall one of
the records you marked for deletion and physically remove the
other record from the file with the PACK command. List the file
again to check on the results of these actions. Finally, delete the
TEMP file from the disk.

Changing the Structure of Records

Another important way that you may wish to change your database is to
change the *structure* of the records in a file. For example, you may wish to
add or delete a field, or change the width of a field in your records. Figure
A4–19 is an example of how this is done. Let's add a seventh PAY field to the
structure of each record in the PAY1 file.

- ☐ You begin the process by selecting the DATABASE FILE option
  from the MODIFY pull-down menu. This brings up a screen that
  displays the specifications of each field in the file.
- ☐ You then modify the structure of the PAY1 file by entering the
  specifications of a seventh data field. PAY is a numeric field that
  will show an employee's weekly earnings. Pressing the CONTROL-
  END keys then copies all data from the original file to the modified
  file and saves it on your disk.
- ☐ Use the LIST option from the RETRIEVE menu. Notice that the
  new PAY field in every employee record shows a zero value. You
  have to use the REPLACE option from the UPDATE menu to
  automatically insert the product of mutiplying the hours worked
  times the hourly rate (RATE*HOURS) into the PAY field of each
  record. Figure A4–20 displays the final results of this operation.

HANDS–ON EXERCISE A4–11

Adding a Data Field

Add a seventh data field (PAY) to the employee records in the
PAY1 file. This should be an eight-position numeric data field
with two positions after the decimal point. Then automatically
insert the result of multiplying the hours worked by the hourly
rate into the PAY field of each record.

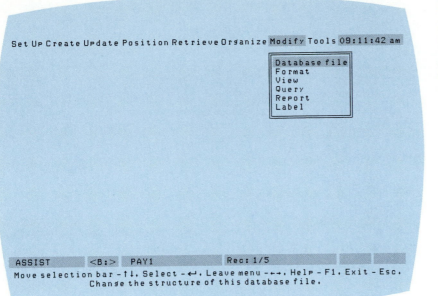

Set Up Create Update Position Retrieve Organize Modify Tools 09:11:42 am

```
                                        ┌─────────────────┐
                                        │ Database file   │
                                        │ Format          │
                                        │ View            │
                                        │ Query           │
                                        │ Report          │
                                        │ Label           │
                                        └─────────────────┘
```

ASSIST   <B:>   PAY1   Rec: 1/5
Move selection bar – ↑↓. Select – ↵. Leave menu – ←→. Help – F1. Exit – Esc.
            Change the structure of this database file.

Bytes remaining: 3952

```
┌──────────────────┬──────────────────┬──────────────────┬──────────────────────┐
│ CURSOR  <---->   │    INSERT        │   DELETE         │ Up a field:      ↑   │
│ Char:    ← →     │ Char:    Ins     │ Char:    Del     │ Down a field:    ↓   │
│ Word: Home End   │ Field:   ^N      │ Word:    ^Y      │ Exit/Save:    ^End   │
│ Pan:    ^← ^→    │ Help:    F1      │ Field:   ^U      │ Abort:        Esc    │
└──────────────────┴──────────────────┴──────────────────┴──────────────────────┘
```

	Field Name	Type	Width	Dec		Field Name	Type	Width	Dec
1	NAME	Character	15						
2	SSNO	Character	9						
3	GENDER	Character	1						
4	DEPT	Character	14						
5	RATE	Numeric	5	2					
6	HOURS	Numeric	4	1					
7	PAY	Numeric	8	2					

MODIFY STRUCTURE <B:> PAY1   Field: 1/7
                    Enter the field name.
Field names begin with a letter and may contain letters, digits, and
                        underscores.

Figure A4-19 Changing the structure of the PAY1 file. The first screen shows how you select the DATABASE FILE option from the MODIFY menu. The second screen shows how the PAY field is added to the structure of the records in the file.

Figure A4–20 Displaying the revised PAY1 file. Notice how using the MODIFY option has added a PAY field to each record. Also notice how using the REPLACE option has calculated the amounts earned by each employee.

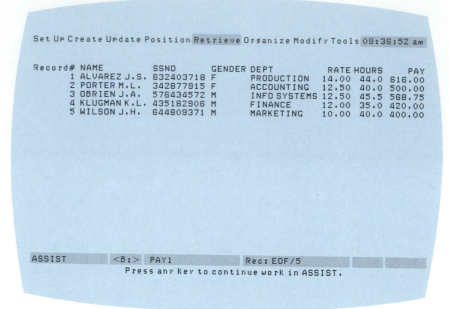

```
Set Up Create Update Position Retrieve Organize Modify Tools 09:36:52 am


Record# NAME          SSNO      GENDER DEPT          RATE HOURS     PAY
      1 ALVAREZ J.S. 632403718 F      PRODUCTION   14.00  44.0  616.00
      2 PORTER M.L.  342877915 F      ACCOUNTING   12.50  40.0  500.00
      3 OBRIEN J.A.  576434572 M      INFO SYSTEMS 12.50  45.5  568.75
      4 KLUGMAN K.L. 435182906 M      FINANCE      12.00  35.0  420.00
      5 WILSON J.H.  644809371 M      MARKETING    10.00  40.0  400.00










ASSIST           <B:>   PAY1                    Rec: EOF/5
            Press any key to continue work in ASSIST.
```

GENERATING REPORTS

Most database management packages have commands like DISPLAY and LIST for quick database inquiries. Responses can be quickly displayed on the video screen of your computer or printed on your system printer. However, what if you want output printed in a report format that you can use repeatedly, with features such as titles, columns, headings, and totals? Then you should use the **report generation** capabilities provided by the report generator module that is part of most database management packages.

Creating a Report Form

The first thing you must do is create a **report form.** This report form should specify the title and column headings of the report. It should specify what data fields from your database will be included, and whether subtotals and totals are required. Once this report form is created, it can be stored on your magnetic disk for use whenever you wish this particular report to be printed.

For example, suppose you wanted to produce a payroll report that gives information on employees organized into male and female categories. This report would use data from the PAY1 file such as employee name, gender, department, and hours worked. You could ask for subtotals of hours worked by male and female employees as well as total hours worked by all employees. Here's how you could produce this report:

☐ First, you should select the REPORT option from the CREATE pull-down menu. Then select the B: drive and enter a name for your report file, such as PAYREP1. See the first screen in Figure A4–21.

☐ An OPTIONS report format screen will then be displayed. See the second screen in Figure A4–21. This screen allows you to specify various report format options. First let's enter a report title. Press

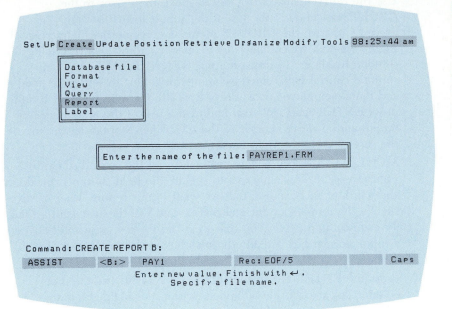

Figure A4–21 Creating a report format. The first screen shows how you select the REPORT option from the CREATE menu and specify a file name (PAYREP1.FRM) for the report form. The second screen show you the OPTIONS menu that allows you to enter a report title (PAYROLL HOURS REPORT) and specify various options.

ENTER to display a highlighted box. We could enter up to four lines of titles. Type in **PAYROLL HOURS REPORT** and press CONTROL–END. We can ignore the rest of the options and accept the *default specifications* shown for such options as page width, margins, lines per page, and so on.

☐ Use the right cursor control key to move the cursor to the GROUPS selection at the top of the report format screen. This presents us with the GROUPS menu screen (see the first screen of Figure A4–22), which allows us to specify subtotal control fields and subtotal headings. In this example, GENDER will be our only subtotal control field, since we want this report to segregate male and female employee data. Press ENTER. Type in GENDER and press ENTER again. We can ignore the rest of the options in this screen and move the cursor to the COLUMNS option at the top of the screen using the right cursor control key.

☐ A COLUMNS screen is now displayed (see the second screen of Figure A4–22). This allows us to specify the field contents, heading, and width of each column that we want in our report. We can also specify the number of decimal places, and whether we want a total for each column. *Note:* You can press the F1 key to switch between a report format box and an edit keys box in the lower part of your screen.

☐ Press the ENTER key to specify the CONTENTS of the first column. An arrowhead will appear within the highlighted area, followed by a cursor. You can now type in the name of a data field. Since we want employees' names to be listed in the first column of this report, type the word NAME and press ENTER. Notice that the field width specification immediately changes to 15, and a row of 15 Xs appears in the bottom box. (Don't forget that you can press the F10 key to bring up a field menu from which you can select choices instead of typing in a field name.)

☐ Next press the down cursor control key to highlight the HEADING entry in the top box. Press ENTER and type in the heading you want for this first column. For example, you can type in the heading NAME into the highlighted box that has appeared. Then press CONTROL–END and the heading of NAME appears in the report format box below.

☐ Since the first field is a character field, you do not have to specify the decimal places and total for this column. Therefore, press the PgDn key and begin specifying the next report column. Now we can specify the GENDER field for the second column and the DEPARTMENT field for the third column, just as we did for the NAME field in the first column.

☐ Now you should specify the HOURS field for the contents of the fourth column. Notice that the width, decimal places, and total entries in the top box are automatically entered. Also notice that pound or number sign (#) characters separated by a decimal are automatically entered into the report format box at the bottom of the screen. Now highlight HEADING in the top box, press ENTER, type in HOURS in the box that appears, and press CONTROL–END. Notice that the HOURS heading appears in the report format box below.

☐ After all columns are specified, you can move the cursor to the EXIT option on the menu line at the top of the screen. Then select

```
Options        Groups        Columns       Locate      Exit       09:45:12 am
          ┌──────────────────────────────────────────────────┐
          │ Group on expression        ▶ GENDER              │
          │ Group heading                                    │
          │ Summary report only          No                  │
          │ Page eject after group                           │
          │ Sub-group on expression                          │
          │ Sub-group heading                                │
          └──────────────────────────────────────────────────┘



┌────────────────┬──────────────────────┬──────────────────────┬───────────────────┐
│CURSOR <-- -->  │Delete char:      Del │Insert column:     ^N │Insert:       Ins  │
│Char:    ←   →  │Delete word:       ^T │Report format:     F1 │Zoom in:    ^PgDn  │
│Word: Home End  │Delete column:     ^U │Abandon:          Esc │Zoom out:   ^PgUp  │
└────────────────┴──────────────────────┴──────────────────────┴───────────────────┘

CREATE REPORT <B:>   PAYREP1.FRM      Opt: 1/3                          Caps
        Enter an expression. F10 for a field menu. Finish with ↵.
    Enter a field or expression on which to break for the first level of
                               subtotals.
```

Figure A4–22 Creating a report format (continued). The first screen shows the GROUPS menu that allows you to specify subtotal control fields. In this case we will subtotal on the GENDER field to group male and female employee data. The second screen shows the COLUMNS menu that allows you to specify the contents, headings, and width of each column in the EMPLOYEE HOURS REPORT.

```
Options        Groups        Columns       Locate      Exit       09:46:30 am
┌────────┐  ┌──────────────────────────────────────────────────┐
│NAME    │  │ Contents            ▶ HOURS                      │
│SSNO    │  │ Heading               HOURS                      │
│GENDER  │  │ Width                 5                           │
│DEPT    │  │ Decimal places        1                          │
│RATE    │  │ Total this column     Yes                        │
│HOURS   │  └──────────────────────────────────────────────────┘
└────────┘
            ┌────────────────────────────────────────────────────┐
            │ Field Name        Type         Width     Decimal    │
            │                                                     │
            │ BATCH->REF        Character     30                  │
  ┌─Report Format─────────────────────────────────────────────────
  │>>>>>>>>NAME            GEN DEPARTMENT         HOURS
  │
  │
  │
  │
  │      XXXXXXXXXXXXXXX X    XXXXXXXXXXXXX      ##.#
  └───────────────────────────────────────────────────────────────

CREATE REPORT <B:>   PAYREP1.FRM      Column 4                          Caps
        Position selection bar -↑↓. Select - ↵. Leave menu - ←→.
   Enter a field or expression to display in the indicated report column.
```

a SAVE option from this menu and press the ENTER key. The PAYREP1 report form is then stored on your magnetic disk.

Note: If subtotals are used, the records in the file that provides data for the report (the PAY1 file) must have been sorted or indexed according to the subtotal control field (GENDER in this example).

Printing a Report

To print a report on your printer, you should select the REPORT option in the RETRIEVE pull-down menu. This option allows you to use a previously created report form repeatedly for full or partial reports. Here's what you can do:

☐ First select the REPORT option from the RETRIEVE pull-down menu, specify the B: drive, and select the name of a report form such as PAYREP1 from a submenu of report form files that appears.

☐ Since we want this first report to include all records in the file, we can now select the EXECUTE THE COMMAND option from the submenu. Then display the report on your video monitor and print it on your printer by answering with a Y to the question "Direct the Output to the Printer?"

You can use the PAYREP1 report form to print variations of the PAYROLL HOURS REPORT. You can specify that only selected records from the database file should be used to print the report. For example, you could print a report only for employees that worked more than 40 hours. Just select the report options as you did previously. However, select BUILD A SEARCH CONDITION from the report submenu. Then you can select the HOURS field from a FIELDS submenu and the GREATER THAN OR EQUAL TO option in the SEARCH CONDITION submenu. Finally, enter the numeric value 40.0 into a box that appears, select NO MORE CONDITIONS from another submenu, and then select EXECUTE THE COMMAND.

Figure A4–23 shows the complete payroll report produced by the database management report generator from the employee payroll file. It also shows a variation of the full payroll report that reports the hours worked only by employees who worked overtime.

HANDS–ON EXERCISE A4–12

Printing a Report

Design and print a report that provides information from the PAY1 file, using the CREATE REPORT and RETRIEVE REPORT options. For example, produce a report on the pay rate of employees by male and female categories. Then use RETRIEVE REPORT options to print a report showing similar information for female employees only.

```
Page No.        1
01/01/89

                        PAYROLL HOURS REPORT

    NAME                GEN         DEPARTMENT          HOURS


    **F
    ALVAREZ J.S.        F           PRODUCTION           44.0
    PORTER M.L.         F           ACCOUNTING           40.0
    **Subtotal**
                                                         84.0

    **M
    KLUGMAN K.L.        M           FINANCE              35.0
    OBRIEN J.A.         M           INFO SYSTEMS         45.5
    WILSON J.H.         M           MARKETING            40.0
    **Subtotal**
                                                        120.5

    ***Total***
                                                        204.5
```

Figure A4–23 Reports produced from the PAY1 file. The first version of the PAYROLL HOURS REPORT shows selected data for all employees grouped into female and male categories. The second report shows this information only for employees who worked more than 40 hours.

```
Page No.        1
01/01/89

                        PAYROLL HOURS REPORT

    NAME                GEN         DEPARTMENT          HOURS


    **F
    ALVAREZ J.S.        F           PRODUCTION           44.0
    **Subtotal**
                                                         44.0

    **M
    OBRIEN J.A.         M           INFO SYSTEMS         45.5
    **Subtotal**
                                                         45.5
    ***Total***
                                                         89.5
```

SUMMARY

We have now accomplished the creation, editing, and entry of data into a simple database file, as well as the retrieval and reporting of information from that file. We have also modified the file by sorting, copying, and indexing operations, along with the deletion of records and the changing of the file structure. This should have given you a good introductory understanding of the capabilities and use of database management packages for microcomputers. For additional information, consult books or user's manuals for the dBASE III Plus database management program or similar packages.

KEY TERMS AND CONCEPTS

These are the key terms and concepts of this chapter. The page number of their first explanation is in parentheses.

1. Changing a database (*A–89*)
2. Character (*A–71*)
3. Command-driven (*A–73*)
4. Creating a database (*A–77*)
5. Database (*A–71*)
6. Database management system (*A–71*)
7. Editing a database (*A–83*)
8. Entering data into a database (*A–79*)
9. Field (*A–71*)
10. File (*A–71*)
11. Generating reports (*A–98*)
12. Menu-driven (*A–74*)
13. Record (*A–71*)
14. Report form (*A–98*)
15. Retrieving data from a database (*A–84*)

REVIEW AND APPLICATION QUIZ

Match one of the **key terms and concepts** listed above with one of the brief examples or definitions listed below. Try to find the "best fit" for answers that seem to fit more than one term or concept. Defend your choices.

_____ 1. A single alphabetic, numeric, or other symbol.

_____ 2. You name is an example.

_____ 3. Your name, address, department, and salary.

_____ 4. A collection of employee payroll records.

_____ 5. A collection of interrelated files or records.

_____ 6. A software package that controls the creation, use, and maintenance of a database.

_____ 7. Entering a series of commands to get things done.

_____ 8. Selecting from a series of menus to get things done.

_____ 9. Specifying the characteristics of the fields in the records of a database.

_____ 10. Adding data to a database you have created.

_____ 11. Correcting errors in database entries.

_____ 12. Listing or displaying selected records from a database.

_____ 13. Presenting data organized by columns, headings, and totals.

_____ 14. A predesigned report format is available for repeated use.

_____ 15. Sorting, deleting, and modifying a database.

Now it's time for you to create and manipulate some database files of your own and generate some simple reports. Good luck!

A4.1   If you have not already done so, create, interrogate, manipulate, and generate reports using a simple employee payroll file, as explained in the twelve HANDS–ON EXERCISES of this section.

A4.2   Create a Student Exam Scores file, consisting of student records containing student names, social security numbers, gender, and grades on three different exams. Enter data into this file for five students. Store and print this file.

A4.3   Edit the Student Exam Scores file by changing a student's exam score. Add and delete records to this file. Store, display, and print this revised file.

A4.4   Retrieve selected data from the Student Exam Scores file by using LIST, DISPLAY, and COUNT options. For example, find and count the records of all female students whose scores on the first exam were greater than 85.

A4.5   Sort the records in your Student Exam Scores file by student names. Also create an index consisting of social security numbers and student record numbers. Use this index and the LIST option to display the records in student record number order.

A4.6   Change the structure of the records in your Student Exam Scores file by adding a new field that totals the three exam scores. Hint: Use a MODIFY option to add the new field to the structure of all records. Then use a REPLACE option to automatically insert the sum of all the exams into each student's total point field. List and print both the new file structure and the newly revised file itself.

A4.7   Design and print several reports that provide information from your Student Exam Scores file. For example, produce a report showing the exam scores and total points earned by students segregated into male and female categories. Then use this same report form to print a report showing this type of information only for male students whose total scores exceed 240 points.

A P P E N D I X

B

DEVELOPING SIMPLE PROGRAMS IN BASIC

Appendix Outline

Learning Objectives

The purpose of this appendix is to introduce you to the essentials of software development using the BASIC programming language. Reading this appendix and completing its assignments should allow you to achieve the following results:

1. *Appreciation* of the process of software development using a high-level programming language such as BASIC.
2. *Knowledge* of how to develop simple programs in the BASIC language.
3. *Experience* with developing and executing a few simple programs in BASIC on a computer system.

After you attain these objectives, you will still need further knowledge and experience in order to be more than a beginning programmer. You can gain this knowledge and experience by taking courses or reading textbooks and practicing programming assignments in BASIC or in any other popular programming language.

Section I: Beginning BASIC

BASIC (Beginner's All-Purpose Symbolic Instruction Code) is the most popular programming language for microcomputer systems used by small businesses and for personal computing. It is also widely used for time-sharing applications and interactive programming in mainframe environments. The specifications for the most essential and widely used parts of BASIC are standardized in a version called Standard Minimal BASIC. Versions with more advanced features (frequently called Extended BASIC) are more likely to contain differences in specifications and usage.

This section provides introductory instruction in BASIC programming using Microsoft BASIC, as provided with the IBM Personal Computer and similar microcomputers. However, with minor modifications, the instructions provided here can be used to develop simple programs with most of the BASIC interpreters and compilers used on popular microcomputer systems or on terminals connected to mainframe computers.

SOFTWARE DEVELOPMENT WITH BASIC

The Software Development Process

In Chapter 11, we saw that software development requires the activities of *program analysis* and *program design* before *program coding* can begin. A newly written program must then be *verified*, *documented*, and *maintained*. Therefore, if you want to write a BASIC program, you need to do the following:

1. Analyze your information processing problem. Look especially at the output that you want to produce, and the input data available.
2. Design the processing procedures necessary to produce the desired output. A program flowchart or pseudocode of the program should be developed. This will help you organize and document the input/output, logical, and computational steps required to carry out your information processing assignment.
3. Write the BASIC statements of the program. This is where you write the instructions that tell the computer how to do what you want done.
4. Perform the "debugging" activities of checking, testing, and correcting to ensure that your program runs and produces the correct results.

The focus of this section is on helping you learn how to develop simple programs in BASIC. Therefore, we will show you how to write the BASIC statements for several example programs. Also, a brief description of the programming problem, and a program flowchart or pseudocode of the solution will be provided for each example presented here.

Entering Your Program

Programming in BASIC is usually accomplished using a computer terminal or personal computer. If you are using a terminal of a large computer system you will have to go through a logging on procedure that will ask for your account number and password. If you are using a personal computer you will have to do the following:

1. Load the operating system into the memory of the machine.
2. Request the use of the BASIC compiler or interpreter with an operating system command such as BASIC.
3. If you want to run a previously written program you will then use the LOAD command to bring a copy of the program into memory.
4. When you receive the READY or OK prompt you can begin to key in each statement of your BASIC program. Each line of a program is entered into the computer system via the keyboard of the computer or terminal. (Most systems require that a RETURN or ENTER key be depressed after each entry.)

BASIC is a "friendly" language that is comparatively easy to learn. Writing statements for data input is easy because input is mostly "free form," that is, no rigid input format is necessary. Output formats can be easily provided if desired. Most BASIC compilers are really interactive interpreters that translate each BASIC statement immediately after it is keyed in and provide helpful diagnostics immediately if an error is sensed in a statement. Correcting an erroneous BASIC statement is also easy. Here's what you do:

Correcting Errors

☐ If you have not yet pressed the RETURN key, you can usually press a DELETE or ← key, which moves the cursor on the video screen back to the point on the statement where you noticed an incorrect character or word. You can then key in the required correction.

☐ If you have already pressed the RETURN key, you should key in the line number and a corrected version of the erroneous statement. Refer to the BASIC manual of your computer system for other error correction methods.

When a complete BASIC program has been coded, users may request a corrected listing of the program by using the system command LIST. This results in a complete listing of the program as it exists in the primary memory of the computer. Statements that have been replaced do not appear and the program is listed in line number order. The program is now ready for execution.

Executing the Program

In most systems, the system command RUN is keyed in to signal the computer to execute the program. The computer will then print or display the output of the program. A copy of the program can be saved and stored on secondary storage devices for later use with the system command SAVE.

In Chapter 11, we stressed the importance of a structured, modular approach to programming. It is not possible to illustrate all aspects of structured programming in this brief introduction to BASIC. However, we will illustrate three of the most important elements of structured program-

STRUCTURED BASIC PROGRAMMING

ming in this appendix: (1) the use of a limited set of control structures, (2) modularization of programs, and (3) extensive program documentation.

Structured programming requires that programs use only three basic control structures: *sequence, selection,* and *repetition.* In general, statements in BASIC are executed in sequence, the first statement of a program followed by the second and so on, unless a control statement is encountered. Control statements are used to modify the order in which the statements of a program are executed, and may be used to create either a selection or a repetition structure.

As programs increase in length and complexity, they become increasingly difficult to code and debug unless the programming task is subdivided into modules. These modules are sections of code that are distinct and easily identified. They are designed to accomplish a specific component of the overall programming task. In Microsoft BASIC, modular structure is implemented through the use of a special pair of control statements, the GOSUB and RETURN statements.

Program documentation is also a crucial element of structured programming. Programs should contain statements describing what job each section (module) of the program is designed to do. They should also describe each variable used in the program and how it is used. Remark (REM) statements are used in BASIC to provide this documentation.

BASIC COMMANDS AND STATEMENTS

BASIC System Commands

Writing and using a BASIC program requires the use of BASIC system commands. These are not BASIC program statements but are "commands" to the operating system of the computer. They control the use of the BASIC compiler and the processing of a BASIC program. Figure B1-1 presents system commands used by Microsoft BASIC. Different BASIC compilers

Figure B1-1 Examples of BASIC system commands.

Command	Description
FILES	Lists the names of all saved files.
DELETE x-y	Deletes program lines x through y.
KILL filename	Erases the diskette file with the indicated name.
LIST x-y	A listing of the statements in the program starting with line number x and ending with line number y. If the line numbers are omitted, it will list your entire program.
LLIST x-y	Will list program lines x-y on a printer.
LOAD filename	Will bring the specified program file from disk into memory.
NEW	Indicates that the user wants to write a new program. This command clears memory and in some versions will prompt the user for the name of a program file.
RUN	Tells the computer to execute the program that is currently in memory or, if followed by a file specification, it executes the named file.
SAVE filename	Stores a copy of the specified program as a program file on a secondary storage device.
SYSTEM	Terminates use of the BASIC compiler.

may require different versions of such commands. Note: BASIC system commands are *not* preceded by a line number.

Instructions in a BASIC program are called **statements.** There are four major types of statements in even simple BASIC programs:

1. **Input/Output** statements such as READ, DATA, INPUT, and PRINT.
2. **Control** statements such as GO TO, IF . . . THEN, FOR . . . NEXT, WHILE . . . WEND, GOSUB . . . RETURN, and END.
3. **Assignment** (or arithmetic) statements such as LET.
4. **Documentation** statements such as REM.

Figure B1–2 presents a useful summary of these statements, all of which will be explained in this section of Appendix B.

Before you can write even simple BASIC programs, you must learn a few important features of BASIC statements. If you don't, your programs will contain *syntax* and *logic* errors, and they won't work! So let's take a look at these fundamental concepts.

FEATURES OF BASIC STATEMENTS

Many versions of BASIC, including Microsoft BASIC, require that each BASIC statement have a unique **line number,** which may have from one to five digits. The computer executes the statements in the order specified by the line numbers. Statements are usually not numbered consecutively but are numbered in increasing order in increments of 5 or 10, for example, 10, 20, 30, 40, and so on. This facilitates inserting new statements in a program without having to renumber the statements that follow them. Thus a statement that must be added to a program can be entered at the end of the program as long as its line number correctly indicates its position in the order of execution. Note, however, that some newer versions of BASIC do not have line numbers. In these versions statements are executed in the order that they appear in the program.

If two or more statements have the same line number, only the last one in the program will be compiled and executed. Thus one can correct or replace a statement in a program by writing a new statement with the same line number later in the program. If a statement is too long to fit on one line, it can be continued on another line; however a continuation character must be used. Check your BASIC manual for the proper continuation character.

At least one blank space should be left between a line number and the beginning of a statement. However, spaces in BASIC statements are utilized to improve readability and are ignored by the compiler, unless they are part of a **literal** and are enclosed in quotation marks.

BASIC statements can include the use of **constants.** Constants are known quantities written in numeric or alphanumeric form. Numeric constants can be written as integers or as real numbers in decimal or exponent form. Many

Figure B1-2 A summary of beginning BASIC statements.

Statement	Purpose	Example
Input/Output Statements		
READ	Reads input data provided by the DATA statements of the program.	10 READ A, B, C
DATA	Provides input data to be read by the READ statements.	20 DATA 75, 42, 81.5
INPUT	Accepts input data directly from the keyboard of the terminal or computer. May include a prompt in quotes to be output on the screen.	30 INPUT "ENTER VALUE FOR A, B"; A, B
PRINT	Causes the video display of output. Also allows arithmetic operations to be performed and printed.	40 PRINT "SUM = ";S
LPRINT	Identical to the PRINT statement except that it is printed in hardcopy form.	50 LPRINT "SUM = ";S
Assignment Statement		
LET	Assigns values to variables and specified arithmetic operations to be performed.	140 LET X = Y + Z
Documentation Statement		
REM	Remarks and comments of the programmer that help identify and document the program.	10 REM PAYROLL PROGRAM
Control Statements		
GO TO	Causes a program to jump or branch unconditionally to another statement in the program.	50 GO TO 120
IF . . . THEN {. . . ELSE}	Causes the statement after the word THEN to be executed when the condition following IF is true. The ELSE portion of the statement is optional. If the ELSE clause is specified, the statement following ELSE will be executed when the specified condition is false.	80 IF A>40 THEN B = 25 ELSE B = 10
FOR	Commands the computer to repeatedly execute a series of statements (a program loop) a specified number of times.	125 FOR A = 1 to 100
NEXT	The last statement of program loops formed by FOR statements.	185 NEXT A
WHILE	The beginning statement of a loop formed by a WHILE and a WEND. The statements between the WHILE and the WEND will be executed repeatedly until the condition after the WHILE is no longer true. Then control of the program is transferred to the statement after the WEND statement.	100 WHILE A<999
WEND	The last statement of a loop formed by a WHILE Statement. It returns the program to the WHILE statement to check the condition.	200 WEND
GOSUB	Transfers control of the program to a specified line number. Statements are executed sequentially beginning with the specified number until a RETURN statement is encountered. Then control is transferred to the statement after the GOSUB statement.	300 GOSUB 500
RETURN	Returns the program to the statement following the GOSUB to which it applies.	550 RETURN
END	Terminates program execution.	200 END

BASIC compilers automatically convert numeric constants to the exponent form if they exceed six or seven digits. Some examples are:

Integer constant   463
Real constant:
   Decimal form   463. or 463.0
   Exponent form   4.63E2
In a statement   20 LET X = 463

Alphanumeric constants (also called *literals* or *string constants*) consist of a string of characters (including blanks) enclosed in quotation marks. For example:

```
40 PRINT ''BASIC IS EASY!!!''
50 DATA ''JAMES JONES'', ''MARY McNIGHT''
```

A **variable** is used to represent a symbolic name given to a memory location. The contents of the location are known as the *value* of the variable.

Variables in BASIC

A comparison: You are given assignments by a professor at your college. The assignments are to be placed in a box, with the professor's name on it, at the office of the college. The box is like the memory location. The professor's name is the symbolic *variable name* used to identify the box. Your assignments are the *value* or the contents of the box.

The length of the name of a variable depends on the version of BASIC you are using, so check with your instructor for the specifications of your computer system. In most versions a valid **variable name** must begin with a letter. You should choose a combination of characters that is as descriptive as possible of the memory location and its contents. However, you must be sure that you do not use a variable name that is identical to a BASIC language reserved word. LET, END, or PRINT, for example, could not be used as variable names.

It is recommended that you provide a "variable dictionary" for your program. The variable dictionary is placed in the program with remarks (REM) statements and is a listing of each variable and a complete description of the variable. Variable names also must inform the computer of the type of data that is to be stored in the memory locations. This is done with a type declaration character that must be the rightmost character of the variable name. The following declaration characters are those used in Microsoft BASIC.

Data Type	Declaration Character	Example
String (Alphanumeric)	$	N$
Numeric		
Integer	%	N%
Real		
Single Precision	!	N!
Double Precision	#	N#

Most computer systems will assume that a numeric variable without a declaration character is of single precision.

THE REM, LET, PRINT, AND END STATEMENTS

We are now ready to briefly review four BASIC statements that we can use to write our first simple BASIC program. These include the documentation statement REM, the assignment statement LET, the output statement PRINT, and the control statement END.

REM Statements

REM statements are not translated by the compiler or executed by the computer. They are merely remarks and comments of the programmer that help document the purpose of the program and only appear in the program listing. The general form of the REM statement is:

Form:

line number REM any comment or set of characters

Example:

```
100 REM PAYROLL PROGRAM
110 REM PROGRAMMED BY JILL GRAY *****
```

LET Statements

LET statements assign values to variables and specify arithmetic operations to be performed. The general form of the LET statement is:

Form:

line number LET variable = expression

Most BASIC compilers allow the word LET to be omitted. As it is used here the equal sign is not a symbol of mathematical equality but means that the *variable* is *assigned* the *value* of the *expression*. Only a single variable name may be on the left of the equal sign, while the right-hand side must be an expression that consists of one or more constants, variables, and appropriate symbols.

Example:

```
10 LET X = Y + Z
```

Explanation:

The current value of X is replaced by the result adding Y and Z.

Example:

```
20 LET SCORE = 82
```

Explanation:

Assigns the value 82 to the variable SCORE.

Example:

```
30 LET COUNT = COUNT + 1
```

Explanation:

Increases the current value of COUNT by one.

Example:

```
40 LET STUDENTNAME$ = ''MARY''
```

Explanation:

Assigns the alphanumeric constant MARY to the alphanumeric variable STUDENTNAME$.

In order to write correct LET statements and other statements involving computations, you must learn how arithmetic operations are accomplished in BASIC. You must know the symbols used, and how to tell the computer *exactly* how you want calculations carried out. If you don't, some very strange and *incorrect* answers will result! So let's take a look at what you should do.

Arithmetic Operations in BASIC

Priority of Arithmetic Operations

Arithmetic operations in a statement are executed from left to right according to the following order of priority (hierarchy):

First priority—exponentiation
Second priority—multiplication and division
Third priority—addition and subtraction

Parentheses must be used in pairs and will overrule the normal order of computation. Thus operations in parentheses are performed first. When a statement contains parentheses inside another set of parentheses, the operations in the innermost parentheses are executed first.

Mathematical Symbols

The mathematical symbols used in arithmetic operations are shown below.

Symbols	Operations
∧ or **	Exponentiation
*	Multiplication
/	Division
+	Addition
−	Subtraction

Let's look at an example of how BASIC determines the order in which computation is performed.

Example 1. The BASIC arithmetic statement:

$$\text{LET X} = \text{Y} + \text{Z} * \text{A/B} \wedge 2 - \text{C}$$

is executed like the mathematical equation:

$$X = Y + \frac{ZA}{B^2} - C$$

If we examine this BASIC statement, we first notice that there are no parentheses, so computation occurs according to the priorities stated above. The first operation to be carried out is exponentiation. B will be raised to the second power. The second priority is multiplication and division. Since operations are executed in order from left to right, multiplication precedes division in this example. Z is multiplied by A and the result is divided by the result of B squared. The two remaining operations are addition and subtraction. They have the same priority. Proceeding from left to right, Y is added to the results above and finally C is subtracted from that result. A summary follows (the numbers underneath indicate the order of operations).

$$\text{LET X} = \text{Y} + \text{Z} * \text{A} / \text{B} \wedge 2 - \text{C}$$
$$\qquad\qquad (4)\ \ (2)\ \ (3)\ \ (1)\ \ (5)$$

Example 2. The BASIC arithmetic statement:

$$\text{LET X} = (\text{Y} + \text{Z}) * (\text{A/B}) \wedge 2 - \text{C}$$

is executed like the mathematical equation:

$$X = (Y + Z)\ (A/B)^2 - C$$

Since there are two sets of parentheses in this LET statement, we proceed from left to right. The value of Y is added to the value of Z. Next the value of A is divided by the value of B. Notice that the execution of both of these operations precedes exponentiation because of the parentheses. The order of the remaining operations is determined by priority order. Exponentiation occurs next—the value of A divided by B is raised to the second power. This result is multiplied by the result of Y + Z. Finally C is subtracted from that result. A summary follows:

$$\text{LET X} = (\text{Y} + \text{Z}) * (\text{A} / \text{B}) \wedge 2 - \text{C}$$
$$\qquad\qquad (1)\qquad (4)\ \ (2)\ \ (3)\ \ (5)$$

PRINT Statements

PRINT statements cause output to be printed on the video display of the computer. They allow arithmetic operations to be performed and the results displayed.

Form:

The PRINT statement can include a *list* of variable names,

constants, arithmetic expressions, or alphanumeric literals. The general form of the PRINT statement is:

line number PRINT list

Examples and Explanations:

The list of a PRINT statement may be:

☐ A list of numeric or alphanumeric variables. This will cause the printing of the current values of the variables. For example:

```
10 PRINT A; B; C
20 PRINT CUSTOMERNAME$, ADDRESS$, BALANCE,
   PAYMENT
```

☐ A list of numeric constants. This will cause the printing of one or more constants. For example:

```
20 PRINT 5; 10; 15
```

☐ Alphanumeric constants or literals. These provide headings, labels, and messages for output and must be enclosed in quotation marks. For example:

```
40 PRINT ''PAYROLL REPORT''
50 PRINT ''THE ANSWER IS''; ANSWER
60 PRINT ''PLEASE ENTER YOUR DATA''
```

☐ One or more mathematical expressions. This will cause the printing of the results of the expressions. For example:

```
30 PRINT Y + Z, B + C
```

☐ Left blank. This results in the skipping of a line (the printing of a blank line). For example:

```
70 PRINT
```

Semicolons or commas can be used to separate the items in the list of PRINT statements. Semicolons will cause output values to be printed close together. Typically, commas cause output values to be printed in *print zones* or columns of 10 to 16 positions each. The print line can typically have up to five print zones for a total of 70 to 80 print positions. If a PRINT statement ends with a comma or semicolon, then the next PRINT statement that is executed will not print its output at the beginning of the next line, but instead will continue to print on the same line if there is space available.

The LPRINT statement is identical in form to the print statement described above. The LPRINT statement can use all of the forms of lists described for the print statement. The only difference is that the LPRINT statement causes output to be printed in hardcopy (paper) form using a printer. In order to use the LPRINT statement you must ensure that a print device is available for your computer, and is set up appropriately.

LPRINT Statements

END Statements

The END statement terminates the execution of a BASIC program.

The END is the last statement executed by a BASIC program. It can appear only once in a program. The general form of an END statement is:

Form:

line number END

Example:

90 END

A Simple BASIC Program Example

We are now ready to examine a simple program that should help you understand how to write a similar program on your own. It will use the REM, LET, PRINT, and END statements we have just explained.

The output of this program is to be a student's total score from two tests. The input is the student's score on each test, and the required processing is simply to add the two scores to produce the desired total. We will call the test scores TEST1 and TEST2, and the resulting sum, TSCORE. The flowchart and BASIC program that accomplishes this is shown in Figure B1–3. Notice the following:

☐ We first ask for the BASIC compiler.

☐ Statement 10 is a REM statement that identifies the program.

☐ Statement 20 assigns to the variable TEST1 the value of 65.

Figure B1–3 A one-shot program: SUM1.

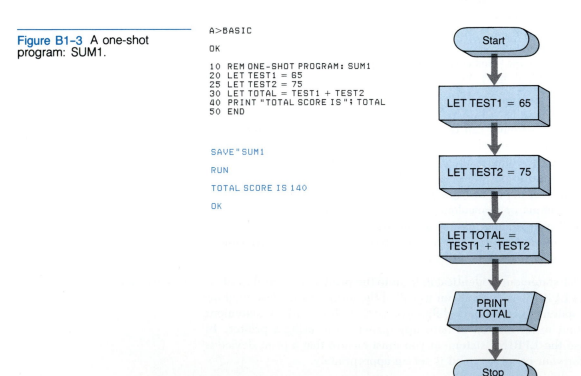

```
A>BASIC

OK

10  REM ONE-SHOT PROGRAM: SUM1
20  LET TEST1 = 65
25  LET TEST2 = 75
30  LET TOTAL = TEST1 + TEST2
40  PRINT "TOTAL SCORE IS "; TOTAL
50  END


SAVE "SUM1

RUN

TOTAL SCORE IS 140

OK
```

☐ Statement 25 assigns to the variable TEST2 the value of 75.

☐ Statement 30 adds TEST1 and TEST2 together to give the result TOTAL.

☐ Statement 40 prints the value of TOTAL as well as a label to identify this answer.

☐ Statement 50 ends the program.

☐ The program is saved on disk using the name SUM1.

☐ The program is executed (RUN).

☐ The output result (TOTAL SCORE IS 140) is printed and the program terminates.

READ, DATA, AND INPUT STATEMENTS

Remember that computer programs typically need to be provided with **data** that they manipulate to produce desired *information output*. We are now ready to describe some BASIC statements (READ . . . DATA and INPUT) that are used to provide input data to a BASIC program.

READ Statements

READ statements read input data provided by the DATA statements of a program.

The READ statement includes a list of variable names separated by commas. The variable names appear on the read statement in the order in which they are to be read. These variable names are assigned (in order) to the next available data values provided by the DATA statements of the program. The general form of the READ statement is:

Form:

line number READ variable, variable, . . .

Examples:

```
10 READ A, B, C
20 READ PRODUCT$, QUANTITY, RETAILPRICE
```

Explanation:

Statement 10 reads the values for the numeric variables A, B, and C from input data provided by the DATA statements of the program. Statement 20 reads the value of the alphanumeric "string" variable PRODUCT$ provided by DATA statements, as well as the values for the numeric variables QUANTITY and RETAILPRICE.

DATA Statements

DATA statements provide input data to be read by READ statements.

The DATA statements include a list of constants separated by commas that are in the order they are to be read. The general form of a DATA statement is:

Form:

line number DATA constant, constant, . . .

Examples:

```
900 DATA 75, 42, 81, 273, 19.50, 968
910 DATA ''Mary H. Brown'', 54191, 100
920 DATA ''John A. Smith'', 63948, 97
```

Explanation:

Provides values for the variables in a READ statement. Note that alphanumeric data is enclosed in quotation marks—some systems require them.

Data values are read in the order of their position in a DATA statement. The first time a READ statement is executed, it reads as many data values from the first DATA statement of a program as it has variable names. The next time the READ statement is executed, it will read the next available data values in the same or subsequent DATA statements. If there are more data entries than are needed by the program's READ statements, the excess values will not be used. If not enough data values are provided in the program DATA statements, the program will terminate with a message such as:

```
OUT OF DATA
```

Since DATA statements are nonexecutable reference statements, they can be placed anywhere in a program, but are usually placed near the end of a program (in front of the END statement) for the convenience of the programmer. This spotlights and documents the data being provided by the program. This also minimizes the renumbering of line numbers if new DATA statements have to be added to a program. Some compilers limit the number of data values that can be provided by a single DATA statement. Therefore, several DATA statements may be necessary for a program that requires a lot of data. Also, many programmers like to have separate DATA statements for each data record that will be processed. Remember that a *data record* consists of several related *data fields*. Thus in our example above, the data records for Mary Brown and John Smith occupy separate DATA statements.

A Revised Program Example

We will now modify our program example to use READ and DATA statements. The flowchart and BASIC program that accomplishes this are shown in Figure B1–4. Notice the following:

☐ Statement 20 will read the values for TEST1 and TEST2 from statement 50.

☐ The variable TEST1 will be assigned the value of 65 and TEST2 will be assigned the value of 75.

INPUT Statements

INPUT statements allow users of a program to provide input data directly from the keyboard of a terminal or computer, instead of through READ and DATA statements. This provides an **interactive** capability since data can be

```
A>BASIC

OK

10  REM ONE-SHOT PROGRAM: SUM2
15  REM WITH READ AND DATA STATEMENTS
20  READ TEST1, TEST2
30  LET TOTAL = TEST1 + TEST2
40  PRINT "TOTAL SCORE IS"; TOTAL
50  DATA 65, 75
60  END


SAVE "SUM2

RUN

TOTAL SCORE IS 140
```

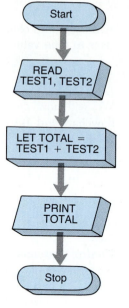

Figure B1-4 A SUM program with READ and DATA statements: SUM2.

entered by users during the execution of the program. The program can then process this data and **prompt** the user for additional data or other responses.

The INPUT statement includes a list of variable names separated by commas that are in the order that input data is to be provided by the program user. The INPUT statement may also include a text prompt to the user describing the information to be supplied. When a prompt is used, it is placed in quotes prior to the first variable name, and is followed by a semicolon. The general form of the INPUT statement is:

Form:

line number INPUT "message"; variable, variable . . .

Example:

30 INPUT ''ENTER 3 NUMBERS''; A, B, C

Explanation:

Writes the message ENTER 3 NUMBERS on the display screen, then accepts as input data values for the variables A, B, and C.

When the INPUT statement is executed, the computer usually types any prompt message supplied, followed by a question mark character (?) on the terminal and waits for the input of data specified in the INPUT statement. The prompt message allows the programmer to indicate the type of data to be input by the user; the prompt should be as descriptive as possible. The user then types in appropriate values (separated by commas) and depresses the RETURN key of the terminal. The computer will then continue with the execution of the program. For example, the statement:

```
30 INPUT ''ENTER 3 NUMBERS''; A, B, C
```

will cause the computer to print the prompt and a ? and then wait for the user to type values for A, B, and C, such as:

```
ENTER 3 NUMBERS? 75, 42, 81
```

Another Revised Program Example

We will now modify our program example to make it interactive. The flowchart and BASIC program that accomplishes this is shown in Figure B1–5. Notice the following:

☐ Statement 20 will cause the printing of the question mark prompt to the CRT for the user.

☐ The user will enter the two numbers separated by a comma and then will press the RETURN or ENTER key.

CONTROL STATEMENTS

Control statements control the order in which a program is executed, perform comparisons and test conditions, change the sequence of a program through a branching process, or stop a program. Important BASIC control statements are IF . . . THEN . . . ELSE, GO TO, WHILE . . . WEND, FOR . . . NEXT, GOSUB . . . RETURN, and END.

IF . . . THEN . . . ELSE Statements

IF . . . THEN . . . ELSE statements are the primary method of implementing the selection control structure in BASIC programming. They cause a statement or set of statements to be executed only if certain conditions are met. They cause a different statement or set of statements to be executed, or cause the next sequential statement to be executed, when the conditions are not met.

The general form of the IF . . . THEN . . . ELSE statement is:

Figure B1–5 A SUM program using the INPUT statement: SUM3.

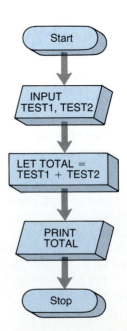

```
A>BASIC

OK

10 REM ONE-SHOT PROGRAM: SUM3
15 REM WITH INPUT STATEMENT
20 INPUT "ENTER TEST SCORES "; TEST1 , TEST2
30 LET TOTAL = TEST1 + TEST2
40 PRINT "TOTAL SCORE IS "; TOTAL
50 END


SAVE"SUM3

RUN

ENTER TEST SCORES? 65 , 75

TOTAL SCORE IS 140

OK
```

Form:

line number IF condition THEN statement {ELSE statement}

where by condition we mean:

expression relation expression

The *expressions* can be numeric or alphanumeric variables and/or constants, or arithmetic formulas, that is, AMT, N$, 100, "THE END", B + 10, and so on. The condition specified consists of a comparison between a variable or expression and another variable, numeric literal, or expression utilizing the "relational comparison operators" outlined below:

=	Equal to
<	Less than
>	Greater than
<>	Not equal to
<=	Less than or equal to
>=	Greater than or equal to

Examples:

```
60 IF CLASS > 2 THEN LET STANDING$ = ''UPPER''
      ELSE LET STANDING$ = ''LOWER''
70 IF G => 80 THEN PRINT N$, G
```

If the variable CLASS has a value greater than 2, then the alphanumeric literal UPPER is placed in the variable STANDING$; if not, the literal LOWER is placed in STANDING$. After executing the statement on either the THEN or the ELSE side, control is transferred to the next sequential statement. In statement 70 the values of the variables N$ and G will be printed only if G has a value greater than or equal to 80. Otherwise control is transferred immediately to the next sequential statement.

Note: IF . . . THEN . . . ELSE statements frequently require more than one physical line on the video screen. However, all of the statement must be associated with the line number that precedes it. This is achieved by using a continuation character at the end of each line of the IF statement. Check with your instructor to determine the continuation character used on your system.

An Interactive Payroll Program

Let's examine a slightly different problem that can serve to illustrate the use of the IF . . . THEN . . . ELSE statement. In this problem we need to calculate the gross pay of a group of employees. An interactive data input mode will be maintained, so that this problem differs from our previous example only in that the input data are hours worked (HRS) and wage rates (WAGE), and the formula used to calculate gross pay (GROSSPAY) differs from that used for total score in the previous examples.

The formula used for gross pay depends on the number of hours worked. If 40 hours per week or less are worked, GROSSPAY is simply WAGE times

HOURS. However, if any overtime hours are worked, an added premium of half the pay rate is paid for those hours beyond 40, so that the formula for GROSSPAY becomes:

$$\text{GROSSPAY} = \text{WAGE} \times \text{HRS} + .5 \times \text{WAGE} \times (\text{HRS} - 40)$$

Thus the appropriate formula for gross pay must be *selected* depending on the number of hours worked. Figure B1-6 shows how this calculation is implemented. Notice the following differences from the previous program.

☐ The variable names have been changed in all statements to reflect the new problem definition.

☐ Statement 30 causes GROSSPAY to be calculated using the formula for overtime if HRS is greater than 40; but GROSSPAY is calculated using just WAGE times HRS if HRS is equal to or less than 40.

☐ Two examples of the execution of the program are presented, one with HRS equal to 40, and one with HRS equal to 48. You can

---

Figure B1-6 An interactive pay program: PAY1.

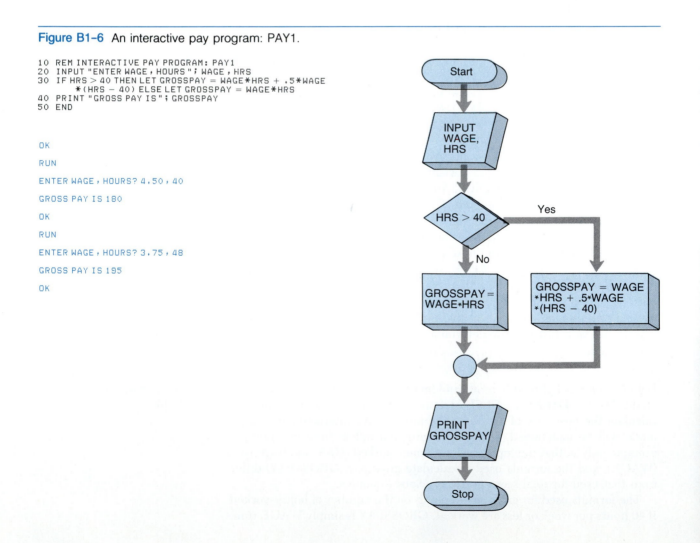

```
10  REM INTERACTIVE PAY PROGRAM: PAY1
20  INPUT "ENTER WAGE, HOURS "; WAGE, HRS
30  IF HRS > 40 THEN LET GROSSPAY = WAGE*HRS + .5*WAGE
        *(HRS - 40) ELSE LET GROSSPAY = WAGE*HRS
40  PRINT "GROSS PAY IS"; GROSSPAY
50  END


OK

RUN

ENTER WAGE, HOURS? 4.50, 40

GROSS PAY IS 180

OK

RUN

ENTER WAGE, HOURS? 3.75, 48

GROSS PAY IS 195

OK
```

verify that the program did use the appropriate formula in each case to compute GROSSPAY.

GO TO Statements

GO TO statements cause a program to *jump* or *branch unconditionally* to another statement in the program that will be executed next.

The general form of the GO TO statement (where n is the statement number of the statement to be executed next) is:

Form:

> line number GO TO n

Example:

> 60 GO TO 45

Explanation:

> Execute statement 45 next.

Note: Great care should be exercised when you use GO TO statements so that you stay within the basic control structures of structured programming. It is possible to write structured code using BASIC and it is also very easy to write extremely poor unstructured code using BASIC. The difference between poor BASIC programming and good structured BASIC programming is not the fault of the language but the programmer. GO TO statements should only be used to help establish needed *selection* or *repetition* control structures. GO TO statements should not be used to jump from one section of code to another in an arbitrary fashion.

We could cause the PAY1 program presented in Figure B1–6 to be executed repeatedly by simply adding the following statement:

> 45 GO TO 20

This would create a loop consisting of the statements 20 through 45. The user would be repeatedly asked to enter hours and pay rate data, and gross pay would be repeatedly calculated and printed. However, the loop created would be an unconditional loop. There is no provision to get out of the loop. The user would be required to press the key combination Ctrl-Alt-Del or turn off the computer to stop execution of the program. An unconditional loop violates the rules of structured programming. All loops created should contain logic within the program causing the loop to be terminated at the appropriate time. Thus our loops will contain selection as well as repetition logic. A loop will be established and a condition will be tested to determine whether we remain within the loop or not.

A Conditional Loop Program

Let's modify the PAY1 program so that it allows the user to calculate the pay for more than one person, and to quit entering data when there are no more pay calculations to be made. There are several ways to do this. Let's use a method that automatically stops execution of a program loop if a specific condition is met. We call that a *conditional loop*. In this method, we use special data values that act as *end-of-data signals* to let the computer know that no more data input values are left. These end-of-data signals are also sometimes referred to as trailer records; a trailer record contains data that is not intended to be processed but is used to tell the computer that there are no more data to be processed.

Let's call the resulting program PAY2. The following flowchart and program are implemented using two INPUT statements. Once we enter the repetition structure we should not jump out of the boundaries of the structure. The boundaries of the structure are the control statements. In this example the control statement that begins the structure is the IF . . . THEN statement. The control statement that ends the structure is the GO TO.

The first INPUT statement is only used to obtain the first record so that the end-of-data condition can be tested prior to entering the loop. The remaining records are entered using the INPUT statement at the bottom of the loop, which allows us to test the end-of-data condition immediately after the data is read. This prevents us from processing the end-of-data record. With this implementation we are able to stay within the control statements of the loop until the condition is no longer valid and we will not process the end-of-data record. Figure B1–7 shows the flowchart, program, and output of program PAY2. Notice the following differences from the previous program:

☐ Statement 30 causes the computer to inspect the input data from statement 20 to see if the first variable (WAGE) is the end-of-data signal (9999). If not, the rest of the statements in the program loop are executed sequentially (there is no ELSE clause on the IF statement) and the program loops back to statement 30 when statement 70 is executed.

☐ When the user has no more pay data to enter, he or she will enter a value of (9999) for WAGE. Statement 25 allows the computer to recognize this (WAGE = 9999) as the end-of-data signal, and it will cause the program to *branch* or *jump* to statement 80, thus terminating the program. This program is an implementation of the repetition structure.

☐ The input statement appears twice, once at statement 20 and again at statement 60. Statement 20 provides an initial value for WAGE so that the IF condition in statement 30 can be tested. After the first pay record has been processed statement 60 allows a new record of pay data to be input before control is transferred back to the IF condition test in statement 30.

The IF . . . THEN . . . ELSE statement has been used in the program PAY2 as a part of a loop or repetition structure. Most popular BASIC compilers in use today also provide alternative sets of statements for looping, the FOR . . . NEXT loop and the WHILE . . . WEND loops, which are felt to provide better structure than the example just presented. In upcoming examples we will examine each of these statements.

Figure B1–7 A conditional loop program: PAY2.

```
10  REM CONDITIONAL LOOP PROGRAM: PAY2
15  REM USING THE IF . . . THEN AND GOTO STATEMENTS
20  INPUT "ENTER WAGE, HOURS (WAGE = 9999 TO QUIT)"; WAGE, HRS
30  IF WAGE = 9999 THEN GOTO 80
40    IF HRS > 40 THEN LET GROSSPAY = WAGES*HRS + .5*WAGE*(HRS − 40)
        ELSE LET GROSSPAY = WAGE*HRS
50    PRINT "GROSS PAY IS"; GROSSPAY
60    INPUT "ENTER WAGE, HOURS (WAGE = 9999 TO QUIT)"; WAGE, HRS
70  GOTO 30
80  END


OK

RUN

ENTER WAGE, HOURS (WAGE = 9999 TO QUIT)? 4.50, 40

GROSS PAY IS 180

ENTER WAGE, HOURS (WAGE = 9999 TO QUIT)? 3.75, 48

GROSS PAY IS 195

ENTER WAGE, HOURS (WAGE = 9999 TO QUIT)? 9999, 0

OK
```

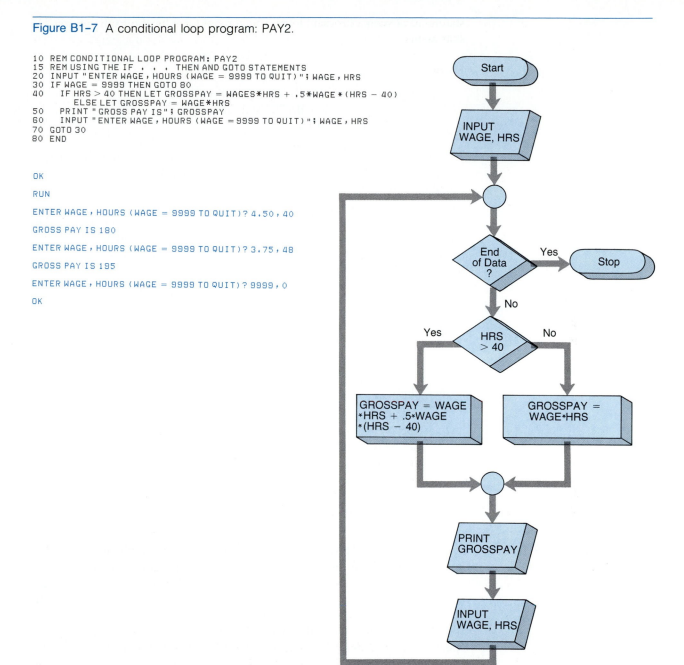

FOR statements command the computer to repeatedly execute a series of statements (a program loop) a specified number of times. The FOR statement is the first statement of the loop and specifies the conditions for executing the statements of the loop. The NEXT statement is the last

FOR and NEXT Statements

statement of such a program loop. The general form for the FOR and NEXT statements is:

Form:

> line number FOR i=j TO k STEP m
>   (other BASIC statements)
> line number NEXT i

The "i" is a variable name that represents the counter or index of the program loop. The "j" is a numeric literal, variable, or expression that establishes the initial value of the loop counter. The "k" is a numeric literal, variable, or expression that is the maximum value that the loop counter can attain. The "m" is a numeric literal, variable, or expression that is the incremental value by which the counter is to be modified for each trip through the program loop. The STEP portion of the statement can be omitted if m has a value of positive 1.

Example:

```
20 FOR A = 1 TO 100
   (other BASIC statements)
80 NEXT A
```

Explanation:

> All statements following the FOR statement up to and including the NEXT A will be executed repeatedly. The initial value of A is set to one and is increased by an increment of one each time the program loop is executed. The loop will be executed for all whole number index values through 100. After executing with an index value of 100 the computer "exits from the loop" and executes the statements that follow the NEXT A statement.

PAY Program with FOR and NEXT Loop

We will modify the PAY2 program to demonstrate the implementation of a loop using the FOR and NEXT statements. The program uses the READ and DATA statements instead of the interactive mode of data entry. In addition, the IF . . . THEN statement has been replaced with the FOR statement and the GO TO statement has been replaced with the NEXT statement. Finally, the initial INPUT statement has been replaced by a special read statement that simply reads the number of times the loop is to be executed (number of records to be processed) into the loop terminating variable. This, of course, requires that the first item in the first data statement be the number of records of data to be processed.

The FOR . . . NEXT loop is the main program loop of program PAY3 (Figure B1–8). Statement 20 reads the number of pay records (N) to be processed (a 2 from statement 80). Statement 30 specifies that the main program loop (from statement 30 to statement 70) will be executed two times (COUNT = 1 to N). Statement 70 causes the program to branch back to statement 30. When COUNT > 2, the program exits from this loop and jumps to statement 80.

Figure B1-8 A PAY program with FOR and NEXT statements: PAY3.

```
10  REM PAY PROGRAM WITH FOR . . . NEXT LOOP: PAY3
20  READ N
30  FOR COUNT = 1 TO N
40     READ WAGE , HRS
50     IF HRS > 40 THEN GROSSPAY = WAGE*HRS + .5*WAGE*(HRS - 40)
             ELSE GROSSPAY = WAGE * HRS
60     PRINT "GROSS PAY IS "; GROSSPAY
70  NEXT COUNT
80  DATA 2
90  DATA 4.50 , 40
100  DATA 3.75 , 48
110  END


OK

RUN

GROSS PAY IS 180
GROSS PAY IS 195

OK
```

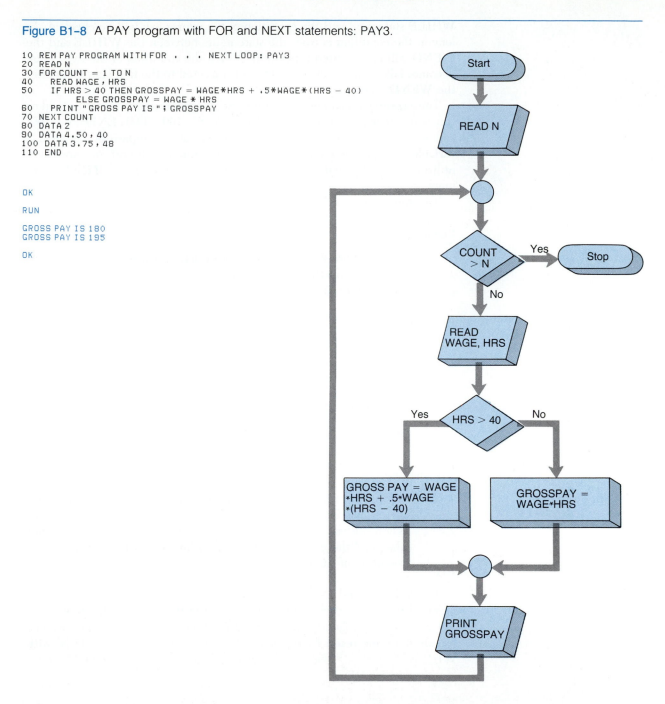

WHILE and WEND statements allow you to repeatedly execute a series of statements (a program loop) as long as the condition of the expression following the WHILE statement is true. If the condition of the expression following the WHILE statement is true, the statements following it up to and including the WEND statement will be executed. When the WEND statement is encountered, control of the program will be returned to the

WHILE and WEND Statements

WHILE statement and the condition of the expression will be checked. As long as the condition is true, the statements between the WHILE and the WEND will be executed repeatedly. When the condition of the expression becomes false, control of the program is directed to the first statement after the WEND statement.

The *expression* can consist of numeric or alphanumeric variables and/or constants, or arithmetic formulas, that is, A, N$, 100, "THE END", B + 100, and so on. The *condition* specified consists of a comparison between a variable or expression and another variable, numeric literal, or expression utilizing the "relational symbols" as outlined with the IF . . . THEN statement.

The general form of the WHILE and WEND statements is:

Form:

>   line number WHILE (expression) relation (expression)
>   (other BASIC statements)
>   line number WEND

Example:

```
 90 READ A
100 WHILE A<> 99
110 PRINT A
120 READ A
130 WEND
130 DATA 12, 18, 16, 99
140 END
```

Explanation:

> The program loop (lines 100–130) will be executed until the value of A equals 99, causing the numbers 12, 18, and 16 to be printed. When the value of A equals 99, the expression A <> 99 becomes false, and the program is directed to line 140, which causes the execution of the program to end.

The WHILE and WEND statements create a loop structure virtually identical to that created by the combination of the IF . . . THEN and GO TO statements. In fact, for program PAY2, Figure B1–7, we could produce exactly the same result by replacing statement 30 (the IF . . .THEN) with WHILE WAGE <> 9999, and replacing statement 80 (the GO TO statement) with WEND.

The PAY Program Revisited

Our pay calculation program would be more useful if it included appropriate title and heading lines, printed the names of the employees whose gross pay is being calculated, and provided a total amount paid to all employees. Several modifications to the program are necessary to produce this type of report. We will need to include print statements to produce the heading and total pay lines of the report, and statements setting up and adding to the accumulator variable will also be required. In addition, we will, of course, change the loop structure to one using WHILE . . . WEND statements. Figure B1–9 shows the flow chart, program, and output of program PAY4. Notice the following features:

☐ The program can logically be divided into three segments: (1) a set of initializing statements that are executed one time before entering the main processing loop; (2) a set of statements that form the main processing loop and are executed once for each record of data processed; and (3) a set of closing statements that are executed one time after the last execution of the main loop has been completed.

☐ Statements 30 through 50 cause a title line and column headings to be printed with one blank line separating them. These lines are printed one time before data for the first employee are processed.

☐ The main processing loop utilizes WHILE and WEND statements, statements 70 and 120, respectively. The WHILE statement tests for the presence of the trailer value "ZZZZ" in the variable EMPNM$. As long as this value is not found, processing continues through the loop to the WEND statement, which transfers control back to the WHILE statement for another pass through the loop. When the trailer value is detected (the condition EMPNM$ <> "ZZZZ" becomes false), statement 130 is executed.

☐ Two READ statements are used. The first is necessary to provide a value to be tested on the first pass through the WHILE statement. The second read is within the main processing loop after all processing and printing within the loop are completed. This ensures that data records will be tested by the WHILE condition before they are processed, so that we will not attempt to process the trailer record.

☐ An alphanumeric variable EMPNM$ is used in the program to process employee names provided by the DATA statements. Note that this variable ends in a dollar sign ($) to indicate that it is alphanumeric. Values of this variable in the DATA statements have been enclosed in quotes (not necessary on some systems).

☐ An accumulator variable, TOTALPAY, is established to record the total pay given to all employees. The accumulator is given an initial value of zero by statement 20. Statement 80, within the main processing loop, adds the value of gross pay for the current employee to the existing amount in total pay. For the first employee, the computed gross pay of $180 is added to the initial value of zero for TOTALPAY, causing the value of TOTALPAY to become $180. On the second pass through the loop, GROSSPAY for the second employee, $195, is added to the $180 already in TOTALPAY, changing its value to $375. Thus pay is accumulated or summed for all of the data records processed.

☐ The accumulated value of TOTALPAY is printed by a statement appearing below the main processing loop, which is executed after all data has been processed.

Figure B1-9 The PAY program revisited: PAY4.

```
10  REM PAY PROGRAM REVISITED: PAY 4
15  REM ********* INITIALIZING STATEMENTS ********************
20  LET TOTALPAY = 0
30  PRINT "WEEKLY PAYROLL FOR XYZ CO."
40  PRINT
50  PRINT "EMP. NAME", "GROSS PAY"
60  READ EMPNM$, WAGE, HRS
65  REM ********* MAIN PROCESSING LOOP ********************
70  WHILE EMPNM$ <> "ZZZZ"
80    IF HRS > 40 THEN LET GROSSPAY = WAGE*HRS + .5*WAGE * (HRS - 40)
             ELSE LET GROSSPAY = WAGE * HRS
90    PRINT EMPNM$, GROSSPAY
100     LET TOTALPAY = TOTALPAY + GROSSPAY
110     READ EMPNM$, WAGE, HRS
120 WEND
125 REM ********* CLOSING STATEMENTS ********************
130 PRINT
140 PRINT "    TOTAL", TOTALPAY
150 DATA "SUSAN", 4.50, 40
160 DATA "ALAN", 3.75, 48
170 DATA "ZZZZ", 0, 0
180 END


RUN

WEEKLY PAYROLL FOR XYZ CO.

EMP.NAME      GROSS PAY
SUSAN            180
ALAN             195
     TOTAL       375

OK
```

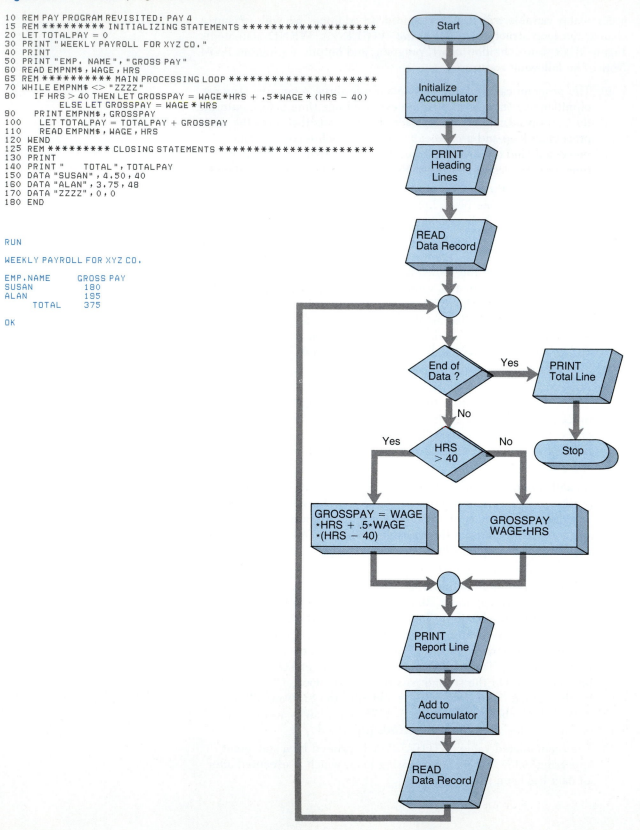

□ Note that the print statements utilize commas to separate variable names and column heading names in statements 50, 90, and 140. This causes the appropriate values to be printed left justified within the first and second print zones. More sophisticated methods of formatting output will be discussed later in this appendix.

GOSUB and RETURN Statements

The GOSUB and RETURN statements provide a structured method of dividing a large program into smaller components called modules or subroutines. The form of the GOSUB statement is:

Form:

>   line number GOSUB line number

and the form of the return statement is simply:

>   line number RETURN

The GOSUB causes control to be transferred to the specified line number, where statements are executed sequentially until a return statement is encountered. When the RETURN statement is encountered, control is returned to the statement immediately following the GOSUB statement.

Example:

```
80 LET A = 20
90 GOSUB 200
100 PRINT A
       .
       .
180 END
200 LET A = A*2
210 RETURN
```

Explanation:

>   When statement 90 is encountered, control is transferred to statement 200, which is executed next, doubling the value of A to 40. When statement 210 is executed, control is shifted back to the next sequential statement after the GOSUB statement, statement 100. This causes the value of A, 40, to be printed.

A Structured Version of the PAY Program

Three elements of structured programming were described earlier in this appendix. We have been careful to follow one of these elements by ensuring that in all of our programming examples only *sequence, selection,* and *repetition* control structures have been used. It is now time to address the other two elements: modularization of programs and program documentation.

Remember that in our last example program, PAY4, we said that the program could be divided into three logical parts; (1) a set of statements to be performed initially before entering the main loop, which processes each employee's pay data; (2) a set of statements that constitute the main processing loop; and (3) a set of statements to be processed only after processing of the main loop has been completed. GOSUB statements will be used to divide the program into three modules, or subroutines. The program will now consist of a main, or control, module and the three subroutines. The main module performs a role similar to that of a boss. It does not perform any of the processing work of the program, but serves to manage the flow of work performed by the subroutines. Thus the main module will consist of GOSUB statements to the appropriate subroutines, and control statements used to manage the order in which subroutines are executed.

A number of remark (REM) statements have also been added to the program. The REM statements are used to document the program by providing a variable dictionary, and to delineate and describe the functions of the program's subroutine modules.

Figure B1-10 presents the program, input data, and output results for the structured pay program PAY5. Pseudocode is also presented in place of the flowcharts that have been used in previous examples. Remember that pseudocode uses indentation of lines to indicate the presence of repetition or selection control structures. Notice the following features of the structured pay program:

Figure B1-10 A Structured PAY program: PAY5.

Pseudocode

Begin Program
  GOSUB Initialization Module
  While there is more data
    GOSUB Processing Module
  WEND
  GOSUB Closing Module
End Program
Begin Initialization Module
  Initialize total pay accumulator
  Print heading lines
  Read pay record
End Initialization Module
Begin Processing Module
  IF hours worked > 40 THEN
    compute gross pay with overtime premium
    ELSE compute gross pay without premium
    Add gross pay to total pay accumulator
    Print report detail line
    Read pay record
End Processing Module
Begin Closing Module
  Print report total line
End Closing Module

Figure B1–10 Concluded

Program
```
10 REM STRUCTURED PAY PROGRAM: PAY5
12 REM THIS PROGRAM CALCULATES XYZ COMPANY'S PAYROLL
14 REM PROGRAMMED BY: JOE STUDENT   DATE: 12/5/89
16 REM
20 REM ******* VARIABLE DICTIONARY *************
30 REM EMPNM$ = EMPLOYEE'S NAME
40 REM WAGE = HOURLY WAGE RATE
50 REM HRS = WEEKLY HOURS WORKED
60 REM GROSSPAY = GROSS PAY EARNED
70 REM TOTALPAY = TOTAL PAY EARNED BY ALL EMPLOYEES
80 REM
100 REM *************** MAIN *****************
110 GOSUB 200
120 WHILE EMPNM$ <> ''ZZZZ''
130 GOSUB 300
140 WEND
150 GOSUB 400
160 END
170 REM
190 REM *********** INITIALIZATION *************
200 LET TOTALPAY = 0
210 PRINT ''WEEKLY PAYROLL FOR XYZ CO.''
220 PRINT
230 PRINT ''EMP. NAME'', ''GROSS PAY''
240 READ EMPNM$, WAGE, HRS
250 RETURN
260 REM
290 REM ************ PROCESSING ***************
300 IF HRS > 40 THEN LET GROSSPAY = WAGE*HRS + .5*WAGE*(HRS - 40)
          ELSE LET GROSSPAY = WAGE * HRS
310 PRINT EMPNM$, GROSSPAY
320 LET TOTALPAY = TOTALPAY + GROSSPAY
330 READ EMPNM$, WAGE, HRS
340 RETURN
350 REM
390 REM ************** CLOSING ***************
400 PRINT
410 PRINT ''  TOTAL'', TOTALPAY
420 RETURN
500 REM *********** DATA STATEMENTS ***********
510 DATA ''SUSAN'', 4.50, 40
520 DATA ''ALAN'', 3.75, 48
530 DATA 'ZZZZ', 0, 0
540 REM
```

Output
```
RUN
WEEKLY PAYROLL FOR XYZ CO.
EMP. NAME      GROSS PAY

SUSAN            180
ALAN             195
   TOTAL         375
OK
```

☐ A set of remark statements precede the main, control module. These statements indicate the purpose of the program, tell who programmed it and when it was programmed, and provide a dictionary of all variables used in the program along with a description of each.

☐ Remark statements are used before and after each module of the program to describe the module and allow its beginning and ending points to be easily identified.

☐ The main module consists entirely of GOSUB and control statements.

☐ Statement 110 causes the INITIALIZATION subroutine, statements 200 through 250, to be executed one time. When the RETURN at statement 250 is encountered, statement 120 is executed next.

☐ Statement 120 initiates a WHILE loop, which causes the PROCESSING subroutine, statements 300 through 340, to be executed repeatedly until the trailer record is detected. Each time the RETURN at statement 340 is executed, control is returned to the WEND at 140, which in turn returns control to the WHILE statement at 120 to test the condition.

☐ Once the condition on the WHILE statement at 120 becomes false, statement 150 causes the CLOSING subroutine, statements 400 through 420, to be executed one time.

☐ The END statement at 160 causes the execution of the program to terminate. It is important that the END statement be encountered at the conclusion of the main module to prevent the program from falling into a subroutine, in this case reexecuting the initialization routine. When a modular structure is used, the programmer must ensure that subroutines are accessed only through the execution of GOSUB statements.

☐ The subroutines of this program are identical to the blocks of statements in the previous program that were identified as INITIALIZING, MAIN PROCESSING, and CLOSING statements, respectively, with two exceptions. First, the statement numbers have been changed so that the first statement of each block is at an even hundred. This is not necessary, but does make identification of the beginning of subroutines easier. Secondly, the WHILE and WEND statements marking the beginning and end of the main processing loop have been moved to the MAIN module.

☐ The data statements form a separate section at the end of the program, though these statements could have been placed at any point in the program.

More on Structured Programming

Structured techniques provide a number of advantages when you are working on sizable programs. They make debugging or modifying a program easier. For instance, if an error is found in the headings for program PAY5 or it is necessary to change them for some reason, we know that this modification must be made in the initialization subroutine. We can then go directly to that section of the program to make the appropriate changes. In addition, the documentation provided makes it much easier for someone other than the original programmer to make needed modifications to the program. A further advantage is the fact that the modular approach allows more than one programmer to work on a program.

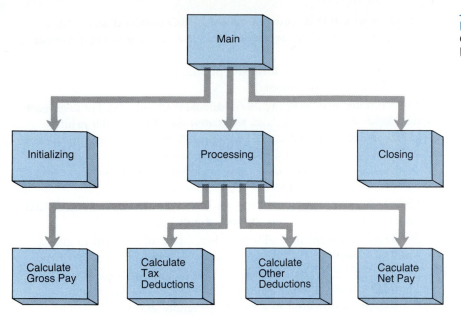

As programs grow in size and complexity, they can be divided into a larger set of modules. Imagine a more complex payroll program, for instance. Some employees may be eligible for commissions or bonuses as well as their hourly pay. Also, net pay must be determined by subtracting from gross pay federal, state, and local tax payments and deductions for retirement, insurance, and the like. Tax deductions and retirement and insurance payment amounts are determined by elaborate and involved computations. Under these circumstances, the main processing subroutine could easily become hundreds of lines long. To avoid this, the main processing subroutine would contain GOSUB statements accessing lower-level subroutines designed to perform specific portions of the processing task. For example, we might create a subroutine to calculate gross pay, a subroutine to calculate tax deductions, a subroutine to calculate deductions for retirement and insurance, and a subroutine to calculate net pay once the other calculations have been completed. A visual table of contents for such a program is shown below in Figure B1-11. We can see that structured programming implements the *top-down* approach to programming described in Chapter 11.

1. If you want to write a program in the BASIC programming language, what command do you use to get the BASIC interpreter?

   _____ .

2. An example of a BASIC command is _____ . An example of a BASIC statement is _____ .

3. Each statement (instruction) in a BASIC program must be preceded by a _____ .

4. If you want a BASIC program to display a prompt and ask for data input with a "?", an _____ statement must be included in your program.

REVIEW AND APPLICATION QUIZ

5. If you want a BASIC program to read data contained in DATA statements, you must include a _____ statement in your program.

6. Data can be included in a BASIC program by the use of a _____ statement.

7. PRINT statements may include semicolons or commas between each data field. A _____ will cause data fields to be printed close together, while a _____ between each output field in a PRINT statement will divide the print line into print zones of _____ spaces each, and a "trailing" comma or semicolon will print the next data output on _____.

8. If the BASIC interpreter detects an error in a BASIC statement that has been keyed in and transmitted, it will _____.

9. A BASIC statement that adds together values of A and B to give a result of C would be _____.

10. A _____ statement is used to include nonexecutable comments in a program, while an _____ statement is the last statement executed in a BASIC program, and terminates its execution.

11. A _____ statement makes part of a computer program repeat itself by an unconditional transfer of control to another statement.

12. The statement that causes one statement or set of statements to be executed when a given condition is true and a different statement or set of statements to be executed when the condition is false, is called an _____ statement.

13. A logical comparison is used to test a condition. The result of the comparison is that the condition tested is either _____ or _____.

14. A BASIC statement that initializes an accumulator named TOTAL would be _____. A BASIC statement that accumulates a running total of SCORE values in the variable TOTAL would be _____.

15. The _____ and _____ serve to begin and terminate a loop that will be executed repeatedly as long as a specified condition is true.

16. A _____ statement commands the computer to repeatedly execute a program loop a specified number of times. A _____ statement is the last statement of such a program loop.

17. A _____ statement causes a transfer of program control to a specified statement number where statements will be executed sequentially until a _____ statement is encountered. This combination of statements is used to implement modular programming.

18. When a FOR . . . NEXT loop has been established, each time the NEXT statement is encountered, the index variable is incremented by the amount specified in the _____ clause of the FOR statement, or by _____ if no increment value has been specified.

19. When GOSUB and RETURN statements have been used to establish a modular program structure, you must ensure that all subroutines in the program are accessed only through _____.

Indicate the order of arithmetic operation for the following statements by placing the appropriate number under each arithmetic operator symbol. For example:

```
LET A = B ∧ 2 − 4 * A * C
          (1)   (4)   (2)   (3)
```

20. LET B2 = B1 − C + S.
21. LET B2 = B1 − (C + S).
22. LET A = B + C / D * C ∧ 4.
23. LET F = (A + (B − C)) / (D * E).

Find the value of F in the following statements, if A = 20, B = 10, C = 2, D = 1, and E = −5:

24. LET F = A / B * C − D + E.
25. LET F = A / (B * C) − (D + E).
26. LET F = A − B * E ∧ C.
27. LET F = A * (1 − B / 100) ∧ (B / C).

Fill in the blanks of the remaining questions based on your analysis of the following program:

```
10 REM LET THE PROGRAM BEGIN
15 PRINT ''A'', ''B'', ''C''
20 READ A, B
30 IF A = 999 THEN GO TO 70
40 C = A − B
50 PRINT A, B, C
55 READ A, B
60 GO TO 30
70 END
75 REM DATA STATEMENTS FOLLOW
80 DATA 25, 15
85 DATA 24, 16
90 DATA 22, 15
95 DATA 21, 15
100 DATA 999, 0
```

28. When statement 20 executes for the first time, the value of A will be _____ and the value of B will be _____.

29. When statement 50 executes for the fourth time, what will be the printed result? _____ _____ _____.

30. Statement number _____ conditionally transfers control of the program to statement number _____.

31. Statement number _____ unconditionally transfers control of the program to statement number _____.

32. This program could be modified to use a WHILE . . . WEND loop by replacing statement _____ with a WHILE statement, and statement _____ with a WEND statement.

HANDS-ON ASSIGNMENTS

The only way to really appreciate and understand computer programming and learn the BASIC programming language is to write and run several simple programs on your own. You should now be ready to write a few simple computer programs in BASIC. Here are a few programming assignments you can try. Good luck.

B1.1. Write a simple BASIC program generally similar to example program SUM2 that does the following:

   a. READS a DATA record containing an employee's hours worked and wage rate.

   b. Calculates the employee's gross pay: gross pay = hours * wage.

   c. Prints the gross pay amount with an appropriate text label.

B1.2. Modify the program you developed in assignment B1.1 so that it uses an INPUT statement rather than READ . . . DATA statements, and prints a "user friendly" prompt message to the user of your program.

B1.3. Modify the program you developed in assignment B1.1 to allow the input data to include the employee's name, and to cause the printed output to include the employee's name as well as gross pay.

B1.4. Write an interactive program (using INPUT statements) that accepts a Fahrenheit temperature, converts it to a Celsius temperature, and prints the result with the appropriate label. The formula for converting a Fahrenheit temperature to Celsius is:

$$\text{Celsius} = (\text{Fahrenheit} - 32) * 5/9$$

B1.5. Write a program that will convert an amount of dollars input by the user of your program into an equivalent amount of German marks, French francs, and Japanese yen, and print out the results for all three currencies. Assume that $1 equals 2.5 marks, 7 francs, and 180 yen, or use current exchange rates.

B1.6.   Modify program PAY4 so that it also calculates and prints the following:
 a. The number of employees who did and did not work overtime.
 b. Total regular pay and total overtime pay for all employees.
 c. The average gross pay earned.

B1.7.   Create a set of hours and wage rate data for the PAY4 program that are in order by hours worked from the lowest to the highest number of hours worked. Based on this data, write a program that will do the following:
 a. Print the required output for employees that worked overtime separately from those that did not, and print appropriate headings for each group.
 b. Compute and print subtotals for those workers with overtime hours and those without, as well as overall totals.

B1.8.   Write a program that reads the names, social security numbers, and test scores of several students and assigns them a letter grade based on the following grading scale: 90 or more = A, 80–89 = B, 65–79 = C, 55–64 = D, 54 or less = F. Print a grade report with the appropriate headings.

B1.9.   Write a program that reads the names, product numbers, beginning quantity, and number of units sold for several items in inventory and calculates the ending quantity. Print an inventory status report with appropriate headings.

B1.10.   Write a program that reads the names, employee numbers, sales quotas, and sales made (in dollars) for several salespersons. Calculate their gross pay based on a 10 percent commission on all sales, and an extra 5 percent commission on sales that exceed their sales quota of $1,000. Print a salesperson gross pay report with appropriate headings.

Section II: Doing More with BASIC

You have now learned the bare essentials of programming in BASIC. At this point you are now ready to learn how to make a computer do more for you by the use of some additional features of BASIC. Figure B2–1 outlines the additional BASIC statements that will be explained in this section. Most of these statements do not vary significantly among the BASIC compilers and interpreters used on many computer systems, including microcomputers. However, you should consult the BASIC manual for the computer you are using to determine if there are any differences in the recommended form of these statements.

PRINTING REPORTS

The PRINT TAB statement uses the TAB function to control the spacing of output. The general form of the PRINT TAB statement is:

The PRINT TAB Statement

Form:

line number PRINT TAB (expression); $\left\{\begin{array}{l}\text{Variable}\\\text{Literal}\end{array}\right\}$; . . .

Examples:

```
100 PRINT TAB(20) ''NAME''; TAB(40) ''BALANCE
    DUE''
220 PRINT TAB(20) CNAME$; TAB(40) BALANCE
```

Figure B2–1 A summary of additional BASIC statements.

Statement	Purpose	Example
Output Statements		
PRINT TAB	Controls the spacing of output.	215 PRINT TAB(10);A
PRINT USING	Directs the printing or display of output according to formats contained in an image statement.	225 PRINT USING I$;A
IMAGE	Provides formats for a PRINT USING statement.	400 I$ = "#####.##"
Control Statements		
STOP	Halts program execution until a user indicates that processing is to continue or terminate.	150 STOP
RESTORE	Allows DATA statements to be reread.	160 RESTORE
ON/GOSUB	Provides conditional transfer of control to alternative statements. When a RETURN statement is read, control is returned to the next statement after the ON/GOSUB statement.	170 ON X GOSUB 260, 310, 420
Array Specifications Statement		
DIM	Specifies the dimensions of arrays and reserves the storage locations needed.	20 DIM A(25), B(10,5)
File Processing Statements		
OPEN	Opens or creates a data file.	40 OPEN ''TEST'' FOR INPUT AS #1
CLOSE	Closes a data file.	900 CLOSE #1

As you can see, the *expression* (which can be a numeric constant, variable, or arithmetic expression) indicates the column number of the column where printing of a variable or literal is to begin (columns 20 and 40 in the example statements). Sample results for the PRINT TAB statements are indicated below. The first line shows the results produced by execution of line 100. The second line shows the results for line 220, assuming the values of CNAME$ and BALANCE are THOMAS and 1234.56, respectively. The third line shows results for line 220 when CNAME$ is SUE and BALANCE is 20.

```
   1                    20              40
1.                      NAME            BALANCE DUE
2.                      THOMAS           1234.56
3.                      SUE              20
```

Note that all variables are printed left justified. Text variables begin at the TAB position while numeric variables start one column to the right, allowing space for a sign position. Since numeric data, such as the values for BALANCE, are normally printed right justified, the PRINT USING statement rather than the PRINT TAB statement is normally used when printing output containing numeric data.

The PRINT USING statement allows programmers to select exact spacing for output. It uses a corresponding **image** statement that specifies how the output should be printed. The general form of the PRINT USING is:

The PRINT USING Statement

> line number PRINT USING print image; list of expressions

or

> line number PRINT USING variable; list of expressions

where the expressions may be variables or text or numeric constants.

Example:

```
120 PRINT USING ''\        \ ######.##'';
    CNAME$, BALANCE
```

The backslash (\) and number sign (#) are replaceable characters when they occur within an image statement. Therefore, when statement 120 is executed, the computer prints the contents of the variable CNAME$ in the portion of the print image between the backslash characters, and the contents of the variable BALANCE in the portion of the print image containing number signs. Thus execution of statement 120 will result in output like the following examples:

```
THOMAS  1234.56
SUE       20.00
```

The previous example could also have been implemented by the following statements:

```
240 IM$ = ''\        \ ######.##''
250 PRINT USING IM$; CNAME$, BALANCE
```

When statement 250 is executed, the computer prints the contents of the variables CNAME$ and BALANCE using the image provided in the contents of the string variable IM$, producing results identical to the previous example.

In all cases, the image statement utilizes the number or pound sign (#) to indicate the maximum number of numeric characters that may be printed for each output variable. Numeric values that exceed this maximum are rounded to fit the number of characters specified by the image statement. The backslash (\) is used for the specification of the size of the field for alphanumeric (string) characters for each output variable or constant. The size of an alphanumeric image is the number of blank spaces between the backslashes plus the two spaces occupied by the beginning and ending backslash.

Examples:

```
100 PRINT USING ''###.##''; M
```

Execution of statement 100 would result in the printing of the current value of the variable M, such as 123.45.

In the second example, the image is defined as a string variable.

```
10 F$ = ''THE MEAN SCORE IS ##.##''
      ⋮
100 PRINT USING F$;M
```

If the value of the numeric variable M is 12.335, execution of statement 100 would result in output such as:

```
THE MEAN SCORE IS 12.34
```

Any characters appearing in an image statement that are not used as replaceable characters will be printed as literals, such as the phrase THE MEAN SCORE IS used in the preceding example.

Replaceable characters include the backslash and number sign characters described above, and the exclamation point (!), which is used to indicate a string variable one character in length.

Example:

```
220 PRINT USING ''YOUR GRADE IS !''; ''B''
```

causes the following output:

```
YOUR GRADE IS B
```

Several additional characters are treated as replaceable only when used in connection with number sign characters to format numeric output. For example, when printing dollar amounts, we would like to have a dollar sign printed to the left of the numeric value, and we would like to have commas printed appropriately when values exceed 1,000. This is accomplished by the following statements:

Examples:

```
330 PRINT USING ''TOTAL $###,###.##''; TOT
360 PRINT USING ''TOTAL $$##,###.##''; TOT
```

If the value of TOT is 1205.5, execution of statement 330 would cause the following output:

```
TOTAL $  1,205.50
```

Execution of statement 360 would cause the following output:

```
TOTAL $1,205.50
```

The presence of the second dollar sign in the image in statement 360 causes the dollar sign to be printed immediately to the left of the most significant digit of the number.

There are several additional characters that may be used to format numeric data for printing with the PRINT USING statement. If you are interested in other types of formatting, consult the BASIC manual for the computer you are using.

The general form of the STOP statement is:

Form:

line number STOP

Example:

```
150 STOP
```

The STOP statement can terminate a program. It is an optional statement that can appear several times in a program. The STOP statement thus causes a break during the execution of a program. Normally when a STOP statement is encountered, a message will appear on the screen informing the user where the break was encountered. The user can then cause the program to terminate or continue with responses such as "END" or "CONT".

The general form of the RESTORE statement is:

Form:

line number RESTORE

Example:

```
260 RESTORE
```

RESTORE statements restart the use of the data provided by DATA statements. A RESTORE statement allows the computer to read the same data several times in a program. It directs the computer to start over at the top of the "data stack" on the next READ statement. Thus the RESTORE

MORE CONTROL STATEMENTS

The STOP and RESTORE Statements

statement is a way of making the same data available for processing more than once. You would need this capability, for example, if you wanted to write a program that first calculated the mean (average) of student scores on an exam, and then had to compare each individual test score to the mean of the exam. A RESTORE statement would allow you to reread the test scores contained in the DATA statements of the program.

The ON/GOSUB Statement

The ON/GOSUB statement causes a program to branch to one of several alternative statements within a program, depending on the value of a specified variable. Thus the ON/GOSUB statement allows a conditional transfer of program control to one of a series of statement numbers (n) depending on the value of a variable, as shown in the following general form and example:

Form:

line number ON variable GOSUB n_1, n_2, n_3 . . .

Example:

```
210 ON X GOSUB 260, 310, 360
```

In the example statement above, if the value of the variable X is 1, the program will branch to the first statement number (260). If the value of X is 2, control will be transferred to the second statement number (310), and so on. Statements 260, 310, and 360 should each begin modules of statements that are terminated by a RETURN statement. When the RETURN statement is executed, control is transferred to the statement immediately following the ON/GOSUB statement.

A Program Example

Let's write a sample program that uses several of the statements described in this section. Suppose salespersons for a company selling apples want to be able to produce reports listing the current balance for any selected customer or a report summarizing the status of all customer accounts. Assume that the following data are available for each customer: the customer's ID number, the customer's name, the type of customer (the company sells both to other businesses and to individuals), and the balance due. We are asked to write an interactive program that will allow the sales staff to see a report for a specified customer, or a summary report for all customers, or both.

Pseudocode for this program is presented in Figure B2–2, while the program itself and sample results are presented in Figure B2–3. Note the following features of this program.

☐ The main module accepts the user's choice about the type of report to be printed, and then statement 290 causes the appropriate section of the program to be executed, depending on the choice. If 1 is chosen, the individual balance subroutine is executed; if 2 is chosen, control is transferred to the summary report subroutine; and if 3 is chosen, control is transferred to the closing subroutine.

☐ In the individual balance subroutine, a customer ID number is input (statement 400) and a loop is established to search for this customer's data (statements 440–470).

Main Module
Set more reports to yes
WHILE more reports = yes
  Display menu choices on screen and accept user's choice
  ON choice execute the appropriate subroutine:
    individual balance, summary report, or closing
WEND
End program

Individual Balance Module
Get customer ID from user
Set found to no
RESTORE the read pointer
READ the number of records
FOR index = 1 to number of records
  READ a customer data record
  IF input customer ID = customer ID read THEN
    GOSUB to the print module
  Endif
NEXT index value
IF found = no THEN print an error message
Endif
RETURN

Print Module
Print customer data report
Set found = yes
Set index to number of records plus one
RETURN

Summary Report Module
Initialize total balance
RESTORE the read pointer
READ the number of records
Set up the print images and print heading lines
FOR index = 1 to number of records
  READ a customer data record
  Add to total balance accumulator
  Print a detail line
NEXT index
Print the total line
RETURN

Closing Module
Set more reports to no
RETURN

Figure B2–2 Pseudocode for a customer balance program.

- □ The RESTORE statement at 420 ensures that data statements will be read beginning with the first data statement. This statement is necessary because more than one report may be printed when this program is run, and the data must be read from the beginning for all reports.
- □ A FOR and NEXT loop is used, assuming that the number of data records is known and can be read from a header record (statement 430).

Figure B2-3 Interactive customer balance program.

```
10 REM ********** INTERACTIVE CUSTOMER BALANCE PROGRAM ***********
20 REM WRITTEN BY: JOE PROGRAMMER   DATE: 12/28/89
30 REM VARIABLE DICTIONARY
40 REM CUSTOMERID = CUSTOMER ID NUMBER
50 REM CNAME$ = CUSTOMER NAME
60 REM CUSTTYPE$ = CUSTOMER TYPE (B: BUSINESS) (I: INDIVIDUAL)
70 REM BALANCE = BALANCE OWED BY CUSTOMER
80 REM TBALANCE = TOTAL BALANCE OWED BY ALL CUSTOMERS
90 REM MORE$ = MORE REPORTS WANTED (Y OR N)
100 REM FOUND$ = CUSTOMER ID FOUND (Y OR N)
110 REM N = NUMBER OF DATA RECORDS
120 REM I_$ = PRINT IMAGE STATEMENT
130 REM ***********************************************************
200 REM ************* MAIN MODULE *******************************
210 LET MORE$ = ''Y''
220 WHILE MORE$ = ''Y''
225 REM ****** DISPLAY SCREEN MENU *****
230 PRINT
240 PRINT ''    CHOOSE THE TYPE OF REPORT YOU WANT''
250 PRINT '' 1   AN INDIVIDUAL CUSTOMER'S BALANCE''
260 PRINT '' 2   A SUMMARY REPORT FOR ALL CUSTOMERS''
270 PRINT '' 3   NO ADDITIONAL REPORTS NEEDED''
275 REM ***** ACCEPT USERS MENU CHOICE *****
280 INPUT ''    (ENTER THE NUMBER OF YOUR CHOICE):''; CHOICE
290 ON CHOICE GOSUB 400, 700, 1000
300 WEND
310 END
320 REM
390 REM ***************** INDIVIDUAL BALANCE MODULE *****************
400 INPUT 'ENTER THE CUSTOMER'S ID NUMBER''; ICUSTID
410 LET FOUND$ = ''N''
420 RESTORE
430 READ N
435 REM ***** SEARCH FOR CUSTOMER'S BALANCE *****
440 FOR I = 1 TO N
450 READ CUSTID, CUSTNM$, CUSTTYPE$, BALANCE
460 IF ICUSTID = CUSTID THEN GOSUB 600
470 NEXT I
480 IF FOUND$ = ''N'' THEN PRINT ''ERROR, CUSTOMER ID NOT ON FILE''
490 RETURN
500 REM
590 REM ****************** PRINT MODULE ***************************
600 PRINT TAB(20); ''CUSTOMER ID NUMBER:''; TAB(40); CUSTID
610 PRINT TAB(20); ''CUSTOMER NAME:''; TAB(40); CUSTNM$
620 PRINT TAB(20); ''CUSTOMER TYPE:''; TAB(40); CUSTTYPE$
630 PRINT TAB(20); ''BALANCE DUE:''; TAB(40); BALANCE
640 LET FOUND$ = ''Y''
650 LET I = N + 1
660 RETURN
670 REM
690 REM ********** SUMMARY REPORT MODULE ***************************
695 REM ********** INITIALIZING SECTION **********
700 LET TBALANCE = 0
710 RESTORE
720 READ N
```

Figure B2–3 Continued

```
725 REM ********** SET PRINT FORMATS **********
730 I1$ = ''     REPORT OF CUSTOMER ACCOUNT BALANCES''
740 I2$ = ''   CUSTOMER   CUSTOMER   CUSTOMER   BALANCE
750 I3$ = ''     ID #       NAME       TYPE       DUE
760 I4$ = ''     #### \          \       !   $##,###.##''
770 I5$ = ''                                $###,###.##''
780 PRINT I1$
790 PRINT
800 PRINT I2$
810 PRINT I3$
815 REM ********** MAIN PROCESSING LOOP **********
820 FOR I = 1 TO N
830   READ CUSTID, CUSTNM$, CUSTTYPE$, BALANCE
840   LET TBALANCE = TBALANCE + BALANCE
850   PRINT USING I4$; CUSTID, CUSTNM$, CUSTTYPE$, BALANCE
860 NEXT I
865 REM ********** CLOSING SECTION **********
870 PRINT
880 PRINT USING I5$; TBALANCE
890 RETURN
895 REM
898 REM ********** CLOSING MODULE **********
1000 LET MORE$ = ''N''
1010 RETURN
1020 REM
1190 REM ********** DATA STATEMENTS ***************************
1200 DATA 6
1210 DATA 1234, ''ED'S APPLES'', B, 1426.25
1220 DATA 2345, ''FRED'S FRUIT'', B, 3824.00
1230 DATA 3456, ''THE APPLE CO.'', B, 3252.50
1240 DATA 4567, ''AL SMITH'', I, 400.00
1250 DATA 5678, ''BOB BROWN'', I, 2247.50
1260 DATA 6789, ''JOY JONES'', I, 1382.00
1270 REM *********************************************************
```

Output

```
RUN
   CHOOSE THE TYPE OF REPORT YOU WANT
1  AN INDIVIDUAL CUSTOMER'S BALANCE
2  A SUMMARY REPORT FOR ALL CUSTOMERS
3  NO ADDITIONAL REPORTS NEEDED
   (ENTER THE NUMBER OF YOUR CHOICE):? 1
ENTER THE CUSTOMER'S ID NUMBER? 3456
    CUSTOMER ID NUMBER:  3456
    CUSTOMER NAME:       THE APPLE CO.
    CUSTOMER TYPE:       B
    BALANCE DUE:         3252.5

   CHOOSE THE TYPE OF REPORT YOU WANT
1  AN INDIVIDUAL CUSTOMER'S BALANCE
2  A SUMMARY REPORT FOR ALL CUSTOMERS
3  NO ADDITIONAL REPORTS NEEDED
   (ENTER THE NUMBER OF YOUR CHOICE):? 2
```

Figure B2–3 Concluded

```
REPORT OF CUSTOMER ACCOUNT BALANCES

CUSTOMER          CUSTOMER          CUSTOMER          BALANCE
  ID#               NAME              TYPE              DUE
  1234            ED'S APPLES          B            $ 1,426.25
  2345            FRED'S FRUIT         B            $ 3,824.00
  3456            THE APPLE CO.        B            $ 3,252.50
  4567            AL SMITH             I            $   400.00
  5678            BOB BROWN            I            $ 2,247.50
  6789            JOY JONES            I            $ 1,382.00
                                    TOTAL           $12,532.25

    CHOOSE THE TYPE OF REPORT YOU WANT
1   AN INDIVIDUAL CUSTOMER'S BALANCE
2   A SUMMARY REPORT FOR ALL CUSTOMERS
3   NO ADDITIONAL REPORTS NEEDED
    (ENTER THE NUMBER OF YOUR CHOICE):? 3
OK
```

☐ Statement 460 causes the subroutine beginning at statement 600 to be executed when the selected customer number has been found.

☐ The print module causes a listing for the selected customer to be printed using PRINT TAB statements. The report is printed one item per line, with the appropriate text description.

☐ The FOUND$ variable is used as a switch that is initially set to "N" (statement 410), and is set to "Y" (statement 640) in the print module. If the print module is never executed, a match for the input ID number is not found, the value of FOUND$ will be "N" when the loop terminates, and statement 480 is executed. Thus, the appropriate error message will be printed.

☐ Statement 650 in the print module sets the index variable I of the FOR and NEXT loop to its terminal value so that the loop will not continue to be executed once the desired data has been found.

☐ The RETURN statement at 660 causes statement 470 to be executed next, the statement after the GOSUB that caused the print module to be executed.

☐ The RETURN statement at 490 causes statement 300 to be executed next, the statement after the ON/GOSUB that caused the individual balance to be executed.

☐ The summary report module is very similar to the PAY5 program in Appendix B, Section I, except for the use of PRINT USING statements.

☐ Statements 730 through 770 provide image statements. Since the image statements for the detail lines (760) and the total line (770) of the report are directly below the image statement for the column headings (750), it is easy to align these image statements properly, or to find them if corrections must be made.

Functions	Description
SQR(X)	Square root of X
RND	A random number between 0 and 1
INT(X)	The integer less than or equal to number X
ABS(X)	The absolute value of X
SGN(X)	The mathematical sign of X
LOG(X)	The natural logarithm (base E) of X
EXP(X)	E raised to the X power
SIN(X)	Trigonometric sine of X
COS(X)	Trigonometric cosine of X
TAN(X)	Trigonometric tangent of X
COT(X)	Trigonometric cotangent of X
ATN(X)	Trigonometric arctangent of X

Figure B2–4 Standard BASIC mathematical functions.

□ The heading lines are printed by statements 780 through 810. PRINT rather than PRINT USING statements are used since the heading lines contain no replaceable characters.

□ The detail line of the report is printed once for each data record when statement 850 is executed. The PRINT USING statement causes the four variables listed to be placed in the appropriate places of the image variable I4$.

□ Statement 880 causes the image variable I5$ to be used to print the total balance once all data has been processed.

USING FUNCTIONS IN BASIC

Most BASIC compilers provide several built-in mathematical functions that perform specific mathematical operations in BASIC statements. Some examples are square root (SQR), logarithmic (LOG), and trigonometric (SIN, COS) functions. These functions free the programmer from having to write the sequence of statements that would be needed to perform such operations. Functions can also be defined by the programmer within a program and referenced by other instructions in the program. Such programmer-defined functions will not be covered in this appendix. Figure B2–4 lists some of the many predefined mathematical functions in BASIC. The general form of a reference to a function in BASIC is:

Form:

    Function name (argument)

For example, the functions shown in Figure B2–4 use the variable X as an *argument*. In BASIC, the argument of a function can be a constant, variable, mathematical expression, or another function. The use of functions in BASIC statements is illustrated by the following examples:

Example:

```
10 LET A = SQR (Y + Z)
```

Explanation:

A equals the square root of Y plus Z.

Example:

```
20 PRINT LOG (A * B)
```

Explanation:

Prints the natural logarithm of A times B.

Example:

```
30 RNUM = RND
40 RVAR = INT(RNUM * 10 + 1)
```

Explanation:

A random number is generated and stored in RNUM by statement 30. Statement 40 multiplies this random number by 10 and adds 1, and then places the largest integer less than that result in RVAR.

USING ARRAYS

The DIM Statement

The DIM statement is used in BASIC to specify the *dimensions* (rows and/or columns) of *arrays* of data items. It reserves the memory locations required to store each data element in an array. An *array* can be defined as an arrangement of items. A *list* of items is a *one-dimensional array*. A *table* or *matrix* of items arranged in rows and columns is a *two-dimensional* array. See Figure B2–5.

The general form of the DIM statement is:

Form:

line number DIM variable (dimensions), . . .

where *variable* is the name of the array, and *dimensions* refers to the maximum number of rows and/or columns for each array specified by the DIM statement. Rules for naming an array usually are the same as naming other program variables. In most cases, only integer constants can be used to specify the dimensions of an array in a DIM statement. Some systems, however, will allow variables to specify the dimensions of an array.

Figure B2–5 Examples of arrays.

12345
67890
54321
09876
21543
76908
32145
89067

123	10.4	2.35
456	12.5	3.45
789	13.6	4.50
801	15.7	5.62
852	16.8	6.73
879	17.3	7.84
902	18.4	8.95
937	19.7	9.24

One-Dimensional Array　　　　Two-Dimensional Array

Example:

```
DIM A(8), B(8,3)
```

Explanation:

> The dimensions of two arrays (named A and B) are specified and the computer is directed to reserve the memory locations required to store each item in the arrays. A is a single list of eight items and B is a *matrix* of eight rows and three columns.

Note that the dimensions of an array are specified by stating the maximum number of rows and columns in the array. For example, array B in the DIM statement above is an *8 by 3 array* or *matrix* since it has eight rows and three columns. (Rows are mentioned first, then columns.) Any item in an array is identified by integer numbers called *subscripts* that indicate the position of the item in an array, that is, the number of its row, and/or column. For example, an item in the *seventh row* and the *third column* of array B would be identified as the *subscripted variable* B(7,3). However, subscripted variable names can also use variables containing integer values as subscripts, such as B(K,L), as well as integer constants.

DIM statements are usually placed at the beginning of a program since a DIM statement must appear before any other statement can reference the array that it defines. However, default array dimensions are specified automatically by many BASIC compilers. For example, the compiler may automatically reserve memory locations for 10 data values when a variable with a single subscription is mentioned in a statement, such as READ A(J). Space for 100 data values (10 by 10) may typically be reserved when a variable with two subscripts is utilized in a statement, such as READ B(K,L).

Occasionally in programming we wish to save the results of one portion of a program so that these results may be used in another portion of the program. In the normal processing cycle, as soon as one record is processed, the information from the previous record is destroyed in memory. For example, suppose four exams are given each semester in a course. Suppose the instructor wishes to calculate each student's average, then calculate an overall class average, and finally compare each student's average with the overall average. If the BASIC statement:

```
STUDAVE = (EXAM1 + EXAM2 + EXAM3 + EXAM4)/4
```

is used in a loop, no permanent record of the average will be available for comparison purposes—as soon as the second average is calculated, the first one will be lost. This problem can be solved by using a DIM statement such as the following:

```
DIM STUDAVE(25)
```

This statement allows us to store 25 exam averages in storage area STUDAVE. In order to distinguish one average from another, a subscript is used. STUDAVE(1) refers to the first average stored in location STUDAVE.

Using the DIM Statement

STUDAVE(2) refers to the second average stored in STUDAVE, and so forth.

Suppose we wanted to store the scores from all four exams in an array. We could create a two-dimensional array or table by using a DIM statement such as:

```
DIM EXAMS(25,4)
```

This statement would create an array of 25 rows and 4 columns in which the scores for 4 exams by 25 students could be stored. Finally, we could combine the creation of the arrays STUDAVE and EXAMS with the creation of an array named STUDID in which 25 student identification numbers could be stored. This can be accomplished by using a DIM statement such as:

```
DIM STUDID(25), EXAMS(25,4), STUDAVE(25)
```

USING DATA FILES

Business computer applications typically involve large amounts of data and frequent use of the same programs. It would not be very practical to store such data or programs in the main memory of the computer or to have to key in such data or programs each time an application has to be processed. Therefore, data and programs are normally stored in the form of *files* on secondary storage devices such as magnetic tapes or disks. In this section we will describe several BASIC statements used in processing of sequential access files. This should give you a good introduction to the use of files in BASIC programs. However, since BASIC file-handling statements can vary significantly among different types of computers, you should consult the manual for the version of BASIC which you are using on your computer.

Opening a File

The first step in using a file is opening or creating the file. This involves creating a name for a file or opening a file that has previously been created. Files to be used by a BASIC program may be created by another BASIC program, or may be created using a text editor program such as a word processor.

On microcomputers like the IBM Personal Computer, the following statement is used:

Examples:

```
20 OPEN ''TESTDATA'' FOR INPUT AS #1
30 OPEN ''OUTDATA'' FOR OUTPUT AS #2
```

Explanation:

The file with the name indicated in quotes is opened. The number following the # is used to refer to the file in other statements within the BASIC program. If the file is opened for INPUT, the file can be read but cannot be modified by the program; if opened for OUTPUT, the program will write results to the file, which will replace any existing file contents.

Once a file has been opened, data can be stored in the file by writing data into it using a WRITE statement as follows:

Writing Data to a File

Form:

> line number WRITE #n, expression

Example:

> 40 WRITE #2 A, B, C

Explanation:

> If file #2 has been opened for output, the contents of the variable A are written to it, followed by a comma, then the contents of B, then another comma, then the contents of C.

The Microsoft version of BASIC used on microcomputers like the IBM Personal Computer also uses a variation of the PRINT statement. This statement is used identically to the print statement discussed earlier, except that the results are written to the designated file:

Form:

> line number PRINT #n, expression

Example:

> 40 PRINT #1, A, B, C

Once a file has been opened, the data stored in it can be accessed by using a variation of the INPUT statement as follows:

Reading Data from a File

Form:

> line number INPUT #n, expression

Example:

> 30 INPUT #1, A, B, C

When reading data from a file in BASIC that does not have a trailer record (a record that is only used to tell the program that the end of the file has been reached), your program must check for the end-of-file mark placed in the file by the system. The form of this end-of-file mark varies from system to system, and will not be discussed in this appendix.

Some computers require that a file that has been opened be closed before processing can terminate. For example, you would close files on the IBM Personal Computer with the following statement:

Closing a File

Form:

> line number CLOSE #n

Example:

```
50 CLOSE #1
```

A Final Program Example

Let's write a program that will use several of the statements we have just described. Suppose a class of students has taken four exams. The instructor has recorded the student's ID numbers and their scores on each exam on a data file. He now wishes to write a program that will compute the average score for each student, calculate a mean for the whole class, and the deviation of each student's average from the class mean. He would also like to save the average scores for later use. Figure B2–6 provides the pseudocode for such a program, while Figure B2–7 displays the input data, program, and output results. Note the following features of this program:

- ☐ Statement 100 sets aside space for three arrays, two 25-position, single-dimension arrays, and a 100-position (25 by 4), two-dimensional array to hold exam scores.

- ☐ Statement 110 opens the data file STUDATA for input and assigns it as file number 1. Statement 120 opens a file to be used for output. The file is given the name STUDATA2 and is assigned the number 2.

- ☐ The FOR and NEXT loop established by statements 200 through 270 allows data for up to 25 students to be read and placed appropriately in the array variables.

- ☐ Statement 210 causes data to be read from the input data file. It is read into the subscripted array variables, and the index variable of the FOR loop is used to determine which row of the array data is placed in.

- ☐ The IF statement at 220 causes the program to jump out of the loop if the trailer record is detected. This allows the program to work correctly for a variable number of records up to 25.

Figure B2–6 Pseudocode for the student average program.

```
Open input and output files
Set up print images and print headings
Initialize record counter and mean score accumulator
FOR index = 1 to 25
    Read a data record from input file
    IF trailer record found THEN drop out of loop
    Calculate student's average score
    WRITE a record to the output file
    Add student's average score to mean score accumulator
    Add 1 to record counter
NEXT index value
Mean score = accumulated mean score divided by record count
FOR Index = 1 to record count
    Deviation = student's average score minus class mean score
    Print detail line
NEXT index value
Print total line
```

Figure B2-7 Student average program.

Contents of Input Data File STUDATA

```
1056,90,93,89,86
1134,76,88,74,70
1278,98,89,90,82
1376,58,68,62,67
1387,94,86,85,85
1465,86,91,100,90
2143,100,100,99,99
2165,66,52,43,42
9999,0,0,0,0
```

Contents of the Student Average Program

```
10 REM STUDENT EXAM REPORT USING FILES AND ARRAYS
20 REM STUCNT = A COUNTER OF THE NUMBER OF STUDENTS
30 REM DEV = DEVIATION OF A STUDENT'S AVERAGE FROM THE CLASS MEAN
40 REM CLMEAN = MEAN OR AVERAGE OF ALL EXAM SCORES
50 REM STUDAVE(25) = AN ARRAY OF THE AVERAGE SCORE ON FOUR EXAMS
60 REM EXAMS(25,4) = AN ARRAY OF THE FOUR EXAM SCORES FOR EACH STUDENT
70 REM STUDID(25) = AN ARRAY OF THE STUDENT ID NUMBERS
90 REM *********** INITIALIZATION *******************
100 DIM STUDID(25), EXAMS(25,4), STUDAVE(25)
110 OPEN ''STUDATA'' FOR INPUT AS #1
120 OPEN ''STUDATA2'' FOR OUTPUT AS #2
130 LET H1$='' STUDENT NO. EXAM SCORES STUDENT AVE. DEVIATION''
140 LET I1$='' #### ### ### ### ### ##.# ###.# ''
150 LET I2$='' CLASS MEAN ##.# ''
160 PRINT H1$
170 LET STUCNT = 0
180 LET CLMEAN = 0
190 REM *********** CALCULATE STUDENT AVERAGES ************
200 FOR R = 1 to 25
210 INPUT #1 STUDID(R),EXAMS(R,1),EXAMS(R,2),EXAMS(R,3),EXAMS(R,4)
220 IF STUDID(R) = 9999 THEN 300
230 STUCNT = STUCNT + 1
240 STUDAVE(R)=(EXAMS(R,1)+EXAMS(R,2)+EXAMS(R,3)+EXAMS(R,4)) /4
250 WRITE #2,STUDID(R),EXAMS(R,1),EXAMS(R,2),EXAMS(R,3),EXAMS(R,4),STUDAVE(R)
260 CLMEAN = CLMEAN + STUDAVE(R)
270 NEXT R
300 REM ********** CALCULATE THE CLASS MEAN **************
310 CLMEAN = CLMEAN /STUCNT
400 REM ********** CALCULATE STUDENT DEVIATIONS **************
410 FOR R = 1 to STUCNT
420 LET DEV = STUDAVE(R) − CLMEAN
430 PRINT USING I1$;STUDID(R),EXAMS(R,1),EXAMS(R,2),EXAMS(R,3), EXAMS(R,4),DEV
440 NEXT R
450 REM ********** CLOSE FILES **********
460 CLOSE #1, #2
500 REM ********** PRINT CLASS MEAN SCORE *****************
510 PRINT USING I2$; CLMEAN
520 END
```

Figure B2-7 Concluded

Printed Output Listing

STUDENT NO.	EXAM SCORES				STUDENT AVE.	DEVIATION
1056	90	93	89	86	89.5	8.3
1134	76	88	74	70	77.0	-4.2
1278	98	88	74	70	89.8	8.6
1376	58	68	62	67	63.8	-17.4
1387	94	86	85	85	87.5	6.3
1465	86	91	100	90	91.8	10.6
2143	100	100	99	99	99.5	18.3
2165	66	52	43	42	50.8	-30.4
		CLASS MEAN			81.2	

Contents of the Output File STUDATA2

```
1056,90,93,89,86,89.5
1134,76,88,74,70,77.0
1278,98,89,90,82,89.8
1376,58,68,62,67,63.8
1387,94,86,85,85,87.5
1465,86,91,100,90,91.8
2143,100,100,99,99,99.5
2165,66,52,43,42,50.8
```

☐ Note that the EXAMS scores and the STUDAVE variable used in statement 240 are subscripted variables.

☐ Once the student's average score has been calculated, results are written to the output file STUDATA2. Its contents are identical to the input file except that the average score for each student has been included.

☐ The loop from statements 410 through 440 allows the average score for each student to be read from the STUDAVE array so that the student's deviation from the class mean can be computed.

☐ Statement 460 causes the files STUDATA and STUDATA2 to be closed.

REVIEW AND APPLICATION QUIZ

1. The _____ statement causes a break in the execution of the program.

2. The _____ statement allows us the option of reprocessing DATA statements.

3. The _____ statement causes a conditional transfer of control to one of a series of alternative statements.

4. The PRINT TAB statement _____ justifies all data, whether it is strictly numeric or alphanumeric.

5. The PRINT USING statement right justifies _____ data and left justifies _____ data.

6. In the statement 150 PRINT USING I$; the string variable
   _____ is provided by an _____ statement.

7. If we want to be able to store 20 values of variable A in addressable
   locations, what BASIC statement would be used? _____.

8. Once a variable has been dimensioned in the program, it can never
   be mentioned again without a _____.

9. After execution of the program, shown below, what number would
   be stored in X(3)? _____. In X(7)? _____.

```
10 DIM X(10)
20 FOR R = 1 TO 10
30 READ X(R)
40 NEXT R
50 DATA 10, 8, 6, 16, 22, 42, 37, 96, 42, 55
60 END
```

10. The statement DIM C(100,5) would create _____
    addressable storage locations for variable C.

11. In what range would X fall if the following statements were used?

Statement	Range
X = RND	_____
X = INT(RND*25 + 1)	_____

12. If you wanted X to be an integer between 1 and 100 inclusive, you
    would write the statement: X = _____.

13. In order to read a data file, it must first be _____. The
    statement that does that is _____.

14. Write a statement that will open a file named SCORES for processing
    _____.

B2.1. Burt's Rent-A-Car has the following rate structure. The standard
rental fee is $12 per day. The first 200 miles are free. For every
mile driven over 200 miles, the customer is charged 12 cents per
mile. This is true regardless of how many days the car is rented.
Produce a report showing the amount due to Burt's Rent-A-Car
for each customer. Also print the total amount due. For each
customer, print the name, type of car, daily charge, mileage
charge, and total charge. Use PRINT USING statements to
format the output. A sample data set follows:

HANDS-ON ASSIGNMENTS

Name	Type of Car	No. of Days	No. of Miles
Allen Benson	Ford Escort	5	3000
Benson Conrad	Chevy S-10	1	150
Conrad Edwards	Pontiac J2000	3	1000
Edwards James	AMC Eagle	4	180
James Roberts	Capri	2	400

B2.2. Calculate the mean and standard deviation of the following test scores: 70, 80, 90, 95, 98, 78, 60, 50, 48, 68, 75, 85, 95, 100, 82, 74, 66. The mean is equal to the total of all scores divided by the number of scores. One formula for the standard deviation is:

$$\text{Standard deviation} = \sqrt{\frac{\Sigma(X - M)^2}{n}}$$

This means that once the mean is calculated, it is subtracted from each score, and the difference is squared. Once these squares have been totaled, the result is divided by the number of scores. The standard deviation is the square root of the quotient.

B2.3. The Economic Order Quantity is a way of determining the optimal number of inventory items to be ordered based on annual demand, ordering cost, and holding cost. Write a program that will allow you to input pertinent data interactively and will output the EOQ. Run at least five trials.

$$\text{EOQ} = \sqrt{\frac{2\,D * S}{H}}$$

where
  D = Annual demand
  S = Cost to order
  H = Holding cost

B2.4. The Pythagorean theorem establishes the following relationships between the legs of a right triangle and the hypotenuse.

$$A^2 + B^2 = C^2$$

where A and B are legs and C is the hypotenuse. Use the random generator to produce 15 pairs of legs. Use the INT function to ensure that all legs have lengths that are whole numbers between 1 and 20, inclusive. Determine the length of the hypotenuse with the Pythagorean theorem and print the lengths of all sides.

B2.5. Use the following formula for compounding interest to determine the value of a dollar compounded annually for a period of 15 years at interest rates varying from 5 to 7.5 percent at increments of .25 of a percent (5%, 5.25%, 5.50%, and so on).

$$\text{Ending balance} = \text{Principal} * (1 + \text{Rate})^n$$

where
  n = Number of years
Print the ending balance at the end of each year for each rate.

B2.6. Modify program B2.5 to compound the interest quarterly, monthly, and daily. Continue to print the results on a yearly basis.

B2.7. Use the random number generator to simulate flips of a coin. Assume that a coin cannot land on its edge so that heads and tails are the only possibilities. Four coins are to be flipped simultaneously in each trial. Simulate 25 trails. There are 16 possibilities if order is important. See how many of the 16 your simulation produces.

B2.8. Have the computer draw a graph of the log function, y = Log x.

B2.9. Use the DIM statement to sort 10 data elements (names, numbers, and so on) in a one-dimensional array. Names should be sorted in alphabetical order; numbers should be arranged from the lowest to highest. Use the *bubble sort* technique, where the lower data elements "bubble up" to the top of an array. You can accomplish this by comparing the first two data elements and interchanging them if the second is smaller than the first. Repeat this process for the second and third elements, the third and fourth elements, and so on, until you have compared the rest of the data elements in the array. Then start at the beginning of the array again and continue to repeat the entire process until a complete *iteration* results in no further exchanges of elements. This process will produce a completely sorted list of data items.

B2.10. Write a program that will accept data interactively and write the data out to a file. Use the data from program B2.1. Add more data if you desire.

B2.11. Modify program B2.1 so that it reads the data sequentially from a file instead of from data statements.

B2.12. Following are a data file and a transaction file. They are both in ascending order according to account number. Write a program that will maintain correct information by adding, changing, or deleting records. Each record in the master file contains an account number, a name, and a balance. Each record in the transaction file contains an account number, a name, an amount, and a transaction code. The transaction codes have the following meanings:

Code Meaning	Master File	Transaction File
1. Change name	1000, Allen Benson, 420	1111, Jan Morgan, 300, 2
2. Add an account	2000, Benson Conrad, 200	2000, Benson Conrad, 0, 3
3. Delete an account	3000, Conrad Edwards, 1000	2345, Dawn Breaks, 500, 2
4. Deposit	4000, Edward James, 1500	5000, James Leonard, 200, 4
5. Withdrawal	5000, James Leonard, 1000	6000, Leonard Morgan, 150, 5
	6000, Leonard Morgan, 600	7000, Morgan Stevens, 0, 1
	7000, Morgan Stevens, 750	9000, Mary June, 200, 4
	8000, Stephanie Mary, 900	
	9000, Mary June, 2000	

GLOSSARY FOR COMPUTER USERS

The following extensive glossary includes terms that are fundamental to effective understanding and communication between *business computer users* and *computer specialists*. Most definitions used are consistent with those published by several official sources. However, the form of such definitions is *not* designed to express exact standards for computer professionals but to assist the beginning computer user in business.

Access Method A technique for moving data between primary storage and input/output and secondary storage devices.

Access Time The time interval between the instant that the CPU requests a transfer of data to or from a storage device and the instant such an operation is completed.

Accumulator A register in which the results of arithmetic operations are accumulated.

Acoustic Coupler A modem that converts digital data into a sequence of tones that are transmitted by a conventional telephone handset to a receiving modem, which transforms the data back to digital form.

Ada A programming language named after Augusta Ada Byron, considered the world's first computer programmer. Developed in 1980 for the U.S. Department of Defense as a standard high-order language. It resembles an extension of Pascal.

Address A name, number, or code that identifies a particular location in storage or any other data source or destination.

ADP: Automatic Data Processing Data processing performed by electronic or electrical machines with a minimum of human assistance or intervention.

ALGOL: ALGOrithmic Language An international procedure-oriented language that is widely used in Europe. Like FORTRAN, it was designed primarily for scientific-mathematical applications.

Algorithm A set of well-defined rules or processes for the solution of a problem in a finite number of steps.

Alphanumeric Pertaining to a character set that contains letters of the alphabet, numeric digits, and special characters such as punctuation marks.

Analog Computer A computer that operates on data by measuring changes in continuous physical variables such as voltage, resistance, and rotation. Contrast with Digital Computer.

APL: A Programming Language A mathematically oriented language originated by Kenneth E. Iverson of IBM. Realtime and interactive versions of APL are being utilized in many time-sharing systems.

Application Development System A system of computer programs that provides interactive assistance to programmers in the development of application programs.

Application Generator A software package that supports the development of an application through an interactive terminal dialogue, where the programmer/analyst defines screens, reports, computations, and data structures using a high-level language.

G

Application Software   Programs that specify the information processing activities required for the completion of specific tasks of computer users. Examples are electronic spreadsheet and word processing programs or inventory or payroll programs.

Arithmetic-Logic Unit (ALU)   The unit of a computing system containing the circuits that perform arithmetic and logical operations.

Array   An arrangement of elements in one or more dimensions.

Artificial Intelligence (AI)   An area of computer science attempting to develop computers that can hear, walk, talk, feel, and think. A major thrust is the development of computer functions normally associated with human intelligence, for example, reasoning, inference, learning, and problem solving.

ASCII: American Standard Code for Information Interchange   A standard code used for information interchange among data processing systems, communication systems, and associated equipment. The coded character set consists of seven-bit coded characters (eight-bits including a parity check bit).

Assemble   To translate a symbolic language program into a machine language program by substituting absolute operation codes for symbolic operation codes and absolute or relocatable addresses for symbolic addresses.

Assembler   A computer program that assembles.

Assembler Language   A programming language that utilizes symbols to represent operation codes and storage locations. Also called a symbolic language.

Asynchronous   Involving a sequence of operations without a regular or predictable time relationship. Thus operations do not happen at regular timed intervals, but an operation will begin only after a previous operation is completed. In data transmission, involves the use of start and stop bits with each character to indicate the beginning and end of the character being transmitted.

Audio-Response Unit   An output device of a computer system whose output consists of the spoken word. Also called a voice synthesizer.

Audit Trail   The presence of media and procedures that allow a transaction to be traced through all stages of information processing, beginning with its appearance on a source document and ending with its transformation into information on a final output document.

Automated Office Systems   Automated systems that combine word processing, data processing, telecommunications, and information systems technologies to automate office communications and activities.

Automatic Teller Machine (ATM)   A special-purpose intelligent terminal used to provide remote banking services.

Automation   The automatic transfer and positioning of work by machines or the automatic operation and control of a work process by machines, that is, without significant human intervention or operation.

Auxiliary Operation   An offline operation performed by equipment not under control of the central processing unit.

Auxiliary Storage   Storage that supplements the primary storage of the computer. Same as Secondary Storage.

Back-End Processor   Typically a smaller general-purpose computer that is dedicated to database processing using a database management system (DBMS). Also called a database machine.

Background Processing   The automatic execution of lower-priority computer programs when higher-priority programs are not using the resources of the computer system. Contrast with Foreground Processing.

Backup   Standby equipment or procedures for use in the event of failure, damage, or overloading of normally used equipment and facilities.

Bar Codes   Vertical marks or bars placed on merchandise, tags, or packaging that can be sensed and read by optical character-reading devices. The width and combination of vertical lines are used to represent data.

BASIC: Beginner's All-Purpose Symbolic Instruction Code   A programming language developed at Dartmouth College that is popular for microcomputer and time-sharing systems.

Batch Processing   A category of data processing in which data is accumulated into "batches" and processed periodically. Contrast with Realtime Processing.

Baud   A unit of measurement used to specify data transmission speeds. It is a unit of signaling speed equal to the number of discrete conditions or signal events per second. In many data communications applications it represents one bit per second.

Binary   Pertaining to a characteristic or property involving a selection, choice, or condition in which there are two possibilities, or pertaining to the number system that utilizes a base of two.

Bit   A contraction of "binary digit" that can have the value of either 0 or 1.

Block   A grouping of contiguous data records or other data elements that are handled as a unit.

Blocking Combining several data records or other data elements into blocks in order to increase the efficiency of input, output, or storage operations.

Bootstrap A technique in which the first few instructions of a program are sufficient to bring the rest of itself into the computer from an input device.

Branch A transfer of control from one instruction to another in a computer program that is not part of the normal sequential execution of the instructions of the program.

Bubble Memory See Magnetic Bubble.

Buffer Temporary storage used to compensate for a difference in rate of flow of data, or time of occurrence of events, when transmitting data from one device to another.

Bug A mistake or malfunction.

Bundling The inclusion of software, maintenance, training, and other products or services in the price of a computer system.

Bus A set of conducting paths for movement of data and instructions that interconnects the various components of the CPU. It may take the form of a cable containing many wires or of microscopic conducting lines on a microcomputer chip.

Business Information System Information systems within a business organization that support one of the traditional functions of business such as marketing, finance, or production. Business information systems can be either operations or management information systems.

Byte A sequence of adjacent binary digits operated on as a unit and usually shorter than a computer word. In many computer systems, a byte is a grouping of eight bits that can represent one alphabetic or special character or can be "packed" with two decimal digits.

C A low-level structured language developed by AT&T–Bell Laboratories as part of the UNIX operating system. It resembles a machine-independent assembler language and is presently popular for system software programming.

Cache Memory A high-speed temporary storage area in the CPU for storing parts of a program or data during processing.

Calculator A data processing device suitable for performing arithmetical operations that requires frequent intervention by a human operator.

Cathode Ray Tube (CRT) An electronic vacuum tube (television screen) that displays the output of a computer system.

CD–ROM An optical disk technology for microcomputers featuring compact disks with a storage capacity of over 500 megabytes.

Cellular Radio A radio communications technology that divides a metropolitan area into a honeycomb of cells to greatly increase the number of frequencies and thus the users that can take advantage of mobile phone service.

Central Processing Unit (CPU) The unit of a computer system that includes the circuits that control the interpretation and execution of instructions. In many computer systems, the CPU includes the arithmetic-logic unit, the control unit, and primary storage unit. The CPU is also known as the central processor or the mainframe.

Chain A list of data records that are linked by means of pointers. Though the data records may be physically dispersed, each record contains an identifier by which the next record can be located.

Channel A path along which signals can be sent. More specifically, a small special-purpose processor that controls the movement of data between the CPU and input/output devices.

Character Printers Slow-speed printers that print serially (one character at a time) as typewriters do.

Charge-Coupled Device (CCD) A slower serial access form of semiconductor memory that uses a silicone crystal's own structure to store data.

Check Bit A binary check digit; for example, a parity bit.

Check Digit A digit in a data field that is utilized to check for errors or loss of characters in the data field as a result of data transfer operations.

Check Point A place in a program where a check or a recording of data for restart purposes is performed.

Chief Information Officer A senior management position that oversees all information technology for a firm, concentrating on long-range information system planning and strategy.

Clock (1) A device that generates periodic signals utilized to control the timing of a synchronous computer. (2) A register whose contents change at regular intervals in such a way as to measure time.

COBOL: COmmon Business Oriented Language A widely used business data processing language.

CODASYL: COnference on DAta SYstems Languages The group of representatives of users and computer manufacturers who developed and maintain the COBOL language.

Code Computer instructions.

Coding Developing the programming language instructions that direct a computer to perform a data processing assignment.

Collate To combine items from two or more ordered sets into one set having a specified order not necessarily the same as any of the original sets.

Communications Carrier An organization that supplies communications services to other organizations and to the public as authorized by government agencies.

Communications Channel The part of a communications system that connects the message source with the message receiver. It includes the physical equipment used to connect one location to another for the purpose of transmitting and receiving information. Frequently used as a synonym for communications link or communications line.

Communications Controller A data communications interface device (frequently a special-purpose mini or microcomputer) that can control a data communications network containing many terminals.

Communications Control Program A computer program that controls and supports the communications between the computers and terminals in a data communications network.

Communications Monitors Computer programs that control and support the communications between the computers and terminals in a data communications network.

Communications Processors Multiplexers, concentrators, communications controllers, and cluster controllers that allow a communications channel to carry simultaneous data transmissions from many terminals. They may also perform error monitoring, diagnostics, and correction, modulation-demodulation, data compression, data coding and decoding, message switching, port contention, buffer storage, and serving as an interface to satellite and other advanced communications networks.

Communications Satellite Earth satellites placed in stationary orbits above the equator that serve as relay stations for communications signals transmitted from earth stations.

Compile To translate a high-level programming language into a machine-language program.

Compiler A program that compiles.

Computer (1) a data processing device that can perform substantial computation, including numerous arithmetic or logic operations, without intervention by a human operator during the processing. (2) A device that has the ability to accept data, internally store, and execute a program of instructions, perform mathematical, logical, and manipulative operations on data, and report the results.

Computer-Aided Design (CAD) The use of computers and advanced graphics hardware and software to provide interactive design assistance for engineering and architectural design.

Computer-Aided Manufacturing (CAM) The use of minicomputers and other computers to automate the operations systems of a manufacturing plant.

Computer-Aided Software Engineering (CASE) Designing, coding, and testing computer programs with the interactive assistance of computer hardware and software. This includes the automation of program code generation using application development systems.

Computer Application The use of a computer to solve a specific problem or to accomplish a particular job for a computer user. For example, common business computer applications include sales order processing, inventory control, and payroll.

Computer-Assisted Data Entry Methods and devices that use the computer itself to assist a user or data entry operator while performing the data input function.

Computer-Assisted Instruction (CAI) The use of computers to provide drills, practice exercises, and tutorial sequences to students.

Computer-Based Information System An information system that uses computer hardware and software to perform its information processing activities.

Computer Industry The industry composed of firms that supply computer hardware, software, and EDP services.

Computer-Integrated Manufacturing A concept that stresses that computer use in manufacturing must be an integrated system of computer-based technologies.

Computer Program A series of instructions or statements, in a form acceptable to a computer, prepared in order to achieve a certain result.

Computer Specialist A person whose occupation is related to the providing of computer services in computer-using organizations or in the computer industry, for example, a systems analyst, programmer, or computer operator.

Computer System Computer hardware as a system of input, processing, output, storage, and control components. Thus a computer system consists of input and output devices, primary and secondary storage devices, the central processing unit, the control unit within the CPU, and other peripheral devices.

Computer User Anyone who uses a computer system or its output. Same as end user.

Concentrator A special-purpose mini or microcomputer that accepts information from many terminals using slow-speed lines and transmits data to a main computer system over a high-speed line.

Concurrent Processing The generic term for the capability of computers to work on several tasks at the same time, that is, concurrently. This may involve specific capabilities such as overlapped processing, multiprocessing, multiprogramming, multitasking, parallel processing, and so on.

Conditional Transfer A transfer of control in the execution of a computer program that occurs if specified criteria are met.

Console That part of a computer used for communication between the operator and the computer.

Control (1) The systems component that evaluates feedback to determine whether the system is moving toward the achievement of its goal and then makes any necessary adjustments to the input and processing components of the system to ensure that proper output is produced. (2) Sometimes synonymous with feedback-control. (3) A management function that involves observing and measuring organizational performance and environmental activities and modifying the plans and activities of the organization when necessary.

Control Program A program that assists in controlling the operations and managing the resources of a computer system. It is usually part of an operating system.

Control Unit A subunit of the central processing unit that controls and directs the operations of the entire computer system. The control unit retrieves computer instructions in proper sequence, interprets each instruction, and then directs the other parts of the computer system in the implementation of a computer program.

Counter A device such as a register or storage location used to represent the number of occurrences of an event.

Cryogenics The study and use of devices utilizing the properties of materials at super cold temperatures. The superconductive nature of such materials provides ultrahigh-speed computer logic and memory circuits.

Cursor A movable point of light displayed on most video display screens to assist the user in the input of data. The cursor may look like a dot, short underline, or other shape that indicates the position of data to be entered or changed.

Cybernetic System A system that uses feedback and control components to achieve a self-monitoring and self-regulating capability.

Cylinder An imaginary vertical cylinder consisting of the vertical alignment of data tracks on each surface of magnetic disks, which are accessed simultaneously by the read/write heads of a disk storage device.

Data Facts or observations about physical phenomena or business transactions.

Data Administration Managing and developing the databases and information resources of an organization.

Data Bank (1) A comprehensive collection of libraries of data utilized by an organization. (2) A centralized common database that supports several major information systems of an organization.

Database A collection of logically related records or files. A database consolidates many records previously stored in separate files so that a common pool of data records serves as a single central file or data bank for many data processing applications.

Database Management System (DBMS) A generalized set of computer programs that controls the creation, maintenance, and utilization of the databases and data files of an organization.

Database Processing System An information system that uses a common database for both the storage and processing of data.

Data Communications Pertaining to the transmitting of data over electronic communication links between a computer system and a number of terminals at some physical distance away from the computer.

Data Dictionary A file containing information about the content, relationships, and structure of one or more databases. It may also refer to the software that supports the creation and maintenance of this file.

Data Entry The process of converting data into a form suitable for entry into a computer system. Also called data capture or input preparation.

Data Flow Diagram A diagramming methodology that expresses the logical data flows in a system.

Data Management Control program functions that provide access to data sets, enforce data storage conventions, and regulate the use of input/output devices.

Data Processing The execution of a systematic sequence of operations performed upon data to transform it into information.

Data Processing System A system that accepts data as input and processes it into information as output.

Debug To detect, locate, and remove errors from a program or malfunctions from a computer.

Decision Support System (DSS) An information system that utilizes decision rules, decision models, a database, and a decision maker's own insights in an interactive computer-based process, leading to a specific decision by a specific decision maker.

Decision Table   A table of all contingencies that are to be considered in the description of a problem, together with the actions to be taken.

Dedicated Computer   Typically, a general-purpose computer that has been "dedicated," or committed, to a particular data processing task or application.

Desktop Publishing   The use of microcomputers, laser printers, and page-makeup software to produce a variety of printed materials, formerly done only by professional printers.

Diagnostics   Messages transmitted by a computer during language translation or program execution that pertain to the diagnosis or identification of errors in a program or malfunctions in equipment.

Digital Computer   A computer that operates on digital data by performing arithmetic and logical operations on the data. Contrast with Analog Computer.

Digitizer   A device that is used to convert drawings and other graphic images on paper or other materials into digital data that is entered into a computer system.

Direct Access   A method of storage where each storage position has a unique address and can be individually accessed in approximately the same period of time without having to search through other storage positions.

Direct Access Storage Device (DASD)   A storage device that can directly access data to be stored or retrieved, for example, a magnetic disk unit.

Direct Data Organization   A method of data organization in which logical data elements are distributed randomly on or within the physical data medium. For example, logical data records distributed randomly on the surfaces of a magnetic disk file. Also called direct organization.

Direct Input/Output   Devices such as terminals that allow data to be input into a computer system or output from the computer system without the use of machine-readable media.

Direct Memory Access (DMA)   A type of computer architecture in which intelligent components other than the CPU (such as a channel) can directly access data in main memory.

Disk Pack   A removable unit containing several magnetic disks that can be mounted on a magnetic disk storage unit.

Display   A visual presentation of data.

Distributed Databases   The concept of distributing databases or portions of a database at remote sites where the data is most frequently referenced. Sharing of data is made possible through a network that interconnects the distributed databases.

Distributed Processing   Also called distributed data processing (DDP). A major form of decentralization of information processing made possible by a network of computers dispersed throughout an organization. Processing of user applications is accomplished by several computers interconnected by a data communication network rather than relying on one large centralized computer facility or on the decentralized operation of several completely independent computers.

Document   (1) A medium on which data has been recorded for human use, such as a report or invoice. (2) In word processing, a generic term for text material such as letters, memos, reports, and so on.

Documentation   A collection of documents or information that describes a computer program, information system, or required data processing operations.

Downtime   The time interval during which a device is malfunctioning or inoperative.

Dump   To copy the contents of all or part of a storage device, usually from an internal device onto an external storage device.

Duplex   In communications, pertaining to a simultaneous two-way independent transmission in both directions.

Dynamic Relocation   The movement of part or all of an active computer program and data from one part or type of storage to another without interrupting the proper execution of the program.

EBCDIC: Extended Binary Coded Decimal Interchange Code   An eight-bit code that is widely used by current computers.

Echo Check   A method of checking the accuracy of transmission of data in which the received data are returned to the sending device for comparison with the original data.

EDI: Electronic Data Interchange   The electronic transmission of source documents between the computers of different organizations.

Edit   To modify the form or format of data, for example, to insert or delete characters such as page numbers or decimal points.

EFT: Electronic Funds Transfer   The development of banking and payment systems that transfer funds electronically instead of using cash or paper documents such as checks.

Electronic Bulletin Board   A service of personal computer networks in which electronic messages can be stored for other subscribers to read and copy.

Electronic Data Processing (EDP)   The use of electronic computers to process data automatically.

Electronic Mail The transmission, storage, and distribution of text material in electronic form over communications networks.

Electronic Spreadsheet Package An application program used as a computerized tool for analysis, planning, and modeling that allows users to enter and manipulate data into an electronic worksheet of rows and columns.

Emulation To imitate one system with another so that the imitating system accepts the same data, executes the same programs, and achieves the same results as the imitated system. Contrast with Simulation.

Encryption To scramble data or convert it, prior to transmission, to a secret code that masks the meaning of the data to unauthorized recipients. Similar to enciphering.

End User See Computer User.

Ergonomics The science and technology emphasizing the safety, comfort, and ease of use of human-operated machines such as computers. The goal of ergonomics is to produce systems that are user friendly, that is, safe, comfortable, and easy to use. Ergonomics is also called human factors engineering.

Executive Information Systems An information system that provides strategic information tailored to the needs of top management.

Expert System A computer-based information system that uses its knowledge about a specific complex application area to act as an expert consultant to users. The system consists of a knowledge base and software modules that perform inferences on the knowledge, and communicates answers to a user's questions.

Facilities Management The use of an external service organization to operate and manage the electronic data processing facilities of an organization.

Facsimile The transmission of images and their reconstruction and duplication on some form of paper at a receiving station.

Feasibility Study Part of the process of systems development that determines the information needs of prospective users and the objectives, constraints, basic resource requirements, cost/benefits, and feasibility of proposed projects.

Feedback (1) Data or information concerning the components and operations of a system. (2) The use of part of the output of a system as input to the system.

Feedback-Control A systems characteristic that combines the functions of feedback and control. Data or information concerning the components and opera-

tions of a system (feedback) is evaluated to determine whether the system is moving toward the achievement of its goal, with any necessary adjustments being made to the system to ensure that proper output is produced (control).

Fiber Optics The technology that uses cables consisting of very thin filaments of glass fibers that can conduct the light generated by lasers at transmission frequencies that approach the speed of light.

Field A subdivision of a data record that consists of a grouping of characters that describe a particular category of data, for example, a name field or a sales amount field. Also sometimes called an item or word.

Fifth-Generation Computer An advanced computer that will be able to see, hear, talk, and think. This would depend on major advances in parallel processing, user input/output methods, and artificial intelligence.

File A collection of related data records treated as a unit. Sometimes called a data set.

File Maintenance The activity of keeping a file up-to-date by adding, changing, or deleting data.

File Processing Utilizing a file for data processing activities such as file maintenance, information retrieval, or report generation.

Firmware The use of microprogrammed read only memory circuits in place of "hardwired" logic circuitry. See also Microprogramming.

Fixed-Length Record A data record that always contains the same number of characters or fields. Contrast with Variable-Length Record.

Fixed Word Length Pertaining to a computer word or operand that always has the same number of bits or characters. Contrast with Variable Word Length.

Flag Any of various types of indicators used for identification.

Flip-Flop A circuit or device containing active elements, capable of assuming either one or two states at a given time. Synonymous with toggle.

Floating-Point Pertaining to a number representation system in which each number is represented by two sets of digits. One set represents the significant digits or fixed-point "base" of the number, while the other set of digits represents the "exponent," which indicates the precision of the radix point.

Floppy Disk A small plastic disk coated with iron oxide that resembles a small phonograph record enclosed in a protective envelope. It is a widely used form of magnetic disk media that provides a direct access storage capability for microcomputer systems.

Flowchart A graphical representation in which symbols are used to represent operations, data, flow, logic, equipment, and so on. A program flowchart illustrates the structure and sequence of operations of a program, while a system flowchart illustrates the components and flows of information systems.

Foreground Processing The automatic execution of the computer programs that have been designed to preempt the use of computing facilities. Contrast with Background Processing.

Format The arrangement of data on a medium.

FORTRAN: FORmula TRANslation A high-level programming language widely utilized to develop computer programs that perform mathematical computations for scientific, engineering, and selected business applications.

Fourth-Generation Languages (4GL) Programming languages that are easier to use than high-level languages like BASIC, COBOL, or FORTRAN. They are also known as nonprocedural, natural, or very high-level languages.

Front-End Processor Typically a smaller, general-purpose computer that is dedicated to handling data communications control functions in a communications network, thus relieving the host computer of these functions.

Function A specific purpose of an entity or its characteristic action.

General-Purpose Application Programs Programs that can perform common information processing jobs for users from all application areas. For example, word processing programs, electronic spreadsheet programs, and graphics programs can be used by individuals for home, education, business, scientific, and many other purposes.

General-Purpose Computer A computer that is designed to handle a wide variety of problems. Contrast with Special-Purpose Computer.

Generate To produce a machine-language program by selecting from among various alternative subsets of coding the subset that embodies the most suitable methods for performing a specific data processing task based on parameters supplied by a programmer or user.

Generator A computer program that performs a generating function.

Gigabyte One billion bytes. More accurately, 2 to the 30th power, or 1,073,741,824 in decimal notation.

GIGO A contraction of "Garbage In, Garbage Out," which emphasizes that information systems will produce erroneous and invalid output when provided with erroneous and invalid input data or instructions.

Graphics Pertaining to symbolic input or output from a computer system, such as lines, curves, and geometric shapes, using video display units or graphics plotters and printers.

Graphics Software A program that helps users generate graphics displays.

Handshaking Exchange of predetermined signals when a connection is established between two communications terminals.

Hard Copy A data medium or data record that has a degree of permanence and that can be read by people or machine.

Hardware (1) Machines and media. (2) Physical equipment, as opposed to computer programs or methods of use. (3) Mechanical, magnetic, electrical, or electronic devices. Contrast with Software.

Hash Total The sum of the numbers in a data field that is not normally added, such as account numbers or other identification numbers. It is utilized as a control total, especially during input/output operations of batch processing systems.

Header Label A machine-readable record at the beginning of a file containing data for file identification and control.

Heuristic Pertaining to exploratory methods of problem solving in which solutions are discovered by evaluation of the progress made toward the final result. It is an exploratory trial-and-error aproach guided by rules of thumb. Contrast with Algorithmic.

Hexadecimal Pertaining to the number system with a radix of 16. Synonymous with sexadecimal.

High-Level Language A programming language that utilizes macro instructions and statements that closely resemble human language or mathematical notation to describe the problem to be solved or the procedure to be used. Also called a compiler language.

HIPO Chart (Hierarchy + Input/Processing/Output) Also known as an IPO Chart. A design and documentation tool of structured programming utilized to record input/processing/output details of the hierarchical program modules.

Hollerith Pertaining to a type of code or punched card utilizing 12 rows per column and usually 80 columns per card. Named after Herman Hollerith, who originated punched card data processing.

Host Computer Typically a larger central computer that performs the major data processing tasks in a computer network.

Icon A small figure on a video display that looks like a familiar office or other device such as a file folder (for storing a file), a wastebasket (for deleting a file), or a calculator (for switching to a calculator mode).

Impact Printers   Printers that form images on paper through the pressing of a printing element and an inked ribbon or roller against the face of a sheet of paper.

Index   An ordered reference list of the contents of a file or document together with keys or reference notations for identification or location of those contents.

Index Register   A register whose contents may be added to or subtracted from the operand address prior to or during the execution of a computer instruction.

Index Sequential   A method of data organization in which records are organized in sequential order and also referenced by an index. When utilized with direct access file devices, it is known as index sequential access method or ISAM.

Information   (1) Data that has been transformed into a meaningful and useful form for specific human beings. (2) The meaning that a human assigns to data by means of the known conventions used in its representation.

Information Center   A support facility for the computer users of an organization. It allows users to learn to develop their own application programs and to accomplish their own information processing tasks. The users are provided with hardware support, software support, and people support (trained user consultants).

Information Processing   A concept that covers both the traditional concept of processing numeric and alphabetic data, and the processing of text, images, and voices. It emphasizes that the production of information products for users should be the focus of processing activities.

Information Processing System   Same as Data Processing System.

Information Resource Management (IRM)   A management concept that views data, information, and computer resources (computer hardware, software, and personnel) as valuable organizational resources that should be efficiently, economically, and effectively managed for the benefit of the entire organization.

Information Retrieval   The methods and procedures for recovering specific information from stored data.

Information System   A system that uses the resources of hardware (machines and media), software (programs and procedures), and people (users and specialists) to perform input, processing, output, storage, and control activities that transform data resources into information products.

Information Theory   The branch of learning concerned with the likelihood of accurate transmission or communication of messages subject to transmission failure, distortion, and noise.

Initialize   To set counters, switches, addresses, and variables to zero or other starting values at the beginning of or at prescribed points in a computer program.

Input   Pertaining to a device, process, or channel involved in the insertion of data into a data processing system. Opposite of Output.

Input/Output (I/O)   Pertaining to either input or output, or both.

Input/Output Control System (IOCS)   Programs that control the flow of data into and out of the computer system.

Input/Output Interface Hardware   Devices such as I/O ports, I/O busses, buffers, channels, and input/output control units, which assist the CPU in its input/output assignments. These devices make it possible for modern computer systems to perform input, output, and processing functions simultaneously.

Inquiry   A request for information from a computer system.

Installation   (1) The process of installing new computer hardware or software. (2) A data processing facility such as a computer installation.

Instruction   A grouping of characters that specifies the computer operation to be performed and the values or locations of its operands.

Instruction Cycle   The phase in the execution of a computer instruction during which the instruction is called from storage and the required circuitry to perform the instructions is readied.

Integer   A whole number, as opposed to a real number, that has fractional parts.

Integrated Circuit   A complex microelectronic circuit consisting of interconnected circuit elements that cannot be disassembled because they are placed on or within a "continuous substrate" such as a silicon chip.

Integrated Packages   Software that combines the ability to do several general-purpose applications (such as word processing, electronic spreadsheet, and graphics) into one program.

Intelligent Terminal   A terminal with the capabilities of a microcomputer or minicomputer, which can thus perform many data processing and other functions without accessing a larger computer.

Interactive Processing   A type of realtime processing in which users at online terminals can interact with the computer on a realtime basis. This may take the form of inquiry/response, conversational computing, online data entry, or interactive programming.

Interactive Program   A computer program that permits data to be entered or the flow of the program to be changed during its execution.

Interface   A shared boundary, such as the boundary between two systems, for example, the boundary between a computer and its peripheral devices.

Interpreter   A computer program that translates and executes each source language statement before translating and executing the next one.

Interrupt   A condition that causes an interruption in a data processing operation during which another data processing task is performed. At the conclusion of this new data processing assignment, control may be transferred back to the point where the original data processing operation was interrupted or to other tasks with a higher priority.

Inverted File   A method of data organization in which a data element identifies a record in a file instead of the original identifier or key.

Iterative   Pertaining to the repeated execution of a series of steps.

Job   A specified group of tasks prescribed as a unit of work for a computer.

Job Control Language (JCL)   A language for communicating with the operating system of a computer to identify a job and describe its requirements.

Joystick   A small lever set in a box used to move the cursor on the computer's display screen.

Justify   (1) To adjust the printing positions of characters toward the left- or right-hand margins of a data field or page. (2) To shift the contents of a storage position so that the most or the least significant digit is at some specified position.

K   An abbreviation for the prefix "kilo," which is 1,000 in decimal notation. When referring to storage capacity it is equivalent to 2 to the 10th power, or 1,024 in decimal notation.

Key   One or more characters within an item of data that are used to identify it or control its use.

Keyboarding   Using the keyboard of a typewriter, word processor, or computer terminal.

Keypunch   (1) A keyboard-actuated device that punches holes in a card to represent data. Also called a card punch. (2) The act of using a keypunch to record data in a punched card.

Key-to-Disk   Data entry using a keyboard device to record data directly onto a magnetic disk.

Key-to-Tape   Data entry using a keyboard device to record data directly onto magnetic tape.

Knowledge Base   A computer-accessible collection of knowledge about a specific complex application area. It is a vital component of expert systems and other knowledge-based systems.

Label   One or more characters used to identify a statement or an item of data in a computer program or the contents of the data file.

Language   A set of representations, conventions, and rules used to convey information.

Language Translator Program   A program that can convert the programming language instructions of computer programs into machine language instructions. Also called language processors. Major types include assemblers, compilers, and interpreters.

Large-Scale Integration (LSI)   A method of constructing electronic circuits in which thousands of circuits can be placed on a single semiconductor chip.

Library   A collection of related files or programs.

Library Routine   A proven routine that is maintained in a program library.

Light Pen   A photoelectronic device that allows data to be entered or altered on the face of a video display terminal.

Line Printer   A device that prints all characters of a line as a unit. Contrast with Character Printer.

Linkage   In programming, the coding that connects two separately coded routines.

Liquid Crystal Displays (LCDs)   Electronic visual displays that form characters by applying an electrical charge to selected silicon crystals.

List   (1) An ordered set of items. (2) A method of data organization that uses indexes and pointers to allow for nonsequential retrieval.

List Processing   A method of processing data in the form of lists.

Load   To enter data or program instructions into primary storage or working registers.

Local Area Network (LAN)   A communications network that typically connects computers, terminals, and other computerized devices within a limited physical area such as an office building, manufacturing plant, or other worksite.

Log   A record of the operations of a data processing system.

Logical Data Elements   Data elements that are independent of the physical data media on which they are recorded.

LOGO   An interactive graphical language used as a tool for learning a variety of concepts (color, direction, letters, words, sounds, etc.) as well as learning to program and use the computer. Forms and figures are used (sprites and turtles) that a child learns to move around on the screen to accomplish tasks.

Loop A sequence of instructions in a computer program that is executed repeatedly until a terminal condition prevails.

Machine Cycle The timing of a basic CPU operation as determined by a fixed number of electrical pulses emitted by the CPU's timing circuitry or internal clock.

Machine Instruction An instruction that a computer can recognize and execute.

Machine Language A programming language where instructions are expressed in the binary code of the computer.

Macro Instruction An instruction in a source language that is equivalent to a specified sequence of machine instructions.

Magnetic Bubble An electromagnetic storage device that stores and moves data magnetically as tiny magnetic spots that look like bubbles under a microscope as they float on the surface of a special type of semiconductor chip.

Magnetic Core Tiny rings composed of iron oxide and other materials strung on wires that provide electrical current that magnetizes the cores. Data is represented by the direction of the magnetic field of groups of cores. Widely used as the primary storage media in second- and third-generation computer systems.

Magnetic Disk A flat circular plate with a magnetic surface on which data can be stored by selective magnetization of portions of the flat surface.

Magnetic Drum A circular cylinder with a magnetic surface on which data can be stored by selective magnetization of portions of the curved surface.

Magnetic Ink An ink that contains particles of iron oxide that can be magnetized and detected by magnetic sensors.

Magnetic Ink Character Recognition (MICR) The machine recognition of characters printed with magnetic ink. Contrast with Optical Character Recognition.

Magnetic Tape A tape with a magnetic surface on which data can be stored by selective magnetization of portions of the surface.

Mag Stripe Card A plastic wallet-size card with a strip of magnetic tape on one surface; widely used for bank credit cards.

Mainframe (1) Same as central processing unit. (2) A larger-size computer system, typically with a separate central processing unit, as distinguished from microcomputer and minicomputer systems.

Management Information System (MIS) An information system that pro-vides the information needed to support management functions.

Manual Data Processing (1) Data processing requiring continual human operation and intervention that utilizes simple data processing tools such as paper forms, pencils, and filing cabinets. (2) All data processing that is not automatic, even if it utilizes machines such as typewriters and calculators.

Mark-Sensing The electrical sensing of manually recorded conductive marks on a nonconductive surface.

Mass Storage (1) Devices having a large storage capacity, such as magnetic disks or drums. (2) Secondary storage devices with extra-large storage capacities (in the hundreds of millions of bytes) such as magnetic strip and card units.

Master File A data file containing relatively permanent information, which is utilized as an authoritative reference and is usually updated periodically. Contrast with Transaction File.

Mathematical Model A mathematical representation of a process, device, or concept.

Matrix A two-dimensional rectangular array of quantities.

Media All tangible objects on which data are recorded.

Megabyte One million bytes. More accurately, 2 to the 20th power, or 1,048,576 in decimal notation.

Memory Same as Storage.

Menu A displayed list of items (usually the names of data processing jobs) from which a video terminal operator makes a selection.

Menu Driven A characteristic of most interactive processing systems that provides menu displays and operator prompting to assit a video terminal operator in performing a particular job.

Merge To combine items from two or more similarly ordered sets into one set that is arranged in the same order.

Message An arbitrary amount of information whose beginning and end are defined or implied.

Microcomputer A very small computer, ranging in size from a "computer on a chip" to a small typewriter-size unit.

Micrographics The use of microfilm, microfiche, and other microforms to record data in greatly reduced form. The use of computers in the field of micrographics involves computer output microfilm or COM, in which microfilm is used as a computer output medium; computer input microfilm or CIM, where microfilm is used as an input medium; or computer-assisted retrieval or CAR, in which special-purpose computer terminals or minicomputers are used as micrographics terminals to locate and retrieve a document stored on microfilm.

Microprocessor (MPU)   A microcomputer central processing unit (CPU) on a chip and without input/output or primary storage capabilities in most types.

Microprogram   A small set of elementary control instructions called microinstructions or microcodes.

Microprogramming   The use of special software (microprograms) to perform the functions of special hardware (electronic control circuitry). Microprograms stored in a read-only storage module of the control unit interpret the machine language instructions of a computer program and decode them into elementary microinstructions, which are then executed.

Microsecond   A millionth of a second.

Millisecond   A thousandth of a second.

Minicomputer   A small (for example, the size of a desk) electronic, digital, stored-program, general-purpose computer.

Mnemonic   The use of symbols that are chosen to assist the human memory, typically abbreviations or contractions such as "MPY" for multiply.

Modem: MOdulator-DEModulator   A device that converts the digital signals from input/output devices into appropriate frequencies at a transmission terminal and converts them back into digital signals at a receiving terminal.

Module   A unit of hardware or software that is discrete and identifiable and designed for use with other units.

Monitor   Software or hardware that observes, supervises, controls, or verifies the operations of a system.

Mouse   A small device that is electronically connected to a computer and is moved by hand on a flat surface in order to move the cursor on a video screen in the same direction. Buttons on the mouse allow users to issue commands and make responses or selections.

Multiplex   To interleave or simultaneously transmit two or more messages on a single channel.

Multiplexor   An electronic device that allows a single communications channel to carry simultaneous data transmission from many terminals.

Multiprocessing   Pertaining to the simultaneous execution of two or more instructions by a computer or computer network.

Multiprocessor Computer System   Computer systems that use a multiprocessor architecture in the design of their central processing units. The CPU may contain several instruction processing units, support microprocessors, or multiple arithmetic-logic and control units.

Multiprogramming   Pertaining to the concurrent execution of two or more programs by a computer by interleaving their execution.

Multitasking   The concurrent use of the same computer to accomplish several different information processing tasks. Each task may require the use of a different program, or the concurrent use of the same copy of a program by several users.

Nanosecond   One billionth of a second.

Natural Language   A programming language that is very close to human language. Also called very high-level language.

Nest   To embed subroutines or data in other subroutines or data at different hierarchical levels.

Network   An interconnection of computers, terminals, and communications channels and devices.

Network Architecture   A master plan designed to promote an open, simple, flexible, and efficient data communications environment through the use of standard protocols, standard communications hardware and software interfaces, and the design of a standard multilevel data communications interface between end users and computer systems.

Node   A terminal point in a communications network.

Noise   (1) Random variations of one or more characteristics of any entity such as voltage, current, or data. (2) A random signal of known statistical properties of amplitude, distribution, and special density. (3) Any disturbance tending to interfere with the normal operation of a device or system.

Nonimpact Printers   Printers that use specially treated paper that form characters by laser, thermal (heat), electrostatic, or electrochemical processes.

Nonprocedural Languages   Programming languages that allow users and professional programmers to specify the results they want without specifying how to solve the problem.

Numeral   A discrete representation of a number.

Numeric   Pertaining to numerals or to representation by means of numerals. Synonymous with numerical.

Numerical Control   Automatic control of a process performed by a device that makes use of all or part of numerical data, generally introduced as the operation is in process. Also called machine control.

Object Program   A compiled or assembled program composed of executable machine instructions. Contrast with Source Program.

Octal   Pertaining to the number representation system with a radix of eight.

OEM: Original Equipment Manufacturer A firm that manufactures and sells computers by assembling components produced by other hardware manufacturers.

Offline Pertaining to equipment or devices not under control of the central processing unit.

Online Pertaining to equipment or devices under control of the central processing unit.

Operand That which is operated upon. That part of a computer instruction that is identified by the address part of the instruction.

Operating System The main control program of a computer system. It is a system of programs that controls the execution of computer programs and that may provide scheduling, debugging, input/output control, system accounting, compilation, storage assignment, data management, and related services.

Operation A defined action, namely, the act of obtaining a result from one or more operands in accordance with rules that specify the result for any permissible combination of operands.

Operation Code A code that represents specific operations. Synonymous with instruction code.

Operations Information System An information system that collects, processes, and stores data generated by the operations systems of an organization and produces data and information for input into a management information system or for the control of an operations system.

Operations System A basic subsystem of the business firm that constitutes its input, processing, and output components. Also called a physical system.

Optical Character Recognition (OCR) The machine identification of printed characters through the use of light-sensitive devices.

Optical Disks A secondary storage medium using laser technology to read tiny pits on a plastic disk. The disks are currently capable of storing billions of characters of information.

Optical Scanner A device that optically scans printed or written data and generates their digital representations.

Output Pertaining to a device, process, or channel involved with the transfer of data or information out of a data processing system.

Overlapped Processing Pertaining to the ability of a computer system to increase the utilization of its central processing unit by overlapping input/output and processing operations.

Pack To compress data in a storage medium by taking advantage of known characteristics of the data in such a way that the original data can be recovered.

Packet A group of data and control information in a specified format that is transferred as an entity.

Packet Switching A data transmission process that transmits addressed packets such that a channel is occupied only for the duration of transmission of the packet.

Page A segment of a program or data, usually of fixed length, that has a fixed virtual address but can in fact reside in any region of the internal storage of the computer.

Paging A process that automatically and continually transfers pages of programs and data between primary storage and direct access storage devices. It provides computers with advanced multiprogramming and virtual memory capabilities.

Parallel Pertaining to the concurrent or simultaneous occurrence of two or more related activities in multiple devices or channels.

Parallel Processing Executing many instructions at the same time, that is, in parallel. Performed by advanced computers using many instruction processors organized in clusters or networks.

Parity Bit A check bit appended to an array of binary digits to make the sum of all the binary digits, including the check bit, always odd or always even.

Parity Check A check that tests whether the number of ones or zeros in an array of binary digits is odd or even.

Pascal A high-level, general-purpose, structured programming language named after Blaise Pascal. It was developed by Niklaus Wirth of Zurich in 1968.

Pass One cycle of processing a body of data.

Patch To modify a routine in a rough or expedient way.

Pattern Recognition The identification of shapes, forms, or configurations by automatic means.

PCM: Plug Compatible Manufacturer A firm that manufactures computer equipment that can be plugged into existing computer systems without requiring additional hardware or software interfaces.

Peripheral Equipment In a data processing system, any unit of equipment, distinct from the central processing unit, that may provide the system with outside communication.

Personal Computing The use of microcomputers by individuals for educational, recreational, professional, and other personal applications.

PERT: Program Evaluation and Review Technique A network analysis technique utilized to find the most efficient scheduling of time and resources when developing a complex project or product.

Physical Data Element The physical data medium that contains one or more logical data elements. For example, a punched card is a single physical record that may contain several logical records.

Picosecond One trillionth of a second.

PILOT: Programmed Inquiry, Learning Or Teaching A special-purpose language designed to develop CAI (computer-aided instruction) programs. It is a simple interactive language that enables a person with minimal computer experience to develop and test interactive CAI programs.

PL/1: Programming Language 1 A procedure-oriented, high-level, general-purpose programming language designed to combine the features of COBOL, FORTRAN, and ALGOL.

Plasma Display Output devices that generate a visual display with electrically charged particles of gas trapped between glass plates.

Plotter A hard-copy output device that produces drawings and graphical displays on paper or other materials.

Pointer A data item associated with an index, a record, or other set of data that contains the address of a related record.

Point-of-Sale (POS) Terminal A computer terminal used in retail stores that serves the function of a cash register as well as collecting sales data and performing other data processing functions.

Port (1) Electronic circuitry that provides a connection point between the CPU and input/output devices. (2) A connection point for a communications line on a CPU or other front-end device.

Private Branch Exchange (PBX) A switching device that serves as an interface between the many telephone lines within a work area and the local telephone company's main telephone lines or trunks. Computerized PBXs can handle the switching of both voice and data in the local area networks that are needed in such locations.

Privileged Instruction A computer instruction whose use is restricted to the operating system of the computer and is not available for use in ordinary programs.

Problem-Oriented Language A programming language designed for the convenient expression of a given class of problems.

Procedure-Oriented Language A programming language designed for the convenient expression of procedures used in the solution of a wide class of problems.

Procedures Sets of instructions used by people to complete a task.

Process A systematic sequence of operations to produce a specified result.

Process Control The use of a computer to control an ongoing physical process such as industrial production.

Processor A hardware device or software system capable of performing operations upon data.

Program (1) A series of actions proposed in order to achieve a certain result. (2) An ordered set of computer instructions that cause a computer to perform a particular process. (3) The act of developing a program.

Program Library A collection of available computer programs and routines.

Programmed Decision A decision that can be automated by basing it on a decision rule that outlines the steps to take when confronted with the need for a specific decision.

Programmer A person mainly involved in designing, writing, and testing computer programs.

Programming The design, writing, and testing of a program.

Programming Language A language used to prepare computer programs.

Prompt Messages that assist the operator in performing a particular job. This would include error messages, correction suggestions, questions, and other messages that guide an operator.

Protocol A set of rules and procedures for the control of communications in a communications network.

Prototyping A "quick and dirty" type of systems development where an actual working model (a prototype) of the information system needed by a user is quickly developed using an application generator and an interactive process between a systems analyst and a user.

Pseudocode An informal design language of structured programming that expresses the processing logic of a program module in ordinary English-language phrases.

Punched Card A card punched with a pattern of holes to represent data.

Punched Tape A tape on which a pattern of holes or cuts is used to represent data.

Query A request for specific data or information.

Query Language   A high-level, English-like language provided by a database management system that enables users to easily extract data and information from a database.

Queue   (1) A waiting line formed by items in a system waiting for service. (2) To arrange in or form a queue.

Random Access   Same as Direct Access.

Random Access Memory (RAM)   One of the basic types of semiconductor memory used for temporary storage of data or programs during processing. Each memory position can be directly sensed (read) or changed (write) in the same length of time, irrespective of its location on the storage medium.

Random Data Organization   See Direct Data Organization.

Read   To acquire or interpret data from a storage device, a data medium, or any other source.

Read Only Memory (ROM)   A basic type of semiconductor memory used for permanent storage. Can only be read, not "written," that is, changed. Variations are Programmable Read Only Memory (PROM) and Erasable Programmable Read Only Memory (EPROM).

Realtime   Pertaining to the performance of data processing during the actual time a process transpires, in order that results of the data processing can be used in guiding the process.

Realtime Processing   Data processing in which data is processed immediately rather than periodically. Contrast with Batch Processing.

Record   A collection of related items or fields of data treated as a unit.

Register   A device capable of storing a specified amount of data such as one word.

Relative Address   The number that specifies the difference between the absolute address and the base address.

Remote Access   Pertaining to communication with the data processing facility by one or more stations that are distant from that facility.

Remote Job Entry (RJE)   Entering jobs into a batch processing system from a remote facility.

Reproduce   To prepare a duplicate of stored data or information.

Reprographics   Copying and duplicating technology and methods.

Robotics   The technology of building machines (robots) with computer intelligence and humanlike physical capabilities.

Routine   An ordered set of instructions that may have some general or frequent use.

RPG: Report Program Generator   A problem-oriented language that utilizes a generator to construct programs that produce reports and perform other data processing tasks.

Run   A single continuous performance of a computer program or routine.

Scan   To examine sequentially, part by part.

Schema   An overall conceptual or logical view of the relationships between the data in a database.

Secondary Storage   Storage that supplements the primary storage of a computer. Synonymous with Auxiliary Storage.

Sector   A subdivision of a track on a magnetic disk surface.

Semiconductor Secondary Storage (RAM Disk)   A method that uses software and control circuitry to make the main processor and the operating system program treat part of the computer's semiconductor storage (RAM) as if it were another disk drive. This offers the advantages of being faster and less expensive than magnetic disk units but has smaller storage capacities and is a volatile storage medium.

Sequence   An arrangement of items according to a specified set of rules. Contrast with Random.

Sequential Access   A sequential method of storing and retrieving data from a file. Contrast with Random Access.

Sequential Data Organization   Organizing logical data elements according to a prescribed sequence.

Serial   Pertaining to the sequential or consecutive occurrence of two or more related activities in a single device or channel.

Serial Access   Pertaining to the process of obtaining data from or placing data into storage, where the access time is dependent on the location of the data most recently obtained or placed in storage. Contrast with Direct Access.

Service Bureau   A firm offering computer and data processing services. Also called a computer service center.

Service Program   A program that provides general support for the operation of a computer system, such as input/output, diagnostic, and other "utility" routines.

Setup Time   The time required to set up the devices, materials, and procedures required for a particular data processing application.

Sign Position A position, normally located at one end of a numeral, that contains an indication of the algebraic sign of the number.

Simplex Pertaining to a communications link that is capable of transmitting data in only one direction. Contrast with Duplex.

Simulation The representation of certain features of the behavior of a physical or abstract system by the behavior of another system. Contrast with Emulation.

Smart Products Industrial and consumer products, with "intelligence" provided by built-in microcomputers or microprocessors that significantly improve the performance and capabilities of such products.

Software Computer programs and procedures concerned with the operation of an information system. Contrast with Hardware.

Software Package A computer program supplied by computer manufacturers, independent software companies, or other computer users. Also known as canned programs, proprietary software, or packaged programs.

Solid State Pertaining to devices whose operation depends on the control of electric or magnetic phenomenon in solids such as transistors and diodes.

Sort To segregate items into groups according to some definite rules.

Source Data Automation The use of automated methods of data entry that attempt to reduce or eliminate many of the activities, people, and data media required by traditional data entry methods.

Source Document The original written record of an activity, such as a purchase order or sales invoice.

Source Program A computer program written in a language that is an input to a translation process. Contrast with Object Program.

Special Character A graphic character that is neither a letter, a digit, nor a space character.

Special-Purpose Computer A computer that is designed to handle a restricted class of problems. Contrast with General-Purpose Computer.

Spooling Simultaneous peripheral operation online. Storing input data from low-speed devices temporarily on high-speed secondary storage units, which can be quickly accessed by the CPU. Also, writing output data at high speeds onto magnetic tape or disk units from which it can be transferred to slow-speed devices such as a card punch or printer.

Statement In computer programming, a meaningful expression or generalized instruction in a source program, particularly in high-level programming languages.

Storage Pertaining to a device into which data can be entered, in which they can be held, and from which they can be retrieved at a later time.

Storage Allocation The assignment of blocks of data to specified blocks of storage.

Storage Protection An arrangement for preventing access to storage for either reading or writing or both.

Store To enter or retain data in a storage device. Sometimes synonymous with storage device.

Stored Program Computer A computer controlled by internally stored instructions that can synthesize, store, and in some cases alter instructions as though they were data, and that can subsequently execute these instructions.

String A linear sequence of entities such as characters or physical elements.

Structure Chart A design and documentation technique used in structured programming to show the purpose and relationships of the various modules in a program.

Structured Programming A programming methodology that uses a top-down program design and a limited number of control structures in a program to create highly structured modules of program code.

Structured Walk-Throughs A structured programming methodology that requires a peer review by other programmers of the program design and coding to minimize and reveal errors in the early stages of programming.

Subroutine A routine that can be part of another routine.

Subschema A subset or transformation of the logical view of the database schema that is required by a particular user application program.

Subsystem A system that is a component of a larger system.

Supercomputer A special category of large mainframe computer systems that are the most powerful available. They are designed to solve massive computational problems.

Superconductor Materials which can conduct electricity with almost no resistance. This allows the development of extremely fast and small electronic circuits. Formerly only possible at super cold temperatures near absolute zero. Recent developments promise superconducting materials at room temperatures.

Supervisor The main control program of an operating system.

Switch (1) A device or programming technique for making a selection. (2) A computer that controls message switching among the computers and terminals in a data communications network.

Symbol A representation of something by reason of relationship, association, or convention.

Synchronous A characteristic in which each event, or the performance of any basic operation, is constrained to start on, and usually to keep in step with, signals from a timing clock. Contrast with Asynchronous.

Synergism A system characteristic where the whole of the system is equal to more than the sum of its component parts.

System (1) A group of interrelated or interacting elements forming a unified whole. (2) A group of interrelated components working together toward a common goal by accepting inputs and producing outputs in an organized transformation process. (3) An assembly of methods, procedures, or techniques united by regulated interaction to form an organized whole. (4) An organized collection of people, machines, and methods required to accomplish a set of specific functions.

Systems Analysis (1) Analyzing in detail the components and requirements of a system. (2) Analyzing in detail the information needs of an organization, the characteristics and components of presently utilized information systems, and the requirements of proposed information systems.

Systems Development (1) Conceiving, designing, and implementing a system. (2) Developing information systems by a process of investigation, analysis, design, implementation, and maintenance.

Systems Development Generator A software tool that allows analysts to define the inputs, outputs, processing, storage, and control requirements of an information system in a high-level, structured-type language. The requirements are analyzed by the system that will generate specifications for programs and hardware necessary to meet the requirements of the system.

Systems Software Programs that control and support operations of a computer system. System software includes a variety of programs such as operating systems, database management systems, communications control programs, service and utility programs, and programming language translators.

Table A collection of data in which each item is uniquely identified by a label, by its position relative to the other items, or by some other means.

Tabulate To form data into a table or to print totals.

Telecommunications Pertaining to the transmission of signals over long distances, including not only data communications but also the transmission of images and voices using radio, television, and other communications technologies.

Telecommuting The use of telecommunications to replace commuting to work from one's home.

Teleconferencing The use of video communications to allow business conferences to be held with participants who are scattered across a country, continent, or the world.

Teleprocessing See Data Communications.

Terabyte One trillion bytes. More accurately, 2 to the 40th power, or 1,009,511,627,776 in decimal notation.

Terminal A point in a system or communication network at which data can either enter or leave. Also, an input/output device at such a point in a system.

Text Data Words, phrases, sentences, and paragraphs used in documents and other forms of communication.

Throughput The total amount of useful work performed by a data processing system during a given period of time.

Time-Sharing Providing computer services to many users simultaneously while providing rapid responses to each.

Top-Down Design A methodology of structured programming in which a program is organized into functional modules, with the programmer designing the main module first and then the lower-level modules.

Touch-Sensitive Screen An input device that accepts data input by the placement of a finger on or close to the CRT screen.

Track The portion of a moving storage medium, such as a drum, tape, or disk, that is accessible to a given reading head position.

Trackball A rollerball device set in a case used to move the cursor on a computer's display screen.

Transaction An event that occurs as part of doing business, such as a sale, purchase, deposit, withdrawal, refund, transfer, payment, and so on.

Transaction File A data file containing relatively transient data to be processed in combination with a master file. Contrast with master file.

Transaction Processing System An information system that processes data arising from the occurrence of business transactions.

Transaction Terminal Terminals used in banks, retail stores, factories, and other worksites that are used to capture transaction data at its point of origin. Examples are point-of-sale (POS) terminals and automated teller machines (ATMs).

Transducer A device for converting energy from one form to another.

Transform Algorithm Performing an arithmetic computation on a record key and using the result of the calculation as an address for that record. Also known as key transformation.

Translator A device or computer program that transforms statements from one language to another, such as a compiler or assembler.

Transmit To send data from one location and to receive the data at another location.

Truncate (1) To terminate a computational process in accordance with certain rules. (2) To remove characters from the beginning or ending of a data element, especially digits at the beginning or ending of a numeric quantity.

Turnaround Document Output of a computer system that is normally printed in a special font (such as utility and telephone bills) and returned to the organization as machine-readable input.

Turnaround Time The elapsed time between submission of a job to a computing center and the return of the results.

Turnkey Systems Computer systems where all of the hardware, software, and systems development needed by a user are provided.

Unbundling The separate pricing of hardware, software, and other related services.

Unconditional Transfer Pertaining to an unconditional departure from the normal sequence of execution of instructions in a computer program.

Unit Record Pertaining to a single physical record that contains a single logical record.

Universal Product Code (UPC) A standard identification code using bar coding, printed on products which can be read by the optical supermarket scanners of the grocery industry.

Update To incorporate into a master file the changes required to reflect the most current status of the records in the file.

User Friendly A characteristic of human-operated equipment and systems that makes them safe, comfortable, and easy to use.

Utility Program A standard set of routines that assists in the operation of a computer system by performing some frequently required process such as sorting or merging.

Variable A quantity that can assume any of a given set of values.

Variable-Length Record Pertaining to data records that contain a variable number of characters or fields.

Variable Word Length Pertaining to a machine word or operand that may consist of a variable number of bits or characters. Contrast with Fixed Word Length.

Verify To determine whether a transcription of data or other operation has been accomplished accurately.

Videotex An interactive information service provided over phone lines or cable TV channels. Users can select specific video displays of data and information (such as electronic *Yellow Pages* or their own personal bank checking account register).

Virtual Machine Pertaining to the simulation of one type of computer system by another computer system.

Virtual Memory The use of secondary storage devices as an extension of the primary storage of the computer, thus giving the appearance of a larger main memory than actually exists.

VLSI Very Large-Scale Integration. Semiconductor chips containing hundreds of thousands of circuits.

Voice Mail A variation of electronic mail where digitized voice messages rather than electronic text are accepted, stored, and transmitted.

Voice Recognition Direct conversion of spoken data into electronic form suitable for entry into a computer system. Also called voice data entry.

Volatile Memory Memory (such as electronic semiconductor memory) that loses its contents when electrical power is interrupted.

Wand A handheld optical character recognition device used for data entry by many transaction terminals.

Wide Area Network (WAN) A data communications network covering a large geographic area.

Window One section of a computer's multiple section display screen, each of which can have a different display.

Word (1) A string of characters considered as an entity. (2) An ordered set of bits (usually larger than a byte) handled as a unit by the central processing unit.

Word Processing The automation of the transformation of ideas and information into a readable form of communication. It involves the use of computers to manipulate text data in order to produce office communications in the form of documents.

Write To record data on a data medium.

ILLUSTRATION CREDITS

Chapter 1

Figure 1–1: Adapted from James Martin, *Application Development without Programmers* (Englewood Cliffs, N.J.: Prentice-Hall, 1982), p. 109. Reprinted with permission. **Page 8 top:** Courtesy Unisys Corp.; **bottom:** Courtesy Hewlett-Packard Co. **Page 9 top:** Courtesy Cincinnati Milicron; **bottom:** Courtesy IBM Corporation. **Page 10 top:** Courtesy NCR Corporation; **bottom:** Courtesy Hewlett-Packard Co. **Page 11 top:** Courtesy Apple Computer, Inc.; **bottom:** Courtesy Hewlett-Packard Co. **Page 12 top:** Courtesy Unisys Corp.; **bottom:** Courtesy of Management Science America, Inc. (MSA). **Page 13 top:** Courtesy IBM Corporation; **bottom:** Courtesy Honeywell-Bull Co. **Page 14 top:** Courtesy Intel Corporation; **bottom:** Courtesy AT&T Bell Laboratories. **Page 15 top:** Courtesy IBM Corporation; **bottom:** Courtesy COMPAQ Computer Corporation. **Page 16 top:** Courtesy Apple Computer, Inc.; **bottom:** Courtesy Hewlett-Packard Co. **Page 17 top:** Courtesy of Prime Computer Inc.; **bottom:** Courtesy IBM Corporation. **Page 18 top:** Courtesy IBM Corporation; **bottom:** Courtesy Cray Research Inc. **Page 19 top:** Courtesy AT&T Bell Laboratories; **bottom:** Courtesy Apple Computer, Inc. **Page 20 top:** Courtesy Hewlett-Packard Co.; **bottom:** Courtesy Hewlett-Packard Co. **Page 21 top:** Courtesy of Prime Computer Inc.;

bottom: Courtesy of MSI Incorporated. **Page 22 top:** Courtesy NCR Corporation; **bottom:** Courtesy Unisys Corp. **Page 23 top:** Courtesy Hewlett-Packard Co.; **bottom:** Courtesy IBM Corporation. **Page 24 top:** Courtesy Motorola; **bottom:** Courtesy IBM Corporation. **Page 25 top:** Courtesy Unisys Corp.; **bottom:** Courtesy Apple Computer, Inc. **Page 26 top:** Courtesy IBM Corporation; **bottom:** Courtesy 3-M Company. **Page 27 top:** Courtesy WordPerfect Corporation; **bottom:** Courtesy Lotus Development Corporation. **Page 28 top:** Courtesy Ashton-Tate; **bottom:** Courtesy Microsoft Corporation. **Page 29 top:** Courtesy IBM Corporation; **bottom:** Courtesy PERSOFT, Inc. **Page 30 top:** Courtesy Software Publishing Co.; **bottom:** Courtesy Dow Jones & Company, Inc. **Figure 1–2:** Adapted from James Martin, *Application Development without Programmers* (Englewood Cliffs, N.J.: Prentice-Hall, 1982), p. 3. Reprinted with permission. **Page 51 all photos:** Courtesy IBM Corporation. **Page 53 top left:** Courtesy IBM Corporation; **top right:** The Bettman Archives; **bottom left:** Courtesy Unisys; **bottom right:** The Bettman Archives. **Page 55 top:** Courtesy Unisys; **bottom:** Courtesy Unisys and AT&T Bell Laboratories. **Page 57 top:** Courtesy IBM Corporation. **Page 59 top:** Adapted from Monte Phister, Jr., *Data Processing Technology and*

Electronics, 2nd ed. (Bedford, Mass.: Digital Press, 1980); **bottom:** Courtesy Intel Corporation.

Chapter 2

Figure 2–4: Courtesy IBM Corporation. **Figure 2–6:** Courtesy IBM Corporation. **Figure 2–7:** Courtesy IBM Corporation. **Figure 2–8:** Courtesy IBM Corporation. **Figure 2–12:** Courtesy IBM Corporation. **Figure 2–9:** Courtesy Duncan-Atwell Computerized Technologies, Inc. **Figure 2–10:** Courtesy Hewlett-Packard Co. **Figure 2–13:** Courtesy of Digital Equipment Corporation. **Figure 2–14:** Courtesy Cray Research Inc.

Chapter 3

Figure 3–7: Courtesy Ashton-Tate. **Figure 3–8:** Courtesy Ashton-Tate. **Figure 3–13:** Courtesy Business and Professional Software, Inc. **Figure 3–14:** Courtesy Context Management Systems. **Figure 3–15:** Courtesy Microsoft Corporation.

Chapter 4

Figure 4–1: Courtesy Intel Corporation.

Chapter 5

Figure 5–2: John K. Murphy, "Office Automation," *Mini-Micro Systems,* December 1983, p. 222. Reprinted with permission. **Figure 5–6:** Courtesy of

C

Management Science America, Inc. (MSA). **Figure 5–7:** Courtesy Apple Computer, Inc. **Figure 5–9:** Courtesy ISSCO Corporation. **Figure 5–10:** Courtesy Honeywell Information Systems, 3-M Company, Calcomp Inc., and IBM Corporation. **Figure 5–11:** Courtesy Hewlett-Packard Co. **Figure 5–13:** Courtesy Quadram Corporation, Hewlett-Packard Co., Texas Instruments, and Honeywell-Bull. **Figure 5–14:** Courtesy Calcomp Inc. **Figure 5–15:** Courtesy Texas Instruments. **Figure 5–16:** Jeffery Rothfeder, "A Few Words about Voice Technology," *PC Magazine,* September 30, 1986, p. 192–93. Reprinted with permission. **Figure 5–17:** Tom Stanton, Diane Burns, and S. Venit, "Page-to-Disk Technology," *PC Magazine,* September 30, 1986, p. 134. Reprinted with permission. **Figure 5–18:** Courtesy NCR Corporation. **Figure 5–20:** Courtesy NCR Corporation. **Figure 5–21:** Courtesy of Datacorp.

Chapter 6

Figure 6–6: Courtesy IBM Corporation. **Figure 6–8:** CLICK/Chicago. **Figure 6–10:** Courtesy Apple Computer, Inc., Unisys Corp., and IBM Corporation. **Figure 6–11:** Courtesy Vertex Peripherals. **Figure 6–13:** Courtesy Unisys Corp. **Figure 6–16:** Courtesy IBM Corporation. **Figure 6–17:** Courtesy IBM Corporation. **Figure 6–18:** Courtesy IBM Corporation. **Figure 6–19:** Courtesy Intel Corporation. **Figure 6–20:** 3-M Company.

Chapter 7

Figure 7–15: Courtesy Artificial Intelligence Corporation, Ashton-Tate, and Microrim Inc. **Figure 7–16:** Courtesy Applied Data Research and Microrim Inc. **Figure 7–17:** Courtesy Index Technology Corp. **Figure 7–20:** Courtesy Applied Data Research. **Figure 7–23:** Courtesy Hewlett-Packard Co.

Chapter 8

Figure 8–3: Courtesy Quadram Corporation. **Figure 8–4:** Courtesy Racal-Milgo. **Figure 8–6:** Courtesy AT&T. **Figure 8–7:** Courtesy American

Satellite Company. **Figure 8–8:** Adapted from Myles E. Walsh, *Database and Data Communications Systems* (Reston, Va.: Reston Publishing Co., 1983), p. 103. Reprinted with permission. **Figure 8–9:** Courtesy The Source. **Figure 8–11:** "Linking Office Computers: The Market Comes of Age," *Business Week,* May 14, 1984, p. 144. Used with permission. **Figure 8–12:** Courtesy of CompuServe. **Figure 8–16:** Courtesy of Formation, Inc. **Figure 8–17:** Courtesy Hewlett-Packard Co. **Figure 8–18:** Courtesy IBM Corporation. **Figure 8–19:** Adapted from Eric D. Steel, "Your Pocket Protocol Primer," *Datamation,* March 1984, p. 152. Used with permission. **Figure 8–20:** Courtesy Digital Equipment Corporation.

Chapter 9

Figure 9–4: Adapted from Jerome Kanter, *Management-Oriented Management Information Systems,* 3rd ed., 1984, p. 176. Reprinted by permission of Prentice-Hall, Inc., Englewood Cliffs, New Jersey. **Figure 9–12:** Courtesy IBM Corporation. **Figure 9–14:** Courtesy IBM Corporation. **Figure 9–20:** Robert K. Elliot and John A. Kielich, "Expert Systems for Accountants," *Journal of Accountancy,* September 1985, p. 128. Reprinted with permission. **Figure 9–21:** Harvey P. Newquist III, "Expert Systems," *Computerworld,* January 13, 1986, p. 43.

Chapter 10

Figure 10–3: Courtesy Index Technology Corp. **Figure 10–4:** Adapted from James Martin, *Application Development without Programmers* (Englewood Cliffs, N.J.: Prentice-Hall, 1982), pp. 66–67. Used with permission. **Figure 10–6:** Adapted from Henry Lucas, *Information Systems Concepts for Management* (New York: McGraw-Hill, 1982). Copyright © 1982 by McGraw-Hill Book Company. Used with the permission of McGraw-Hill Book Company.

Chapter 11

Figure 11–14: Courtesy of Software AG, Cincom, and Applied Data Research.

Chapter 12

Figure 12–2: John K. Murphy, "Office Automation," *Mini-Micro Systems,* December 1983, p. 224. Reprinted with permission. **Figure 12–4:** Courtesy IBM Corporation. **Figure 12–5:** Courtesy IBM Corporation. **Figure 12–6:** Courtesy Software Publishing Corporation. **Figure 12–7:** Courtesy MCI. **Figure 12–8:** Courtesy Martin Marietta Data Systems. **Figure 12–9:** Courtesy TRW Inc. **Figure 12–10:** Courtesy Lotus Development Corporation.

Chapter 13

Figure 13–2: Adapted from Donald Cox and Robert Good, "How to Build a Marketing Information System," *Harvard Business Review* 45, no. 3, p. 46. **Figure 13–3:** Courtesy IBM Corporation. **Figure 13–9:** Courtesy IBM Corporation. **Figure 13–11:** Courtesy IBM Corporation. **Figure 13–12:** Adapted from Jerome Kanter, *Management-Oriented Management Information Systems,* 3rd ed., © 1984. Reprinted by permission of Prentice-Hall, Inc., Englewood Cliffs, New Jersey.

Chapter 14

Figure 14–5: John Vacca, "Money on the Move," *Computerworld,* May 2, 1984, p. 85. **Figure 14–6:** Courtesy Dow Jones & Company, Inc. **Figure 14–7:** Courtesy IBM Corporation. **Figure 14–8:** Courtesy MECA Inc. **Figure 14–11:** Courtesy IBM Corporation. **Figure 14–13:** Courtesy IBM Corporation. **Figure 14–15:** Courtesy IBM Corporation. **Figure 14–16:** Courtesy IBM Corporation. **Figure 14–18:** Courtesy IBM Corporation. **Figure 14–19:** Courtesy IBM Corporation. **Figure 14–21:** Courtesy IBM Corporation. **Figure 14–23:** Courtesy IBM Corporation. **Figure 14–24:** Courtesy IBM Corporation. **Figure 14–26:** Courtesy IBM Corporation. **Figure 14–27:** Courtesy IBM Corporation. **Figure 14–28:** Courtesy IBM Corporation.

Chapter 15

Figure 15–1: Adapted from "CW Profile," *Computerworld,* October 13,

1986, p. 1. **Figure 15–3:** Adapted from "Information Power," *Business Week,* October 14, 1985, pp. 108–9. **Figure 15–4:** Adapted from James C. Wetherbee, *Systems Analysis and Design,* 2nd ed. (St. Paul, Minn.: West Publishing Co., 1984), p. 327. Reprinted with permission. **Figure 15–8:** Adapted from "Hot Buttons," *Computerworld,* September 29, 1986, p. 65. **Figure 15–11:** Adapted from Parker Hodges, "What Are You Worth?" *Datamation,* October 1, 1987, p. 88. **Figure 15–12:** Adapted from Matthew Chatterly, "Keys to Motivation," *Arizona Republic,* January 19, 1987, p. C5. **Figure 15–16:** Courtesy Source-EDP. **Figure 15–21:** Courtesy Johnson Systems, Inc.

Chapter 16

Figure 16–2: Adapted from "The Datamation 100," *Datamation,* June 15, 1987, pp. 30–31. **Figure 16–3:** Adapted from Parker Hodges, "1987 DP Budget Survey," *Datamation,* April 1, 1987, p. 70. **Figure 16–6:** Courtesy Datapro Reports. **Figure 16–11:** Adapted from Jim Bartino, "Buying Smarter," *Personal Computing,* April 1986, p. 64. **Figure 16–12:** Adapted from Jim Bartino, "Buying Smarter," *Personal Computing,* April 1986, p. 63.

Chapter 17

Figure 17–3: Courtesy IBM Corporation. **Figure 17–4:** Adapted from James A. Schweitzer, *Computer Crime and Business Information* (New York: Elsevier Science Publishing Co., 1986), p. 113. **Figure 17–5:** Courtesy Cullinet Corporation. **Figure 17–7:** Adapted from J. J. Bloombecker, "New Federal Law Bolsters Computer Security Efforts," *Computerworld,* October 27, 1986, pp. 55–59. **Figure 17–8:** Adapted from J. J. Bloombecker, "New Federal Law Bolsters Computer Security Efforts," *Computerworld,* October 27, 1986, pp. 55–59. **Figure 17–9:** Adapted from James A. Schweitzer, *Computer Crime and Business Information* (New York: Elsevier Science Publishing Co., 1986), p. 17. **Figure 17–10:** Courtesy Association for Computing Machinery.

Appendix A

Figure A1–2: Courtesy IBM Corporation. **Figure A2–1:** Courtesy MicroPro International Corporation. **Figure A2–2:** Courtesy MicroPro International Corporation. **Figure A2–17:** Courtesy MicroPro International Corporation. **Figure A3–1:** Courtesy Lotus Development Corporation. **Figure A3–2:** Courtesy Lotus Development Corporation. **Figure A4–4:** Courtesy Ashton-Tate.

INDEX